George Rawlinson

History of Herodotus

George Rawlinson

History of Herodotus

ISBN/EAN: 9783741182327

Manufactured in Europe, USA, Canada, Australia, Japa

Cover: Foto ©Andreas Hilbeck / pixelio.de

Manufactured and distributed by brebook publishing software (www.brebook.com)

George Rawlinson

History of Herodotus

POETS

HISTORY

OF

HERODOTUS.

A NEW ENGLISH VERSION, EDITED WITH COPIOUS NOTES AND APPENDICES,
ILLUSTRATING THE HISTORY AND GEOGRAPHY OF HERODOTUS, FROM THE
MOST RECENT SOURCES OF INFORMATION; AND EMBODYING
THE CHIEF RESULTS, HISTORICAL AND ETHNOGRAPHICAL,
WHICH HAVE BEEN OBTAINED IN THE PROGRESS
OF CUNEIFORM AND HIEROGLYPHICAL
DISCOVERY.

BY GEORGE RAWLINSON, M.A.,
CAMDEN PROFESSOR OF ANCIENT HISTORY IN THE UNIVERSITY OF OXFORD;
LATE FELLOW AND TUTOR OF EXETER COLLEGE.

ASSISTED BY
COL. SIR HENRY RAWLINSON, K.C.B., AND SIR J. G. WILKINSON, F.R.S.

IN FOUR VOLUMES.—VOL. III.

WITH MAPS AND ILLUSTRATIONS.

NEW EDITION.

LONDON:
JOHN MURRAY, ALBEMARLE STREET.
1862.

LONDON PRINTED BY W. CLOWES AND SONS, STAMFORD STREET
AND CHARING CROSS.

CONTENTS OF VOL. III.

HISTORY OF HERODOTUS.

THE FOURTH BOOK, ENTITLED MELPOMENE.

Expedition of Darius against Scythia—its pretext (1). Previous history of the Scythians—their war with their slaves (2-4). Traditions of their origin— 1. Their own account (5-7). 2. Greek version of the same (8-10). 3. Account preferred by the author (11, 12). Story of Aristeas (13-16). Description of Scythia (17-20). Neighbouring nations, Sauromatæ, Budini, Argippæi, Issedones, and Arimaspi (21-27). Climate of Scythia (28-31). Stories of the Hyperboreans (32-36). Universal geography—1. Description of Asia (37-41). 2. Circumnavigation of Libya (42, 43). 3. Voyage of Scylax (44). Origin of the names, Europe, Asia, Libya (45). Remarkable features of Scythia— the people (46, 47). The rivers—the Ister and its affluents (48-50). The Tyras (51). The Hypanis (52). The Borysthenes (53). The Panticapes, Hypacyris, Gerrhus, Tanais, &c. (54-58). Religion of the Scyths—Gods (59). Sacrifices (60, 61). Worship of Mars, &c. (62, 63). War-customs (64-66). Soothsayers (67-69). Oaths (70). Burial of the kings, &c. (71-73). Use of hemp (74, 75). Hatred of foreign customs—stories of Anacharsis and Scylas (76-80). Population (81). Marvels (82). Preparations of Darius (83-85). Size of the Euxine, Propontis, &c. (86). March of Darius to the Ister (87-92). Customs of the Thracians (93-96). Darius at the Ister (97, 98). Size and shape of Scythia (99-101). Description of the surrounding nations, Tauri, &c. (102-117). Consultation of the kings (118, 119). Plans of the Scyths (120). March of Darius through Scythia, and return to the Ister (121-141). Passage of the Ister and return to the Hellespont (141, 143). Saving of Megabazus (144). Libyan expedition of Aryandes—Founding of Thera (145-149). Thereans required by the oracle to colonise Libya—two accounts (150-155). Occupation of Platea (156). Settlement at Aziris (157). Colonisation of Cyrene (158). History of Cyrene from its foundation to the death of Arcesilaus III. (159-164). Application of Pheretima to Aryandes (165). Fate of Aryandes (166). Expedition against Barca (167). Account of the Libyan tribes from Egypt to Lake Tritonis (168-181). The three regions of Northern Libya (182-185). Customs of the Libyans (186-190). Contrast of eastern and western Libya (191, 192). Account of the western tribes (193-196). Four nations of Libya (197). Productiveness of Libya (198, 199). Account of the expedition against Barca (200-203). Fate of the Barceans (204). Death of Pheretima (205) .... Page 1

a 2

CONTENTS OF VOL. III.

APPENDIX TO BOOK IV.

ESSAY I.

ON THE CIMMERIANS OF HERODOTUS AND THE MIGRATIONS OF THE CYMRIC RACE.

1. Early importance of the Cimmerians—their geographical extent. 2. Identity of the Cimmerii with the Cymry—close resemblance of the two names. 3. Historical confirmation of the identity—connecting link in the Cimbri. 4. Comparative philology silent but not adverse. 5. Migrations of the Cimmerians—westward, and then eastward. Existing Cimbric and Celtic races .... Page 130

ESSAY II.

ON THE ETHNOGRAPHY OF THE EUROPEAN SCYTHS.

1. Supposed Mongolian origin of the Scyths—grounds of the opinion twofold. 2. Resemblance of physical characteristics, slight. 3. Resemblance of manners and customs, not close. 4. True test, that of language. 5. Possibility of applying it. 6. The application—Etymology of Scythic common terms. 7. Explanation of the names of the Scythian gods. 8. Explanation of some names of men. 9. Explanation of geographical names. 10. Result, that the Scythians of Herodotus were an Indo-European race. 11. Further result, that they were a distinct race, not Slaves, nor Celts, nor Teutons; and that they are now extinct 152

ESSAY III.

ON THE GEOGRAPHY OF SCYTHIA.

1. Necessity of examining Niebuhr's theory of the Scythia of Herodotus. 2. The theory stated. 3. Its grounds. 4. Considerations which disprove it. 5. Real views of Herodotus. 6. His personal knowledge of the region. 7. His correctness as to leading facts, and mistakes as to minutiæ. 8. Possibility of changes since his time. 9. Identification of rivers and places 168

NOTE A.—On the words Thyssagetæ and Massagetæ 175

HISTORY OF HERODOTUS.

THE FIFTH BOOK, ENTITLED TERPSICHORE.

Thracian conquests of Megabazus (1, 2). Customs of the Thracians (3-8). Region north of Thrace (9, 10). Cöes and Histiæus rewarded (11). Story of Pigres and Mantyes (12-14). Megabazus reduces the Pæonians (15). Customs of the Pæonians (16). Submission of Macedonia—story of the ambassadors (17-21). Hellenism of the royal family of Macedon (22). Recall of Histiæus

THE FIFTH BOOK—*continued*.

(23, 24). Appointment of Artaphernes and Otanes (25). Conquests of Otanes (26, 27). Troubles arise in Ionia—previous history of Miletus (28, 29). Aristagoras' expedition against Naxos (30-34). Message of Histiaeus (35). Revolt of Aristagoras (36). Fate of the tyrants (37, 38). Aristagoras goes to Sparta—Recent history of Sparta (39-48). Aristagoras fails to persuade Cleomenes (49-54). He goes to Athens—Recent history of Athens—Murder of Hipparchus—Expulsion of Hippias—Clisthenes—attempts of Sparta; Theban and Eginetan wars, &c. (55-96). Aristagoras obtains aid from Athens (97). Escape of the Paeonians (98). Attack on Sardis, which is taken and burnt (99-101). Retreat and defeat of the Greeks (102). Spread of the revolt to Caria and Caunus (103). Revolt and reduction of Cyprus—Darius and Histiaeus (104-115). Persians recover the Hellespont (116, 117). War in Caria (118-121). Persian successes in Æolia and Ionia (122, 123). Aristagoras resolves on flight (124). Advice of Histiaeus (125). Flight and death of Aristagoras (126) .... Page 176

APPENDIX TO BOOK V.

ESSAY I.

ON THE EARLY HISTORY OF SPARTA.

1. Spartans, immigrants into the Peloponnese. 2. Supposed migrations of the Dorians. 3. Their occupation of the Peloponnese according to the ordinary legend. 4. The true history unknown. 5. Probable line of march. 6. Date of the occupation. 7. The conquest gradual. 8. Spartan Dorians—Sparta and Amyclae—early wars. 9. Internal history—origin of the double monarchy—troubles of the early period. 10. Condition of Sparta before Lycurgus—the three classes—(i.) Spartans—(ii.) Periœci—(iii.) Helots. 11. Succession of the early kings. 12. Original constitution of Sparta.— Kings—Senate—Ecclesia. 13. Constitutional changes of Lycurgus, slight 14. His discipline—question of its origin. 15. Causes of its adoption. 16. Supposed equalisation of landed property. 17. Arguments which disprove it. 18. Effects of Lycurgus' legislation—conquests, and increase of Periœci. 19. Messenian wars. 20. Causes of the rupture. 21. Outline of the first war. 22. Date and duration. 23. Internal changes consequent on the first war—"Peers" and "Inferiors"—"Small" and "Great Assembly"— colonisation of Tarentum. 24. Interval between the wars. 25. Outline of the second war. 26. Its duration. 27. War with Pisatis. 28. War with Arcadia. 29. Gradual diminution of the kingly power at Sparta, and continued rise of the Ephors. 30. Rapid decrease in the number of Spartan citizens 229

ESSAY II.

ON THE EARLY HISTORY OF THE ATHENIANS.

1. Obscurity of early Athenian history. 2. Primitive inhabitants of Attica unwarlike. 3. Causes of her weakness—no central authority—Pelasgic

CONTENTS OF VOL. III.

ESSAY II.—continued.

blood. 4. First appearance of the Athenians in history—stories of Melanthus and Codrus. 5. Blank in the external history. 6. Ionian migration conducted by sons of Codrus. 7. Internal history. 8. Early tribes—*Teleontes, Hopletes, Ægikoreis,* and *Argadeis*. 9. Clans and phratries—importance of this division. 10. Trittyes and Naucraries. 11. Political distribution of the people—*Eupatridæ, Geomori,* and *Demiurgi*. 12. First period of the aristocracy—from Codrus to Alcmæon, B.C. 1050-752. 13. Second period—from Alcmæon to Eryxias—B.C. 752-684—rapid advance. 14. Mode in which the usurpations were made—substitution of the Eupatrid assembly for the old Agora. 15. Power of the old Senate. 16. Full establishment of oligarchy, B.C. 684. 17. First appearance of the democratical spirit—legislation of Draco. 18. Revolt of Cylon, crushed. 19. Sacrileges committed — widespread discontent. 20. Solon chosen as mediator—his proceedings. 21. Date of his archonship. 22. His recovery of Salamis. 23. His connexion with the Sacred War. 24. His legislation—the *Seisachtheia* and debasement of the currency. 25. Prospective measures. 26. Constitutional changes—introduction of the four classes, *Pentacosiomedimni, Hippeis, Zeugitæ,* and *Thetes*. 27. Arrangement of burthens — income-tax — military service. 28. Pro-Bouleutic council. 29. Importance of these changes—Isocrates. 30. Solon the true founder of the democracy. 31. Solon confined citizenship to the tribes. 32. Laws of Solon—(i.) Penalties for crimes—(ii.) Stimulus to population—(iii.) Law against political neutrality. 33. Results of his legislation—time of repose—revival of discontent—Solon leaves Athens. 34. Reappearance of the old parties — Pedieis, &c. — return of Solon — his courage. 35. Tyranny of Pisistratus . . . . Page 390

HISTORY OF HERODOTUS.

THE SIXTH BOOK, ENTITLED ERATO.

Histiæus comes down to the coast (1-3). Conspiracy discovered at Sardis (4). Histiæus sails to the Hellespont (5). Miletus threatened by the Persians—the two fleets—battle of Ladé (6-15). Misfortunes of the Chians (16). Dionysius the Phocæan commander (17). Fall of Miletus (18). Punishment of the Milesians (19, 20). Sorrow of Athens (21). Fate of the Samians—seizure of Zancle (22-25). Fate of Histiæus (26-30). Punishment of the rebels (31, 32). Phœnician fleet ravages the Chersonese (33). Chersonesite kingdom of the Cimonidæ (34-40). Flight of Miltiades to Athens (41). New settlement of Ionia by the Persians (42). Expedition of Mardonius fails (43-45). Suspected revolt of Thasos (46, 47). Envoys of Darius demand earth and water—submission of Egina and the islands generally (48, 49). Cleomenes attempts to punish the Eginetans (50). Cleomenes' feud with Demaratus (51). The double royalty at Sparta—descent—privileges of the kings (52-59). Spartan customs (60). Story of Ariston (61-63). Demaratus, deprived of his crown, flies to Persia (64-70). Leotychides made king (71). Fate of Leotychides (72). Eginetans forced to give hostages (73). Fate of Cleomenes (74, 75). Various causes assigned for his insanity (76-84). Eginetans demand back their hostages—story of Glaucus (85, 86). War between Egina and Athens (87-93). Expedition of Datis and Artaphernes (94). Course of the expedition (95-99). Preparations of the Eretrians—siege

THE SIXTH BOOK—*continued.*

and surrender of Eretria (100, 101). Persians land at Marathon (102). Account of Miltiades (103, 104). Pheidippides sent to Sparta—appearance of Pan (105, 106). Dream of Hippias (107). Plataeans join the Athenians—previous connexion of the two nations (108). Division among the Athenian generals—Miltiades and Callimachus (109, 110). Preparations for battle (111). Battle of Marathon (112-114). Attempt to surprise Athens (115, 116). Story of Epizelus (117). Return of the expedition to Asia (118, 119). Spartans visit Marathon (120). Charge made against the Alcmaeonidae (121-124). Previous history of the family—favours of Croesus (125). Marriage of Megacles with Agariste (126-130). Descent of Pericles (131). Expedition of Miltiades against Paros (132-135). Trial of Miltiades—his death (136). His capture of Lemnos—previous history of the inhabitants (137-140) Page 335

APPENDIX TO BOOK VI.

ESSAY I.

ON THE CIRCUMSTANCES OF THE BATTLE OF MARATHON.

1. Difficulties in the description of Herodotus. 2. Number of Persians engaged. 3. Numbers of the Greeks. 4. Proportion, five or six to one. 5. Landing of the army of Datis, and disposition of the troops. 6. Position occupied by the Greeks. 7. Motives inducing the Persians to delay the attack. 8. Causes of the original inaction of the Greeks, and of their subsequent change of tactics. 9. Miltiades' preparations for battle. 10. Description of the battle — re-embarkation of the invading army 426

ESSAY II.

ON THE TRADITIONS RESPECTING THE PELASGIANS.

1. Original population of Greece and Italy, homogeneous. 2. Kindred races in Asia Minor and the islands. 3. Characteristics of this ethnic group. 4. Position of the Pelasgi in it. 5. Extent of country occupied by the Pelasgians. 6. Their general movement from east to west. 7. Etymology of their name. 8. Lines of passage. 9. Migrations of the Tyrrheno-Pelasgians. 10. Pelasgic walls. 11. Absorption of the Pelasgians in other races 437

NOTE A.—On the Derivation and Meaning of the Proper Names of the Medes and Persians 444

(viii)

LIST OF MAPS AND ILLUSTRATIONS.

Map of the Scythia of Herodotus	To face Title-page.
Scythian Warriors, Stringing the bow	Page 3
Ancient Scythian Whip, and modern Nogais	ib.
Coins of Olbia	14
Chart of the Chersonesus Trachea	15
Greek Griffin	20
Plan of the World according to Hecatæus	26
Scythian horseman	34
Scythian archer	35
Waggons of the Calmucks and other Tatars	ib.
Coin of Olbia (head of Cybele)	41
Scythian god (supposed to be Hercules)	43
Tomb of a Scythian king. Ground plan	50
Section of ditto	51
Scythian drinking-cups	52
Head-dress of the Scythians	58
Scythian arrow-heads	61
Bronze bowl found in the tomb of a Scythian king	ib.
View of the Tauric Mountains from the Steppe region	74
Chart of the island of Thera (Santorin)	100
View of Cyrene, the Forum and Fountain of Apollo	108
Plan of Cyrene (after Beechey)	110
Coin of Cyrene	112
View of the Necropolis of Cyrene	113
Representation of the Silphium on the coins of Cyrene and Barca	121
Egyptian shields	126
Dress of the Ethiopian girls—fringe of thongs	137
Fringe of thongs (enlarged view)	138
Map of the Scythia of Herodotus according to Niebuhr	169
Ruins of Susa—1. Ground plan of the mounds; 2. Plan of the great palace; 3. Base and capital of columns	207
View of the ruins of Sardis	252
Chart of the country about Argos	379
Chart of the plain of Marathon	396
Cave of Pan, as seen on coins of Athens	398

THE
HISTORY OF HERODOTUS.

THE FOURTH BOOK, ENTITLED MELPOMENE.

1. AFTER the taking of Babylon, an expedition was led by Darius into Scythia.[1] Asia abounding in men, and vast sums flowing into the treasury, the desire seized him to exact vengeance from the Scyths, who had once in days gone by invaded Media, defeated those who met them in the field, and so begun the quarrel. During the space of eight-and-twenty years, as I have before mentioned,[2] the Scyths continued lords of the whole of Upper Asia. They entered Asia in pursuit of the Cimmerians, and overthrew the empire of the Medes, who till they came possessed the sovereignty. On their return to their homes after the long absence of twenty-eight years,[3] a task awaited them little less troublesome than their struggle with the Medes. They found an army of no small size prepared to oppose their entrance. For the Scythian women, when they saw that time went on, and their husbands did not come back, had intermarried with their slaves.

2. Now the Scythians blind all their slaves, to use them in preparing their milk. The plan they follow is to thrust tubes made of bone, not unlike our musical pipes, up the vulva of the mare,[4] and then to blow into the tubes with their mouths, some

---

[1] It has been supposed that the notice in the Behistun Inscription (col. v. par. 4), of an expedition of Darius against the Sacæ (Sakā), refers to this invasion (Blakesley, not. ad loc.). But the scanty fragments of the text, which alone remain, and the representation of the leader in the train of captured rebels, lead rather to the conclusion that Asiatic Scyths—old subjects of the Persian monarchy (Beh. Ins. col. i. par. 6, and col. ii. par. 2)—are intended.

[2] Vide supra, i. 103-106.

[3] Some writers ascribed this war with the slaves to quite a different occasion. It was, they said, after the Scythians had been engaged in a long struggle with the Thracians and other tribes south of the Danube (Callistrat. Fr. 3).

[4] Niebuhr the traveller (Description de l'Arabie, p. 146) relates that a somewhat similar practice obtains in Arabia:—"J'entendis et vis moi-même à Basra," he says, "que lorsqu'on Arabe

milking while the others blow. They say that they do this because when the veins of the animal are full of air, the udder is forced down. The milk thus obtained is poured into deep wooden casks, about which the blind slaves are placed, and then the milk is stirred round.⁵ That which rises to the top is drawn off, and considered the best part; the under portion is of less account. Such is the reason why the Scythians blind all those whom they take in war; it arises from their not being tillers of the ground, but a pastoral race.⁶

3. When therefore the children sprung from these slaves and the Scythian women, grew to manhood, and understood the circumstances of their birth, they resolved to oppose the army which was returning from Media. And, first of all, they cut off a tract of country from the rest of Scythia by digging a broad dyke⁷ from the Tauric mountains to the vast lake of the Mæotis. Afterwards, when the Scythians tried to force an entrance, they marched out and engaged them. Many battles were fought, and the Scythians gained no advantage, until at last one of them thus addressed the remainder: "What are we doing, Scythians? We are fighting our slaves, diminishing our own number when we fall, and the number of those that belong to us when they fall by our hands. Take my advice—lay spear and bow aside,⁸ and let each man fetch his horse-

---

trait la femelle du buffle, un autre lui fourre la main, et le bras jusqu'au coude, dans le *vulva*, parceqn'on prétend avoir par expérience qu'étant chatouillée de la sorte, elle donne plus de lait. Cette méthode, "he observes," resembles beaucoup à celle des Scythes." [In India, while they milk the buffaloes, the tail is generally coiled up, and thrust into the vulva for the same purpose.—H. C. R.]

Mares' milk constituted the chief food of the ancient Scythians, who are therefore called γαλακτοφάγοι and Ἱππημολγοί by Homer (Il. xiii. 5) and other writers (Callim. Hymn. ad Dian. 252; Nic. Dam. Frag. 123, &c.). It is still the principal support of the Calmuck hordes which wander over the vast steppes north and west of the Caspian.

⁵ It is apparent from this circumstance that it was *koumiss*, and not cream, on which the Scythians lived. *Koumiss* is still prepared from mares' milk by the Calmucks and Nogais, who during the process of making it keep the milk in constant agitation (Clarke's Travels, vol. I. p. 313; De Hell, p. 274, E. T.).

⁶ That is, eyesight which is requisite for agricultural pursuits is not needed for the offices which a pastoral people requires of its slaves. The Scythians therefore, being a pastoral people, could manage with blind slaves; and by blinding their slaves they rendered it impossible for them either to revolt or to run away.

⁷ On the position of this dyke, vide infra, ch. 20.

⁸ The spear and the bow were the national weapons of the European Scyths (see note on ch. 70), the bow on the whole being regarded as the more essential (infra, ch. 46; Æsch. P. V. 730,). Arrow-heads are found in almost all the Scythian tombs in Southern Russia, while spear-heads have been found only occasionally. The spear used was short, apparently not more than five feet in length, whence in ch. 70 Herodotus terms it a javelin (*ἀκόντιον*). According to the Greeks, the bow was made in a single piece, and when unstrung bent backwards (cf. note on Book vii. ch. 64); but the representations on Scythian

whip,' and go boldly up to them. So long as they see us with arms in our hands, they imagine themselves our equals in birth and bravery; but let them behold us with no other weapon but the whip, and they will feel that they are our slaves, and flee before us."

4. The Scythians followed this counsel, and the slaves were so astounded, that they forgot to fight, and immediately ran away. Such was the mode in which the Scythians, after being for a time the lords of Asia, and being forced to quit it by the Medes, returned and settled in their own country. This inroad of theirs it was that Darius was anxious to avenge, and such was the purpose for which he was now collecting an army to invade them.

5. According to the account which the Scythians themselves give, they are the youngest of all nations.[1] Their tradition is

monuments make this questionable. See the subjoined woodcut, which is taken from a vase found in a Scythian tomb, and exhibits a curious mode of stringing the bow. [This is the common method of stringing the bow in the East. I have seen it among the Bheels, the Huzarehs, and the Kurds.—H. C. R.]

[1] The ancient Scythian whip seems to have closely resembled the nagaik of the modern Cossacks. It had a short handle and a single lash, with a round flat piece of leather at the end (see the subjoined woodcuts). How universally it was carried is indicated by the fact that a whip was buried in the tomb of a Scythian king, with his other arms and implements. (See below, ch. 71.)

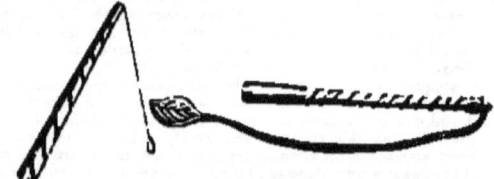

Ancient Scythian Whip (from Dubois). Modern Nogais (from Oliphant).

[1] Justin's assertion, so directly contradictory of this ("Scytharum gentem semper habitam fuisse antiquissimam," ii. 1), is remarkable. We must understand, however, by the Scyths of Herodotus in this place, the single nation of European Scyths with which the Greeks of the Pontus were acquainted.

as follows. A certain Targitaüs' was the first man who ever lived in their country, which before his time was a desert without inhabitants. He was a child—I do not believe the tale, but it is told nevertheless—of Jove and a daughter of the Borysthenes. Targitaüs, thus descended, begat three sons, Leipoxais, Arpoxais, and Colaxais, who was the youngest born of the three. While they still ruled the land, there fell from the sky four implements, all of gold,—a plough, a yoke, a battle-axe, and a drinking-cup. The eldest of the brothers perceived them first, and approached to pick them up; when lo! as he came near, the gold took fire, and blazed. He therefore went his way, and the second coming forward made the attempt, but the same thing happened again. The gold rejected both the eldest and the second brother. Last of all the youngest brother approached, and immediately the flames were extinguished; so he picked up the gold, and carried it to his home. Then the two elder agreed together, and made the whole kingdom over to the youngest born.

6. From Leipoxais sprang the Scythians of the race called Auchatæ; from Arpoxais, the middle brother, those known as the Catiari and Traspians; from Colaxais, the youngest, the Royal Scythians, or Paralatæ. All together they are named Scoloti,² after one of their kings: the Greeks, however, call them Scythians.⁴

7. Such is the account which the Scythians give of their origin. They add that from the time of Targitaüs, their first king, to the invasion of their country by Darius, is a period of one

---

Justin intends the Scythic or Turanian race generally, which was really older than either the Semitic or the Indo-European. (See vol. I. Essay xi. pp. 530-533.)

² The conjectures which would identify Targitaüs, the mythic progenitor of the Scythians, with Togarmah, the son of Gomer, and grandson of Japhet (Gen. x. 3), are even more fanciful than the ordinary run of Biblico-historical speculations. (See Rennell's Geograph. of Herod. p. 410; and Von Hammer's (Osech. v. Osm. I. p. 1.) Were they admitted, the further identification of these two words with the ethnic appellative "Turk" might still be questioned.

³ Nothing is known of these names, though they afford an ample field for speculation. Dr. Donaldson recognises in the Scoloti, the "Am-Galatæ" or "Celts of Asia" (Varronian. p. 41;—a possible, but scarcely a probable derivation. In "Traspians" it may be conjectured that we have the root αςπα, "horse;" while Paralatæ (Παραλάται) recalls the *Paradise* mountain-chain. Mere speculation, however, is in etymology worse than futile. It is apt to be misleading.

⁴ The Greek word Σκύθης is probably nothing but the Asiatic *Saka* (Σάκαι) with an ethnic adjectival ending -θης, equivalent to the ordinary -της or -της found in so many names of peoples—*e. g.* Κελτός, Γαλάτης, Σαυρομάτης, Θεσπρωτός, Βοιωτής, Φθιώτης, κ.τ.λ. The first vowel has been dropt, and Σακθης contracted into Σκύθης. Whether *Saka* is connected with the Old Norse *skyta*, Swedish *skyta*, German *schützen*, and English *shot*, it is quite impossible to say. The connexion is at any rate open to very great doubt.

thousand years, neither less nor more.¹ The Royal Scythians guard the sacred gold with most especial care, and year by year offer great sacrifices in its honour. At this feast, if the man who has the custody of the gold should fall asleep in the open air, he is sure (the Scythians say) not to outlive the year. His pay therefore is as much land as he can ride round on horseback in a day. As the extent of Scythia is very great, Colaxais gave each of his three sons a separate kingdom,² one of which was of ampler size than the other two: in this the gold was preserved. Above, to the northward of the furthest dwellers in Scythia, the country is said to be concealed from sight and made impassable by reason of the feathers which are shed abroad abundantly. The earth and air are alike full of them, and this it is which prevents the eye from obtaining any view of the region.³

8. Such is the account which the Scythians give of themselves, and of the country which lies above them. The Greeks who dwell about the Pontus⁴ tell a different story. According

---

¹ It is curious to find this assertion made the foundation of serious chronological calculations. (Larcher, Table Chronologique; Bähr ad loc.) The number of 1000 represents, palpably enough, an indefinite period; and indeed it is impossible that a nation in the condition of the Scythians should have had more than a vague notion of its origin, and the time it had lasted.

² This tradition, and the triple command at the time of the invasion (infra, ch. 120), indicate, apparently, a permanent division of the Royal Horde into three distinct tribes.

³ Vide infra, ch. 31, where Herodotus explains that the so-called feathers are snow-flakes.

⁴ The principal Greek cities upon the Pontus were the following:—1. On the south coast, Heraclea Pontica (the modern *Erekli*, a colony of the Megarians; Sinope, which retains its name, a colony of the Milesians; Trapezus (*Trebizond*) and Cotyora (*Ordu*), colonies from Sinope itself; and Amisus (*Samsun*), a colony of the Phocaeans re-established by the Athenians (cf. Strab. xii. p. 792, with Scymnus Chius, Fr. 161; and Arrian, Peripl. P. Eux. p. 126. 2. On the east coast, Phasis (*Poti*) and Dioscurias (near *Sukhum Kaleh*), colonies of the Milesians (Steph. Byz. ad voc. Φᾶσις; Arrian, Peripl. P. Eux. p. 123). 3. On the north, Panticapaeum and Phanago-

reia, guarding the Straits of Kertch—the former a colony of the Milesians, and in later times the capital of the kingdom of the Bosphorus—the latter a colony of the Teians (Anon. Peripl. P. E. p. 174; Scymn. Ch. Fr. 153); Theodosia, at the site of the modern *Kaffa*, also a colony of the Milesians (Arrian, Peripl. P. Eux. p. 131; Anon. Peripl. p. 141); Chersonesus at *Kamiesch*, near Hebastopol, a colony from Heraclea Pontica (Scymn. Ch. Fr. 75; Anon. Peripl. p. 148); and Olbia, or Borysthenes, on the right bank of the *Bug*, a little above its junction with the *Dnieper*, a colony of the Milesians (infra, ch. 78). 4. On the west, Tyras, near the mouth of the *Dniester*; Istrus, or Istria, a little south of the lowest mouth of the Danube; Tomi, 30 miles further south; Odessus, near the modern *Varna*; and Apollonia, now *Sizeboli* (infra, ch. 90), colonies of the Milesians (see Herod. ii. 33; Scymn. Ch. ll. 19, 24, 56; Anon. Peripl. pp. 153, 157, 158, 160, and 162); Callatis and Mesembria (*Mesevri*), colonies respectively of the Heracleots and the Chalcedonians (Scymn. Ch. 10; and Anon. Peripl. pp. 158, 161). Besides these, there were a number of smaller settlements, especially along the southern coast. One or two colonies were likewise planted on the shores of the Sea of Azov, as Tanais at the mouth of the Tanais (*Don*), and Tyto them, Hercules, when he was carrying off the cows of Geryon, arrived in the region which is now inhabited by the Scythins, but which was then a desert. Geryon lived outside the Pontus, in an island called by the Greeks Erytheia,[1] near Gades,[1] which is beyond the Pillars of Hercules upon the Ocean. Now some say that the Ocean begins in the east, and runs the whole way round the world; but they give no proof that this is really so.[2] Hercules came from thence into the region now called Scythia, and, being overtaken by storm and frost, drew his lion's skin about him, and fell fast asleep. While he slept, his mares, which he had loosed from his chariot to graze, by some wonderful chance disappeared.

9. On waking, he went in quest of them, and, after wandering over the whole country, came at last to the district called "the Woodland,"[3] where he found in a cave a strange being, between a maiden and a serpent, whose form from the waist upwards was like that of a woman, while all below was like a snake. He looked at her wonderingly; but nevertheless inquired, whether she had chanced to see his strayed mares anywhere. She answered him, "Yes, and they were now in her keeping; but never would she consent to give them back, unless he took her for his mistress." So Hercules, to get his mares back, agreed; but afterwards she put him off and de-

---

rambd above the northernmost mouth of the Κώρα river (Strabo, xi. p. 755).

[1] The island of Erytheia, near Gades (Cadiz), is mentioned both by Strabo and Pliny. The former says it was distant one stade, the latter 100 paces from the above (Strab, iii. p. 233; Plin. iv. 22). Probably Erytheia was one of the two islands included commonly by the Greeks in the name of Gades (Γάδειρα). See the Voyage of Scylax, sub voc. "Ιβηρία". It is thought by some (Bähr ad loc.) that Erytheia was the little isle of Trocadero, which intervenes between St. Leon and the mainland; but perhaps Mariana is right (Hist. Hispan. L. 21) in supposing that the deposits of the Guadalquivir have joined both Erytheia and the island on which Gades was built to the continent.

[1] The name, Gades or Gadira (τὰ Γάδειρα), has been supposed to be Κύδιοι, "the holy," or Α'ώιτ, "powerful." It is rather Α'ώιω, "an enclosure," which agrees with Pliny's meaning of "Gadir," "in Punic an enclosure" (sepem). Of the then two islands (the E., one was

called Erytheia, or Aphrodisias, or "by the natives 'of Juno,' and according to Timæus the larger (W.) one was called the greater Cotinusa, by the Romans Tartessos, by the Pœni Gadir. The name Erytheia was owing to the Tyrians having originally come from the Red Sea." (Plin. iv. 22; cp. Solin. Hisp. c. 23.) Hesiod, as well as Pliny, mentions Erytheia as the island of Geryon. Strabo describes Gades as inferior in size to Rome alone; it had many large ships trading in the Mediterranean and the outer sea. Pomp. Mela (iii. 6) speaks of "Gades and the temple of the Egyptian (Tyrian!) Hercules there," and of Erytheia inhabited by Geryon, as of a different island (v. Plin. ib.).— [G. W.]

[2] Herodotus considered that the eastern and northern boundaries of the earth were unknown, and that the general belief that the sea encompassed the land was a pure conjecture resting on no certain data. (Supra, iii. 116, and infra, chs. 36 and 45.)

[3] Vide infra, ch. 18.

layed restoring the mares, since she wished to keep him with her as long as possible. He, on the other hand, was only anxious to secure them and to get away. At last, when she gave them up, she said to him, "When thy mares strayed hither, it was I who saved them for thee: now thou hast paid their salvage; for lo! I bear in my womb three sons of thine. Tell me therefore when thy sons grow up, what must I do with them? Wouldst thou wish that I should settle them here in this land, whereof I am mistress, or shall I send them to thee?" Thus questioned, they say, Hercules answered, "When the lads have grown to manhood, do thus, and assuredly thou wilt not err. Watch them, and when thou seest one of them bend this bow as I now bend it, and gird himself with this girdle thus, choose *him* to remain in the land. Those who fail in the trial, send away. Thus wilt thou at once please thyself and obey me."

10. Hereupon he strung one of his bows—up to that time he had carried two—and showed her how to fasten the belt. Then he gave both bow and belt into her hands. Now the belt had a golden goblet attached to its clasp.[4] So after he had given them to her, he went his way; and the woman, when her children grew to manhood, first gave them severally their names. One she called Agathyrsus, one Gelônus, and the other, who was the youngest, Scythes. Then she remembered the instructions she had received from Hercules, and, in obedience to his orders, she put her sons to the test. Two of them, Agathyrsus and Gelônus, proving unequal to the task enjoined, their mother sent them out of the land; Scythes, the youngest, succeeded, and so he was allowed to remain. From Scythes, the son of Hercules,[5] were descended the after kings of Scythia; and from the circumstance of the goblet which hung from the belt, the Scythians to this day wear goblets at their girdles.[6] This was the only thing which the mother of Scythes did for him. Such is the tale told by the Greeks who dwell around the Pontus.

---

[4] Among the Greeks the belt was worn round the loins at the bottom of the cuirass or breastplate, to which it was commonly attached, and which it served to fasten. It was usually closed by a clasp or hooks of metal. (See Hom. Il. iv. 132.)

[5] Diodorus substitutes Jupiter for Hercules (H. 43), which is a trace of the genuine Scythian legend (supra, ch. 5).

[6] It is plain that the whole story as told by the Pontic Greeks (chs. 8-10) is a mere Grecised version of the Scythic tradition (chs. 5-7).

[7] The Scythians represented on the vase figured below (ch. 81), have all belts round their middle, but none appear to have goblets attached. Herodotus, however, would be an unexceptionable witness to the fact.

11. There is also another different story, now to be related, in which I am more inclined to put faith than in any other. It is that the wandering Scythians once dwelt in Asia, and there warred with the Massagetæ, but with ill success; they therefore quitted their homes, crossed the Araxes,[f] and entered the land of Cimmeria. For the land which is now inhabited by the Scyths was formerly the country of the Cimmerians.[g] On their coming, the natives, who heard how numerous the invading army was, held a council. At this meeting opinion was divided, and both parties stiffly maintained their own view; but the counsel of the Royal tribe was the braver. For the others urged that the best thing to be done was to leave the country, and avoid a contest with so vast a host; but the Royal tribe advised remaining and fighting for the soil to the last. As neither party chose to give way, the one determined to retire without a blow and yield their lands to the invaders; but the other, remembering the good things which they had enjoyed in their homes, and picturing to themselves the evils which they had to expect if they gave them up, resolved not to flee, but rather to die and at least be buried in their fatherland. Having thus decided, they drew apart in two bodies, the one as numerous as the other, and fought together. All of the Royal tribe were slain, and the people buried them near the river Tyras, where their grave is still to be seen.[h] Then the rest of the Cimmerians departed, and the Scythians, on their coming, took possession of a deserted land.

12. Scythia still retains traces of the Cimmerians; there are

---

[f] It seems impossible that the Araxes can here represent any river but the Wolga. (Cf. Heeren, As. Nat. ii. p. 258.) To imagine it either the Aras or the Jaxartes leads to inextricable confusion. Araxes (Aras) seems to have been a name common in the days of Herodotus to all the great streams flowing into the Caspian, just as Don has been to all the great Scythian rivers (Tanais, Dnieper or Dniepr, Dniester or Dniestr, Doman, Donaub or Danube, &c., and as Avon is to so many English streams. Whether Herodotus was aware of the fact that there were several rivers Araxes is a different question. Probably he was not. Hence the vagueness and unsatisfactoriness of his geography of the Caspian regions.

That the Wolga was sometimes called the Araxes is evident from the tradition reported by Aristotle (Meteorol. I. 13), Scymnus Chius (l. 128), and the author of the Periplus (p. 138), that the Tanais branched off from the Araxes. This Araxes could only be the Wolga. [Ara or Aras signified in primitive Scythic the same as Wolga in Arian Slavonic, viz. "great;" and the name was thus applied to any great river.—H. C. R.]

[g] On the Cimmerians, see the Essays appended to this Book, Essay I.

[h] Niebuhr thinks that the Cimmerians, whose tombs might be seen in the time of Herodotus near the Tyras, fell in a last encounter with the invading Scyths; and he uses this as an argument to prove that the Cimmerians fled, not eastward, but westward; entering Asia, not by the route of the Phasis, but by the passage of the Bosphorus. (Scythia, p. 32, E. T.)

Cimmerian castles, and a Cimmerian ferry,¹ also a tract called Cimmeria, and a Cimmerian Bosphorus.² It appears likewise that the Cimmerians, when they fled into Asia to escape the Scyths, made a settlement in the peninsula where the Greek city of Sinôpé was afterwards built.³ The Scyths, it is plain, pursued them, and missing their road, poured into Media. For the Cimmerians kept the line which led along the sea-shore, but the Scyths in their pursuit held the Caucasus upon their right, thus proceeding inland, and falling upon Media.⁴ This account is one which is common both to Greeks and barbarians.

13. Aristeas also, son of Caÿstrobius, a native of Proconnêsus,⁵ says in the course of his poem that rapt in Bacchic fury he went as far as the Issedones. Above them dwelt the Arimaspi, men with one eye; still further, the gold-guarding Griffins;⁶ and beyond these, the Hyperboreans, who extended to the sea. Except the Hyperboreans, all these nations, beginning with the Arimaspi, were continually encroaching upon their neighbours.

Hence it came to pass that the Arimaspi drove the Issedonians from their country, while the Issedonians dispossessed the Scyths; and the Scyths, pressing upon the Cimmerians, who dwelt on the shores of the Southern Sea,¹ forced them to leave their land." Thus even Aristeas does not agree in his account of this region with the Scythians.

14. The birthplace of Aristeas, the poet who sung of these things, I have already mentioned. I will now relate a tale which I heard concerning him both at Proconnêsus and at Cyzicus. Aristeas, they said, who belonged to one of the noblest families in the island, had entered one day into a fuller's shop, when he suddenly dropt down dead. Hereupon the fuller shut up his shop, and went to tell Aristeas' kindred what had happened. The report of the death had just spread through the town, when a certain Cyzicenian, lately arrived from Artaca,² contradicted the rumour, affirming that he had met Aristeas on his road to Cyzicus, and had spoken with him. This man, therefore, strenuously denied the rumour; the relations, however, proceeded to the fuller's shop with all things necessary for the funeral, intending to carry the body away. But on the shop being opened, no Aristeas was found, either dead or alive.¹ Seven years afterwards he reappeared, they told me, in Proconnêsus, and wrote the poem called by the Greeks 'The Arimaspeia,'² after which he disappeared a second time. This is the tale current in the two cities above mentioned.

---

¹ That is, the Euxine, in contradistinction from the Northern Sea, on the shores of which dwelt the Hyperboreans, according to Aristeas. Herodotus himself questioned the existence of this Northern Sea. (Supra, iii. 115, and infra, ch. 45.)

² The poem of Aristeas may have had no special historical foundation, but it indicated an important general fact, viz. the perpetual pressure on one another of the nomadic hordes which from time immemorial have occupied the vast steppes of Central and Northern Asia, and of Eastern Europe. Scythians, Sarmatians, Huns, Tatars, and Turkomans, have in turn been precipitated upon Europe by this cause, while Mongols, Kirghis, Eleuths, Calmucks, and Cossacks, have disputed the possession of Asia.

³ Artaca is mentioned again in the sixth Book (ch. 33). It was a small seaport town on the west side of the peninsula of Cyzicus (Strab. xiii. p. 812, and xiv. p. 910; Scyl. Peripl. p. 84), opposite to Priapus. Stephen calls it a colony of the Milesians (Steph. Byz. ad voc.). The name remains in the modern Erdek, which has taken the place of Cyzicus (Bal Kis), now in ruins, and is the see of an archbishop. Erdek is a town of about 12,000 houses. (Hamilton's Asia Minor, vol. ii. p. 98.)

¹ In later times the story went that Aristeas could make his soul quit his body and return to it whenever he pleased (Suidas, i. s. a.; Hesych. Miles. Fr. 7, A). Here the power ascribed to him is rather that of appearing and disappearing at his pleasure. In the basis of this last, the mere fact of the alternate appearance and disappearance of an enterprising traveller ?

² According to Suidas (ad voc. 'Apισreas), the Arimaspeia was a poem in three books, containing a history of the Arimaspi. Longinus (De Subl‡m. 10,

15. What follows I know to have happened to the Metapontines of Italy, three hundred and forty years[3] after the second disappearance of Aristeas, as I collect by comparing the accounts given me at Proconnêsus and Metapontum.[4] Aristeas then, as the Metapontines affirm, appeared to them in their own country, and ordered them to set up an altar in honour of Apollo, and to place near it a statue to be called that of Aristeas the Proconnêsian. "Apollo," he told them, "had come to their country once, though he had visited no other Italiots; and he had been with Apollo at the time, not however in his present form, but in the shape of a crow."[5] Having said so much, he vanished. Then the Metapontines, as they relate, sent to Delphi, and inquired of the god, in what light they were to regard the appearance of this ghost of a man. The Pythoness, in reply, bade them attend to what the spectre said, "for so it would go best with them." Thus advised, they did as they had been directed: and there is now a statue bearing the name of Aristeas, close by the image of Apollo in the market-place of Metapontum, with bay-trees standing around it.[6] But enough has been said concerning Aristeas.

16. With regard to the regions which lie above the country whereof this portion of my history treats, there is no one who possesses any exact knowledge. Not a single person can I find who professes to be acquainted with them by actual observation. Even Aristeas, the traveller of whom I lately spoke, does not claim—and he is writing poetry—to have reached any farther than the Issedonians. What he relates concerning the regions

beyond is, he confesses, mere hearsay, being the account which the Issedonians gave him of those countries. However, I shall proceed to mention all that I have learnt of these parts by the most exact inquiries which I have been able to make concerning them.

17. Above the mart of the Borysthenites,[1] which is situated in the very centre of the whole sea-coast of Scythia,[2] the first people who inhabit the land are the Callipedæ, a Græco-Scythic race. Next to them, as you go inland, dwell the people called the Alazonians.[3] These two nations in other respects resemble the Scythians in their usages, but sow and eat corn, also onions, garlic, lentils, and millet.[4] Beyond the Alazonians reside Scythian cultivators, who grow corn, not for their own use,[5] but for sale.[6]

Still higher up are the Neuri.⁴ Northwards of the Neuri the continent, as far as it is known to us, is uninhabited.⁵ These are the nations along the course of the river Hypanis,⁶ west of the Borysthenes.⁷

18. Across the Borysthenes, the first country after you leave the coast is Hylæa (the Woodland).⁸ Above this dwell the Scythian Husbandmen, whom the Greeks living near the Hypanis call Borysthenites, while they call themselves Olbiopolites.⁹ These Husbandmen extend eastward a distance of

---

Dem. {p PolycL p. 1211). It is evident that various other Greek states besides Athens were engaged in the trade; for Demosthenes praises Leucon as giving a preference to Athens over others (Leptin. L. s. c.). If it be inquired what the Scythians got in exchange for their corn, the answer will be wine certainly ; for wine-casks marked ΘΑΣΙ, which had evidently contained Thasian wine, were found in the tomb of the Scythian king at Kertch ; oil probably, and utensils and manufactured goods of all kinds (cf. Strab. xi. p. 494). They may also have taken gold and silver to a considerable extent; for these commodities, which are not productions of Scythia proper, abound in the tumuli throughout the Ukraine. The fertility of the country and the habits of the people remain nearly the same, and the trade of England with Odessa at the present time is the counterpart of that which twenty-three centuries ago was carried on between Athens ' and the Scyths of the Pontus. (See Papers by MM. Hogg and Burgon in the Journal of the Royal Society of Literature for 1835-6, on the pottery of the Greek colonies in the Euxine, stamped amphoræ, &c.; where many interesting particulars will be found with regard to the trade of Athens with Olbia and its sister cities.)

⁴ Vide infra, ch. 105.

⁵ So Ephorus, as reported by Scymnus Chius:—

Ηρώτοι δὲ παρὰ τὸν Ἴστρον εἶσιν Καρπίδαι
Ἔπειτ' Ἀρόται, εἶτεν Ἀροτῆρες, ἐφεξῆς
Νευροὶ τ', ἄχρι γῆς πάσης ἐρήμου διὰ κρύος.
(103-105.)

⁶ The modern Bug or Bouy. See note on ch. 53.

⁷ The modern Dnieper. See note on ch. 53.

⁸ Portions of this country are still thickly wooded, and contrast remarkably with the general bare and arid character of the steppe. " In the vicinity of the great rivers," Madame de Hell says, " the country assumes a different aspect; and the wearied eye at last enjoys the pleasure of encountering more limited horizons, a more verdant vegetation, and a landscape more varied in its outlines. Among these rivers the Dnieper claims one of the foremost places. . . . . After having spread out to the breadth of nearly a league, it parts into a multitude of channels that wind through forests of oaks, alders, poplars, and aspens, whose vigorous growth bespeaks the richness of a virgin soil. . . . These plavnikes of the Dnieper, seldom touched by the woodman's axe, have all the wild majesty of the forests of the new world." (Travels, p. 56.) The woody district extends to a considerable distance towards the east. In the tract occupied by the Mennonite colonies upon the Molochnia Vodi, trees abound. They grow along the banks of all the streams. In former times, when the Dnieper spread out into many more channels than it does at present, it is likely that they were much more numerous than they now are. Still the peculiarly bare and treeless character of the steppe must be taken into account. In order to understand how a region which, after all, is upon the whole somewhat scantily wooded, came to be called Hylæa.

⁹ Herodotus means to say that the Greeks of Olbia gave themselves the name of Olbiopolites, rejecting that of Borysthenites, which others applied to them, but which they applied to the Scythians along the left bank of the river. Concerning the site, &c., of Olbia, vide infra, ch. 78. Like so many of the settlements in these parts (as Phasis, Tanais, Tyras, Istrus, &c.), it seems to have been originally given merely the native name of the river, Borysthenes. (Strab. vii. p. 445.) When, in consequence of its flourishing condi-

three days' journey to a river bearing the name of Panticapes,[1] while northward the country is theirs for eleven days' sail up the course of the Borysthenes. Further inland there is a vast tract which is uninhabited. Above this desolate region dwell the Cannibals,[2] who are a people apart, much unlike the Scythians. Above them the country becomes an utter desert; not a single tribe, so far as we know, inhabits it.[3]

19. Crossing the Panticapes, and proceeding eastward of the Husbandmen, we come upon the wandering Scythians, who neither plough nor sow. Their country, and the whole of this region, except Hylæa, is quite bare of trees.[4] They extend

---

[1] tion, it came to be known as Olbia, the original appellation was disused by the inhabitants, and applied by them to the Scyths of the neighbourhood. Borysthenes is never found upon the coins,

Coins of Olbia.

which have always Olbia for the town, Olbiopolitæ (abbreviated into 'ΟΛΒιο) for the inhabitants. (See Kühler's Remarques sur un ouvrage intitulé "Antiquités Grecques," &c., p. 14.) The name Borysthenes is however still applied to Olbia by many of the later writers, as Dio Chrysostom (Or. xxxvi.), Scymnus Chius, and the anonymous author of the 'Periplus Ponti Euxini,' who copies him (p. 151). Mela wrongly distinguishes between the names, and supposes them to belong to two different towns (ii. 1). Pliny says that Olbiopolis, as he terms it, was called also Miletopolis (H. N. iv. 12); but this title is otherwise unknown. Stephen of Byzantium identifies Borysthenes with Olbia, and notes that the latter was the name used by the inhabitants, the former that commonly in vogue through Greece: thus there is nothing strange in Dio Chrysostom ignoring the native term.

[1] Here the description of Herodotus, which has been hitherto excellent, begins to fail. There is at present no river which at all corresponds with the Panticapes. Either the face of the country must have greatly altered since his time, as Professor Malden (see Murchison's Siberian System, p. 574, note) and others have supposed, or he must have obtained a confused and incorrect account from the Olbiopolites. As Sir R. Murchison observes, " There is no indication of Herodotus having crossed the Dnieper." He is unacquainted with the Isthmus of Perecop and with the true shape of the Crimea. Perhaps, as the accounts of Strabo are "not inconsistent with the present state of the country," it is best to suppose Herodotus mistaken. The real Panticapes may have been the small stream in the peninsula of Kertch, from which the Milesian settlement of Panticapæum derived its name (Steph. Byz. ad voc. Παντικαπαῖον. Eustath. ad Dionys. Perieg. 314).

[2] Infra, ch. 106.

[3] Compare the account of Ephorus (Fr. 78):—

Πῶν ἀνατολὰς ἐχδόντες τὴν Σαυροτίκην
γῆν, τὴν Λογγαῖεν 'Υλαίαν (ἢ, Ὑλαίαν) οἰκοδόντων
Σκυθῶν·
Εἶναι δὲ γεωργοὺς γειτόνων ἐκεῖνον ἄλλους,
Σκυθῶν μὲν ἔχθρους ἀπὸ τοῦ καθ' αὐτοῖς·
γαῖα δὲ σπείρου ζῶντα Ἀσβοκάγων Σκυθῶν,
ἔπειτα δὲ πολὺν ὁμοῦ τοπτακοῦ ἔχουσιν,
Τὴν Παντικαποῦ ποδήρη, κ.τ.λ.

[4] The general treeless character of the steppes is noticed by all travellers. De Hell says—" In the steppes" (those of the Ukraine) " there are indeed here and there a few depressions where the grass retains its verdure during a part of the year, and some stunted trees spread their meagre branches over a less unkindly soil than that of the steppe; but these are unusual circumstances, and one must often travel hundreds of versts to find a single shrub'" (p. 58). The country between the Molochnia Vodi and the Don is particularly flat and bare of trees (see Pallas, vol. i. pp. 512, 504, &c., E. T.).

towards the east a distance of fourteen[3] days' journey, occupying a tract which reaches to the river Gerrhus.[4]

20. On the opposite side of the Gerrhus is the Royal district, as it is called: here dwells the largest and bravest of the Scythian tribes, which looks upon all the other tribes in the light of slaves.[5] Its country reaches on the south to Taurica,[6] on the east to the trench dug by the sons of the blind slaves,[7] the mart upon the Palus Mæotis, called Cremni (the Cliffs), and in part to the river Tanais.[1] North of the country of the Royal Scythians are the Melanchlæni (Black-Robes),[2] a people of

[3] Rennell proposes to read "four days' journey" (Geography, &c. p. 71) —and indeed without some such alteration the geography of this part of Scythia is utterly inexplicable.
[4] Vide infra, ch. 56.
[5] The analogous case of the Golden Horde among the Mongols has been adduced by many writers. (Niebuhr, Vorträge, vol. i. p. 188; Grote, Hist. of Greece, iii. p. 320, &c.) Grote notices that in Algeria some of the native tribes are noble, some enslaved.

[6] Taurica appears here to be nothing but the high tract along the southern coast of the Crimea, from Sebastopol to Kaffa. The steppe country to the north of this belongs to the Royal Scythians.
[7] It is not quite clear how Herodotus considered this trench to run. It did not, according to him, extend from sea to sea, but *from the Tauric Mountains* to the Palus Mæotis (supra, ch. 3). Perhaps the position assigned to it by Dubois (from whom the accompanying Chart is taken)

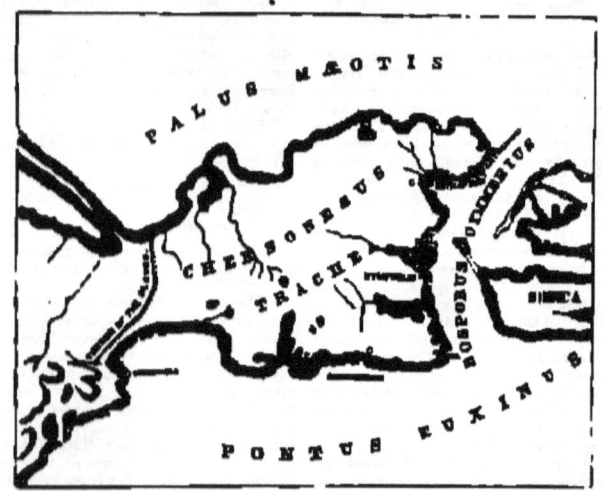

is that which most nearly agrees with the words of our author. But it must be borne in mind, in all comments on his Scythian Geography, that he had no personal acquaintance with the country east of the Borysthenes.
[1] Now the *Ina* (vide infra, note on ch. 57).
[2] Vide infra, ch. 107.

quite a different race from the Scythians. Beyond them lie marshes and a region without inhabitants, so far as our knowledge reaches.

21. When one crosses the Tanais, one is no longer in Scythia; the first region on crossing is that of the Sauromatæ,[3] who, beginning at the upper end of the Palus Mæotis, stretch northward a distance of fifteen days' journey, inhabiting a country which is entirely bare of trees, whether wild or cultivated.[4] Above them, possessing the second region, dwell the Budini,[5] whose territory is thickly wooded with trees of every kind.

22. Beyond the Budini, as one goes northward, first there is a desert, seven days' journey across; after which, if one inclines somewhat to the east, the Thyssagetæ[6] are reached, a numerous nation quite distinct from any other, and living by the chace. Adjoining them, and within the limits of the same region, are the people who bear the name of Iyrcæ;[7] they also support themselves by hunting, which they practise in the following manner. The hunter climbs a tree, the whole country abounding in wood, and there sets himself in ambush; he has a dog at hand, and a horse, trained to lie down upon its belly, and thus make itself low; the hunter keeps watch, and when he sees his game, lets fly an arrow; then mounting his horse, he gives the beast chace, his dog following hard all the while. Beyond these people, a little to the east, dwells a distinct tribe of Scyths, who revolted once from the Royal Scythians, and migrated into these parts.

---

[3] Vide infra, ch. 110.

[4] The ancient country of the Sauromatæ or Sarmatæ (Sarmatians) appears to have been nearly identical with that of the modern Don Cossacks, the northern and western portion of which, along the courses of the Don and the Donetz, is flat indeed and bare of trees, but a good pasture country; while the southern and eastern regions on the left bank of the Don, towards the Wolga and the Manitch, are described as "the Russian desert in all its uniformity." (De Hell, p. 147.)

[5] Vide infra, ch. 108.

[6] The Thyssa-getæ appear to be a branch of the Gothic family, "the lesser Goths" as distinguished from the Massa-getæ, "the greater Goths." They are placed in the same region by Pliny (H. N. iv. 12) and Mela i. 19. See Note A at the end of the Appendix to this Book.

[7] Pliny and Mela (l. s. c.) turn the Iyrcæ of Herodotus into Turcæ, or Turks. But we cannot suppose Herodotus to have meant the Turks, unless we change the reading. [It is, moreover, exceedingly doubtful if the name of Türk is of this antiquity, or at any rate if the name could have been known so early in Europe. To all appearance Türk is a contraction of Türükta, which again is the Pali form of Turushka, the Sanscrit name for the Tartar inhabitants of the snowy range and the plains beyond. In the native traditions of Central Asia the name of Türk is supposed to be derived from Tü'ü, "a helmet," and there is some show of probability in this etymology, as the term of Tirkh'eri, or "helmet-bearers," is applied in the Inscriptions of Darius as an ethnic title to the Asiatic Greeks. —H. C. R.]

23. As far as their country, the tract of land whereof I have been speaking is all a smooth plain, and the soil deep; beyond you enter on a region which is rugged and stony. Passing over a great extent of this rough country, you come to a people dwelling at the foot of lofty mountains,[1] who are said to be all—both men and women—bald from their birth,[2] to have flat noses, and very long chins.[3] These people speak a language of their own, but the dress which they wear is the same as the Scythian. They live on the fruit of a certain tree, the name of which is Ponticum;[4] in size it is about equal to our fig-tree, and it bears a fruit like a bean, with a stone inside. When the fruit is ripe, they strain it through cloths; the juice which runs off is black and thick, and is called by the natives "aschy." They lap this up with their tongues, and also mix it with milk for a drink; while they make the lees, which are solid, into cakes, and eat them instead of meat; for they have but few sheep in their country, in which there is no good pasturage. Each of them dwells under a tree, and they cover the tree in winter with a

---

[1] These mountains can be no others than the chain of the Ural; and thus we obtain the general direction of this line of nations, which is seen to extend from the Palus Mæotis towards the north-east, and to terminate in the Ural chain, probably about latitude 55°. It is an ingenious conjecture of Heeren's (As. Nat. ii. p. 289), strongly supported by the words of our author in ch. 24, that the Greeks of the Pontus carried on a regular trade (chiefly for furs) with these nations, and that the line described by Herodotus is the route of the caravans.

With respect to the exact districts inhabited by the Budini, Thyssagetæ, Iyrcæ, and Argippæi, I agree with Mr. Grote that "it is impossible to fix with precision the geography of these different tribes." (Hist. of Greece, vol. ii. p. 328.)

[2] Although a race of men absolutely without hair may be a fable, yet it is a fact that scanty hair characterises several of the wandering tribes of Northern Asia. (See Prichard's Nat. Hist. of Man, p. 48.)

[3] Some scholars translate γένεια in this place, not "chins," but "beards." Schweighæuser (Lex. Herod. ad voc.) inclines to this. Col. Mure (Lit. of Greece, iv. p. 380) adopts it positively. But γένειον is most properly "the chin; γένεια "the beard." (See Etym. Mag. ad voc. γένειον. "Γένειάδες, αἱ μετὰ τῶν γενείων γινόμεναι τρίχες.")

[4] Heeren (As. Nat. ii. p. 279) conjectures that this is the Prunus Padus of Linnæus, a species of cherry, which is eaten by the Calmucks of the present day in almost the same manner. "The Calmucks," he says, quoting as his authority Neumich's Polyglot Dictionary of Natural History, "dress the berries of this tree with milk, then press them in a sieve, and afterwards form them into a thick mass, which is called moiwn chai, a small piece of which, mixed with water, makes a nutritious and palatable soup." [A similar process is pursued in the manufacture of "brick tea," which forms one of the chief luxuries of the Turcoman and Calmuck "cuisine."—H. C. R.] To conclude from this that the Argippæi were Calmucks, is, however, somewhat over bold. There is little resemblance between the portraiture given of the Argippæi by our author, and that which Pallas and other writers have furnished of the Calmucks. These last have no tendency to baldness, and though their nose is depressed in the upper part, it is not what the word ϭιμὸς indicates, which is the flat nose of the negro; their chin also is remarkably short. (See Pallas, as quoted by Dr. Prichard, Natural Hist. of Man, p. 215.)

cloth of thick white felt, but take off the covering in the summertime. No one harms these people, for they are looked upon as sacred,—they do not even possess any warlike weapons. When their neighbours fall out, they make up the quarrel; and when one flies to them for refuge, he is safe from all hurt. They are called the Argippæans.³

24. Up to this point the territory of which we are speaking is very completely explored, and all the nations between the coast and the bald-headed men are well known to us. For some of the Scythians are accustomed to penetrate as far, of whom inquiry may easily be made, and Greeks also go there from the mart on the Borysthenes,⁴ and from the other marts along the Euxine. The Scythians who make this journey communicate with the inhabitants by means of seven interpreters and seven languages.⁵

25. Thus far therefore the land is known; but beyond the bald-headed men lies a region of which no one can give any exact account. Lofty and precipitous mountains, which are never crossed, bar further progress.⁶ The bald men say, but it does not seem to me credible, that the people who live in these mountains have feet like goats; and that after passing them you find another race of men, who sleep during one half of the year.⁷ This latter statement appears to me quite unworthy of credit.

---

³ Pliny (H. N. vi. 14) and Mela (i. 19, call the Argippæans by the name of Arimphæans. In their account of them they simply follow Herodotus.
⁴ Vide supra, ch. 17. note.
⁵ Herodotus probably intends the languages of the Scythians, the Sauromatæ, the Budini, the Geloni, the Thyssagetæ, the Iyrcæ, and the Argippæans. But it may be questioned whether the traders would have had to pass through all these tribes.
⁶ Heeren considers the mountains here spoken of to be the Altai (As. Nat. ii. p. 272); but to me it seems that Herodotus in these chapters speaks only of a single mountain-chain, and that is the Ural. The country is flat and deep-soiled all the way from the Palus Mæotis to the Refugee Scythians; then it begins to be rough and stony. Passing this rough country, which cannot, I think, represent the Ural, we come to the Argippæans, who dwell at the base of a lofty mountain-range. Here we have the first mention of mountains. Separated from the Argippæans by the

inaccessible peaks of this chain dwell the Issedonians. I should therefore place the Argippæans to the east, and the Issedonians to the west of the Ural range, in lat. 54° to 56°. This agrees with the statements of Book I. ch. 201, that the Issedonians are "opposite,"—that is, in the same longitude as the Massagetæ.
⁷ The remark of Heeren, that "in this tradition we can perceive a ray of truth, inasmuch as we know that the polar regions continue for six months, more or less, without having the light of the sun" (As. Nat. l. s. c.), is not altogether happy. It does not seem likely that any account could have reached Herodotus of what only takes place very near the pole. A different explanation will be found in the Appendix (Essay iii. § 7). [The Orientals, however, have the same idea of the zodiac, or region of darkness, in the far north, which was supposed to be visited by Alexander the Great, and which is alluded to in the Koran.— H. C. R.]

The region east of the bald-headed men is well known to be inhabited by the Issedonians,* but the tract that lies to the north of these two nations is entirely unknown, except by the accounts which they give of it.

26. The Issedonians are said to have the following customs. When a man's father dies, all the near relatives bring sheep to the house; which are sacrificed, and their flesh cut in pieces, while at the same time the dead body undergoes the like treatment. The two sorts of flesh are afterwards mixed together, and the whole is served up at a banquet. The head of the dead man is treated differently: it is stripped bare, cleansed, and set in gold.⁵ It then becomes an ornament on which they pride themselves, and is brought out year by year at the great festival which sons keep in honour of their fathers' death, just as the Greeks keep their Genesia.¹ In other respects the Issedonians are reputed to be observers of justice: and it is to be remarked that their women have equal authority with the men.² Thus our knowledge extends as far as this nation.

27. The regions beyond are known only from the accounts of the Issedonians, by whom the stories are told of the one-eyed race of men and the gold-guarding griffins.³ These stories are

---

* Damastes, the contemporary of Herodotus, placed the Issedonians immediately above the Scythians. Above them were the Arimaspi, extending to the Riphaean mountains. Beyond these were the Hyperboreans, reaching to the Northern Sea (Fr. 1). The Issedonians were also mentioned by Hecataeus (Fr. 168).

⁵ Compare the Scythian custom with respect to the skulls of enemies (infra, ch. 65). A similar practice to theirs is ascribed by Livy to the Boii, a tribe of Gauls (xxiii. 24). Rennell relates that he had himself seen drinking-cups made in this fashion, which had been brought from temples in the country which he assigns to the Issedonians (Geography of Herodotus, p. 164).

¹ These were ceremonial observances at the tombs of the departed, annually, on the day of the deceased person's birth. They are to be distinguished from the νεκύσια, which were similar observances on the anniversary of the death. (Hesych. ad voc. γενέσια.)

² It has been usual to except as fabulous all stories of Amazons, or even of any established equality in any nation of women with men. But the travels of Dr. Livingstone have proved that in parts of Southern Africa such a position is actually occupied by the female sex to this day (pp. 622, 623); [and among the Nairs of Malabar the institutions all incline to a gynocracy, each woman having several husbands, and property passing through the female line in preference to the male.—H. C. R.] It is certain also that some nations have affected the government of Queens, as the Idumaean Arabs (see vol. i. p. 385), and compare the account in 2 Kings, ch. x. of the "Queen of the South", and perhaps the Ethiopians.

³ German critics (as Bähr, Völcker, Rhode, Wahl, &c.) have regarded this tale as deserving of serious attention, and have given various explanations of its meaning, which may be found in Bähr's Excursus (vol. ii. pp. 653-5). To me it seems to be a mere Arabian Nights' story, of a piece with those many others wherein large birds play an important part (supra, note¹, on Book iii. ch. 111). Aristeas picked up the tale in Scythia, and from him it passed both to Aeschylus (P. V. 822) and Herodotus. Later writers merely copy from them. The only truth con-

received by the Scythians from the Issedonians, and by them passed on to us Greeks: whence it arises that we give the one-eyed race the Scythian name of Arimaspi, "*arima*" being the Scythic word for "one," and "*spú*" for "the eye."[4]

28. The whole district whereof we have here discoursed has winters of exceeding rigour. During eight months the frost is so intense, that water poured upon the ground does not form mud, but if a fire be lighted on it mud is produced. The sea freezes,[5] and the Cimmerian Bosphorus is frozen over. At that season the Scythians who dwell inside the trench make warlike expeditions upon the ice, and even drive their wagons[6] across to the country of the Sindians.[7] Such is the intensity of the cold during eight months out of the twelve; and even in the

---

tained in the tale is the productiveness of the Siberian gold-region (Murchison's Geology of Russia, vol. I. pp. 476-491), and the jealous care of the natives to prevent the intrusion of strangers. The griffin has been found as an ornament in Scythian tombs, the drawing, however, being Greek. It was the special emblem of Panticapæum, and is often met with on the coins. The Greek griffin is curiously like the Persepolitan (Ker Porter, vol. I. p. 673, pl. 52), and both are apparently derived from the winged lion of the Assyrians, which was the emblem of the god *Nergal*, or Mars.

[4] On these and other Scythic words, see the Essay at the close of this Book, "On the Ethnography of the Scythians."

[5] Macrobius (Saturn. 7) ignorantly reproves Herodotus for saying that the sea freezes.—[G. W.]

[6] See note on ch. 46.

[7] The Sindi are not unfrequently mentioned in the inscriptions of the Leuconidæ, whose subjects they appear to have been (Dubois, 4me Série, pl. xxvi.). They dwelt on the Asiatic side of the Bosporus or Straits of Kertch, in the immediate neighbourhood of Phanagoria (Scylax, Peripl. p. 75; Strab. xi. p. 723; Plin. H. N. vi. 5; Dionys. Perieg. 681; Steph. Byz. ad voc. Ἰνδοί).

remaining four the climate is still cool.* The character of the winter likewise is unlike that of the same season in any other country; for at that time, when the rains ought to fall in Scythia, there is scarcely any rain worth mentioning, while in summer it never gives over raining; and thunder, which elsewhere is frequent then, in Scythia is unknown in that part of the year, coming only in summer, when it is very heavy. Thunder in the winter-time is there accounted a prodigy; as also are earthquakes,* whether they happen in winter or summer. Horses bear the winter well, cold as it is, but mules and asses are quite unable to bear it; whereas in other countries mules and asses are found to endure the cold, while horses, if they stand still, are frost-bitten.

29. To me it seems that the cold may likewise be the cause which prevents the oxen in Scythia from having horns.¹ There is a line of Homer's in the Odyssey which gives a support to my opinion :—

"Lybia too, where horns bud quick on the foreheads of lambkins."²

He means to say, what is quite true, that in warm countries the horns come early. So too in countries where the cold is severe animals either have no horns, or grow them with difficulty —the cold being the cause in this instance.

They are coupled in the Inscriptions with the Mœotæ (Μαίται), the Torctæ, and the Dandarii.

* The clearing of forests and the spread of agriculture have tended to render the climate of these regions less severe than in the time of Herodotus. Still, even at the present day, the south of Russia has a six months' winter, lasting from October to April. From November to March the cold is, ordinarily, very intense. The great rivers are frozen over, and remain icebound from four to five months. The sea freezes to a considerable distance from the shore. The harbours are blocked up, and all commerce ceases till the return of spring.

The summer is now intensely hot. "In these countries there are really but two seasons; you pass from intense cold to a Senegal heat... The sea-breezes alone make it possible to endure the heat, which in July and August almost always amounts to 94° or 95°." (De Hell, pp. 49-50.)

That Herodotus gives a true account of the state of things in his own day is

apparent from the concurrent testimony of Hippocrates (De Aëre, Aquâ, et Locis, § 96) and Ovid (Tristia, and Epist. ex Ponto passim), both eye-witnesses.

² There was a smart shock of earthquake in the winter which M. de Hell passed on the banks of the Dnieper (1838-9). See his Travels, p. 45. Still the description on the whole suits the present day. (See Appendix, Essay iii. § 7, ad fin.)

¹ Pallas is said to have noticed the lack of horns in these regions as extending also to rams, goats, &c. (Mustoxidi's Nove Muse di Erodoto tradotte, &c., not. ad loc.) But it is certainly not the cold which checks their growth. The vast size of the horns of the elk and reindeer is well-known. Indeed heat rather than cold would seem to check the growth of horns. When cattle were introduced from Spain and Portugal into Paraguay, which is 15 degrees nearer the equator, they lost their horns in a few generations (Prichard's Nat. Hist. of Man, p. 48).

² Odyss. iv. 85.

30. Here I must express my wonder—additions being what my work always from the very first affected[3]—that in Elis, where the cold is not remarkable, and there is nothing else to account for it, mules are never produced. The Eleans say it is in consequence of a curse;[4] and their habit is, when the breeding-time comes, to take their mares into one of the adjoining countries, and there keep them till they are in foal, when they bring them back again into Elis.

31. With respect to the feathers which are said by the Scythians to fill the air,[5] and to prevent persons from penetrating into the remoter parts of the continent, or even having any view of those regions, my opinion is, that in the countries above Scythia it always snows—less, of course, in the summer than in the winter-time. Now snow when it falls looks like feathers, as every one is aware who has seen it come down close to him. These northern regions, therefore, are uninhabitable, by reason of the severity of the winter; and the Scythians, with their neighbours, call the snow-flakes feathers because, I think, of the likeness which they bear to them. I have now related what is said of the most distant parts of this continent whereof any account is given.

32. Of the Hyperboreans nothing is said either by the Scythians or by any of the other dwellers in these regions, unless it be the Issedonians. But in my opinion, even the Issedonians are silent concerning them; otherwise the Scythians would have repeated their statements, as they do those concerning the one-eyed men. Hesiod, however, mentions them,[6] and Homer also in the Epigoni, if that be really a work of his.[7]

---

[3] These *thrą* is more properly an *addition* than a *digression*. Probably this chapter was added at Thurii (see the Introductory Essay, vol. I. ch. I, p. 27).

[4] According to Plutarch (Quæst. Græc. vol. II. p. 303) Œnomaüs, king of Elis, out of his love for horses, laid heavy curses on the breeding of mules in that country. Both he, and Pausanias (v. v. § 2) vouch for the continued observance of the practice which Herodotus goes on to mention. Larcher (ad loc.) conjectures that the curse of Œnomaüs was the cause of the abolition of the chariot-race at Olympia, in which the cars were drawn by mules. But as (Œnomaüs, according to the tradition, preceded Pelops (Strabo, viii. p. 515) his curse should rather have prevented the introduction of the mule chariot-race.

[5] Supra, ch. 7, ad fin.

[6] No mention of the Hyperboreans appears in any extant work of Hesiod. The passage referred to by Herodotus was probably contained in the lost poem, entitled Γῆς περίοδος. (Cf. Strabo, vii. p. 436.)

[7] Modern critics consider the Epigoni to have been composed a little later than the time of Hesiod, i. e. about B.C. 750-700. (Vide Clinton's F. H. vol. I. p. 384.) It was an epic poem, in hexameter verse, on the subject of the second siege of Thebes by the sons of those killed in the first siege. It was a sequel to another very ancient epic, the Thebais, which was upon the first Theban war. The first line of the

33. But the persons who have by far the most to say on this subject are the Delians. They declare that certain offerings, packed in wheaten straw, were brought from the country of the Hyperboreans* into Scythia, and that the Scythians received them and passed them on to their neighbours upon the west, who continued to pass them on, until at last they reached the Adriatic. From hence they were sent southward, and when they came to Greece, were received first of all by the Dodonæans. Thence they descended to the Maliac Gulf, from which they were carried across into Eubœa, where the people handed them on from city to city, till they came at length to Carystus. The Carystians took them over to Tenos, without stopping at Andros; and the Tenians brought them finally to Delos. Such, according to their own account,* was the road by which the

---

Epigoni is preserved, and proves this. It ran thus—

Νῦν αὖθ' ὁπλοτέρων ἀνδρῶν ἀρχώμεθα, Μοῦσαι. (Cert. Hom. et Hes.)

Many very ancient writers, among others, Callinus (Pausan. ix. ix. 9), ascribed the poem to Homer. In the judgment of Pausanias (l. s. c.) it was next to the Iliad and the Odyssey, the best of the ancient Epics.

* Very elaborate accounts have been given of the Hyperboreans both in ancient and modern times. Hecatæus of Abdera, a contemporary of Alexander the Great, wrote a book concerning them (see Müller's Fr. Hist. Gr. vol. ii. pp. 384-8). They are, however, in reality not a historical, but an ideal nation. The North Wind being given a local seat in certain mountains called Rhipæan (from ῥιπή, "a blast"), it was supposed there must be a country above the north wind, which would not be cold, and which would have inhabitants. Ideal perfections were gradually ascribed to this region. According to Pindar, Hercules brought from it the olive, which grew thickly there about the sources of the Danube (Ol. iii. 249). When the country had been made thus charming, it was natural to attach good qualities to the inhabitants. Accordingly they were made worshippers of Apollo (Pindar, l. s. c.), observers of justice (Hellan. Fr. 96), and vegetarians (Ibid.). As geographical knowledge grew, it was necessary to assign them a distinct position, or to banish them to the realms of fable. Herodotus preferred the latter alternative, Damastes the former. Damastes placed them greatly to the north of Scythia, from which they were separated by the countries of the Issedones and the Arimaspi. Southward their boundary was the (supposed) Rhipæan mountain-chain; northward it was the ocean. (Fr. 1.) This arrangement sufficed for a time. When, however, it was discovered that no mountain-chain ran across Europe above Scythia, and that the Danube, instead of rising in the north (compare Pind. Ol. iii. 25, with Isth. vi. 34), rose in the west, a new position had to be sought for the Hyperboreans, and they were placed near the Italian Alps (Posidon. Fr. 80, and compare below, note *), and confounded with the Gauls (Heraclid. Pont. ap. Plut. Cam. 22) and the Etruscans or Tarquinians (Hierocl. Fr. 3). A different, and probably a later tradition, though found in an earlier writer, is that which assigned them an island as large as Sicily, lying towards the north, over against the country of the Celts, fertile and varied in its productions, possessed of a beautiful climate, and enjoying two harvests a year (Hecat. Abder. Fr. 2). In this island it is not difficult to recognise our own country.

* Callimachus (Hymn. in Delum, 284, &c.) follows the same tradition as Herodotus. Pausanias records a different one. According to him, the offerings passed from the Hyperboreans to the Arimaspi, from them to the Issedonians, thence to the Scyths, who conveyed them to Sinope, whence the Greeks passed them on to Attica, from which they were brought to Delos. (Pausan. i. xxxi. § 2.) Athenian vanity seems to have invented this story, which

offerings reached the Delians. Two damsels, they say, named Hyperoché and Laodicé, brought the first offerings from the Hyperboreans; and with them the Hyperboreans sent five men, to keep them from all harm by the way; these are the persons whom the Delians call "Perpherees," and to whom great honours are paid at Delos. Afterwards the Hyperboreans, when they found that their messengers did not return, thinking it would be a grievous thing always to be liable to lose the envoys they should send, adopted the following plan:—they wrapped their offerings in the wheaten straw, and bearing them to their borders, charged their neighbours to send them forward from one nation to another, which was done accordingly, and in this way the offerings reached Delos. I myself know of a practice like this, which obtains with the women of Thrace and Pæonia. They in their sacrifices to the queenly Diana bring wheaten straw always with their offerings. Of my own knowledge I can testify that this is so.

34. The damsels sent by the Hyperboreans died in Delos; and in their honour all the Delian girls and youths are wont to cut off their hair. The girls, before their marriage-day, cut off a curl, and twining it round a distaff, lay it upon the grave of the strangers. This grave is on the left as one enters the precinct of Diana, and has an olive-tree growing on it. The youths wind some of their hair round a kind of grass, and, like the girls, place it upon the tomb. Such are the honours paid to these damsels by the Delians.[1]

35. They add that, once before, there came to Delos by the same road as Hyperoché and Laodicé, two other virgins from the Hyperboreans, whose names were Argé and Opis. Hyperoché and Laodicé came to bring to Ilithyia the offering which they had laid upon themselves, in acknowledgment of their quick labours;[2] but Argé and Opis came at the same time as

---

accords with the geographical scheme of Danaster.

Niebuhr (Roman Hist. vol. I. p. 85, F. T.) regards the Herodotean account as the genuine tradition, and conjectures that the Hyperboreans were "a Pelasgian tribe in Italy," and so of the same religion as the Greeks—their offerings were passed round the Adriatic, and so the Greeks might imagine they came from the far north. He remarks on the traces of the existence of Hyperboreans in Italy (Steph. Byz. in voc. Ταραντία.

Heraclides in Plut. Camill. 22;; and notes that the title of the carriers, Περφερέες (from περφέρω,, is almost a Latin word.

[1] Callimachus and Pausanias differ somewhat from Herodotus, but only in unimportant particulars.

[2] The Greek will not bear Larcher's translation—" Celles-ci apportaient à Ilithye le tribut qu'elles étoient chargées d'offrir pour le prompt et heureux accouchement des femmes de leur pays." It is undoubtedly their own δωτίνη (a

the gods of Delos,³ and are honoured by the Delians in a different way. For the Delian women make collections in these maidens' names, and invoke them in the hymn which Olen, a Lycian, composed for them; and the rest of the islanders, and even the Ionians, have been taught by the Delians to do the like. This Olen, who came from Lycia, made the other old hymns also which are sung in Delos.⁴ The Delians add, that the ashes from the thigh-bones burnt upon the altar are scattered over the tomb of Opis and Argé. Their tomb lies behind the temple of Dinna, facing the east, near the banqueting-hall of the Ceians. Thus much then, and no more, concerning the Hyperboreans.

36. As for the tale of Abaris,⁵ who is said to have been a Hyperborean, and to have gone with his arrow all round the world without once eating, I shall pass it by in silence. Thus much, however, is clear: if there are Hyperboreans, there must also be Hypernotians.⁶ For my part, I cannot but laugh when I see numbers of persons drawing maps of the world without having any reason to guide them; making, as they do, the ocean-stream to run all round the earth, and the earth itself to

---

that is intended. Why in that case they are termed not only κόραι, but παρθένοι (ch. 34), it is difficult to conceive. Perhaps Herodotus means that they were unmarried. Compare the expression παρθένιοι ἄδεσι in Pind. Ol. vi. 51, and the Parthenia at Sparta (Arist. Pol. v. 7).

³ Apollo and Diana. (Cf. Callimach. Hymn. in Delum.)

⁴ Olen, according to Pausanias (IX. xxvii. 2), was the most ancient composer of hymns, preceding even Pamphōs and Orpheus. No fragments of his hymns remain, but their general character may be conjectured from the Homeric hymns, as well as from the fragments ascribed to Orpheus and Pamphōs. (Plat. Cratyl. p. 402, D.; Philostrat. Hercle. p. 693.) They were in hexameter verse, and continued to be sung down to the time of Pausanias (I. xviii. 5). It is curious that his Lycian origin should be so strongly attested as it is (Pausan. IX. xxvii. 2; Suidas ad voc.), since his poems were undoubtedly Greek.

⁵ Many ancient writers (as Plato, Strabo, Jamblichus, Celsus, &c.) allude to the story of Abaris the Hyperborean; but none of them throw any particular light on its meaning or origin. He was said to have received from Apollo, whose priest he had been in his own country, a magic arrow, upon which he could cross streams, lakes, swamps, and mountains (Jamblich. de Vit. Pyth. xix. § 91). This arrow he gave to Pythagoras, who in return taught him his philosophy (ibid.). Oracles and charms under his name appear to have passed current among the Greeks (Schol. ad Aristoph. Eq. 725; Villoison's Anecd. Gr. i. p. 20; Plat. Charm. p. 158, B.) According to Pindar (ap. Harpocrat.; cf. Suidas in voc. Ἄβαρις), he came into Greece in the reign of Crœsus. Eusebius (Chron. Can. ii. p. 332) places him a little earlier. Probably he was, like Anacharsis, a Scythian, who wished to make himself acquainted with Greek customs. [It has been conjectured that the arrow of Abaris is a mythical tradition of the magnet, but it is hardly possible that if the polarity of the needle had been known it should not have been more distinctly noticed.—H. C. R.]

⁶ Eratosthenes noticed the weakness of this argument (ap. Strab. i. p. 91). Herodotus cannot, even while combating, escape altogether from the prevalent notion that in geography there was some absolute symmetry and parallelism.

be an exact circle, as if described by a pair of compasses,¹ with Europe and Asia just of the same size. The truth in this matter I will now proceed to explain in a very few words, making it clear what the real size of each region is, and what shape should be given them.

37. The Persians inhabit a country upon the southern or Erythræan sea; above them, to the north, are the Medes; beyond the Medes, the Saspirians;² beyond them, the Colchians, reaching to the northern sea, into which the Phasis empties itself. These four nations fill the whole space from one sea to the other.³

38. West of these nations there project into the sea two

---

¹ That there is a special allusion to Hecatæus here seems very probable. (Vide supra, II. 21, note.) The belief which Herodotus ridicules is not that of the world's spherical form, which had not yet been suspected by the Greeks, but a false notion of the configuration of the land on the earth's surface. The subjoined plan of the world according to Hecatæus, taken from Klausen, represents with tolerable accuracy the view which Herodotus censures.

Plan of the World according to Hecatæus. From Klausen.

² Vide supra, Book I. ch. 104, note ².
³ Niebuhr (Geography of Herod. p. 25, and map) supposes that these four nations must have been regarded by Herodotus as dwelling in a *direct line* from *south to north*. This is to take his words too strictly. Even if he never visited Ecbatana, he could scarcely be ignorant that Media lay *north-west* of Persia.

tracts¹ which I will now describe; one, beginning at the river Phasis on the north, stretches along the Euxine and the Hellespont to Sigeum in the Troas; while on the south it reaches from the Myriandrian gulf,² which adjoins Phœnicia, to the Triopic promontory.³ This is one of the tracts, and is inhabited by thirty different nations.⁴

39. The other starts from the country of the Persians, and stretches into the Erythræan sea, containing first Persia, then Assyria, and after Assyria, Arabia. It ends, that is to say it is considered to end, though it does not really come to a termination,⁵ at the Arabian gulf—the gulf whereinto Darius conducted the canal which he made from the Nile.⁶ Between Persia and Phœnicia lies a broad and ample tract of country, after which the region I am describing skirts our sea,⁷ stretching from Phœnicia along the coast of Palestine-Syria till it comes to Egypt, where it terminates. This entire tract contains but three nations.⁸ The whole of Asia west of the country of the Persians is comprised in these two regions.

40. Beyond the tract occupied by the Persians, Medes, Saspirians, and Colchians, towards the east and the region of the

¹ We have no single word for the Greek ἀκτή, which means a tract jutting out to a considerable distance into the sea, with one side joining the mainland. Attica (named probably from its shape, Ἀττικὴ being for Ἀκτική) and Iapygia were ἀκταί—peninsulas joined to the main by an isthmus were χερρόνησοι.
² Or Bay of Issus. Myriandrus was a small Phœnician settlement on the southern side of the gulf. It is mentioned by Xenophon as πόλις οἰκουμένη ὑπὸ Φοινίκων Anab. t. iv. § 6, and by Scylax as Μυριάνδρος Φοινίκων (Peripl. p. 9). Though the reading in Herodotus is conjectural, it may, I think, be regarded as certain.
³ Concerning the Triopic promontory, see note ⁹ on Book I. ch. 144, and note ¹ on Book I. ch. 174.
⁴ The thirty nations intended by Herodotus would seem to be the following:—The Moschi, Tibareni, Macrones, Mossynœci, Mares, Alarodii, Armenians, Cappadocians, Matieni, Paphlagonians, Chalybes, Mariandynians, Bithynians, Thynians, Æolians, Ionians, Magnesians, Dorians, Mysians, Lydians, Carians, Caunians, Lycians, Milyans, Cabalians, Lasonians, Hygennes, Phrygians, Pamphylians, and Cilicians. See

l. 28, iii. 90-94, and vii. 72-78.) Or perhaps we should retrench the Hygennes, read very doubtfully in iii. 90, and add the Ligyes from vii. 72.
⁵ Since Egypt adjoins Arabia. (See ch. 41.)
⁶ This was the completion of the canal which Neco found it prudent to desist from re-opening, through fear of the growing power of Babylon. It was originally a canal of Rameses II., which had been filled up by the sand, as happened occasionally in after times. (See n.⁹ on Book ii. ch. 158.) Macrisi says very justly that it was re-opened by the Greek kings, Ptolemies; and it is singular that, though Herodotus expressly says it was open in his time, some have fancied that the Egyptians, the people most versed in canal-making, were indebted to the Greeks for the completion of this one to the Red Sea. The notion of Macrisi, that Adrian also re-opened this canal, was owing to a fresh supply of water having been conducted to it by the Amnis Trajanus.—(G. W.)
⁷ The Mediterranean. (See Book i. ch. 185.)
⁸ The Assyrians (among whom the Palestine Syrians were included), the Arabians, and the Phœnicians.

sunrise, Asia is bounded on the south by the Erythræan sea, and on the north by the Caspian and the river Araxes, which flows towards the rising sun." Till you reach India the country is peopled; but further east it is void of inhabitants,¹ and no one can say what sort of region it is. Such then is the shape, and such the size of Asia.

41. Libya belongs to one of the above-mentioned tracts, for it adjoins on Egypt. In Egypt the tract is at first a narrow neck, the distance from our sea to the Erythræan not exceeding a hundred thousand fathoms, or, in other words, a thousand furlongs;² but from the point where the neck ends, the tract which bears the name of Libya is of very great breadth.

42. For my part I am astonished that men should ever have divided Libya, Asia, and Europe as they have, for they are exceedingly unequal. Europe extends the entire length of the other two,³ and for breadth will not even (as I think) bear to be compared to them. As for Libya, we know it to be washed on all sides by the sea, except where it is attached to Asia. This discovery was first made by Necôs,⁴ the Egyptian king,

---

° Niebuhr (Geograph. of Herod. p. 25-26) concludes from this passage, combined with ch. 202 of Book I., that Herodotus imagined the Araxes (*Aras*) to send a branch into the Caspian, while at the same time the main stream flowed onwards in an easterly direction below and beyond the Caspian, and terminated on the confines of India in a marsh. I incline to suspect a more *lapsus*, by which Herodotus has made the river run east, when he meant to say that it ran west.

¹ Vide supra, iii. 98, note.

² In like manner Pliny (Hist. Nat. v. 11) reckons 125 Roman miles (= 1000 stades) from Pelusium to Arsinoë, which occupied the site of Suez. Modern surveys show that the direct distance across the isthmus is not so much as 80 miles English, or under 700 stades. (See note ⁶ on Book ii. ch. 158.)

³ Herodotus made the Phasis, Caspian, and Araxes, the boundary between Europe and Asia. In this he departed from Hecatæus, who, as is clear from his Fragments, regarded the Tanais as the boundary-line. (See especially Fragm. 166 and 168.) The later geographers, Scylax (Peripl. p. 74, Strabo (xi. 1, § 1), &c., followed Hecatæus—and so the moderns' generally. Recently, however, the Russians have determined to consider the Ural River, the Caspian, and their own Georgian frontier as the boundary.

⁴ We may infer, from Neco's ordering the Phœnicians to come round by the "Pillars of Hercules," that the form of Africa was *already* known, and that this was not the first expedition which had gone round it. The fact of their seeing the sun rise on their right as they returned northwards, which Herodotus doubted, is the very proof of their having gone round the Cape, and completed the circuit. He afterwards mentions (ch. 43) another expedition which set out by the Mediterranean, but which was given up. But the Phœnicians sent by Neco were not the only successful circumnavigators of Africa; and Hanno, a Carthaginian, went round it, going through the Pillars of Hercules, and touching at Gades (Cadiz), and returning by the end of the Arabian Gulf. (Plin. ii. 67; and Arrian, Rer. Indic. at end.) He founded several towns on the coast, none of which remained in the time of Vespasian. Major Rennell (p. 738) thinks that he only navigated the western coast of Africa, and that the term of his voyage was "at Sierra Leone, or at Sherbro', and far more probably the latter."

who on desisting from the canal which he had begun between the Nile and the Arabian Gulf,³ sent to sea a number of ships manned by Phœnicians, with orders to make for the Pillars of Hercules,⁴ and return to Egypt through them, and by the Mediterranean.⁵ The Phœnicians took their departure from Egypt by way of the Erythræan Sea, and so sailed into the southern ocean. When autumn came, they went ashore, wherever they might happen to be, and having sown a tract of land with corn, waited until the grain was fit to cut.⁶ Having reaped it, they again set sail; and thus it came to pass that two whole years went by, and it was not till the third year that they doubled the Pillars of Hercules, and made good their voyage home. On their return, they declared—I for my part do not believe them, but perhaps others may—that in sailing round Libya they had the sun upon their right hand.⁷ In this way was the extent of Libya first discovered.

Pliny also mentions a certain Eudoxus, a contemporary of Ptolemy Lathyrus, by whom he was probably sent, rather than "cum Lathoram regem fugeret," who went round from the Arabian Gulf to Gades; and others were reported to have performed the same voyage for commercial purposes (Plin. ib.). The expedition of Hanno dates some time after that of Neco, who has the credit of discovering the Cape and the form of Africa, 21 centuries before Diaz and Vasco de Gama. The former was for commercial purposes connected with India, the latter to settle a geographical question, as is our modern "N.W. passage."—(G. W.)

³ Vide supra, ii. 158.

⁴ They were so called, not from the Greek hero, but from the Tyrian deity, whose worship was always introduced by the Phœnicians in their settlements. Some suppose the two pillars in the Temple of Hercules (on the Spanish coast) had their name transferred by mistake to the two hills of Calpe and Abyla, on each side of the straits. Herodotus evidently considers them on the African as well as Spanish coast (iv. 181, 185; see Dion. Perieg. 64, seq. 73, and comp. Eustath. Plin. iii. Proem.; Strab. iii. 116 seq.).

Strabo says the Pillars were thought by some to be at the end of the straits, by others at Gades (Γάδειρα), by some even beyond this; by others to be Calpe (Gibraltar), and Abila ('Αβίλη, 'Αβίλη, or 'Αβιλυξ. Abila (now Apes-

hill', being the African mountain opposite Calpe. Many say these hills are at the straits; others that they are two brazen columns, 8 cubits high, in the Temple of Hercules at Gades, which Posidonius thinks most probable, Strabo not. Plato (Tim. p. 469) speaks of that mouth called Pillars of Hercules; Strabo (iii. 96) of the influx of the sea at the Pillars and the town of Calpe. (Cp. the Gaditanum fretum of Pliny, iii. 1.) The dollars of Spain have hence been called *columnatæ*, and have two columns on them. Strabo says the Temple of Hercules at Gades was on the east side of the island nearest the mainland.—(G. W.)

⁷ In the original, "the northern sea"—so called here as washing Libya upon the north, and in contrast with the "southern" or Indian Ocean. (Compare ii. 11.)

⁶ This is less surprising in an African climate, where barley, *dura* (holcus sorghum), peas, &c., are reaped in from 3 months to 100 days after sowing, and vegetables in 50 or 60 days. Even Tamerlane (as Rennell observes), in his preparations for marching into China, included corn for sowing the lands.—(G. W.)

⁷ Here the faithful reporting of what he did not himself imagine true has stood our author in good stead. Few would have believed the Phœnician circumnavigation of Africa had it not been vouched for by this discovery. When Herodotus is blamed for repeat-

43. Next to these Phœnicians the Carthaginians, according to their own accounts, made the voyage. For Sataspes, son of Teaspes the Achæmenian, did not circumnavigate Libya, though he was sent to do so; but, fearing the length and desolateness of the journey, he turned back and left unaccomplished the task which had been set him by his mother. This man had used violence towards a maiden, the daughter of Zopyrus, son of Megabyzus,[1] and King Xerxes was about to impale him for the offence, when his mother, who was a sister of Darius, begged him off, undertaking to punish his crime more heavily than the king himself had designed. She would force him, she said, to sail round Libya and return to Egypt by the Arabian Gulf. Xerxes gave his consent; and Sataspes went down to Egypt, and there got a ship and crew, with which he set sail for the Pillars of Hercules. Having passed the Straits, he doubled the Libyan headland, known as Cape Soloeis,[2] and proceeded southward. Following this course for many months over a vast stretch of sea, and finding that more water than he had crossed still lay ever before him, he put about, and came back to Egypt. Thence proceeding to the court, he made report to Xerxes, that at the farthest point to which he had reached, the coast was occupied by a dwarfish race,[3] who wore a dress made from the palm-tree.[4] These people, whenever he landed, left their towns and fled away to the mountains; his men, however, did them no wrong, only entering into their cities and taking some of their cattle. The reason why he had not sailed quite round Libya was, he said, because the ship stopped, and would not go any further.[5] Xerxes, however, did not accept this account

---

ing the absurd stories which he had been told. It should be considered what we must have had he made it a rule to reject from his History all that he thought unlikely. (See the Introductory Essay, vol. i. pp. 81-82.)

[1] Vide supra, iii. 160.

[2] The modern Cape Spartel. (See n. ch. 32, Book ii.)

[3] This is the second mention of a dwarfish race in Africa (see above, ii. 32). The description is answered by the Roujowas and the Dokos, who may have been more widely extended in early times.

[4] So Larcher and Schweighæuser. Bähr and Beloe translate φοινικήϊον by "red" or "purple." But Herodotus always uses φοινίκεος, never φοινικήϊος, in that sense.

[5] It has been conjectured (Schlichthorst, p. 184), with much reason, that Sataspes reached the coast of Guinea in the early part of the summer, and there fell in with the well-known southerly trade-wind, to avoid which our vessels on going out stand across to the South American continent. These winds continuing for many months without cessation, he at last gave up his voyage in despair, and returned home. The previous circumnavigation of Africa had been in the opposite direction, from Suez round the Cape to the Straits of Gibraltar, and had therefore been advantaged, not impeded, by the "trades."

for true; and so Sataspes, as he had failed to accomplish the task set him, was impaled by the king's orders in accordance with the former sentence.⁶ One of his eunuchs, on hearing of his death, ran away with a great portion of his wealth, and reached Samos, where a certain Samian seized the whole. I know the man's name well, but I shall willingly forget it here.

44. Of the greater part of Asia Darius was the discoverer. Wishing to know where the Indus (which is the only river save one⁷ that produces crocodiles) emptied itself into the sea, he sent a number of men, on whose truthfulness he could rely, and among them Scylax of Caryanda,⁸ to sail down the river. They started from the city of Caspatyrus,⁹ in the region called Pactyica, and sailed down the stream in an easterly direction¹ to the sea. Here they turned westward, and, after a voyage of thirty months, reached the place from which the Egyptian king, of whom I spoke above, sent the Phœnicians to sail round Libya.² After this voyage was completed, Darius conquered

---

⁶ The fate of Sir Walter Raleigh furnishes a curious parallel to this. (See Hume's History of England, vol. v. ch. iv.)

⁷ That is, the Nile. Vide supra, ii. 67.

[He does not reckon the river in Central Africa, though it had crocodiles (Book ii. ch. 32), since it was supposed by some to be the same as the Nile.—G. W.]

⁸ Caryanda was a place on or near the Carian coast. (Scyl. Peripl. p. 91; Strabo, xiv. p. 641; Steph. Byz. in voc. Καρύανδα.) It has been supposed that there were two cities of the name (Dict. of Greek and Roman Geogr. vol. i. p. 555), one on the mainland, the other on an island opposite; but the best authorities know only of one, which is on an island off the coast. The continental Caryanda is an invention of Pliny's (H. N. v. 29), whom Mela follows (i. 16). Caryanda was a native city, not a Greek settlement, as Col. Mure supposes. (Lit. of Greece, vol. iv. p. 140. See Scylax, Καρύανδα πόλις καὶ νῆσος καὶ λιμὴν οὗτοι Κᾶρες.) The island lay between Myndus and Bargylia, on the north coast of the Myndian or Halicarnassian Peninsula. It is said to be now a peninsula, being "joined to the main by a narrow sandy isthmus." There is a fine harbour, called by the Turks Pasha Limani (Leake's Asia Minor, p. 227).

The Periplus, which has come down to us under the name of Scylax, is manifestly not the work of this early writer, but of one who lived about the time of Philip of Macedon. (See Niebuhr's paper in the Denkschrift. d. Berlin. Acad. 1844-1811, p. 83, and his Kleine Hist. Schrift. i. p. 105; also Klausen's work, Hecat. Mil. fragmenta, Scylacis Caryand. Periplus, Berlin, 1831, p. 259.) A very few fragments remain of the genuine Scylax. (See vol. i. p. 40, note ⁴.)

⁹ Vide supra, iii. 102.

¹ The real course of the Indus is somewhat west of south. The error of Herodotus arises perhaps from the Cabul river being mistaken for the true Indus. The course of this stream, before its junction with the Indus at Attock, is from N.W. by W. to S.E. by E. Herodotus's informants probably knew this, and imagined the easterly bearing of the river to continue. Still both they and Herodotus must have known that the main direction of the stream was southerly; otherwise it could never have reached the Erythræan or Southern Sea (supra, ch. 37). Niebuhr's map (Geography of Herod.) is particularly unsatisfactory on this point. According to it, Scylax on reaching the sea must have turned, not westward, but southward.

² Vide supra, ch. 42.

the Indians,³ and made use of the sea in those parts. Thus all Asia, except the eastern portion, has been found to be similarly circumstanced with Libya.⁴

45. But the boundaries of Europe are quite unknown, and there is not a man who can say whether any sea girds it round either on the north⁵ or on the east, while in length it undoubtedly extends as far as both the other two. For my part I cannot conceive why three names, and women's names especially, should ever have been given to a tract which is in reality one, nor why the Egyptian Nile and the Colchian Phasis (or according to others the Mæotic Tanais and Cimmerian ferry)⁶ should have been fixed upon for the boundary lines;⁷ nor can I even say

---

³ The conquest of the Indians, by which we are to understand the reduction of the Punjaub, and perhaps (though this is not certain) of Scinde, preceded (as may be proved by the inscriptions) the Scythian expedition. India, which is not contained among the subject-provinces enumerated at Behistun, appears in the list upon the great platform of Persepolis, where there is no mention of the Western Scythians. These last are added upon the tomb-inscription at Nakhsh-i-Rustam, under the designation of "the Sacæ beyond the sea." (Compare Beh. Inscr. col. i. par. 6, with Lassen's Inscript. I. p. 42, and Sir H. Rawlinson's Inscr. No. 6, pages 197, 260, and 294 of the 1st volume of Sir H. Rawlinson's Behistun Memoir.)

⁴ Limited, that is, and circumscribed by fixed boundaries.

⁵ See Book iii. ch. 115, sub fin.

⁶ Here again, as in ch. 12, Larcher translates "la ville de Porthmies Cimmériennes." How a town can serve as a boundary-line he omits to explain. Herodotus undoubtedly intends the Strait of Jenikaleh.

⁷ The earliest Greek geographers divided the world into two portions only, Europe and Asia, in the latter of which they included Libya. This was the division of Hecatæus. (See Muller's Preface to the Fr. Hist. Gr. vol. i. p. x., and compare Mure's Lit. of Greece. vol. iv. p. 547. See also above, ch. 36, and note ad loc.) Traces of it appear among Greeks later than Herodotus, as in the Fragments of Hippias of Elis, who seems to have made but these two continents (Fr. 4), and in the Panegyric of Isocrates (p. 179, ed. Baiter). The threefold division was, however, far more generally received both in his day and afterwards. (Vide supra, ii. 16, 17, and see the geographers, passim.) It is curious that in Roman times we once more find the double division, with the difference that Africa is ascribed to Europe. (Sallust. Bell. Jug. 17. § 3. Comp. Varro de Ling. Lat. v. 31, and Agathemer, li. 2, ad fin.)

With respect to the boundaries of the continents, it appears that in the earliest times, when only Europe and Asia were recognised, the Phasis, which was regarded as running from the Caspian—a gulf of the circumambient ocean—into the Euxine, was accepted as the true separator between the two continents. Agathemer calls this "the ancient view" (I. 1), and it is found, not only in Herodotus, but in Æschylus (Prom. Solut. Fr. 2, τῇ μὲν δίδυμον χθονὸς Εὐρώπης μέγαν ἠδ᾽ Ἀσίας τέρμονα Φάσιν). We may gather from Dionysius (Perieg. 20, 21) that it continued among the later Greeks to dispute the ground with the more ordinary theory, which Herodotus here rejects—that the Palus Mæotis and the Tanais were the boundary. This latter view is adopted, however, almost exclusively by the later writers. (Cf. Scylax, Peripl. p. 72; Strabo, ii. p. 166; Plin. II. N. iii. 1; Arrian. Peripl. P. E. p. 131; Ptolem. II. 1; Dionys. Perieg. 14; Mela, i. 3; Anon. Peripl. P. E. p. 133; Agathemer, ii. 6; Armen. Geograph. § 10, &c.) Ptolemy, with his usual accuracy, adds to it, that where the Tanais fails the boundary is the meridian produced thence northwards. In modern times Europe has recovered a portion of what it thus lost to Asia, being extended eastward first to the Wolga, and more

who gave the three tracts their names, or whence they took the epithets. According to the Greeks in general, Libya was so called after a certain Libya, a native woman,¹ and Asia after the wife of Prometheus. The Lydians, however, put in a claim to the latter name,² which, they declare, was not derived from Asia the wife of Prometheus, but from Asies, the son of Cotys, and grandson of Manes, who also gave name to the tribe Asias at Sardis. As for Europe, no one can say whether it is surrounded by the sea or not, neither is it known whence the name of Europe was derived,¹ nor who gave it name, unless we say that Europe was so called after the Tyrian Europé,² and before her time was nameless, like the other divisions. But it is certain that Europé was an Asiatic, and never even set foot on the land which the Greeks now call Europe, only sailing from Phœnicia to Crete, and from Crete to Lycia. However let us quit these matters. We shall ourselves continue to use the names³ which custom sanctions.

---

recently to the Ural river. The question of the boundary-line between Asia and Africa has been already treated (see Book ii. ch. 17, note ᵇ).

¹ Of the Libya here mentioned as a "native woman" we have no other account. Andron of Halicarnassus made Libya, like Asia and Europé, a daughter of Oceanus (Fr. 1). Others derived the three names from three men, Europus, Asius, and Libyus (Eustath. ad Dion. Per. 170). There was no uniform tradition on the subject.

² See vol. i. Essay i. p. 288, 789. This was the view of Lycophron (Eustath. ad Dionys. Perieg. 270).

¹ The name of Europe is evidently taken from the Semitic word ereb (the Arabic gharb), the "western" land sought for and colonised from Phœnicia. (See n. ¹ on Book ii. ch. 44.) [G. W.]

² According to Hegesippus (Fr. 6) there were three Europés—one a daughter of Ocean, another a Phœnician princess, the daughter of Agenor, and the third a native of Thrace. In search of whom Cadmus left Asia. He derives the name of Europe from the last; Hipplas (Fr. 4; and Andron (l. s. c.) derive it from the first; Herodotus and Eustathius from the second. (See Eustath. ad Dion. Per. l. s. c.)

³ The question of whence these names, two of which still continue in use, were really derived, is one of some interest.

There are grounds for believing Europe and Asia to have originally signified "the west" and "the east" respectively. Both are Semitic terms, and probably passed to the Greeks from the Phœnicians. Europe is the Hebrew ערב, the Assyrian *ereb*, the Greek Ἔρεβος, the Arabic *ghurb* and *Arab*. It signifies "setting," "the west," "darkness." Asia is from the Hebrew איצא (whence יצא, "the east"), Assyrian *aru*, "to rise," or "go forth". It is an adjectival or participial form from this root (comp. מוצא, 2 Chr. xxxii. 21); and thus signifies "going forth," "rising," or "the east." The Greeks first applied the title to that portion of the eastern continent which lay nearest them, and with which they became first acquainted—the coast of Asia Minor opposite the Cyclades; whence they extended it as their knowledge grew. Still it had always a special application to the country about Ephesus. With regard to Libya, it is perhaps most probable that the Greeks first called the south or south-west wind λίψ, because it brought moisture (λίβα, comp. λείβω), and then when they found a land from which it blew, called that land Libya; not meaning "the moist land," which would be a misnomer, but "the southern land." The connexion with the Hebrew *Lubim*, לובים (Dan. xi. 43; Nahum iii. 9), who are probably

46. The Euxine sea, where Darius now went to war, has nations dwelling around it, with the one exception of the Scythians, more unpolished than those of any other region that we know of. For, setting aside Anacharsis and the Scythian people, there is not within this region a single nation which can be put forward as having any claims to wisdom, or which has produced a single person of any high repute. The Scythians indeed have in one respect, and that the very most important of all those that fall under man's control, shown themselves wiser than any nation upon the face of the earth. Their customs otherwise are not such as I admire. The one thing of which I speak, is the contrivance whereby they make it impossible for the enemy who invades them to escape destruction, while they themselves are entirely out of his reach, unless it please them to engage with him. Having neither cities nor forts, and carrying their dwellings with them wherever they go; accustomed, moreover, one and all of them, to shoot from horseback; and

living not by husbandry but on their cattle, their wagons the only houses that they possess,[1] how can they fail of being unconquerable, and unassailable even?

47. The nature of their country, and the rivers by which it is intersected, greatly favour this mode of resisting attacks. For the land is level, well watered, and abounding in pasture;[2] while the rivers which traverse it are almost equal in number to the canals of Egypt. Of these I shall only mention the most famous and such as are navigable to some distance from the sea. They are the Ister, which has five mouths;[3] the Tyras, the

archer, although they show the mode in which the Scyths used the javelin on horseback, and in which they shot their arrows on foot.

[1] Compare the earlier description of Æschylus:—

Σκύθας .... εὐνόμους, οἱ πλεκτὰς στέγας
πεδάρσιοι ναίουσ' ἐπ' εὐκύκλοις ὄχοις,
ἐκηβόλοις τόξοισιν ἐξηρτυμένοι.
From Vinct. 734–736.

Hippocrates, who visited Scythia a generation later than Herodotus, gave a similar account, adding the fact that the Scythian wagons were either four-wheeled or six-wheeled. (De Aëre, Aquâ, et Locis, § 44, p. 353.)

It may be doubted whether the ancient Scythians really lived entirely in their wagons. More probably their wagons carried a tent, consisting of a light framework of wood covered with felt or matting (Fig. 1), which could be readily transferred from the wheels to the ground, and vice versâ. This at least is the case with the modern Nogai and Kundure Tatars, who however use also a sort of covered cart

Fig. 1.

(Figs. 2 and 3), not very unlike the caravans of our wealthy gypsies. The subjoined representations of Tatar vehicles are from the works of Pallas (Figs. 1 and 2), and of Mr. Oliphant (Fig. 3).

Fig. 2.

Fig. 3.

[2] The pasture is now not good, excepting in the immediate vicinity of the rivers; otherwise the picture drawn of the country accords exactly with the accounts given by modern travellers. The extreme flatness of the whole region is especially noted. De Hell speaks of the "cheerless aspect of these vast plains, with nothing to vary their surface but the tumuli, and with no other boundaries than the sea." (Travels, p. 36, E. T.) Dr. Clarke says, "All the south of Russia, from the Dnieper to the Volga, and even to the territories of the Kirgisian and Thibet Tartars (?), with all the north of the Crimea, is one flat uncultivated desolate waste, forming, as it were, a series of those deserts bearing the name of steppes." (Travels in Russia, &c., p. 306.)

[3] So Ephorus (Fr. 77), Arrian (Peripl. P. E. p. 135), and the Anonymous Peripl. P. E. (p. 155); but Pliny (H. N. iv. 12) and Mela (ii. 7) mention six mouths, while Strabo (vii. p. 441) and Sallust (c. 19) have seven. There would no doubt be perpetual changes. At present the number is but four.

Hypanis, the Borysthenes, the Panticapes, the Hypacyris, the Gerrhus, and the Tanais.¹⁰ The courses of these streams I shall now proceed to describe.

48. The Ister is of all the rivers with which we are acquainted the mightiest. It never varies in height, but continues at the same level summer and winter. Counting from the west it is the first of the Scythian rivers, and the reason of its being the greatest is, that it receives the waters of several tributaries. Now the tributaries which swell its flood are the following: first, on the side of Scythia, these five—the stream called by the Scythians Porata, and by the Greeks Pyretus, the Tiarantus, the Ararus, the Naparis, and the Ordessus.¹ The first-mentioned is a great stream, and is the easternmost of the tributaries. The Tiarantus is of less volume, and more to the west. The Ararus, Naparis, and Ordessus fall into the Ister between these two. All the above-mentioned are genuine Scythian rivers, and go to swell the current of the Ister.

49. From the country of the Agathyrsi comes down another river, the Maris,² which empties itself into the same; and from the heights of Hæmus descend with a northern course three mighty streams,³ the Atlas, the Auras, and the Tibisis, and pour their waters into it. Thrace gives it three tributaries, the Athrys, the Noës, and the Artanes, which all pass through the country of the Crobyzian Thracians.⁴ Another tributary is furnished by Pæonia, namely, the Scius; this river, rising near

---

¹⁰ For the identification of these rivers see below, chs. 51-57.
¹ For the etymology of these names, see the Appendix, Essay ii. 'On the Ethnography of the European Scyths.' With respect to the identification of the rivers, that the Porata is the *Pruth*, would seem to be certain. Probably the Tiarantus is the *Aluta*, in which case the Ararus will be the *Serrth*, the Naparis the *Pruova* or *Jalomnitsa*, and the Ordessus the *Arditch*. (See Niebuhr's Scythia, p. 39, E. T.) The names *Arditch* and *Serrth* may be corruptions of the ancient appellations.
² This must certainly be the modern *Maruch*, a tributary of the *Theiss*, which runs with a course almost due west from the eastern Carpathians, through Transylvania into Hungary. The Theiss apparently was unknown to Herodotus, or regarded as a tributary of the Maris.
³ Mannert (Geograph. vii. p. 8) proposes to read οὐ μεγάλοι; and certainly it is untrue to say that any great rivers descend from the northern skirts of Mount Hæmus (the modern *Balkan*). It is almost impossible to decide to which of the many small streams running from this mountain range the names in Herodotus apply. The Scius, however, which is no doubt the Oscius of Thucydides (ii. 96), and the Œscus of Pliny (Hist. Nat. iii. 26), may be identified, both from its name and position, with the *Isker*. The six rivers, therefore — the Atlas, Auras, Tibisis, Athrys, Noës, and Artanes—have to be found between the *Isker* and the sea. They may be conjectured to represent the *Tuhra, Pristu, Kara Lom, Jantra, Osma*, and *Vid*.
⁴ The Crobyzi are supposed to be a Slavic population, and the same mentioned by Strabo, vii. 401, and Plin. iv. 12. The name is thought to be retained in the Krivitshi, a tribe of Russia.—[G. W.]

Mount Rhodopé, forces its way through the chain of Hæmus,⁵ and so reaches the Ister. From Illyria comes another stream, the Angrus, which has a course from south to north, and after watering the Triballian plain, falls into the Brongus, which falls into the Ister.⁶ So the Ister is augmented by these two streams, both considerable. Besides all these, the Ister receives also the waters of the Carpis⁷ and the Alpis⁸, two rivers running in a northerly direction from the country above the Umbrians. For the Ister flows through the whole extent of Europe, rising in the country of the Celts⁹ (the most westerly of all the nations of Europe, excepting the Cynetians¹), and thence running across the continent till it reaches Scythia, whereof it washes the flanks.

50. All these streams, then, and many others, add their waters to swell the flood of the Ister, which thus increased becomes the mightiest of rivers; for undoubtedly if we compare the stream of the Nile with the *single* stream of the Ister, we must give the preference to the Nile,² of which no tributary

river, nor even rivulet, augments the volume. The Ister remains at the same level both summer and winter—owing to the following reasons, as I believe. During the winter it runs at its natural height, or a very little higher, because in those countries there is scarcely any rain in winter, but constant snow. When summer comes, this snow, which is of great depth, begins to melt, and flows into the Ister, which is swelled at that season, not only by this cause but also by the rains, which are heavy and frequent at that part of the year. Thus the various streams which go to form the Ister are higher in summer than in winter, and just so much higher as the sun's power and attraction are greater; so that these two causes counteract each other, and the effect is to produce a balance, whereby the Ister remains always at the same level.[3]

51. This, then, is one of the great Scythian rivers; the next to it is the Tyras,[4] which rises from a great lake separating Scythia from the land of the Neuri, and runs with a southerly course to the sea. Greeks dwell at the mouth of the river, who are called Tyritae.[5]

52. The third river is the Hypanis.[6] This stream rises

---

tary in Ethiopia and Egypt, there is of course no reason for its becoming larger towards its mouth. The broadest part is the White River, which is sometimes miles across, and divided into several broad but shallow channels. In Egypt its general breadth is about one-third of a mile, and the rate of its mid-stream is generally from 1¼ to about 2 knots, but during the inundation more rapid, or above 3 miles an hour.—[G. W.]

[3] Too much force is here assigned to the attracting power of the sun. The "balance" of which Herodotus speaks is caused by the increased volume of the southern tributaries during the summer (which is caused by the melting of the snows along the range of the Alps), being just sufficient to compensate for the diminished volume of the northern tributaries, which in winter are swelled by the rains. It is not true that the rains of summer are heavier than those of winter in the basin which the Danube drains: rather the exact reverse is the case. Were it otherwise, the Danube, like the Nile, would overflow in the summer; for the evaporating power of the sun's rays on the surface of a river in the latitude of the Danube is very trifling.

[4] The Tyras is the modern Dniestr (= Danas-Tor), still called, according to Heeren (As. Nat. vol. ii. p. 257, note[1]), the Tyral near its mouth. Its main stream does not rise from a lake, but one of its chief tributaries, the Sered, which rises near Zloczow in Galicia, does flow from a small lake. There is also a largish lake on the Worryacz, near Lowberg, in the same country, which communicates with the main stream of the Dniestr, not far from its source. Heeren regards this as the lake of which Herodotus had heard. (As. Nat. l. s. o.)

[5] A Greek town called Tyras, and also Ophium (Plin. Hist. Nat. iv. 11; Steph. Byz. ad voc.), lay at the mouth of the Dniestr on its right bank. (Ophium in Scylax, Peripl. p. 70; Tyras in the Anon. Peripl. Pont. Eux. p. 153.) It was a colony of the Milesians. (Anon. Peripl. l. s. o.) When the Goths (Getæ) conquered the region about this river, they received the name of Tyri-getæ. (Strab. vii. p. 442.)

[6] The Hypanis is undoubtedly the Bog, a main tributary of the Dniepr. The marshes of Volhynia, from which flow the feeders of the Pripet, are in this direction; but it is scarcely possible that the Bog can at any time have flowed out of them.

within the limits of Scythia, and has its source in another vast lake, around which wild white horses graze. The lake is called, properly enough, the Mother of the Hypanis.' The Hypanis, rising here, during the distance of five days' navigation is a shallow stream, and the water sweet and pure; thence, however, to the sea, which is a distance of four days, it is exceedingly bitter. This change is caused by its receiving into it at that point a brook the waters of which are so bitter that, although it is but a tiny rivulet, it nevertheless taints the entire Hypanis, which is a large stream among those of the second order. The source of this bitter spring is on the borders of the Scythian Husbandmen,² where they adjoin upon the Alazonians; and the place where it rises is called in the Scythic tongue *Exampæus*,³ which means in our language, "The Sacred Ways." The spring itself bears the same name. The Tyras and the Hypanis approach each other in the country of the Alazonians,⁴ but afterwards separate, and leave a wide space between their streams.

53. The fourth of the Scythian rivers is the Borysthenes.⁵ Next to the Ister, it is the greatest of them all; and, in my judgment, it is the most productive river, not merely in Scythia, but in the whole world,⁶ excepting only the Nile, with which no stream can possibly compare. It has upon its banks the loveliest

---

⁷ Compare below, ch. 86.
² Herodotus appears to have penetrated as far as this fountain (infra, ch. 81), no traces of which are to be found at the present day. The water of the Scythian rivers is brackish to a considerable distance from the sea, but there is now nothing peculiar in the water of the Hypanis.
³ The etymology of this term is discussed in the Appendix, Essay ii. "On the Ethnography of the European Scyths."
⁴ That is, between the 47th and 48th parallels. The fact here noticed by Herodotus strongly proves his actual knowledge of the geography of these countries.
⁵ The Borysthenes is the Dnieper. It had got the name as early as the compilation of the anonymous Periplus Pont. Eux. (See p. 150.)
⁶ Something of the same enthusiasm which appears in the description of Herodotus breaks out also in modern travellers when they speak of the Dnieper. "Among the rivers of Southern Russia," says Madame de Hell, "the Dnieper claims one of the foremost places, from the length of its course, the volume of its waters, and the deep bed which it has excavated for itself across the plains; but nowhere does it present more charming views than from the height I have just mentioned, and its vicinity. After having spread out to the breadth of nearly a league, it parts into a multitude of channels that wind through forests of oaks, alders, poplars, and aspens, whose vigorous growth bespeaks the richness of a virgin soil. The groups of islands, capriciously breaking the surface of the waters, have a melancholy beauty and a primitive character scarcely to be seen except in those vast wildernesses where man has left no traces of his presence. Nothing in our country at all resembles this land of landscape. . . . . . For some time after my arrival at Deutchina I found an endless source of delight in contemplating these majestic scenes." (Travels, pp. 56, 57. E. T.)

and most excellent pasturages for cattle; it contains abundance of the most delicious fish; its water is most pleasant to the taste; its stream is limpid, while all the other rivers near it are muddy; the richest harvests spring up along its course, and where the ground is not sown, the heaviest crops of grass; while salt forms in great plenty about its mouth without human aid,[4] and large fish are taken in it of the sort called Antacæi, without any prickly bones, and good for pickling.[5] Nor are these the whole of its marvels. As far inland as the place named Gerrhus, which is distant forty days' voyage from the sea,[6] its course is known, and its direction is from north to south; but above this no one has traced it, so as to say through what countries it flows. It enters the territory of the Scythian Husbandmen after running for some time across a desert region, and continues for ten days' navigation to pass through the land which they inhabit. It is the only river besides the Nile the sources of which are unknown to me, as they are also (I believe) to all the other Greeks. Not long before it reaches the sea, the Borysthenes is joined by the Hypanis, which pours its waters into the same lake.[7] The land that lies between them, a narrow point like the beak of a ship,[8] is called Cape Hippolaüs. Here is a temple dedicated to Ceres,[9] and opposite the temple upon the Hypanis

---

[4] Dio Chrysostom notes the value of this salt as an article of trade with the other Greeks and with the Scyths of the interior (Or. xxxvi. p. 43). The salines of Kinburn, at the extremity of the promontory which forms the southern shore of the liman of the Dniepr, are still of the greatest importance to Russia, and supply vast tracts of the interior. (See Dr. Clarke's Russia, Appendix, No. VIII. p. 759.)

[5] The sturgeon of the Dnièpr have to this day a great reputation. Cavièr (the τάμγος Ἀντακαῖος of Athenæus) is made from the roes of these fish at Kherson and Nicolaef. For a scientific description of the sturgeon of the Dnièpr, see Kirby's Bridgewater Treatise, vol. i. p. 107.

[6] The Dnièpr is navigable for barges all the way from Smolensko to its mouth, a distance of not less than 1500 miles. The navigation is indeed greatly impeded by the rapids below Ekaterinoslav; but still for a month or six weeks in the spring, at the time of the spring floods, they are passed by boats. (See Dr. Clarke's Russia, App. VIII. p. 756; and De Hell's Travels, p. 20,

E. T.) Herodotus does not seem to have been aware of the rapids, which may possibly have been produced by an elevation of the land since his time. (See Murchison's Geology of Russia, vol. i. p. 571.) It is uncertain what distance he intended by a day's voyage up the course of a river, but there seems to be no sufficient reason for altering the number forty in the text, as Malthus and Larcher suggest.

[7] The word in the Greek (λίμνη) is rather "marsh" than "lake," and the liman of the Dnièpr is in point of fact so shallow as almost to deserve the name. "In summer it has hardly six feet water." (Report of Russian Engineers; Clarke, l. s. c.)

[8] This description, which is copied by Dio (Or. xxxvi. p. 437), and which would exactly suit the promontory of Kinburn, applies but ill to the land as it now lies between the two rivers. Has the author's memory played him false, or are we to suppose that the form of the land has changed since his time?

[9] Or "Cybèle," for the reading is doubtful. Bähr gives Μητρὶ for Δήμητρι on the authority of many of

54. Next in succession comes the fifth river, called the Panticapes,² which has, like the Borysthenes, a course from north to south, and rises from a lake. The space between this river and the Borysthenes is occupied by the Scythians who are engaged in husbandry. After watering their country, the Panticapes flows through Hylæa, and empties itself into the Borysthenes.

55. The sixth stream is the Hypacyris, a river rising from a lake, and running directly through the middle of the Nomadic Scythians. It falls into the sea near the city of Carcinitis,³ leaving Hylæa and the course of Achilles⁴ to the right.

the best MSS.; and among the coins found on the site of Olbia, the head of Cybele, with the well-known crown of towers, occurs frequently. 'See Mionnet's Description des Médailles, &c.' Supplément, tom. ii. pp. 14-15.)

¹ Olbia, called also Borysthenes (supra, ch. 18, note ⁹), was on the western or right bank of the Hypanis, as sufficiently appears from this passage. Its site is distinctly marked by mounds and ruins, and has been placed beyond a doubt by the discovery of numerous coins and inscriptions. (Clarke, pp. 614-623; Choix des Médailles Antiques d'Olbiopolis ou Olbia, faisant partie du cabinet du Conseiller d'Etat De Klaramberg, Paris, 1822.) It is now called Stomoyli, "the Hundred Mounds," and lies about 12 miles below Nicolaef, on the opposite side of the Bog. 3 or 4 miles from the junction of the Bog with the limen of the Dniepr. (De Hell, p. 34, E. T.)

It is curious to find Olbia placed on the wrong bank of the Hypanis by Major Rennell in his great map of Western Asia, published so late as 1831.

² On the Panticapes, see ch. 18, note ⁹. This and the next two rivers defy identification with any existing stream. Great changes have probably occurred in the physical geography of Southern Russia since the time of Herodotus. (Murchison's Geology of Russia, pp. 573-577.) The Dniepr in his time seems

to have had a large delta, enclosed within the mouth which he knew as the Borysthenes, and that called by him the Gerrhus, though this latter can scarcely have parted from the main stream at so great a distance from the sea as he imagined. It is possible that there have been great changes of level in Southern Russia since his time, and the point of departure may perhaps have been as high as Kryloe, in lat. 49°, as represented in the map prefixed to this volume; but perhaps it is more probable that the delta did not begin till about Katofka, where the Borysthenes may have thrown off a branch which passed into the Gulf of Perekop by Krimitchik (see Murchison, p. 574, note); or, finally, Herodotus may have been completely at fault, and the true Gerrhus of his day may, like that of Ptolemy (iii. 5), have really fallen into the Palus Mæotis, being the modern Molotchnai, as Rennell supposes. (Geography of Herod. p. 71.)

³ This place is called Carcine by Pliny (H. N. iv. 12) and Mela (ii. 1), Carcina by Ptolemy (l. s. c.), Carcinitis by Hecatæus (Fr. Hist. Gr. vol. i. p. 10, Fr. 153) and Herodotus, Carcinites, or Carcinites, by the anonymous author of the Peripl. Pont. Eux. (p. 148). It gave name to the bay on the western side of the Tauric Chersonese (Plin. l. s. a.; Mel. l. s. c., &c.), the modern Gulf of Perekop. It does not appear to have been a Greek settlement. Perhaps it may have been a Cimmerian town, and have contained the Cymric Carr in its first syllable.

⁴ This is the modern Kosa Tendra and Kosa Djaritgatsch, a long and narrow strip of sandy beach extending about 80 miles from nearly opposite Kolan-

56. The seventh river is the Gerrhus, which is a branch thrown out by the Borysthenes at the point where the course of that stream first begins to be known, to wit, the region called by the same name as the stream itself, viz. Gerrhus. This river on its passage towards the sea divides the country of the Nomadic from that of the Royal Scyths. It runs into the Hypacyris.

57. The eighth river is the Tanais, a stream which has its source, far up the country, in a lake of vast size,[3] and which empties itself into another still larger lake, the Palus Mæotis, whereby the country of the Royal Scythians is divided from that of the Sauromatæ. The Tanais receives the waters of a tributary stream, called the Hyrgis.[4]

58. Such then are the rivers of chief note in Scythia. The grass which the land produces is more apt to generate gall in the beasts that feed on it than any other grass which is known to us, as plainly appears on the opening of their carcases.

59. Thus abundantly are the Scythians provided with the most important necessaries. Their manners and customs come now to be described. They worship only the following gods, namely, Vesta, whom they reverence beyond all the rest, Jupiter, and Tellus, whom they consider to be the wife of Jupiter; and after these Apollo, Celestial Venus, Hercules, and Mars.[7] These

---

tchał to a point about 12 miles south of the promontory of A*iulum*, and attached to the continent only in the middle by an isthmus about 12 miles across. Strabo (vii. p. 445) and Eustathius (ad Dionys. Perieg. 306) compare it to a fillet, Pliny (N. N. iv. 12) and Mela (ii. 1) to a sword. It is carefully described by Strabo, Eustathius, and the anonymous author of the Periplus, less accurately by Mela. Various accounts were given of the name. At the western extremity there was a grove sacred to Achilles (Strab. p. 446), or, according to others, to Hecate (Anon. Peripl. P. E. p. 149). Marcianus Capella placed here the tomb of Achilles (vi. p. 214), who was said by Alcæus to have "ruled over Scythia" (Fr. 49, Bergk.) The worship of Achilles was strongly affected by the Pontic Greeks. He had a temple in Olbia (Strab. l. s. c.), on the coins of which his name is sometimes found (Mionnet, Supplément, tom. ii. p. 32); another in the present Isle of Serpents (Arrian, Peripl. P. Eux. p. 135); a third on the Asiatic side of the Straits of Kertch, at the narrowest point Strab. xi. p. 756); and, as some think, a fourth on a small island at the mouth of the Borysthenes, dedicated to him by the Olbiopolitæ. (See Köhler's Mémoire sur les îles et la course commerciale à Achille; and comp. Dio Chrysost. Or. xxxvi. p. 439.) His head also appears occasionally on the coins of Chersonesus (Mionnet, ut supra, pp. 1 and 3); and in an inscription found at Olbia, and given accurately in Köhler's Remarques sur un ouvrage, &c. p. 12, he is (apparently) entitled "Ruler of the Pontus" (ΠΟΝΤΑΡΧΗΣ).

[3] The Tanais (the modern *Don*) rises from a *small* lake, the lake of *Ivan-Ozero*, in lat. 54° 2'. long. 38° 3'. The Volga flows in part from the *great* lake of Onega.

[4] There are no means of identifying this river. Mr Blakesley regards it as the *Seviersty*, in which he finds "some vestige of the ancient title." I should be inclined rather to look on it as representing the Donetz, if any dependence could be placed on this part of our author's geography. He calls it in another place the Syrgis (infra, ch. 123).

[7] The religion of the Scythians appears by this account to have consisted chiefly in the worship of the elements. Jupiter

gods are worshipped by the whole nation: the Royal Scythians offer sacrifice likewise to Neptune. In the Scythic tongue Vesta is called *Tabiti*, Jupiter (very properly, in my judgment) *Papœus*, Tellus *Apia*, Apollo *Œtosyrus*, Celestial Venus *Artimpasa*, and Neptune *Thamimasadas*.[5] They use no images, altars, or temples, except in the worship of Mars; but in his worship they do use them.

60. The manner of their sacrifices is everywhere and in every case the same; the victim stands with its two fore-feet bound together by a cord, and the person who is about to offer, taking his station behind the victim, gives the rope a pull, and thereby throws the animal down; as it falls he invokes the god to whom he is offering; after which he puts a noose round the animal's neck, and, inserting a small stick, twists it round, and so strangles him. No fire is lighted, there is no consecration, and no pouring out of drink-offerings; but directly that the beast is strangled the sacrificer flays him, and then sets to work to boil the flesh.

61. As Scythia, however, is utterly barren of firewood,[6] a plan

(*Papœus*), while he was the father of the gods, was also perhaps the air; Vesta (*Tabiti*) was fire, Tellus (*Apia*) earth, Neptune (*Thamimasadas*) water, Apollo (*Oïtosyrus*) the sun, and celestial Venus (*Artimpasa*) the moon. The supposed worship of Mars was probably the mere worship of the scymitar (cf. Grote's Hist. of Greece, vol. iii. p. 323). What that of Hercules may have been it is impossible to determine; but it is worthy of remark that Herodotus has no Scythian name for Hercules, any more than he has for Mars. The subjoined representation of a Scythian god is not uncommon in the tombs. M. Dubois calls it "the Scythian Hercules," but there is nothing which determinately fixes its character. It has rather the appearance of a god of drinking.

[5] The probable etymology of these names is given in the Appendix, Essay ii. "On the Ethnography of the European Scyths."

[6] The scarcity of firewood in the steppes gives rise to a number of curious contrivances. In Southern Russia, and also in Mongolia and Eastern Tartary, almost the only firing used is the dung of animals. This is carefully collected, dried in the sun, and in Russia made into little bricks, in Mongolia piled in its natural state about the tents. The Tatars call this species of fuel *argols*, the Russians *kirbick*. (Huc's Voyage dans la Tartarie, tom. i. p. 65; Pallas, vol. i. p. 538; De Hell, pp. 41 and 96.) A similar scarcity in Northern Africa renders the dung of the camel so precious that on journeys a bag is placed under the animal's tail to catch the fuel on which the evening meal depends. (Pacho's Voyage dans la Marmorique, p. 180.)

has had to be contrived for boiling the flesh, which is the following. After flaying the beasts, they take out all the bones, and (if they possess such gear) put the flesh into boilers made in the country, which are very like the cauldrons of the Lesbians, except that they are of a much larger size; then placing the bones of the animals beneath the cauldron, they set them alight, and so boil the meat.[10] If they do not happen to possess a cauldron, they make the animal's paunch hold the flesh, and pouring in at the same time a little water, lay the bones under and light them. The bones burn beautifully; and the paunch easily contains all the flesh when it is stript from the bones, so that by this plan your ox is made to boil himself, and other victims also to do the like. When the meat is all cooked, the sacrificer offers a portion of the flesh and of the entrails, by casting it on the ground before him. They sacrifice all sorts of cattle, but most commonly horses.[1]

62. Such are the victims offered to the other gods, and such is the mode in which they are sacrificed; but the rites paid to Mars are different. In every district, at the seat of government,[2] there stands a temple of this god, whereof the following is a description. It is a pile of brushwood, made of a vast quantity of fagots, in length and breadth three furlongs; in height somewhat less,[3] having a square platform upon the top, three sides of which are precipitous, while the fourth slopes so that men may walk up it. Each year a hundred and fifty wagon-loads of brushwood are added to the pile, which sinks continually by reason of the rains. An antique iron sword[4] is planted on the top of every such mound, and serves as the image of Mars;[5]

---

[10] It may be gathered from Ezekiel (xxiv. 5; that a similar custom prevailed among the Jews. The bones of the ox are said to be used for fuel in Eastern Nepaul at the present day. (Hooker's Notes of a Naturalist, vol. I. p. 213.)

[1] Vide supra, ch. I. 216, where the same is related of the Massagetæ. Horses have always abounded in the steppes, and perhaps in ancient times were more common than any other animal. In the province of Tchakar, north of the Great Wall, the emperor of China has, it is said, between 400,000 and 500,000 horses. (Huc's Voyage, tom. I. p. 57.) De Hell estimates the horses of the Calmucks at from 250,000 to 300,000, their sheep at 1,000,000, but their kine only at 180,000.

(Travels, p. 241, E. T.)

[2] Mr. Blakesley well observes (not. ad loc.) that the expression here used is scarcely appropriate to Scythia, where the people had no fixed abodes.

[3] These measures are utterly incredible. We gather from them that Herodotus had not seen any of these piles, but took the exaggerated accounts of certain mendacious Scythians. How a country almost ἄξυλος was to furnish such enormous piles of brushwood, he forgot to ask himself.

[4] In the Scythian tombs the weapons are usually of bronze; but the sword in the great tomb at Kertch was of iron, so that Herodotus is perhaps not mistaken.

[5] This custom is also ascribed to the Scythians by Lucian (Jov. Trag. § 42, p. 275), Mela (ii. 1, sub fin.), Solinus

yearly sacrifices of cattle and of horses are made to it, and more victims are offered thus than to all the rest of their gods. When prisoners are taken in war, out of every hundred men they sacrifice one, not however with the same rites as the cattle, but with different. Libations of wine are first poured upon their heads, after which they are slaughtered over a vessel; the vessel is then carried up to the top of the pile, and the blood poured upon the scymitar. While this takes place at the top of the mound, below, by the side of the temple, the right hands and arms of the slaughtered prisoners are cut off, and tossed on high into the air. Then the other victims are slain, and those who have offered the sacrifice depart, leaving the hands and arms where they may chance to have fallen, and the bodies also, separate.

63. Such are the observances of the Scythians with respect to sacrifice. They never use swine for the purpose, nor indeed is it their wont to breed them in any part of their country.

64. In what concerns war, their customs are the following. The Scythian soldier drinks the blood of the first man he overthrows in battle. Whatever number he slays, he cuts off all their heads,[6] and carries them to the king; since he is thus entitled to a share of the booty, whereto he forfeits all claim if he does not produce a head. In order to strip the skull of its covering, he makes a cut round the head above the ears, and, laying hold of the scalp, shakes the skull out; then with the rib of an ox he scrapes the scalp clean of flesh, and softening it by rubbing between the hands, uses it thenceforth as a napkin.[7] The Scyth

is proud of these scalps, and hangs them from his bridle-rein; the greater the number of such napkins that a man can show, the more highly is he esteemed among them.[1] Many make themselves cloaks, like the capotes of our peasants, by sewing a quantity of these scalps together. Others flay the right arms of their dead enemies, and make of the skin, which is stripped off with the nails hanging to it, a covering for their quivers. Now the skin of a man is thick and glossy, and would in whiteness surpass almost all other hides. Some even flay the entire body of their enemy, and stretching it upon a frame carry it about with them wherever they ride. Such are the Scythian customs with respect to scalps and skins.

65. The skulls of their enemies, not indeed of all, but of those whom they most detest, they treat as follows. Having sawn off the portion below the eyebrows, and cleaned out the inside, they cover the outside with leather. When a man is poor, this is all that he does; but if he is rich, he also lines the inside with gold: in either case the skull is used as a drinking-cup.[2] They do the same with the skulls of their own kith and kin if they have been at feud with them, and have vanquished them in the presence of the king. When strangers whom they deem of any account come to visit them, these skulls are handed round, and the host tells how that these were his relations who made war upon him, and how that he got the better of them; all this being looked upon as proof of bravery.

66. Once a year the governor of each district, at a set place in his own province, mingles a bowl of wine, of which all Scythians have a right to drink by whom foes have been slain; while they who have slain no enemy are not allowed to taste of the bowl, but sit aloof in disgrace. No greater shame than this can happen to them. Such as have slain a very large number of foes, have two cups instead of one, and drink from both.

67. Scythia has an abundance of soothsayers, who foretell the future by means of a number of willow wands. A large bundle of these wands is brought and laid on the ground. The soothsayer unties the bundle, and places each wand by itself, at the same time uttering his prophecy: then, while he is still speaking, he gathers the rods together again, and makes them up once

---

[1] The resemblance of these customs to those of the Red Indians will strike every reader.

[2] Ammianus Marcellinus relates the same of the Scordisci, most probably a Teutonic people (xxvii. 4); "Hostils captivorum Bellonæ litant et Marti, humanumque sanguinem in ossibus capitum cavis bibunt aviditis."

more into a bundle. This mode of divination is of home growth in Scythia.¹ The Enarees, or woman-like men,² have another method, which they say Venus taught them. It is done with the inner bark of the linden-tree. They take a piece of this bark, and, splitting it into three strips, keep twining the strips about their fingers, and untwining them, while they prophesy.

68. Whenever the Scythian king falls sick, he sends for the three soothsayers of most renown at the time, who come and make trial of their art in the mode above described. Generally they say that the king is ill, because such or such a person, mentioning his name, has sworn falsely by the royal hearth. This is the usual oath among the Scythians, when they wish to swear with very great solemnity. Then the man accused of having forsworn himself is arrested and brought before the king. The soothsayers tell him that by their art it is clear he has sworn a false oath by the royal hearth, and so caused the illness of the king—he denies the charge, protests that he has sworn no false oath, and loudly complains of the wrong done to him. Upon this the king sends for six new soothsayers, who try the matter by soothsaying. If they too find the man guilty of the offence, straightway he is beheaded by those who first accused him, and his goods are parted among them: if, on the contrary, they acquit him, other soothsayers, and again others, are sent for, to

---

¹ It was not, however, confined to Scythia. The Scholiast on Nicander (Theriaca, 613) observes that the Magi, as well as the Scythians, divine by means of a staff of tamarisk-wood (μάγοι δὲ καὶ Σκύθαι μυρικίνῃ μαντεύονται ῥάβδῳ); and his statement with respect to the Magi is confirmed by a reference to Dino. There is also distinct allusion to such a mode of divination in Hosea (ii. 12): "My people ask counsel of their stocks, and their staff declareth unto them." So Tacitus tells us of the Germans: "Sortium consuetudo simplex: virgam, frugiferæ arbori decisam, in surculos amputant, eosque, notis quibusdam discretos, super candidam vestem temere ac fortuito spargunt; mox . . . precatus Deos, cœlumque suspiciens, ter singulos tollit; sublatos secundum impressam ante notam interpretatur." (German. c. 10.) Ammianus Marcellinus notes a similar practice among the Alani (xxxi. 2), and Saxo Grammaticus among the Slaves near the Baltic (Hist. Dan. xiv. p. 288). The superstition with respect to the number three appears in this last, as in so many other instances. (See Mr. Blakesley's not. ad loc.)

² Vide supra, L 105. The existence of this class of persons in Scythia, and the religious interpretation placed upon their physical infirmity, is witnessed to by Hippocrates (De Aere, Aquis, et Locis, vi. § 106-109; see also Arist. Eth. vii. 7, § 6), who calls them ἀναριεῖς. This is probably the exact rendering of the Scythic word, which I should be inclined to derive from *en* (= *an*), the negative (Greek and Zend *an*, Latin *in*- or *ne*, our *un*-), and *oior* (Lat. *vir*, Greek ἥρως, ἀλθηρ, Ἄρης), "a man." This at least appears to me a more probable etymology than Mr. Blakesley's of 'Erdpars' quasi Ferdpoes, arwvi, Venus, according to Herodotus, was in Scythic "Artimpasa" (ch. 59).

Reinegg says that a weakness like that here described is still found among the Nogai Tatars who inhabit this district. (Cf. Adelung's Mithridates, L p. 472.)

try the case. Should the greater number decide in favour of the man's innocence, then they who first accused him forfeit their lives.

69. The mode of their execution is the following: a wagon is loaded with brushwood, and oxen are harnessed to it; the soothsayers, with their feet tied together, their hands bound behind their backs, and their mouths gagged, are thrust into the midst of the brushwood; finally the wood is set alight, and the oxen, being startled, are made to rush off with the wagon. It often happens that the oxen and the soothsayers are both consumed together, but sometimes the pole of the wagon is burnt through, and the oxen escape with a scorching. Diviners—lying diviners, they call them—are burnt in the way described, for other causes besides the one here spoken of. When the king puts one of them to death, he takes care not to let any of his sons survive: all the male offspring are slain with the father, only the females being allowed to live.

70. Oaths among the Scyths are accompanied with the following ceremonies: a large earthern bowl is filled with wine, and the parties to the oath, wounding themselves slightly with a knife or an awl, drop some of their blood into the wine; then they plunge into the mixture a scymitar, some arrows, a battle-axe, and a javelin, all the while repeating prayers; lastly the two contracting parties drink each a draught from the bowl, as do also the chief men among their followers.

BURIAL OF THE KINGS.

71. The tombs of their kings are in the land of the Gerrhi, who dwell at the point where the Borysthenes is first navigable. Here, when the king dies, they dig a grave, which is square in shape, and of great size. When it is ready, they take the king's corpse, and, having opened the belly, and cleaned out the inside, fill the cavity with a preparation of chopped cyperus, frankincense, parsley-seed, and anise-seed, after which they sew up the opening, enclose the body in wax, and, placing it on a wagon, carry it about through all the different tribes. On this procession each tribe, when it receives the corpse, imitates the example which is first set by the Royal Scythians; every man chops off a piece of his ear, crops his hair close,[7] makes a cut all round his arm, lacerates his forehead and his nose, and thrusts an arrow through his left hand. Then they who have the care of the corpse carry it with them to another of the tribes which are under the Scythian rule, followed by those whom they first visited. On completing the circuit of all the tribes under their sway, they find themselves in the country of the Gerrhi, who are the most remote of all, and so they come to the tombs of the kings. There the body of the dead king is laid in the grave prepared for it, stretched upon a mattrass;[8] spears are fixed in the ground on either side of the corpse, and beams stretched across above it to form a roof, which is covered with a thatching of ozier twigs.[9]

In the open space around the body of the king they bury one of his concubines, first killing her by strangling, and also his cup-

from which the subjoined plan and section are taken, was opened at Kertch (the ancient Panticapæum) about twenty years ago. It appeared to be that of a Scythian king, and answered in most respects to the description given by Herodotus. The tumulus which contained it was 165 feet in diameter, formed partly of earth and partly of rough stones. In the centre was a sepulchral chamber 15 feet by 14, with a vestibule (A) about 6 feet square. Both were built of hewn stones 3 feet long and 9 feet high. The vestibule was empty, but the chamber contained a number of most curious relics. The chief place was occupied by a large sarcophagus of yew wood, divided into two compartments, in one of which (B) lay a skeleton of unusual size, shown by its ornaments—especially a golden crown or mitre—to be that of a king—while in the other (FE) were a golden shield, an iron sword, with a hilt richly ornamented and plated with gold, a whip, the remains of a bow and bow-case, and five small statuettes. By the side of the sarcophagus, in the "open space" of the tomb were, first, the bones of a female (G), and among them a diadem and other ornaments in gold and electrum, showing that she was the queen ; secondly, the bones of an attendant (I), and thirdly, in an excavation in one corner, the bones of a horse (H). There were also found arranged along the wall, a number of arrow-heads (J), two spear-heads (K), a vase in electrum (L), beautifully chased (see the next note and compare woodcut in note⁴ on ch. 3), two silver vases (MM, containing drinking-cups, four amphoræ in earthenware (N , which had held Thasian wine, a large bronze vase (O), several drinking-cups, and three large bronze cauldrons (P), containing mutton bones. There was sufficient evidence to show that suits of clothes had been hung from the walls, and even fragments of musical instruments were discovered,

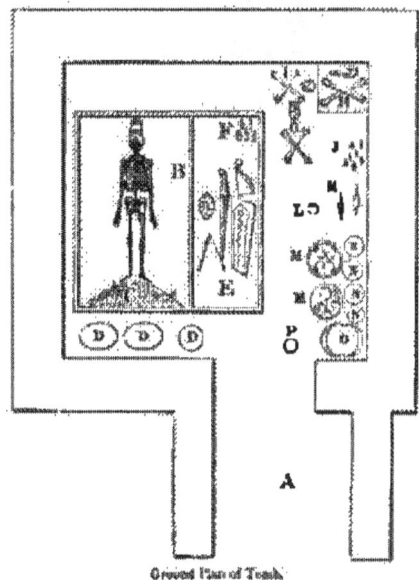

Ground Plan of Tomb.

bearer, his cook, his groom, his lacquey, his messenger, some of

proving that all the king's tastes had been taken into account.

It must be confessed that the tomb above described belongs to a later era than our author, probably to about B.C. 400-350; and that there are abundant traces of Greek influence in the furniture and ornaments of the place. Still the general ideas are purely Scythic, and there can be little doubt that the tomb belongs to one of those native kings, who from B.C. 438 to B.C. 304 held the Greeks of Panticapaeum in subjection (Clinton, F. H. vol. ii. App. ch. 13). Greek ideas had apparently modified the old barbarism, so far as to reduce the number of victims at a king's death from six to two, and Greek skill had improved the method of constructing a tomb; but otherwise the description of Herodotus accords almost exactly with the modern discovery. There is not indeed such an abundance of gold as be describes, and there are implements both in silver and bronze; but here we may either consider that time had brought about a change, or (more probably, that our author indulged in his favourite exaggeration (see Introductory Essay, ch. iii. pp. 82-93). The accompanying plan and section are taken from the magnificent work of Dubois. (Voyage autour du Caucase, &c., Atlas, 4me Série, Pl. XVIII.)

Many other tombs more or less resembling this have been found at different times in various parts of Russia and Tartary. The ornaments are generally of silver and gold, the weapons of bronze, and horses are usually buried with the chief. In the second volume of the Archaeologia (Art. XXVIII.) a description is given of a barrow opened by the Russian authorities, which contained the skeletons of a man, a woman, and a horse, with weapons, and many rich ornaments. The human remains were laid on sheets of pure gold, and covered with similar sheets; the entire weight of the four sheets being 40 lbs. The ornaments were some of them set with rubies and emeralds.

The thirtieth volume of the Archaeologia contains another description of a similar tomb (Art. XXL). This was near Astarabad, and was opened by the Bey in 1841. It contained human and horses' bones; heads of spears, axes, and maces, forks, rods, &c., all of bronze, a vase and cup of pale yellow stone; two mutilated female figures; and a number of utensils in gold. These were a goblet weighing 36 ounces; a lamp (70 oz.); a pot (11 oz.); and

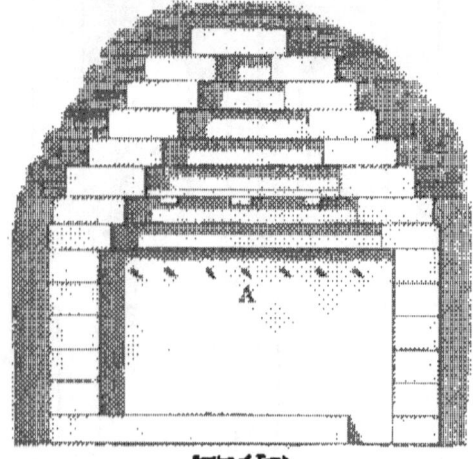

Section of Tomb.

his horses, firstlings of all his other possessions,[1] and some golden cups;[2] for they use neither silver nor brass. After this they set

---

two small trumpets. A portion of the contents was commonly reported to have been secreted by the Key.

The excavations of Dr. M'Pherson in the neighbourhood of Kertch in 1856 were curious, but produced no very important results, as far as Scythian antiquity is concerned. He found the burial of the horse common, not only in Scythic, but in much later times. The great shaft, which he believed to be the burial-place of a Scythian king, and to which he assigned the date of about B.C. 500, appears to me to contain traces of Roman influence, and therefore to be later than the time of Pompey. (See his 'Antiquities of Kertch,' London, 1857.)

A tomb closely answering to the description of Herodotus is said to have been opened very recently near Alexandropol, in the province of Ekaterinoslav (M'Pherson, p. 86), but I have been unable to obtain any account of it.

[1] A very similar custom still prevails in Tartary and Mongolia. "Pour dire toute la vérité sur le compte des Tartares," says M. Huc, "nous devons ajouter, que leurs rois usent parfois d'un système de sépulture qui est le comble de l'extravagance et de la barbarie : on transporte le royal cadavre dans un vaste édifice construit en briques, et orné de nombreuses statues en pierre, représentant des hommes,

des lions, des éléphants, des tigres, et divers sujets de la mythologie Bouddhique. Avec l'illustre défunt, on enterre dans un large caveau, placé au centre du bâtiment, de grosses sommes d'or et d'argent, des habits royaux, des pierres précieuses, enfin *tout ce dont il pourra avoir besoin dans une autre vie.* Ces enterrements monstrueux coûtent quelquefois la vie à un grand nombre d'esclaves. On prend des enfants de l'un et de l'autre sexe, remarquables par leur beauté, et on leur fait avaler du mercure jusqu'à ce qu'ils soient suffoqués ; de cette manière, ils conservent, dit-on, la fraîcheur et le coloris de leur visage, au point de paraître encore vivants. Ces malheureuses victimes sont placées debout, autour du cadavre de leur maître, continuant en quelque sorte de le servir comme pendant sa vie. Elles tiennent dans leurs mains la pipe, l'éventail, la petite fiole de tabac à priser, et tous les autres colifichets des majestés Tartares." (Voyage dans la Tartarie, pp. 115-6.)

[2] The Kertch tomb above described contained eight drinking-cups in silver, and one in electrum, or a mixture of silver and gold (fig. 1). They were principally shaped like the electrum vase, but some were of a still more elegant form, particularly one terminating in the head of a ram (fig. 2). The only implement of pure gold in the

Fig. 1.

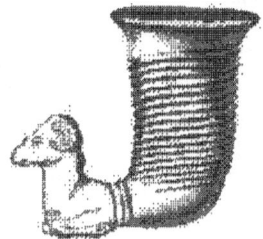

Fig. 2.

to work, and raise a vast mound above the grave, all of them vying with each other and seeking to make it as tall as possible.

72. When a year is gone by, further ceremonies take place. Fifty of the best of the late king's attendants are taken, all native Scythians—for as bought slaves are unknown in the country, the Scythian kings choose any of their subjects that they like, to wait on them—fifty of these are taken and strangled, with fifty of the most beautiful horses. When they are dead, their bowels are taken out, and the cavity cleaned, filled full of chaff, and straightway sewn up again. This done, a number of posts are driven into the ground, in sets of two pairs each, and on every pair half the felly of a wheel is placed archwise; then strong stakes are run lengthways through the bodies of the horses from tail to neck, and they are mounted up upon the fellies, so that the felly in front supports the shoulders of the horse, while that behind sustains the belly and quarters, the legs dangling in midair; each horse is furnished with a bit and bridle, which latter is stretched out in front of the horse, and fastened to a peg.³ The fifty strangled youths are then mounted severally on the fifty horses. To effect this, a second stake is passed through their bodies along the course of the spine to the neck; the lower end of which projects from the body, and is fixed into a socket, made

---

place was the shield, which was of small size.

There was, however, a second tomb below that which has been described, in which gold was much more plentiful. This tomb was plundered, and its contents never scientifically examined, but it is said to have contained not less than 120 lbs. of gold! (See Dubois, vol. v. p. 218, and Seymour's Russia on the Black Sea, p. 288. On the general subject of the riches found in Scythian tombs, see l'ellas's Travels, vol. i. p. 197.)

³ The practice of impaling horses seems to have existed in three regions. It was found, however, among the Tatars so late as the 14th century. See the passage quoted by Mr. Blakesley from Ibn Batuta, the Arabian traveller (not. ad loc.). In Patagonia a practice very like the Scythian prevails. There "the favourite horse of the deceased is killed at the grave. When dead it is skinned and stuffed, then supported by sticks (or set up) on its legs, with the head propped up as if looking at the grave. Sometimes more horses than one are killed. At the funeral of a

cacique four horses are sacrificed, and one is set up at each corner of the burial-place." (Fitzroy's Narrative of the Beagle, vol. ii. p. 155.)

The slaughter and burial of the horse with its owner was "common to the Germans (Tacit. Germ. 27), the Tschuds of the Altai (Ledebour, Reim. I. 231), the Tartars of the Crimea (Lindner, p. 92), the Celtic tribes in Gaul and Britain; the Franks, as evidenced in Childeric's grave; the Saxons, as proved by constant excavation; and the Norsemen, as we read in all the Norse Sagas, and find in innumerable Norse graves. It was common also to the Slavonic nations; to the Russ in the 10th century (see Frahn's edition of Ibn Foslan's travels, pp. 104, 105); to the Lithuanians, Letts, Wends, and the Ugrian population of the Finns." (Mr. Kemble in Dr. M'Pherson's Kertch, pp. 77, 78.)

A horse was killed and interred with the owner so late as 1781. (See the account of the funeral of Frederic Casimir, Commander of Lorraine, in the Hänisische Antiquarius, I Abtheil, I Band, p. 206.)

in the stake that runs lengthwise down the horse. The fifty riders are thus ranged in a circle round the tomb, and so left.

73. Such, then, is the mode in which the kings are buried: as for the people, when any one dies, his nearest of kin lay him upon a wagon and take him round to all his friends in succession: each receives them in turn and entertains them with a banquet, whereat the dead man is served with a portion of all that is set before the others; this is done for forty days, at the end of which time the burial takes place. After the burial, those engaged in it have to purify themselves, which they do in the following way. First they well soap and wash their heads; then, in order to cleanse their bodies, they act as follows: they make a booth by fixing in the ground three sticks inclined towards one another,⁴ and stretching around them woollen felts, which they arrange so as to fit as close as possible: inside the booth a dish is placed upon the ground, into which they put a number of red-hot stones, and then add some hemp-seed.

74. Hemp grows in Scythia: it is very like flax; only that it is a much coarser and taller plant: some grows wild about the country, some is produced by cultivation:⁵ the Thracians make garments of it which closely resemble linen; so much so, indeed, that if a person has never seen hemp he is sure to think they are linen, and if he has, unless he is very experienced in such matters, he will not know of which material they are.

75. The Scythians, as I said, take some of this hemp-seed, and, creeping under the felt coverings, throw it upon the red-hot stones; immediately it smokes, and gives out such a vapour as no Grecian vapour-bath can exceed; the Scyths, delighted, shout for joy, and this vapour serves them instead of a water-

---

⁴ Here we see tent-making in its infancy. The tents of the wandering tribes of the steppes, whether Calmucks and Khirgis in the west, or Mongols in the east, are now of a much more elaborate construction. These *kibitka*, as the Russians call them, are circular; they are at bottom cylindrical, with a conical top, supported on a framework of small spars resembling in their arrangement the rods of a parasol. (Huc, tom. i. p. 62; De Hell, p. 245.) The material is still felt. Further south, in the plain of *Moghan*, towards the mouth of the combined Kur and Aras, Pallas found the Kurds using a method almost as simple as that here mentioned by Herodotus:—"They place," he says,
"two long bent poles transversely, fasten them at the centre above, and fix their ends in the ground; they then cover them with felt, or mats of sedge." (Travels, vol. i. p. 173, note.) May not this last be the material intended by Æschylus when he speaks of the πλεκτὰς στέγας of the Scythians, rather than an osier framework, as Niebuhr supposes? (Geography of Scythia, E. T. p. 47).

⁵ Hemp is not now cultivated in these regions. It forms, however, an item of some importance among the exports of Southern Russia, being brought from the north by water-carriage. It would seem from the text that in the time of Herodotus the plant was grown in Scythia proper. He speaks like an eye-witness.

bath;⁶ for they never by any chance wash their bodies with water.⁷ Their women make a mixture of cypress, cedar, and frankincense wood, which they pound into a paste upon a rough piece of stone, adding a little water to it. With this substance, which is of a thick consistency, they plaster their faces all over, and indeed their whole bodies. A sweet odour is thereby imparted to them, and when they take off the plaster on the day following, their skin is clean and glossy.

76. The Scythians have an extreme hatred of all foreign customs, particularly of those in use among the Greeks, as the instances of Anacharsis, and, more lately, of Scylas, have fully shown. The former, after he had travelled over a great portion of the world, and displayed wherever he went many proofs of wisdom, as he sailed through the Hellespont on his return to Scythia, touched at Cyzicus.⁸ There he found the inhabitants celebrating with much pomp and magnificence a festival to the Mother of the Gods,⁹ and was himself induced to make a vow to the goddess, whereby he engaged, if he got back safe and sound to his home, that he would give her a festival and a night-procession in all respects like those which he had seen in Cyzicus. When, therefore, he arrived in Scythia, he betook himself to the district called the Woodland,¹⁰ which lies opposite the Course of Achilles, and is covered with trees of all manner of different kinds, and there went through all the sacred rites with the tabour in his hand, and the images tied to him.¹¹ While thus employed, he was noticed by one of the Scythians, who went and told king Saulius what he had seen. Then king Saulius came in person, and when he perceived what Anacharsis was about, he shot at him with an arrow and killed

---

⁶ Herodotus appears in this instance to have confounded together two things in reality quite distinct, viz., intoxication from the fumes of hemp-seed, and indulgence in the vapour-bath. The addiction of the Russians to the latter is well-known, the former continues to be a Siberian custom. (See Clarke's Russia, pp. 142-7; Niebuhr's Scythia, p. 47. E. T.) Compare the account in Book i. ch. 202.

⁷ In Russia they had still in Clarke's time "only vapour-baths." (Travels, p. 147.)

⁸ For the site of Cyzicus see note on Book vi. ch. 33.

⁹ Cybèlè or Rhea, whose worship (common throughout Asia; passed from the Phrygians to the Ionian Greeks, and thence to their colonies, among which were Cyzicus and Olbia. (Vide supra, ch. 53.)

¹⁰ Vide supra, chs. 18, 19, and 54.

¹¹ The use of the tabour in the worship of Rhea is noticed by Apollonius Rhodius:—

"μήτηρ καὶ ῥοιηδῷ Ῥείην θυρεοῖς ἰλάσκοντο."
(Argonaut. t. 1139.)

Euripides ascribes the invention of the instrument to Bacchus and Rhea (Bacch. 59). Polybius, Dionysius of Halicarnassus, and Clement of Alexandria, allude to the images, which seem to have been small figures hung around the neck. They were called σφραγίδια. (See Polyb. xxii. 20; Dion. Hal. ii. 19; Clem. Al. Protrept. vol. i. p. 20.)

him.[1] To this day, if you ask the Scyths about Anacharsis, they pretend ignorance of him, because of his Grecian travels and adoption of the customs of foreigners. I learnt, however, from Timnes, the steward[2] of Ariapithes, that Anacharsis was paternal uncle to the Scythian king Idanthyrsus, being the son of Gnurus, who was the son of Lycus and the grandson of Spargapithes. If Anacharsis were really of this house, it must have been by his own brother that he was slain, for Idanthyrsus was a son of the Saulius who put Anacharsis to death.[3]

77. I have heard, however, another tale, very different from this, which is told by the Peloponnesians: they say, that Anacharsis was sent by the king of the Scyths to make acquaintance with Greece—that he went, and on his return home reported, that the Greeks were all occupied in the pursuit of every kind of knowledge, except the Lacedæmonians; who, however, alone knew how to converse sensibly. A silly tale this, which the Greeks have invented for their amusement! There is no doubt that Anacharsis suffered death in the mode already related, on account of his attachment to foreign customs, and the intercourse which he held with the Greeks.

78. Scylas, likewise, the son of Ariapithes, many years later, met with almost the very same fate. Ariapithes, the Scythian

---

[1] Diogenes Laertius says that there were two accounts of the death of Anacharsis—one that he was killed while celebrating a festival, another (which he prefers) that he was shot by his brother while engaged in hunting. He calls his brother, Caduidas (Vit. Anach. i. § 101-2).

[2] The Greek word (ἐπίτροπος) might mean "Regent." But it is unlikely that Herodotus could have conversed with a man who had been regent for the father of Scylas, his own contemporary. A steward or man of business employed by Ariapithes need not have been much older than Herodotus himself. (See Niebuhr's Scythia, p. 38, note 9. E. T.) Mr. Blakesley's conjecture that Timnes was a "functionary representing the interests of the barbarian sovereign at the factory which was the centre of the commercial dealings between the merchants and the natives," i.e. at Olbia, is not improbable.

[3] Herodotus is the earliest writer who mentions Anacharsis. There is no sufficient reason to doubt the fact of his travels, although what Herodotus here relates of his family history is very difficult to reconcile with their supposed date. According to Sosicrates (Fr. 15) he was at Athens in A.C. 592, almost 90 years before the date of his nephew's contest with Darius. But the chronology of Sosicrates is too pretentious to be depended on. Diogenes Laertius (i. 101) tells us that the mother of Anacharsis was a Greek, which would account for his Greek leanings—for his comparative refinement and wish to travel. That the Scythian kings married Greeks we learn by the case of Ariapithes (infra, ch. 78). We may doubt whether Anacharsis deserved the compliment of being reckoned among the Seven Sages (Ephor. Fr. 101; Nic. Dam. Fr. 123). Comp. Hermipp. Fr. 17 and Dicæarch. Fr. 28); but we may properly regard him as an intelligent half-caste, who made a very favourable impression on the Greeks of his day, an impression the more remarkable, as the Greeks were not usually very liberal in their estimate of foreigners. The anecdotes in Diog. Laertius (i. § 103-5) do not show much more than tolerable shrewdness.

TALE OF SCYLAS.

king, had several sons, among them this Scylas, who was the child, not of a native Scyth, but of a woman of Istria.[4] Bred up by her, Scylas gained an acquaintance with the Greek language and letters. Some time afterwards, Ariapithes was treacherously slain by Spargapithes, king of the Agathyrsi; whereupon Scylas succeeded to the throne, and married one of his father's wives,[5] a woman named Opœa. This Opœa was a Scythian by birth, and had brought Ariapithes a son called Oricus. Now when Scylas found himself king of Scythia, as he disliked the Scythic mode of life, and was attached, by his bringing up, to the manners of the Greeks, he made it his usual practice, whenever he came with his army to the town of the Borysthenites,[6] who, according to their own account, are colonists of the Milesians,— he made it his practice, I say, to leave the army before the city, and, having entered within the walls by himself, and carefully closed the gates,[7] to exchange his Scythian dress for Grecian garments, and in this attire to walk about the forum, without guards or retinue. The Borysthenites kept watch at the gates, that no Scythian might see the king thus apparelled. Scylas, meanwhile, lived exactly as the Greeks, and even offered sacrifices to the Gods according to the Grecian rites. In this way he would pass a month, or more, with the Borysthenites, after which he would clothe himself again in his Scythian dress,[8] and

---

[4] Istria, Ister, or Istropolis, at the mouth of the Danube or Ister, was a colony of the Milesians, founded about the time of the Cimmerian invasion of Asia Minor. (Peripl. Pont. Eux. p. 157.) Its name remains in the modern *Wisteri* (vide supra, note * on ii. 33), but its site was probably nearer to *Kostendje*.

[5] Compare Adonijah's request to be given one of his father's (David's) wives (1 Kings ii. 17-25). Such marriages were forbidden by the Jewish law (Lev. xviii. 8, &c.), but they were no doubt common among other nations.

[6] Olbia (vide supra, ch. 53, note.)

[7] It appears from this passage that the native princes of Western Scythia exercised nearly the same authority in Olbia that their brethren in the East enjoyed over Panticapæum and Theodosia. The Scythian dynasty of the Leuconidæ, which bore sway in the country on either side of the straits of Yeni-kaleh, from about B.C. 438 to B.C. 304, had a qualified dominion in the Greek town of which they did not claim to be kings, but only rulers. (See the formula common in the inscriptions of Kertch,

Ἄρχοντος ...... Βοσπόρου καὶ Θεοδοσίης, καὶ Βασιλεύοντος Σινδῶν, καὶ Μαιτῶν, κ. τ. λ. Dubois, 4me Série, Pl. 26; Köhler's Remarques, p. 10, &c.) The position of Scylas in Olbia was perhaps not quite on a par with this; still his coming with an army, stationing it in the suburb, entering the town, and commanding the gate to be closed, are indicative of his having the real rights of sovereignty. The coins of Olbia however did not, like those of Panticapæum, bear the head of a Scythian king; nor did the public acts run in the name of a prince, but in those of a number of archons, who seem to have been usually Greeks (see Köhler, p. 12).

[8] Herodotus never distinctly mentions what the costume of the European Scyths was. It appears, by the representations of it upon the remains found at Kertch and elsewhere, not to have differed greatly from that of their Asiatic brethren (infra, vii. 64). The ordinary head-dress was a cap, or hood, coming to a point at the top, and projecting somewhat in the fashion of the Phrygian bonnet (compare the woodcut

so take his departure. This he did repeatedly, and even built himself a house in Borysthenes,[2] and married a wife there who was a native of the place.

79. But when the time came that was ordained to bring him woe, the occasion of his ruin was the following. He wanted to be initiated in the Bacchic mysteries,[3] and was on the point of obtaining admission to the rites, when a most strange prodigy occurred to him. The house which he possessed, as I mentioned a short time back, in the city of the Borysthenites, a building of great extent and erected at a vast cost, round which there stood a number of sphinxes and griffins[4] carved in white marble, was struck by lightning from on high, and burnt to the ground. Scylas, nevertheless, went on and received the initiation. Now the Scythians are wont to reproach the Greeks with their Bacchanal rage, and to say that it is not reasonable to imagine there is a god who impels men to madness. No sooner, therefore, was Scylas initiated in the Bacchic mysteries than one of the Borysthenites went and carried the news to the Scythians— "You Scyths laugh at us," he said, "because we rave when the god seizes us. But now our god has seized upon your king, who raves like us, and is maddened by the influence. If you think

---

in notes [3] and [4] on chs. 3 and 71); the material being, apparently, felt. On the

body was worn a loose coat, trimmed with fur, and gathered in at the waist with a belt. Loose trousers protected the legs, and the feet were encased in short boots of a soft leather, which generally covered the bottom of the trouser. In the case, at any rate, of the richer classes, all the garments were thickly ornamented with spangles and coins, sewn on to them in rows, throughout. The most common colour, at least near Olbia, seems to have been black (Dio

Chrysost. Or. xxxvi. p. 439).

[2] The town bore the two names of Borysthenes and Olbia (vide supra, ch. 18, note [9]); the former, which Herodotus evidently prefers, being the appellation best known among the Greeks generally, while the latter was affected by the inhabitants. The two names are used, not only by Herodotus, but by Pliny (H. N. iv. 12), Ptolemy (iii. 5), the anonymous author of the Periplus P. Euxini (p. 151), Scymnus Chius (Fr. II. 59-60), and Stephen (ad voc. Βορυσθένης). Strabo (vii. p. 470) and Arrian (Peripl. P. Eux. p. 132) give only the name Olbia. Dio Chrysostom (Or. xxxi.) and Martianus Capella (vi. p. 214) confine themselves to the term Borysthenes.

[3] The Milesian colonists seem to have carried the worship of the Phrygian Bacchus (Sabazius) to Olbia. Hence Olbia was itself called Σαβία, or Σαβία (Peripl. P. Eux. p. 151).

[4] Griffins are common in the ornamentation of objects discovered in Scythian tombs (Dubois, 4ᵐᵉ Série, Pls. 11, 20, 22, and 24), and sometimes adorn the tombs themselves (Pl. 25). Sphinxes have not, so far as I am aware, been found.

REVOLT OF OCTAMASADAS.

I do not tell you true, come with me, and I will show him to you." The chiefs of the Scythians went with the man accordingly, and the Borysthenite, conducting them into the city, placed them secretly on one of the towers. Presently Scylas passed by with the band of revellers, raving like the rest, and was seen by the watchers. Regarding the matter as a very great misfortune they instantly departed, and came and told the army what they had witnessed.

80. When, therefore, Scylas, after leaving Borysthenes, was about returning home, the Scythians broke out into revolt. They put at their head Octamasadas, grandson (on the mother's side) of Teres. Then Scylas, when he learned the danger with which he was threatened, and the reason of the disturbance, made his escape to Thrace. Octamasadas, discovering whither he had fled, marched after him, and had reached the Ister, when he was met by the forces of the Thracians. The two armies were about to engage, but before they joined battle, Sitalces[3] sent a message to Octamasadas to this effect—" Why should there be trial of arms betwixt thee and me? Thou art my own sister's son, and thou hast in thy keeping my brother. Surrender him into my hands, and I will give thy Scylas back to thee. So neither thou nor I will risk our armies." Sitalces sent this message to Octamasadas, by a herald, and Octamasadas, with whom a brother of Sitalces[4] had formerly taken refuge, accepted the terms. He surrendered his own uncle to Sitalces, and obtained in exchange his brother Scylas.[5] Sitalces took his brother with him and

---

[3] Vide infra, vii. 137. Sitalces was contemporary with Herodotus. He died B.C. 424 (Thucyd. iv. 101). Teres, his father, founded the great kingdom of the Odrysæ in the generation after the Scythian expedition of Darius (Ibid. ii. 29). The following table will show the relationship of the several members of this royal house, and the alliances contracted by them with neighbouring monarchs:—

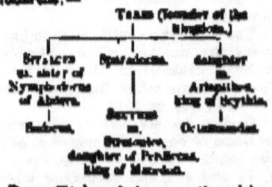

From Sitalces being mentioned here without any explanation of who he was, it has been argued that this passage was written after the first year of the Peloponnesian War (Dahlmann's Life of Herod. p. 29, E.T.; Blakesley ad loc., &c.). But this is at least doubtful. (See Introductory Essay, ch. i. p. 21, note [5].)

[4] Perhaps Sparadocus, the father of Seuthes.

[5] The following genealogical table of the Scythian kings may be drawn out from these chapters:—

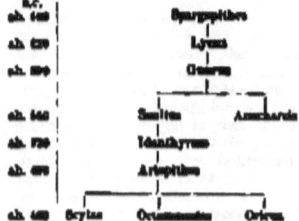

withdrew; but Octamasades beheaded Scylas upon the spot. Thus rigidly do the Scythians maintain their own customs, and thus severely do they punish such as adopt foreign usages.

81. What the population of Scythia is, I was not able to learn with certainty; the accounts which I received varied from one another. I heard from some that they were very numerous indeed; others made their numbers but scanty for such a nation as the Scyths.[4] Thus much, however, I witnessed with my own eyes. There is a tract called Exampæus between the Borysthenes and the Hypanis. I made some mention of it in a former place, where I spoke of the bitter stream which rising there flows into the Hypanis, and renders the water of that river undrinkable.[7] Here then stands a brazen bowl, six times as big as that at the entrance of the Euxine, which Pausanias, the son of Cleombrotus, set up.[4] Such as have never seen that vessel may understand me better if I say that the Scythian bowl holds with ease six hundred amphoræ,[5] and is of the thickness of six fingers' breadth. The natives gave me the following account of the manner in which it was made. One of their kings, by name Ariantas, wishing to know the number of his subjects, ordered them all to bring him, on pain of death, the point off one of their arrows. They obeyed; and he collected thereby a vast heap of arrow-heads,[1] which he resolved to form into a memorial

CHAP. 80-82.   FOOT-MARK OF HERCULES.   61

that might go down to posterity. Accordingly he made of them this bowl,² and dedicated it at Exampæus. This was all that I could learn concerning the number of the Scythians.

82. The country has no marvels except its rivers, which are larger and more numerous than those of any other land. These, and the vastness of the great plain,³ are worthy of note, and one thing besides, which I am about to mention. They show a foot-mark of Hercules,⁴ impressed on a rock, in shape like the print of a man's foot, but two cubits in length.⁵ It is in the neighbour-

---

able for the skilful manner in which they are barbed. They are triangular and usually made of bronze.

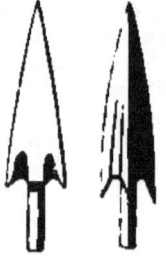

² Very elegant bronze bowls (see the woodcut below) have been found in the Scythian tombs—undoubtedly of Greek workmanship—but none at all of the size of this.
³ Concerning the great plain of Southern Russia, vide supra, ch. 47, note ⁹.
⁴ This does not prove that the Scythians recognised Hercules as a god, for the persons who showed the footprints may have been Greeks. The Greek traditions of these parts brought Hercules into Scythia : supra, chs. 8-10).
⁵ Cf. ii. 91. These supposed foot-prints of giants are pointed out in all countries. They form no sufficient ground for presuming, with Ritter (Vorhalle, pp. 332-348) that Buddhism was

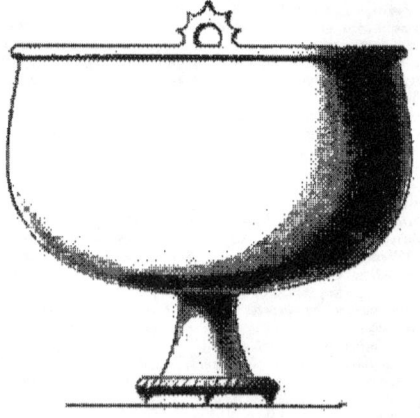

the religion of the Cimmerians. Indeed, as Buddha Sakya was not born till B.C. 623, and the last remnant of the Cimmerians was driven out by the Scyths before

B.C. 637 (supra, vol. I. p. 301), it is simply impossible that the Cimmerians of these parts should have been Buddhists.

hood of the Tyras. Having described this, I return to the subject on which I originally proposed to discourse.

83. The preparations of Darius against the Scythians had begun, messengers had been despatched on all sides with the king's commands, some being required to furnish troops, others to supply ships, others again to bridge the Thracian Bosphorus, when Artabanus, son of Hystaspes and brother of Darius, entreated the king to desist from his expedition, urging on him the great difficulty of attacking Scythia.[5] Good, however, as the advice of Artabanus was, it failed to persuade Darius. He therefore ceased his reasonings; and Darius, when his preparations were complete, led his army forth from Susa.

84. It was then that a certain Persian, by name Œobazus, the father of three sons, all of whom were to accompany the army, came and prayed the king that he would allow one of his sons to remain with him. Darius made answer, as if he regarded him in the light of a friend who had urged a moderate request, "that he would allow them all to remain." Œobazus was overjoyed, expecting that all his children would be excused from serving; the king however bade his attendants take the three sons of Œobazus and forthwith put them to death. Thus they were all left behind, but not till they had been deprived of life.[7]

85. When Darius, on his march from Susa, reached the territory of Chalcedon[8] on the shores of the Bosphorus, where the bridge had been made, he took ship and sailed thence to the Cyanean islands,[9] which, according to the Greeks, once floated. He took his seat also in the temple[1] and surveyed the Pontus, which is indeed well worthy of consideration. There is not in the world any other sea so wonderful: it extends in length

---

[5] The cautious temper of Artabanus again appears, vii. 10.

[7] Compare the similar story told of Xerxes, infra. vii. 39.

[8] Chalcedon was situated on the Asiatic side, at the point where the Bosphorus (Canal of Constantinople) opens into the Propontis, or Sea of Marmora (Scyl. Peripl. p. 83; Strab. xii. p. 843). The modern village of Kadi Keui, a few miles south of Scutari, marks the place (vide infra, ch. 144, note).

[9] Otherwise called the Symplegades. According to Strabo (vii. p. 492) they were two in number, and lay, one on the European, the other on the Asiatic side of the mouth of the strait. And so

Pindar, the earliest writer who notices them, says, Βόσπορον ἴσως. (Pyth. iv. 371.) Compare the Κυανέας δίσσας δίω of Apollonius Rhodius (ii. 318). They were, Strabo tells us, 20 stadia apart from one another. Moderns remark two rocks off the two coasts in this position (Clarke, p. 674).

The legend of the Symplegades will be found in Pindar (l. s. c.), Apollonius Rhodius l. s. c.), and Apollodorus (Bibliothec. I. ix. 23.). We need not seek to discover a matter-of-fact explanation of it.

[1] The temple at the mouth of the strait mentioned below, ch. 87. See note.

eleven thousand one hundred furlongs, and its breadth, at the widest part, is three thousand three hundred.² The mouth is but four furlongs wide;³ and this strait, called the Bosphorus, and across which the bridge of Darius had been thrown, is a hundred and twenty furlongs in length,⁴ reaching from the Euxine to the Propontis. The Propontis is five hundred furlongs across,⁵ and fourteen hundred long.⁶ Its waters flow into

---

² These measurements are extremely incorrect. The distance from the mouth of the Bosphorus to the Phasis, which Herodotus regards as the extreme length of the Pontus, instead of being 11,100 stades (1280 miles), is, by the most direct course, about 3500 stades, or little more than 630 miles. Even following the sinuosities of the coast, it does not exceed 7000 stades, or 800 miles. Again, the distance across from the Thermodon (Thermeh) to the Sindic peninsula (and here the coast-line cannot be meant, instead of being 3300 stades (380 miles), is about 2340 stades, or 270 miles.

It has been supposed by Larcher and others, that Herodotus here uses a different stade from that which he commonly employs, but this is a mere gratuitous assumption to escape a difficulty. Dahlmann (Life of Herod. p. 71, E. T.) has well exposed the absurdity of such a theory.

Herodotus is manifestly in error. The question is, how was he misled? In the first place he over-estimated the rate of speed of sailing vessels. He had probably been himself from the Bosphorus to the Phasis in a sailing vessel, and knew that he had made an average voyage, and that the time was, as he gives it, 9 days and 8 nights. In this voyage of his he had followed the coast-line, landing occasionally, as it appears (ii. 104). He was told that the vessel made 1300 stades a-day, when its real rate was little more than 800 stades. Further, at Themiscyra on the Thermodon, he probably heard that vessels sailed thence to Sindica in 2½ days, and applying in this case the same rate of sailing, he supposed the distance to be 3300 stades. But either an occasional high speed was given to him as his average rate, or the vessels which adventured into the open sea were better sailors than the ordinary coasters; so that here he did not make an estimate so greatly exceeding the truth. The ships which crossed from Themiscyra to Sindica in 2½ days must have attained a speed but little short of

the 1000 stadia per diem, which seems to have been the estimate made by Ptolamy, and again by Strabo, of the powers of sailing-vessels in their time. (See the note of Larcher, quoting Casaubon, vol. iii. p. 433, note 164.)

³ Moderns generally estimate the width of the canal of Constantinople at three-quarters of a mile, which would be rather more than six stadia. As Strabo, Pliny, Eustathius, and other writers agree with Herodotus, it is conjectured that the opening has gradually widened (Kruse, Ueber Herodots Aumessung des Pontus, Breslau, 1819, p. 41). The strong current would eventually tend to produce this effect. It must be noted, however, that Col. Chesney calls the width only 800 yards, or less than 3 stades (Euphrat. Exped. vol. i. p. 326).

⁴ This is under the true length, which is about 18 miles, or 140 stades. It was however the usual estimate in ancient times (Polyb. iv. 39; Arrian's Peripl. ad fin.), and most have been taken from the rate of vessels sailing with the current.

⁵ Herodotus appears to have measured the width of the Propontis by a line running nearly north and south, from the European shore near Perinthus to the Asiatic about Placia. The distance is there nearly 50 miles, or about 440 stades. Strabo, on the other hand, measured by a line running nearly east and west from Bisanthe to the innermost recess of the Gulf of Cius, and so made the breadth about equal the length (ii. p. 187).

⁶ By the length of the Propontis we must understand here (as in Strabo, ii. p. 188) the distance from the lower mouth of the Bosphorus to the upper end of the Hellespont. This, if we regard the strait as commencing at Gallipoli, is, in a direct line, rather more than 115 miles, or about 1000 stades. Along the western coast the distance would amount to 135 miles, or 1170 stades. Strabo estimates it at 1500 stades (l. s. c.).

the Hellespont, the length of which is four hundred furlongs, and the width no more than seven.¹ The Hellespont opens into the wide sea called the Egean.

86. The mode in which these distances have been measured is the following. In a long day a vessel generally accomplishes about seventy thousand fathoms, in the night sixty thousand. Now from the mouth of the Pontus to the river Phasis, which is the extreme length of this sea,² is a voyage of nine days and eight nights, which makes the distance one million one hundred and ten thousand fathoms, or eleven thousand one hundred furlongs. Again, from Sindica,³ to Themiscyra⁴ on the river Thermôdon, where the Pontus is wider than at any other place,⁵ is a sail of three days and two nights; which makes three hundred and thirty thousand fathoms, or three thousand three hundred furlongs. Such is the plan on which I have measured the Pontus, the Bosphorus, and the Hellespont, and such is the account which I have to give of them. The Pontus has also a lake belonging to it, not very much inferior to itself in size.⁶

---

¹ The length of the Dardanelles, from Gallipoli to the open sea, is, as nearly as possible, 40 miles (about 345 stades). Its breadth at the narrowest part is probably about one mile (8½ stades). Moderns differ considerably in their estimates (see Grote's Hist. of Greece, vol. v. p. 26, note). Strabo (ii. p. 164) and Pliny (Hist. Nat. iv. 12) agree with Herodotus.

The table on the opposite page gives at a glance the several measurements of Herodotus, Strabo, and Pliny, together with the (probable) actual distances. It will be seen that our author's errors do not very greatly exceed those of the best geographers of five centuries later.

Again, it will be seen, that (excepting as regards the width of the straits, which is very uncertain, and which may not improbably be somewhat greater now than in his day) the measurements of Herodotus, all but one, exceed the reality. This arises from his over estimate of the rate of sailing vessels. Secondly, it will be observed that his errors are far greater in the Euxine than elsewhere. This is consequent upon the less acquaintance which the Greeks had with that sea. Thirdly, it is worthy of remark, that except in respect of the length of the Euxine, his errors are not very considerable, varying from one-eighth to two-fifths upon the actual distance. The less width of the straits is

not to be regarded as altogether an error, but as arising in part from the wear of the coasts at the narrowest point.

² The real greatest axis, or extreme length, of the Euxine is from the Gulf of Burghaz (long. 27° 30′, lat. 42° 30′) to the Phasis. This is about 700 miles, or above 6000 stadia.

³ The Sindica of Herodotus is the region at the mouth of the Palus Mæotis, on the eastern side of the Cimmerian Bosphorus, the modern "Island of Taman" (vide supra, ch. 28). All the ancient geographers agree in placing a people of the name of Sindi in this region (Scylax, Peripl. p. 75; Strabo, xi. p. 723; Anon. Peripl. Pont. Eux. p. 134; Arrian, Peripl. Pont. Eux. p. 131); and to their evidence may be added that of the inscriptions of the Leuconidæ (vide supra, ch. 78, note 7).

⁴ Themiscyra is mentioned by Scylax (Peripl. p. 80) as a Greek city at the mouth of the Thermodon. According to Æschylus (Prom. V. 744) it was founded by the Amazons. Herodotus had been in these parts (ii. 104).

⁵ This is a mistake. The Black Sea is widest between the mouths of the Telepsi, and that of the Sakharieh or Sangarius (long. 31°). It is there about 400 miles across (3460 stades.)

⁶ It is commonly supposed that Herodotus fell here into a very gross mistake, since the Sea of Azof is not now much more

CHAP. 86.

TABLE OF LENGTHS AND WIDTHS OF THE EUXINE, BOSPHORUS, PROPONTIS, AND HELLESPONT.

	Herodotus	Strabo	Pliny	Real Distance	Error of Herodotus		Error of Strabo		Error of Pliny	
					Excess	Defect	Excess	Defect	Excess	Defect
	Stadia	*Stadia*	*Stadia*	*Stadia*						
Length of Euxine ...	11,100	7000	Not given	5400	Double	...	3-11ths	...	...	...
Width of Euxine* ...	3,300	2300	1360	2340	2-5ths	...	2-50ths	...	...	1-6th (nearly.)
Length of Bosphorus ...	120	Not given	165	140	...	1-7th	...	...	1-6th	...
Width of Bosphorus ...	4	4½	4	6½	...	3-13ths	...	...	...	3-13ths
Length of Propontis ...	1,400	1500	1123	1000	2-5ths	...	One-half	...	1-8th	...
Width of Propontis ...	500	1500½	Not given	435	1-7th	...	5-6ths	...	...	...
Length of Hellespont ...	400	Not given	698	345	1-6th	...	...	...	Double	...
Width of Hellespont ...	?	?	?	8½	...	1-6th	...	1-8th	...	1-6th

* Herodotus gives the width of the Euxine from *Themis* to the mouth of the Cimmerian Bosphorus. Strabo and Pliny give the shortest distance, from the south-western point of the Crimea (Criu-metopon) to Cape Acrompd (Carambis), which they estimate as above, but which is really less than 160 miles, or about 1500 stadia. Their error is calculated from this limit.

† This is Strabo's estimate in one place (ii. p. 165), but in another he calls the distance 5 stadia (vii. p. 463).

‡ Strabo (1 presume) means the heaped distance from Asia to Europe, which would be that from the inner recess of the gulf of Mendeleia to the European coast, about Rhodius. The actual distance here is not more than 95 miles, or about 820 stadia.

VOL. III.   F

The waters of this lake run into the Pontus: it is called the Mæotis, and also the Mother of the Pontus.

87. Darius, after he had finished his survey, sailed back to the bridge, which had been constructed for him by Mandrocles a Samian. He likewise surveyed the Bosphorus, and erected upon its shores two pillars of white marble, whereupon he inscribed the names of all the nations which formed his army—on the one pillar in Greek, on the other in Assyrian characters. Now his army was drawn from all the nations under his sway; and the whole amount, without reckoning the naval forces, was seven hundred thousand men, including cavalry. The fleet consisted of six hundred ships. Some time afterwards the Byzantines removed those pillars to their own city, and used them for an altar which they erected to Orthosian Diana. One block

more than one-twelfth of the size of the Euxine; but it is possible that the Palus Mæotis may have been very greatly larger in the time of Herodotus than it is at present. Pallas and other writers have speculated on the former existence of a connexion between the Caspian and the Euxine. (*Pallas's Travels*, vol. i. p. 78, E. T.; Rennell's *Western Asia*, vol. ii. p. 394.) These speculations are grounded chiefly on the appearance of the country eastward of the Sea of Azof, which is low and flat, only very slightly elevated above the level of that sea, and strongly impregnated with salt. Now without advancing any such violent hypothesis as that of these writers, we may well believe that the sea did once cover the great plains to the east as far as the 42nd or 43rd degree of longitude, and that the deposits brought down by the rivers—together with an actual elevation of a considerable tract of country—have formed new land out of what was formerly the bed of the sea. The filling up of the Sea of Azof still continues, and it has long been in summer not more than 14 feet deep at its greatest depth. (Heber's MS. Journal, quoted in Clarke, p. 329.) The Palus Mæotis may thus at the time of Herodotus have had an area four or five times as great as it has at present, so as to have better admitted of comparison with the Euxine than it now does. (Compare the very sensible remarks of Polybius, iv. 40, and note that Scylax makes the Palus Mæotis *half* the size of the Euxine, p. 72.)

It may be questioned whether the Mæotis derived its name from this idea, or whether it was not rather so called from the Mæta (Mæται), who were certainly a people in these parts, and are frequently mentioned in the inscriptions. They may be reasonably connected with the Sauro-Matæ.

It was natural that the Persians, who set up trilingual inscriptions in the central provinces for the benefit of their Arian, Semitic, and Tatar populations, should leave bilingual records in other places. Thus in Egypt they would have their inscriptions in the hieroglyphic as well as the Persian character, of which the vase in St. Mark's, at Venice, is a specimen. In Greece they would use, besides their own, the Greek language and character. Herodotus, however, is no doubt inaccurate when he speaks hard of *Assyrian letters*. The language and character used in the inscription would be the Persian, and not the Assyrian. But as moderns, till recently, have been accustomed to speak of "*the cuneiform language*," not distinguishing between one sort of cuneiform writing and another, so Herodotus appears to have been ignorant that in the arrowheaded inscriptions which he saw, both the letters and the languages varied. There are, in point of fact, at least six different types of cuneiform writing, viz., the old Scythic Babylonian, the Susianian, the Armenian, the Scythic of the trilingual tablets, the Assyrian, and the Achæmenian Persian. Of these the first four are to a certain extent connected; but the Assyrian and Achæmenian Persian differ totally from them and from each other.

That is, Diana, who had established or *preserved* their city. (Compare the Latin "*Jupiter Stator*.")

remained behind: it lay near the temple of Bacchus at Byzantium, and was covered with Assyrian writing. The spot where Darius bridged the Bosphorus was, I think, but I speak only from conjecture, half-way between the city of Byzantium and the temple at the mouth of the strait.[1]

88. Darius was so pleased with the bridge thrown across the strait by the Samian Mandrocles, that he not only bestowed upon him all the customary presents, but gave him ten of every kind. Mandrocles, by way of offering firstfruits from these presents, caused a picture to be painted which showed the whole of the bridge, with King Darius sitting in a seat of honour, and his army engaged in the passage. This painting he dedicated in the temple of Juno at Samos, attaching to it the inscription following:—

> "The fish-fraught Bosphorus bridged, to Juno's fane
> Did Mandrocles this proud memorial bring;
> When for himself a crown he'd skill to gain,
> For Samos praise, contenting the Great King."

Such was the memorial of his work which was left by the architect of the bridge.

89. Darius, after rewarding Mandrocles, passed into Europe, while he ordered the Ionians to enter the Pontus, and sail to the mouth of the Ister. There he bade them throw a bridge across the stream and await his coming. The Ionians, Æolians, and Hellespontians were the nations which furnished the chief strength of his navy. So the fleet, threading the Cyanean Isles, proceeded straight to the Ister, and, mounting the river to the point where its channels separate,[2] a distance of two days'

---

[1] Here, and above in ch. 85, the temple of Jupiter Urius (Οὔριος) is supposed to be meant. (Bähr ad loc.) This temple certainly was considered in later times to mark the mouth of the strait (see Arrian, Peripl. Pont. Eux. p. 124; Strabo, vii. p. 164; Anon. Peripl. p. 165-7), but it is very uncertain whether Herodotus alludes to it; for, first, it was on the Asiatic side (see the Peutingerian Table; Polyb. iv. 39, &c.), and we should expect, after the mention of Byzantium, a second place on the European coast; and further, we have no evidence that the temple of Jupiter Urius was built so early. The Byzantines had a temple directly opposite to the temple of Jupiter Urius, if, as generally supposed, it is that whereof Strabo speaks (l. s. c.) as "the temple of the Chalcedonians."

[2] The Danube divides at present near Isatcha, between Braîlow and Ismail; but we cannot be certain that the division was always at this place. Although the recent surveys have shown that no branch can ever have been thrown out from the angle near Rassova (see Geogr. Journ. vol. xxvi. p. 210), yet we do not know enough about the Dobrudscha to say whether there is not some other line by which a stream may have passed considerably to the south of all the present mouths. It seems clear that a navigable branch must once have reached the sea at or near Istria (see above, Book ii. ch. 33, note [9]), which was certainly as far south as Karupiak.

voyage from the sea, yoked the neck of the stream. Meantime Darius, who had crossed the Bosphorus by the bridge over it, marched through Thrace; and happening upon the sources of the Tearus,[9] pitched his camp and made a stay of three days.

90. Now the Tearus is said by those who dwell near it, to be the most healthful of all streams, and to cure, among other diseases, the scab either in man or beast. Its sources, which are eight and thirty in number, all flowing from the same rock, are in part cold, in part hot. They lie at an equal distance from the town of Heræum near Perinthus,[1] and Apollonia on the Euxine,[2] a two days' journey from each.[3] This river, the Tearus, is a tributary of the Contadesdus, which runs into the Agrianes, and that into the Hebrus.[4] The Hebrus empties itself into the sea near the city of Ænus.[5]

91. Here then, on the banks of the Tearus, Darius stopped and pitched his camp. The river charmed him so, that he caused a pillar to be erected in this place also, with an inscription to the following effect: "The fountains of the Tearus afford the best and most beautiful water of all rivers: they were visited, on his march into Scythia, by the best and most beautiful of men, Darius, son of Hystaspes, king of the Persians, and of the

[9] The Tearus has generally been supposed to be the modern *Tekedere*, which runs into the *Kirishtiran*, near *Eski Baba*. It appears, however, to be rather the *Simerdere*, which rises from the western side of the woody range called *Stranja Dagh*, or the *Little Balkan*, near the villages of *Yene* and *Bunarhissar*. Here "the 38 sources of the Tearus mentioned by Herodotus may easily be made out. All are cold during the summer, but many of them become so warm during the winter that snow or ice thrown into them immediately melts." (Geog. Journ. vol. xxiv. p. 45.) The springs are not now supposed to have any healing efficacy.

[1] Perinthus (afterwards Heraclea) lay upon the Propontis, in lat. 41°, long. 28°, nearly. Its site is marked by the modern *Erekli* (vide infra, v. 1). Heræum or Heræon-tichos (Ἡραῖον τεῖχος) as it is called by Demosthenes (Olynth. iii. § 5) and others (Steph. Byz. ad voc. Suidas, &c.) was an unimportant place near Perinthus. Its exact site is unknown. According to the Etym. Mag. it was a Samian colony.

[2] There were several cities of this name. The most famous was that on the coast of Illyria, of which Herodotus speaks (infra, ix. 92). Apollonia upon the *Euxine* is mentioned by Scylax among the Greek cities of Thrace. (Peripl. p. 68.) According to the anonymous author of the Periplus Ponti Euxini, who follows here Scymnus Chius, it was founded by the Milesians 50 years before the accession of Cyrus (about B.C. 609). The same writer informs us that Apollonia in his time had become Sozopolis, which determines its site to be that of the modern *Sizeboli*, on the south side of the Gulf of *Burghas*.

[3] The village of *Yene* is nearly equidistant from *Erekli* (Perinthus) and *Sizeboli* (Apollonia), but a little further from the latter. The distance, however, even as the crow flies, is above 50 miles to the nearer (*Erekli*), and would be 70 by any practicable route; thus the estimate of two days is too little.

[4] The Agrianes is undoubtedly the modern *Erkene*, which runs into the *Maritza* (Hebrus) to the north of the range of Rhodope (*Despoto Dagh*). The Contadesdus is the river of *Kirishtiran*.

[5] Concerning the site of Ænus, vide infra, vii. 58.

whole continent."⁶ Such was the inscription which he set up at this place.⁷

92. Marching thence, he came to a second river, called the Artiscus,⁸ which flows through the country of the Odrysians.⁹ Here he fixed upon a certain spot, where every one of his soldiers should throw a stone as he passed by. When his orders were obeyed, Darius continued his march, leaving behind him great hills formed of the stones cast by his troops.

93. Before arriving at the Ister,¹ the first people whom he subdued were the Getæ,² who believe in their immortality. The Thracians of Salmydessus,³ and those who dwelt above the cities of Apollonia and Mesembria⁴—the Scyrmiadæ and Nipsæans,

---

⁶ Vide supra, l. 4. " τὴν Ἀσίαν ἁπ- ασαν οἱ Πέρσαι."

⁷ There is some reason to believe that a portion of this inscription was in existence a few years ago. When General Jochmus visited Bunarhissar in 1847, he was informed by an old Turk that an inscription in "old Syrian" (esti Suriani), written with "letters like nails," had been lying uncared for not many years previously near his house. Search was of course made, but unfortunately it proved vain; and the inscription is believed to have been either burnt for lime, or possibly built into the wall of a farm-house. (Geograph. Journ. vol. xxiv. p. 44.)

⁸ This river has been supposed to be the Arda (Gatterer, p. 42), which joins the Maritza from the west, not much below Adrianople; but it is not at all probable that Darius went so far to the left as to touch this stream. The Artiscus is most likely the Teke-derch, which is crossed several times on the present high road to the Balkan. Here General Jochmus observed on an eminence near the road six large tépés or tumuli. He also remarked in the winding bed of the river and the adjoining low grounds, "innumerable large loose stones," which may have caused Darius to give the order to his soldiers that Herodotus here mentions. (See Geogr. Journ. vol. xxiv. p. 47.)

⁹ The country of the Odrysæ was the great plain included within the chains of Rhodope, Hæmus, and the Little Balkan (Thucyd. ii. 96), in the centre of which now stands the city of Adrianople.

¹ It is not quite clear by which route Darius crossed the Balkan; but the probability is that, passing the Little Balkan between Dolci and Faki, he descended to the shore about Burghas, and thence proceeded by the defiles nearest to the sea-coast, which lie between Missivria and Tosun-Dervish. He would thus have followed the route pursued by Generals Roth and Rudiger in 1828, and by Marshal Diebitsch in 1829.

² The identity of the Getæ with the Goths of later times is more than a plausible conjecture. It may be regarded as historically certain (see note on Book v. ch. 8). Moreover the compounds, Massa-getæ, Thyssa-getæ, Tyri-getæ, have a striking analogy to the later names of Visi-goths and Ostro-goths.

³ Salmydessus, or Halmydessus, was a strip of shore (αἰγιαλός, Scymn. Ch. I, 723) in the neighbourhood of a river of the same name, which emptied itself into the Euxine 70 miles from the opening of the Bosphorus. (Arrian, Peripl. ad fin.; Anon. Peripl. p. 164.) It is mentioned by Xenophon (Anab. vii. 5, § 12), who visited it, and was witness to the barbarous conduct of the Thracian inhabitants towards the persons wrecked upon the coast. A fragment of the old appellation appears to survive in the modern Turkish town of Midjeh (long. 28° 10', lat. 41° 35'). The name Salmydessus seems compounded of the root Salm (found also in Zalm-oxis and Solym-bris), and of the word Odessus, the name of another town upon this coast.

⁴ Mesembria is mentioned by Scylax among the Greek cities upon the Thracian coast. (Peripl. p. 68.) According to Scymnus Chius (ll. 740, 741) it was founded by the Chalcedonians and Me-garians about the time of Darius' expe-

as they are called—gave themselves up to Darius without a struggle; but the Getæ obstinately defending themselves, were forthwith enslaved, notwithstanding that they are the noblest as well as the most just of all the Thracian tribes.

94. The belief of the Getæ in respect of immortality is the following. They think that they do not really die, but that when they depart this life they go to Zalmoxis,[5] who is called also Gebeleïzis[6] by some among them. To this god every five years they send a messenger, who is chosen by lot out of the whole nation, and charged to bear him their several requests. Their mode of sending him is this. A number of them stand in order, each holding in his hand three darts; others take the man who is to be sent to Zalmoxis, and swinging him by his hands and feet, toss him into the air so that he falls upon the points of the weapons. If he is pierced and dies, they think that the god is propitious to them; but if not, they lay the fault on the messenger, who (they say) is a wicked man: and so they choose another to send away. The messages are given while the man is still alive. This same people, when it lightens and thunders, aim their arrows at the sky, uttering threats against the god;[7] and they do not believe that there is any god but their own.

95. I am told by the Greeks who dwell on the shores of the Hellespont and the Pontus, that this Zalmoxis was in reality a man, that he lived at Samos, and while there was the slave[8] of

---

dition against the Scyths. Strabo (vii. p. 462) calls it a colony of the Megarenses only. Arrian (Peripl. p. 136) and the anonymous author of the Periplus Ponti Euxini sufficiently mark its site. It lay at the base of Mount Hæmus, a little to the south. The name remains in the modern *Missivria* (long. 27° 45′, lat. 42° 35′).

"The Thracians of Salmydessus, and those who dwelt above the cities of Apollonia and Mesembria," would represent the inhabitants of the entire tract between the Little Balkan and the Black Sea.

[5] That Zalmoxis or Zamolxis was the chief object of worship among the Getæ is witnessed also by Mnaseas of Batræ (Fr. 23), by Strabo (vii. p. 430), Jamblichus (Vit. Pythag. § 173.), and Diogenes Laertius (viii. 1). Mnaseas regarded him as identical with the Chronus of the Greeks. Porphyry (Vit. Pythag. § 14) derives the name from a Thracian word *salmus*, which, he says,

signified "a skin;" but this does not seem a very probable origin. May we connect the name with that of Selm, the son of Feridun, who in Arian romance inherited from his father the western third of the world? Plato mentions Zalmoxis in conjunction with Abaris in the Charmides (p. 158, B as a master of incantation. Vide supra, ch. 36.

[6] A Lithuanian etymology '*Gyra leyvis*, "giver of rest") has been suggested for this word (Bayer's Origin. Sinic. p. 283). Zalmoxis or Zamolxis might, it is said, in the same language signify "Lord of the earth."

[7] Compare the customs of the Calymdians (i. 172), and the Psylli (iv. 173).

[8] Thracian slaves were very numerous in Greece. The Thracians often sold their children into slavery (infra, v. 6). In the times of the later comedy, *Geta* and *Davus* (Δάος, Δᾶος) were the most common names for slaves. (See the comedies of Terence, *passim*.)

Pythagoras son of Mnesarchus. After obtaining his freedom he grew rich, and leaving Samos, returned to his own country. The Thracians at that time lived in a wretched way, and were a poor ignorant race; Zalmoxis, therefore, who by his commerce with the Greeks, and especially with one who was by no means their most contemptible philosopher, Pythagoras to wit, was acquainted with the Ionic mode of life and with manners more refined than those current among his countrymen, had a chamber built, in which from time to time he received and feasted all the principal Thracians, using the occasion to teach them that neither he, nor they, his boon companions, nor any of their posterity would ever perish, but that they would all go to a place where they would live for aye in the enjoyment of every conceivable good. While he was acting in this way, and holding this kind of discourse, he was constructing an apartment underground, into which, when it was completed, he withdrew, vanishing suddenly from the eyes of the Thracians, who greatly regretted his loss, and mourned over him as one dead.[9] He meanwhile abode in his secret chamber three full years, after which he came forth from his concealment, and showed himself once more to his countrymen, who were thus brought to believe in the truth of what he had taught them. Such is the account of the Greeks.

96. I for my part neither put entire faith in this story of Zalmoxis[10] and his under-ground chamber, nor do I altogether discredit it: but I believe Zalmoxis to have lived long before the time of Pythagoras. Whether there was ever really a man of the name, or whether Zalmoxis is nothing but a native god of the Getae, I now bid him farewell. As for the Getae themselves, the people who observe the practices described above, they were now reduced by the Persians, and accompanied the army of Darius.[1]

97. When Darius, with his land forces, reached the Ister, he made his troops cross the stream, and after all were gone over gave orders to the Ionians to break the bridge, and follow him

---

[9] This story was told also by Hellanicus (Fr. 173,), who seems to have simply copied Herodotus. (Comp. Porphyr. ap. Euseb. P. E. x. p. 466, B.)

[10] Dahlmann (Life of Herod. p. 115, E. T.) conjectures that this whole story sprung out of the name, which was as often written Zamolxis as Zalmoxis. The Greeks of the Pontus imagined that Zamo-laïs must have been a native of Samos; and the belief of the Getae, who worshipped him, in the immortality of the soul, must have come, they thought, from Pythagoras.

[1] The whole tract between the Balkan (Hæmus) and the Danube, the modern Bulgaria, seems to have been at this time in the possession of the Getae, who reached up the river almost to the confines of Servia. (Thucyd. ii. 96.)

with the whole naval force in his land march. They were about to obey his command, when the general of the Mytilenæans, Coës son of Erxander, having first asked whether it was agreeable to the king to listen to one who wished to speak his mind,[1] addressed him in the words following:—"Thou art about, Sire, to attack a country no part of which is cultivated, and wherein there is not a single inhabited city. Keep this bridge, then, as it is, and leave those who built it to watch over it. So if we come up with the Scythians and succeed against them as we could wish, we may return by this route; or if we fail of finding them, our retreat will still be secure. For I have no fear lest the Scythians defeat us in battle, but my dread is lest we be unable to discover them, and suffer loss while we wander about their territory. And now, mayhap, it will be said, I advise thee thus in the hope of being myself allowed to remain behind;[2] but in truth I have no other design than to recommend the course which seems to me the best; nor will I consent to be among those left behind, but my resolve is, in any case, to follow thee." The advice of Coës pleased Darius highly, who thus replied to him:—"Dear Lesbian, when I am safe home again in my palace, be sure thou come to me, and with good deeds will I recompense thy good words of to-day."

98. Having so said, the king took a leathern thong, and tying sixty knots in it, called together the Ionian tyrants, and spoke thus to them:—"Men of Ionia, my former commands to you concerning the bridge are now withdrawn. See, here is a thong: take it, and observe my bidding with respect to it. From the time that I leave you to march forward into Scythia, untie every day one of the knots. If I do not return before the last day to which the knots will hold out, then leave your station, and sail to your several homes. Meanwhile, understand that my resolve is changed, and that you are to guard the bridge with all care, and watch over its safety and preservation. By so doing ye will oblige me greatly." When Darius had thus spoken, he set out on his march with all speed.

99. Before you come to Scythia, on the sea coast, lies Thrace. The land here makes a sweep, and then Scythia begins, the Ister falling into the sea at this point with its mouth facing the east. Starting from the Ister I shall now describe the measure-

---

[1] Compare the Inquiry of Crœsus (i. 88). The fear of giving offence to the Great King is strongly marked by this practice.

[2] After the punishment of Œobazus (supra, ch. 84), it was important to guard against this suspicion.

ments of the sea-shore of Scythia. Immediately that the Ister is crossed, Old Scythia⁴ begins, and continues as far as the city called Carcinitis, fronting towards the south wind and the midday. Here upon the same sea, there lies a mountainous tract⁵ projecting into the Pontus, which is inhabited by the Tauri, as far as what is called the Rugged Chersonese,⁶ which runs out into the sea upon the east. For the boundaries of Scythia extend on two sides to two different seas, one upon the south, and the other towards the east, as is also the case with Attica. And the Tauri occupy a position in Scythia like that which a people would hold in Attica, who, being foreigners and not Athenians, should inhabit the highland⁷ of Sunium, from Thoricus to the township of Anaphlystus,⁸ if this tract projected into the sea somewhat further than it does. Such, to compare great things with small, is the Tauric territory. For the sake of those who may not have made the voyage round these parts of Attica, I will illustrate in another way. It is as if in Iapygia a line were drawn from Port Brundusium to Tarentum, and a people different from the Iapygians inhabited the promontory.⁹ These two in-

---

⁴ Herodotus considers that the Cimmerians maintained themselves in parts of Eastern Scythia, as, *e. g.* in the Rugged Chersonese, long after they were forced to relinquish the rest of their territory. Old Scythia is the part from which they were driven at the first.

⁵ The mountains lie only along the southern coast of the Crimea. All the rest of the peninsula belongs to the steppes. "We beheld towards the south," says Dr. Clarke, "a ridge of mountains upon the coast; but unless a traveller follows the sinuosity of the southern shore of the Crimea, all the rest of the peninsula is as flat as Salisbury Plain." (Travels, p. 401. See the view overleaf.)

⁶ By the "rough" or "rugged" Chersonese, Herodotus plainly intends the eastern part of the Crimea, called the Peninsula of Kertch, which in his day, and for many centuries later, formed the kingdom of the Bosphorus. This tract is hilly and uneven, presenting a strong contrast with the steppe, but it scarcely deserves an epithet applied also to Western Cilicia—a truly rugged country. Probably the general character of the south coast of the Crimea was considered to extend along its whole length.

⁷ This seems to be the meaning of the rare word, γουνός, here. See the authorities quoted by Schweighæuser (not. ad loc.). In this sense it is an apa descriptio of the place. Comp. Soph. Aj. ἰὼ θᾶσσον ἴσχοντι πάντων ἐράσθλαν ἀλλάσσοντος, ἄκραν ὑπὸ πλάκα Σούνιον. And Dr. Chandler's description : " We now approach Cape Sunium, which is steep, abrupt, and rocky. On it is the ruin of the temple of Minerva Sunias, overlooking from its lofty situation the subject deep." (Travels, vol. ii. p. 7.)

⁸ The sites of Thoricus and Anaphlystus are marked by the villages of *Thorico* and *Anaphiso*, the former on the east, the latter on the west side of the peninsula. They were both fortified posts in later times, for the protection of the neighbouring silver-mines. (Xen. de Redit. iv. § 43.)

⁹ This passage, as Mitford and Dahlmann have observed, was evidently written in Magna Græcia. (Mitford's Greece, vol. ii. p. 356; Dahlmann's Life of Herod. p. 35.) Herodotus at Thurii would have Iapygia (the *Terra di Otranto*) before his eyes, as it were. Writing from Ionia, or even from Greece Proper, he would never have thought of such an illustration. Brundusium and Tarentum remain in the *Brindisi* and *Taranto* of the present day. From

The Tauric Mountains, from the Steppe.

CUSTOMS OF THE TAURI.

stances may suggest a number of others where the shape of the land closely resembles that of Taurica.

100. Beyond this tract, we find the Scythians again in possession of the country above the Tauri and the parts bordering on the eastern sea, as also of the whole district lying west of the Cimmerian Bosphorus and the Palus Mæotis, as far as the river Tanais, which empties itself into that lake at its upper end. As for the inland boundaries of Scythia, if we start from the Ister, we find it enclosed by the following tribes, first the Agathyrsi, next the Neuri, then the Androphagi, and last of all, the Melanchlæni.

101. Scythia then, which is square in shape, and has two of its sides reaching down to the sea, extends inland to the same distance that it stretches along the coast, and is equal every way. For it is a ten days' journey from the Ister to the Borysthenes, and ten more from the Borysthenes to the Palus Mæotis, while the distance from the coast inland to the country of the Melanchlæni, who dwell above Scythia, is a journey of twenty days. I reckon the day's journey at two hundred furlongs. Thus the two sides which run straight inland are four thousand furlongs each, and the transverse sides at right angles to these are also of the same length, which gives the full size of Scythia.[10]

102. The Scythians, reflecting on their situation, perceived that they were not strong enough by themselves to contend with the army of Darius in open fight. They, therefore, sent envoys to the neighbouring nations, whose kings had already met, and were in consultation upon the advance of so vast a host. Now they who had come together were the kings of the Tauri, the Agathyrsi, the Neuri, the Androphagi, the Melanchlæni, the Geloni, the Budini, and the Sauromatæ.

103. The Tauri have the following customs. They offer in sacrifice to the Virgin all shipwrecked persons, and all Greeks compelled to put into their ports by stress of weather. The mode of sacrifice is this. After the preparatory ceremonies, they strike the victim on the head with a club. Then, according to some accounts, they hurl the trunk from the precipice whereon

---

From both comparisons it may be gathered that Herodotus did not look upon the Tauric Peninsula as joined to the continent by a narrow isthmus, but as united by a broad tract. (Niebuhr's Scythia, p. 39, E. T.) What if changes in the land have taken place, and the Putrid Sea did not exist in his time? Scylax calls the tract an ἀπορθμως (p. 70), and Strabo is the first who speaks of it as a χερρόνησος or peninsula (vii. p. 445.).

[10] See the Appendix, Essay lii., "On the Geography of Scythia."

the temple stands,[1] and nail the head to a cross. Others grant that the head is treated in this way, but deny that the body is thrown down the cliff—on the contrary, they say, it is buried. The goddess to whom these sacrifices are offered the Tauri themselves declare to be Iphigenia,[2] the daughter of Agamemnon. When they take prisoners in war they treat them in the following way. The man who has taken a captive cuts off his head, and carrying it to his home, fixes it upon a tall pole, which he elevates above his house, most commonly over the chimney. The reason that the heads are set up so high, is (it is said) in order that the whole house may be under their protection. These people live entirely by war and plundering.[3]

104. The Agathyrsi are a race of men very luxurious, and very fond of wearing gold on their persons.[4] They have wives in common, that so they may be all brothers,[5] and, as members of one family, may neither envy nor hate one another. In

---

[1] This temple occupied a promontory on the south coast of the Crimea, not far from Criumetopon (Cape Aia). The promontory itself was named by the Greeks Parthenium, from the temple (Strab. vii. p. 446; Plin. H. N. iv. 12; Mela, ii. l. &c.). It is thought that the monastery of St. George occupies the site.

[2] The virgin goddess of the Tauri was more generally identified by the Greeks with their own Artemis: hence Artemis got the epithet of Ταυροπόλος. (Cf. Diod. Sic. iv. 44; Etym. Mag. ad voc. Scholiast. ad Soph. Aj. 172.) The legend of Iphigenia is probably a mere Greek fancy, having the Tauric custom of offering human sacrifices as its basis. In the time of Herodotus the Tauri were not averse to admitting the legend, and identifying their national goddess with the virgin worshipped by the Greeks.

[3] The conjecture that the Tauri were a remnant of the Cimmerians (Grote, vol. III. p. 327; Heeren's As. Nat. vol. II. p. 260, E. T.) has little more than its internal probability to rest upon. We do not know their language, and there is scarcely anything in their manners and customs to distinguish them from the Scythians. As, however, it is declared by Herodotus that they were not Scythians, and we must therefore seek for them some other ethnic connexion, the Cimmerian theory may be accepted as probable. It is clear that the strong and mountainous region extending along the south coast of the Crimea would offer just that refuge in which a weak nation, when driven from the plains, is able to maintain itself against a strong one. It is noticeable also that the tradition made the last resting-place of the Cimmerians to be the Crimea (supra, ch. 12), where they left their name so firmly fixed that it has clung to the country till the present day. Names also closely resembling that of the Tauri are found in a clearly Cimbric, or at any rate Celtic, connexion, as those of the Taurisks and Taurisci, who were called Gauls by Posidonius (Fr. 75); and that of the city Taurœsis or Tauroentium (cf. Apollnd. Fr. 105, with Strab. iv. p. 247), a Celtic town, according to Stephen (ad voc. Ταυρόεις). It may be questioned also whether the Taurini, whose name remains in the modern Turin, were not really Gauls, though called Ligurians by Strabo (iv. p. 286). At least it is strange, if they were really different from the Taurisci, who are acknowledged to be Gauls (Polyb. ii. 15, § 8, and who afterwards dwelt in these parts.

[4] The country of the Agathyrsi is distinctly marked 'sup. 49 as the plain of the Maros (Maris). This region, enclosed on the north and east by the Carpathian Alps, would be likely to be in early times auriferous.

[5] This anticipation of the theory of Plato (Rep. v.) is curious. Was Plato indebted to Herodotus?

other respects their customs approach nearly to those of the Thracians.

105. The Neurian customs are like the Scythian. One generation before the attack of Darius they were driven from their land by a huge multitude of serpents which invaded them. Of these some were produced in their own country, while others, and those by far the greater number, came in from the deserts on the north. Suffering grievously beneath this scourge, they quitted their homes, and took refuge with the Budini. It seems that these people are conjurors: for both the Scythians and the Greeks who dwell in Scythia say, that every Neurian once a year becomes a wolf for a few days, at the end of which time he is restored to his proper shape. Not that I believe this, but they constantly affirm it to be true, and are even ready to back their assertion with an oath.

106. The manners of the Androphagi are more savage than

those of any other race. They neither observe justice, nor are governed by any laws. They are nomads, and their dress is Scythian; but the language which they speak is peculiar to themselves. Unlike any other nation in these parts, they are cannibals.

107. The Melanchlæni² wear, all of them, black cloaks, and from this derive the name which they bear. Their customs are Scythic.

108. The Budini are a large and powerful nation: they have all deep blue eyes, and bright red hair.³ There is a city in their territory, called Gelônus, which is surrounded with a lofty wall, thirty furlongs each way, built entirely of wood.⁴ All the houses in the place and all the temples are of the same material. Here are temples built in honour of the Grecian gods, and adorned after the Greek fashion with images, altars, and shrines, all in wood. There is even a festival, held every third year in honour

---

(Ross's Fur-Hunters of the Far West, vol. i. p. 249.)

² Or "Black-cloaks." This is probably a translation of the native name. There is at present a tribe in the Hindoo Koosh, who call themselves *Siah-push*, which is an exact equivalent of Μελαγχλαῖνοι. (Rennell's Geograph. of Herod. p. 87.) There is also a tribe of "Black-robes" among the North-American Indians (Ross, vol. i. p. 305). Such titles are common among barbarous people.

The dress of the Melanchlæni is noted by Dio Chrysostom (Orat. xxxvi. p. 439), who says it had been adopted by the Olbiopolites. He describes the cloak as "small, black, and thin" (μικρὸν, μέλαν, λεπτόν). Probably the dress was the more remarked, as the other nations of those parts, like the modern Calmucks and Tatars generally, may have affected bright colours.

The Melanchlæni had been mentioned by Hecatæus (Fr. 154) as "a Scythian nation." They continue to figure in the Geographies (Plin. vi. 5; Mela, i. 19; Dionys. Perieg. 309; Ptol. v. 19, &c.), but appear to be gradually pressed eastward. By Ptolemy they are placed upon the Rha or Wolga.

Their position in the time of Herodotus seems to be the country between the Donetz and the Don, or Tanais.

³ These physical characteristics of the Budini are very remarkable, and would give them a far better title to be considered the ancestors of the German race, than the Androphagi and Melan-

chlæni, to whom Heeren grants that honour. (As. Nat. ii. p. 265, E. T.) The nomade races which people the entire tract from the Don to the North Pacific, have universally dark eyes and hair. May not the Budini have been a remnant of the Cimmerians, to whom the woody country between the upper Don and the Wolga furnished a protection? In that case *Gel-oni* (compare "*Gmel*," and "*Galil*") might be their true ethnic title, as the Greeks generally maintained. (Vide infra, ch. 109.)

⁴ Heeren (As. Nat. ii. p. 292, E. T.) sees in this city, or *slobode*, a staple for the fur-trade, founded expressly for commercial purposes by the Greeks of the coast. Schafarik regards it as not of Greek, but of barbaric origin, and grounds upon it an argument that the Budini were a Sclavonic people. (Slavische Alterth. i. 10, pp. 185-95.) This last view, of which Mr. Grote speaks with some favour (Hist. of Greece, vol. iii. p. 325, note) is utterly at variance with the statements in Herodotus. Heeren is probably right, that the place became a staple, for it lay in the line of the trade carried on by the Greeks with the interior (supra, chs. 21-24); but as we know no other instance of the Greeks founding a factory for trading purposes at a distance from the coast, it is perhaps best simply to accept the narrative of Herodotus, that it was a place where certain fugitive Greeks happened to settle.

of Bacchus, at which the natives fall into the Bacchic fury. For the fact is that the Gelôni were anciently Greeks, who, being driven out of the factories along the coast, fled to the Budini and took up their abode with them. They still speak a language half Greek, half Scythian.

100. The Budini, however, do not speak the same language as the Gelôni, nor is their mode of life the same. They are the aboriginal people of the country, and are nomads; unlike any of the neighbouring races, they eat lice. The Gelôni, on the contrary, are tillers of the soil, eat bread, have gardens, and both in shape and complexion are quite different from the Budini. The Greeks notwithstanding call these latter Gelôni; but it is a mistake to give them the name.[3] Their country is thickly planted with trees of all manner of kinds.[4] In the very woodiest part is a broad deep lake, surrounded by marshy ground with reeds growing on it. Here otters are caught, and beavers, with another sort of animal which has a square face. With the skins of this last the natives border their capotes:[7] and they also get from them a remedy,[8] which is of virtue in diseases of the womb.

110. It is reported of the Sauromatæ, that when the Greeks fought with the Amazons,[9] whom the Scythians call *Oior-pata*

---

[3] It has been conjectured that the name *Budini* is a religious title, and marks that the people who bore it were Buddhists. (Ritter, Vorhalle, p. 25.) But as Buddha or Sakya did not begin to spread his doctrines till about B.C. 600, and then taught in India and Thibet, it is extremely improbable that his religion could have reached European Scythia by the days of Herodotus. Perhaps the name is best connected with the ethnic appellative *Wend*, which is from *wend*, "water," Sclav. *woda*, Phryg. βέδυ, &c. (See Smith's Dict. of Gr. and R. Geography, s. v. BUDINI.)

[4] This part of the description seems to fix the locality of the Budini to the region about Zadonsk and Novosil, which offers so remarkable a contrast to the rest of Russia. (Clarke, i. p. 194.) The mention, however, of the lake, containing otters and beavers, and especially of the "square-faced animals"—if these are seals, would seem to require a position further to the east. There are no lakes in the Woroneti country, and though seals are found in the Caspian, at the mouths of the Wolga, and in some of the Siberian lakes (Heeren, As. Nat. II. p. 291, note, E. T.), they do not mount the Wolga, nor are they found in the Tanais. It may be doubted whether seals are really intended.

[7] A border of fur is commonly seen to edge the coat worn by the Scythians on the sepulchral vases and other remains. See woodcuts in notes [6] and [7] on chs. 46 and 59. It is also frequent at the present day. (Pallas, vol. II. pl. 23; Dubois, vol. v. p. 202.)

[8] "Horum *testiculis* remedium obtinent, quod in morbis uterinis unul est." This has been thought by some to show that *Castor oil* was in the pharmacopœia of these nations. Herodotus might have been misinformed as to which of the three animals furnished the remedy, and the other mistake prevailed till comparatively modern times. Mr. Blakesley, however, supposes that the "bags of the musk-deer" are meant (note ad loc.).

[9] Some Amazons were supposed to live in Asia, others in Africa. Diodorus (iii. 51) says the latter were much the most ancient, having lived many ages before the Trojan war (those of the

or "man-slayers," as it may be rendered, *Oior* being Scythic for "man," and *pata* for "to slay"—it is reported, I say, that the Greeks after gaining the battle of the Thermôdon, put to sea, taking with them on board three of their vessels all the Amazons whom they had made prisoners; and that these women upon the voyage rose up against the crews, and massacred them to a man. As however they were quite strange to ships, and did not know how to use either rudder, sails, or oars, they were carried, after the death of the men, where the winds and the waves listed. At last they reached the shores of the Palus Mæotis and came to a place called Cremni or "the Cliffs,"[1] which is in the country of the free Scythians. Here they went ashore, and proceeded by land towards the inhabited regions; the first herd of horses which they fell in with they seized, and mounting upon their backs, fell to plundering the Scythian territory.

111. The Scyths could not tell what to make of the attack upon them—the dress, the language, the nation itself, were alike unknown—whence the enemy had come even, was a marvel. Imagining, however, that they were all men of about the same age,[2] they went out against them, and fought a battle. Some of the bodies of the slain fell into their hands, whereby they discovered the truth. Hereupon they deliberated, and made a resolve to kill no more of them, but to send against them a detachment of their youngest men, as near as they could guess equal to the women in number, with orders to encamp in their neighbourhood, and do as they saw them do—when the Amazons advanced against them, they were to retire, and avoid a fight—when they halted, the young men were to approach and pitch their camp near the camp of the enemy. All this they did on account of their strong desire to obtain children from so notable a race.

Thermodon only a little before it), and their queen, Myrina, was the friend of Horus the son of Isis. The numerous body-guard of the king of the Behrs, on the White Nile, is to this day composed entirely of women (his ministers only having access to him when he is about to die, to prevent his leaving the world by a vulgar natural death); and a similar custom may have been the origin of the fable of the Amazons. It is found again in Western Africa. The name is probably African, not Greek. V. note [4], ch. 191.—[G. W.]

[1] Vide supra, ch. 20. This place appears to have been a Greek port, and was probably a colony from Panticapæum. Its name is clearly Greek, and marks that it was in the neighbourhood of some high cliffs, which are difficult to find on the shores of the Sea of Azof. Perhaps the most probable site is near *Marinpol* (see Pul. iii. 5), where the coast attains some elevation. Cremnisci is not to be confounded with Cremni. It was on the Euxine, between the Dniestr and the Danube. (Anon. Peripl. P. E. p. 153; Plin. H. N. iv. 12.)

[2] That is to say, as they were all alike beardless, they took them for an army of youths.

STORY OF THE AMAZONS.

112. So the youths departed, and obeyed the orders which had been given them. The Amazons soon found out that they had not come to do them any harm; and so they on their part ceased to offer the Scythians any molestation. And now day after day the camps approached nearer to one another; both parties led the same life, neither having anything but their arms and horses, so that they were forced to support themselves by hunting and pillage.

113. At last an incident brought two of them together—the man easily gained the good graces of the woman, who bade him by signs (for they did not understand each other's language) to bring a friend the next day to the spot where they had met—promising on her part to bring with her another woman. He did so, and the woman kept her word. When the rest of the youths heard what had taken place, they also sought and gained the favour of the other Amazons.

114. The two camps were then joined in one, the Scythians living with the Amazons as their wives; and the men were unable to learn the tongue of the women, but the women soon caught up the tongue of the men. When they could thus understand one another, the Scyths addressed the Amazons in these words,—" We have parents, and properties, let us therefore give up this mode of life, and return to our nation, and live with them. You shall be our wives there no less than here, and we promise you to have no others." But the Amazons said—" We could not live with your women—our customs are quite different from theirs. To draw the bow, to hurl the javelin, to bestride the horse, these are our arts—of womanly employments we know nothing. Your women, on the contrary, do none of these things; but stay at home in their wagons, engaged in womanish tasks, and never go out to hunt, or to do anything. We should never agree together. But if you truly wish to keep us as your wives, and would conduct yourselves with strict justice towards us, go you home to your parents, bid them give you your inheritance, and then come back to us, and let us and you live together by ourselves."

115. The youths approved of the advice, and followed it. They went and got the portion of goods which fell to them, returned with it, and rejoined their wives, who then addressed them in these words following:—" We are ashamed, and afraid to live in the country where we now are. Not only have we stolen you from your fathers, but we have done great damage to

Scythia by our ravages. As you like us for wives, grant the request we make of you. Let us leave this country together, and go and dwell beyond the Tanais." Again the youths complied.

116. Crossing the Tanais they journeyed eastward a distance of three days' march from that stream, and again northward a distance of three days' march from the Palus Mæotis.[3] Here they came to the country where they now live, and took up their abode in it.[4] The women of the Sauromatæ have continued from that day to the present, to observe their ancient customs,[5] frequently hunting on horseback with their husbands, sometimes even unaccompanied; in war taking the field; and wearing the very same dress as the men.

117. The Sauromatæ speak the language of Scythia,[6] but have never talked it correctly, because the Amazons learnt it imperfectly at the first. Their marriage-law lays it down that no girl shall wed till she has killed a man in battle.[7] Sometimes it happens that a woman dies unmarried at an advanced age, having never been able in her whole lifetime to fulfil the condition.

118. The envoys of the Scythians, on being introduced into

---

[3] Here we have an indication of the belief of Herodotus, that the Palus Mæotis extended some considerable distance eastward of the place where the Tanais fell into it. It has been already observed that a great portion of what is now the government of the Caucasus, as well as part of the country of the Don Cossacks, was probably once under water, and included in the Sea of Azof. Vide supra, ch. 86, note [8], and infra, Appendix, Essay ii.

[4] According to this description the country of the Sauromatæ did not touch the Mæotis, but began about the 48th parallel. Compare however the statement in ch. 21. In later times, as we find by the Periplus of Scylax (p. 74), they certainly reached to the sea.

[5] This is of course the origin of the myth narrated above. That the Sarmatian women had these habits seems to be a certain fact. (Compare Nic. Damasc. Fr. 122; Hippocr. de Aer. Aq. et Loc. § 42; Ephor. Frag. 78; Scylax, Peripl. p. 74.) Yet Niebuhr (Researches, p. 68, note 78, E. T.) regarded the whole matter as a tale without foundation. For modern instances of Amazonian habits, vide supra, ch. 26, note [9], and

ch. 110, note [9].

[6] That the Sauromatæ of Herodotus are the Sarmatians of later times does not appear to admit of a doubt. Niebuhr (Researches, pp. 74-81, traces their gradual progress from the steppes of the Don to the rich plains of Hungary. Thence, under the name of Slaves they overspread Poland and Russia. In them we seem to have a link, elsewhere desiderated, between the Arian and the modern European races. Their name, Sauromatæ (Sauro-Medes or Northern Medes), as well as their locality and language (Boeckh, Corp. Inscr. part xi. pp. 107-117,) connect them with the Median nation, and their identity with the Slaves is a matter of historic certainty. Whether we may presume from the declaration of Herodotus, that the Sauromatæ spoke bad Scythian, to regard the Scyths as Slaves is a distinct question. An analysis of the Scythian language leads to a different result. See Appendix, Essay iii.

[7] Nicholas of Damascus repeats this statement (Fr. 122), but it is not certain that he does more than follow Herodotus.

the presence of the kings of these nations, who were assembled to deliberate, made it known to them, that the Persian, after subduing the whole of the other continent, had thrown a bridge over the strait of the Bosphorus, and crossed into the continent of Europe, where he had reduced the Thracians, and was now making a bridge over the Ister, his aim being to bring under his sway all Europe also. "Stand ye not aloof then from this contest," they went on to say, "look not on tamely while we are perishing—but make common cause with us, and together let us meet the enemy. If ye refuse, we must yield to the pressure, and either quit our country, or make terms with the invaders. For what else is left for us to do, if your aid be withheld from us? The blow, be sure, will not light on you more gently upon this account. The Persian comes against you no less than against us: and will not be content, after we are conquered, to leave you in peace. We can bring strong proof of what we here advance. Had the Persian leader indeed come to avenge the wrongs which he suffered at our hands when we enslaved his people,* and to war on us only, he would have been bound to march straight upon Scythia, without molesting any nation by the way. Then it would have been plain to all, that Scythia alone was aimed at. But now, what has his conduct been? From the moment of his entrance into Europe, he has subjugated without exception every nation that lay in his path. All the tribes of the Thracians have been brought under his sway, and among them even our next neighbours, the Getae."

119. The assembled princes of the nations, after hearing all that the Scythians had to say, deliberated. At the end opinion was divided—the kings of the Geloni, Budini, and Sauromatae were of accord, and pledged themselves to give assistance to the Scythians; but the Agathyrsian and Neurian princes, together with the sovereigns of the Androphagi, the Melanchlaeni, and the Tauri, replied to their request as follows:—"If you had not been the first to wrong the Persians, and begin the war, we should have thought the request you make just; we should then have complied with your wishes, and joined our arms with yours. Now, however, the case stands thus—you, independently of us, invaded the land of the Persians, and so long as God gave you the power, lorded it over them: raised up now by the same God, they are come to do to you the like. We, on our part, did no

---
* Alluding to the Scythian invasion of Asia in the time of Cyaxares. See Book I. chs. 103-105, and supra, ch. 1.

wrong to these men in the former war, and will not be the first to commit wrong now. If they invade our land, and begin aggressions upon us, we will not suffer them; but, till we see this come to pass, we will remain at home. For we believe that the Persians are not come to attack us, but to punish those who are guilty of first injuring them."

120. When this reply reached the Scythians, they resolved, as the neighbouring nations refused their alliance, that they would not openly venture on any pitched battle with the enemy, but would retire before them, driving off their herds, choking up all the wells and springs as they retreated, and leaving the whole country bare of forage. They divided themselves into three bands, one of which, namely that commanded by Scopasis, it was agreed should be joined by the Sauromatæ, and if the Persians advanced in the direction of the Tanais, should retreat along the shores of the Palus Mæotis and make for that river; while if the Persians retired, they should at once pursue and harass them. The two other divisions, the principal one under the command of Idanthyrsus, and the third,[9] of which Taxacis was king, were to unite in one, and, joined by the detachments of the Gelôni and Budini, were, like the others, to keep at the distance of a day's march from the Persians, falling back as they advanced, and doing the same as the others. And first, they were to take the direction of the nations which had refused to join the alliance, and were to draw the war upon them: that so, if they would not of their own free will engage in the contest, they might by these means be forced into it.[1] Afterwards, it was agreed that they should retire into their own land, and, should it on deliberation appear to them expedient, join battle with the enemy.

121. When these measures had been determined on, the Scythians went out to meet the army of Darius, sending on in front as scouts the fleetest of their horsemen. Their wagons, wherein their women and their children lived, and all their cattle, except such a number as was wanted for food, which they kept with them, were made to precede them in their retreat, and

---

[9] These three divisions, and the three kings, Idanthyrsus, Taxacis and Scopasis, recall the ancient triple division of the nation under the mythic Leipoxais, Arpoxais, and Colaxais (supra, ch. 5). Possibly there were at all times three great tribes among the Royal Scythians whose chiefs had a special dignity.

[1] It is to be observed, that, according to the narrative of Herodotus, the nations who assisted the Scythians had the war drawn upon them as much as those who refused. The Sauromatæ, Budini, and Gelôni are even the first sufferers. (Infra, chs. 122, 123.)

departed, with orders to keep marching, without change of course, to the north.

122. The scouts of the Scythians found the Persian host advanced three days' march from the Ister, and immediately took the lead of them at the distance of a day's march, encamping from time to time, and destroying all that grew on the ground. The Persians no sooner caught sight of the Scythian horse than they pursued upon their track, while the enemy retired before them. The pursuit of the Persians was directed towards the single division of the Scythian army,[1] and thus their line of march was eastward toward the Tanais. The Scyths crossed the river, and the Persians after them, still in pursuit. In this way they passed through the country of the Sauromatæ, and entered that of the Budini.

123. As long as the march of the Persian army lay through the countries of the Scythians and Sauromatæ, there was nothing which they could damage, the land being waste and barren; but on entering the territories of the Budini, they came upon the wooden fortress above mentioned,[2] which was deserted by its inhabitants and left quite empty of everything. This place they burnt to the ground; and having so done, again pressed forward on the track of the retreating Scythians, till, having passed through the entire country of the Budini, they reached the desert, which has no inhabitants,[3] and extends a distance of seven days' journey above the Budinian territory. Beyond this desert dwell the Thyssagetæ, out of whose land four great streams flow. These rivers all traverse the country of the Mæotians, and fall into the Palus Mæotis. Their names are the Lycus, the Oarus, the Tanais, and the Syrgis.[4]

124. When Darius reached the desert, he paused from his pursuit, and halted his army upon the Oarus.[5] Here he built eight large forts, at an equal distance from one another, sixty furlongs apart or thereabouts, the ruins of which were still remaining in my day.[6] During the time that he was so occupied,

---

[1] The division of Scopasis (supra, ch. 120).
[2] That is, the town Gelonus. Vide supra, ch. 108.
[3] Mentioned above, ch. 22.
[4] This appears to be the stream called the Hyrgis in ch. 57. It is there said to run into the Tanais. Ptolemy however makes the Hyrgis, as well as the Lycus, run into the Palus Mæotis, between Cremni and the mouth of the Tanais.

[5] The Oarus is generally supposed to represent the Wolga (Ritter, Erdkunde, ii. p. 765; Rennell, p. 90; Mannert, iv. p. 79); but the geography of this region, as described by Herodotus, is so utterly unlike the present conformation of the country, that no positive identifications are possible.
[6] The conjecture is probable that these supposed "forts" were ruined barrows—perhaps of larger size and

the Scythians whom he had been following, made a circuit by the higher regions, and re-entered Scythia. On their complete disappearance, Darius, seeing nothing more of them, left his forts half finished, and returned towards the west. He imagined that the Scythians whom he had seen were the entire nation, and that they had fled in that direction.

125. He now quickened his march, and entering Scythia, fell in with the two combined divisions of the Scythian army,[1] and instantly gave them chase. They kept to their plan of retreating before him at the distance of a day's march; and, he still following them hotly, they led him, as had been previously settled, into the territories of the nations that had refused to become their allies, and first of all into the country of the Melanchlæni. Great disturbance was caused among this people by the invasion of the Scyths first, and then of the Persians. So, having harassed them after this sort, the Scythians led the way into the land of the Androphagi, with the same result as before; and thence passed onwards into Neuris, where their coming likewise spread dismay among the inhabitants. Still retreating they approached the Agathyrsi; but this people, which had witnessed the flight and terror of their neighbours, did not wait for the Scyths to invade them, but sent a herald to forbid them to cross their borders, and to forewarn them, that, if they made the attempt, it would be resisted by force of arms. The Agathyrsi then proceeded to the frontier, to defend their country against the invaders. As for the other nations, the Melanchlæni, the Androphagi, and the Neuri, instead of defending themselves, when the Scyths and Persians overran their lands, they forgot their threats, and fled away in confusion to the deserts lying towards the north. The Scythians, when the Agathyrsi forbade them to enter their country, refrained;[2] and led the Persians back from the Neurian district into their own land.

---

better material than common. Herodotus would hear of them from the Greek traders. His words do not necessarily imply that he had himself seen them; while that he should have penetrated so far into the interior is in the highest degree improbable. Of course we may believe in the existence of the ruins without accepting the tradition connecting them with Darius's invasion. It is, as Dahlmann observes (Life, p. 130, E. T.), extremely unlikely that any forts were built in Scythia by Darius.

[1] The divisions of Idanthyrsus and Taxacis (supra, ch. 120).

[2] The Agathyrsi, having the Carpathians for their frontier, would be better able to defend themselves than the nations which lay further to the east. As "luxurious" and "fond of wearing gold" (supra, ch. 104), the Agathyrsi would also have more to lose than their neighbours.

126. This had gone on so long, and seemed so interminable, that Darius at last sent a horseman to Idanthyrsus, the Scythian king, with the following message:—"Thou strange man, why dost thou keep on flying before me, when there are two things thou mightest do so easily? If thou deemest thyself able to resist my arms, cease thy wanderings and come, let us engage in battle. Or if thou art conscious that my strength is greater than thine—even so thou shouldest cease to run away—thou hast but to bring thy lord earth and water, and to come at once to a conference."

127. To this message Idanthyrsus, the Scythian king, replied:—"This is my way, Persian. I never fear men or fly from them. I have not done so in times past, nor do I now fly from thee. There is nothing new or strange in what I do; I only follow my common mode of life in peaceful years. Now I will tell thee why I do not at once join battle with thee. We Scythians have neither towns nor cultivated lands, which might induce us, through fear of their being taken or ravaged, to be in any hurry to fight with you. If, however, you must needs come to blows with us speedily, look you now, there are our fathers' tombs [1]—seek them out, and attempt to meddle with them—then ye shall see whether or no we will fight with you. Till ye do this, be sure we shall not join battle, unless it pleases us. This is my answer to the challenge to fight. As for lords, I acknowledge only Jove my ancestor,[2] and Vesta, the Scythian queen.[3] Earth and water, the tribute thou askedst, I do not send, but thou shalt soon receive more suitable gifts. Last of all, in return for thy calling thyself my lord, I say to thee, 'Go weep.'" (This is what men mean by the Scythian mode of speech.)[4] So the herald departed, bearing this message to Darius.

128. When the Scythian kings heard the name of slavery they were filled with rage, and despatched the division under

---

[1] The tombs of the kings, which were at the place called Gerrhus (supra, chs. 56 and 71), seem to be meant. These were probably defended by a wattled enclosure (γέρρον) behind which the Scythians would have fought. Common barrows covered, no doubt, as they still cover, the whole country.

[2] Supra, ch. 5.

[3] We may gather from this, that while the Scythians acknowledged a number of deities (vide supra, ch. 59), they paid special honours to Jove and Vesta, the king and queen of Heaven.

[4] Diogenes Laertius (vit. Anachars. l. p. 26) makes Anacharsis the origin of this Greek proverb, and seems to apply it to all free and bold speaking. (Πάρεχε δὴ, he says, ὁ Ἀνάχαρσις καὶ ἀφορμὴν παροιμίας, διὰ τὸ παρρησιαστικὸς εἶναι, Ἡ ἀπὸ Σκυθῶν ῥῆσις.) The remark of Herodotus must therefore be understood of the whole reply of Idanthyrsus, not only of the last words.

Scopasis to which the Sauromatæ were joined, with orders that they should seek a conference with the Ionians, who had been left at the Ister to guard the bridge. Meanwhile the Scythians who remained behind resolved no longer to lead the Persians hither and thither about their country, but to fall upon them whenever they should be at their meals. So they waited till such times, and then did as they had determined. In these combats the Scythian horse always put to flight the horse of the enemy; these last, however, when routed, fell back upon their foot, who never failed to afford them support; while the Scythians, on their side, as soon as they had driven the horse in, retired again, for fear of the foot. By night too the Scythians made many similar attacks.

129. There was one very strange thing which greatly advantaged the Persians, and was of equal disservice to the Scyths, in these assaults on the Persian camp. This was the braying of the asses and the appearance of the mules. For, as I observed before, the land of the Scythians produces neither ass nor mule, and contains no single specimen of either animal, by reason of the cold.[5] So, when the asses brayed, they frightened the Scythian cavalry; and often, in the middle of a charge, the horses, hearing the noise made by the asses, would take fright and wheel round, pricking up their ears, and showing astonishment. This was owing to their having never heard the noise, or seen the form, of the animal before: and it was not without some little influence on the progress of the war.

130. The Scythians, when they perceived signs that the Persians were becoming alarmed, took steps to induce them not to quit Scythia, in the hope, if they stayed, of inflicting on them the greater injury, when their supplies should altogether fail. To effect this, they would leave some of their cattle exposed with the herdsmen, while they themselves moved away to a distance: the Persians would make a foray, and take the beasts, whereupon they would be highly elated.

131. This they did several times, until at last Darius was at his wits' end; hereon the Scythian princes, understanding how

---

[5] The same statement is made by Aristotle (De Generat. An. ii. ad fin.), who agrees with Herodotus as to the cause. M. de Buffon remarks that the ass is originally an inhabitant of warm countries, and has only been recently introduced into colder ones, where he always degenerates. (Histoire des Quadrupèdes, vol. i. p. 160.) The notion of the Hyperboreans sacrificing asses (Pind. Pyth. x. 51) was connected with the belief that they inhabited a warm country (supra, ch. 33, note ⁶).

matters stood, despatched a herald to the Persian camp with presents for the king: these were, a bird, a mouse, a frog, and five arrows. The Persians asked the bearer to tell them what these gifts might mean, but he made answer that he had no orders except to deliver them, and return again with all speed. If the Persians were wise, he added, they would find out the meaning for themselves. So when they heard this, they held a council to consider the matter.

132. Darius gave it as his opinion, that the Scyths intended a surrender of themselves and their country, both land and water, into his hands. This he conceived to be the meaning of the gifts, because the mouse is an inhabitant of the earth, and eats the same food as man, while the frog passes his life in the water; the bird bears a great resemblance to the horse, and the arrows might signify the surrender of all their power. To the explanation of Darius, Gobryas, one of the seven conspirators against the Magus, opposed another which was as follows:—"Unless, Persians, ye can turn into birds and fly up into the sky, or become mice and burrow under the ground, or make yourselves frogs, and take refuge in the fens, ye will never make escape from this land, but die pierced by our arrows." Such were the meanings which the Persians assigned to the gifts.[6]

133. The single division of the Scyths, which in the early part of the war had been appointed to keep guard about the Palus Mæotis,[7] and had now been sent to get speech of the Ionians stationed at the Ister, addressed them on reaching the bridge, in these words;—"Men of Ionia, we bring you freedom, if ye will only do as we recommend. Darius, we understand, enjoined you

---

[6] This story was told, with some not very important alterations, by Pherecydes of Lerus. (See Clem. Alex. Strom. v. pp. 671, 672, where Ἀγρίου should be read for Ἴρων). It is uncertain whether he wrote before or after Herodotus see Müller's Fr. Hist. Gr. vol. i. pp. xxxv.-vl.; Mure's Lit. of Greece, vol. iv. p. 183; Dahlmann's Life of Herodotus, ch. vi. § 7, p. 98, E. T.). As however, he may possibly have written earlier, and Herodotus may have had the passage in question under his eye, it seems worth subjoining in an English dress. "Pherecydes relates," says Clemens, "that Idanthuras the Scythian king, when Darius had crossed the Ister, threatened him with war, sending him not a letter, but a symbol, which was a mouse, a frog, a bird, an arrow, and a plough. When there was —not unnaturally—much doubt concerning the meaning of this message, Orontopagus, the chiliarch, maintained that it was a surrender of the empire; for he conjectured the mouse to mean their dwellings, the frog their waters, the bird their air, the arrows their arms, and the plough their country. But Xiphodres interpreted it differently; for he explained it thus:—'Unless like birds we fly aloft, or like mice burrow under-ground, or like frogs betake ourselves to the water, we shall never escape their weapons; for we are not masters of their country.'" The story in Herodotus is more Scythian, in omitting any mention of dwellings.

[7] Vide supra, ch. 120.

to keep your guard here at this bridge just sixty days; then, if he did not appear, you were to return home. Now, therefore, act so as to be free from blame, alike in his sight, and in ours. Tarry here the appointed time,* and at the end go your ways." Having said this, and received a promise from the Ionians to do as they desired, the Scythians hastened back with all possible speed.

134. After the sending of the gifts to Darius, the part of the Scythian army, which had not marched to the Ister, drew out in battle array horse and foot' against the Persians, and seemed about to come to an engagement. But as they stood in battle array, it chanced that a hare started up between them and the Persians, and set to running; when immediately all the Scyths who saw it, rushed off in pursuit, with great confusion, and loud cries and shouts. Darius, hearing the noise, inquired the cause of it, and was told that the Scythians were all engaged in hunting a hare. On this he turned to those with whom he was wont to converse, and said:—"These men do indeed despise us utterly: and now I see that Gobryas was right about the Scythian gifts. As, therefore, his opinion is now mine likewise, it is time we form some wise plan, whereby we may secure ourselves a safe return to our homes." "Ah! sire," Gobryas rejoined, "I was well nigh sure, ere I came here, that this was an impracticable race—since our coming I am yet more convinced of it, especially now that I see them making game of us. My advice is, therefore, that, when night falls, we light our fires as we are wont to do at other times, and leaving behind us on some pretext that portion of our army which is weak and unequal to hardship, taking care also to leave our asses tethered, retreat from Scythia, before our foes march forward to the Ister and destroy the bridge, or the Ionians come to any resolution which may lead to our ruin."

---

* It is evident that the sixty days ought to have expired long ere this. Scythia is a square of 20 days' journey each way (ch. 101). Darius had marched along one side, and had skirted two others. He had also gone so far out of the direct course as to reach the Oarus, and he had tarried there long enough to build eight great forts. He had begun to descend the fourth side of Scythia, when the Scythians, under Scopasis, set off for the Ister, and they had to complete that side of Scythia before they could reach the Ionians. Altogether the time consumed, according to Herodotus's own showing, ought to have been 90 or 100 days.

' We now hear for the first time of the Scythians having infantry. It is scarcely possible that they really possessed any such force. The nomade nations of these countries have always lived on horseback, and are utterly helpless on foot. (Compare Hommaire de Hell, Travels, p. 243, E. T., and Herodotus's own words, supra, ch. 46, and infra, ch. 136.) If they had had a force of foot-soldiers, Darius might have compelled them to a general engagement.

135. So Gobryas advised; and when night came, Darius followed his counsel, and leaving his sick soldiers, and those whose loss would be of least account, with the asses also tethered about the camp, marched away. The asses were left that their noise might be heard: the men, really because they were sick and useless, but under the pretence, that he was about to fall upon the Scythians with the flower of his troops, and that they meanwhile were to guard his camp for him. Having thus declared his plans to the men whom he was deserting, and having caused the fires to be lighted, Darius set forth, and marched hastily towards the Ister. The asses, aware of the departure of the host, brayed louder than ever; and the Scythians, hearing the sound, entertained no doubt of the Persians being still in the same place.

136. When day dawned, the men who had been left behind, perceiving that they were betrayed by Darius, stretched out their hands towards the Scythians, and spoke as befitted their situation. The enemy no sooner heard, than they quickly joined all their troops in one, and both portions of the Scythian army,—alike that which consisted of a single division, and that made up of two,[1]—accompanied by all their allies, the Sauromatæ, the Budini, and the Geloni, set off in pursuit, and made straight for the Ister. As, however, the Persian army was chiefly foot, and had no knowledge of the routes, which are not cut out in Scythia;[2] while the Scyths were all horsemen and well acquainted with the shortest way; it so happened that the two armies missed one another, and the Scythians, getting far ahead of their adversaries, came first to the bridge. Finding that the Persians were not yet arrived, they addressed the Ionians, who were aboard their ships, in these words:—"Men of Ionia, the number of your days is out, and ye do wrong to remain. Fear doubtless has kept you here hitherto: now, however, you may safely break the bridge, and hasten back to your homes, rejoicing that you are free, and thanking for it the gods and the Scythians. Your former lord and master we undertake so to handle, that he will never again make war upon any one."

137. The Ionians now held a council. Miltiades the Athenian, who was king of the Chersonesites upon the Hellespont,[3] and

---

[1] Vide supra, ch. 120.
[2] Even at the present day Southern Russia possesses but few made roads. The turf of the steppes is smooth and firm, and is traversed, at discretion, by the carts of the peasantry. (See Clarke's Russia, pp. 186, 187, 212, 213, &c. De Hell, Travels, p. 19, E. T.)
[3] Concerning the mode in which this sovereignty came into the family of

their commander ⁴ at the Ister, recommended the other generals to do as the Scythians wished, and restore freedom to Ionia.⁵

Miltiades, vide infra, Book vi. chs. 34-36. The dominion of Miltiades was over the whole of the peninsula, as far as the wall which stretched across from Pactya to Cardia.

³ "The Chersonesites upon the Hellespont" are here distinguished from the inhabitants of the Heracleotic Chersonesus, which occupied the peninsula between the port of Balaclava and the great harbour of Sebastopol. See below vii. 33.

⁴ Mr. Blakesley (note 365 on ch. 141) supposes Herodotus to mean that Miltiades commanded the whole fleet, and endeavours to explain in what sense; but Herodotus certainly does not say that Miltiades commanded any besides his own subjects.

⁵ Dr. Thirlwall has called in question the truth of this story (Hist. of Greece, vol. ii. Append. ii. p. 480), which he considers to have been fabricated by Miltiades on his return to Attica, B.C. 493. Mr. Grote (History, vol. iv. p. 368, note) maintains the credit of the great Athenian. The difficulty in connexion with the story is, to understand how Miltiades could have remained undisturbed in his sovereignty (as he appears to have done, Herod. vi. 40) during the campaigns of Megabazus and Otanes (Herod. v. 1-2, and 26), if he had taken the part against Darius which is ascribed to him. Mr. Grote cuts the Gordian knot, by assuming that he did not remain, but fled to Attica at once, as Cornelius Nepos asserts. (Milt. § 3.) The flight which Herodotus ascribes to fear of the Scythians (vi. 40), Mr. Grote considers to have been caused in reality by fear of the Persians.

The objections to this are, first, that it "contradicts Herodotus in a matter of fact very conspicuous"—the enemy before whom Miltiades fled; and secondly, that it is incompatible with the chronology. Mr. Grote says that "the chronological data in Herodot. vi. 40 are exceedingly obscure and perplexed," and therefore he sets them aside altogether. But one thing is sufficiently clear from them, viz. that the Scythian invasion of the Chersonese and flight of Miltiades happened only three years before his final return to Attica; that is, nearly twenty years after the Scythian expedition. Surely Herodotus cannot have confounded a flight from the Persians in B.C. 514 or 513, with one from the Scythians in B.C. 493, the undoubted year of the Scythian inroad. (See note ad loc.)

Mr. Grote, however, shows good reasons for rejecting Dr. Thirlwall's hypothesis. There would have been too many witnesses to the true facts of the case for a fabrication to have had any chance of success. And Herodotus's inquiries would have been made chiefly on the Asiatic side, among those whose fathers had been present at the bridge, and who had no interest in exaggerating the patriotism of Miltiades. We must therefore accept the fact of Miltiades having advocated the breaking up of the bridge.

How then may the fact that, notwithstanding this advocacy, he escaped the Persian vengeance during the campaigns of Megabazus and Otanes be accounted for? I conjecture, *because it was then unknown*. The matter would be debated by the Greek princes *in secret conclave*. It would be a point of honour on the part of all present not to divulge what had been proposed at the meeting, especially when to do so would be to bring ruin on one of their own body. Darius would know that the Ionians had been urged by the Scythians to break the bridge, and that Histiæus had been very active in persuading his colleagues not to listen to them. But he need not have known that any of the despots had actually proposed complying with the entreaties of the Scyths. His special gratitude to Histiæus may also in part have been owing to the fact, of which there are indications (chs. 136 and 141), that Histiæus held a higher rank than his brother despots, and had the *special* charge of the bridge.

When the Ionian revolt broke out, and Miltiades joined in it, as is evident by his attack on Lemnos, a Persian dependency (Herod. v. 27), there would be no longer any need of concealment. Miltiades would boast of what he had formerly done, and it would become known generally.

That the Scythians, twenty years afterwards, did not spare the Chersonese on this account, does not seem to me at all strange. Their incursions were not wars undertaken from motives of policy, but plundering inroads. Further, they might not know that Miltiades had been

But Histiæus the Milesian opposed this advice. "It is through Darius," he said, "that we enjoy our thrones in our several states. If his power be overturned, I cannot continue lord of Miletus, nor ye of your cities. For there is not one of them which will not prefer democracy to kingly rule." Then the other captains, who, till Histiæus spoke, were about to vote with Miltiades, changed their minds, and declared in favour of the last speaker.

138. The following were the voters on this occasion—all of them men who stood high in the esteem of the Persian king: the tyrants of the Hellespont,—Daphnis of Abydos, Hippoclus of Lampsacus, Herophantus of Parium, Metrodôrus of Proconnêsus, Aristagoras of Cyzicus, and Ariston of Byzantium;[6] the Ionian princes— Strattis of Chios, Æaces of Samos,[7] Laodamas of Phocæa, and Histiæus of Miletus, the man who had opposed Miltiades. Only one Æolian of note was present, to wit, Aristagoras[8] of Cymê.[9]

139. Having resolved to follow the advice of Histiæus, the Greek leaders further determined to speak and act as follows. In order to appear to the Scythians to be doing something, when in fact they were doing nothing of consequence, and, likewise to prevent them from forcing a passage across the Ister by the bridge, they resolved to break up the part of the bridge which abutted on Scythia, to the distance of a bowshot from the river bank; and to assure the Scythians, while the demolition was proceeding, that there was nothing which they would not do to pleasure them. Such were the additions made to the resolu-

---

on their side; and if they did, the gratitude of a barbarous people does not often last twenty years.

[6] Except Byzantium, all these places are on the Asiatic side. Byzantium had no doubt been compelled to submit at the time of the passage of the Bosphorus. Why Miltiades, whose kingdom lay so much out of Darius's route, had submitted, is not so apparent.

[7] Sylosōn, it appears, did not long enjoy the throne, which he had recovered by Persian aid iii. 149. He had now been succeeded by his son, Æaces (vide infra, vi. 13).

[8] Of whom we hear again, infra, v. 37-8.

[9] This list is remarkable, both for what it omits, and for what it contains. The absence of the Lesbians, who a few years later furnished 70 ships to the combined fleet at Ladê, is the most unaccountable omission of all. Teos also

on that occasion supplied 17 ships, Priênê 12, and Erythræ 8; while Phocæa could give but three. Yet here the Phocæan leader appears as possessing a vote, while Lesbos, Teos, Priênê, and Erythræ, are unmentioned. One cannot but suspect that the list of Herodotus is imperfect, and that more contingents were present than he names. It may be conjectured that the list came from a Hellespontine source (from the family of Miltiades, most probably); and thus, while the catalogue of the Hellespontine cities is tolerably complete, there being no important omission but that of Chalcêdon, only those Ionian and Æolian leaders who were of particular repute obtained any mention. Phocæa, though so weak in ships, might still possess a leader of eminence, as was found to be the case in the Ionian struggle, when the entire command was placed in the hands of Dionysius (vi. 11).

tion of Histiæus; and then Histiæus himself stood forth and made answer to the Scyths in the name of all the Greeks:—
"Good is the advice which ye have brought us, Scythians, and well have ye done to come here with such speed. Your efforts have now put us into the right path; and our efforts shall not be wanting to advance your cause. Your own eyes see that we are engaged in breaking the bridge; and, believe us, we will work zealously to procure our own freedom. Meantime, while we labour here at our task, be it your business to seek them out, and, when found, for our sakes, as well as your own, to visit them with the vengeance which they so well deserve."

140. Again the Scyths put faith in the promises of the Ionian chiefs, and retraced their steps, hoping to fall in with the Persians. They missed, however, the enemy's whole line of march; their own former acts being to blame for it. Had they not ravaged all the pasturages of that region, and filled in all the wells, they would have easily found the Persians whenever they chose. But, as it turned out, the measures which seemed to them so wisely planned were exactly what caused their failure. They took a route where water was to be found and fodder could be got for their horses, and on this track sought their adversaries, expecting that they too would retreat through regions where these things were to be obtained. The Persians, however, kept strictly to the line of their former march, never for a moment departing from it; and even so gained the bridge with difficulty. It was night when they arrived, and their terror, when they found the bridge broken up, was great; for they thought that perhaps the Ionians had deserted them.

141. Now there was in the army of Darius a certain man, an Egyptian, who had a louder voice than any other man in the world. This person was bid by Darius to stand at the water's edge, and call Histiæus the Milesian. The fellow did as he was bid; and Histiæus, hearing him at the very first summons, brought the fleet to assist in conveying the army across, and once more made good the bridge.

142. By these means the Persians escaped from Scythia, while the Scyths sought for them in vain, again missing their track.[1] And hence the Scythians are accustomed to say of the

---

[1] This seems to be the proper place for reviewing the entire history of this expedition, which almost all moderns agree in thinking absolutely incredible (Niebuhr, Vortrage über alte Geschichte, i. pp. 189-191; Grote, iv. pp. 354-361; Thirlwall, ch. xiv. p. 723, 8vo. ed.; Dahlmann's Life, p. 120, E. T.).

Ionians, by way of reproach, that, if they be looked upon as freemen, they are the basest and most dastardly of all mankind—

That Darius led an expedition into Scythia, across the Canal of Constantinople and the Danube, may be regarded as historically certain: it is a point in which Ctesias himself did not venture to contradict Herodotus. (Excerpt. ap. Photium, § 17.) The passage of the Straits, and of the river, by bridges made by Greeks of Greek ships, and the presence of Miltiades, on both occasions, must be taken to be facts as assured as the battle of Marathon itself.

Again, the general result of the expedition—negative rather than positive —that Darius penetrated to some distance into Scythia, and returned without obtaining any remarkable success, or experiencing any very overwhelming loss, may be regarded as ascertained. Ctesias agrees sufficiently, though he represents the matter less favourably to the Persians than Herodotus; but the proof is to be found in the course of events—the safe return of the king—his ability to detach 80,000 men under Megabazus (ch. 143)—and the permanent hold which he obtained on Europe by his attack. The incredulity of the moderns attaches to the circumstances of the campaign in Scythia—to the line of route and length of march—as well as to the period of time (above two months) during which the army is supposed to have remained in the enemy's country. It is regarded as impossible, first, that Darius should have been able to effect the passage of such great rivers as the Dniestr, the Dniepr and the Don, without his fleet and in the summer (Grote, p. 355; Niebuhr, p. 191); and secondly, that the army should have been able to exist for so long a time, and to traverse so vast a territory, when the country was itself so barren, and had moreover been purposely exhausted before his coming. (Grote, ib.; Niebuhr, p. 190; Thirlwall, p. 225.) But these difficulties are not so formidable as they appear; and if they were greater, it would perhaps be better to accept the narrative with them, than to suppose either that Herodotus failed to obtain any knowledge of the real course of the campaign, or that he purposely gave us a grand graphic sketch in lieu of history. This latter seems to be what Mr. Grote imagines (p. 358, and again, p. 359), without seeing, apparently, what a fatal blow is thereby dealt to the general credibility of the historian. For my own part I cannot conceive it possible either that Herodotus should fail utterly to obtain a general notion of the march of the Persians, or that, knowing it, he should set it aside and give us instead a grand "illustrative fiction."

If we accept the existence of the town Gelonus, and the semi-Greek character of its inhabitants (accepted by Niebuhr, p. 193), the burning of that town by Darius would be a plain matter of fact, which could not but have been known to the Pontic Greeks, if it really happened, and which could scarcely have been believed by them if it did not. But if, with Rennell (Geography, p. 103), and, I believe, Klaproth and Reichard, we allow this expedition to have reached thus far, and to have returned, we may almost as well accept the line of march mentioned by Herodotus as assume any other—the length of the way and difficulties of the route being much the same in any case, supposing the army to have reached Gelonus. The question seems to be, can we conceive the Pontic Greeks, in 50 or 60 years' time, losing all recollection of the real course of the invasion, or not? If we cannot, and they distinctly declared that their staple, Gelonus, was burnt by the invader, then we have an ascertained point, certainly beyond the Don (ch. 21, and again chs. 122, 123), and deep in the interior of the country, to which the expedition reached; and the difficulties as to how the army obtained supplies, and how the great rivers were crossed, must admit of explanation, whether the true explanation has as yet been hit upon, or no.

Even the tradition that the curious old walls, which were to be seen between the Wolga and the Don (τῶν ἐν δὲ ἐπὶ τὰ ἑπτέρα σὺν ἦν, ch. 124), owed their origin to Darius, although probably untrue as a matter of fact (see note on the place), yet would scarcely have arisen so soon after the event, if his expedition had never approached the region in which they lay.

With respect to the difficulties which have induced so many historical critics to reject the narrative of Herodotus, it may be observed, first, that the Persians were probably very skilful in the passage of rivers, from the frequent occasion which they had to cross the

but if they be considered as under servitude, they are the faithfullest of slaves, and the most fondly attached to their lords.

143. Darius, having passed through Thrace, reached Sestos in the Chersonese, whence he crossed by the help of his fleet into

Asia, leaving a Persian, named Megabazus,[2] commander on the European side. This was the man on whom Darius once conferred special honour by a compliment which he paid him before all the Persians. He was about to eat some pomegranates, and had opened the first, when his brother Artabanus asked him "what he would like to have in as great plenty as the seeds of the pomegranate?" Darius answered—"Had I as many men like Megabazus as there are seeds here, it would please me better than to be lord of Greece." Such was the compliment wherewith Darius honoured the general to whom at this time he gave the command of the troops left in Europe, amounting in all to some eighty thousand men.[3]

144. This same Megabazus got himself an undying remembrance among the Hellespontians, by a certain speech which he made. It came to his knowledge, while he was staying at Byzantium, that the Chalcedonians made their settlement seventeen years earlier than the Byzantines. "Then," said he, "the Chalcedonians must at that time have been labouring under blindness—otherwise, when so far more excellent a site was open to them, they would never have chosen one so greatly inferior."[4] Megabazus now, having been appointed to take the command upon the Hellespont, employed himself in the reduction of all those states which had not of their own accord joined the Medes.

145. About this very time another great expedition was

---

[2] Or *Megabyrus*, according to one MS., a reading confirmed by Eustathius (ad Il. ii. p. 182, 27), and to a certain extent by Plutarch, who tells the story of Megabyzus's son, Zopyrus (Apophthegm. vol. ii. p. 173, A.). But it is not likely that Herodotus intends the conspirator. He would not speak of him merely as ἀνὴρ Πέρσης.

[3] Hence the absurdity of Rennell's supposition (Geogr. p. 114), that the number in ch. 87 ought to be 70,000 instead of 700,000. Hence too the certainty which we have that Darius fared infinitely better than most of those who have made similar attempts, as Cræsus, Julian, and Napoleon.

[4] Strabo says (vii. p. 464) that as early as the time of the founding of Byzantium, this reproach was made against the Chalcedonians. According to him, the Delphian oracle advised certain Greeks, who wished to found a colony, and asked to have a site recommended them, "to build their city over against the *blind men*"—by which the Chalcedonians were understood to be meant. Tacitus follows this tale (Annal. xii. 63), with which Herodotus is evidently unacquainted.

The great advantages of the position occupied by Byzantium are elaborately set forth by Polybius (iv. 38). Gibbon's description (Decline and Fall, ch. xvii. pp. 6-10) is excellent. Considering how unimportant a place Byzantium was when Herodotus wrote, and how great a city it has become, it is interesting to see that its capabilities had *really* been observed as early, *at least*, as the time of our author.

Chalcedon was founded by the Megareans (Thucyd. iv. 75) about the year B.C. 674. (Clinton's F. H. vol. i. p. 186.) Byzantium, founded seventeen years later, B.C. 657, was likewise a Megarean colony. (Scymn. Ch. 717; Steph. Byz. ad voc.)

undertaken against Libya,⁴ on a pretext which I will relate when I have premised certain particulars. The descendants of the Argonauts in the third generation,⁵ driven out of Lemnos by the Pelasgi who carried off the Athenian women from Brauron,⁶ took ship and went to Lacedæmon, where, seating themselves on Mount Taygetum,⁷ they proceeded to kindle their fires. The Lacedæmonians, seeing this, sent a herald to inquire of them "who they were, and from what region they had come;" whereupon they made answer, "that they were Minyæ,⁸ sons of the heroes by whom the ship Argo was manned; for these persons had stayed awhile in Lemnos, and had there become their progenitors." On hearing this account of their descent, the Lacedæmonians sent to them a second time, and asked, "what was their object in coming to Lacedæmon, and there kindling their fires?" They answered, "that, driven from their own land by the Pelasgi, they had come, as was most reasonable, to their fathers;¹ and their wish was to dwell with them in their country, partake their privileges, and obtain allotments of land.² It seemed good to the Lacedæmonians to receive the Minyæ among them on their own terms; to assign them lands, and enrol them in their tribes.³ What chiefly moved them to this was the con-

---

⁴ Vide infra, ch. 167. Herodotus looks upon the expedition of Aryandes as undertaken in reality against all the independent African nations.

⁵ The myth ran, that in Lemnos at the time of the Argonautic expedition there were no males, the women having revenged their ill-treatment upon the men by murdering them all. The Argonauts touched at the island, and were received with great favour. They stayed some months, and the subsequent population of the island was the fruit of this visit. Hypsipyle, the queen, had twin sons by Jason. (Apollod. i. 9, 17; Apollon. Rhod. i. 609-915; Herodes. Fr. 44.) Sophocles wrote a tragedy (the Λήμνιαι), which is lost, upon this piece of ancient story.

⁶ Vide infra, vi. 1:18.

⁷ Taygetum or Taygetus (Pliny) is the high mountain-range west of the valley of the Eurotas, the modern Pentedactylon.

⁸ The Argonauts generally were called Minyæ (Pind. Pyth. iv. 69). This was said by some to be on account of Jason's descent from Minyas (Apollon. Rhod. i. 229-233); but there is reason to believe that the Minyæ were in early times a very powerful race in Greece, having settlements in Thessaly (Plin. H. N. iv. 8), and Magnesia (Strab. ix. p. 601; Schol. ad Ap. Rhod. i. 763), as well as about Orchomenos. Strabo (l. s. c.) says that, according to some writers, Iolcus was a colony from Orchomenus.

¹ According to some, Hercules himself was one of the Argonauts (Apollod. i. 9, § 19); and accompanied the expedition beyond Lemnos. But the reference here is evidently to Castor and Pollux, the two great heroes of Sparta, who are always enumerated among the companions of Jason (Apoll. Rhod. i. 146-147; Pind. Pyth. iv. 305; Apollod. i. 9, § 10).

² It may be reasonably conjectured that these fugitives were in reality Minyans of Orchomenus driven out a little earlier by the irruption of the Boeotians from Arne (Thucyd. i. 12), and that they invented this story, in order to claim kindred with the Spartans. Or perhaps, as K. O. Müller supposes, it was invented for them in after times. The expelled Minyans went chiefly to Asia Minor. (Supra, i. 146.)

³ K. O. Müller (Orchom. p. 313) thinks it incredible that the Minyans should really have been received into full citizenship; and supposes that they

sideration that the sons of Tyndarus[4] had sailed on board the Argo. The Minyæ, on their part, forthwith married Spartan wives, and gave the wives, whom they had married in Lemnos, to Spartan husbands.

146. However, before much time had elapsed, the Minyæ began to wax wanton, demanded to share the throne, and committed other impieties: whereupon the Lacedæmonians passed on them sentence of death, and, seizing them, cast them into prison. Now the Lacedæmonians never put criminals to death in the daytime, but always at night. When the Minyæ, accordingly, were about to suffer, their wives, who were not only citizens, but daughters of the chief men among the Spartans, entreated to be allowed to enter the prison, and have some talk with their lords; and the Spartans, not expecting any fraud from such a quarter, granted their request. The women entered the prison, gave their own clothes to their husbands, and received theirs in exchange: after which the Minyæ, dressed in their wives' garments, and thus passing for women, went forth. Having effected their escape in this manner, they seated themselves once more upon Taÿgetum.[5]

147. It happened that at this very time Theras, son of Autesion (whose father Tisamenus was the son of Thersander, and grandson of Polynices), was about to lead out a colony from Lacedæmon. This Theras, by birth a Cadmeian, was uncle on the mother's side to the two sons of Aristodêmus,[6] Procles and

---

were admitted among the Pericœci. It is certain that in later times the Spartans were excessively chary of bestowing their citizenship (Arist. Pol. ii. 6, § 12). Herodotus himself says, in another place ('ix. 33, 34), that they never imparted it but to two men. However we cannot argue from their practice at a later period what they might have done in early times, especially so soon after their first settlement, and when they may have been glad to receive an increase of strength from any quarter. It is quite possible therefore that the Minyans may have been received into actual citizenship. (Compare the reception of the Sabine refugees into the Roman people, Liv. ii. 16.) This is certainly what Herodotus intends.

[4] Castor and Pollux. Vide supra, ch. 145, note [1].

[5] Plutarch (de Virt. Mulier. tom. ii. p. 247) tells this story with remarkable variations from the Herodotean narrative. According to him, the fugitives were not the Minyæ driven out by the Pelasgi, but the Pelasgi driven out in their turn by the Athenians. They were not received into citizenship, but rebelled on account of being refused civil rights. They did not finally settle in Thera and Elis, but in Melos and Crete. We may learn from this the extreme uncertainty of the ancient stories, even when their character is least mythic. Polyænus gave both narratives. (Strat. vii. ch. 49, viii. ch. 61.)

[6] Vide infra, vi. 52. The authors of this genealogy, which may be thus exhibited—

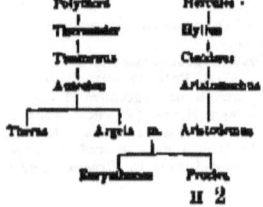

Eurysthenes, and, during their infancy, administered in their right the royal power. When his nephews, however, on attaining to man's estate, took the government, Theras, who could not bear to be under the authority of others after he had wielded authority so long himself, resolved to leave Sparta, and cross the sea to join his kindred. There were in the island now called Thera,[*]

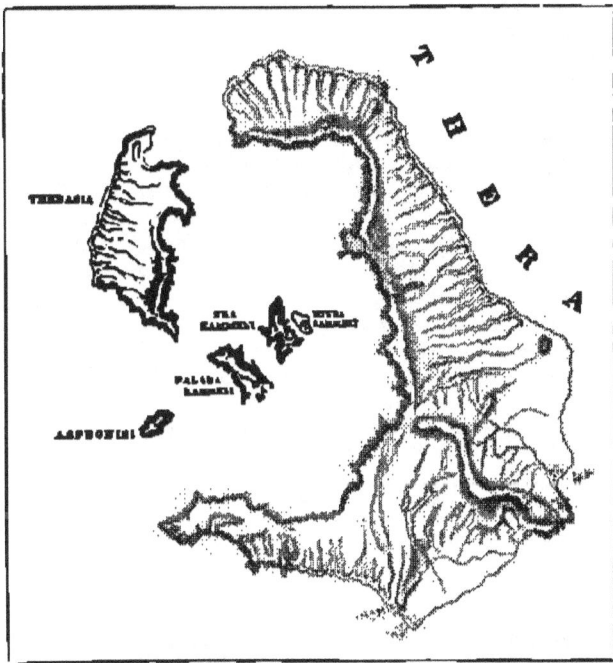

intended probably to represent the history thus. Aristodemus, son of Aristomachus, married Argeia, daughter of Autesion, great-grandson of Polynices, and king of Thebes, while the Cadmeians were still unconquered. On the invasion of the Bœotians, Theras, her brother, who had succeeded his father Autesion, was driven out and took refuge with Aristodemus, his brother-in-law, at Sparta. Aristodemus dying while his sons, Eurysthenes and Procles, were under age, Theras, their uncle, naturally became their guardian.

[*] Thera is the island, or group of islands, now known by the name of Santorin, lying to the south of the other Cyclades. Pliny (H. N. ii. 87) says that it first appeared in the fourth year of the 135th Olympiad (B.C. 237). This must evidently be a mistake. It is conjectured that a great volcanic change took place at this date, by which the original Thera was broken up into the three islands of Thera, Therasia, and Aspronisi. (See Capt. Graves's article in the Journal of the Geograph. Society, vol. xx. Art. 1.) Capt. Graves supposes that the name Calliste, "the most beautiful," properly applied to it "before the eruption" which left it almost in its present state (p. 1). His own descrip-

but at that time Callisté, certain descendants of Membliarus, the son of Pœciles, a Phœnician. (For Cadmus, the son of Agenor, when he was sailing in search of Europé, made a landing on this island; and, either because the country pleased him, or because he had a purpose in so doing, left there a number of Phœnicians, and with them his own kinsman Membliarus. Callisté had been inhabited by this race for eight generations of men, before the arrival of Theras from Lacedæmon.)

148. Theras now, having with him a certain number of men from each of the tribes, was setting forth on his expedition hitherward. Far from intending to drive out the former inhabitants, he regarded them as his near kin, and meant to settle among them. It happened that just at this time the Minyæ, having escaped from their prison, had taken up their station upon Mount Taÿgetum; and the Lacedæmonians, wishing to destroy them, were considering what was best to be done, when Theras begged their lives, undertaking to remove them from the territory. His prayer being granted, he took ship, and sailed, with three triaconters, to join the descendants of Membliarus. He was not, however, accompanied by all the Minyæ, but only

by some few of them.⁴ The greater number fled to the land of the Paroreats,⁵ and Caucons,⁶ whom they drove out, themselves occupying the region in six bodies, by which were afterwards built the towns of Lepreum, Macistus, Phryxæ, Pyrgus, Epium, and Nudium;⁷ whereof the greater part were in my day demolished by the Eleans.⁸

148. The island was called Thera after the name of its founder. This same Theras had a son, who refused to cross the sea with him; Theras therefore left him behind, "a sheep," as he said, "among wolves." From this speech his son came to be called Œolycus, a name which afterwards grew to be the only one by which he was known. This Œolycus was the father of Ægeus, from whom sprang the Ægidæ, a great tribe⁹ in Sparta. The men of this tribe lost at one time all their children, whereupon they were bidden by an oracle to build a temple to the furies of

---

⁴ Three triaconters could not have accommodated more than about 350 or 360 men. The Minyæ were probably much more numerous. Their colonization of Thera in conjunction with the Lacedæmonians, had been already celebrated by Pindar:—

Λακεδαιμονίων μυχίατοι δι᾽ ἡμῶν
ὅσων τὰν ποτε Καλλίστας ἀνέμωσαν ἀχθον
νᾶσον.—Pyth. iv. 261, ed. Dissen.

Apollonius Rhod. (iv. 1760-1764), and Pausanias (Lacon. iii. l. § 7) gave nearly the same account. According to the Cyrenaic historians, Theocrastus and Acesander, the head of the Minyan colonists was a certain Samæus (Schol. ad Apollon. Rhod. iv. 1750).

⁵ Paroreatæ is a geographical, not an ethnic appellation. It may be applied to any "dwellers on the mountain-sides." The Lemnians, who are here said to have fled to the Paroreatæ, are themselves called Paroreatæ in the eighth book (ch. 73). The tract of land intended seems to have been the mountainous district between the Neda and the Alpheus, called by Strabo (viii. p. 504) Triphylia, which is sometimes reckoned to Elis, but improperly, as is evident from Herod. viii. 73, and again from Thucyd. v. 34, where Lepreum appears as an independent city. (See Müller's Dorians, ii. p. 465, E. T.)

⁶ The Caucons (Καύκωνες) appear to have been among the most ancient inhabitants of Greece. They are placed upon a par with the Pelasgi and Leleges

(vide supra, Bk. l. ch. 147, note ⁸), from whom they probably did not much differ. The district here mentioned was always looked upon as one of their earliest seats. (Strabo, viii. pp. 495-502.)

⁷ The site of these places can only be fixed conjecturally. Lepreum is probably the Palæokastro near Strovitzi, Macistus Mositzæ, Pyrgus the acropolis near the sea, a little to the north of the Neda. (Cf. Müller, l. s. c. and Leake's Morea, vol. i. p. 56.)

⁸ Lepreum is the only one of the six which can be shown to have maintained its independence. (Thucyd. l. s. c.) Probably it was always the chief town; whence its position at the head of the list. Two hundred Lepreans are named among the confederates at Platæa (infra, ix. 28). Dahlmann correctly observes that the war of the Eleans and Minyans is fixed by Herodotus to his own day. (Life, p. 44, E. T.)

⁹ Herodotus uses the word "tribe" (φυλή), but it seems impossible that the Ægidæ can have been more than a family. (Cf. Müller's Orchomenus. p. 329.) There was another account of their origin entirely unlike that given by Herodotus. They were said to have been Thebans, who accompanied Aristodemus in his last expedition (Ephor. Fr. 13). This seems to be the view of Pindar (Pyth. v. 102; Isth. vii. 21), who claims connexion with the Cyrenæans through the Ægidæ, calling them his own ancestors.

Laïus and Œdipus;[1] they complied, and the mortality ceased. The same thing happened in Thera to the descendants of these men.[2]

150. Thus far the history is delivered without variation both by the Theræans and the Lacedæmonians; but from this point we have only the Theræan narrative. Grinus (they say), the son of Æsanius, a descendant of Theras, and king of the island of Thera, went to Delphi to offer a hecatomb on behalf of his native city. He was accompanied by a large number of the citizens, and among the rest by Battus, the son of Polymnestus, who belonged to the Minyan family of the Euphemidæ.[3] On Grinus consulting the oracle about sundry matters, the Pythoness gave him for answer, "that he should found a city in Libya." Grinus replied to this: "I, O king! am too far advanced in years, and too inactive, for such a work. Bid one of these youngsters undertake it." As he spoke, he pointed towards Battus; and thus the matter rested for that time. When the embassy returned to Thera, small account was taken of the oracle by the Theræans, as they were quite ignorant where Libya was, and were not so venturesome as to send out a colony in the dark.

151. Seven years passed from the utterance of the oracle, and not a drop of rain fell in Thera: all the trees in the island, except one, were killed with the drought. The Theræans upon this sent to Delphi, and were reminded reproachfully, that they had never colonised Libya. So, as there was no help for it, they sent messengers to Crete, to inquire whether any of the Cretans, or of the strangers sojourning among them, had ever travelled as far as Libya: and these messengers of theirs, in their wanderings about the island, among other places visited Itanus,[4] where they fell in with a man, whose name was Corô-

---

[1] Herodotus here employs the less usual form Œdipodes; in v. 60 he has the commoner Œdipus.
[2] That is, of the Minyans who accompanied Theras. The cause in both instances may have been their intermarrying only with one another.
[3] This is a conjectural reading. The MSS. have Εὐθυμίδης or Εὐθυμίδης. Euphemus, son of Neptune, is reckoned among the companions of Jason. (Apollod. I. 9, 16; Apollon. Rhod. I. 179.) The royal family of the Battiadæ traced their descent to him. Hence Pindar calls them γένος Εὐφάμου (Pyth. iv. 256, ed. Dissen.). Compare the passage of Apollonius Rhodius, where the island of Callisté or Thera is styled νᾶσον ἱερὴν τροφὸν Εὐφήμοιο (iv. 17:9).
[4] Itanus lay at the eastern extremity of Crete, near the promontory of the same name (mentioned by Scylax, Peripl. p. 47), which is now Cape Salomone or Cape Itaro. It was a place of some importance, as appears from the coins, which are numerous. The Palæokastro, near Itagnia, probably marks the site. (See Dict. of Greek and Roman Geogr. s. v. Itanus.)

bius, a dealer in purple. In answer to their inquiries, he told them that contrary winds had once carried him to Libya, where he had gone ashore on a certain island which was named Platea.[6] So they hired this man's services, and took him back with them to Thera. A few persons then sailed from Thera to reconnoitre. Guided by Corobius to the island of Platea, they left him there with provisions for a certain number of months, and returned home with all speed to give their countrymen an account of the island.

152. During their absence, which was prolonged beyond the time that had been agreed upon, Corobius' provisions failed him. He was relieved, however, after a while by a Samian vessel,[6] under the command of a man named Colæus, which, on its way to Egypt, was forced to put in at Platea. The crew, informed by Corobius of all the circumstances, left him sufficient food for a year. They themselves quitted the island; and, anxious to reach Egypt, made sail in that direction, but were carried out of their course by a gale of wind from the east. The storm not abating, they were driven past the pillars of Hercules, and at last, by some special guiding providence, reached Tartessus. This trading town was in those days a virgin port, unfrequented by the merchants. The Samians, in consequence, made by the return-voyage a profit greater than any Greeks before their day, excepting Sostratus, son of Laodamas, an Eginetan, with whom no one else can compare. From the tenth part of their gains, amounting to six talents,[7] the Samians made a brazen vessel, in shape like an Argive wine-bowl, adorned with the heads of griffins standing out in high relief.[8] This bowl, supported by three kneeling colossal figures in bronze, of the height of seven cubits, was placed as an offering in the temple of Juno at Samos. The aid given to Corobius was the original cause of that close friendship which afterwards united the Cyrenæans and Theræans with the Samians.[9]

---

[5] There can be little doubt that Platea is the small island of Bomba, which lies off the African coast in the gulf of the same name, lat. 32° 20′, long. 23° 15′. (Cf. Rennell, p. 609, and Pacho, Voyage dans la Marmorique, pp. 51, 52, where the arguments are fully stated.)

[6] The tale which follows is of some consequence, as showing the character of the Samians for naval enterprise. Samos and Phocæa are the only Greek states reported to have reached so far west in their voyages. (Vide supra, i. 163.)

[7] About 1460l. of our money. The entire profit was therefore between 14,000l. and 15,000l.

[8] Concerning the eminence of Samos in the arts, vide supra, Bk. iii. ch. 60, notes [8] and [9].

[9] Of this alliance no traces appear, unless we are to consider in that light the flight of Arcesilaus III. to Samos, and his success in collecting an armament there (infra, chs. 162, 163).

153. The Theræans who had left Corôbius at Platea, when they reached Thera, told their countrymen that they had colonised an island on the coast of Libya. They of Thera, upon this, resolved that men should be sent to join the colony from each of their seven districts, and that the brothers in every family should draw lots to determine who were to go. Battus was chosen to be king and leader of the colony. So these men departed for Platea on board of two pentoconters.[1]

154. Such is the account which the Theræans give. In the sequel of the history their accounts tally with those of the people of Cyrênê; but in what they relate of Battus these two nations differ most widely. The following is the Cyrenaic story. There was once a king named Etearchus, who ruled over Axus,[2] a city in Crete, and had a daughter named Phronima. This girl's mother having died, Etearchus married a second wife; who no sooner took up her abode in his house than she proved a true step-mother to poor Phronima, always vexing her, and contriving against her every sort of mischief. At last she taxed her with light conduct; and Etearchus, persuaded by his wife that the charge was true, bethought himself of a most barbarous mode of punishment. There was a certain Theræan, named Themison, a merchant, living at Axus. This man Etearchus invited to be his friend and guest, and then induced him to swear that he would do him any service he might require.[3] No sooner had he given the promise, than the king fetched Phronima, and, delivering her into his hands, told him to carry her away and throw her into the sea. Hereupon Themison, full of indignation at the fraud whereby his oath had been procured, dissolved forthwith the friendship, and, taking the girl with him, sailed away from Crete. Having reached the open main, to acquit himself of the obligation under which he was laid by his oath to Etearchus, he

---

[1] Justin (xlii. 7) reduces the two ships of Herodotus to one. Even the larger number would have furnished but a poor colony, since a pentoconter can scarcely have accommodated more than about 200 men. The numerical accuracy affected in the Theræan narrative is remarkable (supra, chs. 148, 151, 152, &c.).

[2] This place, called Axus by Herodotus, Oaxus and Saxus on its coins (comp. Steph. Byz. ad voc. ῎Αξος), is not mentioned by Strabo among the cities of Crete. It appears, however, in Scylax, where (as Voss observes) ῎Οαξος should be read for Πάξος (Peripl. p. 42). It lay on the north side of Ida, not far from Cnossus, and retains its name to the present day (Pashley's Travels, vol. i. p. 143). A coin belonging to it may be seen in Chishull (Antiq. As. p. 125). The name is said to have been given from the precipices (ἄξοι = ἄγμοί) among which the town was built (Steph. Byz. ad voc. ῎Οαξος). It furnishes almost a solitary instance of the replacement of the digamma by an omicron.

[3] Of this practice we have another instance, infra, vi. 62.

fastened ropes about the damsel, and, letting her down into the sea, drew her up again, and so made sail for Thera.

155. At Thera, Polymnéstus, one of the chief citizens of the place, took Phronima to be his concubine. The fruit of this union was a son, who stammered and had a lisp in his speech. According to the Cyrenæans and Theræans, the name given to the boy was Battus: in my opinion, however, he was called at the first something else,⁴ and only got the name of Battus after his arrival in Libya, assuming it either in consequence of the words addressed to him by the Delphian oracle, or on account of the office which he held. For, in the Libyan tongue, the word "Battus" means "a king."⁵ And this, I think, was the reason why the Pythoness addressed him as she did: she knew he was to be a king in Libya, and so she used the Libyan word in speaking to him. For after he had grown to man's estate, he made a journey to Delphi, to consult the oracle about his voice; when, upon his putting his question, the Pythoness thus replied to him:—

"Battus, thou camest to ask of thy voice; but Phœbus Apollo
Bids thee establish a city in Libya, abounding in fleeces;"

which was as if she had said in her own tongue, "King, thou camest to ask of thy voice." Then he replied, "Mighty lord, I did indeed come hither to consult thee about my voice, but thou speakest to me of quite other matters, bidding me colonise Libya —an impossible thing! what power have I? what followers?" Thus he spake, but he did not persuade the Pythoness to give him any other response; so, when he found that she persisted in her former answer, he left her speaking, and set out on his return to Thera.

156. After a while, everything began to go wrong both with Battus and with the rest of the Theræans, whereupon these last, ignorant of the cause of their sufferings, sent to Delphi to inquire for what reason they were afflicted. The Pythoness in reply told them, "that if they and Battus would make a settlement at Cyrêné in Libya, things would go better with them."

---

⁴ It is curious that Herodotus was ignorant of the name given in the myth to the first Battus, before he received that appellation from the oracle, especially as it had already been celebrated by a poet whose works he knew. (Pind. Pyth. v. 81, ed. Dissen.) The name was Aristotle, which appears not only in Pindar, but likewise in the works of the Cyrenaic poet, Callimachus (Hymn. ad Apoll. 75), in Heraclides Ponticus (Fr. iv.), Eusebius (Chron. Can. ii. p. 320), and in the Scholiasts passim.

⁵ Hesychius states this likewise (ad voc.); but he can hardly be considered a distinct witness from Herodotus.

SETTLEMENT AT AZIRIS.

Upon this the Theræans sent out Battus with two penteconters, and with these he proceeded to Libya, but within a little time, not knowing what else to do, the men returned and arrived off Thera. The Theræans, when they saw the vessels approaching, received them with showers of missiles, would not allow them to come near the shore, and ordered the men to sail back from whence they came. Thus compelled to return, they settled on an island near the Libyan coast, which (as I have already said) was called Platea. In size it is reported to have been about equal to the city of Cyréné, as it now stands.

157. In this place they continued two years, but at the end of that time, as their ill luck still followed them, they left the island to the care of one of their number, and went in a body to Delphi, where they made complaint at the shrine, to the effect that, notwithstanding they had colonised Libya, they prospered as poorly as before. Hereon the Pythoness made them the following answer:—

"Knowest thou better than I, fair Libya abounding in fleeces?
Better the stranger than he who has trod it? Oh! clever Theræans!"

Battus and his friends, when they heard this, sailed back to Platea: it was plain the god would not hold them acquitted of the colony till they were absolutely in Libya. So, taking with them the man whom they had left upon the island, they made a settlement on the mainland directly opposite Platea, fixing themselves at a place called Aziris, which is closed in on both sides by the most beautiful hills, and on one side is washed by a river.

158. Here they remained six years, at the end of which time the Libyans induced them to move, promising that they would

---

Menecles of Barca, who lived about B.C. 120, gave a much more prosaic account of these matters. According to him, there were violent factions at Thera, and Battus, who was the leader of one, being worsted, was driven into banishment with his partisans. Under these circumstances he applied to the Delphic oracle, and asked whether he should renew the struggle or lead out a colony. The oracle, thus appealed to, recommended the latter course; and suggested Africa by advising a settlement "on the continent." (See Müller's Fr. Hist. Gr. vol. iv. p. 449.)

This comparison seems to be accurate enough. The ruins of Cyrene cover a space very nearly equal to the whole area of Bomba. (See Kiepert's Atlas von Hellas, map xaii.)

If Platea is Bomba, the Aziris of Herodotus must be sought in the valley of the Temineh, the ancient Paliurus. Kiepert appears to think that there was both a district and a port of the name (see the map referred to above), and places the port to the westward of the Ras-it-Tyn. This view is founded seemingly on the statement of Scylax (Peripl. p. 107), a statement which is too corrupt and too vague to be of any service. The district about the Temineh is said by Pacho to suit exactly the description of Herodotus (Voyage dans la Marmarique, p. 53.)

108 APOLLO'S FOUNTAIN. Book IV.

Cyrus from the west.—The Forum and Fountain of Apollo.

lead them to a better situation." So the Greeks left Aziris and were conducted by the Libyans towards the west, their journey being so arranged, by the calculations of their guides, that they passed in the night the most beautiful district of that whole country, which is the region called Irasa.¹ The Libyans brought them to a spring, which goes by the name of Apollo's fountain,² and told them—"Here, Grecians, is the proper place for you to settle; for here the sky leaks."³

159. During the lifetime of Battus,⁴ the founder of the colony,

---

⁹ The friendly terms on which the Greeks stand towards the natives at the first, is here very apparent. Their position resembles that of the first English settlers in America. They minister to the wants of the inhabitants, and are felt as benefactors. The natives do not wish to give them their best lands, but they willingly place them in a very favourable situation. The Greeks also exhibit confidence by placing themselves at some distance from the sea. Both Cyrene and Barca are inland towns. After a while the feeling changes, as it did towards the English settlers. A struggle ensues, and the humble traders become lords of the country.

¹ Irasa is mentioned by Pindar (Pyth. iv. 106, ed. Dissen,) as a city in the neighbourhood of Cyrene. Its situation is very doubtful. Pacho supposes (Voyage, &c., pp. 84-5) that it lay at the north-eastern foot of the great Cyrenaic table-land (which extends from Cyrene a full degree towards the east), in a district which is still remarkable for its fertility, and where a fountain called *Erazen* or *Erasem* by the Arabs, appears to contain a trace of the old name. Hamilton (Wanderings in N. Africa, Introduction, p. xlii.) suggests *El-Kubbrh*, on the road to *Derna*, as the true site. There are many remains of buildings there, and a copious stream, in which he recognises the fountain of *Theste* (see the next chapter).

² The fountain of Apollo is celebrated by Pindar (Pyth. iv. 294, ed. Dissen.). It is thought to be the same with the fountain of *Cyré*, mentioned both by Callimachus and Stephen. (Callim. Hymn. ad Apoll. 81; Steph. Byz. ad voc. *Κυρήνη*), after which, according to one account, Cyrene was named. Modern travellers have recognised it in a copious spring on the road from the necropolis to the plateau whereon the town stood. Della Cella, p. 146, E. T.; Pacho, p. 217; Beechey, p. 423; Hamilton, p. 37). The view (p. 108) is from Beechey's work.

³ Literally, "Here the sky is pierced." Eustathius (ad Hom. Il. p. 742, 22) explains the expression to mean "that the sky is a sort of reservoir, which in other parts of the world is sound and holds water, but at this place leaks." (Compare 2 Kings vii. 2, " If the Lord would make windows in heaven.") The reference is not therefore to the fountain, but to rain, which in most parts of N. Africa is of extreme rarity. (See note on ch. 185.) That abundant rain falls in the Cyrenaica, and along much of the northern coast of Africa, is a well-known fact. Mr. Hamilton says (Wanderings in N. Africa, ch. vii. p. 92): "The rains set in usually about the middle of November, and then come down with a violence which no tent can resist." He himself experienced them at *Teukra* (Tauchira), and speaks of them as "descending every night in torrents, and frequently lasting all day" (p. 150). Advantage is taken of them to sow the corn immediately after the first have fallen, which is sometimes as early as the latter part of October. From the beginning of spring till this time there is rarely a drop of rain, though from the middle of August the sky is almost always cloudy (ibid. p. 94).

No doubt the real circumstance that fixed the exact site of the city was the copious spring or fountain mentioned above, which is still the most abundant in the neighbourhood (Hamilton, p. 38), and which in a country so scant of water as N. Africa would constitute a most strong attraction. The principal public buildings of the town were grouped about this fountain. See the plan overleaf.

⁴ If we might believe the stories told of this Battus by others, the prosperity of Cyrene should date from his time. A scholiast on Aristophanes says that the Libyans brought to his notice the

who reigned forty years, and during that of his son Arcesilaüs, who reigned sixteen, the Cyrenæans continued at the same level, neither more nor fewer in number than they were at the first. But in the reign of the third king, Battus, surnamed the Happy, the advice of the Pythoness brought Greeks from every quarter

valuable *silphium* (infra, ch. 169), and put his image upon their coins (Plut. 425). Another relates that his own citizens, in return for the great benefits which he had conferred on them, made a statue of him in gold, with the silphium in his right hand. The proverb, "Βάττου σίλφιον," which was used for all that was expensive and honourable, is referred by common consent to him. (Suidas ad voc.; Schol. ad Arist. Plut. l. s. c.; Bekker, Anecd. I. p. 224, &c.) As this drug seems certainly to have been the great cause of the wealth and power of Cyrene, if the trade in it is rightly referred to the *first* Battus, Cyrenæan prosperity should begin with him.

into Libya, to join the settlement.* The Cyrenæans had offered to all comers a share in their lands; and the oracle had spoken as follows:—

> "He that is backward to share in the pleasant Libyan acres,
> Sooner or later, I warn him, will feel regret at his folly."

Thus a great multitude were collected together to Cyrênê, and the Libyans of the neighbourhood found themselves stripped of large portions of their lands. So they, and their king Adicran, being robbed and insulted by the Cyrenæans, sent messengers to Egypt, and put themselves under the rule of Apries, the Egyptian monarch; who, upon this, levied a vast army of Egyptians,⁷ and sent them against Cyrênê. The inhabitants of that place left their walls and marched out in force to the district of Irasa, where, near the spring called Thestê, they engaged the

---

* If we may regard as historical the part said to have been taken by the oracle in the founding and establishment of this colony, it will appear that an influence over the destinies of Greece was exercised by the Delphian priests in early times which has seldom been fully recognised. The want of a settlement on the African coast, for the general interests of Greece, is felt; the Delphians determine to have it supplied. They fix on Thera, a Dorian settlement, and the most southern of all the Cyclades, as the point from which the colonisation will most conveniently proceed. They order the colony to be sent out, refuse to be content with anything short of a settlement upon the mainland, watch the progress of the settlement when it is made, and at the fitting moment cause the redundant population of Greece to flow towards it. The powerful and flourishing Greek state of Cyrene is, according to this statement, the absolute creation of the priests of Delphi.

There are not wanting other instances of a somewhat similar influence. We may gather from what is said of Dorieus (infra, v. 42), that he "did not inquire of the Delphic oracle in what land he should settle, or go through any of the customary preparations;" that, at any rate in Dorian states, when a colony was determined on, the choice of the site was habitually left to the oracle. Other examples of this practice are—the settlement of the Æginæans in Southern Thessaly (Plut. Qu. Gr. ii. p. 294,¹ A.), of the Chalcidians at Rhegium (Strab. vi.

p. 370), of the Spartans and Achæans at Crotona (Paus. iii. iii. § 1; Strab. vi. p. 376), and of the Megareans (if the account be true) at Byzantium (Strab. vii. 464). See on this subject Müller's Dorians, i. pp. 282-294, E. T.

⁴ The beauty and fertility of the Cyrenaica are celebrated by all who visit it. Hamilton says (p. 78), "In the neighbourhood of Grennah, the hills abound with beautiful scenes.... Some of them exceed in richness of vegetation, and equal in grandeur, anything that is to be found in the Apennines.... The Wady Shelaleh presents a scene beyond my powers of description. The olive is here contrasted with the fig, the tall cypress and the dark juniper with the arbutus and myrtle, and the pleasant breeze which always blows through the valley is laden with balmy perfumes." Again, on approaching from the west, he observes, "The rest of the journey was over a range of low undulating hills, offering perhaps the most lovely sylvan scenery in the world. The country is like a most beautifully-arranged jardin Anglais, covered with pyramidal clumps of evergreens, variously disposed, as if by the hand of the most refined taste; while bosquets of junipers and cedars, relieved by the pale olive and the bright green of the tall arbutus-tree, afford a most grateful shade from the mid-day sun." (p. 31.)

⁷ Apries had probably not thought it prudent to take his Greek auxiliaries against the Cyrenæans. (See n. ⁸ on Book ii. ch. 163.)—[G. W.]

Egyptian host, and defeated it. The Egyptians, who had never before made trial of the prowess of the Greeks, and so thought but meanly of them, were routed with such slaughter that but a very few of them ever got back home. For this reason, the subjects of Apries, who laid the blame of the defeat on him, revolted from his authority.

160. This Battus left a son called Arcesilaüs, who, when he came to the throne, had dissensions with his brothers, which ended in their quitting him and departing to another region of Libya, where, after consulting among themselves, they founded the city, which is still called by the name then given to it, Barca. At the same time they endeavoured to induce the

---

* Vide supra, ii. 161.
* The quarrel was said to have resulted from the "ill temper" of Arcesilaüs II., who was therefore called ὁ χαλεπός. The brothers here spoken of seem to be the "Perseus, Zacynthus, Aristomedon, and Lycus," by whom Barca was founded, according to Stephen (ad voc. Βάρκη).

¹ There is no difficulty in determining the exact site of Cyrene. The Arabic name Grennah (Κυρήνη, or in the Doric Greek of the place, Κυράνα, sounded A'prāna) is sufficiently close to mark the identity of the ruined city, which is so called, with the Cyrene of former times. Inscriptions and coins dug up on the spot confirm the identification. Della Cella figures one of the latter thus:—

(See his Narrative, p. 143, E. T.) The situation of Grennah likewise corresponds very exactly with the accounts of Cyrene in the geographers. Grennah, according to Beechey, stands on the edge of a high plateau or table-land, 1800 feet above the level of the sea, which is at no great distance, being very distinctly visible, except in hazy weather. (Beechey's Expedition, pp. 434, 435.) This account recalls very remarkably the description in Strabo, who had seen Cyrene as he sailed along the coast: πόλεις μεγάλας ἐν τραπεζώδεσι πεδίοις κειμένας, οἷ ἐκ τοῦ πελάγους ἐφαίνετο πάντα. (xvii. p. 1181.)
The country around Grennah is celebrated for its fertility. The upper plateau, at the edge of which Cyrene stood, is cultivated in wheat and other cereals; the lower one, on which the town looks down, a thousand feet above the sea-level, is richly wooded, and diversified with meadows and corn-fields (see the view, p. 113). The best account will be found in Beechey (pp. 434–437).

The site of Barca is not so readily fixed. Ptolemaïs indeed, with which it has sometimes been confounded (Steph. Byz. in voc. Βάρκη; Strab. xvii. p. 1181; Plin. H. N. v. 5), still exists in the modern Dolmeita, or Ptolemeta, a town of some importance upon the coast, nearly in long. 21°. But that the original Barca was not at Ptolemaïs appears both from Scylax, who places it 11½ miles away from the shore (Peripl. p. 109), and from Ptolemy, who distinguishes the two cities (Geograph. iv. 4). Ptolemaïs undoubtedly arose, not upon the ancient Barca, but upon its port, the Λιμὴν κατὰ Βάρκην of Scylax. Barca has therefore to be sought in the interior, 11 or 12 miles from this place. All recent travellers agree that the extensive plain of Merdj, which lies at the required distance from the coast, is connected with Ptolemeta by two ravines affording a ready communication, and corresponds moreover with the descriptions of Barca left by the Arabian geographers, is the most probable site. It is an objection, however, that the ruins at this place are inconsiderable. (See Della Cella, p. 217, E. T.; Pacho, pp. 175–177; Beechey, pp. 386–402; Hamilton, p. 134.)

² Barca was evidently an African word, and probably the previous name of the place at which the Greeks now

Chap. 100. GENERAL VIEW OF CYRENE. 113

Cyrene—The Acropolis.

Libyans to revolt from Cyrêné. Not long afterwards Arcesilaüs made an expedition against the Libyans who had received his brothers and been prevailed upon to revolt; and they, fearing his power, fled to their countrymen who dwelt towards the east. Arcesilaüs pursued, and chased them to a place called Leucon,³ which is in Libya, where the Libyans resolved to risk a battle. Accordingly they engaged the Cyreneans, and defeated them so entirely that as many as seven thousand of their heavy-armed were slain in the fight. Arcesilaüs, after this blow, fell sick, and, whilst he was under the influence of a draught which he had taken, was strangled by Learchus, one of his brothers.⁴ This Learchus was afterwards entrapped by Eryxo, the widow of Arcesilaüs, and put to death.⁵

161. Battus, Arcesilaüs' son, succeeded to the kingdom, a lame man, who limped in his walk. Their late calamities now induced the Cyreneans to send to Delphi and inquire of the god what form of government they had best set up to secure themselves prosperity. The Pythoness answered by recommending them to fetch an arbitrator from Mantinea in Arcadia.⁶ Accord-

---

settled. It is traced by some to the root *bar*, which is "desert" in Arabic (Bochart, Phaleg, L. 20, p. 496); but this scarcely seems a satisfactory account, as it ignores the third consonant, and does not well apply to the country, which is not desert. May not Barca, as the name of a town, have arisen from some word like the Hebrew בְּרֵכָה, *b'rekah*, "a reservoir," the place having grown up around an attraction of that kind? It must be regarded as doubtful whether the epithet Barca, assumed by Hamilcar at Carthage, was really at all connected with the name of the city. [As applied to him, the term signified lightning, being analogous to the *fulmen* adopted by Hajazet. — G. W.] The town Barca long outlived Cyrene. It was an important place during the Mahometan period; and the name still attaches to the neighbourhood, the whole of the Cyrenaica being known to the Turks as the province of *Barka*.

³ Leucon is not mentioned by any other author; but Ptolemy places a city which he calls Leucoë in those parts. (Geogr. IV. ch. v. p. 121.) Kiepert conjectures this town to have lain between Cyrene and Irasa. (See his map.)

⁴ Nicolas of Damascus seems to have understood the account of Herodotus differently. According to him, Arcesilaüs tried to poison himself in consequence of the defeat of his army; but dying hard in this way, was strangled by his sympathising brother (Fr. 52). Plutarch (b. p. 160) makes Learchus not the brother, but only the friend of Arcesilaüs, and says that he killed him by poison in order to get the crown.

⁵ See, for a full account of this matter, Plutarch (De Virt. Mul. ii. p. 260) and Polyænus (viii. 41). The former is the original narrative. It appears that Learchus governed for a time in the name of his nephew, who was a minor. Eryxo put Learchus to death by the help of her brother Polyarchus, who then became regent and seems to have been the person under whose authority Democax acted. (τὴν ἀν' ἀρχῆς πολιτείαν ὁ Πολύαρχος ἀνέλαβε τοῖς Κυρηναίοις.)

⁶ Mantinea was situated near the eastern frontier of Arcadia, in the high plateau west of the range of Mænalus, the waters of which have no outlet through the hills, but collect in lakes, or disappear in subterranean passages (katavothras). It is now called *Paleopoli*, and lies about 8 miles nearly due north of *Tripolitza*. There are abundant remains, "the circuit of the walls being entire." (Leake's Morea, vol. i. pp. 103-105.)

It is remarkable that the Delphic

ingly they sent; and the Mantineans gave them a man named Demônax,¹ a person of high repute among the citizens; who, on his arrival at Cyrênê, having first made himself acquainted with all the circumstances,* proceeded to enrol the people in three tribes.³ One he made to consist of the Theræans and their vassals; another of the Peloponnesians and Cretans; and a third of the various islanders.⁴ Besides this, he deprived the king

Battus of his former privileges, only reserving for him certain sacred lands and offices;² while, with respect to the powers which had hitherto been exercised by the king, he gave them all into the hands of the people.

162. Thus matters rested during the lifetime of this Battus, but when his son Arcesilaüs came to the throne, great disturbance arose about the privileges. For Arcesilaüs, son of Battus the lame and Pheretima, refused to submit to the arrangements of Demonax the Mantinean, and claimed all the powers of his forefathers. In the contention³ which followed Arcesilaüs was worsted, whereupon he fled to Samos,⁴ while his mother took refuge at Salamis⁵ in the island of Cyprus. Salamis was at that time ruled by Evelthon, the same who offered at Delphi the censer which is in the treasury of the Corinthians,⁶ a work deserving of admiration. Of him Pheretima made request, that he would give her an army, whereby she and her son might regain Cyréné. But Evelthon, preferring to give her anything rather than an army, made her various presents. Pheretima accepted them all, saying, as she took them: "Good is this too, O king! but better were it to give me the army which I crave at thy hands." Finding that she repeated these words each time that he presented her with a gift, Evelthon at last sent her a golden spindle and distaff, with the wool ready for spinning. Again she uttered the same speech as before, whereupon Evelthon rejoined—"These are the gifts I present to women, not armies."

163. At Samos, meanwhile, Arcesilaüs was collecting troops by the promise of granting them lands.⁷ Having in this way

---

² The early kings of the various Grecian states, like those of Rome, were uniformly priests likewise. (Hermann, Pol. Antiq. of Greece, § 56, note 10.) At Sparta we find them still so regarded. (Infra, vi. 56.) Aristotle says (Polit. iii. 8) that it was their usual fate to be left nothing but their priestly character. Compare the institution of the ἄρχων βασιλεὺς at Athens, and the *rex sacrificulus* at Rome. (Livy, ii. 2.)

³ This is most likely the contention (στάσις) of which Aristotle speaks (Pol. vi. 2), and which he ascribes to the want of moderation on the part of those who established the democracy, whereby the nobles (γνώριμοι) were exasperated, and driven to attempt a counter-revolution. According to his view, Demonax had extended the rights of citizenship too far, and had thereby introduced disorders.

⁴ Vide supra, ch. 152, note ⁶.

⁵ Concerning the site of Salamis, vide infra, v. 104, note. Pheretima may perhaps have applied for aid in this quarter on account of its Graeco-Phœnician character.

⁶ See note ⁸ on Book i. ch. 14, and note ⁷ on Book ii. ch. 167. It is not very clear why the offering should have been put into the treasury of the Cypselids.

⁷ It does not appear to me that ἀναδασμός, either in this place or where it occurred before (ch. 159), has the sense which Müller assigns to it. (Dorians, ii. p. 63, E. T.) It does not signify "a new division of their lands,"

drawn together a vast host, he sent to Delphi to consult the oracle about his restoration. The answer of the Pythoness was this: "Loxias grants thy race to rule over Cyrêné, till four kings Battus, four Arcesilaüs by name,⁴ have passed away. Beyond this term of eight generations of men, he warns you not

but simply an allotting of land. On the former occasion the land to be allotted to the new colonists was land previously unoccupied by Greeks, and considered by the nomade Libyans to belong to them (vide supra, ch. 159). On this occasion the estates of the opposite party would furnish the means of fulfilling the promise under which persons were enlisted.

⁴ That the Battiadae continued to reign at Cyrene till the eighth generation is confirmed by Pindar, who calls the Arcesilaüs of his day (Arcesilaüs IV.) ὄγδοον μέρος Ἀρκεσίλας. (Pyth. iv. 65, ed. Dissen.) The Scholiast (ad loc.) states the fact historically, declaring that "four kings Battus, and four Arcesilaüs by name" τέσσαρες μὲν Βάττοι τέσσαρες δὲ Ἀρκεσίλαοι, actually reigned—that the line of descent was uninterrupted from father to son—and that the reign of the fourth Arcesilaüs was followed by a democracy. It may be conjectured that these events had already happened before Herodotus wrote this portion of his History. Heraclides Ponticus (Fr. 4) confirms the Scholiast, adding that Battus, who appears to have been the son of Arcesilaüs IV., was compelled to fly, and took refuge at Euesperides.

The chronology of the reigns presents, however, certain difficulties. According to Solinus, Cyrene was founded B.C. 597 (xxvii. 44); but in that case Battus the Happy, who ascended the throne 56 years later (Herod. iv. 159), would be contemporary, not with Apries, but Amasis. Eusebius gives a better date, viz. B.C. 631. This will make Battus the Happy ascend the throne B.C. 575 and be contemporary therefore with the last six years of the reign of Apries, who was succeeded by Amasis in B.C. 569. It will also accord tolerably with the statements, 1. of Theophrastus, that Cyrene was founded close upon 300 years before B.C. 311 (Hist. Plant. vi. iii. 3), and 2. of the Scholiast on Pind. Pyth. iv.), that the dynasty continued for 200 years. These periods are manifestly round numbers; but they will perhaps enable us to approximate to the true chronology.

DYNASTY OF THE BATTIADAE AT CYRENE.

	B.C.	B.C.	
Battus I. (founder of the city, reigned 40 years)	631	to 591	
Arcesilaüs I. (his son, reigned 16 years)	591	to 575	
Battus II. (the Happy, his son)	575	to 545 (?)	Amasis, king of Egypt, married Ladice, the daughter of one or other of these 2 kings.
Arcesilaüs II. (the ill-tempered, his son)	545 (?)	to 540 (?)	
Battus III. (the Lame, his son)	540 (?)	to 530 (?)	Legislation of Demonax.
Arcesilaüs III. (his son)	530 (?)	to 515 (?)	Becomes tributary to Cambyses.
(Pheretima, regent)	515 (?)	to 514 (?)	Expedition of Aryandes.
Battus IV. (the Fair, son of Arcesilaüs III.)	514 (?)	to 470 (?)	
Arcesilaüs IV. (his son) succeeded the throne about 470, gained a Pythian victory 466, and perhaps till nearly		431 (?)	

Thus Herodotus would be still adding touches to his history after the murder of Arcesilaüs IV., and the expulsion of his son Battus. Arcesilaüs IV. would be a young man in B.C. 466 (Pind. Pyth. v. 102, 103, ἐπίσσαμα μὲν ἁλικίας ῥόδον φέροντι, and might continue to reign for five-and-thirty years. Battus IV. being, as is evident from the position assumed by Pheretima, a minor at the death of his father, would be likely to have a long reign (44 years). The 200 years of Theophrastus would be a little exceeded; but his words are not precise. (μάλιστα περὶ τριακόσια (fr. i. s. c.)

Compare Boeckh's Dissertations (ch. xii.), and Clinton's F. H., Years 631, 597, 591, 575, 466, &c.

It has been recently argued, from a Cyrenaic coin in the British Museum, that the monarchy came to an end at least as early as B.C. 450. The coin is thought by its style to be "not later" than that date; and, as it bears the inscription Κ Κ (Κυρηναῖον κοινόν), it must have been struck under the republic. (See a paper by Mr. Stuart Poole on a coin from the Cyrenaica.) The doubt, however, remains, whether the style of a coin can accurately fix a date.

to seek to extend your reign. Thou, for thy part, be gentle,
when thou art restored. If thou findest the oven full of jars,
bake not the jars; but be sure to speed them on their way. If,
however, thou heatest the oven, then avoid the island—else thou
wilt die thyself, and with thee the most beautiful bull."[1]

164. So spake the Pythoness. Arcesilaüs upon this returned
to Cyrênê, taking with him the troops which he had raised in
Samos. There he obtained possession of the supreme power;
whereupon, forgetful of the oracle, he took proceedings against
those who had driven him into banishment. Some of them fled
from him and quitted the country for good; others fell into his
hands and were sent to suffer death in Cyprus. These last happening on their passage to put in through stress of weather at
Cnidus, the Cnidians rescued them, and sent them off to Thera.
Another body found a refuge in the great tower of Aglômachus,
a private edifice, and were there destroyed by Arcesilaüs,
who heaped wood around the place, and burnt them to death.
Aware, after the deed was done, that this was what the Pythoness
meant when she warned him, if he found the jars in the oven,
not to bake them, he withdrew himself of his own accord from
the city of Cyrênê, believing that to be the island of the oracle,[1]
and fearing to die as had been prophesied. Being married to a
relation of his own, a daughter of Alazir,[2] at that time king of
the Barcæans, he took up his abode with him. At Barca, however, certain of the citizens, together with a number of Cyrenæan exiles, recognising him as he walked in the forum, killed
him; they slew also at the same time Alazir, his father-in-law.
So Arcesilaüs, wittingly or unwittingly, disobeyed the oracle,
and thereby fulfilled his destiny.

---

[1] This oracle is given in prose, but evidently contains fragments of the hexameters in which it was delivered; *e. g.*, Ἢν μέντοι ἧκοντος εἴσω—ἀνόπισθε κατ' οὖρον—μὴ ἐς τὴν ἀμφίρρυτον ἔλθῃς; and the last line, which may be restored with an approach to certainty; αὐτὸς γὰρ θανέαι, καὶ ταῦρος ὁ καλλιστεύων. The allusion here seems to be to Alazir, the father-in-law of Arcesilaüs. (See the next chapter.)

[1] It is not very easy to see how either Cyrene or Barca could be regarded as islands. Perhaps the existence of springs on several sides of Cyrene may have been considered, in a country so scant of water, as what the word ἀμφίρρυτον pointed at. At Barca there would not be even this approach to an insular character, for water is scarce there, if at least the site was at *Merdj*.

[2] This name is remarkable. It is clearly not Greek, and therefore is pro-
bably African. Hence it would seem that not only was Barca originally an African town (see note [?] on ch. 160), but that while falling under Greek influence in the reign of Arcesilaüs II., it had still retained its native princes, who in-
termarried with the Battiadæ. It is no objection to this view that the daughter of Alazir is called a "relation" of Arce-
silaüs, for she may have been so on her mother's side. However, it is certainly possible that, as Mr. Blakesley thinks, the Greek princes of Barca may have adopted African names to conciliate their native subjects. Battus, it must be remembered, was an African word.

105. Pheretima, the mother of Arcesilaüs, during the time that her son, after working his own ruin, dwelt at Barca, continued to enjoy all his privileges at Cyrênê, managing the government, and taking her seat at the council-board. No sooner, however, did she hear of the death of her son at Barca, than leaving Cyrênê, she fled in haste to Egypt. Arcesilaüs had claims for service done to Cambyses, son of Cyrus; since it was by him that Cyrênê was put under the Persian yoke, and a rate of tribute agreed upon.[3] Pheretima therefore went straight to Egypt, and presenting herself as a suppliant before Aryandes, entreated him to avenge her wrongs. Her son, she said, had met his death on account of his being so well affected towards the Medes.[4]

106. Now Aryandes had been made governor of Egypt by Cambyses. He it was who in after times was punished with death by Darius for seeking to rival him. Aware, by report and also by his own eyesight, that Darius wished to leave a memorial of himself, such as no king had ever left before,[5] Aryandes resolved to follow his example, and did so, till he got his reward. Darius had refined gold to the last perfection of purity in order to have coins struck of it: Aryandes, in his Egyptian government, did the very same with silver, so that to this day there is no such pure silver anywhere as the Aryandic.

---

[3] Vide supra, III. 13 and 91.

[4] It is not likely that there was any ground at all for this statement which however was plausible enough, and might easily impose upon the Persian governor, who would not care to investigate it. He would consider it his business to uphold the royal family which had treated with Cambyses, even apart from any such special claim; for the Persians, until after the Ionian revolt, everywhere maintained and supported the Greek despots. (See below, vi. 43; and compare the cases of Syloson, III. 141-149, and Hippias, v. 96.) As an ambitious satrap, he may also have been glad of the opportunity for gaining territory.

[5] Two conclusions have been drawn from this passage:—1. That Darius was "the first Persian king who ever coined money" (Grote, iv. p. 319); 2. That he was actually the first person who ever performed that feat 'Rahr ad loc.}. The words of Herodotus justify neither statement. He tells us himself elsewhere that the Lydians were the first who coined money (L 94,) and here all that he asserts is that Darius coined gold *of superior purity* to any which had been known before. It is said to have been from the purity of his gold coinage that the expression "Darius's gold" came to be used for gold without any alloy. (See Plutarch, Pactolus, p. 1152, A.) Of course it is quite possible that Darius may, in point of fact, have been the first to coin Persian money; and the name "daric" (vide infra, vii. ch. 28) favours this view; but no statement to this effect is here made by Herodotus.

[6] Some silver coins have been found which are supposed to be of Aryandes: on the obverse is a Persian archer on a hippocampus, beneath which is a *zyger* (or water with a dolphin; on the reverse an owl) traversed by the two sceptres of Osiris, and dates in hieroglyphics of the years 5, 6, and 7. Another has a dolphin instead of the hippocampus, and being of older style throws a doubt on these coins being of Aryandes.—[G. W.] There are also some coins of a different type from either of these, which have been ascribed to this satrap. (See note on Book vii. ch. 28.)

Darius, when this came to his ears, brought another charge,¹ a charge of rebellion, against Aryandes, and put him to death.

167. At the time of which we are speaking Aryandes, moved with compassion for Pheretima, granted her all the forces which there were in Egypt, both land and sea. The command of the army he gave to Amasis, a Maraphian;² while Badres, one of the tribe of the Pasargadæ, was appointed to lead the fleet. Before the expedition, however, left Egypt, he sent a herald to Barca to inquire who it was that had slain king Arcesilaus. The Barcæans replied 'that they, one and all, acknowledged the deed—Arcesilaus had done them many and great injuries.' After receiving this reply, Aryandes gave the troops orders to march with Pheretima. Such was the cause which served as a pretext for this expedition: its real object was, I believe, the subjugation of Libya.³ For Libya is inhabited by many and various races, and of these but a very few were subjects of the Persian king, while by far the larger number held Darius in no manner of respect.

168. The Libyans dwell in the order which I will now describe. Beginning on the side of Egypt, the first Libyans are the Adyrmachidæ.¹ These people have, in most points, the same customs as the Egyptians, but use the costume of the Libyans. Their women wear on each leg a ring made of bronze;² they let their hair grow long, and when they catch any vermin on their persons, bite it and throw it away. In this they differ from all the other Libyans. They are also the only tribe with whom the custom

---

¹ There would be no need of "another charge." Issuing a coinage, whether good or bad, would be considered, and indeed would be, an act of rebellion. The ostentatious imitation of Darius might make the offence of the act still more apparent.

² The Maraphians were the Persian tribe next in dignity to the Pasargadæ. Vide supra, i. 125. It is curious to find the Egyptian name of Amasis in such a connexion.

³ Dahlmann's remark is just: "Here a human infirmity seems to have stolen upon Herodotus. . . . An exaggerated representation, which does not correspond with the truth, of the real importance of this affair has imposed itself upon Herodotus, who was anxious to collect together his information concerning the Libyan nations. (Life, p. 123, E. T.) No attempt to subjugate Libya appears in the expedition itself.

¹ The Adyrmachidæ appear in Scylax in the same position, but are reckoned to Egypt (Peripl. pp. 105, 106). They extend from the Canopic mouth of the Nile to Apis, which, according to Strabo (xvii. p. 1138), is 114 miles west of Paretonium (now Bartova). They are mentioned likewise by Ptolemy (p. 117), Pliny (v. 6), and Silius Italicus (iii. 279; ix. 224). The last of these calls them "gens accola Nili," and says their arms were a variegated shield and a curved scymitar.

² Bronze and silver bangles are often found in the Egyptian tombs, and they were very generally worn, as they still are, by the Egyptian, Ethiopian, Moorish, and other women of Africa.—[G.W.]

Mr. Hamilton, speaking of the women of Benghazi (the ancient Euesperides), says—"The silver bracelets and anklets which complete their adornment, are sometimes of great weight. A Jewess in Benghazi wears a pair of anklets which weigh five pounds." (Wanderings, p. 13.)

obtains of bringing all women about to become brides before the king, that he may choose such as are agreeable to him.³ The Adyrmachidæ extend from the borders of Egypt to the harbour called Port Plynus.⁴

169. Next to the Adyrmachidæ are the Gilligammæ,⁵ who inhabit the country westward as far as the island of Aphrodisias.⁶ Off this tract is the island of Platea, which the Cyrenæans colonised. Here too, upon the mainland, are Port Menelaüs,⁷ and Aziris, where the Cyrenæans once lived. The Silphium⁸

³ Compare the middle age *droit de cuiss op.*

⁴ Plynus, according to Scylax, is two days' sail west of Apis, and belongs to Marmarica (Peripl. p. 108). It is generally thought to be identical with the Panormus of Ptolemy (*Port Bardeah*). Thus the Adyrmachidæ extend *a degree further west* in Herodotus than in Scylax. Herodotus, it is to be remarked, makes no mention of the Marmaridæ, who are reckoned the chief nation in these parts by Scylax, Strabo, and Ptolemy.

⁵ The Gilligammæ are unknown to any other independent geographer. Stephen merely echoes Herodotus. They appear to represent the Marmaridæ.

⁶ Aphrodisias appears both from Scylax (Peripl. p. 108, and Ptolemy (iv. 4, to be the little island which lies off the coast due north of Cyrene, opposite the ruins of Apollonia. Thus the Gilligammæ dwelt partly within the Cyrenaica, where they were held in vassalage by the Greek inhabitants. (Vide supra, ch. 151, note ⁴.) Kiepert, following Rennell (Geograph. p. 609), places Aphrodisias near *Derna*, marking the island off Cyrene as Lela (Map XXII.). But Lela and Aphrodisias were two names of the same island (Ptolemy. l. s. c).

⁷ In the eastern part of the tract, not very far from Plynus Scylax, Peripl. p. 108. By Ptolemy's time the port seems to have been blocked up, as the town is by him considered an inland one (p. 117).

⁸ This famous plant, the *laserpitium* of the Romans, which is figured upon most of the Cyrenæan and Barcæan coins, was celebrated both as an article of food and also for its medicinal virtues. It formed an important element in the ancient commerce of Cyrene. It was probably a royal monopoly, and a main source of the great wealth of the Battiadæ (Pind. Pyth. v. 1, &c.); as there is a representation of king Arcesilaüs upon an ancient vase, in the act of weighing out the drug to his customers (Annali dell' Inst. Archeolog. di Roma, vol. v. p. 5). Hence the expression in Aristophanes (Plut. 921), 'τὸ βάττου σίλφιον.' A description of it is given at great length in Theophrastus Hist. Plant. vi. 3, and another in Pliny H. N. xxii. 21. Della Cella, Pacho, and Beechey, all considered that they recognised the silphium in a plant called by the Arabs *drids* or *derris*—an umbelliferous plant, three feet in height, resembling the laserus or wild carrot. This flower is first met with about *Merdj*, and extends eastward a little beyond *Derna* (Darnis). It is injurious to the cattle which feed on it (Della Cella, pp. 126, 127; Pacho, ch. xviii.; Beechey, pp. 409-420; Hamilton, p. 27).

The identity of this plant with the silphium has been questioned on account of the manner in which the latter is figured upon the coins. The stem is not nearly so thick as represented; and altogether the figure is far from being a good likeness. Still, as Mr. Hamilton observes, (p. 28), the plant, as given upon the coins, is a very fair " *conventional* silphium," and the inexactness of

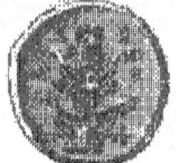 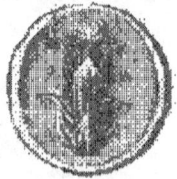

begins to grow in this region, extending from the island of Platea on the one side to the mouth of the Syrtis on the other. The customs of the Gilligammæ are like those of the rest of their countrymen.

170. The Asbystæ¹ adjoin the Gilligammæ upon the west. They inhabit the regions above Cyrêné, but do not reach to the coast, which belongs to the Cyrenæans. Four-horse chariots are in more common use among them than among any other Libyans. In most of their customs they ape the manners of the Cyrenæans.²

171. Westward of the Asbystæ dwell the Auschisæ,³ who possess the country above Barca, reaching, however, to the sea at the place called Euesperides.⁴ In the middle of their territory is the little tribe of the Cabalians,⁵ which touches the coast near

Tauchira,[4] a city of the Barcæans. Their customs are like those of the Libyans above Cyrênê.

172. The Nasamonians,[1] a numerous people, are the western neighbours of the Auschisæ. In summer they leave their flocks and herds upon the sea-shore, and go up the country to a place called Augila,[2] where they gather the dates from the palms,[3] which in those parts grow thickly,[4] and are of great size, all of them being of the fruit-bearing kind. They also chase the locusts, and, when caught, dry them in the sun, after which they grind them to powder, and, sprinkling this upon their milk, so drink it. Each man among them has several wives, in their intercourse with whom they resemble the Massagetæ. The following are their customs in the swearing of oaths and the practice of augury. The man, as he swears, lays his hand upon the tomb of some one considered to have been pre-eminently just and good, and so doing swears by his name. For divination they betake themselves to the sepulchres of their own ancestors, and, after praying, lie down to sleep upon their graves; by the dreams which then come to them they guide their conduct. When they pledge their faith to one another, each gives the other to drink out of his hand;[5] if there be no liquid to be had, they take up dust from the ground,[6] and put their tongues to it.

---

ing. This "little tribe" escaped the notice of all other geographers. It would seem to exist still in the *Cabyles* of modern Algeria, a true Berber race.

[4] Tauchira retains its name as *Taukra*, *Tokrai*, or *Terkera*. Considerable ruins mark the site (Della Cella, p. 209, E. T.; Pacho, pp. 164-186; Beechey, pp. 367-376). The walls, according to Beechey, are a mile and a half round.

[1] All the geographers speak of the Nasamonians, and agree in their locality (Scylax, Peripl. p. 111; Strab. xvii. p. 1193; Plin. H. N. v. 5). They dwelt around the shores of the Greater Syrtis (vide supra, ii. 32). In the Roman times they had the character of being wreckers (Quint. Curt. iv. 7; Lucan's Pharsal. ix. 438-444).

[2] This place retains its name unchanged. It lies on the great route from Egypt to Fezzan and Mauritania, almost due south of Cyrene, between the 29th and 30th parallels. It was visited by Hornemann and Pacho, and more recently by Hamilton. Pacho declares the account of Herodotus to be in all respects true (pp. 272-280). His descriptions are, he says, "tellement fidèles, qu'elles pourraient encore servir à décrire l'Augile moderne."

[3] See below, note [1] on ch. 182.

[4] Mr. Hamilton estimates the number of date-trees in the oasis of Augila at 16,000 (p. 190). Those of Jala, which was probably included in the Augila of Herodotus, at 100,000! Dates continue to be the sole product of the place and the source whence the inhabitants draw all their subsistence. A brisk trade is carried on between them and the natives of the coast, chiefly those of *Bengházi*, who bring them corn and manufactured articles of all kinds, and receive dates in exchange. In the time of Leo Africanus (the 15th century) a similar trade was carried on with Egypt (vi. p. 246).

[5] Shaw mentions a custom exactly like this in Algeria. In the marriage ceremony the form of plighting troth is by drinking out of each other's hands (Travels, p. 303).

[6] So the Mahometan law of ablution allows sand to be used where water cannot be procured.

173. On the country of the Nasamonians borders that of the Psylli,[1] who were swept away under the following circumstances. The south-wind had blown for a long time and dried up all the tanks in which their water was stored. Now the whole region within the Syrtis is utterly devoid of springs. Accordingly, the Psylli took counsel among themselves, and by common consent made war upon the south-wind—so at least the Libyans say, I do but repeat their words—they went forth and reached the desert; but there the south-wind rose and buried them under heaps of sand:[2] whereupon, the Psylli being destroyed, their lands passed to the Nasamonians.[3]

174. Above the Nasamonians, towards the south, in the district where the wild beasts abound, dwell the Garamantians,[1] who avoid all society or intercourse with their fellow-men, have no weapon of war, and do not know how to defend themselves.[2]

175. These border the Nasamonians on the south: westward along the sea-shore their neighbours are the Macae,[1] who, by

letting the locks about the crown of their head grow long, while they clip them close everywhere else, make their hair resemble a crest. In war these people use the skins of ostriches for shields.² The river Cinyps³ rises among them from the height called "the Hill of the Graces," and runs from thence through their country to the sea. The Hill of the Graces is thickly covered with wood, and is thus very unlike the rest of Libya, which is bare. It is distant two hundred furlongs from the sea.⁴

176. Adjoining the Macæ are the Gindanes,⁵ whose women wear on their legs anklets of leather. Each lover that a woman has gives her one; and she who can show the most is the best esteemed, as she appears to have been loved by the greatest number of men.

177. A promontory jutting out into the sea from the country of the Gindanes is inhabited by the Lotophagi,⁶ who live en-

---

furnished mercenaries to the Carthaginians (Polyb. iii. 33).

² Compare vii. 70. Ostriches are still found in great numbers in this part of Africa, but at some distance from the coast (Lyon's Travels, p. 66).

³ The river Cinyps, or Cinyphus, is commemorated by all the geographers (Scylax, Peripl. p. 112; Ptol. iv. 3; Strab. xvii. p. 1179; &c.). It ran into the sea a little to the east of Leptis, the present Lebda (Strab. l. s. c.). Moderns do not find any river of consequence on this coast, which is intersected by torrents courses dry during the summer months. Perhaps the Wád el Khāhan has the best right to be considered the ancient Cinyps. It has "more pretensions to the title of river" than any of the other torrents upon this coast (Bombay, p. 82. Compare Barth's Wanderungen, vol. i. p. 317.—it is in the right position, a little to the east of Lebeda—it has marshes upon its right bank crossed by a causeway, agreeably to Strabo's description (xvii. p. 1179) —and the surrounding country corresponds with the descriptions of Scylax (Peripl. p. 112) and Herodotus (infra, ch. 198, and cf. note ad loc.). The only objection to the identification is that the Uharián falls from which it flows, are not more than 4 miles from the sea (Bombay, l. s. c.). But this objection would lie equally against all the other streams.

⁴ The Hill of the Graces, which was likewise mentioned by Callimachus (ap. Schol. ad Pind. Pyth. v. 32), must be looked for in the Gharián range. This range however is not now more than 4, or at most 5 miles distant from the shore. It is possible that Herodotus was misinformed as to the distance; but it is likewise possible that the occurrence of the discrepancy may be the encroachment of the sea upon this low shore, which is very perceptible in places. (See Beechey, pp. 493-494, and Map of Apollonia. Compare Hamilton, p. 32, &c., who thinks that the whole of this coast has subsided.) The Gharián chain is said to "preserve the character given of it by the historian, as being covered with trees, contrasting by their verdure with the scorched and arid soil of Libya." (Della Cella, p. 37, E. T.).

⁵ The Gindanes are mentioned by no other ancient writer, if we except Stephen, whose knowledge comes from Herodotus. It may be suspected that the ethnic appellative of Gindanes was superseded by the descriptive name of Lotophagi (Lotus-eaters). Stephen identifies the two; and Scylax places the Lotophagi immediately to the west of the Cinyps (Peripl. 113). The Gindanes are rightly placed by Kiepert (Map II.) upon the coast.

⁶ The country of the Lotophagi is evidently the Peninsula of Zarzis, which is the only tract projecting from this part of the coast. They are thus brought into the position usually assigned them, the neighbourhood of the Lesser Syrtis, or Gulf of Khobs (Scylax, Peripl. p. 113; Strabo, xvii. 1178).

tirely on the fruit of the lotus-tree.[7] The lotus fruit is about the
size of the lentisk berry, and in sweetness resembles the date.
The Lotophagi even succeed in obtaining from it a sort of
wine."

178. The sea-coast beyond the Lotophagi is occupied by the
Machlyans,[8] who use the lotus to some extent, though not so
much as the people of whom we last spoke. The Machlyans
reach as far as the great river called the Triton, which empties
itself into the great lake Tritonis.[1] Here, in this lake, is an is-

[7] The lotos or lotus tree was either the *Rhamnus Zizyphus* (the *Eh. Nabeca* of Forsk.), or the *Cordia Myxa*; which last, very common in the Oases, is called *Nothiyl* in Arabic, and has a sweet fruit growing in clusters, as described by Theophrastus, "περικαρπιον θερμον ἁδυτατον." But the lotus is evidently the *Rhamnus*, now called in Arabic *Sidr*, the fruit *Nebk*. It looks and tastes rather like a bad crab-apple. It has a single stone within it. To Ulysses it was as inconvenient as modern "gold-diggings" to ship captains, since he had the greatest difficulty in keeping his sailors to the ship when they had once tasted it (Hom. Od. ix. 84 to 96). Pliny (xiii. 32) thinks the tree a species of *Celtis*, differing from that of Italy — the *Celtis Australis* of Linnæus. He says, "It has the size of a pear tree, though Cornelius Nepos calls it low." He also alludes to its fruit being very delicious, and to strangers forgetting their country who tasted it (xxii. 21). He also mentions the lotos herb, or *Faba Greca* (xxiv. 2; the *lotometra* (xxii. 21), "of whose grains the Egyptian shepherds make bread;" and the lotus lily (*Nymphæa Lotus*, in ponds after the inundation (xiii. 17); also the *Melilotus* (xxi. 20), which is a trifoliated herb, supposed by some to be the *Trigonella fœnum-grœcum*; but none of these four last have anything to do with Homer's lotophagi. (See notes on Book ii. chs. 92 and 96, and compare Major Rennell, p. 628 to 650.)—[G. W.]

[8] Perhaps this is the origin of the Homeric myth (Od. ix. 74 et sqq.).

[9] Pliny calls the Machlyans neighbours of the Nasamonians. No other geographer mentions them under the same name; but they are probably represented by the Machryi of Ptolemy, who dwelt on the Lesser Syrtis (iv. 3); or by their neighbours, the Machryans (Ib.). It may be suspected that the Macæ, Masyes, or Maxyes, and Mach-

lyes of our author, and likewise the Machyni, Machryes, Macæi, Mimaces, and Macæ-tutæ of Ptolemy, belonged to the same stock. The physical type and customs of the Machlyans were noticed by Calliphanes, Aristotle (Fr. 249, and Nic. Damasc. (Fr. 136.)

[1] No great river exists in these parts. Small streams only empty themselves into the Lesser Syrtis; and the brooks which flow into the *Shibkah Loudeah*, or lose themselves among the sands that border it, do not deserve the name of rivers. Dr. Shaw believed that he recognised the Triton in the *Wad 'el Hammah*, or river of Kabes, a stream of some width, which has its source in the hills to the west of that city, and reaches the sea a little south of it. (Travels, p. 197.) Bähr accepts this view, while Kiepert (Map II.) appears to make the *Wady Acrroude*, or *Akarrih*, which is not even a perennial stream, the Triton. In this he follows Sir Greville Temple (Excursions in the Mediterranean, p. 185). Rennell's arguments, however, have never been answered. (See his Geography, pp. 659-667.) And the probability seems to be greatly in favour of his views, which are that the Lake Tritonis of Herodotus includes both the *Shibkah Loudeah* and the Lesser Syrtis, between which he supposes there to have been anciently a communication by a narrow and shallow channel; and that the Triton must be sought for among the rivulets which run into, or lose themselves in the sands of the *Shibkah*. Herodotus, it must be observed, makes the river Triton run into the Lake Tritonis, and says not a word of its running out of it; and the Lake Tritonis is with him a part of the sea, for Jason's vessel is driven by the north wind into it.

The description in Scylax (Peripl. pp. 115-117), and the brief notice in Ptolemy (iii. 4), are strongly confirmatory of these views. We may trace the land called Phla,² which it is said the Lacedæmonians were to have colonised, according to an oracle.

179. The following is the story as it is commonly told. When Jason had finished building the Argo at the foot of Mount Pelion, he took on board the usual hecatomb, and moreover a brazen tripod. Thus equipped, he set sail, intending to coast round the Peloponnese, and so to reach Delphi.³ The voyage was prosperous as far as Malea; but at that point a gale of wind from the north⁴ came on suddenly, and carried him out of his course to the coast of Libya; where, before he discovered the land, he got among the shallows of Lake Tritônis. As he was turning it in his mind how he should find his way out, Triton (they say) appeared to him, and offered to show him the channel, and secure him a safe retreat, if he would give him the tripod. Jason complying, was shown by Triton the passage through the shallows; after which the god took the tripod, and, carrying it to his own temple, seated himself upon it, and, filled with prophetic fury, delivered to Jason and his companions a long prediction. "When a descendant," he said, "of one of the Argo's crew should seize and carry off the brazen tripod, then by inevitable fate would a hundred Grecian cities be built around Lake Tritônis." The Libyans of that region, when they heard the words of this prophecy, took away the tripod and hid it.

180. The next tribe beyond the Machlyans is the tribe of the Auseans.⁵ Both these nations inhabit the borders of Lake Tritônis,

---

gradual blocking-up of the mouth of the inner sea, which stood to the Lesser Syrtis as the Sea of Asof (or *Lake Mæotis*) to the Euxine—then the drying up of the water by evaporation, and the separation of the original Lake Triton into several seas or meres—lastly the desiccation of all these with one exception, and the transformation of the ancient Lake of Triton into the modern *Shibkah-el-Loudeah.*

² Probably the same as Scylax's Isle of Triton. Shaw (p. 213) identified it with a sand-bank in the *Shibkah-el-Loudeah*, which sand-bank has since become a peninsula (Temple, p. 164). Rennell, with more probability, conjectures that Phla is now part of the flat tract of sand which intervenes between the Shibkah and the sea (p. 663).

³ Various modes were adopted of bringing Jason to Lake Tritônis. Some made the visit take place on the return of the expedition from Colchis, after a storm sent by Jupiter as a punishment for the murder of Apsyrtus. (Apoll. Rhod. iv. 557, &c.) Others made the Argonauts, when commanded to expiate this murder by sailing to Italy, coast along the African and Celtic (Iberian?) shores voluntarily. (Apollodor. l. p. 65.) These divergences prove sufficiently the unreal and poetic character of the entire narrative. (See Grote, vol. L pp. 316-348.)

⁴ Hypercritics observe that a north wind springing up at Malea (the Capo St. Angelo) should have carried the vessel to the Greater, and not the Lesser Syrtis (Müller, Orchom., p. 354; Pacho, p. 173). But Herodotus is here only reporting the story as it was told by some poet, who was not perhaps very well skilled in geography. He seems however, himself, to have compressed Africa too much between Egypt and the Lake Tritonis (vide infra, ch. 181, note ⁴).

⁵ The Auseans are not mentioned by any other ancient writer, unless we may

being separated from one another by the river Triton. Both also wear their hair long, but the Machlyans let it grow at the back of the head, while the Auseans have it long in front. The Ausean maidens keep year by year a feast in honour of Minerva, whereat their custom is to draw up in two bodies, and fight with stones and clubs. They say that these are rites which have come down to them from their fathers, and that they honour with them their native goddess, who is the same as the Minerva (Athené) of the Grecians.* If any of the maidens die of the wounds they receive, the Auseans declare that such are false maidens. Before the fight is suffered to begin, they have another ceremony. One of the virgins, the loveliest of the number, is selected from the rest; a Corinthian helmet and a complete suit of Greek armour are publicly put upon her; and, thus adorned, she is made to mount into a chariot, and led around the whole lake in a procession. What arms they used for the adornment of their damsels before the Greeks came to live in their country, I cannot say. I imagine they dressed them in Egyptian armour, for I maintain that both the shield and the helmet came into Greece from Egypt.⁷

regard them as identical with the Ausuriæs of Synesius, who, in the 5th and 6th centuries of our era, devastated the Cyrenaica. (Op. p. 298-303.) Their temple of Athené seems to be that mentioned by Scylax (p. 116), as 'Αθηνᾶς Τριτωνίτος ἱερόν (vide infra, ch. 188).

* The Athené of the Greeks was identified with the Neith or Nit of the Egyptians (Plat. Tim. p. 21, E.), whose worship was common to all the African nations. Herodotus appears to regard the worship as indigenous in this part of Africa, and as having passed from hence into Egypt, and from Egypt into Greece (vide supra, ii. 50, and infra, ch. 188).

⁷ Plato notices the resemblance of the Greek and Egyptian arms (Tim. p. 24, B.), and ascribes the invention of them to the latter people.

[There is, however, very little resemblance between the shield and helmet of Egypt and those of Greece; though the κυνέη of Homer (Il. x. 258), without a crest, may not have looked unlike the head-piece of the Egyptians. The Shairetana, a northern people, with whom the Pharaohs were at one time in alliance, had a helmet with horns, and a round shield like that of Greece (see woodcut in n. on Book vii., ch. 61;) and the custom of adorning the helmet with horns was introduced into Greece from Asia, whence κέρας, "horn," was used to signify a "crest." The σαυρωτός was of bull's hide. The original κυνέη, or Greek helmet,

The Auseans declare that Minerva is the daughter of Neptune and the Lake Tritônis¹—they say she quarrelled with her father, and applied to Jupiter, who consented to let her be his child; and so she became his adopted daughter. These people do not marry or live in families, but dwell together like the gregarious beasts. When their children are full-grown, they are brought before the assembly of the men, which is held every third month, and assigned to those whom they most resemble.²

181. Such are the tribes of wandering Libyans dwelling upon the sea-coast. Above them inland is the wild-beast tract: and beyond that, a ridge of sand, reaching from Egyptian Thebes to the Pillars of Hercules.³ Throughout this ridge, at the distance of about ten days' journey from one another,⁴ heaps of salt

was probably of a similar material, and it is supposed to have taken its name from being of dog's skin. The Carians are said by Herodotus (i. 171) to have been the first to introduce the use of crests, and "to put devices on shields, and to invent handles for shields; in the earlier times their wearers managed them by the aid of a leathern thong, by which they were slung round the neck and left shoulder." This invention of the handle was evidently known long before in Egypt, at least as early as 2000 B.C. In the time of the Osirtasens of the 12th, and apparently of the kings of the 6th dynasty. The Egyptian shields had no emblems on them. They were also furnished with a thong for suspending them on the soldier's back, while using his left hand for some other purpose.—G. W.]

² This is the earliest form of the legend, and hence the epithet, Τριτογενεια, so frequently applied to this goddess (Hes. Theog. 924; Hom. Hymn. 28, 4; Arist. Eq. 1189; &c.) The philosophical *μυθος* which brought Athene from the head of Jove, was a later refinement.

³ Compare Arist. Pol. ii. 1.

¹ This division of Northern Africa had been already made (ii. 32). Niebuhr (Geogr. of Herod. p. 16, E. T.) regards it as artificial and imaginary. Heeren, more justly, as a near approximation to the truth 'African Nat. vol. i. p. 6, E. T.). There are, in fact, three tracts, which stretch across the continent from Egypt to the Atlantic ocean; first, the coast-tract, or Barbary, the country of the Berbers, comprising the modern provinces of Morocco, Fez, Algiers,

Tunis, Tripoli and Barka, which is comparatively fertile: next, the hill-region, or, *Bürdulgerid*, "the land of dates," as the Arabs call it, which, especially in its more western parts, is greatly infested with wild-beasts; and thirdly, the Great Sahara. These are not indeed, exactly, "parallel belts of land." The fertility of the coast is interrupted in places, as between Tunis and Tripoli, and again between Cape *Mezurata* and *Bengbasi*; and the hilly tract varies greatly in width, and sometimes sinks almost to a level with the desert; but speaking in a general way, it would be right to distinguish the regions as Herodotus does, and to regard them as running across Africa; and so we find them regarded by Ritter in his Erdkunde (vol. i. p. 897), and Humboldt in his Aspects of Nature (vol. i. p. 58, E. T.).

² No doubt there is here somewhat too much of "regularity" and "symmetry" for truth. (Niebuhr's Geograph. of Herod. p. 17, E. T.) It is to be remarked, however, that Herodotus uses the expression, "about 10 days' journey from one another" (μάλιστα διὰ δέκα ἡμερέων ὁδοῦ), which shows that he did not intend an exact regularity, such as his critics have assumed him to mean. Heeren has shown the general measurements not to err greatly. (Af. Nat. vol. i. pp. 202-215, E. T.) His conjecture that Herodotus here describes the caravan route across the desert, between Egypt and Western Africa, is one of those happy thoughts which seem obvious as soon as they are uttered, yet which occur only to genius.

130   THE FOUNTAIN OF THE SUN.   Book IV.

in large lumps lie upon hills. At the top of every hill there gushes forth from the middle of the salt a stream of water, which is both cold and sweet.[3] Around dwell men who are the last inhabitants of Libya on the side of the desert, living, as they do, more inland than the wild-beast district. Of these nations the first is that of the Ammonians, who dwell at a distance of ten days' journey from Thebes,[4] and have a temple derived from that of the Theban Jupiter. For at Thebes likewise, as I mentioned above,[5] the image of Jupiter has a face like that of a ram.[6] The Ammonians have another spring besides that which rises

---

[3] In the Oases salt is in great abundance, and sometimes a large space is covered with an incrustation of it, which breaks like frozen mud or shallow water, under the feet. Springs frequently rise from the sand in that desert, and sometimes on the top of hillocks of sand; where the water, as Herodotus says, is always cool and sweet; the coolness being caused by the evaporation. One of the most remarkable of the latter that I have seen is on the road from the Little Oasis to Faráfreh; and water rises from the sand in other places between Farâfreh and the Oasis of Dakhleh. Though there is much salt in the plain, these hillocks are free from it.—[G. W.]

Minutoli, however (pp. 174, 175), describes a district near the oasis of Ammon (Siwah), where the salt, with which Northern Africa everywhere abounds, "rises in masses above the ground." "There are," he says, "patches above a mile long, so covered with this substance as to have the appearance of a field of snow." (Compare Hamilton, pp. 183 and 193; and Denham, vol. I. pp. 128, 129.) "Out of the midst of these," Minutoli adds, "springs of fresh water sometimes gush forth." Mr. Hamilton speaks of a spring of remarkably sweet water near Augila, which springs from sand "mixed with crystals of common salt, admirably white and pure" (p. 223). The general character of these salt-tracts, however, is rather that of plains than of hills.

[4] Siwah, which is undoubtedly where the temple of Ammon stood (vide supra, iii. 26), lies at the distance of 400 geographical miles, or not less than 20 days' journey, from Thebes. Heeren thinks that a station was here omitted, or that the Great Oasis - El Wah) was reckoned to Thebes. (Afr. Nat. I. p. 212, E. T.) This may have been the origin of the erroneous statement in the text; but Herodotus was himself deceived, and led to contract unduly the extent of eastern Africa (vide supra, ch. 179).

[5] Vide supra, ii. 42.

[6] The Theban Jupiter had the head of a man, and wore a cap with two long feathers, to which Q. Curtius seems to allude when he says, the head-dress of the God of the Oasis of Ammon was "umbraculo maxime similis." The Ethiopians, however, looked upon the ram-headed God, Noum or Nef, as Jupiter, though they also worshipped the Amun of Thebes; and both these Deities are found in the temples of the Oases. The ram-headed God, however, is called "Amunebis," i.e. Amun-Nef, at Kasr Zián in the Great Oasis; but this temple was only built in the late time of Antoninus, and the neighbouring one at Kasr Ain el Gowyta was dedicated under Ptolemy Euergetes I. to the Theban triad of Amun, Maut, and Khons. The confusion between Amun and the ram-headed Noum was first made by the Ethiopians, and it was only prevalent in Egypt subsequently to the age of the Pharaohs; though a few instances occur in Egypt of the ram-headed deity being called Amun, even in the 19th dynasty. (See n. [6] on Book ii. ch. 42.) It is possible that Amun, or Amun-Re, was originally a title, rather than the name of a God, as Atin-re was added to the name of Noum, who in the earliest legends is often called Noum-Atin-re. This Atin-re was taken up as a God by those "stranger kings" (probably from the title resembling Adoni, or Atin, "the sun," and from Atin-re being the solar disk; and Amun was banished by them. Atin, Atys, or Attin, was the sun (Macrob. Saturn. I. 26), or nature, and was both male and female. Atin-re was not a new God, but an Egyptian title given to one or more Gods (being on

from the salt.' The water of this stream is lukewarm at early dawn; at the time when the market fills it is much cooler; by noon it has grown quite cold; at this time, therefore, they water their gardens. As the afternoon advances the coldness goes off, till, about sunset, the water is once more lukewarm; still the heat increases, and at midnight it boils furiously. After this time it again begins to cool, and grows less and less hot till morning comes. This spring is called "the Fountain of the Sun."

182. Next to the Ammonians, at the distance of ten days' journey along the ridge of sand, there is a second salt-hill like the Ammonian, and a second spring. The country round is inhabited, and the place bears the name of Augila.

Hither it is that the Nasamonians come to gather in the dates.¹

183. Ten days' journey from Augila there is again a salt-hill and a spring; palms of the fruitful kind grow here abundantly, as they do also at the other salt-hills. This region is inhabited by a nation called the Garamantians,² a very powerful people, who cover the salt with mould, and then sow their crops.³ From thence is the shortest road to the Lotophagi, a journey of thirty days.⁴ In the Garamantian country are found the oxen which,

as they graze, walk backwards. This they do because their horns curve outwards in front of their heads, so that it is not possible for them when grazing to move forwards, since in that case their horns would become fixed in the ground.⁵ Only herein do they differ from other oxen, and further in the thickness and hardness of their hides.⁶ The Garamantians have four-horse chariots, in which they chase the Troglodyte Ethiopians,⁷ who of all the nations whereof any account has reached our ears are by far the swiftest of foot.⁸ The Troglodytes feed on serpents, lizards, and other similar reptiles. Their language is unlike that of any other people; it sounds like the screeching of bats.⁹

184. At the distance of ten days' journey from the Garamantians there is again another salt-hill and spring of water; around which dwell a people, called the Atarantians,¹ who alone of all

---

stopping, however, exactly six days at Soles. The Lotophagi, including in them the Gindanians, commenced about *Lebda*. (Vide supra, ch. 178, note ².)

⁵ No oxen of this kind have been observed by modern travellers, though the same account is given by many of the ancients. (Alex. Mynd. ap. Athen. v. 20, p. 221, E.; Plin. H. N. viii. 45; Mela, I. 8.) Heeren conjectures that the horns were *made* to grow in this way. The neatherds of Africa, he says, frequently amuse themselves in giving an artificial form to the horns of their cattle, by continually bending them. (Af. Nat. i. p. 222, E. T.) But it is difficult to assign a motive for their giving them so inconvenient a shape.

⁶ The thickness and hardness of the hides of the cattle in this part of Africa are noticed by modern travellers. (Horneman, p. 127.)

⁷ It is usual to regard the word Troglodyte here as a proper name. But perhaps it would be better to translate "the Ethiopians who dwell in holes." Troglodytes have always abounded in Africa. The most notorious are those along the shores of the Red Sea, of whom Strabo gives a full account (xvi. p. 1102). There were others upon the Nile. (Strab. xvii. p. 1159.) Those here spoken of must be distinguished from both. They dwelt probably in the region south of Fezzan, in the mountains of the Tibesti range, where the *Tibboo Irshad*, or *Rock Tibboos*, are still said to live in caves. (Horne-

man, p. 107; Denham, vol. i. p. 140.)

⁸ Great slave-hunts (*Grassie* in the language of the country) are still common in Fezzan. Armed bodies of 800 or 1000 men set forth on these expeditions, and sweep the countries to the southward of their inhabitants, returning after an absence of months, with a band of captives, often more numerous than the captors. (See, among others, Hamilton, p. 196.) These are usually *Tibboos*. The *Tibboos* are described as "a timid race, in such dread of a gun or horse, that the bare sight of an Arab, and particularly a mounted one, is sufficient to put a number of them to flight." (Lyon, p. 254.) Their "agility" is said to be "proverbial," and their neighbours call them, by way of distinction, "the Birds" (ib. p. 227).

⁹ "The people of Augila, in speaking of those tribes (the *Tibboos*)," observes Horneman, "say that their language is like the whistling of birds." (Journal, &c. p. 119.)

¹ All the MSS. have *Atlantians*, which was read evidently by Pliny (v. 8), and Mela (i. 8). The reading Atarantians is recovered from Eustathius ad Dionys. Perieg. 66). The locality of this people is very uncertain. Heeren conjectures that the route described by Herodotus turns southward at the Garamantian station, and that the Atarantians are the *Bornoos* of *Tegerry*; but this view is quite incompatible with the words of Herodotus in chs. 181 and 185. We must regard him as proceeding west-

known nations are destitute of names. The title of Atarantians is borne by the whole race in common; but the men have no particular names of their own.¹ The Atarantians, when the sun rises high in the heaven, curse him, and load him with reproaches, because (they say) he burns and wastes both their country and themselves. Once more at the distance of ten days' journey there is a salt-hill, a spring, and an inhabited tract. Near the salt is a mountain called Atlas, very taper and round; so lofty, moreover, that the top (it is said) cannot be seen, the clouds never quitting it either summer or winter.² The natives call this mountain "the Pillar of Heaven;"³ and they themselves take their name from it, being called Atlantes. They are reported not to eat any living thing, and never to have any dreams.

185. As far as the Atlantes the names of the nations inhabiting the sandy ridge are known to me; but beyond them my knowledge fails. The ridge itself extends as far as the Pillars of Hercules, and even further than these;⁵ and throughout the whole distance, at the end of every ten days' journey, there is a salt-mine, with people dwelling round it who all of them build their houses with blocks of the salt. No rain falls in these parts of Libya; if it were otherwise, the walls of these houses could not

---

ward, and seek for the Atarantians among the Tuariks of the Western Sahara. Oudney found salt-plains and springs in this country, towards Gadamis (pp. 96-99).

¹ Leo Africanus says of the Borneus —"Quantum ä quodam mercatore intelligere potui, qui longam cum his habuerat consuetudinem, nullum hic proprium nomen indicio, sed omnes vel a longitudine, vel pinguitudine, aut alio quovis accidente nomen habent" (vii. p. 255, A. Salt (Travels in Abyssinia, p. 379) notices a similar custom among the negroes south and west of Abyssinia; but it does not by any means amount to the entire absence of names which is spoken of by Herodotus. He probably misunderstood his informant.

² Ideler has shown (see Humboldt's Aspects of Nature, vol. I. pp. 144-146, E. T.; that there was a confusion in the Greek mind with respect to Atlas. The earlier writers 'Homer, Hesiod, &c.) intended by that name the Peak of Teneriffe, of which they had some indistinct knowledge derived from Phœnician sources. The later, unacquainted with the great Western Ocean, placed Atlas in Africa, first regarding it as a single mountain, and then, as their geographical knowledge increased, and they found there was no very remarkable mountain in North-western Africa, as a mountain chain. Herodotus is a writer of the transition period. His description is only applicable to the Peak, while his locality is Africa—not, however, the western coast, but an inland tract, probably south-eastern Algeria. Thus his mountain, if it is to be considered as having any foundation at all on fact, must represent the eastern, not the western, extremity of the Atlas chain.

⁴ So Æschylus says of the giant Atlas—

ὅπου δορίγομφι τάλαντα
ἱστηκί, κίων οὐρανοῦ τε καὶ χθονός
ὠμοῖν ἐρείδων, ἄχθος οὐκ εὐάγκαλον.—P. V. 351.

And Pindar, in like manner, calls Etna, κίων οὐρανία. (Pyth. I. 19, ed. Diss.) The supposed height of the "pillar" may be gathered from the Scholiast on Plato, who reports that its shadow extended to the distance of 5000 stades (ad Plat. Tim. p. 426, ed. Bekker).

⁵ Herodotus, it should be observed, knows that the African coast projects beyond the pillars.

stand.' The salt quarried is of two colours, white and purple.' Beyond the ridge, southwards, in the direction of the interior, the country is a desert,' with no springs, no beasts, no rain, no wood, and altogether destitute of moisture.'

186. Thus from Egypt as far as Lake Tritônis Libya is in-

habited by wandering tribes,¹ whose drink is milk² and their food the flesh of animals. Cow's flesh however none of these tribes ever taste, but abstain from it for the same reason as the Egyptians, neither do they any of them breed swine. Even at Cyrênê, the women think it wrong to eat the flesh of the cow, honouring in this Isis, the Egyptian goddess, whom they worship both with fasts and festivals.³ The Barcæan women abstain, not from cow's flesh only, but also from the flesh of swine.

187. West of Lake Tritônis the Libyans are no longer wanderers,⁴ nor do they practise the same customs as the wandering people, or treat their children in the same way. For the wandering Libyans, many of them at any rate, if not all—concerning which I cannot speak with certainty—when their children come to the age of four years, burn the veins at the top of their heads with a flock from the fleece of a sheep: others burn the veins about the temples.⁵ This they do to prevent them from being plagued in their after lives by a flow of rheum from the head; and such they declare is the reason why they are so much more healthy than other men. Certainly the Libyans

---

¹ Herodotus here indicates that he is about to resume the account of the sea-coast tribes, which was broken off at the end of ch. 180.

² The water in Northern Africa is for the most part so strongly impregnated with salt that milk forms the only palatable beverage. It is however at the present day a rarity. (See Denham's Travels, vol. i. p. 42.)

³ The Greeks, on settling in Africa, appear to have adopted many customs from their "barbarian" neighbours. As their monarchs took the name of Battus, the native term for "king" (supra, ch. 155), so the citizens generally conformed to African manners. The Cyrenæan Greeks took the costume of the country. Pacho observes upon the "striking analogy" between the dresses depicted in the tombs and the modern costume of Fezzan (p. 210). The four-horse chariot was used commonly at Cyrene while it was still rare in Greece (infra, ch. 189). The habit of burning the dead was abandoned, and rock-tombs were excavated with vast toil (which are often of striking beauty) as receptacles wherein to lay up the bodies of the departed. (See Hamilton's Wanderings, p. 65.) There are no urns, nor places for them, but many miles of necropolis extending all round the city—the monuments and sarcophagi rising in terraces of ten and even twelve rows, one above the other. (Ibid. p. 86. Compare the view of the ruins, supra, p. 113.) It appears from the passage in the text that a portion, at any rate, of the Egyptian ritual was adopted both in Cyrene and Barca, the latter being even more African than the former. (See above, ch. 164, note ¹.)

⁴ West of Lake Tritonis the Libyans are no longer wanderers, as the Nasamones and others between it and Egypt were. Those west of the Tritonis lived by agriculture (ch. 191). This is still the case, except upon the coast.—[G. W.]

⁵ Burning with a red-hot iron is still practised in these countries for the cure of diseases. (Lyon, p. 343; Hamilton, p. 90.) See also Denham's Travels, who calls this mode of cure "the sovereign Arab remedy for almost every disorder." (Vol. i. p. 173.) Mr. Layard notices its use among the Arabs of Mesopotamia (Nineveh and Babylon, p. 291); and Lieut. Burton among the Egyptians (Pilgrimage to El-Medineh, vol. i. p. 80). A similar notion prevailed in Scythia in ancient times. (Hippocrat. de Aëre, Aquâ, et Locis, § 47.)

are the healthiest men that I know;[6] but whether this is what makes them so, or not, I cannot positively say—the healthiest certainly they are. If when the children are being burnt convulsions come on, there is a remedy of which they have made discovery. It is to sprinkle goat's water upon the child, who thus treated, is sure to recover. In all this I only repeat what is said by the Libyans.

188. The rites which the wandering Libyans use in sacrificing are the following. They begin with the ear of the victim, which they cut off and throw over their house: this done, they kill the animal by twisting the neck. They sacrifice to the Sun and Moon, but not to any other god. This worship is common to all the Libyans. The inhabitants of the parts about Lake Tritônis worship in addition Triton, Neptune,[7] and Minerva, the last especially.

189. The dress wherewith Minerva's statues are adorned, and her Ægis, were derived by the Greeks from the women of Libya. For, except that the garments of the Libyan women are of leather,[8] and their fringes made of leathern thongs[9] instead of serpents, in all else the dress of both is exactly alike.

[6] Vide supra, ii. 77. The Tuaricks have, of all existing tribes, the best right to be regarded as the descendants of Herodotus's Libyans. . They are free from the intermixtures which have changed the character of the tribes upon the coast. They speak the Berber, or old African language. (Lyon, p. 111.) They are not a black race, nor have they the negro features. (Humboldt, i. p. 87; Prichard, Nat. Hist. of Man, p. 264.) Lyon says of them, "They are the finest race of men I ever saw: tall, straight, and handsome, with a certain air of independence and pride which is very imposing" (p. 109). By the amusing account which he gives (pp. 115, 110) of their application for medicines, it appears that there was but little illness among those with whom he became acquainted.

[7] Vide supra, ii. 50.

[8] The inhabitants of Northern Africa, and even the tribes of the desert, wear at the present day chiefly woollen and cotton garments. In the interior, however, that is in Soudan or Nigritia, "the general dress is leather." (Lyon, p. 127.) Among the desert tribes, the Tuaricks not unfrequently wear leathern shirts over the rest of their dress. Lyon gives a representation of this costume (p. 110).

[9] Leathern dresses of women, with fringes of thongs, have always been common in Africa; and these last being the origin of the snakes of the Ægis is very probable. The unmarried girls of Ethiopia now only wear an apron of thongs, not unlike that on the nose of a charger. It is called Rahát, and is sometimes ornamented with cowries.—[G. W.]

138 ORIGIN OF THE ÆGIS. Book IV.

The name too itself shows that the mode of dressing the Pallas-statues came from Libya. For the Libyan women wear over their dress goat-skins stript of the hair, fringed at their edges, and coloured with vermilion;[1] and from these goat-skins the Greeks get their word Ægis (goat-harness). I think for my part that the loud cries uttered in our sacred rites[2] came also

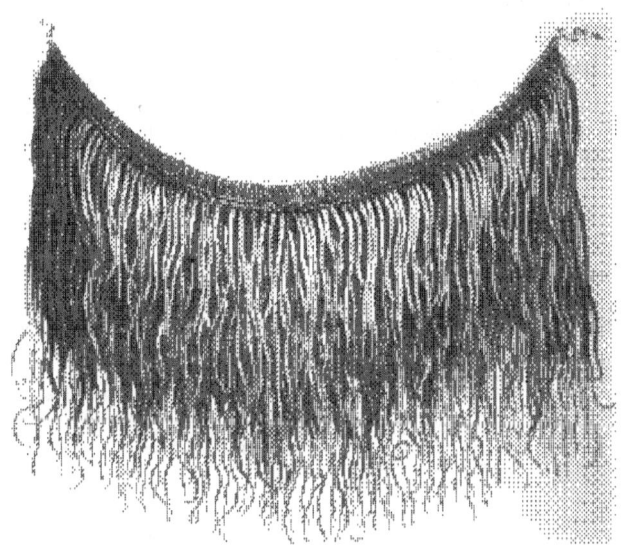

[1] Vermilion is abundant in North Africa. (Pacho, p. 59.) Red shoes are commonly worn at Tripoli. (Lyon, p. 7.) Red shawls and mantles are frequent in the interior. (Ibid. pp. 153-155.) The African nations, too, continue to excel in the dressing and dyeing of leather. The superiority of Morocco leather is universally acknowledged. Even the barbarous tribes of the interior possess the arts; and Lyon tells us that in A'aë́es "the people are excellent workers in wood and leather, which they prepare equally well as Europeans, dyeing it of very fine colours." (Travels, p. 139.) These colours are elsewhere stated to be chiefly yellow, red, and black (p. 155). Hemsley (Afric. Assoc. 1790) says that the skins are those of the goat.

Rennell (Geograph. of Herod. p. 669) conjectures that the tanning and dyeing of leather was first practised by the Libyans, passing from them into Egypt and the East, while it was likewise carried across the sea directly into Greece. He notices the "rams' skins dyed red," which covered the tabernacle in the wilderness (Exod. xxv. 5, &c.), as possibly the manufacture of Libyan tribes. They must have been brought from Egypt, and Egypt has always imported leather from the interior. (Maillet, p. 199; Lyon, p. 158.)

[2] These cries, according to the Scholiast on Æschylus (Sept. c. Th. 274), were solely in honour of Minerva (Athené). They were not howling cries, but rather triumphal shouts. Ὀλολύζειν (= ἀλαλάζειν) is to shout the interjection ἀλ, or ἐλ, an exclamation of joy and triumph. Ἐλελίζειν (= ululare)

from thence; for the Libyan women are greatly given to such cries and utter them very sweetly. Likewise the Greeks learnt from the Libyans to yoke four horses to a chariot.³

190. All the wandering tribes bury their dead according to the fashion of the Greeks, except the Nasamonians. They bury them sitting, and are right careful when the sick man is at the point of giving up the ghost, to make him sit and not let him die lying down.⁴ The dwellings of these people are made of the stems of the asphodel, and of rushes wattled together.⁵ They can be carried from place to place. Such are the customs of the afore-mentioned tribes.

191. Westward of the river Triton and adjoining upon the Auseans,⁶ are other Libyans who till the ground, and live in houses: these people are named the Maxyans.⁷ They let the hair grow long on the right side of their heads,⁸ and shave it close on

---

is to shout *ἰὰ* (Lat. ul), or *ἰαλεῦ*, a cry of lamentation. Homer speaks of the *ὀλολυγή* as proper to the worship of Athené:—

Αἱ δ' ὅτε νηὸν ἵκανον Ἀθήνης ἐν πόλει ἄκρῃ,
Τῇσι θύρας ὤϊξε θεανὼ καλλιπάρῃος...
Αἱ δ' ὀλολυγῇ πᾶσαι Ἀθήνῃ χεῖρας ἀνέσχον.
Il. vi. 297—301.

³ It is difficult to understand what is intended by this assertion. Herodotus can scarcely mean that the Cyrenaeans, having learnt the practice from the Libyans, communicated it to their countrymen; for not only was the four-horse chariot known in Greece half a century before the founding of Cyrene, when it was first introduced into the games at Olympia (Paus. v. 8, § 3), but it was even known to Homer, and according to him, used by the Greeks in war in the very earliest ages. (Il. viii. 185; Od. xiii. 81.) Can Herodotus intend to assert a connection between Greece and Libya Proper in the ante-Homeric times?

The fact probably is that the four-horse chariot first came into use in Egypt (Minutoli, Abhandl. Vermischt. Inhalts. B. I., pp. 129–139), and passed thence both into Libya Proper and into Greece. The Cyrenaeans, however, may not have begun to employ the four-horse chariots for common use till they settled in Africa, and may have adopted the custom from the Libyans.

⁴ We may compare with this the custom of the Guanches, the primitive inhabitants of the Canary Isles, a genuine African people, who buried their dead *standing*, some with a staff in their hands. (Prichard, Nat. Hist. of Man, p. 267.)

[The Shulluks of the White River bury their dead upright. The ancient Britons often buried them in a sitting posture, the hands raised to the neck, and the elbows close to the knees.—G. W.]

⁵ Hellanicus (Fragm. Hist. Gr. I. p. 57, Fragm. 93), in relating this same feature, mentions that these "houses" were merely "to keep off the sun" (*ἴσον σκιᾶς ἕνεκα*), by which they would appear to have been little more than huge parasols.

⁶ Vide supra, ch. 180. Herodotus here proceeds in his enumeration of the tribes of the coast.

⁷ This people had been mentioned under the same name by Hecataeus. (Fr. 304). It is doubtful whether they are distinct from the Machlyans of ch. 180. Some writers called them Mazyans. (Steph. Bys. ad voc.) The word, especially in this latter form, may be connected with the term *Amazigh*, which is the name given by the *Siwah*, or Berbers of the Northern Atlas, to their dialect of the Berber language. *Amazigh* means "noble." (Prichard's Nat. Hist. of Man, p. 263.)

⁸ The Egyptians left a tuft of hair on the forehead of their children, and another sometimes on the back of their heads, as they still do; but the long lock left on the right side of the head was the real emblem of childhood. (Comp. Macrob. Saturn. i. 26, and see n. on Book ii. ch. 65.)—[G. W.]

the left; they besmear their bodies with red paint; and they say that they are descended from the men of Troy.[1] Their country and the remainder of Libya towards the west is far fuller of wild beasts, and of wood, than the country of the wandering people. For the eastern side of Libya, where the wanderers dwell, is low and sandy, as far as the river Triton; but westward of that the land of the husbandmen is very hilly, and abounds with forests and wild beasts.[1] For this is the tract in which the huge serpents[2] are found, and the lions, the elephants, the bears, the aspicks, and the horned asses.[3] Here too are the dog-faced creatures, and the creatures without heads, whom the Libyans declare to have their eyes in their breasts; and also the wild

---

[1] The tradition was, that Antenor, on his way to Italy, coasted along the African shore, and planted colonies. (Cf. Pind. Pyth. v. 78, ed. Diss.)

[1] It would be impossible, even with our present knowledge, to describe more accurately the *general* differences between the eastern and western regions of North Africa. While the western region, containing the countries of Morocco, Algiers, and Tunis, is mountainous, well wooded, and well watered, and consequently abounds with wild beasts (Humboldt's Aspects, l. p. 115), the eastern, comprising Tripoli and Barka, is a low, flat, sandy tract, almost destitute of perennial streams, and admitting of cultivation only in certain favoured spots. It contains few wild animals, and those chiefly of a harmless character.

The *cause* of this difference is to be found in the sudden sinking and contraction of the mountain range which runs across North Africa, at about the 8th or 9th degree of longitude (E. from Greenwich). The continuation of Atlas, which under the names of *Soulat* and *Harudsh* extends from the borders of Tunis to the Egyptian Natron lakes, is a low hamitic range of hills, rather than mountains, quite insufficient to collect moisture and form rivers. The consequence is that the desert extends north of this line, and is only prevented from reaching the sea by the abundant rains which fall upon the coast in consequence of the vicinity of the Mediterranean. (See Beechey's Narrative, pp. 17, 37, 41, 48, 59, &c.; Della Cella, p. 46, E. T.; Lyon, p. 232.)

[2] These are of the Python tribe, still found in Africa (noted of old from one of them having stopped the army of Regulus), and common in our modern museums. The Greek name Python was probably Egyptian, Pi-Tan, and may be traced in the Tan, or Tanin of Hebrew, translated "serpent," Exod. vii. 10; or "dragon," Psa. xliv. 19; Isa. xiii. 22 and xxvii. 1; Jer. ix. 11; and "whale," in Gen. i. 21; Job vii. 12; Ezek. xxxii. 2; but which in Genesis might rather apply to the Saurian monsters in the early state of the world. It is singular that the Egyptians even believed that it was inhabited by large monsters. (See Lyell's Pr. Geology, i. p. 22.) The Python evidently corresponded to the Giant "Aphophis," or Apap, of Egypt, represented as the "great serpent," who was sin, and was pierced by the spear of Horus (Apollo) and other gods. The last syllable of Satan (Shaytán) is not related to Tan, as some might imagine, the t being a ט, not a ת, in the Hebrew: but Titan may be related to it.—(G. W.)

[3] Elephants are not now found in the countries north of the desert. It is doubted whether they could ever have been indigenous in those regions, but the testimony of Pliny ("Elephantes fert Africa ultra Syrticas solitudines, et in Mauritaniâ," H. N. viii. 11) would seem to settle the question. Hanno's voyage likewise mentions them as seen near Cape Soloeis (p. 6). Bears are rare, and are not mentioned by Leo among the animals of Africa. Shaw however speaks of them as occasionally found in Barbary (Travels, p. 249). Serpents, both great and small, and lions, are common. It is uncertain what animal Herodotus intends by his "horned ass;" probably some kind of antelope.

men, and the wild women,[4] and many other far less fabulous beasts.

192. Among the wanderers are none of these, but quite other animals; as antelopes, gazelles, buffaloes, and asses, not of the horned sort, but of a kind which does not need to drink;[5] also oryxes,[6] whose horns are used for the curved sides of citherns, and whose size is about that of the ox; foxes, hyænas, porcupines, wild rams, dictyes,[7] jackals, panthers, boryes, land-crocodiles about three cubits in length,[8] very like lizards, ostriches, and little snakes, each with a single horn. All these animals are found here, and likewise those belonging to other countries, except the stag and the wild-boar; but neither stag nor wild-boar are found in any part of Libya.[9] There are, however, three sorts

of mice in these parts; the first are called two-footed;[1] the next, zegeries,[2] which is a Libyan word meaning "hills;" and the third, urchins.[3] Weasels also are found in the Silphium-region,[4] much like the Tartessian. So many, therefore, are the animals belonging to the land of the wandering Libyans, in so far at least as my researches have been able to reach.[5]

193. Next to the Maxyan Libyans are the Zavecians;[6] whose wives drive their chariots to battle.

194. On them border the Gyzantians;[7] in whose country a vast deal of honey is made by bees; very much more, however, by the skill of men.[8] The people all paint themselves red, and eat monkeys, whereof there is inexhaustible store in the hills.[9]

---

[1] The jerboa (*Dipus jaculus* of Linnæus), is undoubtedly intended. This animal is common in Northern Africa (Shaw's Travels in Barbary, p. 321; Lyon, p. 272; Hamilton, p. 170). Its fore-legs are very diminutive, and, like the kangaroo and the squirrel, it usually sits upright.
[The jerboa has the habit of sitting up on its hind legs, using its small forepaws as hands; it even drinks water as a man sometimes does, raising it to its mouth with both hands. The "mouse," or עכבר of Lev. xi. 17, and Levit. xl. 29, is supposed to be this animal.—G. W.]

[2] Perhaps the *Gundiko*, described by Lyon as "an animal of the rat species, having a bushy tail, and head resembling that of a badger" (p. 272.) The native name, *zegeries*, has been derived from *ziger*, a kind of root (Bochart's Phaleg. li. 4), and again compared with the Fezzanian *dsideira* or *zereero*, which is applied to spots on the desert where palm-trees grow (Lyon, p. 345; Jahn, Annal, viii. 3, p. 286); but no satisfactory explanation of it has really yet been discovered.

[3] These three kinds of African "mice" are described in nearly the same terms by Theophrastus (ap. Phot. Bibl. cclxxviii.), and Ælian (Hist. An. xv. 26).

[4] The weasel is sometimes found on the Cyrenaic coins below the representation of the Silphium.

[5] How accurate these researches were, will appear sufficiently from a single comparison. Lyon says, "The animals found in Fezzan are, the tiger-cat, hyæna, jackal, fox, buffalo (of three kinds), antelope, wild cat, porcupine, hedgehog, rat, *gundiko*, mouse (of two kinds), jerboa, rabbit, hare, and camel" (Travels, pp.

271, 272). Here the additions are unimportant, except the camel, which was probably introduced at a later period. The only omissions from the list of Herodotus worth notice are, the wild ass, the wild ram, the panther, and the great lizard or land-crocodile. Three of these are borne out by Leo Africanus, who notices the "Asinus sylvaticus," the "adimain," of which he says, "aristem formâ refert," and the leopard, which is constantly confused with the panther (see Leo's Africa, pp. 292-294). The fourth—the great lizard or monitor —also really belongs to the country (see above, note [5]).

[6] The Zavecians (or Zabycians, according to some MSS.) are not mentioned by any other extant writer. They were known, however, to Hecatæus (Steph. Byz. in voc.). It seems to have been from them that a great portion of the Roman province of Africa, extending north as far as to the 36th parallel, was called *Byzacium* (Pliny, v. 4). A similar transposition has occurred in the case of their neighbours, the Gyzantians, or Zygantians.

[7] Many of the MSS. have "Zygantians," which was the form preferred by Hecatæus (Steph. Byz. in voc. Ζυγαντίς). They gave name to the northern division of the Roman Africa, which reached from the river Tusca (the *Zaine*) to Hermolus (*Herbis*), and was called Zeugitania (Plin. l. s. c.). It contained Carthage, Hippo, and Utica.

[8] Bees still abound in this country, and honey is an important article of commerce (Della Cella, p. 198, K. T.). A substitute for honey is likewise prepared from the juice of the palm (Shaw, p. 225).

[9] Monkeys have always abounded in the Western division of North Africa

195. Off their coast, as the Carthaginians report, lies an island, by name Cyraunis, the length of which is two hundred furlongs, its breadth not great, and which is soon reached from the mainland.[1] Vines and olive-trees cover the whole of it, and there is in the island a lake, from which the young maidens of the country draw up gold-dust, by dipping into the mud birds' feathers smeared with pitch. If this be true, I know not; I but write what is said.[2] It may be even so, however; since I myself have seen pitch drawn up out of the water from a lake in Zacynthus.[3] At the place I speak of there are a number of lakes; but one is larger than the rest, being seventy feet every way, and two fathoms in depth. Here they let down a pole into the water, with a bunch of myrtle tied to one end, and when they raise it again, there is pitch sticking to the myrtle, which in smell is like to bitumen, but in all else is better than the pitch of Pieria.[4] This they pour into a trench dug by the lake's side; and when a good deal has thus been got together, they draw it off and put it up in jars. Whatever falls into the lake passes underground, and comes up in the sea, which is no less than four furlongs distant.[5] So then what is said of the island off the Libyan coast is not without likelihood.

(cf. Diod. Sic. xx. 58; Leo Afric. p. 294, R.). Diodorus says that there were three places named Pithecusæ (Ape-town), because the houses were as full of apes as of men.

[1] Niebuhr (Geograph. of Herod. p. 20, E. T.) supposes Cyraunis to be the Cerne of Hanno, Scylax, and other writers, an island in the Atlantic, beyond Cape Sulosis, commonly regarded as the modern Isle of Arguin. But probably Rennell (p. 638) is right in looking upon the Cyraunis of Herodotus as the Cercinna of Strabo (xvii. p. 1178), and Pliny (v. 7), which is undoubtedly the Kardenah or Kerkenes of the present day. The length given by Pliny (25 Roman miles) exactly corresponds with the 200 stadia of Herodotus. Kiepert takes this view (Map II.).

[2] Achilles Tatius (li. 14), has the same story; but he is of no weight as an authority.

[3] Zante still produces large quantities of mineral pitch. Dr. Chandler thus describes the "tar-springs" (as he calls them) of that island:—

"The tar is produced in a small valley, about two hours from the town, by the sea, and encompassed with mountains, except towards the bay. The spring, which is most distinct and apt for inspection, rises on the farther side, near the foot of the hill. The well is circular, and 4 or 5 feet in diameter. A shining film like oil, mixed with scum, swims on the top. You remove this with a bough, and see the tar at the bottom, 3 or 4 feet below the surface.... The water is limpid, and runs off with a smart current.... We filled some vessels with tar by letting it trickle into them from the boughs which we immersed; and this is the method used to gather it from time to time into pits, where it is hardened by the sun to be barrelled, when the quantity is sufficient" (Travels, vol. ii. pp. 367, 368).

[4] The pitch of Pieria was considered the best in Greece. Pliny says "Asia piceam Idæam maximè probat, Græcia Piericam" (H. N. xiv. 20)). The quality of the Zante pitch is said now to be bad. It is unsuited for cordage; and can only be applied to the outside of boats when mixed with a better article.

[5] The sea has, apparently, encroached upon the coast in the vicinity of the "tar-springs." They are now only separated from it by a narrow morass and

196. The Carthaginians also relate the following:—There is a country in Libya, and a nation, beyond the Pillars of Hercules,⁵ which they are wont to visit, where they no sooner arrive but forthwith they unlade their wares, and, having disposed them after an orderly fashion along the beach, leave them, and, returning aboard their ships, raise a great smoke. The natives, when they see the smoke, come down to the shore, and, laying out to view so much gold as they think the worth of the wares, withdraw to a distance. The Carthaginians upon this come ashore and look. If they think the gold enough, they take it and go their way; but if it does not seem to them sufficient, they go aboard ship once more, and wait patiently. Then the others approach and add to their gold, till the Carthaginians are content. Neither party deals unfairly by the other: for they themselves never touch the gold till it comes up to the worth of their goods, nor do the natives ever carry off the goods till the gold is taken away.⁷

197. These be the Libyan tribes whereof I am able to give the names; and most of these cared little then, and indeed care little now, for the king of the Medes. One thing more also I can add concerning this region, namely, that, so far as our knowledge reaches, four nations, and no more, inhabit it; and two of these nations are indigenous, while two are not. The two indigenous are the Libyans and Ethiopians, who dwell respectively in the north and the south of Libya. The Phœnicians and the Greeks are in-comers.⁸

---

a thin strip of shingle (Walpole's Turkey, vol. ii. pp. 1, 2). The re-appearance in the sea of substances thrown into the lake is not confirmed by modern travellers.

⁵ The trade of the Carthaginians with the western coast of Africa (outside the Straits of Gibraltar) has been fully proved; and some suppose the glass objects still found there were brought by them.

The name Carthage has been noticed in n. ⁹ to Book ii. ch. 32. The derivation Cartha-hrdith (or hedes) "new town," seems the most probable one.—[G. W.]

⁷ The "dumb commerce" of the African nations is now matter of notoriety. It exists not only upon the western coast, but also to a considerable extent in the interior (see Rennell, p. 717). Lyon thus describes it:—"An invisible nation, according to our informant, in-habit near this place (Soudan), and are said to trade by night. Those who come to traffic for their gold, lay their merchandise in heaps, and retire. In the morning they find a certain quantity of gold-dust placed against every heap, which if they think sufficient, they leave the goods; if not, they let both remain till more of the precious ore is added" (p. 149). Shaw gives a similar account (Travels, p. 302). For further instances, see the Journal of the Asiatic Society, vol. xviii. p. 348.

⁸ The Egyptians are omitted, because Egypt is reckoned to Asia (supra, ii. 17, iv. 39 and 41). Taking the Ethiopians to represent that type of man, which starting from the characteristics of the Egyptian, develops into the Negro, we shall find no reason to cavil at the enumeration of races in our author. The Libyans, the indigenous inhabitants of the northern parts, are

198. It seems to me that Libya is not to compare for goodness of soil with either Asia or Europe, except the Cinyps-region,[1] which is named after the river that waters it. This piece of land is equal to any country in the world for cereal crops, and is in nothing like the rest of Libya. For the soil here is black, and springs of water abound; so that there is nothing to fear from drought; nor do heavy rains (and it rains in that part of Libya[2]) do any harm when they soak the ground. The returns of the harvest come up to the measure which prevails in Babylonia.[2] The soil is likewise good in the country of the Euesperites;[3] for there the land brings forth in the best years a hundredfold. But the Cinyps-region yields three hundred-fold.

---

the modern Berbers, who, under various names, Berbers, Shuluhs, Cabyles, and Tuariks, continue to form an important element in the population of North Africa, stretching from the mountains of Morocco to the oasis of Ammon. Southward of this race dwell an entirely different people. From Senegambia to Nubia, a type of man approaching more or less nearly to the Negro, is found to prevail (Prichard, Nat. Hist. of Man, p. 269). Even the southern races, Caffres and Hottentots, appear to belong to this same family ibid. p. 314). In these we have the Ethiopians of Herodotus. The other two Herodotean races have been absorbed, as likewise have the Romans and the Vandals. The only existing element in the population of Africa which does not appear in Herodotus, is the Arabian, the introduction of which is fixed historically to the period of the Mahometan conquests, A.D. 649-710.

[1] Della Cella says of this region, "The extensive plain, which about an hour's march from the torrent (Cinyps), stretches out to the east as far as Cape Mesurata, is abundantly productive.... This extraordinary degree of fruitfulness is not owing to the industry of the inhabitants, but proceeds from the generous nature of the soil, spontaneously covered with palm and olive-trees, which there require no sort of cultivation" (p. 37). Beechey expresses himself still more strongly: "From the summit appears," he says, "the whole plain of Lebida, stretching down in a gentle slope from the high ground to the sea; and a more beautiful scene can scarcely be witnessed than that which is presented by this fine tract of country. Thick groves of olive and date-trees are seen rising above the villages which are scattered over its surface, and the intermediate spaces are either covered with the most luxuriant turf, or rich with abundant crops of grain" (Narrative, p. 51). Hence the force of the line in Ovid (Pont. ii. 7, 25):—

"Cinyphiæ segetis citius numerabis aristas."

[1] The "heavy rains" of this region are noticed by Beechey (pp. 37, 41, 48, &c.); Lyon (p. 332); Della Cella (p. 40); and Hamilton (p. 150). They fall chiefly in the month of November. Compare note on ch. 158.

[2] Vide supra, i. 193.

[3] The Euesperites are the inhabitants of a town, called Hesperides by Scylax (p. 111), Euesperides by Herodotus (supra, ch. 171), and Hesperis by Stephen (ad voc.). It was situated at the eastern extremity of the Greater Syrtis, between the Berean or Northern Promontory (Cape Tejounes) and Teuchira. The Ptolemies changed its name to Berenice (Strab. xvii. p. 1181; Plin. H. N. v. 5), which has since been corrupted into Benghazi. It has been supposed that the famous gardens of the Hesperides were at this place; but Pacho has observed (p. 173) that this is unlikely, as the whole country about Benghazi is bare of trees. He places the gardens considerably further to the east, near Cape Phycus (the modern Ras Sem), and not far from Cyrene. The account in Scylax bears out this view (pp. 110, 111).

Benghazi is still famous for its cereal crops, great quantities of which are carried to Augila and there offered for sale, year by year (Horneman, p. 39). Mr. Hamilton says of the tract cultivated by the Benghazini:—"The soil is a rich loam, yielding, without any sort of til-

199. The country of the Cyrenæans, which is the highest tract within the part of Libya inhabited by the wandering tribes,[1] has three seasons that deserve remark. First the crops along the sea-coast begin to ripen, and are ready for the harvest and the vintage; after they have been gathered in, the crops of the middle tract above the coast-region (the hill-country, as they call it) need harvesting; while about the time when this middle crop is housed, the fruits ripen and are fit for cutting in the highest tract of all.[2] So that the produce of the first tract has been all eaten and drunk by the time that the last harvest comes in. And the harvest-time of the Cyrenæans continues thus for eight full months. So much concerning these matters.

200. When the Persians sent from Egypt by Aryandes to help Pheretima, reached Barca, they laid siege to the town, calling on those within to give up the men who had been guilty of the murder of Arcesilaüs. The townspeople, however, as they had one and all taken part in the deed, refused to entertain the proposition. So the Persians beleaguered Barca for nine months, in the course of which they dug several mines[3] from their own lines to the walls, and likewise made a number of vigorous assaults. But their mines were discovered by a man who was a worker in brass, who went with a brazen shield all round the fortress, and laid it on the ground inside the city. In other places the shield, when he laid it down, was quite dumb; but

where the ground was undermined, there the brass of the shield rang. Here, therefore, the Barcæans countermined, and slew the Persian diggers. Such was the way in which the mines were discovered; as for the assaults, the Barcæans beat them back.

201. When much time had thus been consumed, and great numbers had fallen on both sides, nor had the Persians lost fewer than their adversaries, Amasis, the leader of the land-army, perceiving that, although the Barcæans would never be conquered by force, they might be overcome by fraud, contrived as follows. One night he dug a wide trench, and laid light planks of wood across the opening, after which he brought mould and placed it upon the planks, taking care to make the place level with the surrounding ground. At dawn of day he summoned the Barcæans to a parley: and they gladly hearkening, the terms were at length agreed upon. Oaths were interchanged upon the ground over the hidden trench, and the agreement ran thus—"So long as the ground beneath our feet stands firm, the oath shall abide unchanged; the people of Barca agree to pay a fair sum to the king, and the Persians promise to cause no further trouble to the people of Barca." After the oath, the Barcæans, relying upon its terms, threw open all their gates, went out themselves beyond the walls, and allowed as many of the enemy as chose, to enter. Then the Persians broke down their secret bridge, and rushed at speed into the town—their reason for breaking the bridge being, that so they might observe what they had sworn; for they had promised the Barcæans that the oath should continue "so long as the ground whereon they stood was firm." When, therefore, the bridge was once broken down, the oath ceased to hold.

202. Such of the Barcæans as were most guilty the Persians gave up to Pheretima, who nailed them to crosses all round the walls of the city.[7] She also cut off the breasts of their wives, and fastened them likewise about the walls. The remainder of the people she gave as booty to the Persians, except only the Battiadæ, and those who had taken no part in the murder, to whom she handed over the possession of the town.

203. The Persians now set out on their return home, carrying with them the rest of the Barcæans, whom they had made their slaves. On their way they came to Cyrêné; and the Cyrenæans, out of regard for an oracle, let them pass through the town.

---

[7] Compare the punishment of the Babylonians by Darius (supra, iii. 150), and see note ad loc.

During the passage, Bares, the commander of the fleet, advised to seize the place; but Amasis, the leader of the land-force, would not consent; "because," he said, "they had only been charged to attack the one Greek city of Barca." When, however, they had passed through the town, and were encamped upon the hill of Lycæan Jove, it repented them that they had not seized Cyrênê, and they endeavoured to enter it a second time. The Cyrenæans, however, would not suffer this; whereupon, though no one appeared to offer them battle, yet a panic came upon the Persians, and they ran a distance of full sixty furlongs before they pitched their camp. Here as they lay, a messenger came to them from Aryandes, ordering them home. Then the Persians besought the men of Cyrênê to give them provisions for the way, and, these consenting, they set off on their return to Egypt. But the Libyans now beset them, and, for the sake of their clothes and harness, slew all who dropped behind and straggled, during the whole march homewards.

204. The furthest point of Libya reached by this Persian host was the city of Euesperides. The Barcæans carried into slavery

---

This whole account of the danger and escape of Cyrene is exceedingly improbable. If Cyrene was not in rebellion, the Persians would pass through it, as a matter of course, on their way to and from Barca. If it was, they would have orders to reduce it no less than Barca. If the Cyrenæans regarded their coming as hostile, they would not have been induced by an oracle to open their gates. If they had opened their gates and suffered no punishment, it is not likely that a hostile attack would directly afterwards have been made on them. Again the panic is suspicious. And the presence of Bares, the commander of the fleet, is an improbability. Probably the Cyrenæans, who were under the government of Battus IV., established king by his grandmother before she sought the assistance of Aryandes (Menecles, Fr. 2), received the Persians with due submission, both on their way to Barca and on their return; and incurred no further danger or loss, than was involved in the necessity of furnishing supplies to the host. In after times vanity might induce them to declare that they had assumed an attitude of defiance.

Lycæan Jove was worshipped especially in Arcadia (Pausan. VIII. ii. § 3); and we may suppose that his worship at Cyrene is a trace of the influence of Demonax (supra, i. 161). It is possible, however, that among the settlers who came to Cyrene from Peloponnesus in the reign of Battus II. (chs. 159 and 161), some considerable number may have been Arcadians. No remains have as yet been identified as those of this temple.

Although the wild tribes had submitted to Cambyses (supra, iii. 13), and continued to be reckoned in the sixth satrapy (iii. 91), yet it seems they could not resist the temptation to plunder afforded by the hasty return to Egypt of an army summoned thither by the governor. We are not however to suppose a disastrous retreat, but only the loss of a number of stragglers. If there had been anything more than this, the Barcæan prisoners would no doubt have escaped.

This place is said to have been first colonised by Arcesilaüs IV. (supra, ch. 171, note). Perhaps Herodotus only means that the Persians proceeded to the point afterwards occupied by Euesperides. Or perhaps Arcesilaüs IV. in reality only collected a fresh body of colonists to strengthen an already existing settlement. Euesperides lay about 820 stades (72 miles) W. of Barca (Scylax, Peripl. p. 109). It is certainly surprising that the Persians should have penetrated so far.

were sent from Egypt to the King; and Darius assigned them a village in Bactria for their dwelling-place.³ To this village they gave the name of Barca, and it was to my time an inhabited place in Bactria.

205. Nor did Pheretima herself end her days happily. For on her return to Egypt from Libya, directly after taking vengeance on the people of Barca, she was overtaken by a most horrid death. Her body swarmed with worms, which ate her flesh while she was still alive.⁴ Thus do men, by over-harsh punishments, draw down upon themselves the anger of the gods. Such then, and so fierce, was the vengeance which Pheretima, daughter of Battus, took upon the Barcæans.

---

³ The transplantation of nations was largely practised by the Persians, as it had been at an earlier date by the Assyrians and Babylonians. Besides this instance, we find noticed in Herodotus, the removal of the Pæonians to Asia Minor (v. 15), of the Milesians to Ampé (vi. 20), of the Eretrians to Susiana (vi. 119), and the proposed removal of the Phœnicians to Ionia, and of the Ionians to Phœnicia (vi. 3); which last, if not really contemplated, was at least sufficiently probable to be believed.

⁴ Pheretima seems to have been afraid of remaining in the Cyrenaica, and to have considered herself insecure except under Persian protection. The manner of her death cannot fail to recall the end of Herod Agrippa (Acts xii. 23). For the succession of Cyrenæan kings after Arcesilaüs III., see ch. 163, note ⁵.

(150)

APPENDIX TO BOOK IV.

ESSAY I.

ON THE CIMMERIANS OF HERODOTUS AND THE MIGRATIONS OF THE CYMRIC RACE.

1. Early importance of the Cimmerians — their geographical extent. 2. Identity of the Cimmerii with the Cymry — close resemblance of the two names. 3. Historical confirmation of the identity — connecting link in the Cimbri. 4. Comparative philology silent but not adverse. 5. Migrations of the Cimmerians — westward, and then eastward. Existing Cimbric and Celtic races.

1. THAT a people known to their neighbours as Cimmerii, Gimiri,[1] or (probably) Gomerim, attained to considerable power in Western Asia and Eastern Europe, within the period indicated by the date B.C. 800-600, or even earlier, is a fact which can scarcely be said to admit of a doubt. If the information gained by Herodotus in Scythia were considered as not sufficiently trustworthy for the establishment of such a conclusion, yet the confirmation which his statements derive from Homer, from Æschylus, from Callinus, from Aristotle, and from geographical nomenclature, must be held to remove all uncertainty on the point. The Cimmerians of Homer have not indeed a very definite locality: they dwell "at the furthest limit of the ocean stream, immersed in darkness, and beyond the ken of the light-giving sun,"[2] — words which might perhaps be understood of a region outside the Pillars of Hercules; but considering the condition of Greek geographical knowledge and Greek navigation in Homer's day, it is far more likely that he intended by them some part of the northern coast of the Black Sea.[3] Here

---

[1] The ethnic name of Gimiri first occurs in the Cuneiform records of the time of Darius Hystaspes, as the Semitic equivalent of the Arian name Saka (Sacæ). The nation spoken of contained at this time two divisions, the Eastern branch, named Humurgu (Ἀμύργιοι of Herodotus and Hellanicus), and the Tigrakhuda, or "archers," who were conterminous with the Assyrians. Whether at the same time three Gimiri or Saka are really Cymric Celts we cannot positively say. Josephus identified the גמר of Genesis with the Galati of Asia Minor (Ant. Jud. I. 6), in evident allusion to the ethnic title of Cymry, which they, as so many other Celtic races, gave themselves. But it must be observed, that the Babylonian title of Gimiri, as applied to the Saka, is not a vernacular but a foreign title, and that it may simply mean "the tribes"; generally, corresponding thus to the Hebrew גוים, and the Greek Πάμφυλοι. In this case it would prove nothing concerning the ethnic character of the race designated by it. — [H. C. R.]

[2] Odyss. xi. 13-22.

³Ἡ δ᾽ ἐς πείρας ἵκανε βαθυρρόου Ὠκεανοῖο Ἔνθα δὲ Κιμμερίων ἀνδρῶν δῆμός τε πόλις τε, Ἠέρι καὶ νεφέλῃ κεκαλυμμένοι· οὐδέ ποτ᾽ αὐτοὺς Ἠέλιος φαέθων καταδέρκεται ἀκτίνεσσιν, κ.τ.λ.

³ Comp. Eustath. ad Hom. Od. loc. cit. and Nizol Dissert. Homeric. p. 432. See also Mr. Gladstone's 'Homer and the Homeric Age,' vol. iii. p. 294.

Æschylus places Cimmeria* in close proximity to the Palus Mæotis and the Bosphorus; and here in the time of Herodotus were still existing a number of names, recalling the fact of the former settlement in those regions of the Cimmerian nation.* The Greek colonists of the various towns planted upon the northern coast of the Black Sea, in the seventh and eighth centuries before our era, could not fail to form an acquaintance with the inhabitants of those parts, and would spread the knowledge of them among their countrymen. Further, there are grounds for believing that during the period of which we are speaking, frequent invasions of the countries towards the south were made by this same people, who, crossing the Danube and the Thracian Bosphorus, sometimes alone, sometimes in combination with plundering Thracian tribes,* carried their arms far and wide over Asia Minor, and spread the terror of their name throughout the whole of that fertile region. Of one at least of these incursions the poet Callinus appears to have been a witness.* It was universally recognised by the Greeks that these incursions proceeded from a people dwelling north of the Danube, in the tract between that river and the Tanais, and there seems no reason to doubt this location.

From the Cimmerians of this region it appears to have been that certain permanent settlements of the same race in Asia Minor were derived. Sinópé, on occasion of one of their raids, was seized and occupied,* while probably on another the town of Antandros fell into their possession.* In the first-mentioned of these two places the Cimmerians were after a while superseded by Greek colonists; but it is conjectured, with some reason,* that they still, under the name of Chalybes (or " Iron-workers"), remained the principal race in the vicinity. In Antandros they retained their position for a century,* when the Æolians recovered it from them.

Further, there is evidence to show that more to the east, in Armenia and Central Persia, a race known nearly by the same name existed about this same time—a race whom we may *probably* connect with the Cimmerians of our author. The Prophet Ezekiel, who writes about B.C. 600, speaks of Gomer as a nation,* and couples it with Togarmah, which he places in " the north quarter," *i. e.* Armenia; and similarly the Armenian historians speak of *Gamir* as the ancestor of their Haichian race of kings.* It is also very remarkable that in the Achæmenian inscriptions the Sacan or Scythic population, which was widely spread over the Persian empire, receives in the Babylonian transcripts the name of *Gimiri*,[1] which looks as if this were the Semitic equivalent for the Arian name of *Sala* or Scyths. Perhaps both names originally meant "nomads" or "wanderers,"[2] and only came in course of time to be used as ethnic appellatives. It is clear, however, that by Herodotus the term "Cimmerian" is used distinctly in an ethnic sense; and the point to be now considered is, who these Cimmerians were, to what ethnic family they belonged, and whether they can be identified with any still existing race. When these questions have been settled, it will be interesting to trace the history and migrations of a people which has an antiquity of above twenty-five hundred years, and has spread from the steppes of the Ukraine to the mountains of Wales.

2. To build an ethnographical theory upon a mere identity of name is at all times, it must be allowed, a dangerous proceeding. The Jazyges of modern Hungary are a completely different race from the Jazyges Metanastæ who in ancient times occupied the very same country; the Wends are distinct from the Veneti, the Permian Germanii from the Germans, the Iberi of Spain from those of Georgia—yet still identity of name, even alone, is an argument which requires to be met, and which, unless met by positive objections, establishes a presumption in favour of connexion of race. Now certainly there is the very closest possible resemblance between the Greek name Κιμμέριοι and the Celtic *Cymry*; and the presumption thus raised, instead of having objections to combat, is in perfect harmony with all that enlightened research teaches of the movements of the races which gradually peopled Europe.

3. The Cimmerians, when the Scythians crossed the Tanais, and fell upon them from the east, must have gradually retreated westward. The hordes which from time to time have issued from Asia, and exerted a pressure upon the population of Europe, have uniformly driven the previous inhabitants before them in that direction.[3] Wave has followed wave; and the current, with the exception of an occasional eddy,[4] has set constantly from east to west. If the Cimmerians therefore fled westward about B.C. 650-600, where did they settle, and under what name are they next met with in history? Herodotus knows but of three nations inhabiting central and western Europe—the Sigynnæ,[5] the Cynetians,[6] and the Celts.[7] Of these the Sigynnæ and Cynetians, weak tribes who so soon disappear altogether from history, can scarcely be the great nation of the Cimmerii, which, until driven from the Ukraine by the force of the

---

[1] See Sir H. Rawlinson's Memoir on the Babylonian and Assyrian Inscriptions in the Journal of the Asiatic Society, vol. xiv. part i. p. xxi., and compare above, note 1 on § 1.

[2] According to Festus and Plutarch the name "Cimbri," which we shall find reason to identify with Cimmerii, in the old Celtic and German tongues meant "robbers" (Fest. de Verb. Signif. lib. p. 77, "Cimbri lingua Gallica latrones dicuntur." Plut. vit. Mar. c. 11, "Κίμβρους ἐπονομάζουσι Γερμανοὶ τοὺς λῃστάς"). But this meaning may have grown out of the other, just as "robber" is connected with "rover."

[3] See Niebuhr's Researches, &c. p. 52.

[4] Such as the Cimmerian inroad into Asia by the Caucasus, and the after wanderings of the Gauls.

[5] Herod. v. 9.

[6] Ibid. iv. 49.

[7] Ibid. ii. 33, and iv. 49.

Scythian torrent, was wont to extend its ravages over large tracts of Asia Minor.¹ If then we are to find the Cimmerii, driven westward B.C. 650-600, among the known nations of central or western Europe in B.C. 450-430, we must look for them among the Celts. Now the Celts had an unvarying tradition that they came from the east;² and it is a fact, concerning which there can be no question, that one of the main divisions of the Celtic people has always borne the name of Cymry as its special national designation.³ Celts were undoubtedly the primitive inhabitants of Gaul, Belgium, and the British Islands—possibly also of Spain and Portugal. In all these countries Cymry are found either as the general Celtic population, or as a leading section of it.⁴ These Cymry, or Cimbri (as the Romans called them⁵), play on several occasions an important part in history: notices of them meet us constantly as we trace the progress of the European peoples; and in more than one place they have left their name to the country of their occupation as an enduring mark of their presence in it.⁶ Though the march of events, and especially the pressure upon them of the great Gothic or Teutonic race, has for the most part wiped out at once their nationality, their language, and their name, yet they continue to form the substratum of the population in several large European countries;⁷ while in certain favoured situations they remain to the present day unmixed with any other people, retaining their ancient tongue unchanged, and, at least in one instance,⁸ their ancient appellation. The identity of the Cymry of Wales with the Cimbri of the Romans seems worthy of being accepted as an historic fact

154   TOTAL LOSS OF THE CIMMERIAN LANGUAGE.   App. Book IV.

upon the grounds stated by Niebuhr and Arnold." The historical connexion of these latter with the Cimmerii of Herodotus has strong probabilities, and the opinion of Posidonius,¹ in its favour; but cannot, it must be admitted, in the strict sense of the word, be proved.

4. It is to be regretted that we have no means of submitting the question of this connexion to the test of comparative philology. Of the Cimmerian language we know absolutely nothing beyond the single word Cimmerii. No names of Cimmerians even, on which any reliance can be placed,² have come down to us; and although some of the Scythian river-names, which have a close connexion with Celtic roots,³ may be conjectured to belong to Cimmerian rather than Scythic times, yet this is only a surmise; and though an argument of some slight weight, as it accords with what we should have expected if the people driven out by the Scyths were Celts, yet it is scarcely sufficient to put forward as a distinct ground on which to rest the identification. All perhaps that can be said is that comparative philology is *not adverse* to the identification, which, if regarded as historically probable, would help to explain the formation of certain words, whereof it would otherwise be difficult to give a satisfactory account.⁴

5. It is probable that when the Cimmerians fled westward before the Scyths,⁵ they found the central and western countries of Europe either without inhabitants, or else very thinly peopled by a Tatar race. This race, where it existed, everywhere yielded to them, and was gradually absorbed,⁶ or else driven towards the north,⁷ where it is found at the present day in the persons of the Finns, Esths, and Lapps. The Cymry, or rather the Celtic hordes gene-

rally (for in the name of Cimmerii may have been included many Celtic tribes not of the Cymric branch), spread themselves by degrees over the vast plains of central Europe, lying between the Alps on the one side, and the Baltic Sea and German Ocean on the other. It probably required a fresh impulsion from the east to propel the Celts yet further westward, and to make them occupy the remoter regions of Gaul, Spain, and Britain. This impulsion seems to have been given by the Goths and other Teutons, who by degrees possessed themselves of the countries between the Danube and the Baltic. The Celts found central and northern Gaul occupied by a Tatar population, while towards the south coast they came in contact with the Ligurians, most probably an Illyrian race.[1] In the Spanish peninsula it is not quite certain whether on their arrival they found Iberians or no; but if not, these latter must have shortly crossed over from the African main, and it was in consequence of the gradual pressure exerted by this people upon the Celts in Spain that the further migrations of the Celtic tribes took place.[2] The struggle in Spain was probably of long duration; but at length the Celts were compelled to cross the Pyrenees in vast numbers, and to seek a refuge with their kinsmen in Gaul. These, however, were themselves too numerous and too closely packed to offer more than a temporary asylum to the refugees, who consequently had to seek a permanent abode elsewhere. Hereupon they crossed the Alps into Italy, and made themselves masters of the whole plain of the Po; after which they separated into two streams, and overran, on the one hand, the whole of middle and lower Italy, even reaching Sicily, according to some accounts;[3] while, on the other hand, crossing the Alps to the north of the Adriatic,[4] and following down the streams which run into the Danube, they spread over the great central European plain, the modern kingdom of Hungary. Here for a time they found ample room, and the torrent of emigration paused awhile upon its course;[5] but a century later fresh movements of the Celtic tribes took place. About the year B.C. 280 vast hordes of Gauls from these regions entered Macedonia, and pressing towards the south threatened Greece with destruction. Repulsed, however, from Delphi, they returned northwards; and crossing the Dardanelles, invaded Asia Minor, the whole of which for many years they ravaged at their pleasure.[6] In course of time the native inhabitants recovered from them most of their conquests; but the Gauls permanently maintained themselves in the heart of Phrygia, and gave their name to the northern portion, which became known as *Galatia*. They also, during this same period, carried their victorious arms into Scythia, and avenged themselves on their former conquerors, whom they subdued, and with whom they intermixed,

---

[1] Niebuhr (Roman Hist. vol. I. p. 165, E. T.) connects them with the Liburnians of the Adriatic, and these with the Venetians, who were Illyrians according to Herodotus (l. 196).

[2] Niebuhr's Rom. Hist. vol. ii. p. 520, E. T. The Iberians are thought to remain in the modern Basques.

[3] Justin. xx. 5.

[4] Part stayed between the Alps and the Adriatic (Scylac. Peripl. p. 1:3).

[5] From these Celts came the ambassadors to Alexander (Arrian, Exp. Alex. l. 4).

[6] Livy, xxxviii. 16.

forming thereby the people known in history as Celto-Scythians. At this period they warred with the Greek town of Olbia; and advanced as far as the Mæotis, from which they had been driven by the Scyths five hundred years earlier. Here, however, they were met and overpowered by a movement of nations from the east. The progress of the Sarmatic tribes commenced; and the Celts fell back along the valley of the Danube, leaving traces of their presence in the names *Wallachia* and *Gallicia*, but everywhere sinking and disappearing before the antagonism of more powerful nations. In Eastern and Central Europe the Celtic race has been either absorbed or destroyed; in the West, as has been observed already, it still remains. Northern Italy deserves its German appellation of *Wallachland*; for neither the Roman nor the Lombard conquest, nor the ravages of Goths, Huns, or Vandals, ever rooted out the offspring of those Gallic hordes which settled in the plain of the Po four centuries before our era. France is still mainly Gallic. Rome indeed imposed her language there as elsewhere, except in one remote corner of the land, where the Celtic is still spoken; but the people continued *Gauls*, and the country *Gallia*. The Teutonic bands, Franks, Normans, Burgundians, caused the name of Gaul to disappear; but the conquerors, as a race, were absorbed among the conquered. In the British Islands, the Anglo-Saxon Teutons, in their earlier conquests, displaced the Cymry, and drove them beyond their borders; but these last maintained themselves in various places—in Cornwall, Wales, the Scotch Highlands, and Ireland— until the inauguration of a new policy. When the Cymry of Wales and Cornwall, the Gaels in Scotland, and the Erse in Ireland, submitted to Anglo-Saxon supremacy, they retained their lands, their language, and even their name. Amalgamation of race has since been effected to a certain extent; but still in many parts of Wales, Scotland, and Ireland, the mass of the population is mainly or entirely Celtic. Four Celtic dialects—the Manx, the Gaelic, the Erse, and the Welsh—are spoken in our country; and the pure Celtic type survives alike in the Bretons, the Welsh, the native Irish, the people of the Isle of Man, and the Scottish Highlanders, of whom the two former represent the Cimbric, and the three latter the non-Cimbric branch of the nation.

Strabo, L. p. 48.

See the Inscription of Protogenes, edited by Köhler.

Strabo, vii. p. 425.

The modern Wallachs and Gallicians may not indeed be descendants of the ancient Gauls; but the names can scarcely have come from any other source. The theory which would derive them from the old German use of *walachen*, *walli*, for "strangers, foreigners," is somewhat fanciful.

Brittany. See Prichard's "Celtic Nations," § 3; and Michelet's "Histoire de France," vol. i. pp. 139-143.

Cornwall was the country of the *Cern-Walli*, or Welsh of the Horn. A Celtic dialect was spoken in Cornwall till late in the last century.

The Welsh is akin to the Breton and the Cornish dialects; the Gallic and the Erse, which are closely allied, differ considerably from the three first-mentioned. In the former we have the Cimbric, in the latter the more ordinary Celtic tongue.

ESSAY II.

ON THE ETHNOGRAPHY OF THE EUROPEAN SCYTHS.

1. Supposed Mongolian origin of the Scyths — grounds of the opinion twofold. 2. Resemblance of physical characteristics, slight. 3. Resemblance of manners and customs, not close. 4. True test, that of language. 5. Possibility of applying it. 6. The application — Etymology of Scythic common terms. 7. Explanation of the names of the Scythian gods. 8. Explanation of some names of men. 9. Explanation of geographical names. 10. Result, that the Scythians of Herodotus were an Indo-European race. 11. Further result, that they were a *distinct* race, not Slaves, nor Celts, nor Teutons; and that they are now extinct.

1. A LARGE number of the best scholars of Germany,[1] among them the great historian Niebuhr,[2] have maintained that the Scythians of Herodotus were a Tatar or Mongolian race, the earliest specimen known to us of that powerful people which, under the name of Huns, Bulgarians, Magyars, and Turks, has so often carried desolation over Europe, and which in Asia, as Mongols, Calmucks, Eleuths, Khirgis, Nogais, Turcomen, Thibetians, and (perhaps) Chinese, extends from the steppes of the Don to the coasts of the Yellow Sea. This opinion has also been adopted by the most eminent of our own historians,[3] who regard it as certain, or at least as most highly probable, that the Scythians of Herodotus were a Mongol nation.

The grounds upon which the opinion rests are twofold: first, it is maintained that the physical characteristics of the Scythians, as recorded by Hippocrates (who himself visited Scythia), are such as to place it beyond a doubt that the people so described belong to the Mongolian family; and, secondly, it is contended that such an identity of manners and customs can be made out as would alone suffice to prove the same point.

2. The description of Hippocrates, on which reliance is placed, is the following: "Their bodies," says the great physician, "are gross and fleshy; the joints are loose and yielding; the belly flabby; they have but little hair, and they all closely resemble one another."[4] "This," Niebuhr observes, "is a picture of the native tribes of Northern Asia, for whom there is no more suitable name

---

[1] As Boeckh (Corpus Inscrip. Gr. Introduct. ad Inscript. Sarmat. pars xi. p. 81., Schafarik (Slavische Alterthümer, vol. I. xli. 6), and Hack (Samml. Abhandl. I. 314).

[2] See his "Untersuchungen über die Geschichte der Skythen, Geten, und Sarmaten," published in the "Kleine Schriften," p. 362, and compare the "Vorträge über alte Geschichte" (vol. I. p. 179).

[3] Thirlwall, History of Greece, vol. ii. ch. xiv. p. 239, 8vo. edition; Grote, History of Greece, vol. III. p. 322, 2nd ed.

[4] "Τὰ εἴδεα αὐτῶν παχέα ἐστὶ καὶ σαρκώδεα, καὶ ἄρθρα καὶ ὑγρὰ καὶ ἄτονα, αἵ τε κοιλίαι ὑγρόταται πασέων... διὰ τε μολθὸν καὶ ψιλὸν τὴν σάρκα, τά τε εἴδεα ἑωυτοῖ ἀλλήλοισιν, τά τε ἄρσενα τοῖς ἄρσεσιν, καὶ τὰ θήλεα τοῖς θήλεσιν." De Aëre, Aquâ, et Locis, c. 6, p. 558, ed. Kühn.

than that of *Mongols.*"¹ The description of Hippocrates, however, does not very closely resemble the accounts which travellers give either of the strictly Mongolian, or of the cognate Turkish or Tatar race. Dr. Prichard, in his Natural History of Man, selects the following as the most accurate description of the Mongols which had come to his knowledge. "The Kalmucks (Mongols) are generally of a moderate height. We find them rather small than large. *They are well made;* and I do not remember to have seen a deformed person. They entirely abandon their children to nature; hence they are all healthy, and have their bodies *well proportioned.* They are generally *slender and delicate in their limbs and figure. I never saw a single man among them who was very fat.*"² It is evident that this description contrasts remarkably with that of Hippocrates, and indeed in nothing do the Mongols of the present day appear to resemble the ancient Scythians, except in the scantiness of hair³ and the general likeness of individuals to one another.⁴

The account given by eye-witnesses of the physical peculiarities of the nomadic Turkish tribes more nearly approaches to the ancient Scythic type. Dr. Prichard thus describes them:—"In stature they are under the middle size; of a kyl numbering seven men, the tallest was 5 feet 5¼ inches in height. Their countenances is disagreeable . . . , their cheeks, large and bloated, look as if pieces of flesh had been daubed upon them; a slender beard covers their chin, and in those individuals who have more luxuriant hair the beard has a natural curl. Their persons are not muscular."⁵ Still even here there is no such exact conformity as would warrant us in assuming the identity of the two races.

Mr. Grote, who adopts the theory of Niebuhr, confesses that many nomadic hordes, whom no one would refer to the same race, may have exhibited an analogy of characteristics equal to that between the Scythians and Mongols.⁶ And indeed it is manifest that the chief points of the analogy are such as extend to a vast number of unconnected tribes. Scantiness of hair is common to the Kamtschatkans,⁷ the Samoieides,⁸ the Chinese,⁹ the Mexicans,¹⁰ and the American nations generally;¹¹ while the absence of discriminating features among the individuals of the race appears to mark a certain low condition of civilisation and of national development rather than any special ethnic variety.¹² It would seem therefore that the

---

¹ Untersuchungen, &c., p. 66, English translation.
² Physical History of Man, p. 215. The passage is quoted by Dr. Prichard from the writings of the traveller Pallas.
³ Pallas notices that the "eyebrows are black and woolly" (Prichard, l. s. c.). De Hell says, "The Kalmucks have eyes set obliquely, with eyelids little opened, scanty black eyebrows, nose deeply depressed near the forehead, prominent cheek-bones, spare beards, thin moustaches, and a brownish-yellow skin." (Travels, ch. xxv. p. 242, E. T.)
⁴ "Paint one individual," says De Hell,

"and you paint the whole nation." And he relates an anecdote of the Calmuck prince Tumene, who, growing tired of sitting to an artist for his portrait, had it finished from one of his attendants. The picture was a striking likeness. (Travels, l. s. c.)
⁵ Physical History, pp. 210, 211. Dr. Prichard quotes from the travels of Lieutenant Wood.
¹ History of Greece, vol. iii. p. 322, note ².
² Prichard, p. 221.   ³ Ibid. p. 225.
⁴ Ibid. p. 212.   ⁵ Ibid. p. 372.
⁶ Ibid. p. 98.
⁷ Nations in the savage, like animals in the wild state, are devoid of any striking

supposed resemblance of the picture drawn by Hippocrates to the present characteristics of the Mongols, is a very insufficient ground for presuming the ethnic identity of the two races.

3. The remaining ground on which the opinion rests, the close resemblance of the Scythian manners and customs, as described by Hippocrates and Herodotus, to the known habits of the Mongols, possesses (it must be confessed) very considerable claims upon our attention. The adoration of the scymitar,[?] the ceremonies at the funeral of a king,[?] the use of burning as a remedy,[?] the production of intoxication by placing hemp seeds upon red-hot stones,[?] the use of mare's milk,[?] the general filthiness,—all these are features thoroughly Mongolian;[?] and some of them are so strange and peculiar as to indicate at least connexion, if not absolute identity. Humboldt, who rejects the ethnic affinity of the Scyths and Mongols, nevertheless observes that the "cruelties practised at the funeral of the grand khans of the Mongols *bear a complete resemblance* to those which Herodotus describes as obtaining among the Scyths of the Borysthenes;"[?] and M. Huc bears witness to the continuance of similar customs to the present day.[?] And the worship of the naked scymitar, another most remarkable custom, very strongly indicative of a connexion of one kind or another between the races practising it, was certainly in use among the Huns (who were true Mongols) in the days of Attila.[?] Identity of race, however, is not proved by similarity of manners and customs, even when it extends much further than can be shown in this instance. Nations, especially those which are in immediate contact with one another, adopt each other's usages; and if the Mongolians, as is probable, absorbed the ancient race of the Scyths at the time of their great migration westward,[?] they may well have begun the practice of certain Scythic customs at that period. At any rate, however we may account for the resemblance which undoubtedly exists between the manners

---

individual differences. Where the life is the same for all, and no variety of external influences calls forth various powers and qualities in the sentient being, a sameness pervades the class. (See Ruskin's Modern Painters, vol. ii. p. 106.) Negroes, Cadiz, Esquimaux, Calmucks, Bushmen, have the peculiarity in common. Even among the Arabs of the Desert a far higher type of humanity) the same fact is verified. " I was now," says the gifted author of Eothen, " amongst the true Bedouins: *almost every man of this race closely resembles his brethren*, almost every man has large and finely formed features, &c." (Ch. xvii. p. 180, 5th ed.)

[?] Herod. iv. 62; Lucian. Toxar. xxxviii. (vol. vi. p. 101.)

[?] Herod. iv. 71.

[?] Hippocrat. De Aere, Aquâ, et Locis, c. 47 (p. 559, ed. Kühn).

[?] Herod. iv. 75.

[?] Ibid. ch. 2; Eph. Fr. 76; Nic. Dam. Fr. 123.

[?] Herod. iv. 75.

[?] See Niebuhr's Untersuchungen, pp. 46, 47, E. T.

[?] "Les cruautés lors de la pompe funèbre des grand-khans *ressemblent entièrement à celles que nous trouvons décrites par Hérodote* . . . . chez les Scythes du Gerrhus et du Borysthène." Asie Centrale, vol. i. p. 244.

[?] See note [?] to Book iv. ch. 71, where the passage is quoted at length. As, however, customs very similar are found in Southern Africa and in Patagonia, it is plain that similarity in this regard does not prove connexion. Mr. Blakesley well observes (note 205 on Book iv.) that " such proceedings were not merely a traditional custom, but rested on that common feeling of humanity which ascribes to the departed similar tastes and pursuits to those which have been valued by them in their lifetime."

[?] Jornandes de Rebus Geticis, c. 35.

[?] About A.D. 1235-1245. See Gibbon's Decline and Fall, vol. vi. ch. 64.

and customs of the Mongols and the Scyths, it is decidedly (as Mr. Grote confesses[1]) insufficient to establish a real ethnic connexion.

4. One thing only will enable us to decide the ethnographical position of the ancient Scythic people, and that is their *language*. It is only by an accurate analysis of the remains of the ancient Scythic speech which have come down to us that any satisfactory conclusion can be drawn.

And this also is confessed by Mr. Grote. "To enable us to affirm," he observes, "that the Massagetæ, or the Scythians, or the Alani, belonged to the Indo-European family, it would be requisite that we should know something of their language."[2] But, he maintains, "the Scythian language may be said to be wholly unknown" to us, and therefore this test cannot be applied in the present instance. "A very few words" have indeed been brought to our knowledge; but these, he thinks, "do not tend to aid the Indo-European hypothesis."

5. It is the opinion, however, of the best comparative philologists[3] that the fragments of the Scythic language which remain to us are amply sufficient to determine the family of nations to which the people who spoke it must have belonged. Dr. Donaldson in his 'Varronianus,'[4] and more recently Jacob Grimm, in his 'History of the German Language,'[5] have shown by an elaborate examination of Scythic roots that there are the strongest grounds for believing the Scythians of Herodotus to have been an Indo-European people. As the weight of this argument depends entirely on the number and character of the instances, and as independently of their value in determining the question of ethnography, speculations upon the language of an ancient nation possess intrinsically a high interest, the following analysis of Scythic words, drawn chiefly from the two writers above mentioned, is appended as sufficient evidence of the position here maintained, viz., that the Scythians of Herodotus belonged ethnically to the Indo-European, and not to the Mongolian family of nations.

6. The Scythic words of which the meaning is certainly known to us are the following: *Oior, pata, arima, spu, temerinda, graurasus, exampæus, brimön, phrysa, araxa, halinda,* and *sarrium* or *satrium.* These will be first considered.

Oior,[6] "a man," is undoubtedly the Sanscrit *vîra,* the Zend *vairya,* the Greek Ἥρως, the Latin *vir,* Gothic *vair,* Celtic *gwr,* Lithuanian *vyras.*[7] It may be connected likewise with the ancient Persian *ariya,* which primarily signified "men," "heroes," and thence was adopted as an ethnic appellative by the great Medo-Bactric or Arian race.[8]

Pata,[9] "to kill," is probably the Sanscrit *vadha,* "to strike, kill,

---

[1] History of Greece, vol. iii. p. 321, note.
[2] Ibid. l. s. c.
[3] To the names mentioned in the text may be added that of the late lamented Dr. Trithen, Professor of Modern Languages in the University of Oxford, who privately expressed to me the same conviction.
[4] Pp. 39-40.
[5] Geschichte der Deutschen Sprache, Leipzig, 1848.
[6] Herod. iv. 110. οἰὸρ γὰρ καλέουσι τὸν ἄνδρα (Σκύθαι).
[7] See Sir H. Rawlinson's Ancient Persian Vocabulary, sub voc. *Ariya,* note 6.
[8] Herod. iv. 110. τὰ κατὰ στείλειν (καλέουσι Σκύθαι).

destroy;" for the Scythian language, as is plain from the *Thesmophoriazusæ* of Aristophanes, affected the Ionis in the place of the aspirate. It may also be compared with the Latin "*butyrum*," and so with our verbs "to beat," "to batter;" perhaps also with "to pat."

Arima,[2] "one," would seem to be for Γάριμα, a form almost identical with the Latin, Gothic, and Lithuanian ordinals, *primus*, *frums*, *pirmà*, and connected with the Sanscrit *prathamá*, Zend *frathema*, Greek πρῶτος. The initial sound may have been dropped by Herodotus, because in his time the Greeks had no letter to express it; or it may have been absent from the Scythic word just as it is from the old High German *èrister* and the modern German *erst*, which are nevertheless identical with the Gothic *frumist* and our *first*.[1]

Spu,[3] "the eye," is manifestly cognate to the Latin *spic-* or *spec-*, the root of the words *specio*, *specto*, *speculor*, *auspicio*, &c., and may be compared with the German *spähen*, French *épier* (*espier*), and our own *spy*.

Temerinda,[2] "mother of the sea," is a compound word, the analysis of which is uncertain. It is probable that the ending *-inda* is a mere feminine termination, which is found again in *hulinda*,[4] and has a parallel in the Anglo-Saxon termination *-ende*, which appears occasionally in the later period of that language.[5] If then we are to seek for "mother of the sea" in *Temer*, it may be conjectured that *Te* was "mother" in Scythic, and *mer* "sea." *Te* would then resemble the gipsy *dei*, *dai*, and the Greek θεῖα, "aunt;"[6] and *mer* would be the Latin *mare*, German *meer*, French *mer*, our *mere* or *meer*.

Graucasus,[7] "white with snow," was the name by which the Scythians knew the Caucasus, and may be regarded as the true original of that word. There can be little doubt that the *Grau* here is the Greek κρυ- in κρύος, κρύσταλλος, κρυμός, whence perhaps the Latin *cruor*, *crudelis*, the German *graus*, *grausam*, our *crud*, &c.; and also by the change of *r* into *l*, the Latin *gelu*, *glacies*; Germ. *kalt*; our *cool*, *cold*. It will therefore mean "snow," and *casus* will be the Scythic word for "white." Compare with this latter the Sanscrit *kas-*, Greek καθαρός, Latin *castus*, *casus*, *candidus*, perhaps the Oscan *casnar*, and the German *keusch*.

Exampæus,[8] "holy ways," the name, according to Herodotus, of a bitter spring near the Hypanis, divides probably into the two roots *exau* or *hexau*, and *pai* or *pais*, the former of which may be connected with the Sanscrit *accha*, which (according to Grimm) is the Greek

---

[2] Herod. iv. 27. Ἄριμα γὰρ ἓν καλοῦσι Σκύθαι.

[2] See Bopp's Comparative Grammar, vol. I. p. 416 (English translation).

[3] Herod. iv. 27. Σποῦ τὸν ὀφθαλμὸν [καλοῦσι Σκ.].

[2] Plin. Hist. Nat. vi. 7. "Mæotis [Scythæ] Temerinda [vocant], quo significant matrem maris."

[4] See the next page.

[5] Grimm quotes from an Anglo-Saxon document of later times the formula "on land and on *orands*" as equivalent to *terrâ ma-*

ríque. (Geschichte, vol. I. p. 234, note.)

[6] It is possible that *Te* may be the final syllable of μήτηρ. Sansc. *mâtâ*. Initial syllables sometimes, though rarely, disappear. Compare γε-λαστος, lac—av-unculum, uncle, oncle—ex-put, pute, &c.

[7] Plin. Hist. Nat. vi. 17. "Scythæ Caucasum montem, Graucasum, i. e. nive candidum [appellarunt]."

[8] Herod. iv. 52. Οὔνομα δὲ τῇ κρήνῃ καὶ, ὅθεν ῥέει, τῷ χώρῳ, Ἐξαμπαῖοι, κατὰ δὲ τὴν Ἑλλήνων γλῶσσαν, ἱραὶ ὁδοί.

άγία and the Latin *sacra*; while the latter is manifestly the Sanscrit *patha*, Greek πάτος, German *pfad*, and our own *path*.¹

Briraba,¹ "a ram's forehead," seems to be composed of *brir*, "a ram," and *aba*, "the head or forehead." *Brir* appears in the Latin *berbex* or *vervex*, Italian *berbice*, Provençal *berbitz*, French *brebis*. Also in *caput* (Sanscrit *kapala*, German *haupt*), without the initial guttural, which is lost also in *holiwla* = "*caulis*."

Phryxa,¹ "hater of evil," compared with *araxa*, "hater of damsels," gives *xa* as the verb "to hate," and *phry* or *phru* as "evil." *Xa* is compared by Dr. Donaldson with the German *schou*² (our *shy*); but this identification is a very doubtful one. *Phru* may with more confidence be connected with the Latin *pravus*, and the German *frevel*, *freuler*.

Araxa,¹ "hater of damsels," contains the roots *xa*, "to hate," and *ara*, "a maiden." This latter word appears in the Greek Ἄρτεμις, Etruscan *Aritimis*, the virgin goddess. It occurs also in the Scythic name for Celestial Venus, *Artimpasa*.

Halinda,¹ "a species of cabbage," may be the Latin *caulis* (our "*cauli-flower*"), the initial guttural having become an aspirate, and the feminine suffix *-inda* (compare *Temerinda*) having taken the place of the Latin *-is*.

Salrium,¹ "amber," if it may be read for *sacrium*, will be the Lettish *sihters*, or *duinters*, which is the Lithuanian *gintaras* or *gentaras*, and the Russian *jantar*.

In addition to these words with determined meanings we possess a number of Scythian appellations, the probable meaning of which may to some extent be surmised. These likewise tend to bear out the Indo-European theory. They may be divided into (1), names of gods; (2), names of men; (3), geographical names.

7. The names of the Scythian gods, according to Herodotus, are the following:—Tabiti, Papæus, Apia, Oitosyrus, Artimpasa, and Thamimasadas. These he identifies respectively with the Grecian Vesta, Jupiter, Earth, Apollo, Aphrodite, and Poseidon.⁷

Tabiti (Vesta), the fire-goddess, derived her name apparently from the root *tap*, "to burn," which is found both in Sanscrit and Zend, and which runs through a vast number of the Indo-European languages, forming *tep-idus*, *tep-ere*, in Latin, *teply* in Bohemian, *cieply* in Polish, *täften* and *täbau* in Persian, θάπ-τειν (πυρί θάπτειν, Hom.) in Greek, and so ταφ-ος, and also τέφρα, "cinis."

Papæus (Zeus, or Jupiter) was the *father* of gods and men, as Herodotus plainly indicates.⁸ The root *pa-* or *pi-*, with or without

---

¹ It may be doubted whether *Hecatæus'd*, "witches' path," be not the truer reading of the Scythic *Exampæus*. (Cf. Rüter's Vorhalle, p. 345; Issukhn's Varronianæ, p. 39; Bähr ad Herod. iv. 52.) But *Hesse* itself (Spanish *hechizera*, our "hag") is perhaps only a variant of the same root, *ac-, sac-, sep-*, signifying primarily a sacred person.

¹ Plutarch, ii. p. 1156.
² Ibid.

³ Varronianæ, l. s. c.
⁴ Plutarch, b. p. 1167.
⁵ Ibid. p. 1158.
⁶ Plin. Hist. Nat. xxxvii. 2. Schafarik proposed this reading, and Grimm approves of it.
⁷ Herod. iv. 59.
⁸ This is the meaning of his remark, that "Jupiter is called very properly in his judgment (ὀρθότατα, κατὰ γνώμην γε τὴν ἐμήν), Papæus," iv. 59. Compare the ordinary Greek address to the Supreme Being.

the suffix *ter, tri*, expresses the paternal relationship in almost all the Indo-European tongues.² The reduplicated form *Papæus* is closely akin to *Papias* and *Papas*, titles under which the supreme God was worshipped in Asia Minor in very early times,¹ and appears likewise in the Phrygian BABA,² the Greek πάππας, the Latin *papa*, German *Papst*, our "pope," and again in the familiar *papa* of so many modern languages.

Apia (Earth) would seem to be nothing but another form of the Latin *Ops* (*Opis*), who is identical with Rhea or Tellus. *Apis, Opis, Apia*, were forms common to the early Greek and Italian nations, and signified "earth, land, country." Hence Mesa-apia, Dry-opia, &c.; and the many names of tribes ending in *-opes*, Dolopes, Meropes, Cecropes, and the like. Hence also the old name *Apia* for the Peloponnese, derived afterwards from the mythic king Apis.³

Oitosyrus (Apollo) appears to be a compound word, formed of the two elements *oito*, and *syrus* or *surus*. About the meaning of the latter term there can be little doubt. It is plainly the Sanscrit *súrya*, "the sun." The other element may connect either with the Latin *vitu* and Greek *aisa*, or, perhaps better, with αἶθος, αἴθων, *citrum, weiss*, "white." The word will thus mean "the bright shining sun."

Artimpasa (Urania, or Celestial Venus) is the most obscure of all the names of the Scythian deities. It is not even certain what attributes Herodotus intended to assign to her. If she was, as is probable,⁴ the Moon, we may compare the title with the Greek Ἄρτεμις, in which the root *arn*, "a virgin," is to be recognised. The remainder of the word has as yet received no satisfactory explanation.

Thamimasadas (Poseidon, or Neptune), "the Water God," is a name which may be analysed, with an approach to certainty, into the two parts *Thami* and *masadas*. Of these the former, *Thami*, would seem to be the *Teme* of Pliny's *Temerinda*, which has been already explained, and which may well have been a general designation for lakes and rivers.⁵ The latter, *masadas*, occurs in the royal title,

---

Ζεὺ πάντερ. Lat. Ju-piter, Dies-piter; and the Homeric πατὴρ ἀνδρῶν τε θεῶν τε; Virgil's "hominum pater atque Deorum;" also Aratus, as quoted by St. Paul, τοῦ ἡ. c. Ζηνὸς) γὰρ καὶ γένος ἐσμέν. (Acts xvii. 28.)

² Sanscr. *pitá, pitri*; Ancient Persian, *pitá*; Greek, πατήρ; Latin, *pater*; Italian, *padre*; German, *vater*; our *father*, &c.

¹ Leake (Asia Minor, p. 20) gives an inscription which he found in Asia Minor, near Doganlu, addressed to Papias the Saviour (ΠΑΠΙΑΔΙ ΣΩΤΗΡΙ). Arrian (ap. Eustat. ad Il. v. 429) mentioned that Jupiter was worshipped under the name of *Papas* in Bithynia.

² See the Phrygian inscription on the great tomb of Midas near Doganlu (supra, vol. i. p. 547). BABA appears there as a title of honour borne by the person who erected the monument. *Papas* occurs in this same in other Asiatic inscriptions. (See Perocke's Ins. Ant. ch. ii. § 6, p. 13.)

³ Æschyl. Suppl. 255-265 (ed. Scholef.).

⁴ The Alitta or Alilat of the Arabians, whom Herodotus (l. 131; iii. 8) identifies with Urania, is thought to have been the Moon by some of the best authorities. (See Bochart's Phaleg, II. 19, and Seldon de Dis Syris, ii. 2.)

¹ *Temer*, or *Teme*, if it meant "mother of the sea," may easily have come to be applied widely to rivers and to lakes at their mouths (Herod. iv. 46). Rivers were often looked on in this light. (Cf. Stasho, v. p. 214; and see Grimm's Geschichte der Deutschen Sprache, p. 234.) Hence perhaps the *Temer-ites* and *Timer-ates* of the ancients, the latter of which, Strabo expressly says (l. s. c.), was regarded by the dwellers on its banks as

M 2

Octa-masulas,ᵃ and may be identified with the *-mas-das* (ancient Pers. *-mazda*) of the Arian god Oromasdes (*Auramazdá*). Etymologically *mazdas* seems to mean "great giver;"ᵇ but it probably passed at an early time into the more general sense of "god." Thus Thamima-sadas would be, as stated above, "the Water-God," or more fully and literally, "the great Giver of lakes and streams."

8. The Scythian names of men are these: Spargapithes, Aria-pithes, Octamasadas, Idanthyrsus, Anacharsis, Taxacis, Saulius, Lycus, Gnurus, Scylas, Scopasis, Scolopitus, Oricus:—to which perhaps should be added the mythic personages Targitaus, Lipoxais, Arpoxais, and Colaxais. Among these there are two or three which present very palpable etymologies.

Spargapithes (or *Spargapises*ᶜ) is probably the Sanscrit *Svargapati*, "lord of heaven," a title of the god Indra in the Vedas, and hence we obtain a clue to the name of *Ariapithes* (which may be compared with the Persian names *Ariaramnes*, *Arvamardus*, *Ariabignes*, and the like), formed probably from the two roots *ariya*, originally "manly," and thence "noble, excellent," and *pati*, "lord," as in the preceding. In *Octamasadas* the root *masdas* recurs, of which an account has been given: and in Idanth-*yrsus*, Anach-*arsis*, we seem to have the Persian (and Armenian) *Arses*, which appears as the initial element in the names *Arsames* and *Arsaces*, and occurs as a final in the old Persian *Khshay-árshá* (Xerxes), and in *Dad-arses*, a general of Darius.ᵈ The root *arses* (in Persian *arshá*, or *arsha*) is clearly the same with the Sanscrit *drshá*, "venerable;" while in *Anach-* we can hardly fail to recognise the Persian *naqa*ᵉ and Greek ἄναξ. The remaining names do not admit of any very distinct identification. Some, as *Lycus*, *Scylas*, *Saulius*, are Greek in their general character. Others (*Lipoxais*, *Arpoxais*, *Colaxais*) have a Slavonic look. In the *Scolopitus* of Justin the root *pati* may again be recognised: and if in the first part of the word we may consider that we have the national appellation *Scoloti*, the term would be equivalent to "king of the Scoloti or Scyths;" and it may, like Brennus, Pharaoh, &c., have been a mere title, mistaken by foreigners for the actual name of a monarch.

9. The *geographical* terms which Scythia furnishes are few in number. They consist almost entirely of the names of rivers:—these are, the Ister, with its tributaries the Porata, Tiarantus, Ararus, Naparis, and Ordessus; the Tyras, the Hypanis, the Borysthenes, the Panticapes, the Gerrhus, the Hypacyris, the Syrgis, and the Tanais. These names mostly admit of explanation from Indo-Germanic roots.

The word *Ister* is made up of two elements (*is* and *ter*), both of which seem to have signified, in different Indo-European dialects,

---

ᵃ "μυρίων ὑδάτων;" and hence too, it may be, our rivers *Thamer*, *Tamar*, and *Thames* or *Thamesa*. (Cf. Donaldson's Varr. p. 38.)

ᵇ Herod. iv. 8).

ᶜ From the Sanscrit roots *mas*, "great" (compare μείζων), and *dá*, "to give" (= Heb. נתן, *dare*, &c.) See Sir H. Rawlinson's Vocabulary of the Ancient Persian language, ad voc. *Auramazda*.

ᵈ As it is read in Book i. ch. 211.

ᵉ Mentioned in the Behistun Inscription, col. i. par. 7, § 2.

ᶠ "*Naqa*" is a doubtful reading, and may perhaps be an Egyptian title. (See Sir H. Rawlinson's Memoir on the Beh. Ins. vol. ii. p. 316.)

"river" or "water."* We may trace the element *Is* in the names of rivers from the vicinity of the Euphrates to the banks of the Thames. In the *Is* of Herodotus (i. 179) and Herodianus (p. 19, ed. Dindorf) we have the word in its simple and most primitive form—in the *Is-auros*, *Is-apis*, *Is-aras*, in the many rivers *Isar* (*Isere*) and *Isel* we find the same root combined with a second element; in *Isis* and *Tham-isis* (Thames) it occurs reduplicated. The other element, *ter*, is less widely spread, but it appears again in the two Scythian rivers, the *Tyr-as* and *Tiar-antus*; it is found in the word *Dnies-tr*, the modern name of the Tyras; it appears in the Sicilian *Ter-ias*, and the Sardinian *Ter-mus*; and it may perhaps be traced in *Trebia* (= *Ter-ab-ia*, compare Drave), *Trasimene*, *Trerus*, *Trinium*, *Truentus* (= *Tiarantus*, our *Trent*), and other similarly commencing names.

The *Poruta* (now the *Pruth*) seems to have been named from a root connected with the Greek πόρος, German *furth*, our "ford." The Scottish river *Forth* is apparently the same word.

The *Tarantus* (= *Ter-antus*) contains the root *Ter*, and a suffix *antus*, which may be compared with the *ander* of *Scam-ander*, *Mæ-ander*, and the *entus* or *ento* of *Tru-entus*, *Casu-entus*, *Frento*, &c. Tiarantus, Truentus, Tronto, Trent, are different forms of the same word.

In the *Ar-aras* and the *Nap-aris* we may recognise the root *aras* (reduplicated in *Ar-aras*, combined with a distinct element, *Nap*, in *Nap-aris*), which was widely used in the regions about the Caspian as a river name, where indeed it still lingers. Araxes in ancient times seems to have been a name common to the modern *Aras*, the *Jaxartes*, the *Wolga*, and many other streams. Its ultimate base is perhaps *Ra* or *Rha*, a name which the Wolga still bears, and which may be traced throughout Europe, in the *Rho-danus*, *Rhe-nus*, *Eri-danus*, *Rho-danax*, &c. The *Oarus* of Herodotus is merely a digammated form of *Aras*.

The *Hypanis* (*Hypan-is*) introduces us to a new element, *Hypan*, the Celtic *Apan*, our *Avon*, which may be traced in two other Scythian rivers, the *Hypa-cyris* and the *Pan-ticapes*. The remaining portion of each of these names is extremely obscure. We are reminded, however, by the element *cyris* (-κυρις) of the Atrapatenian river *Cyrus*, the *Kur* of the present day. Perhaps this same root may be the base of another Scythian stream, the *Ger-rhus* (Kur-rha?).

The *Tyr-as* (now the Danas-ter or Dniestr) contains the same two roots as *Is-ter*, only in the reverse order. It is sufficiently explained by what has been said concerning the name of that stream.

The Borysthenes furnishes us with another specimen of inversion. It has become the Danas-per, Dana-per, or Dnie-pr. The form Borys-thenes is manifestly Grecized—the native name, in all proba-

---

* "Local names," in Dr. Donaldson observes (Varronius, p. 33), "very often consist of synonymous elements," Wick-ham, Hamp-ton-wick, Wans-beck-water, Dan-ube, Nag-pour are cases in point. The first occupants of a country call a stream by their generic word for river; the next comers regard this as a proper name, and add to it their own generic term; later immigrants take this whole compound word for the true name of the stream.

bility, approached nearly to Porus-danus. If this be allowed, the *Borys* of *Borys-thenes* may be identified with the word *Porata*, and *-thenes* will be *Danas*, *Dana-is*, or *Tana-is*.

In the word *Tanais* (*Tana-is*) the medial *d* has become a tenuis, *t*; just as we find *Tun-owe* in the *Nibelungen-lied* for *Dan-ube*. In the modern name *Don* the *d* is restored to its place.[c]

10. It results from this entire investigation, that the Scythians were not Mongolians, but members of the Indo-European race. Language, as Mr. Grote correctly observes, is the only sure test; and language pronounces unmistakeably in favour of the Indo-European, and against the Mongol theory. The small number of Scythic words which remain to us present from thirty to forty roots capable of identification with well-known Indo-European terms. A very few words, and those, almost all of them, the names, real or supposed, of men, are not distinctly referable to known roots belonging to this family of languages. These data are fully sufficient to establish the ethnic connexion of the Scythians of Herodotus with the great bulk of the nations who have peopled Europe.[d]

11. When we attempt to go beyond this, and to inquire to which of the great divisions of the Indo-European race the Scyths belonged, we find ourselves at a loss to determine in favour of one branch more than another. The analogies which have been pointed out do not connect the Scythic language specially with any single Indo-European dialect. The Scyths, as their language exhibits them, were neither Medes, nor Slaves, nor Goths, nor Celts, nor Pelasgians; but their tongue possessed affinities to the speech of all these nations. We must not therefore be led away by doubtful etymologies[e] to identify the Scythians with any special Indo-European race. They were probably a branch of this ethnic family as distinct from all other branches as Celts, Germans, and Slaves from one another. Their supposed connexion with the Sauromatæ or Sarmatians[f] does not disprove this; for while it is not quite certain that the Sarmatians were Slaves, it is extremely questionable whether there was really any very close *ethnic* connexion between the Scyths and the Sauromatæ.[g] At any rate it is clear that the fragments of the Scythic language are no more Slavonic than they are Celtic, or Medo-Persian, or Pelasgian; and the argument of Lindner,[h] that the Slavonians

---

[c] No great weight can be attached to the Indo-European character of these names, as it is very probable that they may have been adopted by the Scyths from the Cimmerians, and so may be really indicators of the ethnic character of that people. In this point of view it is interesting to observe among them the Celtic river-names, Avon, Don, Tivat, Forth, &c.

[d] It is not, however, impossible, nor even improbable, that there may have been a Mongolian element among the European Scyths. The language of which we have specimens may be that of the Royal Tribe only; the rest of the nation was perhaps Turanian.

[e] Such as Dr. Donaldson's identification of Σκύθαι with Τίτας, Goth, "Goths" (Var- ron, p. 271), or his equally doubtful deriva- tion of Ἐσθονοι from Ἀσπαλαθοι (p. 41).

[f] Niebuhr regards this connexion as indubitable (Researches, &c., p. 83, E. T.) Boeckh likewise maintains it (Corp. Inscript. Sarmat. Introduct. pars al. p. 83). But Schafarik (Slaveche Alterthümer, vol. i. ch. xvi.) has called it in question on strong grounds.

[g] Pliny (Hist. Nat. vi. 7) and Pomponius Mela (i. 19) differ on this point from Herodotus (iv. 117), whose personal observations do not appear to have extended eastward of Olbia.

[h] Skythien und die Skythen des Herodots, Stuttgart, 1841.

must be the descendants of the Scythians because no other nation can have descended from them, is absurd, since the Scythians may easily have had no descendants. Indeed if we trace historically the after-fortunes of the Scythic people, we shall find reason to suspect that they were crushed between their two neighbours, the Getæ and the Sarmatians.[1] By the time of Pliny they had disappeared from the coasts of the Pontus; and the name of Scythia, which had once denoted a definite tract between the Danube and the Tanais, inhabited by a people with whose language, physical type, religious and other customs, the Greeks and Romans were perfectly familiar, had come to be applied vaguely and indefinitely to the remote and unknown regions of Northern Asia and Europe.[2] It is probable that about this time the Scyths altogether perished; or if they lingered anywhere, as a weakly and expiring tribe, in the forests of the far interior, the Mongol ravages of later times completed their destruction. In vain we look for their descendants at the present day. While the Cimmerians, whom they drove before them with such ease on their first passage of the Tanais, continue to exist as Cymry in the mountains of Wales,[3] and the Getæ, their neighbours upon the west, have their descendants among the great Gothic or Teutonic family by which nearly one-half of Europe is still occupied, the Scyths have disappeared from the earth. Like the Mexican Aztecs, whom they resembled in some degree, they have been swept away by the current of immigration, and, except in the mounds which cover their land and in the pages of the historian or ethnologist, not a trace remains to tell of their past existence.

---

[1] See Niebuhr's Researches, &c., pp. 66-84.
[2] Plin. Hist. Nat. iv. 25. "Scytharum nomen usquequaque transiit in Sarmatas atque Germanos: nec aliis prisca illa duravit appellatio, quam qui extremi gentium harum, ignoti prope cæteris mortalibus degunt."
[3] See the preceding chapter.

ESSAY III.

ON THE GEOGRAPHY OF SCYTHIA.

1. Necessity of examining Niebuhr's theory of the Scythia of Herodotus. 2. The theory stated. 3. Its grounds. 4. Considerations which disprove it. 5. Real views of Herodotus. 6. His personal knowledge of the region. 7. His correctness as to leading facts, and mistakes as to minutiæ. 8. Possibility of changes since his time. 9. Identification of rivers and places.

1. BEFORE entering upon any direct statements as to the actual shape and extent of Scythia, or attempting to identify any of the geographical features pointed out by Herodotus, and explain his real or apparent errors, it is necessary to examine that theory on the subject which was first broached by Niebuhr in his 'Kleine Schriften' about the year 1828, and which has recently been brought a second time before the public, only slightly modified, in his 'Vorträge über alte Geschichte,' published in 1847.[1] The authority of Niebuhr is so great, and his conjectures, even when not correct, are always so ingenious, that his view cannot be put aside without distinct and formal examination.

2. Now Niebuhr's view is, that Herodotus regarded Scythia as a *square bounded on two sides by the sea*; that he looked upon its southern coast as extending in a straight line from the mouth of the Danube to the Palus Mæotis, a distance of 4000 stades, its eastern as reaching an equal distance from thence to the embouchure of the Tanais (Don), its western frontier as parallel to this, and formed by the Lower Danube (which river he thinks Herodotus supposed to make a sudden bend at the north-western angle of Scythia, and to run thence with a southerly course to the Euxine), and its northern frontier as marked by a line drawn from this sharp bend in the Danube to the mouth of the Tanais.[2] The annexed plan, which is taken from his 'Map of the World according to Herodotus,' will more plainly show his meaning.

3. This account he gathers chiefly from chs. 99-101; but he conceives it to be confirmed by various scattered notices, as by the comparison between the Nile and the Danube in Book ii.,[3] by what is said in Book v. of the great size of Thrace,[4] and of the countries north of the Danube being desert,[5] as well as by other casual remarks.

4. The following considerations appear to be fatal to the scheme in question:—

(1.) Its derangement of the course of the Danube, in favour of which nothing can be brought but a supposed analogy, and which

---

[1] See pp. 182, 183. [2] Geography of Herod. p. 29, E. T. Scythians, pp. 39-41, E. T. [3] Chs. 33, 34. [4] Ch. 3. [5] Ch. 10.

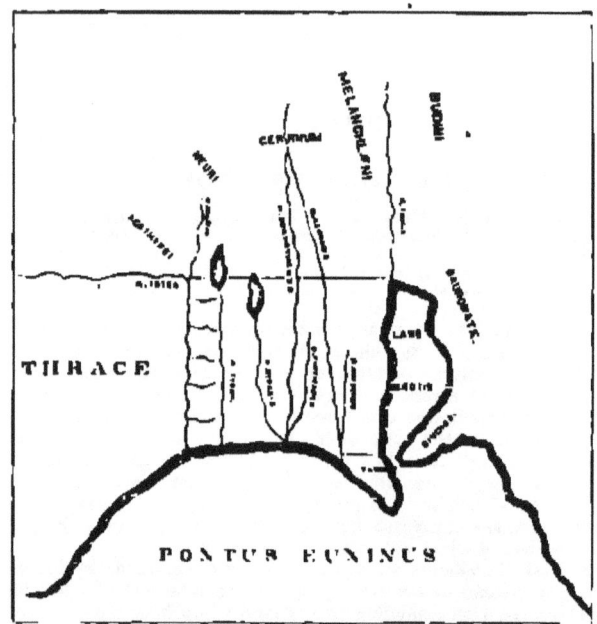

is contradicted by the whole account, so very consonant with facts, which Herodotus gives of that river and its tributaries. The Danube, he says, runs *from the west* right through Europe,[a] and falls into the Black Sea, "*with its mouth facing the east.*"[b] It receives many great tributaries on both sides: from the side of Scythia five—the Porata, Ararus, Naparis, Ordessus, and Tiarantus, of which the Porata (*Pruth*) is the most *easterly*, the Tiarantus (*Aluta*) most *towards the west*; from the mountain-chain of Thrace and Illyria eight others, which all run "*with a northern course*" into it.[c] This whole account is exactly in accordance with the real geography, and cannot possibly be made to square with the scheme of Niebuhr, in which the mouth of the Danube *fronts the south*; and the five Scythian tributaries, if they can be imagined to exist at all, must be interposed between the sea and the Maris, according to the dotted lines inserted in the accompanying plan to represent them, in which case the terms "most eastern," "most western," would cease to be applicable.

(ii.) The assertion of Herodotus that "the mart of the Borysthenites is situated in the very centre of the *whole sea-coast* of Scythia."[d] Niebuhr's view places it in the centre of the south side only, while the east, according to him, is also washed by the sea.

[a] Book iv. ch. 49. [b] Ibid. ch. 99. [c] Herod. chs. 48, 49. [d] Ibid. ch. 17.

(iii.) The impossibility of reconciling Herodotus's account of the Persian campaign with the supposed figure of Scythia. The division of Scythians with which Darius first fell in, had orders to retreat "*along the shores of the Palus Mæotis*" to the Tanais,[1] orders which appear to have been duly executed. Darius, following in their track, is said to have marched "*eastward*" to that stream.[1] Niebuhr's plan would make this march at least as much north as east. Arrived at the Tanais, they cross into the country of the Sauromatæ, which they traverse from south to north, a distance of 15 days' journey;[2] whence they pass on to the Budini, the next nation to the north, whose country they likewise traverse. According to Niebuhr, they would now be nearly 20 days' journey beyond the borders of Scythia, and separated from Scythia by the entire country of the Melanchlæni. Yet here the Scythians, suddenly giving Darius the slip, make a *détour* through the country *above* the Budini, and at once return *into Scythia*;[3] while Darius, missing them, turns *westward*, and is shortly within the Scythian borders, where he falls in with the other division of the Scythian army, and is led for the first time into the country of the Melanchlæni. All this is absolutely impossible upon Niebuhr's theory, where the Budini lie *north* of Scythia, at a vast distance, and separated by the tract in which the Melanchlæni live. It is indifferent, so far as this argument is concerned, whether we admit the expedition into these parts as a reality or no, since all that we are at present considering is how Herodotus himself conceived of Scythia.

5. The truth seems to be that Herodotus regarded Scythia as having only one of its sides washed by the sea,[4] that he took the coast from the Danube to the Tanais as representing tolerably well a straight line, when the peninsula occupied by the Tauri (the Crimea) was cut off; that he estimated the length of this at 4000 stades (400 miles),[5] 2000 between the Danube and the mouth of the Borysthenes, 2000 between that and the place where the Tanais reached the sea; that he regarded this side of Scythia, thus divided into two parts and fronting towards the south-east, as reaching down to two seas, one of which (the Euxine) might be called "southern," the other (the Sea of Azof), "eastern;" that he thought Scythia extended inland about the same distance as its length along the coast; and that he therefore called it square, meaning thereby not to give its exact figure, but to describe its general shape. He did not regard the Danube as bounding one side of the square, but

---

[1] Herod. ch. 120.   [2] Ibid. ch. 122.
[3] Ibid. ch. 21.   [4] Ibid. ch. 124.
[5] "Scythia," he says, "which is square in shape, and has two of its sides (or parts) reaching down to the sea, extends inland to the same distance that it reaches along the coast, and is equal every way. For it is a ten days' journey from the Ister to the Borysthenes, and ten more from the Borysthenes to the Palus Mæotis, while the distance from the coast inland to the country of the Melanchlæni, who dwell above Scythia, is a journey of twenty days. . . . Thus the two sides which run straight inland (τὰ ἐπὶ τὰ ἐς μεσόγαιαν φέροντα) are 4000 furlongs (stadia) each, and the transverse sides at right angles to these (τὰ ἐπικάρσια) are of the same length." This passage alone would appear to me to settle the controversy. The ἐπὶ τὰ ἐς μεσόγαιαν φέροντα must be parallel sides, not, as in Niebuhr's plan, sides at right angles to one another.

[6] The actual distance of a straight line from the most northern mouth of the Danube to the embouchure of the Tanais is about 40 miles more.

ESSAY III. EXTENT OF HIS PERSONAL OBSERVATION. 171

as meeting it obliquely at a corner. This is implied in the expression ἐς τὰ πλάγια τῆς Σκυθίης ἐσβάλλει.[1] On the other hand he regarded the Tanais as not merely touching an angle of the square, but as washing at least a portion of the eastern side, and so separating the Royal Scythians from the Sauromatæ.[2] His notion is fairly expressed by Heeren nearly in these words:—"The boundaries which Herodotus assigns to Scythia are as follows: on the south, the coast of the Black Sea, from the mouth of the Danube to the Palus Mæotis; on the east, the Don or Tanais to its rise out of the lake Ivan(?); on the north, a line drawn from this lake to that out of which the Tyras or Dniestr flows; and on the west, a line from thence to the Danube."[3] Thus Scythia comprised the modern governments of Kherson, Poltawa, Ekaterinoslav, Kharkov, Koursk, the Don Cossacks, Voronez, Riazan, Orlov, Tula, Mogilev, Tchernigov, Minsk, Volhynia (part), Kiev, and Podolsk, together with the provinces of Bessarabia, Moldavia, and Wallachia; and consisted of the two great basins of the Don and Dniepr, the minor basins of the Dniestr and the Boug, and the northern half of the basin of the Lower Danube from Orsova to the sea.

6. Of this region Herodotus personally knew but little. He had made the coast voyage from the Straits of Constantinople to the town of Olbia, situated on the right bank of the Hypanis (*Boug*), near the point at which that river falls into the sea. He had likewise penetrated into the interior as far as Exampæus, four days' journey up the course of the same stream; but it does not appear that he had ever crossed the Borysthenes (*Dniepr*), nor that he had any personal acquaintance with the country east of that river. He regarded the Tauric Chersonese, not as a peninsula, but as a great promontory like Attica or Iapygia, and was unaware of the existence of the *Sibachd Moré* or Putrid Sea. He imagined the Palus Mæotis to be a sea not very much smaller than the Euxine, and thought the Tanais (*Don*) ran into it with a *south* course. He had also notions with respect to the rivers east of the Borysthenes which it is very difficult to reconcile with existing geographical facts. Still his description of the general features of the region is remarkably accurate, and might almost pass for an account of the same country at the present day. A recent traveller,[4] whose journeys took him pretty

---

[1] Ch. 49. Yet the Danube separated between Scythia and Thrace because in this place the square was particularly irregular, there being a projection from it consisting of the country between the Black Sea and the Carpathian chain, the modern province of Wallachia. The general course of the Danube was rightly apprehended by Herodotus, and its tributaries up to Belgrade were known with an approach to accuracy. Above Belgrade his knowledge was less exact. He confounded the *Marosch* (Maris) with the Theiss, and the two great streams flowing in from the south side of the Danube at about the same point, of which he had heard from the inhabitants of the lower part of the river, and which were really the Drave and the Save, he confounded with the two Alpine streams of which he had heard the Umbrians of Northern Italy discourse as flowing into the Danube from the country just beyond their borders. These were the Salga and the Inn, or possibly the latter stream and the Rhine, which in its upper course has nearly the same direction as the Inn, and would flow into the Danube if it did not make a right angle at the Lake of Constance.

[2] Herod. iv. chs. 20, 21.

[3] "Asiatic Nations," vol. ii. p. 257, note [4], E. T.

[4] The Rev. W. Palmer, whose observations, made upon the spot, have been kindly communicated to me by his brother, the Rev. E. Palmer, Fellow of Balliol.

nearly over the entire extent of Herodotus's Scythia, notices the following particulars as among those which most strike a person on traversing the region:—

"First, the size of the rivers and their abundance in good fish. (Cf. Herod. iv. 53.) Secondly, the general flatness of the country. Thirdly, the total absence of wood over the southern part of Herodotus's square; while, as one gets beyond it, or near its borders, there is wood. Fourthly, that the bare country, or steppes, up the *Boug* (Hypanis) and the *Dnieper* (Borysthenes) is still a corn-growing country, and the parts to the east of these still abound rather in cattle, so corresponding with the situation of the agricultural and nomade Scythians of Herodotus's time. Fifthly, that the abundance of light carts moving in all directions, with or without tracks, reminds one of Herodotus's observation that the nature of the country made the tribes inhabiting it what they were."

7. We seem to see in Herodotus a remarkable knowledge of leading geographical facts, combined, either really or apparently, with mistakes as to minutiæ. Niebuhr[*] observed long ago upon the superiority of our author to later geographers in his implied denial of that Rhipæan mountain-chain supposed generally to bound Scythia upon the north; and further noticed his acquaintance (indicated by what he says of the sources of the Hypanis) with the great marshy district of Vollhynia. The writer to whom reference was made above, adds other similar points:—

"What Herodotus says of the Don rising in a vast lake seems to show that there were rumours in the south of the existence and size of the great lakes of North Russia, out of the largest of which (the Onega) the Volga, not the Don, does in fact rise. So Herodotus knew that the Caspian was an inland sea, which later writers did not; he knew, which they did not either, that the bare plains of the nomade Scythians did not extend to the ocean, but that northwards beyond them the country became woody; that in one part of this further country the people 'became wolves' for some days annually, that is, wore wolf-skins in winter (as they do still), there being no wood to shelter wolves, and consequently few wolves to furnish skins in the south; that in another part there were people who lived by hunting in a woody country: that going to the north-east, above the royal Scythians and across the Don, one arrived after a time at the roots of high and rugged mountains, namely, of the Ural range (which was also unknown to later writers); he knew also that from the Ural Mountains it was that the gold came which so abounded in Scythia, while iron and silver were wanting. With regard to the parts more to the north, he rightly understood the figure of the air being full of feathers to mean that there was more and more snow as one went northwards, and that it lay longer, till one could go no further for the want of people and means of subsistence. He speaks of people who slept (*i. e.* lived in-doors) in comparative darkness) half the year (which is not the same as if he had said that the *night* lasted half the year, as it does nearer the pole). He had heard not

---

[*] See his "Researches into the History of the Scythians, Getæ, &c.," p. 42, E. T.

only of the great lakes in the north, but of the ocean being beyond all. His remarks on the climate, especially concerning the abundance of rain and thunder in summer, and the extreme rareness of both in winter, contrary to what one is used to in the Levant, and again concerning the extreme rareness of earthquakes, are such as still strike people who go to the north."

8. This general accuracy inclines one to suspect that possibly where Herodotus appears to be in error, he may have given a true account of the state of things in his own day, which account is now inapplicable in consequence of changes that have occurred since his time. Professor Pallas[2] was among the first to conjecture that vast alterations in the levels of the countries about the Black Sea and Palus Maeotis have taken place in comparatively recent times. Sir R. Murchison, in his 'Geology of Russia,' expresses himself as of the same opinion.[3] It is possible that the Putrid Sea has been formed by a late depression of the land, and that the *Kosa Arabatskaia* marks the line of the ancient coast. The Taurida would then have deserved to be called a promontory (ἄκρη), and not a peninsula (χερσόνησος). The courses of the rivers from the Borysthenes (*Dnieper*) to the Don may have been completely altered, many (as the Panticapes, Hypacyris, and Gerrhus) having been dried up, and others (as the Donetz and the Dnieper itself) having formed themselves new beds. The Palus Maeotis may have had its limits greatly contracted, partly by the deposits of the rivers, partly by an elevation of the countries along the line of the *Manitch*; and may have been in former times not so very unworthy of being compared for size with the Euxine.[4] On the other hand, it must not be forgotten that the personal observation of Herodotus did not extend beyond the Borysthenes; and that it is exactly in the parts of Scythia which he had not visited that his descriptions cease to be applicable to the existing condition of things. This circumstance favours the notion that the divergence of his descriptions from fact arose from insufficient information.

9. With respect to the identification of the several rivers and places mentioned by Herodotus, it may be considered as absolutely certain that the Ister is the *Danube*, the Porata the *Pruth*, the Tyras the *Dniestr* (= Danas-Tyr), the Hypanis the *Boug*, the Borysthenes the *Dnieper* (= Dana-Bor), and the Tanais the *Don*. The other rivers of Scythia—the Gerrhus, the Panticapes, the Hypacyris, the Lycus, the Hyrgis or Syrgis, and the Oarus—cannot so readily be determined. We may be certain, however, that the Gerrhus was not the *Molochnia Vadi*, as Rennell supposes (Geography, p. 71), since it fell into the Euxine near Carcinitis; and that the Panticapes was neither the *Desna*, nor the *Psol*,[5] since it joined the Borysthenes at its embouchure. The little stream which enters the sea by *Kalantchak* would seem to represent either the Gerrhus or the Hypacyris. The

---

[2] "Travels," vol. i. pp. 78–87, and 302–307.
[3] See pp. 573–575.
[4] Herodotus extends the Palus to a distance of three days' journey east of the Tanais (ch. 116), which would make it cover a good deal of the country supposed by Pallas to have been formerly submerged.
[5] Heeren's A. Nal. ii. p. 262.

Donetz may be the Syrgis. The Oarus is perhaps the *Volga*. There is, however, the utmost uncertainty with respect to all identifications east of the Isthmus of *Perekop*.

Of places, Herodotus notices but few in Scythia. Olbia, at the mouth of the Hypanis, is the only town mentioned by him. Its site is marked by ruins and mounds, and determined beyond a question by coins and inscriptions. It lies on the right bank of the river, near its embouchure in the *liman* of the Dniepr, and is now called *Nomogil*, or "the Hundred Mounds."[1] Opposite is the promontory called by Herodotus Cape Hippolaüs, where in his time was a temple of Ceres. Further east is the Course of Achilles, the *Kosa Tendra* and *Kosa Djarilgatch* of our maps. The site of Carcinitis is occupied probably by the modern town of *Kalantchak*. The Crimea is Herodotus's Taurica; the peninsula of Kertch his "rugged Chersonese." Further inland we may identify Podolia as the country of the Alazonians; Transylvania as that of the Agathyrsi, whose river Maris must be the *Maruch*; Volhynia and Lithuania as the habitation of the Neuri; part of Tambov as that of the Budini and Geloni; and the steppe between the Don and the Volga as that of the Sauromatæ. The situations of the Thyssagetæ, Iyrcæ, Argippæi, and Issedones, it is impossible to fix with any exactitude. The 'Map of the Scythia of Herodotus' prefixed to this volume gives the probable position of these nations.

[1] Vide supra, note 1 on Book iv. ch. 53.

NOTE A.

ON THE WORDS THYSSAGETÆ AND MASSAGETÆ.

The etymology of the names of these tribes is of some interest in its bearing on their ethnic classification. It has been generally supposed that the Getæ, whether compared with the Jāts of India or the Goths of Europe, must be of the Arian stock, and *Massa* for "great" belongs to the same family of languages; but it may be doubted if any of the Arian dialects furnish a correspondent for *Thyssa*, with the signification of "small" or "lesser." That term seems to be Scythic. At any rate, in primitive Babylonian *tur* or *tús* (compare interchange of δυρ and δυς) has two significations, one "a chief," and the other "small" or "lower," and in each of these senses the term has been preserved to modern times. Thus, the Cuneiform *Tur*, used as the determinative of rank, is to be recognised in the Biblical *Tartan*, *Tirsatha* (for *Tartan*, *Tursatha*), in the Chaldee *Targús*, "a general," and in the modern Lur *Túshmál* تو ش مال (Persian *Ketkhoda*) "chief of the house," the ordinary title of the "white beards" of the mountain tribes; while *Tur* for "lower," which in Cuneiform is used as the standard monogram for "a son," and which is translated in Assyrian by *Zikhir* (Heb. צער, Arab. صغير) is still found in the title of *Turkhan* given to the "Heir Apparent" or "Crown Prince" by the Uzbegs of Khiva.

Massa also for "greater," although closely resembling the Zend *mas* (for Sanscrit *maha*), which was actually in use in Persia within modern times (as in ماس‌مغان , *Mas-mughán*, "Chief of the Magi," the title of the kings of Mazenderan at the time of the Arab conquest), may perhaps with equal reason be compared with the Babylonian Scythic term *mus* or *mis*, which signified "much" or "many" (Assyrian *mudut*), and the monogram for which was thus ordinarily used as the sign of the plural number (compare the Scythic name Παρθαμασπάτης, "chief of the Parthians"). To illustrate the connexion of *mudut*, "much," with *mis*, "greater," we may compare "multus" and "magis."
—[H. C. R.]

THE FIFTH BOOK

OF THE

HISTORY OF HERODOTUS,

ENTITLED TERPSICHORE.

1. THE Persians left behind by King Darius in Europe, who had Megabazus for their general,[1] reduced, before any other Hellespontine state, the people of Perinthus,[2] who had no mind to become subjects of the king. Now the Perinthians had ere this been roughly handled by another nation, the Pæonians.[3] For the Pæonians from about the Strymon were once bidden by an oracle to make war upon the Perinthians, and if these latter, when the camps faced one another, challenged them by name to fight, then to venture on a battle, but if otherwise, not to make the hazard. The Pæonians followed the advice. Now the men of Perinthus drew out to meet them in the skirts of their city; and a threefold single combat was fought on challenge given. Man to man, and horse to horse, and dog to dog, was the strife waged; and the Perinthians, winners of two combats out of the three, in their joy had raised the pæan; when the Pæonians, struck by the thought that this was what the oracle had meant, passed the word one to another, saying, "Now of a surety has the oracle been fulfilled for us; now our work begins." Then the Pæonians set upon the Perinthians in the midst of their pæan, and defeated them utterly, leaving but few of them alive.

2. Such was the affair of the Pæonians, which happened a long time previously. At this time the Perinthians, after a brave

---

[1] Vide supra, iv. 143.
[2] Perinthus, called afterwards Heraclea (Ptolem. iii. 11), is the modern *Erekli*, a place of some consequence on the sea of Marmora (lat. 41°, long. 28° nearly). Scylax mentions it p. 68). It was a Samian colony (Plut. Q. G. 56; Scym. Ch. l. 713).
[3] Concerning the Pæonians, vide infra, ch. 13, note ⁹, and ch. 16, note ⁹. It is surprising to find that they ever penetrated so far east as Perinthus.

struggle for freedom, were overcome by numbers, and yielded to Megabazus and his Persians. After Perinthus had been brought under, Megabazus led his host through Thrace, subduing to the dominion of the king all the towns and all the nations of those parts.' For the king's command to him was, that he should conquer Thrace.

3. The Thracians are the most powerful people in the world, except, of course, the Indians;' and if they had one head, or were agreed among themselves, it is my belief that their match could not be found anywhere, and that they would very far surpass all other nations.' But such union is impossible for them, and there are no means of ever bringing it about. Herein therefore consists their weakness. The Thracians bear many names in the different regions of their country,' but all of them have like usages in every respect, excepting only the Getæ,'

' This must be understood with the limitation supplied at the end of ch. 10. The conquests of Megabazus were confined to the tracts along the coast.

' Alluding to what he had said before (Bk. iii. ch. 94).

' Thucydides makes almost the same remark of the Scythians (ii. 97). There is a curious parallelism between his expressions and those of Herodotus.

' Strabo said that the Thracians consisted of 22 different tribes (vii. Fr. 40), and no doubt enumerated them, but this part of his work is lost. Herodotus himself names 18 tribes; the Bessi (vii. 111), Bisaltæ (viii. 116), Bistones (vii. 110), Brygi (vi. 45), Cicones (vii. 110), Crobyzi (iv. 49), Dersæi (vii. 110), Dolonci (vi. 34), Edoni (vii. 110), Getæ (iv. 93), Nipsæi (ibid.), Odomanti (vii. 112), Odrysæ (iv. 92), Pæti (ib.), Sapæi (vii. 110), Satræ (ibid.), Scyrmiadæ (iv. 93), and Trausi (v. 3). The fragments of Hecatæus supply 12 or 13, of which only two—the Satræ and the Crobyzi—are mentioned by Herodotus. The remainder are the Bantii, Darsii, Datylepti, Danili, Disorse, Entribæ, Sairocentæ, Sindonæi, Trispæ, and Trizi. Of these the Darsii may be Herodotus's Dersæi, but the remainder are clearly new names. Thucydides adds the Dii (= Dai or Daei), the Treres, and the Tilatæi (ii. 96); Strabo, the Breuc, Corpili, Mædi, Mæsi or Mysi, Sinti, and Triballi. Pliny augments the list by above 20 more names; the Adræi, Benæ, Botilæi, Dryæ, Cænici, Carbilesi, Car-

bileta, Clarim, Cœlete, Densiletæ, Digeri, Diobessi, Drageri, Elethi, Gaudæ, Hypsaltæ, Moriseni, Priantæ, Pyrogeri, Belletæ, Sithonii, and Thyni (H. N. iv. 11). He also notices that the tribes were occasionally subdivided, as that of the Bessi, which included under it a number of names. His list undoubtedly contains repetitions, as Carbilesi, Carbileti—Digeri, Drugeri—and the Thracian character of some of his tribes (e. g. the Bottiæi) may be questioned; but after making allowances on these grounds, we shall find that the number of Thracian tribes known to us exceeds fifty! Of these the most important in the earlier times were the Getæ, the Treres, the Odrysæ, the Triballi, and the Odomanti, while the Daci and the Mæsi obtained ultimately the preponderance.

With regard to the military strength of the Thracians, it may be observed, that Sitalces, king of the Odrysæ, who had a very widely extended influence over the various tribes, invaded Macedonia in the year B.C. 429, at the head of 150,000 men, of whom 50,000 were cavalry (Thucyd. ii. 98). But his army was in part composed of Pæonians. Strabo estimates the military strength of the nation in his own times at 215,000 men—15,000 horse, and 200,000 foot (vii. Fr. 48). The want of union, of which Herodotus speaks, continued; and was a source of enduring weakness.

' Concerning the Getæ, vide supra, Bk. iv. ch. 93.

the Trausi,² and those who dwell above the people of Creston.¹

4. Now the manners and customs of the Getæ, who believe in their immortality, I have already spoken of.² The Trausi in all else resemble the other Thracians, but have customs at births and deaths which I will now describe. When a child is born all its kindred sit round about it in a circle and weep for the woes it will have to undergo now that it is come into the world, making mention of every ill that falls to the lot of humankind; when, on the other hand, a man has died, they bury him with laughter and rejoicings, and say that now he is free from a host of sufferings, and enjoys the completest happiness.

5. The Thracians who live above the Crestonæans observe the following customs. Each man among them has several wives;³ and no sooner does a man die than a sharp contest ensues among the wives upon the question, which of them all the husband loved most tenderly; the friends of each eagerly plead on her behalf, and she to whom the honour is adjudged, after receiving the praises both of men and women, is slain over the grave by the hand of her next of kin, and then buried with her husband.⁴ The others are sorely grieved, for nothing is considered such a disgrace.

6. The Thracians who do not belong to these tribes have the customs which follow. They sell their children to traders.⁵ On their maidens they keep no watch, but leave them altogether

---

² The Trausi occur in Livy as a Thracian people ("gens et ipsa Thracum," 39, 41). Nicolas of Damascus repeats concerning them the story of Herodotus (Fr. 119). Stephen of Byzantium confounds them with the Agathyrsi (Steph. ad voc.). They seem not to be mentioned by any other ancient writer. Bähr connects their name with the river Travus (Τραῦος) mentioned in the seventh Book (ch. 109), which appears to be the modern Karutch. This would place them in the range of Despoto Dagh, between the 25th and 26th degrees of longitude.

¹ Concerning Creston, vide supra, i. 57.

² Supra, iv. 94.

³ Three or four commonly, according to Heraclides Ponticus, but sometimes as many as 30! Their treatment, as is usually the case where polygamy prevails, was harsh and degrading (Fr. xxviii.). Arrian ascribed the introduction of polygamy among the Thracians to a king, Dolonchus (Fr. 37).

⁴ Stephen of Byzantium gives this as a special custom of the Getæ (in voc. Γέται). It is scarcely necessary to compare with it the suttecism of the Hindoos. Belief in a happy future state is clearly the pervading principle of almost all these Thracian customs. Suttee has been practised by various nations. It existed among the Teutons (Val. Max. vi. 1), the Wends (S. Bonifac. Ep. ad Ethelbald.), and the Heruli (Procop. B. Goth. ii. 14), as well as the Indians. [It was also an ancient Slavonian and Scandinavian custom.—G. W.]

⁵ [As the Circassians now do for the "foreign" market.—G. W.] Hence Geta and Davus (Δᾶος) came to be the commonest names for slaves at Athens (see the comedies of Terence, which were adaptations of Menander, and comp. Schol. ad Arist. Acharn. 231).

free, while on the conduct of their wives they keep a most strict watch. Brides are purchased of their parents for large sums of money. Tatooing among them marks noble birth, and the want of it low birth. To be idle is accounted the most honourable thing, and to be a tiller of the ground the most dishonourable. To live by war and plunder is of all things the most glorious. These are the most remarkable of their customs.

7. The gods which they worship are but three, Mars, Bacchus, and Dian. Their kings, however, unlike the rest of the citizens, worship Mercury more than any other god, always swearing by his name, and declaring that they are themselves sprung from him.

8. Their wealthy ones are buried in the following fashion. The body is laid out for three days; and during this time they kill victims of all kinds, and feast upon them, after first bewailing the departed. Then they either burn the body or else bury it in the ground. Lastly, they raise a mound over the grave, and hold games of all sorts, wherein the single combat is awarded the highest prize. Such is the mode of burial among the Thracians.

9. As regards the region lying north of this country no one can say with any certainty what men inhabit it. It appears that you no sooner cross the Ister than you enter on an interminable wilderness.³ The only people of whom I can hear as dwelling beyond the Ister are the race named Sigynnæ,⁴ who wear, they say, a dress like the Medes, and have horses which are covered entirely with a coat of shaggy hair, five fingers in length. They are a small breed, flat-nosed, and not strong enough to bear men on their backs; but when yoked to chariots, they are among the swiftest known,⁵ which is the reason why the people of that country use chariots. Their borders reach down almost to the

expressive of race. Nothing conclusive is to be gathered from the customs here assigned to the Thracians; and to decide the ethnic family to which they belong, we must avail ourselves of the light thrown upon the subject by subsequent history, as well as by comparative philology. Now it is almost certain that the Getæ—one of the principal Thracian tribes, according to Herodotus—are the Gothi or Gothones of the Romans, who are the old German *Gutha* or *Guthans*, and our *Goths* (see Grimm's Geschichte der Deutschen Sprache, vol. i. pp. 178-184). The one name supplanted the other *in the same country*, and there are not wanting ancient writers who expressly identify the two forms (Philostorgius, Hist. Eccl. ii. 5; Enneadius, p. 321, &c.). Grimm has shown that the change from Γέτης to Goth is according to the analogy of the Teutonic and Græco-Roman forms of speech; instancing such words as *deus*, *θεὸς* = "tumulus," *frater* = "brother," &c. (p. 179). Little is left to us of the Thracian language; but one or two striking analogies to the Teutonic may be pointed out. The *βρία*, for instance, which is so common an ending of the names of Thracian towns (*e.g.* Mesembria, Selymbria, Poltyombria, &c.), is said by Strabo (vii. p. 462) and Stephen (ad voc. Μεσημβρία), to signify a "city" (ἄστυ). Compare the Anglo-Saxon *borough*, and especially its use as a termination to the names of towns, in such names as Edinburgh, Peterborough, Glastonbury, &c. Again, the name of the Drygi or Brigæ, a Thracian tribe (Herod. vi. 45), is said by Hesychius to signify "freemen." Compare the Gothic *freis*, German *frei*, and our *free*. It is not pretended that these analogies are of much weight; but they point in the same direction as the history, tending to connect the Thracians with the Teutonic family.

There is some little confirmation of this view to be gathered from the Thracian customs. A good many points of resemblance may be traced between the German customs described by Tacitus, and those assigned by Herodotus to the Thracians. Common to the two people are—1. the special worship of Mercury and Mars (Tacit. Germ. 9); 2. the contempt of agriculture, and delight in war (ibid. 14); 3. the purity of married life (ibid. 19); 4. the purchase of wives (ib. 18); 5. the practice of burning the bodies of the dead (ib. 27); and 6. the practice of covering graves with mounds (ibid.). Further, those peculiarities which Herodotus relates of the Getæ (iv. 94-96) and the Trausi, bearing upon the great mysteries of life and death, are in harmony with the general characteristics of the "sad" Teutonic race, which has always leant towards the spiritual, and despised this life in comparison with the next.

³ Hungary and Austria seem to be the countries intended in this description. Dense forests and vast morasses would in the early times have rendered them scarcely habitable.

⁴ The Sigynnæ of Europe are unknown to later historians and geographers. Apollonius Rhodius introduces them into his poem as dwellers upon the *Euxine* (iv. 320), and his scholiast calls them ἔθνος Ξανθικόν. Curiously enough, Strabo, whose Sigynni (or Siginni) are in Asia near the Caspian, tells the same story, as Herodotus, of their ponies (xi. p. 757).

⁵ It has been suggested that dogs used in the manner practised by the Esquimaux were the origin of this description; but I should rather understand ponies, like the Shetland.

Eneti upon the Adriatic Sea, and they call themselves colonists of the Medes;⁴ but how they can be colonists of the Medes I for my part cannot imagine. Still nothing is impossible in the long lapse of ages.¹ Sigynnæ is the name which the Ligurians⁶ who dwell above Massilia⁷ give to traders, while among the Cyprians the word means spears.¹

10. According to the account which the Thracians give, the country beyond the Ister is possessed by bees, on account of which it is impossible to penetrate farther.² But in this they seem to me to say what has no likelihood; for it is certain that those creatures are very impatient of cold. I rather believe that it is on account of the cold that the regions which lie under the Bear are without inhabitants. Such then are the accounts given of this country, the sea-coast whereof Megabazus was now employed in subjecting to the Persians.

11. King Darius had no sooner crossed the Hellespont and reached Sardis, than he bethought himself of the good deed of Histiæus the Milesian,³ and the good counsel of the Mytilenean Coës.⁴ He therefore sent for both of them to Sardis, and bade them each crave a boon at his hands. Now Histiæus, as he was already king of Miletus, did not make request for any government besides, but asked Darius to give him Myrcinus⁵ of the Edo-

---

⁶ Perhaps the Sigynnæ retained a better recollection than other European tribes of their migrations westward, and Arian origin.

¹ Herodotus has vague notions of the great antiquity of the world and of mankind. Though in general he only professed to carry history back for some eight or ten centuries, yet he felt no objection to receiving the Egyptian exaggeration, whereby Menes was referred to B.C. 12,000. In one place (ii. 11) he speculates on the world being 20,000 years old.

² Niebuhr has collected together (Hist. of Rome, vol. i. pp. 163-166; compare Prichard, Phys. Hist. of Mankind, iii. ch. 3, § 2, and the excellent article in Smith's Geogr. Dict.) all that is known of the Ligurians. They once extended along the coast from Spain to Etruria, and possessed a large portion of Piedmont. They were certainly not Celts; and it is probable that they may have been an Illyrian race. The name may perhaps be connected with that of the Liburnians on the Adriatic, of which it seems to be a mere variant. Note that Liburnum, near the mouth of the Arno, has become Livorno, and with us Leghorn.

⁷ Massilia, the modern Marseilles, appears to have been founded by the Phocæans about the year B.C. 600. (See Clinton's Fast. Hell. vol. i. p. 220.)

¹ Apollonius Rhodius uses the word σίγυνος for a spear or dart (ii. 99), and σιγύνη occurs in this sense in the Anthology (Anth. Pal. vi. 176). Suidas says that the Macedonians called spears by this name (sub voc. σιγύνη). The Scholiast on Apoll. Rhod., like Herodotus, regards the term in this sense as Cyprian. May we connect it with the Hebrew סֶגֶן ?

² The mosquitos, which infest the valley of the Danube, seem to be here indicated.

³ Supra, iv. 137.

⁴ Supra, iv. 97.

⁵ The site of Myrcinus cannot be fixed with certainty. It was near the Strymon (infra, ch. 23) on the left bank (Appian, Bell. Civ. iv. p. 1041), and not very near the sea. Stephen ad voc. 'Αμφίπολις believed it to have occupied the site of Amphipolis; but it is

nians,⁶ where he wished to build him a city. Such was the choice that Histiæus made. Coës, on the other hand, as he was a mere burgher, and not a king, requested the sovereignty of Mytilênê. Both alike obtained their requests, and straightway betook themselves to the places which they had chosen.

12. It chanced in the meantime that King Darius saw a sight which determined him to bid Megabazus remove the Pæonians from their seats in Europe and transport them to Asia. There were two Pæonians, Pigres and Mantyes, whose ambition it was to obtain the sovereignty over their countrymen. As soon therefore as ever Darius crossed into Asia, these men came to Sardis, and brought with them their sister, who was a tall and beautiful woman. Having so done, they waited till a day came when the king sat in state in the suburb of the Lydians; and then dressing their sister in the richest gear they could, sent her to draw water for them. She bore a pitcher upon her head, and with one arm led a horse, while all the way as she went she spun flax.⁷ Now as she passed by where the king was, Darius took notice of her; for it was neither like the Persians nor the Lydians, nor any of the dwellers in Asia, to do as she did. Darius accordingly noted her, and ordered some of his guard to follow her steps, and watch to see what she would do with the horse. So the spearmen went; and the woman, when she came to the river, first watered the horse, and then filling the pitcher, came back the same way she had gone, with the pitcher of water upon her head, and the horse dragging upon her arm, while she still kept twirling the spindle.

13. King Darius was full of wonder both at what they who had watched the woman told him, and at what he had himself seen. So he commanded that she should be brought before him.

---

clear that this was not the case; for Aristagoras attacked Amphipolis from Myrcinus (compare Herod. v. 126, with Thucyd. iv. 102), and Myrcinus continued to be a town of some consequence after Amphipolis had obtained its greatest extent (Thucyd. iv. 107). Colonel Leake places Myrcinus to the north of Pangæum, and very near Amphipolis (Travels in Northern Greece, iii. p. 18.

⁶ The Edonians appear in history as a very ancient Thracian people (infra, vii. 110; Soph. Ant. 956; Strab. x. p. 686; Apollod. iii. 5. § 1). They seem to have dwelt originally in Mygdonia,

whence they were dislodged by the Macedonians (Thucyd. ii. 99). They possessed at this time a small tract east of the Strymon, where they had the two cities Myrcinus and Ennea-Hodoi (Nine-Ways). Afterwards Drabiscus (Dhrama) is called theirs (Thucyd. i. 100); but it is doubtful if they extended so far at this period.

⁷ Nicolas of Damascus told the same story of a certain Thrasim, who thus exhibited his wife to Alyattes, king of Lydia (Fragm. Hist. Græc. iii. p. 413. The repetition of such tales is a common feature of ancient legendary history.

And the woman came; and with her appeared her brothers, who had been watching everything a little way off. Then Darius asked them of what nation the woman was; and the young men replied that they were Pæonians, and she was their sister. Darius rejoined by asking, "Who the Pæonians were, and in what part of the world they lived? and, further, what business had brought the young men to Sardis"? Then the brothers told him they had come to put themselves under his power, and Pæonia was a country upon the river Strymon, and the Strymon was at no great distance from the Hellespont. The Pæonians, they said, were colonists of the Teucrians from Troy." When they had thus answered his questions, Darius asked if all the women of their country worked so hard? Then the brothers eagerly answered, Yes; for this was the very object with which the whole thing had been done.

14. So Darius wrote letters to Megabazus, the commander whom he had left behind in Thrace,[b] and ordered him to remove the Pæonians from their own land, and bring them into his presence, men, women, and children. And straightway a horseman took the message, and rode at speed to the Hellespont; and, crossing it, gave the paper to Megabazus. Then Megabazus, as soon as he had read it, and procured guides from Thrace, made war upon Pæonia.

15. Now when the Pæonians heard that the Persians were marching against them, they gathered themselves together, and marched down to the sea-coast, since they thought the Persians would endeavour to enter their country on that side. Here then they stood in readiness to oppose the army of Megabazus. But the Persians, who knew that they had collected, and were gone to keep guard at the pass near the sea, got guides, and taking the inland route before the Pæonians were aware, poured down upon their cities, from which the men had all marched out; and

---

[a] Herodotus. It must be remembered, brought the Teucrians with the Mysians out of Europe into Asia, at a time anterior to the Trojan war (vii. 20). He probably therefore intends here to represent the Pæonians as an offshoot from the Teucrians *before* they left their ancient abodes in Europe (cf. Niebuhr, K. H. vol. i. p. 51).

To what ethnic family the Pæonians really belonged is very uncertain. That they were neither Thracians nor Illyrians, we may perhaps, with Niebuhr, consider to be "unquestionable." But can we say, with Mr. Grote (vol. iv. p. 1--, that they were not Macedonians? They may have been a remnant of the ancient Pelasgic race to which the early Macedonians likewise belonged (cf. Niebuhr, L. s. c. and Appendix to lk. vi. Essay I.); or they may have been a remnant of the primitive Turanian population, which first spread over Europe. There are some circumstances which favour this latter view (see below, ch. 16, note *).

[b] Supra, iv. 143; and v. 1.

finding them empty, easily got possession of them. Then the men, when they heard that all their towns were taken, scattered this way and that to their homes, and gave themselves up to the Persians. And so these tribes of the Pæonians, to wit, the Siropæonians,[1] the Pæoplians,[2] and all the others as far as Lake Prasias,[3] were torn from their seats and led away into Asia.

16. They on the other hand who dwelt about Mount Pangæum[4] and in the country of the Doberes,[5] the Agrianians,[6] and the Odomantians,[7] and they likewise who inhabited Lake Prasias, were not conquered by Megabazus. He sought indeed to subdue the dwellers upon the lake, but could not effect his purpose. Their manner of living is the following. Platforms supported

---

[1] The Siropæonians, or Pæonians of Siris, must have dwelt in the fertile plain, which is still known as "the great plain of Serres". (Clarke, iv. p. 404; Leake, Northern Gr. iii. p. 201), lying north of the Strymonic lake. They derived their name from their capital city Siris (Steph. Byz. ad voc.), which is mentioned by Herodotus (viii. 115), and Livy (xlv. 4); the *Seres* or *Serres* of modern geographers, now a town of 20,000 inhabitants (Leake, iii. pp. 199-200).

[2] The Pæoplians are mentioned again (vii. 113, in connexion with the Doberes as dwelling to the north of Mount Pangæum. They probably occupied a portion of the same plain with the Siropæonians (Leake, iii. 212).

[3] Colonel Leake's arguments (N. Gr. iii. pp. 210-212) in proof that Lake Prasias is not Lake Bolbe (*Beshik*) but the Strymonic lake (*Takhino*) seem to me completely satisfactory. The Pæonia of Herodotus is entirely (εἰ τῷ Στρυμόν ποταμῷ) (v. s. ch. 13, and infra, note to ch. 17).

[4] I regard Mount Pangæum as the range which runs parallel to the coast between the valley of the *Anghista* (Angites), or eastern portion of the plain of *Serres*, and the high road from *Orfano* to *Pravista*. It is called in some maps *Pnar Dagh*.

[5] The Doberes dwelt on the northern skirts of Mount Pangæum (infra, vii. 113). They can scarcely be the inhabitants of the Pæonian Doberus mentioned by Thucydides (ii. 98), since that city lay near the Axius, which is more than a degree to the westward.

[6] The Agrianians are regarded with probability as the inhabitants of the upper valley of the Strymon (Gatterer,

p. 114; Leake, iii. p. 210). The notices in Thucydides (ii. 96), Strabo (vii. p. 460), and Stephen (ad voc. 'Αγρίαι, agree with such a position. They continued independent to the time of Alexander, when their king, Langarus, made his submission (Arrian, Exp. Al. i. 5). Afterwards in Alexander's army they formed about the most important portion of his light troops (Ibid. iii. 12, 18, 20, 24, &c.).

[7] We must not confound this people with the Odomanti of Thucydides, who dwelt in a plain beyond the Strymon, far to the north, and moreover were Thracians (ii. 101). They are undoubtedly the Odomanti of Livy (xlv. 4), who gradually encroached on the Siropæonians, and became masters of their chief city ("Sirae terrae Odomanticæ". Colonel Leake places them on the northern slopes of the mountain-chain which closes in the Strymonic plain (plain of Serres) upon the north and north-east, the Mount Orbelus of Herodotus. He observes with respect to this campaign of Megabazus —

"It was very natural that Megabazus should have subdued the Siropæones, who possessed the most fertile and exposed part of the Strymonic plain, while the Odomanti, who were secure in a higher situation, and still more the Agrianes, who dwelt at the sources of the Strymon, were able to avoid or resist him, as well as the Doberes, and the other Pæones of Mount Pangæum, and the amphibious inhabitants of the Lake Prasias" (Travels in Northern Greece, iii. p. 210).

The substance of this remark is very true; but that the Odomanti of Herodotus dwelt in Pangæum, not in Orbelus, as appears from vii. 112.

upon tall piles stand in the middle of the lake, which are approached from the land by a single narrow bridge." At the first, the piles which bear up the platforms were fixed in their places by the whole body of the citizens, but since that time the custom which has prevailed about fixing them is this:—they are brought from a hill called Orbëlus,* and every man drives in three for each wife that he marries. Now the men have all many wives apiece; and this is the way in which they live. Each has his own hut, wherein he dwells, upon one of the platforms, and each has also a trap-door giving access to the lake beneath; and their wont is to tie their baby children by the foot with a string, to save them from rolling into the water. They feed their horses and their other beasts upon fish, which abound in the lake to such a degree that a man has only to open his trap-door and to let down a basket by a rope into the water, and then to wait a very short time, when he draws it up quite full of them.[1] The fish are of two kinds, which they call the paprax and the tilon.[2]

17. The Pæonians[3] therefore—at least such of them as had been conquered—were led away into Asia. As for Megabazus he had no sooner brought the Pæonians under, than he sent into Macedonia an embassy of Persians, choosing for the purpose the seven men of most note in all the army after himself. These persons were to go to Amyntas, and require him to give earth and water to King Darius. Now there is a very short cut from the lake Prasias across to Macedonia. Quite close to the lake is the mine which yielded afterwards a talent of silver a day to

---

[1] The following description of the huso-fishing on the Wolga may serve to illustrate this passage of our author:— "The huso enters the rivers to spawn earlier than the sturgeon, generally about mid-winter, when they are still covered with ice. At this time the natives construct dikes across the river in certain parts, formed with piles, leaving no interval that the huso can pass through; in the centre of the dike is an angle opening to the current, which consequently is an entering angle to the fish ascending the stream; at the summit of this angle is an opening, which leads into a kind of chamber formed with cord or osier hurdles, according to the season of the year. Above the opening is a kind of scaffold, and a little cabin, where the fishermen can retire and warm themselves or repose, when they are not wanted abroad. No sooner is the huso entered into the chamber, which is known by the motion of the water, than the fishermen on the scaffold let fall a door, which prevents its return to seaward; they then, by means of ropes and pulleys, lift the moveable bottom of the chamber, and easily secure the fish." (Kirby's Bridgewater Treatise, vol. i. p. 108.)

[2] These names are untranslatable. No other ancient writer mentions the *Paprax*, and only Aristotle in a single passage the *Tilon*. (Hist. Animal. viii. 20, § 12.). At the present day the fish principally caught in the lake are carp, tench, and sole. (Leake, ili. p. 198.)

[3] Pæonia in ancient times appears to have consisted of two distinct tracts. One, commencing at the sources of the Strymon, the country of the Agrianians, extended down that river to the great lake near its mouth, being bounded to the east by the mountain ridge of Orbelus, and to the south by that of Pangæum. On the west it is not clear how far these Pæonians extended, but probably they held both banks of the Strymon from its source to the commencement of the Strymonic lake. The other Pæonic territory was upon the Axius. It commenced at some distance inland, and in its upper part was a broadish tract, separated by the mountain-range of Cercine from the country of the Medi and Sinti (Thucyd. ii. 0x), which lay west and south-west of the Strymon; but lower down it was confined to a very narrow strip along the course of the river Axius to the sea. (Thuc. ii. 99.) This latter tract had been conquered by the Macedonians before the commencement of the Peloponnesian war (ibid.), but at what time is uncertain. The upper Æaian region continued Pæonian till a much later date.

Herodotus seems to have known only of the Strymonic Pæonia.

Alexander; and from this mine you have only to cross the mountain called Dysōrum to find yourself in the Macedonian territory.'

18. So the Persians sent upon this errand, when they reached the court, and were brought into the presence of Amyntas, required him to give earth and water to King Darius. And Amyntas not only gave them what they asked, but also invited them to come and feast with him; after which he made ready the board with great magnificence, and entertained the Persians in right friendly fashion. Now when the meal was over, and they were all set to the drinking, the Persians said—

"Dear Macedonian, we Persians have a custom when we make a great feast to bring with us to the board our wives and concubines, and make them sit beside us.² Now then, as thou hast received us so kindly, and feasted us so handsomely, and givest moreover earth and water to King Darius, do also after our custom in this matter."

Then Amyntas answered—"O, Persians! we have no such custom as this; but with us men and women are kept apart. Nevertheless, since you, who are our lords, wish it, this also shall be granted to you."

When Amyntas had thus spoken, he bade some go and fetch the women. And the women came at his call and took their seats in a row over against the Persians. Then, when the Persians saw that the women were fair and comely, they spoke again to Amyntas and said, that 'what had been done was not wise; for it had been better for the women not to have come at all, than to come in this way, and not sit by their sides, but remain over against them, the torment of their eyes.' So Amyntas was forced to bid the women sit side by side with the Persians.

---

¹ Dysōrum is probably the mountain-range between Lake Bolbé and Lake Prasias. Herodotus, in making this range the boundary between Pæonia and Macedonia, is thinking of the Macedonia of his own day, which had been extended by the conquests of Perdiccas and others, to the neighbourhood of the Strymon. (See Leake, iii. p. 212.) The whole of this region abounds with mines (infra, vi. 23 and 46; vii. 112; Thucyd. iv. 105; Appian, Bell. Civ. iv. p. 1041). Some, as those of Fidherokópea, are still worked. (Leake, iii. p. 181.) Silver is the ore chiefly obtained. It may be regarded as a confirmation of the statement in the text, that silver coins (tetradrachms) of Alexander I. are found among the earliest specimens in the Macedonian series.

² The ambassadors, if this portion of the tale be true, must have presumed greatly upon the Greek ignorance of Persian customs. The seclusion of the women was as much practised by the Persians as by any other Orientals. The message to Vashti (Esther i. 11) is an act of royal wantonness, and her refusal arises from her unwillingness to outrage the established usages of society. (See Joseph. Ant. Jud. xi. 6; and compare on the subject generally, Brisson, de Regn. Pers. II. pp. 273-276, and Bahr ad loc.)

The women did as he ordered; and then the Persians, who had drunk more than they ought, began to put their hands on them, and one even tried to give the woman next him a kiss.

19. King Amyntas saw, but he kept silence, although sorely grieved, for he greatly feared the power of the Persians. Alexander, however, Amyntas' son, who was likewise there and witnessed the whole, being a young man and unacquainted with suffering, could not any longer restrain himself. He therefore, full of wrath, spake thus to Amyntas:—"Dear father, thou art old and shouldest spare thyself. Rise up from table and go take thy rest; do not stay out the drinking. I will remain with the guests and give them all that is fitting."

Amyntas, who guessed that Alexander would play some wild prank, made answer:—"Dear son, thy words sound to me as those of one who is well nigh on fire, and I perceive thou sendest me away that thou mayest do some wild deed. I beseech thee make no commotion about these men, lest thou bring us all to ruin, but bear to look calmly on what they do. For myself, I will e'en withdraw as thou biddest me."

20. Amyntas, when he had thus besought his son, went out; and Alexander said to the Persians, "Look on these ladies as your own, dear strangers, all or any of them—only tell us your wishes. But now, as the evening wears, and I see you have all had wine enough, let them, if you please, retire, and when they have bathed they shall come back again." To this the Persians agreed, and Alexander, having got the women away, sent them off to the harem, and made ready in their room an equal number of beardless youths, whom he dressed in the garments of the women, and then, arming them with daggers, brought them in to the Persians, saying as he introduced them, "Methinks, dear Persians, that your entertainment has fallen short in nothing. We have set before you all that we had ourselves in store, and all that we could anywhere find to give to you—and now, to crown the whole, we make over to you our sisters and our mothers, that you may perceive yourselves to be entirely honoured by us, even as you deserve to be—and also that you may take back word to the king who sent you here, that there was one man, a Greek, the satrap ⁵ of Macedonia, by whom you were both feasted

---

⁵ The word used in the text is not σατράπης, but ὕπαρχος. This latter has, however, nearly the same force in Herodotus, who does not use the former. (See iii. 128; iv. 166; v. 25; vii. 6; ix. 113; &c.) He intends to mark here an admission on the part of Alexander, that his father only held Macedonia as a fief under the Persian crown.

and lodged handsomely." So speaking, Alexander set by the side of each Persian one of those whom he had called Macedonian women, but who were in truth men. And these men, when the Persians began to be rude, despatched them with their daggers.[7]

21. So the ambassadors perished by this death, both they and also their followers. For the Persians had brought a great train with them, carriages, and attendants, and baggage of every kind — all of which disappeared at the same time as the men themselves. Not very long afterwards the Persians made strict search for their lost embassy; but Alexander, with much wisdom, hushed up the business, bribing those sent on the errand, partly with money, and partly with the gift of his own sister Gygea,[8] whom he gave in marriage to Bubares,[9] a Persian, the chief leader of the expedition which came in search of the lost men. Thus the death of these Persians was hushed up, and no more was said of it.

22. Now that the men of this family are Greeks, sprung from Perdiccas, as they themselves affirm, is a thing which I can declare of my own knowledge, and which I will hereafter make plainly evident.[10] That they are so has been already adjudged by those who manage the Pan-Hellenic contest at Olympia. For when Alexander wished to contend in the games, and had come to Olympia with no other view, the Greeks who were about

to run against him would have excluded him from the contest—saying that Greeks only were allowed to contend, and not barbarians. But Alexander proved himself to be an Argive, and was distinctly adjudged a Greek; after which he entered the lists for the foot-race, and was drawn to run in the first pair. Thus was this matter settled.

23. Megabazus, having reached the Hellespont with the Paeonians, crossed it, and went up to Sardis. He had become aware while in Europe that Histiaeus the Milesian was raising a wall at Myrcinus—the town upon the Strymon which he had obtained from King Darius as his guerdon for keeping the bridge. No sooner therefore did he reach Sardis with the Paeonians than he said to Darius, "What mad thing is this that thou hast done, sire, to let a Greek, a wise man and a shrewd, get hold of a town in Thrace, a place too where there is abundance of timber fit for shipbuilding, and oars in plenty, and mines of silver,[1] and about which are many dwellers both Greek and barbarian, ready enough to take him for their chief, and by day and night to do his bidding? I pray thee make this man cease his work, if thou wouldst not be entangled in a war with thine own followers. Stop him, but with a gentle message, only bidding him to come to thee. Then when thou once hast him in thy power, be sure thou take good care that he never get back to Greece again."

24. With these words Megabazus easily persuaded Darius, who thought he had shown true foresight in this matter. Darius therefore sent a messenger to Myrcinus, who said, "These be the words of the king to thee, O Histiaeus! I have looked to find a man well affectioned towards me and towards my greatness; and I have found none whom I can trust like thee. Thy deeds, and not thy words only, have proved thy love for me. Now then, since I have a mighty enterprise in hand, I pray thee come to me, that I may show thee what I purpose!"

Histiaeus, when he heard this, put faith in the words of the

---

[1] Histiaeus showed excellent judgment in selecting this site. The vicinity of the rich and extensive Strymonic plain, the abundance of timber, the neighbourhood of gold and silver mines (v. s. note * on ch. 17), the ready access to the sea, were all points of the utmost importance to a new settlement. The value set upon the site in later times is indicated by the struggles for its possession (Thucyd. iv. 102). The excellence of the position caused the subsequent greatness of Amphipolis, and in later times of Philippi. It is extolled abundantly by writers both ancient and modern. (Thucyd. iv. 108; Liv. xlv. 30; Appian, de Bell. Civ. iv. p. 1041; Bouć, Voyage en Turquie, i. pp. 196-199; Clarke, iv. pp. 402-403; Leake, iii. pp. 190-201.)

[2] Compare the Behistun Inscription, where obedience is thus described.— "That which has been said to them by me, both by night and by day it has been done by them." (Col. I. par. 7, end.) See also Thucyd. i. 139.

messenger; and, as it seemed to him a grand thing to be the king's counsellor, he straightway went up to Sardis. Then Darius, when he was come, said to him, "Dear Histiæus, hear why I have sent for thee. No sooner did I return from Scythia, and lose thee out of my sight, than I longed, as I have never longed for aught else, to behold thee once more, and to interchange speech with thee. Right sure I am there is nothing in all the world so precious as a friend who is at once wise and true: both which thou art, as I have had good proof in what thou hast already done for me. Now then 'tis well thou art come; for look, I have an offer to make to thee. Let go Miletus and thy newly-founded town in Thrace, and come with me up to Susa; share all that I have; live with me, and be my counsellor."

25. When Darius had thus spoken he made Artaphernes, his brother by the father's side, governor of Sardis, and taking Histiæus with him, went up to Susa. He left as general of all the troops upon the sea-coast Otanes, son of Sisamnes, whose father King Cambyses slew and flayed, because that he, being of the number of the royal judges, had taken money to give an unrighteous sentence. Therefore Cambyses slew and flayed Sisamnes, and cutting his skin into strips, stretched them across the seat of the throne whereon he had been wont to sit when he heard causes. Having so done Cambyses appointed the son of Sisamnes to be judge in his father's room, and bade him never forget in what way his seat was cushioned.

26. Accordingly this Otanes, who had occupied so strange a throne, became the successor of Megabazus in his command, and took first of all Byzantium and Chalcêdon, then Antandrus in

the Troas, and next Lamponium.⁵ This done, he borrowed ships of the Lesbians, and took Lemnos and Imbrus, which were still inhabited by Pelasgians.¹

27. Now the Lemnians stood on their defence, and fought gallantly; but they were brought low in course of time. Such as outlived the struggle were placed by the Persians under the government of Lycarētus, the brother of that Mæandrius² who was tyrant of Samos. (This Lycarētus died afterwards in his government.) The cause which Otanes alleged for conquering and enslaving all these nations was, that some had refused to join the king's army against Scythia, while others had molested the host on its return. Such were the exploits which Otanes performed in his command.

28. Afterwards, but for no long time,³ there was a respite from suffering. Then from Naxos and Miletus troubles gathered anew about Ionia. Now Naxos at this time surpassed all the other islands in prosperity;⁴ and Miletus had reached the height

---

Pelasgic town (vii. 42), and by Alcæus a city of the Leleges ap. Strab. l. s. c.). Its foundation must therefore be ascribed to a period prior to the first Greek colonies upon the coast. The occupation of Antandrus for a hundred years by the Cimmerians has been already noticed (vol. i. p. 300, note ⁴, and supra, p. 151, note ⁹).

⁵ This was an unimportant place on the same coast, the exact site of which cannot be fixed. It is said to have been an Æolian colony (Strab. xiii. p. 877). Hecatæus and Hellanicus both mentioned it (Steph. Byz. ad voc. Λαμπώνια); but it is omitted by Scylax.

¹ Vide supra, iv. 145.

² Supra, iii. 142-148.

³ The chronology of the events in the reign of Darius depends almost entirely on the question of what we are to understand by this expression. If we regard the battle of Marathon as fixed by the concurrent voice of all the Greek chronologists and historians to the Olympic year, 72, 3 (B.C. 490), we can, from Herodotus alone, determine the dates of the various events in the reign of Darius up to the Naxian revolt, almost with certainty. But the earlier events, as the Thracian and the Scythian campaigns, depend for their date upon the length of the interval here described as "no long time" (οὐ πολλὸς χρόνος). Perhaps Clinton is not far wrong in reckoning it "a tranquillity

of two years." (F. H. vol. ii. ch. 18, App. p. 314.)

Mr. Grote's proposed punctuation, μετὰ δὲ οὐ πολλὸν χρόνον, ἄνεσις κακῶν ἦν, appears to me to give no sense at all.

⁴ Naxos (now Axia, Ross's Inselreise, vol. iii. Pref. p. x.), the largest of the Cyclades, when we last heard of it, was said to have been delivered by Pisistratus into the hands of his follower, Lygdamis (i. 64). It would seem that an oligarchy had succeeded to his tyranny (infra, ch. 30), as was usual in the Greek states. (See Hermann's Pol. Ant. § 65. According to the Pseudo-Plutarch the Lacedæmonians had driven Lygdamis from his post. (De Malign. Herod. vol. ii. p. 859.) This is questioned by Mr. Grote (vol. iv. p. 378, note.; but it is in accordance with the general statements both of Herodotus and Thucydides (Herod. v. 62; Thucyd. I. 18, 122, &c.).

The fertility of Naxos was proverbial in ancient times. Agathemer says that it was called on this account "little Sicily" (I. 5, p. 194). M. de Tournefort gives an agreeable description of its productiveness. (Travels, Letter v. vol. i. pp. 166, 167, E. T.) Ross says (Inselreise, vol. i. p. 42), "Ja, Vater Herodot hat recht; Naxos ist schon jetzt die schönste der Inseln; und was könnte sie vollends durch sorgsamen Anbau werden!"

of her power, and was the glory of Ionia. But previously for two generations the Milesians had suffered grievously from civil disorders, which were composed by the Parians, whom the Milesians chose before all the rest of the Greeks to rearrange their government.

29. Now the way in which the Parians healed their differences was the following. A number of the chief Parians came to Miletus, and when they saw in how ruined a condition the Milesians were, they said that they would like first to go over their country. So they went through all Milesia, and on their way, whenever they saw in the waste and desolate country any land that was well farmed, they took down the names of the owners in their tablets; and having thus gone through the whole region, and obtained after all but few names, they called the people together on their return to Miletus, and made proclamation that they gave the government into the hands of those persons whose lands they had found well farmed; for they thought it likely (they said) that the same persons who had managed their own affairs well would likewise conduct aright the business of the state. The other Milesians, who in time past had been at variance, they placed under the rule of these men. Thus was the Milesian government set in order by the Parians.

30. It was, however, from the two cities above mentioned that troubles began now to gather again about Ionia; and this is the way in which they arose. Certain of the rich men had been banished from Naxos by the commonalty, and, upon their banishment, had fled to Miletus. Aristagoras, son of Molpagoras, the nephew and likewise the son-in-law of Histiæus, son of Lysagoras, who was still kept by Darius at Susa, happened to be regent of Miletus at the time of their coming. For the kingly power belonged to Histiæus; but he was at Susa when the Naxians came. Now these Naxians had in times past been bond-friends of Histiæus; and so on their arrival at Miletus they addressed themselves to Aristagoras and begged him to lend them such

aid as his ability allowed, in hopes thereby to recover their country. Then Aristagoras, considering with himself that, if the Naxians should be restored by his help, he would be lord of Naxos, put forward the friendship with Histiæus to cloak his views, and spoke as follows:—'

"I cannot engage to furnish you with such a power as were needful to force you, against their will, upon the Naxians who hold the city; for I know they can bring into the field eight thousand² bucklers, and have also a vast number of ships of war. But I will do all that lies in my power to get you some aid, and I think I can manage it in this way. Artaphernes happens to be my friend. Now he is a son of Hystaspes, and brother to King Darius. All the sea-coast of Asia is under him,⁹ and he has a numerous army and numerous ships. I think I can prevail on him to do what we require."

When the Naxians heard this, they empowered Aristagoras to manage the matter for them as well as he could, and told him to promise gifts and pay for the soldiers, which (they said) they would readily furnish, since they had great hope that the Naxians, so soon as they saw them returned, would render them obedience, and likewise the other islanders.¹⁰ For at that time not one of the Cyclades was subject to King Darius.

31. So Aristagoras went to Sardis and told Artaphernes that Naxos was an island of no great size, but a fair land and fertile,¹ lying near Ionia,² and containing much treasure and a vast number of slaves. "Make war then upon this land (he said)

---

² In the last century the whole population of the island was estimated at this amount. (Tournefort, vol. i. p. 171.) If Naxos could really at this time bring into the field an army of such a size, she must have been one of the most powerful of the Greek states. Sparta is said (vii. 234) to have been "a city of 8000 men," and Athens, in the Peloponnesian war, could send into the field no more than 13,000 heavy-armed. (Thucyd. ii. 13.)

⁹ This is evidently an exaggeration. As the command of Artaphernes did not extend on the south coast beyond Pamphylia, so northwards it probably stopped at Adramyttium, where the satrapy of Dascyleium began. It suits the purpose of Aristagoras to over-rate the power of his friend.

¹⁰ Naxos would appear by this to have exercised a species of sovereignty over some of the other Cyclades. A προστασία was ascribed to her, which was

said to have lasted 10 years, and which is reckoned apparently from B.C. 510 to B.C. 500, thus covering the 10 years immediately preceding this war (cf. Euseb. Chron. Can. i. p. 30, and ii. p. 336).

¹ Pliny estimates the circumference of Naxos at 75 Roman miles (H. N. iv. 12); Tournefort at a hundred (vol. i. p. 167). It is considerably larger than Jersey, but not more than half the size of the Isle of Wight. Its fertility caused it to be called not only "little Sicily" (see note 4, ch. 28), but also Dionysias ("à vinearum fertilitate"), and Callipolis. (Plin. H. N. l. s. c.) It is still famous for its vineyards, its citrons, and its orange-groves. (Ross, vol. i. p. 38, and p. 41.)

² Naxos is distant from the Ionian coast at least 80 miles. From Samos, however, which was now in the possession of the Persians, it is not more than 65 miles, and in clear weather is visible. (Tournefort, vol. i. p. 175.)

and reinstate the exiles; for if thou wilt do this, first of all, I have very rich gifts in store for thee (besides the cost of the armament, which it is fair that we who are the authors of the war should pay); and, secondly, thou wilt bring under the power of the king not only Naxos but the other islands which depend on it,³ as Paros, Andros, and all the rest of the Cyclades. And when thou hast gained these, thou mayest easily go on against Eubœa, which is a large and wealthy island not less in size than Cyprus,⁴ and very easy to bring under. A hundred ships were quite enough to subdue the whole." The other answered—"Truly thou art the author of a plan which may much advantage the house of the king; and thy counsel is good in all points except the number of the ships. Instead of a hundred, two hundred shall be at thy disposal when the spring comes. But the king himself must first approve the undertaking."

32. When Aristagoras heard this he was greatly rejoiced, and went home in good heart to Miletus. And Artaphernes, after he had sent a messenger to Susa to lay the plans of Aristagoras before the king, and received his approval of the undertaking, made ready a fleet of two hundred triremes and a vast army of Persians and their confederates. The command of these he gave to a Persian named Megabates, who belonged to the house of the Achæmenids, being nephew both to himself and to King Darius. It was to a daughter of this man that Pausanias the Lacedæmonian, the son of Cleombrotus (if at least there be any truth in the tale ⁵), was affianced many years afterwards, when he conceived the desire of becoming tyrant of Greece. Artaphernes now, having named Megabates to the command, sent forward the armament to Aristagoras.

---

³ Larcher (ad loc.) understands this to mean, not that the other Cyclades were generally subject to Naxos, but only that, as they lay so near it, the capture of Naxos might probably lead to that of the rest. But something more seems to be intended. Compare note ᵖ on ch. 30.

⁴ Cyprus is really more than twice the size of Eubœa (*Negropont*). The ancients, however, in general, regarded them as nearly equal. Scylax placed them together, assigning a mere preference to Cyprus. (Peripl. p. 131.) Agathemer allowed a greater interval (ii. 8, p. 283), but even he estimated the length of Eubœa to exceed considerably that of Cyprus (i. 5, p. 195), whereas Cyprus is in reality much (nearly half a degree) the longer of the two. Pliny, according to one measurement of Cyprus, brought them nearly to an equality. (Compare iv. 12, p. 215, with v. 31, p. 302.) The error arose from underestimating the size of Cyprus, not from over-estimating that of Eubœa.

⁵ For the true account of these proceedings of Pausanias, cf. Thucyd. i. 128-130. By the documents there brought forward—which, however, Thucydides shows by a casual phrase (ἐν δευτέρῳ ἀνευρέθη) not to have become known to the Greeks till some time afterwards, and which, therefore, Herodotus may very well never have seen—it appears that the marriage which Pausanias desired to contract was, in reality, with one of the daughters of Xerxes.

33. Megabates set sail, and, touching at Miletus, took on board Aristagoras with the Ionian troops and the Naxians; after which he steered, as he gave out, for the Hellespont; but when he reached Chios, he brought the fleet to anchor off Caucasa,⁶ being minded to wait there for a north wind,⁷ and then sail straight to Naxos. The Naxians however were not to perish at this time; and so the following events were brought about. As Megabates went his rounds to visit the watches on board the ships, he found a Myndian⁸ vessel upon which there was none set. Full of anger at such carelessness, he bade his guards to seek out the captain, one Scylax⁹ by name, and thrusting him through one of the holes in the ship's side,¹⁰ to fasten him there in such a way that his head might show outside the vessel, while his body remained within. When Scylax was thus fastened, one went and informed Aristagoras that Megabates had bound his Myndian friend and was entreating him shamefully. So he came and asked Megabates to let the man off; but the Persian refused him; whereupon Aristagoras went himself and set Scylax free. When Megabates heard this he was still more angry than before, and spoke hotly to Aristagoras. Then the latter said to him—

"What hast thou to do with these matters? Wert thou not sent here by Artaphernes to obey me, and to sail whithersoever I ordered? Why dost meddle so?"

Thus spake Aristagoras. The other, in high dudgeon at such language, waited till the night, and then despatched a boat to Naxos, to warn the Naxians of the coming danger.

34. Now the Naxians up to this time had not had any suspicion that the armament was directed against them; as soon, therefore, as the message reached them, forthwith they brought within their walls all that they had in the open field, and made themselves ready against a siege by provisioning their town both with food

---

⁶ This place does not appear to be mentioned by any other ancient writer. Strabo omits it, though he gives a careful description of the coast (xiv. p. 934).

⁷ Such a wind might be looked for with confidence, as the Etesian gales blew during the greater part of the summer months from this quarter. (Vide supra, ii. 20.)

⁸ Myndus was a town in Caria (Hecat. Fr. 230). It lay upon the coast, between Halicarnassus and Bargylia (Scylax. Peripl. p. 91; Strab. xiv. p. 611), and is probably identified with the ruins at Gumishlu, nearly at the extreme west of the Halicarnassian peninsula (Leake's Asia Minor, p. 228).

⁹ Scylax is known to us altogether as a Carian appellative. The most famous of the name was the navigator mentioned in 44. He was of Caryanda, a city a little north of Myndus (Strab. l. s. c.). Another well-known Scylax, the friend of Panætius, was of Halicarnassus, "on the southern side of the peninsula."

¹⁰ The "holes in the side" of a Greek vessel were, of course, for the oars. The term used by Herodotus (θαλαμίη), is literally "the hole for the oar of a θαλαμίτης," the θαλαμίται being the rowers on the third or lowest benches of the trireme.

and drink. Thus was Naxos placed in a posture of defence; and the Persians, when they crossed the sea from Chios, found the Naxians fully prepared for them. However they sat down before the place, and besieged it for four whole months. When at length all the stores which they had brought with them were exhausted, and Aristagoras had likewise spent upon the siege no small sum from his private means, and more was still needed to insure success, the Persians gave up the attempt, and first building certain forts, wherein they left the banished Naxians,[1] withdrew to the mainland, having utterly failed in their undertaking.

35. And now Aristagoras found himself quite unable to make good his promises to Artaphernes; nay, he was even hard pressed to meet the claims whereto he was liable for the pay of the troops; and at the same time his fear was great, lest, owing to the failure of the expedition and his own quarrel with Megabates, he should be ousted from the government of Miletus. These manifold alarms had already caused him to contemplate raising a rebellion, when the man with the marked head[2] came from Susa, bringing him instructions on the part of Histiæus to revolt from the king. For Histiæus, when he was anxious to give Aristagoras orders to revolt, could find but one safe way, as the roads were guarded, of making his wishes known; which was by taking the trustiest of his slaves, shaving all the hair from off his head, and then pricking letters upon the skin, and waiting till the hair grew again. Thus accordingly he did; and as soon as ever the hair was grown, he despatched the man to Miletus, giving him no other message than this—"When thou art come to Miletus, bid Aristagoras shave thy head, and look thereon." Now the marks on the head, as I have already mentioned, were a command to revolt.[3] All this Histiæus did because it irked him greatly to be kept at Susa, and because he had strong hopes that, if troubles broke out, he would be sent down to the coast to quell them, whereas, if Miletus made no movement, he did not see a chance of his ever again returning thither.

---

[1] This was the common practice in such cases (cf. Thucyd. iii. 85, iv. 52, 75, &c.). The exiles expected either by perpetual warfare to force an accommodation, or to find an opportunity of seizing the town. Does the story told by Parthenius (Erotic. 19,) after Andriscus, relate to this war?

[2] Herodotus introduces this circumstance as one well known to his hearers. The tale is related by Gellius (Noct. Att. xvii. 9), Polyænus (Strat. i. 24), and Tzetzes (Chil. iii. 512,) the two former of whom appear to derive their facts from some other writer besides Herodotus. According to Gellius, the slave's head was shaved and punctured, ostensibly on medical grounds, so that he himself was not aware that he carried any message.

[3] Polyænus professes to give the exact words of the message. "Histiæus to Aristagoras—raise revolt in Ionia." ('Ιστιαῖος 'Αρισταγόρῃ—'Ιωνίην ἀνάστησον.)

36. Such, then, were the views which led Histiæus to despatch his messenger; and it so chanced that all these several motives to revolt were brought to bear upon Aristagoras at one and the same time.

Accordingly, at this conjuncture Aristagoras held a council of his trusty friends, and laid the business before them, telling them both what he had himself purposed, and what message had been sent him by Histiæus. At this council all his friends were of the same way of thinking, and recommended revolt, except only Hecatæus the historian.⁴ He, first of all, advised them by all means to avoid engaging in war with the king of the Persians, whose might he set forth, and whose subject nations he enumerated. As however he could not induce them to listen to this counsel, he next advised that they should do all that lay in their power to make themselves masters of the sea. "There was one only way," he said, "so far as he could see, of their succeeding in this. Miletus was, he knew, a weak state—but if the treasures in the temple at Branchidæ,⁵ which Crœsus the Lydian gave to it,⁶ were seized, he had strong hopes that the mastery of the sea

---

⁴ Vide supra, ii. 143, note ⁸.

⁵ A general description of the Temple of Apollo at Branchidæ has been given in the foot-notes to Book i. (ch. 157, note ¹). In addition to what was there stated, it may be observed that the building was probably of great antiquity, some of its accessories having a peculiarly archaic character. A straight road led from the sea to the temple, "bordered on either side with statues on chairs, of a single block of stone, with the feet close together and the hands on the knees—an exact imitation of the avenues of the temples in Egypt" (Leake's Asia Minor, p. 239, note. Compare the representation of an Egyptian temple, supra, vol. ii. p. 202.) On one of these statues (some of which are now in the British Museum) an inscription was found by Sir W. Gell, also very archaic in type. It was written boustrophedon, and the forms of the letters marked an extremely early period. It is read, a little doubtfully, thus— [Ἐρ]μησίσκος ἐμέσε ἀνέθηκεν (Β)ρα[γχί]-δη τῷ τέλλοντι. On another of the statues—now in the British Museum— are two inscriptions, both evidently very ancient, which seem to show that the practice of scribbling one's name in a conspicuous place can boast a respectable antiquity. One of these inscriptions, written from right to left, may be read thus—Χάρης εἰμί ὁ Κλέσιος, Τειχιούσης ἄρχος. The archaic form ἄρχος is interesting. Τειχιούσης is for Τειχιούσσης—Teichiussa being a well-known place in the Milesian territory. (Thucyd. viii. 26, 28; Athen. Deipn. viii. p. 391; Steph. Byz. ad voc.) Another curious inscription may be seen on a lion brought from the same temple. (See vol. iv. Appendix to Book ix. Note A.) The earliest historical notice which attaches to the building is that contained in Herod. ii. 159, which shows the celebrity of the shrine at the close of the 7th century. The original temple appears to have been burnt by the Persians on putting down this revolt (infra, vi. 19). A second temple was then built, which was plundered and destroyed by Xerxes (Strab. xiv. p. 910). Finally, a third temple (that of which the plan is given, vol. i. p. 236) was erected by the Milesians; but the avenue of statues undoubtedly belongs to the first temple. Strabo speaks of the third temple as still very magnificent in his own day (l. s. c.).

⁶ The name Branchidæ, as the name of a *place*, is curious. The term properly applied to the priestly family to which was committed the superintendence of the oracle, and may be compared with such names as Eumolpidæ, Iamidæ, &c. Hence even Herodotus has in one place οἱ Βραγχίδαι (supra, i. 158; cf. Strab. xiv. p. 910). According to the

might be thereby gained; at least it would give them money to begin the war, and would save the treasures from falling into the hands of the enemy."[1] Now these treasures were of very great value, as I showed in the first part of my History.[2] The assembly, however, rejected the counsel of Hecatæus, while, nevertheless, they resolved upon a revolt. One of their number, it was agreed, should sail to Myus,[3] where the fleet had been lying since its return from Naxos, and endeavour to seize the captains who had gone there with the vessels.

37. Iatragoras accordingly was despatched on this errand, and he took with guile Oliatus the son of Ibanôlis the Mylassian,[1] and Histiæus the son of Tymnes[2] the Termercean,[3]—Coës likewise, the son of Erxander, to whom Darius gave Mytilênê,[4] and Aristagoras the son of Heraclides the Cymæan, and also many others. Thus Aristagoras revolted openly from Darius; and now he set to work to scheme against him in every possible way. First of all,

---

local tradition they were descended from Branchus, a Thessalian, or according to others a Delphian, the original founder and priest of the temple, of whom a legend was told similar to that of Hyacinthus (Strab. ix. p. 611; xiv. p. 910; Metrodor. Fr. 7a; Aristag. Miles. Fr. 11).

[1] Bishop Thirlwall regards this advice as the best that could be given, and reproaches the Ionians with their folly in neglecting it. Mr. Grote sees, that "the seizure of the treasures would have been insupportable to the pious feelings of the people, and would thus have proved more injurious than beneficial." (Vol. iv. p. 392.) May we not say, without taking too high a view of the Greek religion, that it would have been a real act of sacrilege, unless done in the last resort, and then with the intention of restoration? (Compare the unexceptionable advice of Pericles, Thucyd. ii. 13.)

[2] Supra, i. 92. They were (according to our author) of the same weight and value as the offerings made by Crœsus to Delphi (cf. i. 50, 51). We learn from Strabo, that the treasures at Branchidæ did in fact fall a prey to the Persians; not, however, according to him, till after the return of Xerxes to Asia from Greece, and even then with the connivance of the priests. Afraid of the indignation which their sacrilege would excite, they accompanied him to his court, and were settled by him in Bactria, where Alexander found and punished them. (Strab. xi. p. 753, 754, and xiv. p. 910. Cf. Quint. Curt. vii. 5.) The statue of Apollo was carried off at the same time with the treasures, and was found at Agbatana, whence Seleucus sent it back to Miletus (Pausan. viii. 46, § 2).

[3] Myus was one of the twelve cities of Ionia (supra, i. 142). It lay on the Mæander, not far from Miletus. Originally on the coast, in Strabo's time it was three or four miles up the stream of the Mæander (Strab. xiv. p. 912), and is now still further inland. Its site appears to have been correctly determined by Chandler. (Travels, i. p. 213.) Vide supra, i. 142, note [7].

[1] Mylasa or Mylassa was an inland town of Caria (Strab. xiv. p. 942). It is still a large place, and is called Melassa (Chandler, vol. i. p. 234; Leake's Asia Minor, p. 230). Its famous temple to the Carian Jupiter has been mentioned already (i. 171).

[2] This Histiæus afterwards accompanied the expedition of Xerxes (infra, vii. 98).

[3] Termera, like Mylasa, was a Carian city (infra, vii. 98; Pliny, H. N. v. 29, p. 292). It lay on the coast, a little west of Halicarnassus, opposite to the island of Cos (Strab. xiv. p. 940). Stephen of Byzantium has confused the name with the native appellation of the Lycians, Tramilæ, or Termilæ.

[4] Supra, ch. 11.

in order to induce the Milesians to join heartily in the revolt, he gave out, that he laid down his own lordship over Miletus, and in lieu thereof established a commonwealth: after which, throughout all Ionia he did the like; for from some of the cities he drove out their tyrants, and to others, whose goodwill he hoped thereby to gain, he handed theirs over, thus giving up all the men whom he had seized at the Naxian fleet, each to the city whereto he belonged.

38. Now the Mytileneans had no sooner got Coës into their power, than they led him forth from the city and stoned him; the Cymæans, on the other hand, allowed their tyrant to go free; as likewise did most of the others. And so this form of government ceased throughout all the cities. Aristagoras the Milesian, after he had in this way put down the tyrants, and bidden the cities choose themselves captains[5] in their room, sailed away himself on board a trireme to Lacedæmon; for he had great need of obtaining the aid of some powerful ally.

39. At Sparta, Anaxandridas the son of Leo was no longer king:[6] he had died, and his son Cleomenes had mounted the throne, not however by right of merit, but of birth. Anaxandridas took to wife his own sister's daughter,[7] and was tenderly attached to her; but no children came from the marriage. Hereupon the Ephors[8] called him before them, and said—"If thou hast no care for thine own self, nevertheless we cannot allow this, nor suffer the race of Eurysthenes to die out from among us. Come then, as thy present wife bears thee no children, put her away, and wed another. So wilt thou do what is well-pleasing to the Spartans." Anaxandridas however refused to do as they required, and said it was no good advice the Ephors gave, to bid him put away his wife when she had done no wrong, and take to himself another. He therefore declined to obey them.

40. Then the Ephors and Elders[9] took counsel together, and

---

[5] This is the literal rendering of the Greek word; but, no doubt, as Larcher and Dahr observe, the persons so called were, like the στρατηγοί of Athens (infra, vi. 103), civil magistrates no less than military commanders. They had limited powers, and were elected, most probably, for a limited period.

[6] As he was when Spartan affairs were last treated of, at the time of the embassy sent by Cræsus (i. 65-70).

[7] Marriages of this kind were common at Sparta. Leonidas married his niece, Gorgo (infra, vii. 239); Archidamus his aunt, Lampito (infra, vi. 71).

[8] Concerning the Ephors at Sparta, vide supra, i. 65. This passage is very important, as marking their power over the kings. (Compare infra, ch. 40, vi. 82, ix. 9, 10, and Thucyd. i. 131-134.)

[9] The council of twenty-eight, mentioned with the Ephors, in Book i. ch. 65, and again spoken of in Book vi. ch. 57. It seems that when the Ephors and the Elders agreed together, the king had no power to withstand them.

laid this proposal before the king:—"Since thou art so fond, as we see thee to be, of thy present wife, do what we now advise, and gainsay us not, lest the Spartans make some unwonted decree concerning thee. We ask thee not now to put away thy wife to whom thou art married—give her still the same love and honour as ever,—but take thee another wife beside, who may bear thee children."

When he heard this offer, Anaxandridas gave way—and henceforth he lived with two wives in two separate houses, quite against all Spartan custom.[1]

41. In a short time, the wife whom he had last married bore him a son, who received the name of Cleomenes; and so the heir to the throne was brought into the world by her. After this, the first wife also, who in time past had been barren, by some strange chance conceived, and came to be with child. Then the friends of the second wife, when they heard a rumour of the truth, made a great stir, and said it was a false boast, and she meant, they were sure, to bring forward as her own a supposititious child. So they raised an outcry against her; and therefore, when her full time was come, the Ephors, who were themselves incredulous, sat round her bed, and kept a strict watch on the labour.[2] At this time then she bore Dorieus, and after him, quickly, Leonidas, and after him, again quickly, Cleombrotus. Some even say that Leonidas and Cleombrotus were twins. On the other hand, the second wife, the mother of Cleomenes (who was a daughter of Prinetadas, the son of Demarmenus), never gave birth to a second child.

42. Now Cleomenes, it is said, was not right in his mind; indeed he verged upon madness; while Dorieus surpassed all his co-mates, and looked confidently to receiving the kingdom on

---

[1] Pausanias says (iii. 3, § 7) that this was never allowed to any other Spartan. ('Ἀναξανδρίδης Λακεδαιμονίων μόνος γυναῖκας τε δύο ἅμα ἔσχε, καὶ οἰκίας δύο ἅμα ᾤκησε.) The account in Herod. vi. 61-63, does not conflict with these statements, as Col. Mure thinks (Lit. of Greece, vol. iv. p. 542), since Ariston is not said to have had two wives at one and the same time. (See the Introductory Essay, vol. i. p. 87, note ².)

[2] Compare with this, the practice in our own country of summoning the great officers of state to the queen's apartments at the birth of a prince or princess. With the Spartans there was a religious motive at work, in addition to the political one which alone obtains with ourselves. It was necessary for them, in a religious point of view, to preserve the purity of the blood of Hercules. Mr. Grote justly observes of the Spartan kings:—

"Above all, their root was deep in the religious feelings of the people. Their pre-eminent lineage connected the state with a divine paternity. Nay, the chiefs of the Heracleidæ were the special grantees of the soil of Sparta from the gods—the occupation of the Dorians being only sanctified and blest by Zeus for the purpose of establishing the children of Hercules in the valley of the Eurotas." (Vol. ii. p. 476.)

the score of merit. When, therefore, after the death of Anaxandridas, the Spartans kept to the law, and made Cleomenes, his eldest son, king in his room, Dorieus, who had imagined that he should be chosen, and who could not bear the thought of having such a man as Cleomenes to rule over him, asked the Spartans to give him a body of men, and left Sparta with them in order to found a colony. However, he neither took counsel of the oracle at Delphi as to the place whereto he should go,³ nor observed any of the customary usages;⁴ but left Sparta in dudgeon, and sailed away to Libya, under the guidance of certain men who were Thereans.⁵ These men brought him to Cinyps, where he colonised a spot, which has not its equal in all Libya, on the banks of a river;⁶ but from this place he was driven in the third year by the Macians,⁷ the Libyans,⁸ and the Carthaginians.

43. Dorieus returned to the Peloponnese; whereupon Antichares the Eleônian⁹ gave him a counsel (which he got from the oracles of Laïus¹), to "found the city of Heraclea in Sicily; the whole country of Eryx² belonged," he said, "to the Heracleids, since Hercules himself conquered it." On receiving this advice, Dorieus went to Delphi to inquire of the oracle whether he would

---

³ Vide supra. iv. 159, note, and compare Müller's Dorians (iii. p. 282, E. T.), and Hermann's Political Antiquities of Greece (§ 75, note 4). The sanction of some oracle or other was required for every colony; the sanction of the oracle at Delphi, when the colony was Dorian. The passage in Cicero (De Div. II. L. § 3) is important: "Quam vero Græcia coloniam misit in Æoliam, Ioniam, Asiam, Siciliam, Italiam, sine Pythio aut Dodonæo aut Hammonis oraculo?"

⁴ The taking of fire from the Prytaneum of the parent city was one of these. (Hermann, § 74, note 1.) Compare note * on Book I. ch. 146.

⁵ Thera, as a Spartan colony (supra, iv. 147), would be likely to keep up a connexion with the mother country. Again, the connexion of Thera with Cyrene (iv. 150-159) would explain the choice of Cinyps as a settlement.

⁶ This place, which Herodotus regarded as the most fertile spot in Africa, has been already described (iv. 198; compare ch. 175). Scylax only calls it χωρίον καλόν (Peripl. p. 112). Perennial streams are so rare in this part of Africa, that the highest praise was contained in the words, "on the banks of a river."

⁷ Cinyps was in the country of the Macians (iv. 175; Scyl. Peripl. l. s. c.), who would therefore be likely to resist the settlement.

⁸ That is, "the other Libyans." The Macians were Libyans (iv. 168, 175, 197).

⁹ Eleon was a village in the territory of Tanagra (Strabo, ix. pp. 587, 637).

¹ Proposals have been made to change the name here either to Iamus (mentioned Pind. Ol. vi. 74), or to Bacis, a native of Eleon (Schol. Aristoph. Pac. 1071); as we do not hear of any prophet Laïus. But no change is needed. We may understand, with Larcher, "oracles given to Laïus." (Cf. Soph. Œd. T. 906, Ἀλλῳ παλαιὰ θέσφατα.)

² Eryx is said by Thucydides to have been a Trojan settlement (vi. 2). It lay at the western point of the island, a little to the north of Drepanum, the modern Trapani. (See Plin. H. N. iii. 8; Strab. vi. p. 393.) Its site is fixed by the remarkable mountain, the "mons Eryx" of antiquity, which can only be the modern Mount St. Julian. The conquest of this district by Hercules is related at length by Diodorus (iv. 22).

take the place to which he was about to go. The Pythoness prophesied that he would; whereupon Dorieus went back to Libya, took up the men who had sailed with him at the first, and proceeded upon his way along the shores of Italy.

44. Just at this time, the Sybarites say, they and their king Télys were about to make war upon Crotôna, and the Crotoniats, greatly alarmed, besought Dorieus to lend them aid. Dorieus was prevailed upon, bore part in the war against Sybaris, and had a share in taking the town. Such is the account which the Sybarites give of what was done by Dorieus and his companions. The Crotoniats, on the other hand, maintain that no foreigner lent them aid in their war against the Sybarites, save and except Callias the Elean, a soothsayer of the race of the Iamidæ; and he only forsook Télys the Sybaritic king, and deserted to their side, when he found on sacrificing that the victims were not favourable to an attack on Crotôna. Such is the account which each party gives of these matters.

45. Both parties likewise adduce testimonies to the truth of what they say. The Sybarites show a temple and sacred precinct near the dry stream of the Crastis, which they declare that Dorieus, after taking their city, dedicated to Minerva Crastias. And further, they bring forward the death of Dorieus as the

surest proof; since he fell, they say, because he disobeyed the oracle. For had he in nothing varied from the directions given him, but confined himself to the business on which he was sent, he would assuredly have conquered the Erycian territory, and kept possession of it, instead of perishing with all his followers. The Crotoniats, on the other hand, point to the numerous allotments within their borders which were assigned to Callias the Elean by their countrymen, and which to my day remained in the possession of his family; while Dorieus and his descendants (they remark) possess nothing. Yet if Dorieus had really helped them in the Sybaritic war, he would have received very much more than Callias. Such are the testimonies which are adduced on either side; it is open to every man to adopt whichever view he deems the best.*

46. Certain Spartans accompanied Dorieus on his voyage as co-founders, to wit, Thessalus, Parœbates, Celeas, and Euryleon. These men and all the troops under their command reached Sicily; but there they fell in a battle wherein they were defeated by the Egesteans* and Phœnicians, only one, Euryleon, surviving the disaster. He then, collecting the remnants of the beaten army, made himself master of Minôa, the Selinusian colony,¹ and helped the Selinusians to throw off the yoke of their tyrant Peithagoras. Having upset Peithagoras, he sought to become tyrant in his room, and he even reigned at Selinus for a brief

---

* This chapter is clearly the writing of Herodotus *the Thurian*. (Arist. Rhet. iii. 9.) Other specimens of the same intimate knowledge of the cities of Magna Græcia occur, iii. 131, 136-138, iv. 15; infra, chs. 46, 47, vii. 170, &c.

* Egesta, or Segesta (the native name, as appears from the coins) was a sister settlement of Eryx (Thuc. vi. 2). It was situated at some little distance from the sea, and had a port known as Emporium Segestanum. (Strab. vi. p. 393; Ptol. Geograph. iii. 4; Plin. H. N. iii. 8.) The latter seems to have occupied the site of the modern *Castell-à-mare* (lat. 38° 2′ long. 12° 52′). A temple and theatre mark the site of the former, about six miles inland from *Castell-à-mare*.

¹ Minôa was said to have derived its name from Minos (Heracl. Pont. Fr. xiii.), who was reported by tradition to have visited Sicily (infra. vii. 170). But it seems more probable that the Megarians, who colonised Selinus (Thucyd. vi. 4), brought the name with them from their former country (Thucyd. iii. 51). Minôa was afterwards called Heraclea. It is uncertain when this change was made—perhaps on its occupation by Euryleon. Sometimes both names were used ('Ηρακλείαν τὴν Μινῴαν, Polyb. L 25; cf. Liv. xxiv. 35); but commonly we find only Heraclea. The town lay at the mouth of the Halycus (*Platani*), where some slight ruins still remain (Smyth's Sicily, p. 216). Heraclea is mentioned by various writers, among them by Ptolemy (Geograph. iii. 4), Stephen (ad voc.), and Cicero (adv. Verr. ii. 50).

Selinus was founded from Megara Hyblæa, about B.C. 630 (Thucyd. vi. 4). It was a place of great importance until its destruction by Hannibal (Diod. Sic. xiii. 59). From that time it fell into decay (Strab. vi. p. 394). Very extensive ruins mark the site, which is in the *Terra dei Pulci* between the rivers *Modione* and *Belici* (Smyth's Sicily, pp. 219, 220).

space—but after a while the Selinusians rose up in revolt against him, and though he fled to the altar of Jupiter Agoræus,[2] they notwithstanding put him to death.

47. Another man who accompanied Dorieus, and died with him, was Philip the son of Butacides, a man of Crotôna; who, after he had been betrothed to a daughter of Têlys the Sybarite, was banished from Crotôna, whereupon his marriage came to nought; and he in his disappointment took ship and sailed to Cyrênê. From thence he became a follower of Dorieus, furnishing to the fleet a trireme of his own, the crew of which he supported at his own charge. This Philip was an Olympian victor, and the handsomest Greek of his day. His beauty gained him honours at the hands of the Egestæans which they never accorded to any one else; for they raised a hero-temple over his grave, and they still worship him with sacrifices.[3]

48. Such then was the end of Dorieus, who if he had brooked the rule of Cleomenes, and remained in Sparta, would have been king of Lacedæmon; since Cleomenes, after reigning no great length of time, died without male offspring, leaving behind him an only daughter, by name Gorgo.[4]

49. Cleomenes, however, was still king when Aristagoras, tyrant of Miletus, reached Sparta. At their interview, Aristagoras, according to the report of the Lacedæmonians, produced a bronze tablet, whereupon the whole circuit of the earth was engraved, with all its seas and rivers.[5] Discourse began between the two; and Aristagoras addressed the Spartan king in these words following:—"Think it not strange, O King Cleomenes, that I have been at the pains to sail hither; for the posture of affairs, which I will now recount unto thee, made it fitting. Shame and grief is it indeed to none so much as to us, that the sons of the Ionians should have lost their freedom, and come to be the slaves of others; but yet it touches you likewise, O Spartans, beyond the rest of the Greeks, inasmuch as the pre-

---

[2] That is, the altar of Jupiter, Protector of the Forum (ἀγοραῖος). It probably stood in the market-place.

[3] Eustathius reports the same (ad Hom. Il. L.); but he derives his knowledge from Herodotus.

[4] She became the wife of Leonidas, her uncle, according to a usual Spartan custom (infra, vii. 239; compare note [5] on ch. 39 of this Book). The noble character of Gorgo is evidenced by the anecdote related below (ch. 51),

and by the praises of Plutarch (ii. p. 145). Her acuteness appears, vii. 239.

[5] Maps, according to Strabo and others (Strab. i. p. 10; Agathem. i. 1; Diog. Laert. ii. 1), were invented about this time by Anaximander. Hecatæus appears to have made use of them. (Compare iv. 36, and note [1] on the passage.) The map of Aristagoras was probably the first which had been seen in European Greece.

eminence over all Greece appertains to you. We beseech you, therefore, by the common gods of the Grecians, deliver the Ionians, who are your own kinsmen, from slavery. Truly the task is not difficult; for the barbarians are an unwarlike people; and you are the best and bravest warriors in the whole world. Their mode of fighting is the following:—they use bows and arrows and a short spear; they wear trousers in the field, and cover their heads with turbans.* So easy are they to vanquish! Know too that the dwellers in these parts have more good things than all the rest of the world put together—gold, and silver, and brass, and embroidered garments, beasts of burthen, and bondservants—all which, if you only wish it, you may soon have for your own. The nations border on one another, in the order which I will now explain. Next to these Ionians" (here he pointed with his finger to the map of the world which was engraved upon the tablet that he had brought with him) "these Lydians dwell; their soil is fertile,[1] and few people are so rich in silver." Next to them," he continued, "come these Phrygians, who have more flocks and herds than any race that I know,[2] and more plentiful harvests. On them border the Cappadocians, whom we Greeks know by the name of Syrians:[1] they are neighbours to the Cilicians, who extend all the way to this sea, where Cyprus (the island which you see here) lies. The Cilicians pay the king a yearly tribute of five hundred talents.[2] Next to them come the Armenians, who live here—they too have numerous flocks and herds.[3] After them come the Matieni,[4] inhabiting this country; then Cissia, this province, where you see the

---

* Vide infra, vii. 61. A representation of the ordinary Persian dress has been already given, vol. i. p. 221. Their war costume will be seen by reference to the notes on Book vii. ch. 61.

[1] The valleys of the Hermus, Cayster, Caïcus, and Evenus, are all of extreme fertility. (Fellows's Asia Minor, pp. 21, 26, 278; Leake's Tour, pp. 255, 265.) The intermediate country is mountainous and barren, especially the district called Catakecaumenè. (Hamilton's Asia Minor, i. pp. 132-141.).

* Mount Tmolus, ἀργυρέων ὄρος, as Strabo calls it (xiii. p. 897), is said to have produced gold in abundance, but not silver, so far as I am aware. Was the silver the product of those mines between Pergamus and Atarneus, to which some writers ascribed the immense riches of Gyges, Alyattes, and Crœsus? (Strab. xiv. p. 908.)

[2] The high table-land of Phrygia is especially adapted for pasturage. Flocks and herds, even under the present miserable system of government, are numerous (Leake, pp. 19, 36; Hamilton, i. pp. 415-418; ii. pp. 218-221, &c.). The Angora wool has a world-wide reputation. The land is in many places very rich, but is wretchedly cultivated (Leake, p. 94).

[1] Vide supra, i. 72, and infra, vii. 72.

[2] Supra, iii. 90.

[3] Armenia is, even more than Phrygia, a pasture country. Phrygia has many wide plains, capable of bearing ample harvests; but Armenia is all mountain and valley (cf. vol. i. Essay ix. § 10).

[4] Not the Matieni of Asia Minor, but those of the Kurdish hills. (Compare i. 74, 189, 202, &c.)

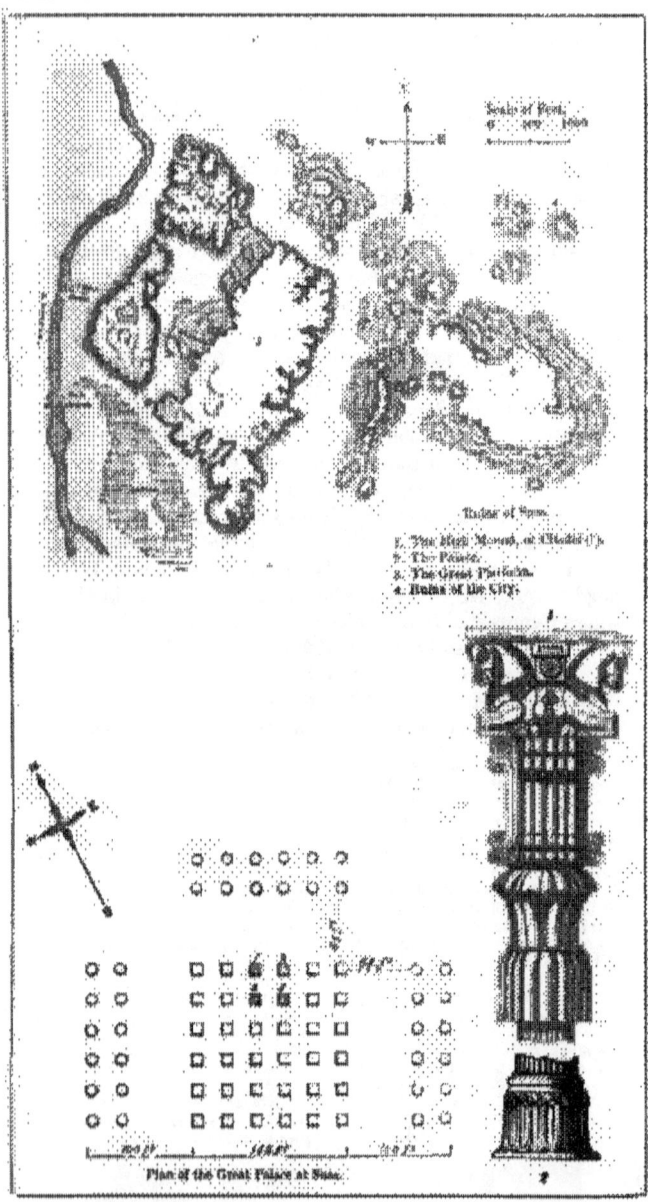

Ruins of Susa.
1. The High Mound, or Citadel (?).
2. The Palace.
3. The Great Platform.
4. Ruins of the City.

Plan of the Great Palace at Susa.

river Choaspes marked, and likewise the town Susa upon its banks, where the Great King holds his court,[5] and where the

[5] That Susa had by this time certainly become the Persian capital, has been already admitted (supra, iii. 30, note⁹). It was the ancient capital of Elam or Susiana, the country between Mount Zagros and the lower Tigris. It was situated on the edge of the great Mesopotamian plain, 25 or 30 miles from the mountains, in a luxuriant region abundantly watered, and famous for its beautiful herbage. The city does not now lie directly upon the Choaspes (*Kerkhah*), but upon a small stream, called the *Shapur*, which rises about 10 miles to the north of the ruins, and flows into the *Karun* near *Ahwaz*. The Choaspes is at present a mile and a half to the west of the town (Journal of Geograph. Society, vol. ix. part i. p. 71; compare Herod. v. 52, and Strab. xv. p. 1032,, and the *Karun* or river of *Dizful*, about six miles to the east. It is thought, however, that anciently the Choaspes bifurcated a little above the ruins of Sedaca, and flowed in part east of Susa (supra, vol. i. p. 467, note⁶.) The citadel, so often noticed (supra, iii. 68; Polyb. v. xlviii. § 14; Strab. xv. p. 1031; Arrian. iii. 16; Plin. H. N. vi. 27, p. 362), lay at the western extremity of the place, close to the *Shapur*, and opposite to the modern "tomb of Daniel." It occupied the highest part of the great mound, which is even now 120 feet above the level of the *Shapur*. The town extended from this point in an easterly direction; it was of an oblong shape, and had a circuit which we find differently estimated at 200 and 120 stades (cf. Strab. l. s. c., and Polyclit. ap. Strab. xv. p 1032). The ruins seem at present to be confined within a circumference of 7 miles or about 60 stades (Geograph. Journ. l. s. c.). They extend considerably beyond the limits of the accompanying plan.

The material used in the construction of the city was baked and sun-dried brick, like the Babylonian. It was probably built originally by the Scythic people whose language is found on all the most ancient of its remains; but it was no doubt enlarged and beautified when Darius transferred to it the seat of empire (cf. Plin. H. N. vi. 27, p. 361). The magnificent palace which had so great a fame in antiquity (infra. ch. 53; Ar. de Mund. p. 398; Strab. l. s. c.; Diod. Sic. xvii. 65; Cassiodorus, vii. Ep. 15), and of which the best account is to be found in the book of Esther (i. 5, 6), occupied the northern portion of the great mound (supra, iii. 68, note⁸), an irregular rectangle, two sides of which measure 1200 feet, while the remaining two fall somewhat short of 1000. It has been recently exhumed in a great measure by Sir W. Williams and Mr. Loftus, and is found to have consisted of a great hall of stone pillars, of the same size and on the same plan as that of Xerxes at Persepolis (Ker Porter, vol. i. Pl. 30, and compare Pl. 45), and of a number of inferior buildings behind the hall, the material of which is brick. The pillars are arranged into a central group of 36, standing in six rows of six each, so as to form an exact square, 145 feet (nearly) each way; and into three outlying groups or porticoes, flanking the central group on three sides, the east, the north, and the west. These porticoes, which are exactly parallel to the sides of the inner square, are formed of two rows of six pillars each, in line with the pillars of the central group, the distance between the outermost pillars of the central group and the inner pillars of the porticoes being 64 feet. The pillars are of two kinds—those of the central group or phalanx have square bases, while those of the porticoes have round or bell-shaped bases, as given in the woodcut (No. 2). Both sorts appear, however, to have been surmounted by the same capital, the form of which is represented in the woodcut (No. 1). The central group is supposed to have been covered with a roof, but the space between that group and the porticoes was probably only shaded by curtains (see Loftus's Chaldæa, pp. 373-375, and compare the description in the book of Esther, i. 5, 6). It appears by a trilingual inscription upon four of the pillars (1, 2, 3, and 4 in the plan) that the palace was commenced by Darius and finished by Artaxerxes Mnemon.

The town is said to have been unwalled (Polyclit. ap. Strab. l. s. c., and certainly appears as an open place in the wars of the successors of Alexander (Polyb. l. s. c.). It is unfortunate that we have no description of ancient Susa from an eye-witness, since it doubtless exceeded in magnificence both Persepolis and Ecbatana.

With regard to the residence of the

treasuries are in which his wealth is stored. Once masters of this city, you may be bold to vie with Jove himself for riches. In the wars which ye wage with your rivals of Messenia, with them of Argos likewise and of Arcadia, about paltry boundaries and strips of land not so remarkably good, ye contend with those who have no gold, nor silver even, which often give men heart to fight and die. Must ye wage such wars, and when ye might so easily be lords of Asia, will ye decide otherwise?" Thus spoke Aristagoras; and Cleomenes replied to him,—"Milesian stranger, three days hence I will give thee an answer."

50. So they proceeded no further at that time. When, however, the day appointed for the answer came, and the two once more met, Cleomenes asked Aristagoras, "how many days' journey it was from the sea of the Ionians to the King's residence?" Hereupon Aristagoras, who had managed the rest so

cleverly, and succeeded in deceiving the king, tripped in his speech and blundered; for instead of concealing the truth, as he ought to have done if he wanted to induce the Spartans to cross into Asia, he said plainly that it was a journey of three months. Cleomenes caught at the words, and, preventing Aristagoras from finishing what he had begun to say concerning the road, addressed him thus:—"Milesian stranger, quit Sparta before sunset. This is no good proposal that thou makest to the Lacedæmonians, to conduct them a distance of three months' journey from the sea." When he had thus spoken, Cleomenes went to his home.

51. But Aristagoras took an olive-bough in his hand, and hastened to the king's house, where he was admitted by reason of his suppliant's guise. Gorgo, the daughter of Cleomenes, and his only child, a girl of about eight or nine years of age, happened to be there, standing by her father's side. Aristagoras, seeing her, requested Cleomenes to send her out of the room before he began to speak with him; but Cleomenes told him to say on, and not mind the child. So Aristagoras began with a promise of ten talents* if the king would grant him his request, and when Cleomenes shook his head, continued to raise his offer till it reached fifty talents; whereupon the child spoke:—"Father," she said, "get up and go, or the stranger will certainly corrupt thee." Then Cleomenes, pleased at the warning of his child, withdrew and went into another room. Aristagoras quitted Sparta for good, not being able to discourse any more concerning the road which led up to the King.

52. Now the true account of the road in question is the following:—Royal stations¹ exist along its whole length, and ex-

---

* On the readiness of the Spartans to yield to bribery, vide supra, iii. 148, note¹.

¹ By "royal stations" are to be understood the abodes of the king's couriers (ἄγγαροι), who conveyed despatches from their own station to the next, and then returned (infra, viii. 98). The route described is probably at once the post-route and the caravan-route between the two capitals. If Herodotus visited Babylon, he would have travelled along this road, at least as far as the Gyndes, where this great highway was crossed by the route leading from Babylon to Agbatana (cf. i. 189). The road is nearly that which would now be followed by travellers between Smyrna and Baghdad. It bears away out of the straight line, towards the north, in order to avoid the vast arid tract between the Upper Tigris and Upper Euphrates, the Great Desert of Sinjar. It also, by this deviation, is able to take in the Armenian capital, Diarbekr. It passes by Sart (Sardis), Allah Shehr (Philadelphia), Afiom Kara Hissar, Ak-Shehr, Kaisariyeh, Gurnn, Malatiyeh, Diarbekr, Jezireh, Mosul (Nineveh), Arbil (Arbela), and Kirkuk. There are two other great roads, or rather routes, connecting Asia Minor with Persia: the Erzeroum route, which leads, however, into what was rather Upper Media, debouching upon Tabriz and Teheran; and the Aleppo route, by far the most direct line, but which runs mainly through the Syrian and Arabian deserts,

cellent caravanserais; and throughout, it traverses an inhabited tract, and is free from danger. In Lydia and Phrygia there are twenty stations within a distance of 94½ parasangs. On leaving Phrygia the Halys has to be crossed; and here are gates through which you must needs pass ere you can traverse the stream. A strong force guards this post. When you have made the passage, and are come into Cappadocia, 28 stations and 104 parasangs bring you to the borders of Cilicia, where the road passes through two sets of gates, at each of which there is a guard posted. Leaving these behind, you go on through Cilicia, where you find three stations in a distance of 15½ parasangs. The boundary between Cilicia² and Armenia is the river Euphrates, which it is necessary to cross in boats. In Armenia the resting-places are 15 in number, and the distance is 56½ parasangs. There is one place where a guard is posted. Four large streams intersect this district,³ all of which have to be crossed by means of boats. The first of these is the Tigris; the second and the third have both of them the same name,⁴ though they are not only different rivers, but do not even run from the same place.⁵ For the one which I have called the first of the two has its source in Armenia, while the other flows afterwards out of the country of the Matieniana. The fourth of the streams is called the Gyndes, and this is the river which Cyrus dispersed by digging for it three hundred and sixty channels.⁶ Leaving Armenia and entering the Matienian country, you have four

---

and so must at all times have been very unsafe, on account of the Arab plunderers.

² This description gives Cilicia an extension towards the north, which no other writer allows to it. I have endeavoured to express this in the Map of the Satrapies which accompanies the present volume.

³ Armenia is here given an extraordinary extension to the south, and so made to include a large tract ordinarily reckoned either to Assyria or Media.

⁴ Undoubtedly the two Zabs, the Greater and the Lesser. These rivers, which gave the appellation of Adiabene to the region watered by them (Ammian. Marcell. xxiii. 6; Bochart, Sac. Geog. iv. 19. p. 243), seem to have retained their names unchanged from the earliest times to the present. The Greater Zab, at any rate, appears under that title in the Assyrian Inscriptions (passim); it is also, undoubtedly, the Zabatus of Xenophon (Anab. ii. v. 5, and iii. iii. 6), and the Diava or Diaba of Ammianus (l. s. c.). The Lesser Zab is a less famous stream; but its continuity of name appears from this passage, combined with the mention of it by Ammianus as the Adiava or Adiaba, and with the fact of its present appellation.

The word Zab, Diab, or Diav באב, according to Bochart (l. s. c.), signifies "a wolf" in Chaldee. Hence the Greater Zab is called Λύκος (Lycus) in Strabo, Ammianus, and Pliny, and Ἀσσύβης (by mistake) in Ptolemy (Geogr. vi. 1.).

⁵ What Herodotus here states is exactly true of the two Zabs. The Greater Zab has its source in Armenia between the lakes of Van and Urumiyeh—the Lesser rises in the Koordish mountains (his Matienian hills) at a distance of nearly two degrees to the S.S.E.

⁶ Vide supra, i. 189, note ², where the Gyndes is identified with the Diyaleh.

stations; these passed you find yourself in Cissia, where eleven stations and 42½ parasangs bring you to another navigable stream, the Choaspes, on the banks of which the city of Susa is built. Thus the entire number of the stations is raised to one hundred and eleven; and so many are in fact the resting-places that one finds between Sardis and Susa.

53. If then the royal road be measured aright, and the parasang equals, as it does, thirty furlongs,[1] the whole distance from Sardis to the palace of Memnon (as it is called), amounting thus to 450 parasangs, would be 13,500 furlongs.[2] Travelling then at the rate of 150 furlongs a day,[3] one will take exactly ninety days to perform the journey.

54. Thus when Aristagoras the Milesian told Cleomenes the Lacedæmonian that it was a three months'-journey from the sea up to the king, he said no more than the truth. The exact distance (if any one desires still greater accuracy) is somewhat more; for the journey from Ephesus to Sardis must be added to the foregoing account; and this will make the whole distance between the Greek Sea and Susa (or the city of Memnon, as it is called[4]) 14,040 furlongs; since Ephesus is distant from Sardis

---

[1] Supra, ii. 6. This was the ordinary estimate of the Greeks. (See Xen. Anab. ii. 2, § 6; Suidas in voc. Hosych. in voc., &c.) Strabo, however, tells us that it was not universally agreed upon, since there were some who considered the parasang to equal 40, and others 60 stades (xi. p. 754). The truth is, that the ancient parasang, like the modern farsakh, was originally a measure of time (an hour), not a measure of distance. In passing from the one meaning to the other, it came to mark a different length in different places, according to the nature of the country traversed. The modern farsakh varies also, but not so much as the parasang, if we can trust Strabo. It is estimated at from 3¼ to 4 miles, or from 30 to 35 stades.

[2] As usual, there is a discrepancy in the numbers. The stations, according to the previous small sums, are 81 instead of 111, and the parasangs or farsakhs, 328 instead of 450, as will be seen by reference to the subjoined table:—

Stations	Parasangs
In Lydia and Phrygia	20 .. 94½
In Cappadocia	28 .. 104
In Cilicia	3 .. 15½
In Armenia	15 .. 56½
In the Matienian country	4 (say) 16
In Cissia	11 .. 42½
Total	81 .. 328

The subsequent arguments of Herodotus are based upon his totals; we must conclude, therefore, that errors have crept into some of the smaller sums. The distance from Sardis to Susa by the Armenian route does not seem to be over-estimated at 13,500 stades (between 1500 and 1600 miles).

[3] Herodotus takes here the rate at which an army would be likely to move. Elsewhere (iv. 101) he reckons the journey of the ordinary pedestrian at 200 stades (about 23 miles). It appears, by the account which Xenophon has left of the expedition of Cyrus the younger (Anab. i.), that a somewhat longer day's march was usual. (The average is about 6 farsakhs or 180 stades.) But this rate, apparently, cannot be continued without resting the army, at intervals, for several days at a time. If the days during which the army of Cyrus rested be counted, the real rate of motion is reduced below the estimate of our author.

[4] The fable of Memnon is one of those in which it is difficult to discover any germs of truth. Memnon, the son of Tithonus and Eôs (Dawn), or Hêmera (Day), is, according to most accounts, an Ethiopian king. His father Tithonus, however, reigns at Susa, and he himself

540 furlongs." This would add three days to the three months' journey.

55. When Aristagoras left Sparta he hastened to Athens, which had got quit of its tyrants in the way that I will now describe. After the death of Hipparchus (the son of Pisistratus, and brother of the tyrant Hippias),³ who, in spite of the clear warning he had received concerning his fate in a dream, was slain by Harmodius and Aristogeiton (men both of the race of the Gephyraeans), the oppression of the Athenians continued by the space of four years;⁴ and they gained nothing, but were worse used than before.

56. Now the dream of Hipparchus was the following :—The night before the Panathenaic festival, he thought he saw in his sleep a tall and beautiful man, who stood over him, and read him the following riddle:—

"Bear thou unbearable woes with the all-bearing heart of a lion;
Never, be sure, shall wrong-doer escape the reward of wrong-doing."

---

leads a combined army of Susianians and Ethiopians to the assistance of his father's brother, Priam, king of Troy (cf. Strabo, xv. p. 1031; Pausan. x. xxxi. 2; Diod. Sic. ii. 72; iv. 75. We seem here to have nothing but the wildest imaginations of pure romancers.

Homer makes very slight and passing allusions to Memnon (Od. iv. 188; xi. 522). Hesiod calls him king of the Ethiopians (Theogr. 984). So Pindar (Nem. iii. 62, 63, Dissen.). This seems to have been the first form of the legend, from which all mention of Susa was omitted. The earliest author who is known to have connected Memnon with Susa is Aeschylus, who made his mother a Cissian woman (Strab. l. s. c.). It is clear, however, that by the time of Herodotus, the story that he built Susa, or his great palace, was generally accepted in Greece. Perhaps the adoption of this account may be regarded as indicating some knowledge of the ethnic connexion which really existed between Ethiopia and Susiana. (See vol. i. p. 396, and pp. 537, 538.)

³ Rennell (Geography of Western Asia, I. p. 290) says that this is "less than the direct distance," which he estimates at 45 geographical (or about 52 English) miles. But if we reckon the stade at its true length of 606 feet 9 inches (English), the distance given will be rather more than 62 miles (English), so that a distance of about 10 miles will be allowed for the deflections of the route.

³ It has been commonly supposed that there is an opposition between Herodotus and Thucydides with respect to the relative age of the two brothers, and to the fact involved in their relative ages, whether Hipparchus was king at the time of his assassination. But if the narrative of Herodotus be carefully examined, it will be found that he confirms, instead of opposing, the well-known view of Thucydides, that Hippias was the elder of the two. Not only is Hipparchus never called king, but here at his first introduction he is brought forward as "brother of the tyrant Hippias."

With respect to the fact, which is disputed by Larcher, I agree with Thirlwall, that "the authority of Thucydides is more convincing than his reasons" (Hist. of Greece, vol. ii. p. 65; cf. Thucyd. vi. 55). His authority, backed as it is by Herodotus, seems to me decisive. Plato (if it be he), the only early writer on the other side (Hipparch.), as a historical authority, is valueless. Clitodemus, who has been quoted against Thucydides by Meursius and others, in reality takes the same view (Frag. Hist. Gr., vol. i. p. 364). As for Heraclides Ponticus and Diodorus Siculus, on such a matter they are writers of no account.

⁴ From B.C. 514 to B.C. 510. Compare Thucyd. vi. 59; Plat. Hipparch. The fourth year was not quite complete (Clinton's F. H. ii. p. 18).

As soon as day dawned he sent and submitted his dream to the interpreters, after which he offered the averting sacrifices, and then went and led the procession in which he perished.[5]

57. The family of the Gephyraeans,[6] to which the murderers of Hipparchus belonged, according to their own account, came originally from Eretria. My inquiries, however, have made it clear to me that they are in reality Phoenicians, descendants of those who came with Cadmus[7] into the country now called Boeotia. Here they received for their portion the district of Tanagra, in which they afterwards dwelt. On their expulsion from this country by the Boeotians (which happened some time after that of the Cadmeians from the same parts by the Argives[8]) they took refuge at Athens. The Athenians received them among their citizens upon set terms, whereby they were excluded from a number of privileges which are not worth mentioning.

58. Now the Phoenicians who came with Cadmus, and to whom the Gephyraei belonged, introduced into Greece upon their arrival a great variety of arts, among the rest that of writing,[9] whereof the Greeks till then had, as I think, been ignorant. And originally they shaped their letters exactly like

---

[5] Full details of this whole transaction are given by Thucydides (vi. 54-58; compare Ar. Pol. v. 8 and 9). The time of the Panathenaic festival was chosen because the citizens might then appear in arms.

[6] Bochart (Geog. Sacr. l. xxi.) believes the Gephyraei to have got their name from the fact that they were settled at the bridge (γέφυρα) over the Cephissus, on the road from Athens to Eleusis. It seems to be certain that there was a village there called Gephyris, and a temple of Ceres, thence said to have been called Gephyraean Ceres (cf. Etym. Mag. ad voc. Γεφυρείς, and Strab. ix. p. 581). But it may be questioned whether the Gephyraeans did not rather bring their name with them into Attica. No ancient writer connects the Gephyraean family with the bridge, or with the village of Gephyris. Nor could the temple of Ceres near Gephyris have been (as Bochart supposes) their temple of Achaean Ceres (mentioned below, ch. 61); for that was in Athens. On the other hand it appears that Tanagra, the city from which the Gephyraeans came to Athens, was anciently called Gephyra, and its inhabitants generally Gephyraeans (Strab. ix.

p. 586; Steph. Byz. ad voc. Γέφυρα; Etym. Magn. ad eund.). The origin of the name was the bridge there over the Asôpus. Gephyraean Ceres meant Tanagraean Ceres, or Ceres whose worship was introduced into Attica from Tanagra. Etym. Magn. ad voc. 'Αχαιά; Steph. Byz. l. s. o.; and infra, ch. 61).

[7] On the reality of this immigration, see note [1] on Bk. ii. ch. 49, and cf. Bochart's Geog. Sac. (I. xvi.-xxi.).

[8] Herodotus alludes here to the legend of the Epigoni. Ten years after the first unsuccessful attack upon Thebes, the sons of the seven chiefs succeeded in taking the city and avenging their fathers (Apollod. III. vii. 2). This was shortly before the Trojan war (Hom. Il. iv. 405). The great invasion of the Boeotians was sixty years after that event (Thuc. L 12). It was this which caused the Gephyraeans to quit their country (vide supra, i. 146; iv. 147).

[9] Homer (Il. vi. 168) shows that in his time the Greeks wrote on folding wooden tablets. On the introduction of letters into Greece from Phoenicia, see end of Ch. v. in the Appendix to Book ii., and on Cadmus, n. on Bk. ii. ch. 44.—[G. W.]

all the other Phœnicians, but afterwards, in course of time, they changed by degrees their language, and together with it the form likewise of their characters.[1] Now the Greeks who dwelt about those parts at that time were chiefly the Ionians. The Phœnician letters were accordingly adopted by them, but with some variation in the shape of a few, and so they arrived at the present use, still calling the letters Phœnician,[2] as justice required, after the name of those who were the first to introduce them into Greece. Paper rolls also were called from of old "parchments" by the Ionians, because formerly when paper was scarce[3] they used, instead, the skins of sheep and goats— on which material many of the barbarians are even now wont to write.[4]

---

[1] That the Greeks derived their letters directly from the Phœnicians is probable on many grounds:—1. A glance at the table given in the Appendix to Bk. ii. (vol. ii. p. 268, App.) will show the close resemblance, almost amounting to identity, between the Greek alphabet (especially in its archaic form) and the Phœnician. It is evident that one is copied from the other. 2. The names of the letters, which are all significative in Semitic tongues of the objects which they were originally intended to represent, but have no meaning in Greek, prove that the Semites are the inventors, the Greeks the copyists. 3. The dropped letters of the early Greek alphabet prove the same. These are found, very distinctly, in the numerals, where they have the place which belongs to them in Phœnician and Hebrew. 4. The traditional late invention of those letters, which the Greeks possessed beyond the Phœnicians, is an additional argument. These points will receive illustration from the subjoined comparative table:—

ORIGINAL GREEK ALPHABET.	A	B	Γ	Δ	E	F	Z	H	Θ	I	K
	alpha	beta	gamma	delta	e (ψιλόν)	van (F)	zeta (ζ)	klieta	theta	iota	kappa
PHŒNICIAN NAME.	aleph	beth	gimel	daleth	he	vau	zain	kheth	theth	yod	koph
SIGNIFICATION.	bull	tent	camel	door	window	hook	lance	paling	serpent	hand	hollow of hand
NUMERICAL POWER IN GREEK.	1	2	3	4	5	6	7	8	9	10	20

ORIGINAL GREEK ALPHABET.	Λ	M	N	Ϡ	O	Π	Ϙ	P	Σ	T
	lambda	mu	nu	sigma	o (μικρόν)	pi	koppa	rho	sas	tau
PHŒNICIAN NAME.	lamed	mem	nun	samech	ain	peh	qoph	rhah	shin	tau
SIGNIFICATION.	prickly stick	water	fish	prop	eye	mouth	ax	head	tooth	bread
NUMERICAL POWER IN GREEK.	30	40	50	60	70	80	90	100	200	300

[2] This is strong evidence to the fact, that European Greeks got its alphabet direct from the Phœnicians. Otherwise, there is so great a similarity between the various alphabets of Western Asia and Southern Europe (the Lycian, Phrygian, Etruscan, Umbrian, &c.), that it would be difficult to prove more than their common origin from a single type, which might be one anterior to the Phœnician.

[3] That is, before the establishment of a regular commerce with Egypt, which was perhaps scarcely earlier than the reign of Amasis.

[4] This is a remarkable statement. Among the "barbarians" alluded to, we may assume the Persians to be

59. I myself saw Cadmeian characters[5] engraved upon some tripods in the temple of Apollo Ismenius[6] in Bœotian[7] Thebes, most of them shaped like the Ionian. One of the tripods has the inscription following:—

"Me did Amphitryon place, from the far Teleboans[8] coming."

---

included, on the authority of Ctesias, who declared that he drew his Persian history "from the royal parchments" (ἐκ τῶν βασιλικῶν διφθερῶν, ap. Diod. Sic. ii. 32). But we have (I believe) no distinct evidence of parchment being used at this early date by any other "barbarous" nation. Stone and clay seem to have been the common material in Assyria and Babylonia; wood, leather, and paper in Egypt; the bark of trees and linen in Italy; stone, wood, and metal among the Jews. Parchment seems never to have been much used, even by the Greeks, till the time of Eumenes II. (B.C. 197-159), to whom the invention was ascribed by Varro (Plin. H. N. xiii. 21).

[5] The old Greek letters, like the Phœnician, were written from right to left, and were nearer in shape to those of the parent alphabet. (See the table in p. 368, Cr. v. of the App. to Bk. ii., and n. ch. 30, Bk. ii.) They continued to be so written till a late time on vases; but this appears to have been then merely the imitation of an old fashion; for already, in the age of Psammetichus, the 7th century B.C., inscriptions were written from left to right, and the double letters Φ, Χ, Ψ, were introduced, as well as the germ of the long vowels, Η, Ω, a century before Simonides. The boustrophedon style succeeded to that from right to left, when the lines were written alternately one way and the other, like the ploughing of oxen—whence the name; and at last the method followed to the present day, from left to right, was adopted. And while the Phœnician method is common to all the Semitic nations, it is curious that the later Greek should have become the same as the Sanscrit method,—the Greek being of the Sanscrit, and not of the Semitic family of languages: see n. p. 267, in App. to Bk. ii. Of the age of Greek vases nothing is certain; so that they lead to no exact conclusion respecting the use of Greek letters, especially as the old form of them continued to be imitated in later times.

In Millingen's monuments (Ancient Unedited Monuments, plate 1) is a very ancient bas-relief, bearing some resemblance in the style of the letters to the inscription at Aboosimbel, but without any double letters, and rather more archaic in character, which he only considers somewhat anterior to the 69th Olympiad, B.C. 500; there is also a prize vase, from its inscription supposed to date before 582 B.C., of which the letters are very similar to those at Aboosimbel, though they are written from right to left. (Millingen, plate 1, Vases.) If the Psammetichus of Aboosimbel were the third, this date would agree very well with 582 B.C.; but he was probably the first (as stated in n. ch. 30, Bk. ii.). The inscription of Menecrates at Corfu is supposed to be about 600 B.C., written from right to left, with the aspirate and digamma, and old form of letters. The introduction of the double letters and long vowels was earlier in some places (as in Asia Minor) than in others. At first ε was used for η, and ο for ω (as ο was for ω in ancient Italy); ϙ was a hard K used in Corinth, Hector, and other names, and afterwards replaced by κ. It was the Latin Q. The aspirate H and the digamma F are both found in archaic inscriptions, the latter answering to the Latin f in many Etruscan names; the former a soft aspirate. The χ was a harder h, like the Arabic ﺡ, but not guttural like the ﺥ, which is proved by its modern Romaic pronunciation, and by the fact of the Copts being obliged to make a new letter ϧ for the guttural kh.—[G. W.]

[6] Cf. i. 52.
[7] Bœotian Thebes is here distinguished from Egyptian.
[8] Strabo identifies the Teleboans with the Taphians, who were among the most ancient inhabitants of Acarnania (vii. p. 466). He mentions the expedition of Amphitryon (x. 694, 673), which is likewise spoken of by Pherecydes (Frag. Hist. Gr. i. p. 77) and Apollodorus (ii. iv. 6, 7).

This would be about the age of Laïus, the son of Labdacus, the son of Polydorus, the son of Cadmus.*

60. Another of the tripods has this legend in the hexameter measure:—

"I to far-shooting Phœbus was offered by Scæus the boxer,
When he had won at the games—a wondrous beautiful offering."

This might be Scæus, the son of Hippocoön;[1] and the tripod, if dedicated by him, and not by another of the same name, would belong to the time of Œdipus, the son of Laïus.

61. The third tripod has also an inscription in hexameters, which runs thus:—

"King Laodamas gave this tripod to far-seeing Phœbus,
When he was set on the throne—a wondrous beautiful offering."

It was in the reign of this Laodamas, the son of Eteocles, that the Cadmeians were driven by the Argives out of their country,[2] and found a shelter with the Encheleans.[3] The Gephyræans at that time remained in the country, but afterwards they retired before the Bœotians,[4] and took refuge at Athens, where they have a number of temples for their separate use, which the other Athenians are not allowed to enter—among the rest, one of Achæan Ceres,[5] in whose honour they likewise celebrate special orgies.

62. Having thus related the dream which Hipparchus saw, and traced the descent of the Gephyræans, the family whereto

---

* It may be doubted whether this tripod belonged really to so early an age as Wolf's Prolegomena, p. iv.). The inscription, at any rate, must have been later, and can at best only have expressed the belief of the priests as to the person who dedicated the tripod. The same remark will apply to the two other inscriptions.

[1] Hippocoön was the brother of Tyndareus and Icarius. Assisted by his twelve sons, he drove his two brothers from Lacedæmon. Afterwards Hercules slew him and his sons, and restored Tyndareus. One of his sons was named Scæus (Apollod. III. x. 5).

[2] Vide supra, ch. 57, note 4. Laodamas succeeded his father Eteocles upon the throne of Thebes. According to the legend, he reigned ten years, and was slain by the Epigoni (Apollod. III. vii. 2).

[3] The Encheleans were an Illyrian tribe. They dwelt on the coast above Epidamnus (Scylax, Peripl. p. 19;

Steph. Byz. ad voc.; Hecatæus, Fr. 73). There was a legend that Cadmus assisted them against the other Illyrians (Apollod. III. v. 4). Hence perhaps it was thought likely that the Cadmeians would take refuge with them.

[4] Thucyd. I. 12; supra, ch. 57.

[5] Bochart believes that the Phœnicians introduced the worship of Ceres into Greece (Geog. Sac. I. xli.), and supposes the Gephyræans to have been the first by whom the worship was brought into Attica (ib. ch. xxi.). Certainly the Eleusinian mysteries appear to have been thoroughly Oriental in their character.

It is difficult to explain the epithet "Achæan" here. The grammarians say that it has no connexion with the well-known Hellenic tribe, but is formed either from ἄχος (grief) or ἠχώ (sound), because Ceres grieved for the loss of Proserpine, or because of the cymbals used in her worship (Etym. Mag. ad voc. 'Αχαιά).

his murderers belonged, I must proceed with the matter whereof I was intending before to speak; to wit, the way in which the Athenians got quit of their tyrants. Upon the death of Hipparchus, Hippias, who was king, grew harsh towards the Athenians;[4] and the Alcmæonidæ,[1] an Athenian family which had been banished by the Pisistratidæ,[2] joined the other exiles, and endeavoured to procure their own return, and to free Athens, by force. They seized and fortified Leipsydrium[3] above Pæonia,[4] and tried to gain their object by arms; but great disasters befell them,[5] and their purpose remained unaccomplished. They therefore resolved to shrink from no contrivance that might bring them success; and accordingly they contracted with the Amphictyons[6] to build the temple which now stands at Delphi, but which in those days did not exist.[7] Having done this, they proceeded, being men of great wealth and members of an ancient and distinguished family, to build the temple much more magnificently than the plan obliged them. Besides other improvements, instead of the coarse stone whereof by the contract the temple was to have been constructed, they made the facings of Parian marble.[8]

63. These same men, if we may believe the Athenians, during

their stay at Delphi persuaded the Pythoness by a bribe[5] to tell the Spartans, whenever any of them came to consult the oracle, either on their own private affairs or on the business of the state, that they must free Athens. So the Lacedæmonians, when they found no answer ever returned to them but this, sent at last Anchimolius, the son of Aster—a man of note among their citizens—at the head of an army against Athens, with orders to drive out the Pisistratidæ, albeit they were bound to them by the closest ties of friendship. For they esteemed the things of heaven more highly than the things of men. The troops went by sea and were conveyed in transports. Anchimolius brought them to an anchorage at Phalerum;[7] and there the men disembarked. But the Pisistratidæ, who had previous knowledge of their intentions, had sent to Thessaly, between which country and Athens there was an alliance,[8] with a request for aid. The Thessalians, in reply to their entreaties, sent them by a public vote 1000 horsemen,[9] under the command of their king, Cineas, who was a Coniæan.[1] When this help came, the Pisistratidæ laid their plan accordingly: they cleared the whole plain about Phalerum so as to make it fit for the

---

[5] The Delphic oracle is again bribed by Cleomenes, infra, vi. 66.

[7] Phalerum is the most ancient, as it is the most natural, harbour of Athens. It is nearer than Piræus to the city (Leake's Demi, § 9, p. 397), and the two rivers (Cephissus and Ilissus), between which Athens is placed, lead into it. The Piræus seems not to have been used as a port until the time of Pericles (Pausan. i. il. 3).

[8] As Bœotia is found generally on the Spartan, so Thessaly appears on the Athenian side. Mutual jealousy of Bœotia would appear to be the chief ground of the alliance. It was broken by the Persian invasion, renewed B.C. 461, when hostilities with Sparta threatened (Thuc. i. 102), infringed by the expedition of B.C. 453 (Thuc. i. 111), renewed partially before B.C. 431 (ibid. il. 22), and fully re-established in B.C. 423 (ibid. iv. 132).

[9] The Thessalians were still in that "early stage of society" mentioned by Arnold, "when the ruling order or class has fought on horseback, their subjects or dependents on foot" (Hist. of Rome, vol. i. p. 71). "The cavalry service under these circumstances has been cultivated, that of the infantry neglected." In Thessaly the bulk of the population were held in the condition of serfs (πενέσται)—the ruling class, however, was large and warlike. Hence we constantly hear of the excellence of the Thessalian horse, while it is seldom that we have any mention of their infantry. (Compare Herod. vii. 28, 29; Thucyd. i. 111; Ephor. Fr. 5; Pausan. x. i. 2; Polyb. iv. 8; Plut. Mor. p. 70, A.; Hipp. Maj. p. 284, A.) The country was favourable for pasturage; and Thessalian horses were of special excellency (vide infra, vii. 196, and note ad loc.).

[1] Wachsmuth proposes to read a "Gonnæan" (Γονναῖον), for a "Coniæan" (Κονιαῖον) here. And certainly there is no known town in Thessaly, from which the word "Coniæan" could be formed. It is impossible to understand, with Larcher, Coelum or Iconium, the modern Κόνιγεh, in Phrygia. I should incline, therefore, to adopt the emendation of Wachsmuth. Gonnus, or Gonal, is a well-known Thessalian town (Strab. ix. p. 638; Porphyr. Tyr. 8; Steph. Byz. ad voc.; Ptol. Geograph. iii. 13; Liv. xlii. 54). It lay north of the Peneus, a little above the commencement of the pass of Tempé in the modern valley of Derrli (Leake's Northern Greece, vol. iii. pp. 381, 382).

movements of cavalry, and then charged the enemy's camp with their horse, which fell with such fury upon the Lacedæmonians as to kill numbers, among the rest Anchimolius, the general, and to drive the remainder to their ships. Such was the fate of the first army sent from Lacedæmon, and the tomb of Anchimolius may be seen to this day in Attica; it is at Alopecæ[2] (Foxtown), near the temple of Hercules in Cynosargos.[3]

64. Afterwards, the Lacedæmonians despatched a larger force against Athens, which they put under the command of Cleomenes, son of Anaxandridas, one of their kings. These troops were not sent by sea, but marched by the mainland. When they were come into Attica, their first encounter was with the Thessalian horse, which they shortly put to flight, killing above forty men; the remainder made good their escape, and fled straight to Thessaly. Cleomenes proceeded to the city, and, with the aid of such of the Athenians as wished for freedom, besieged the tyrants, who had shut themselves up in the Pelasgic fortress.[4]

65. And now there had been small chance of the Pisistratidæ falling into the hands of the Spartans, who did not even design to sit down before the place,[5] which had moreover been well provisioned beforehand with stores both of meat and drink,—nay, it is likely that after a few days' blockade the Lacedæmonians would have quitted Attica altogether, and gone back to Sparta,—had not an event occurred most unlucky for the besieged, and most advantageous for the besiegers. The children of the Pisistratidæ were made prisoners, as they were being removed out of the country. By this calamity all their plans were deranged, and—as the ransom of their children—they consented to the demands of the Athenians, and agreed within five days' time to quit Attica.[6] Accordingly they soon afterwards

---

[2] It is curious to find that the Spartans had passed Athens, and penetrated to this place, which lay to the north-east of the city, at the distance of about a mile and a half (Æsch. Timarch. p. 119). We may suspect that Herodotus has ill-understood the Spartan plan of campaign. The site of Alopecæ is marked by the modern village of Ἀμπελόκηπο (Leake's Demi of Attica, p. 31).

[3] Vide infra, vi. 116, and note ad loc.

[4] That is, the Acropolis, which the Pelasgi were said to have fortified for the Athenians (see below, vi. 137).

According to Cleidemus, all that the Pelasgi did was to level the surface of the rock at the summit, and build a wall round the space so obtained (Frag. 22, ed. Didot.).

[5] Aware, apparently, of their inability to conduct sieges (vide infra, ix. 70). That the acropolis was not at this time very strong appears from the account of its siege by Xerxes (viii. 52, 53). It was afterwards fortified by Cimon (Plut. Vit. Cim. c. 13).

[6] All the chief points of this narrative are confirmed by Aristotle, who relates the contract of the Alcmæo-

left the country, and withdrew to Sigeum on the Scamander,¹ after reigning thirty-six years over the Athenians. By descent they were Pylians, of the family of the Neleids, to which Codrus and Melanthus likewise belonged, men who in former times from foreign settlers became kings of Athens. And hence it was that Hippocrates¹ came to think of calling his son Pisistratus: he named him after the Pisistratus who was a son of Nestor. Such then was the mode in which the Athenians got quit of their tyrants. What they did and suffered worthy of note from the time when they gained their freedom until the revolt of Ionia from King Darius, and the coming of Aristagoras to Athens with a request that the Athenians would lend the Ionians aid, I shall now proceed to relate.

66. The power of Athens had been great before; but, now that the tyrants were gone, it became greater than ever. The chief authority was lodged with two persons, Clisthenes, of the family of the Alcmæonids, who is said to have been the persuader of the Pythoness,² and Isagoras, the son of Tisander, who belonged to a noble house, but whose pedigree I am not able to trace further. Howbeit his kinsmen offer sacrifice to the Carian Jupiter.³ These two men strove together for the mastery; and Clisthenes, finding himself the weaker, called to his aid the common people.⁴ Hereupon, instead of the four

tribes[4] among which the Athenians had been divided hitherto, Clisthenes made ten tribes, and parcelled out the Athenians

ancient landed aristocracy: Clisthenes had taken his father's place at the head of the Parali, or wealthy middle class, who were attached to the timocratical constitution of Solon; while the Diacrii, or democrats, were without a leader, but had strength sufficient to turn the scale either way. Clisthenes, it seems, was not a democrat by choice, but from necessity. It was only when he found himself unable to contend successfully with Isagoras, that he had recourse to the democratical party. (Vide infra, ch. 69, note [1].)

[4] That is, the Geleontes or Teleontes, Hopletes, Ægicoreis, and Argadeis, the ancient hereditary tribes of Attica. Mr. Grote (Hist. of Greece, vol. iii. p. 53) denies that there is any sufficient ground for believing that a division into castes, such as the names of these tribes has been thought to indicate, ever prevailed in Attica. In this he opposes, among the ancients, Plato, Strabo, and Plutarch; among the moderns, almost all who have written upon the subject (C. F. Hermann, § 94; Thirlwall, vol. ii. p. 7; Boeckh, Corp. Inse. 3655; Illgen, p. 38-50; Schömann de Com. Ath. p. 351, &c.). It seems inconceivable that names, three out of four of which read so clearly Warriors (Hopletes), Goatherds (Ægicoreis), and Artisans (Argadeis), can have been given except to classes formed according to professions, or *least of the outset*. The difficulty and uncertainty that attaches to the fourth name, which appears under three forms—Geleontes, Gedeontes, and Teleontes—cannot invalidate the argument derived from the other three. Teleontes, which rests upon decent authority (Eurip. Ion, 1579; Pollux, viii. 109; Steph. Byz. ad voc. Αἰγικορεῖς), is certainly the form most easy of explanation, for this would be etymologically connected with τελέω, τέλος, τελετή, and would give the excellent sense of Priests or Consecrators (cf. Strabo, viii. p. 858). Geleontes, which has by far the greatest weight of authority, since it is the form of the Inscriptions as well as that of the best MSS. of Herodotus, may possibly only be a variant from this, according to the notice which we find in Hesychius, that γελέα was in use for τελέα (Hesych. ad voc. γελέα). The form Gedeontes has the least authority (Plutarch only), and may be safely set aside as having arisen from ill-written MSS., in which ΓΕΛΕΟΝΤΕΣ might easily be mistaken for ΓΕΔΕΟΝΤΕΣ.

It would seem therefore that at Athens in very early times there were four castes: 1. Priests; 2. Warriors; 3. Herdsmen; and 4. Mechanics. This may be considered as tolerably certain from the appellations themselves. It is also confirmed by several writers of fair name and note. The passages in Plato (Timæus, p. 24, A.; Critias, p. 110, C.), where ancient Athens is compared to Egypt in respect of its castes, are well known. They are the more valuable, because, so far as appears, the fact recorded is not based upon the etymology of the names of the tribes, or indeed connected consciously with the tribes at all. Plutarch's statement is distinct and positive (Vit. Solon. ch. 23); and the error in detail—the substitution of husbandmen for priests—arises from his having the false form γεδέοντες, for τελέοντες. Strabo also, who is a respectable authority, has no doubt of the four tribes having been castes. His account exactly accords with the view taken above; for it is of no importance that he uses the term husbandmen (γεωργοί) for goatherds (αἰγικορεῖς), to designate the caste which got its living from the soil.

If we admit the *fact* of the existence of castes in Attica in the earliest times, it becomes a matter of importance to inquire, whence did these castes come?—were they of home growth, or introduced from abroad? They have been regarded as favouring the notion of a special connexion of Athens with Egypt (Diodor. Sic. i. 28; Thirlwall, vol. ii. p. 67); and in Plato they certainly appear in this shape; but it is difficult to say whether this is the true account of them, or whether the fact is not, that the same spirit which prevailed in early times in Egypt and India, also independently sprang up in Greece. The nature of the special connexion, if any, between Egypt and Athens, is not agreed on. Plato gives no account of it; and Phanodemus and Callisthenes, the earliest writers who propounded a theory, derived Saïs from Athens (ap. Procl. Comment. in Plat. Tim. p. 30). The Egyptian colony to Attica seems to have been a late invention of the Egyptians themselves.

among them. He likewise changed the names of the tribes; for whereas they had till now been called after Geleon, Ægicores, Argades, and Hoples, the four sons of Ion,[4] Clisthenes set these names aside, and called his tribes after certain other heroes,[5] all of whom were native, except Ajax. Ajax was associated because, although a foreigner, he was a neighbour and an ally of Athens.[6]

67. My belief is that in acting thus he did but imitate his maternal grandfather, Clisthenes, king of Sicyon.[7] This king, when he was at war with Argos, put an end to the contests of the rhapsodists at Sicyon, because in the Homeric poems Argos and the Argives were so constantly the theme of song. He likewise conceived the wish to drive Adrastus, the son of Talaüs, out of his country,[8] seeing that he was an Argive hero. For Adrastus had a shrine at Sicyon, which yet stands in the market-place of the town. Clisthenes therefore went to Delphi, and asked the

oracle if he might expel Adrastus. To this the Pythoness is reported to have answered—"Adrastus is the Sicyonians' king, but thou art only a robber." So when the god would not grant his request, he went home and began to think how he might contrive to make Adrastus withdraw of his own accord. After a while he hit upon a plan which he thought would succeed. He sent envoys to Thebes in Bœotia, and informed the Thebans that he wished to bring Melanippus,[2] the son of Astacus, to Sicyon. The Thebans consenting, Clisthenes carried Melanippus back with him, assigned him a precinct within the government-house, and built him a shrine there in the safest and strongest part. The reason for his so doing (which I must not forbear to mention) was, because Melanippus was Adrastus' great enemy, having slain both his brother Mecistes and his son-in-law Tydeus.[3] Clisthenes, after assigning the precinct to Melanippus, took away from Adrastus the sacrifices and festivals wherewith he had till then been honoured, and transferred them to his adversary. Hitherto the Sicyonians had paid extraordinary honours to Adrastus, because the country had belonged to Polybus,[4] and Adrastus was Polybus' daughter's son;[5] whence it came to pass that Polybus, dying childless, left Adrastus his kingdom. Besides other ceremonies, it had been their wont to honour Adrastus with tragic choruses, which they assigned to him rather than Bacchus, on account of his calamities.[6] Clisthenes now gave the choruses to Bacchus, transferring to Melanippus the rest of the sacred rites.

68. Such were his doings in the matter of Adrastus. With respect to the Dorian tribes, not choosing the Sicyonians to have the same tribes as the Argives, he changed all the old names for new ones; and here he took special occasion to mock the Sicyonians, for he drew his new names from the words "pig," and "ass," adding thereto the usual tribe-endings; only in the case of his own tribe he did nothing of the sort, but gave them a name

---

[2] A statue of Melanippus is probably intended. See below, ch. 80.

[3] Melanippus, the son of Astacus, is mentioned among the defenders of Thebes by Pherecydes (Fr. 51), Apollodorus (III. vi. § 8), and Pausanias (IX. xviii. § 1). He is said to have lost his own life at the siege, being slain by Amphiaraus (Pherecyd. l. s. c.).

[4] Polybus was king of Corinth, and Sicyon was included in his dominions (Apollod. III. v. § 7).

[5] The Scholiast on Pindar (Nem. ix.) follows the same tradition. According to him Talaus married Lysimache, the daughter of Polybus, and their issue was Adrastus. Apollodorus gives a different account (I. ix. § 13).

[6] Besides the destruction of his army and friends in the first expedition against Thebes, Adrastus was said to have lost his son Ægialeus in the second (Hellanicus, Fr. 11; Apollod. III. vii. § 2).

drawn from his own kingly office. For he called his own tribe the Archelai, or Rulers, while the others he named Hyatæ, or Pig-folk, Oneatæ, or Ass-folk, and Chœreatæ, or Swine-folk.¹ The Sicyonians kept these names, not only during the reign of Clisthenes, but even after his death, by the space of sixty years: then, however, they took counsel together, and changed to the well-known names of Hyllæans, Pamphylians, and Dymanatæ,² taking at the same time, as a fourth name, the title of Ægialeans, from Ægialeus the son of Adrastus.³

69. Thus had Clisthenes the Sicyonian done."⁵⁰ The Athenian Clisthenes, who was grandson by the mother's side of the other, and had been named after him, resolved, from contempt (as I believe) of the Ionians,¹ that his tribes should not be the same as

---

¹ The dynasty of the Orthagoridæ, to which Clisthenes belonged, was not Dorian, but Achæan. Clisthenes aimed at depressing the Doric population, and elevating the Achæans—his own kinsfolk. His arrangement of the Sicyonian tribes may be thus compared with the older (and later) division—

Achæans	..	..	Archelaï	..	..	Ægialeis
			{Hyatæ.			Hylleis.
Dorians	..	..	{Oneatæ.	}		{Pamphylii.
			{Chœreatæ.}			Dymanatæ.

² That these were the three ancient tribes of the Dorians is now universally acknowledged. Müller (Dorians, vol. ii. pp. 76, 78, E. T.) has collected the principal testimonies. The most direct is that of Stephen of Byzantium (ad voc. Δυμᾶν): Δυμᾶν, φυλὸν Δωριέων· ἔστι δὲ τρεῖς, Ὑλλεῖς, καὶ Πάμφυλοι, καὶ Δυμᾶνες. (Compare also the words of the same writer, ad. voc. Ὑλλεῖς.) Homer (Il. ii. 668; Od. xix. 177, Hesiod (Frag. vii. ed. Göttling), Pindar (Pyth. i. 61), and Ephorus (Fr. 10), besides Herodotus, confirm the statement of Stephen. A multitude of inscriptions from the ruins of different Dorian towns lead to the same conclusion.

The names were traceable to Pamphylus and Dyman, the two actual sons, and Hyllus, the adopted son, of Ægimius, who was the traditional king of Doris at the time of the flight of the Heracleidæ.

³ Ægialeans was the ancient name of the primitive Ionians of this tract (vide infra, vii. 94; cf. Apollod. ii. L § 1, and Strabo, viii. p. 555). Pausanias conjectures, with reason, that the term was derived from the common word αἰγιαλός, "coast," and signified "the dwellers along the shore" (vii. L § 1). Compare the Attic τέμαλοι (supra, i. 59). It is not unfrequent to find a tribe or tribes of the aboriginal inhabitants alongside of the Hylleans, Dymanes, and Pamphyles, in a Dorian state. In Argos, and perhaps in Epidaurus, the Hyrnithians was such a tribe (Steph. Byz. ad voces Δυμᾶν et 'Υρνίθιον). In Corinth there appear to have been five such (Müller's Dorians, vol. ii. p. 58, E. T.).

⁵⁰ An interesting account is given by Nicolas of Damascus, of the mode in which Clisthenes obtained the throne. Clisthenes was the youngest of three brothers, and had therefore, in the natural course of things, little hope of the succession. Myron, however, his eldest brother, having been guilty of adultery with the wife of Isodemus the second brother, Clisthenes persuaded the latter to revenge himself by slaying the adulterer. He then represented to him that he could not reign alone, as it was impossible for him to offer the sacrifices; and was admitted as joint king on this account. Finally, he had Isodemus persuaded to go into voluntary exile for a year, in order to purge his pollution; and during his absence made himself sole king (Fr. 61).

¹ There can be no doubt that Clisthenes was actuated by a higher motive. He abolished the old tribes, not because they were Ionic, but because they were exclusive: his intention was to break down an old oligarchical distinction, and to admit the more readily to the franchise fresh classes of the free inhabitants. The old tribes were hereditary, and with their machinery of phratries and clans (γένη), tended to

theirs; and so followed the pattern set him by his namesake of Sicyon. Having brought entirely over to his own side the common people of Athens, whom he had before disdained,² he gave all the tribes new names, and made the number greater than formerly; instead of the four phylarchs he established ten;³ he likewise placed ten demes in each of the tribes;⁴ and he was, now that the common people took his part, very much more powerful than his adversaries.

70. Isagoras in his turn lost ground; and therefore, to counterplot his enemy, he called in Cleomenes the Lacedæmonian, who had already, at the time when he was besieging the Pisistratidæ, made a contract of friendship with him. A charge is even brought against Cleomenes that he was on terms of too great familiarity with Isagoras's wife. At this time the first thing that he did, was to send a herald and require that Clisthenes, and a large number of Athenians besides, whom he called "The Ac-

---

confine within very narrow limits the rights of Athenian citizenship. A free *plebs* had grown up outside the hereditary tribes at Athens, as it did at Rome, and by the same means, except that in Rome the element of forced, in Athens that of free, settlers preponderated. Clisthenes resolved to admit all free Athenians to the franchise, and therefore enrolled the entire free population in *local* tribes. It would have been almost impossible for him to have set up fresh hereditary tribes by the side of the ancient ones; for "a tie of faith and feeling" connected these together, which could not have been "conjured suddenly up as a bond of union between comparative strangers." Mr. Grote views these transactions in their true light (Hist. of Greece, vol. iv. pp. 169-175).

² So we were told before, that when Clisthenes "found himself the weaker, he called to his aid the common people" (ch. 66). On what grounds Mr. Grote supposes it "not unreasonable to give Clisthenes credit for a more forward generous movement than is implied in the literal account of Herodotus," does not appear. We may certainly do so; but then we reject the authority of the writer who is our only guide in the matter, and who, as a lover of democracy (vide infra, ch. 78), would not willingly have spoken evil of one who had done so much for it as Clisthenes. Are democrats alone of all mankind immaculate?

³ Vide supra, ch. 66. By Phylarchs, in this place, Herodotus probably means the ἐπιμελητοὶ τῶν φυλῶν, who took the place of the old φυλοβασιλεῖς, as the heads of the tribes. The Phylarchs proper were, under the Hipparchs, the chief officers of the cavalry (cf. Hermann's Pol. Ant. of Greece, §§ 111 and 132).

⁴ It seems to me quite impossible that this passage can bear the construction given it by Wachsmuth, and adopted by Mr. Grote (vol. iv. p. 176, note), or indeed admit of any sense but that assigned it in the text. Whether Herodotus was mistaken, as Hermann (l. s. c.) supposes, or whether, as Schömann contends (De Com. Att. p. 363), the number of demes was originally 100, and was afterwards increased to the 170 mentioned by Polemo (ap. Strab. ix. p. 375), is an open question. Perhaps scarcely sufficient ground has been shown for questioning the statement of Herodotus.

The fact is quite ascertained, that the demes of which each tribe was composed, were not locally contiguous (Leake's Demi of Attica, p. 13; Grote, vol. iv. p. 177). It is a happy conjecture of Mr. Grote's, that the object in view was the avoidance of those local feuds and jealousies of which we have a trace in the contentions of the Diacrii, the Pedieii, and the Parali (supra, ch. 66, note, and i. 59).

cursed," should leave Athens.⁸ This message he sent at the suggestion of Isagoras: for in the affair referred to, the blood-guiltiness lay on the Alcmæonidæ and their partisans, while he and his friends were quite clear of it.

71. The way in which "The Accursed" at Athens got their name, was the following. There was a certain Athenian called Cylon, a victor at the Olympic games,⁴ who aspired to the sovereignty, and aided by a number of his companions, who were of the same age with himself, made an attempt to seize the citadel.⁵ But the attack failed; and Cylon became a suppliant at the image.⁶ Hereupon the Heads of the Naucraries,⁷ who at

---

⁸ The same demand was made immediately before the breaking out of the Peloponnesian war (Thucyd. I. 126); when it was directed against Pericles, who was connected, through his mother, with the Alcmæonid family (infra, vi. 131).

⁴ Cylon gained the prize for the διαυ-λος, or double foot-race (Pausan. I. xxviii. 1).

⁵ Cylon's enterprise, and the circumstances which led to it, have been better stated by Bishop Thirlwall than by Mr. Grote. The latter does not appear to see any stir of the democratic element at Athens, until the time immediately preceding the legislation of Solon. But, as Dr. Thirlwall well remarks, the legislation of Draco, which tended to limit the authority of the nobles, cannot have proceeded from their own wish, but must have been extorted from them by the growing discontent of the people (vol. ii. p. 18). A popular stir, therefore, began before Draco's legislation—a demand for written laws, like that which at Rome led to the Decemvirate—Draco was appointed to satisfy this demand, but framed his laws in a manner "designed to overawe and repress the popular movement," which had led to his being set up as lawgiver. The insurrection of Cylon was the natural consequence of this attempt at repression; it was a democratic movement, at least it derived its chief strength from the discontent of the masses; and thus, although Cylon was a Eupatrid. Whether Cylon's views were selfish or not, we cannot say. He may have designed what Pisistratus afterwards accomplished, or he may have been really the Spurius Cassius, or Titus Manlius of Athens. His failure left the Athenians to groan

under the weight of a cruel oligarchy for at least eighteen more years (from B.C. 612 to B.C. 594. See on this subject, Hermann's Pol. Antiq. § 103, and the writers there quoted, Meier, Welcker, and Siebelis). It is remarkable that Cylon's statue was preserved in the Acropolis to the days of Pausanias (I. xxviii. § 1), a sign of the gratitude of the people.

⁶ The account in Thucydides (I. 126) is much fuller, and may itself be completed from Plutarch's Solon, c. 12. According to these writers, Cylon himself escaped. His adherents took refuge in the temple of Minerva Polias, and when induced, under promise of being spared, to surrender, fastened themselves with a rope to the statue of the goddess, and so descended into the town. On their way the rope broke, or was cut; and they were immediately set upon. Many fled for refuge to the sanctuary of the Furies, which happened to be near, but were slain at the altars. Megacles, who was chief archon at the time, directed the proceedings (Heracl. P. i. 4); and hence the guilt of the double sacrilege was considered to rest chiefly on him. During the rule of Solon, Epimenides was employed to devise an expiation of the crime; but the measures which he took (Diog. Laert. i. 110) failed to satisfy public opinion.

⁷ The Naucraries were divisions of the ancient tribes: in each tribe there were three Trittyes, and in each Trittys, four Naucraries. Thus the number of these last was 48. According to some writers, each Naucrary was bound to furnish a vessel to the navy; and this was the origin of the name (ναυκραρία ὡσανεὶ ἡ ναυκληρία καὶ ναῦν ἔχον, ἀφ᾽ ἧς ἴσως ὠνόμασται. Pollux, viii. 108).

that time bore rule in Athens, induced the fugitives to remove by a promise to spare their lives. Nevertheless they were all slain; and the blame was laid on the Alcmæonidæ. All this happened before the time of Pisistratus.

72. When the message of Cleomenes arrived, requiring Clisthenes and "The Accursed" to quit the city, Clisthenes departed of his own accord. Cleomenes, however, notwithstanding his departure, came to Athens, with a small band of followers; and on his arrival sent into banishment seven hundred Athenian families, which were pointed out to him by Isagoras. Succeeding here, he next endeavoured to dissolve the council,¹ and to put the government into the hands of three hundred of the partisans of that leader. But the council resisted, and refused to obey his orders; whereupon Cleomenes, Isagoras, and their followers took possession of the citadel. Here they were attacked by the rest of the Athenians, who took the side of the council, and were besieged for the space of two days: on the third day they accepted terms, being allowed—at least such of them as were Lacedæmonians—to quit the country. And so the word which came to Cleomenes received its fulfilment. For when he first went up into the citadel, meaning to seize it, just as he was entering the sanctuary of the goddess, in order to question her, the priestess arose from her throne, before he had passed the doors, and said—"Stranger from Lacedæmon, depart hence, and presume not to enter the holy place—it is not lawful for a Dorian to set foot there." But he answered, "Oh! woman, I am not a Dorian, but an Achæan."² Slighting this warning, Cleomenes made his attempt, and so he was forced to retire, together with his Lacedæmonians.³ The

---

This derivation, however, is rather plausible than probable; and the account of the word which connects it with πρύτανις, and makes the πρύτανεις (= πρυτάνεις), "a householder," is on all accounts to be preferred.

As Thucydides says that the nine archons at this time managed affairs, some writers (as Harpocration) have confounded the Heads (Prytaneis) of the Naucraries with the archons. It is better to suppose that they were the chief military officers, or that they formed a council or court which assisted the chief archons in the decision of criminal causes (Wachsmuth, i. p. 246; Thirlwall, ii. p. 27, note).

¹ The new council of 500, fifty from each local tribe, which Clisthenes had recently substituted for Solon's council of Four Hundred. For the constitution of this council, see the excellent account in the Dictionary of Antiquities pp. 155-159).

² The Heraclidæ were, according to the unanimous tradition, the old royal family of the Peloponnese, when it was yet Achæan. Expelled thence, they had found a refuge in Doris, and been adopted by the Dorians into their nation. Hence in the legend mentioned above 'note' on ch. 68, Hyllus is the adopted son of Ægimius (Ephor. Fr. 10).

³ The Athenians always cherished a lively recollection of this triumph over their great rivals. Even Aristophanes, notwithstanding his peace policy, cannot refrain from indulging in the recollection. According to him Cleomenes

were cast into prison by the Athenians, and condemned to die,—among them Timasitheus the Delphian, of whose prowess and courage I have great things which I could tell.[4]

73. So these men died in prison.[5] The Athenians directly afterwards recalled Clisthenes, and the seven hundred families which Cleomenes had driven out; and, further, they sent envoys to Sardis, to make an alliance with the Persians, for they knew that war would follow with Cleomenes and the Lacedæmonians. When the ambassadors reached Sardis and delivered their message, Artaphernes, son of Hystaspes, who was at that time governor of the place, inquired of them "who they were, and in what part of the world they dwelt,[6] that they wanted to become allies of the Persians?" The messengers told him; upon which he answered them shortly—that "if the Athenians chose to give earth and water to King Darius, he would conclude an alliance with them; but if not, they might go home again." After consulting together, the envoys, anxious to form the alliance, accepted the terms; but on their return to Athens, they fell into deep disgrace on account of their compliance.

74. Meanwhile Cleomenes, who considered himself to have been insulted by the Athenians both in word and deed, was drawing a force together from all parts of the Peloponnese, without informing any one of his object; which was to revenge himself on the Athenians, and to establish Isagoras, who had escaped with him from the citadel,[7] as despot of Athens. Accordingly, with a large army, he invaded the district of Eleusis,[8] while the Bœotians, who had concerted measures with him, took Œnoë[9] and

---

had to surrender his arms, and to retire in a very miserable plight — φμιφλς ἔχων τῶν τραξίων, σιπὸς, ἀυπίς, ἀπωρίλυτι, ἐξ ὅτου ἔλοντος (Lysist. 269).

[4] Pausanias, referring to this passage, relates that Timasitheus was a pancratiast, and had won three victories at the Pythian, and two at the Olympian games (vi. viii. § 4). His statue—the work of Agelades the Argive—was still standing at Olympia when Pausanias wrote (ibid. § 6).

[5] Mr. Blakesley (not. ad loc.) calls in question this severity, but (as it seems to me) without reason. The passage of the Scholiast on Aristophanes (Lysistr. 273), to which he refers, belongs to a later period of the history (see note [8] on ch. 74).

For a similar instance of the cowardly desertion of allies by the Spartans, see Thuc. iii. 109-111.

[6] Vide supra, l. 153, and infra, ch. 103.

[7] Disguised, probably as a Spartan.

[8] According to the Scholiast on Aristophanes (Lysist. l. s. c.), Cleomenes took Eleusis on his way back from Athens, and was aided in so doing by a number of Athenians. These traitors were punished by the confiscation of their goods, the razing of their houses to the ground (cf. Liv. ii. 41), their own condemnation to death, and the public inscription of their names as condemned felons on a brazen pillar in the Acropolis.

Eleusis was the key to Attica on the south, and its possession enabled Cleomenes to invade whenever he chose to do so.

[9] The Œnoë here spoken of, is undoubtedly that near Eleutheræ, which belonged to the tribe Hippothoöntis

Hysiæ,¹ two country-towns upon the frontier; and at the same time the Chalcideans,² on another side, plundered divers places in Attica. The Athenians, notwithstanding that danger threatened them from every quarter, put off all thought of the Bœotians and Chalcideans till a future time,³ and marched against the Peloponnesians, who were at Eleusis.⁴

75. As the two hosts were about to engage, first of all the Corinthians, bethinking themselves that they were perpetrating a wrong, changed their minds, and drew off from the main army. Then Demaratus, son of Ariston, who was himself king of Sparta and joint-leader of the expedition, and who till now had had no sort of quarrel with Cleomenes, followed their example. On account of this rupture between the kings, a law was passed at Sparta, forbidding both monarchs to go out together with the army, as had been the custom hitherto. The law also provided, that, as one of the kings was to be left behind, one of the Tyn-

---

(Harpocration ad voc.). Its vicinity to Hysiæ is sufficient to prove this; for the other (Enoe was close to Marathon, near the eastern coast, 30 miles from Hysiæ (Leake's Demes, p. 83). The exact site is not agreed upon. Kiepert places it at the modern Palæo-kastro, which is not more than six miles from Eleusis (Atlas von Hellas, Blatt X.). Leake regards it as identical with Gyfto-kastro, which lies close under Cithæron, in a narrow valley through which must have passed the road from Athens to Platæa. His arguments appear to me conclusive (Demi of Attica, pp. 129-131).

(Enoe was a place of great importance in the Peloponnesian war (Thucyd. ii. 18, 19, viii. 98). It was taken by the Bœotians, B.C. 411, but probably soon after recovered by Athens.

¹ Hysiæ lay on the north side of Cithæron, in the plain of the Asopus (infra, ix. 15, 25; Strab. ix. p. 387), between Platæa and Erythræ. It belonged naturally and commonly to Bœotia. Homer mentions it, under the name of Hyria, as a Bœotian city. (Il. ii. 496. Compare Strab. l. s. o.) It seems to have been recaptured by Athens soon after this (infra, vi. 108), but to have reverted to Thebes before the time of the Peloponnesian war (Thucyd. iii. 24; viii. 98.

² Chalcis had been one of the most important cities in Greece. It was said to have been originally a colony from Athens (Strab. x. p. 651), but shortly acquired complete independence. In a war which it had maintained with Eretria, some considerable time before this, all Greece had been concerned on the one side or the other (Thucyd. i. 15, and infra, ch. 99). Few cities sent out so many, or such distant colonies. The whole peninsula situated between the Thermaic and Strymonic gulfs, acquired the name of Chalcidice, from the number of Chalcidean settlements (Thucyd. passim). Scriphus, Peparethus, and others of the Cyclades, were Chalcidean (Scym. Chius, l. 583). In Italy and Sicily, the colonies of Chalcis exceeded in number those of any other state. Naxos, Leontini, Catana, Zancle, Rhegium, and Cuma, were among them (Thucyd. vi. 3, 4; Strab. vi. p. 376).

The government of Chalcis was aristocratic (vide infra, ch. 77). Its site is fixed by the fact that it lay exactly at the narrowest part of the channel of the Euripus (Strab. x. p. 648). It is therefore the modern Egripo, or Negropont.

³ Compare the very similar course taken by Pericles in the campaign of B.C. 445 (Thuc. i. 114).

⁴ The situation of Eleusis is very distinctly marked. It lay on the coast (Scylax, Peripl. p. 47; Strab. ix. p. 572), opposite Salamis, at the point where the western Cephissus reached the sea. (Pausan. i. xxxviii. § 7.) It thus commanded the coast route from the Peloponnese into Attica. (Leake's Demi, p. 144). The little village of Lepsina (Λέψινα) marks the site.

daridæ should also remain at home;[1] whereas hitherto both had accompanied the expeditions, as auxiliaries. So when the rest of the allies saw that the Lacedæmonian kings were not of one mind, and that the Corinthian troops had quitted their post, they likewise drew off and departed.

76. This was the fourth time that the Dorians had invaded Attica: twice they came as enemies, and twice they came to do good service to the Athenian people. Their first invasion took place at the period when they founded Megara,[2] and is rightly placed in the reign of Codrus at Athens;[3] the second and third occasions were when they came from Sparta to drive out the Pisistratidæ; the fourth was the present attack, when Cleomenes, at the head of a Peloponnesian army, entered at Eleusis. Thus the Dorians had now four times invaded Attica.[4]

77. So when the Spartan army had broken up from its quarters thus ingloriously, the Athenians, wishing to revenge themselves, marched first against the Chalcideans. The Bœotians, however, advancing to the aid of the latter as far as the Euripus, the Athenians thought it best to attack them first. A battle was fought accordingly; and the Athenians gained a very complete victory, killing a vast number of the enemy, and taking seven

---

[1] By the Tyndaridæ are meant the sacred images, or rather symbols, of Castor and Pollux, which several writers tell us were objects of religious worship at Sparta. Plutarch (De Amor. Frat. p. 478, A.) says they were two oblong blocks of wood, joined together by two transverse spars. It would seem that it was possible to separate them. Examples of the superstitious regard attached by the Greeks to images will be found, infra, chs. 80, 81, and viii. 64, 83. See also above, note [8] on ch. 87.

[2] According to Pausanias (i. xxxix. § 4), Megara existed before the Dorian invasion, and was at that time an Athenian town. According to Strabo (ix. p. 370, and Herodotus, it was first founded, after that invasion, by the Dorians. It is agreed on all hands that the tract of country, afterwards called the Megarid, at this time belonged to Athens, and was taken from them by the invaders.

[3] The story went, that many fugitives from the Peloponnese having fled before the Dorian conquerors, and found a refuge in Attica—among the rest Melanthus and his son Codrus, from Pylos (vide supra, ch. 65)—it was thought necessary to make an attack upon Attica from the Peloponnese (about B.C. 1050). Corinth and Messenia were the chief instigators of the invasion. It resulted in a battle, wherein Codrus devoted himself for his country, in consequence of an oracle which declared that Athens must either be conquered or lose her king. He disguised himself, and was slain, after which victory declared for the Athenians. The Peloponnesians, however, retained their hold upon the Megarid, which thenceforth became a Dorian state. (Pausan. l. s. c.; Strab. l. s. c.; Cic. Tusc. i. 48.)

[4] Some commentators, among them Mr. Blakesley (note 202 ad loc.), have made a difficulty here, which does not exist in the text. The four expeditions, two friendly and two hostile, are—
1. The expedition in the reign of Codrus—(hostile).
2. The attack of Anchimolius on the Pisistratidæ—(friendly).
3. The attack of Cleomenes on the same—(friendly).
4. The expedition under Cleomenes and Demaratus—(hostile).

The coming of Cleomenes to help Isagoras is simply not counted, since it was not a military expedition.

hundred of them alive. After this, on the very same day, they crossed into Euboea, and engaged the Chalcideans with the like success; whereupon they left four thousand settlers* upon the lands of the Hippobotæ,¹—which is the name the Chalcideans give to their rich men. All the Chalcidean prisoners whom they took were put in irons, and kept for a long time in close confinement, as likewise were the Bœotians, until the ransom asked for them was paid; and this the Athenians fixed at two minæ the man.² The chains wherewith they were fettered the Athenians suspended in their citadel; where they were still to be seen in my day, hanging against the wall scorched by the Median flames,³ opposite the chapel which faces the west.⁴ The Athenians made an offering of the tenth part of the ransom-money: and expended it on the brazen chariot drawn by four steeds,⁵ which stands on

* Literally, "allotment-holders" (κληροῦχοι). These allotment-holders are to be carefully distinguished from the ordinary colonists ἄποικοι, who went out to find themselves a home wherever they might be able to settle, and who retained but a very slight connexion with the mother-country. The cleruchs were a military garrison planted in a conquered territory, the best portions of which were given to them. They continued Athenian subjects, and retained their full rights as Athenian citizens, occupying a position closely analogous to that of the Roman coloni in the earlier times. Cf. Boeckh's Economy of Athens, vol. ii. p. 176, E. T.; and Hermann's Pol. Ant. § 117.) This is the first known instance of Athenian cleruchs: afterwards they became very numerous. (Plutarch, Pericl. c. ii. 34; Thucyd. iii. 50; Boeckh's Corp. Ins. i. pp. 150, 297, &c.)

These cleruchs are again mentioned by name, infra, vi. 100, and alluded to, viii. 1, and ix. 28. Mr. Grote supposes the lands they occupied to have been situated "in the fertile plain of Lelantum, between Chalcis and Eretria." (Vol. iv. p. 226.) This is a very probable conjecture.

¹ The Chalcidean Hippobotæ, or "horse-keepers," were a wealthy aristocracy (Strab. x. pp. 651, 652), and correspond to the knights (ἱππεῖς) of most Grecian states, and the "equites," or "celeres," of the Romans. In early times wealth is measured by the ability to maintain a horse, or horses. Compare εἰσὶ τεθριπποτρόφοι (infra, vi. 35).

² From this passage and another (vi. 79) it has been concluded that the ordinary ransom among the Greeks was of this amount. (Wesseling and Ruhr, ad loc.) But, on the principle of "exceptio probat regulam," it may rather be gathered from this passage that the rate of two minæ was unusual, and from the other, that it was only a received rate among the Peloponnesians. A passage of Aristotle (Ethics, v. 7, § 1) makes it clear that the ordinary ransom, at least in his day, was one mina.

³ Infra, viii. 53.

⁴ It is conjectured that this chapel was the temple of Tellus Curotrophus and Ceres Chloë, mentioned by Pausanias (I. xxii. § 3) as opposite the western face of the acropolis (Bähr, ad loc.). Or again, that it was the temple of Victory without wings (Larcher, ad loc.), which seems to have intervened between that of Tellus and Ceres, and the western wall. (See Colonel Leake's plan at the end of his 'Demi of Attica,' vol. i. pl. 2.) But I should rather understand a chapel within than one without the acropolis; and by "facing the west" I should understand "looking westward," and not "facing the western wall of the acropolis." The chapel intended probably occupied the site of the later Pandroseum, which abutted towards the west on the temple of Minerva Pollas. The fetters most likely hung on the northern or Pelasgic wall.

⁵ Pausanias saw this in the same place. Καὶ ἅρμα κεῖται χαλκοῦν, he says, ἀπὸ Βοιωτῶν δεκάτη, καὶ Χαλκιδέων τῶν ἐν Εὐβοίᾳ. (I. xxviii. § 2.)

the left hand immediately that one enters the gateway¹ of the citadel. The inscription runs as follows:—

"When Chalcis and Bœotia dared her might,
Athens subdued their pride in valorous fight;
Gave bonds for insults; and, the ransom paid,
From the full tenths these steeds for Pallas made."

78. Thus did the Athenians increase in strength. And it is plain enough, not from this instance only, but from many everywhere, that freedom is an excellent thing; since even the Athenians, who, while they continued under the rule of tyrants, were not a whit more valiant than any of their neighbours, no sooner shook off the yoke than they became decidedly the first of all. These things show that, while undergoing oppression, they let themselves be beaten, since then they worked for a master; but so soon as they got their freedom, each man was eager to do the best he could for himself. So fared it now with the Athenians.

79. Meanwhile the Thebans, who longed to be revenged on the Athenians, had sent to the oracle, and been told by the Pythoness that of their own strength they would be unable to accomplish their wish: "they must lay the matter," she said, "before the many-voiced, and ask the aid of those nearest them." The messengers, therefore, on their return, called a meeting, and laid the answer of the oracle before the people, who no sooner heard the advice to "ask the aid of those nearest them" than they exclaimed,—"What! are not they who dwell the nearest to us the men of Tanagra, of Coronæa, and Thespiæ?" Yet these men always fight on our side,' and have aided us with a good

---

¹ For a full description of this gateway, the great *Propylæa*, the most magnificent of the works of Pericles, see Leake's *Demi of Attica* (vol. I. pp. 315-318; compare Wordsworth's *Greece*, p. 192, and the article PROPYLÆA, in Smith's Dict. of Antiq. p. 961); It filled up the whole western end of the acropolis, and through it was the only entrance into the fortified enclosure. The cost of the construction was 2012 talents (nearly half a million of our money), and the time which it took in building five years (Harpocrat. ad voc.). The feelings with which it was regarded by the Athenians may be gathered from Aristophanes (Eq. 1226-1428). Epaminondas is said to have threatened that he would carry the whole building to Thebes, to adorn the Cadmeia there. (Æsch. de F. Leg. p. 278, Reiske.)

² A question has been raised, why these three cities should have been singled out, since, at any rate, Coronæa is not one of the nearest neighbours of Thebes. The answer would seem to be, that they are named from combining importance with nearness of locality. The Erythræans, Haliartians, &c., who lay nearer to Thebes, were too weak to deserve mention in such a connexion.

³ Here we may discern the hegemony of Thebes over the other cities of Bœotia, of which there are traces throughout Herodotus, but which only appears plainly in Thucydides (iv. 91). On what the hegemony rested is not very clear. Thebes herself claimed to have *founded* the other cities of Bœotia (Thuc. iii. 61), but probably without any sufficient grounds. The original confederacy is thought to have contained *fourteen* cities (Hermann's Pol. Ant. § 179); but in the Peloponnesian war there seem to

heart all through the war. Of what use is it to ask them? But maybe this is not the true meaning of the oracle."

80. As they were thus discoursing one with another, a certain man, informed of the debate, cried out,—"Methinks that I understand what course the oracle would recommend to us. Asôpus, they say, had two daughters, Thêbé and Egina.[2] The god means that, as these two were sisters, we ought to ask the Eginetans to lend us aid." As no one was able to hit on any better explanation, the Thebans forthwith sent messengers to Egina, and, according to the advice of the oracle, asked their aid, as the people "nearest to them." In answer to this petition the Eginetans said, that they would give them the Æacidæ[1] for helpers.

81. The Thebans now, relying on the assistance of the Æacidæ, ventured to renew the war; but they met with so rough a reception, that they resolved to send to the Eginetans again, returning the Æacidæ, and beseeching them to send some men instead. The Eginetans, who were at that time a most flourishing people,[2] elated with their greatness, and at the same time calling to mind their ancient feud with Athens,[3] agreed to lend

---

have been only ten. The following are sufficiently ascertained: Thebes, Tanagra, Coronæa, Thespiæ, Orchomenus, Haliartus, Copæ, Lebadea, Anthedon, and Plataea. The other four are thought to have been Chæronæa, Chalia, Oropus, and Eleutheræ. (Cf. Clinton, F. H. vol. ii. pp. 486-487, where the list is given correctly, with one exception, viz. the substitution of the district Parasopia for the town Chalia. For this town cf. Steph. Byz. ad voc., and Marm. Oxon. 29, 1. p. 67.)

[2] So **Pindar** (Isth. vii. 15-18, ed. Dissen.)—

Διὸς δ' ἐν ἀντιθέοισιν θρόνοις πραόσσατα
Λίγινα γειτόνων θατρων προσέρρει,
πατρος οὕνεκα διδύμας γένεντι θυγατρας Ασωπίδων, κ. τ. λ.

And compare the allusions in Nem. iii. 3-5, and iv. 19-22. Egina is constantly found as the daughter of Asôpus, Thebé less often. (Cf. Pherecyd. Frag. 78; Apollod. i. ix. 3; iii. xii. 6; Schol. ap. Pind. Nem. iv. 21; Schol. ap. Callimach. Hymn. in Del. 78.) A good understanding seems in fact to have existed between Bœotia and Egina from very early times: the ground of it was a common jealousy of Athens.

[1] The superstitious value attached by the Greeks to the images of the Æacidæ (Peleus and Telamon) appears again

before the battle of Salamis, when these same images were expressly sent for, and the battle was not fought till they arrived (viii. 64, and 83). It is noticeable that Herodotus, with his usual devout faith, identifies the images with the Gods themselves. (Cf. Grote, iv. p. 229, and supra, ch. 75, note [5].)

[2] Eusebius (Chron. Can. 1. xxxvi.) gives the Eginetans the empire of the sea (θαλασσοκρατία) for the ten years immediately preceding the invasion of Xerxes, i. e. from B.C. 490 to B.C. 480. Herodotus apparently would extend the term and make it begin earlier. So far back as the reign of Cambyses they had made a naval expedition to Crete, defeated the Samian settlers at Cydonia (supra, iii. 59), and founded a colony there (Strab. viii. p. 545); and it was probably their naval power and commercial enterprise (supra, iv. 152) which had made them obnoxious to the Samians at a far earlier period (iii. 59). They appear to have been the most enterprising of the Dorians, and in their general character, "oligarchical, wealthy, commercial, and powerful at sea, were more analogous to Corinth than to any other Dorian state." (Grote iv. p. 229; see also Müller's Eginetans for the full early history of this people.)

[3] Related in the next chapter.

the Thebans aid, and forthwith went to war with the Athenians, without even giving them notice by a herald.⁴ The attention of these latter being engaged by the struggle with the Bœotians, the Eginetans in their ships of war made descents upon Attica, plundered Phalerum,⁵ and ravaged a vast number of the townships upon the sea-board, whereby the Athenians suffered very grievous damage.

82. The ancient feud between the Eginetans and Athenians arose out of the following circumstances. Once upon a time the land of Epidaurus would bear no crops; and the Epidaurians sent to consult the oracle of Delphi concerning their affliction. The answer bade them set up the images of Damia and Auxesia,⁶ and promised them better fortune when that should be done. "Shall the images be made of bronze or stone?" the Epidaurians asked; but the Pythoness replied, "Of neither: but let them be made of the garden olive."⁷ Then the Epidaurians sent to Athens and asked leave to cut olive wood in Attica, believing the Athenian olives to be the holiest; or, according to others, because there were no olives at that time anywhere else in all the world but at Athens.⁸ The Athenians answered that they would give them

---

⁴ "Exemptio probat regulam." In Greece, as at Rome (Liv. i. 32), and in modern Europe, war was, by the rules of international law, preceded by a declaration. (Instances occur, Thucyd. ii. 12; v. 41, &c.; cf. Wachsmuth, vol. I. p. 138.)

⁵ The port of Athens at the time. (Vide supra, ch. 83, note ⁷.)

⁶ Damia and Auxesia are undoubtedly Ceres and Proserpine, the "great goddesses," whose most celebrated shrine was at Eleusis. The well-known passage of Pausanias, where reference is made to these chapters in Herodotus, leaves no doubt upon this point (II. xxx. 5, ἵδρυνταί σφισι κατὰ τὰ αὐτὰ, καί ἁ δη καὶ Ἐλευσῖνι θέαν νομίζουσι). What the exact origin of the names may be, is not quite so easy to determine. Auxesia seems clearly to be the Goddess of Increase (αὔξησις), that is, the goddess who blesses the land with increase, which was the office of Proserpine when coupled with Ceres. (Pausan. viii. lill. 3.) Damia has been thought to be Demia, the *people's* goddess (Bähr, ad loc.), or again, Damia, the charioteer (Welcker, Zeitschrift für Geschicht. d. Kunst, I. p. 130); but it appears rather to be Δᾶ-μαῖα, "Earth-mother," and so equivalent to Demeter,

the ordinary Greek name of Ceres. (Cf. Macrob. Saturn. i. xii. p. 245.) The name was in after-times transferred to Rome, where Ceres was known as "Damia," and her priestess as "Damiatrix." (Festus, sub voc. *Damium*.)

⁷ Statues in wood (ξόανα) preceded those in stone and bronze. The material suited a ruder state of the arts. (See Dict. of Antiq. ad voc. "Statuary.")

⁸ This is, of course, not true, for the olive had been cultivated in the east from a very remote antiquity. (Deuteronom. vi. 11; viii. 8, &c.) It is, however, very likely that the olive may have been introduced into Attica from Asia, before it was known to the rest of Greece. Pausanias calls the tree in the Pandroseum (see the next note, "the most ancient in the world" (i. xxx. § 2), and one of those in the Academy the second oldest. The olive was at all times regarded as the special pride of Attica, where (according to Sophocles) it grew spontaneously, and attained a greater size (ὃ τᾷδε θάλλει μέγιστα χώρᾳ, Œd. Col. 700) than elsewhere. A vase of oil from the sacred olives of Academus was the prize given to victors at the Panathenaic games (Aristot. Fr. 266; comp. Pind. Nem. x. 61 et seqq.).

leave, but on condition of their bringing offerings year by year to Minerva Polias and to Erechtheus.⁵ The Epidaurians agreed, and having obtained what they wanted, made the images of olive wood, and set them up in their own country. Henceforth their land bore its crops; and they duly paid the Athenians what had been agreed upon.

83. Anciently, and even down to the time when this took place, the Eginetans were in all things subject to the Epidaurians,¹ and had to cross over to Epidaurus for the trial of all suits in which they were engaged one with another.² After this, however, the Eginetans built themselves ships, and, growing proud, revolted from the Epidaurians. Having thus come to be at enmity with them, the Eginetans, who were masters of the sea, ravaged Epidaurus, and even carried off these very images of Damia and Auxesia, which they set up in their own country, in the interior, at a place called Œa,³ about twenty furlongs from their city. This done, they fixed a worship for the images, which consisted in part of sacrifices, in part of female satiric choruses;⁴ while at the same time they appointed certain men to furnish the choruses, ten for each goddess. These choruses did not abuse men, but only the women of the country. Holy orgies of a similar kind were in use also among the Epidaurians, and likewise another sort of holy orgies, whereof it is not lawful to speak.

---

⁵ By "Minerva Polias" we are to understand the Minerva who presided over the city (πόλις). Her temple in later times was a portion of the building known to the Athenians by the general name of Erechtheium, which stood on the north side of the acropolis, nearly opposite the spot afterwards occupied by the Parthenon, and was traditionally regarded as founded by Erechtheus, the tutelar hero of Attica, and as the place of his burial. This building contained, towards the west, the Pandroseium, or temple of Pandrosus; towards the east, divided only by a party-wall, the temple of Minerva Polias. In the former, most probably in the southern projection, supported by the Caryatides, was the sacred olive (infra, viii. 55). In the latter was an altar to Erechtheus, who was identified with Neptune at Athens. (See Col. Leake's very judicious remarks in his 'Athens and Demi of Attica,' vol. I. pp. 318–345, and Appendix, § 17.)

¹ Egina had been colonised from Epidaurus, infra, viii. 46; Pausan. ii. xxix.

5), but seems to have been less independent than most colonies. (Hermann, Pol. Ant. § 73.)

² Compare the case of the Athenian subject-allies. (Xen. de Rep. Ath. i. 16-18.)

³ No sufficient materials exist for fixing the situation of Œa, which is not mentioned by any other writer. It was probably where Niepert places it, near the centre of the island, on the site of the modern Egina. (Chandler, vol. ii. ch. iv. p. 18.) Lähr is certainly wrong in supposing it to have been near the temple of Minerva, at the north-eastern corner of the island; for that is more than double the proper distance from the capital (45 stades instead of 20).

⁴ Compare the similar customs at the Eleusinian festival, which gave rise to the peculiar meaning of the words τεφυρίζειν, γεφυριστής, and to the expression ἔσπερ ἐξ ἁμάξης. (See Bentley upon Phalaris, p. 180.) There too we hear that the women "abused one another" (ἀλλήλους ἀλλήλαις. Suid. In τὰ ἐξ ἁμαξῶν.)

84. After the robbery of the images the Epidaurians ceased to make the stipulated payments to the Athenians, wherefore the Athenians sent to Epidaurus to remonstrate. But the Epidaurians proved to them that they were not guilty of any wrong:—"While the images continued in their country," they said, "they had duly paid the offerings according to the agreement; now that the images had been taken from them, they were no longer under any obligation to pay: the Athenians should make their demand of the Eginetans, in whose possession the figures now were." Upon this the Athenians sent to Egina, and demanded the images back; but the Eginetans answered that the Athenians had nothing whatever to do with them.

85. After this the Athenians relate that they sent a trireme to Egina with certain citizens on board, and that these men, who bore commission from the state, landed in Egina, and sought to take the images away, considering them to be their own, inasmuch as they were made of their wood. And first they endeavoured to wrench them from their pedestals, and so carry them off; but failing herein, they in the next place tied ropes to them, and set to work to try if they could haul them down. In the midst of their hauling suddenly there was a thunderclap, and with the thunderclap an earthquake; and the crew of the trireme were forthwith seized with madness, and, like enemies, began to kill one another; until at last there was but one left, who returned alone to Phalerum.*

86. Such is the account given by the Athenians. The Eginetans deny that there was only a single vessel:—"Had there been only one," they say, "or no more than a few, they would easily have repulsed the attack, even if they had had no fleet at all; but the Athenians came against them with a large number of ships, wherefore they gave way, and did not hazard a battle." They do not however explain clearly whether it was from a conviction of their own inferiority at sea that they yielded, or whether it was for the purpose of doing that which in fact they did. Their account is that the Athenians, disembarking from their ships, when they found that no resistance was offered, made for the statues, and failing to wrench them from their pedestals, tied ropes to them and began to haul. Then, they say,—and some people will perhaps believe them, though I for my part do not,—

---

* Similar stories are frequent in Pausanias, (See l. xviii. 2; iii. xvi. 6; vii. xix. 3, &c.) Compare also the tale in Athenaeus (xv. xii. p. 672 B., and the story of the preservation of Delphi (infra, viii. 37).

the two statues, as they were being dragged and hauled, fell down both upon their knees; in which attitude they still remain.[6] Such, according to them, was the conduct of the Athenians; they meanwhile, having learnt beforehand what was intended, had prevailed on the Argives to hold themselves in readiness; and the Athenians accordingly were but just landed on their coasts when the Argives came to their aid. Secretly and silently they crossed over from Epidaurus, and, before the Athenians were aware, cut off their retreat to their ships, and fell upon them; and the thunder came exactly at that moment, and the earthquake with it.

87. The Argives and the Eginetans both agree in giving this account; and the Athenians themselves acknowledge that but one of their men returned alive to Attica. According to the Argives, he escaped from the battle in which the rest of the Athenian troops were destroyed by them.[7] According to the Athenians, it was the god who destroyed their troops; and even this one man did not escape, for he perished in the following manner. When he came back to Athens, bringing word of the calamity, the wives of those who had been sent out on the expedition took it sorely to heart, that he alone should have survived the slaughter of all the rest;—they therefore crowded round the man, and struck him with the brooches by which their dresses were fastened—each, as she struck, asking him, where he had left her husband. And the man died in this way. The Athenians thought the deed of the women more horrible even than the fate of the troops; as however they did not know how else to punish them, they changed their dress and compelled them to wear the costume of the Ionians. Till this time the Athenian women had worn a Dorian dress, shaped nearly like that which prevails at Corinth. Henceforth they were made to wear the linen tunic, which does not require brooches.[8]

---

[6] The statues were still shown in the days of Pausanias, who says he saw them 'π. xxx. 5, οἶδα τε τὰ ἀγάλματα, καί σφισι σφάσιν). He does not, however, mention their attitude, which was very unusual.

[7] Doris of Samos (the pupil of Theophrastus) preferred the Argive account. He considered the war to have originated in the naval aggressions of Egina upon Athens. His habitual carelessness has made him call the Argives Spartans. (Cf. Fragm. Hist. Gr. ii. pp. 481 and 488.)

[8] The large horseshoe brooch with which ladies in our times occasionally fasten their shawls, closely resembles the ancient περόνη, which was not a buckle, but "a brooch, consisting of a pin, and a curved portion, furnished with a hook." The Dorian tunic was of woollen; it had no sleeves, and was fastened over both the shoulders by brooches. It was scanty and short, sometimes scarcely reaching the knee. The Ionic tunic was of linen; it had short loose sleeves, as we see in statues of the Muses, and so did not need

88. In very truth, however, this dress is not originally Ionian, but Carian;[2] for anciently the Greek women all wore the costume which is now called the Dorian. It is said further that the Argives and Eginetans made it a custom, on this same account, for their women to wear brooches half as large again as formerly, and to offer brooches rather than anything else in the temple of these goddesses. They also forbade the bringing of anything Attic into the temple, were it even a jar of earthenware,[3] and made a law that none but native drinking vessels should be used there in time to come.[4] From this early age to my own day the Argive and Eginetan women have always continued to wear their brooches larger than formerly, through hatred of the Athenians.

89. Such then was the origin of the feud which existed between the Eginetans and the Athenians. Hence, when the Thebans made their application for succour, the Eginetans, calling to mind the matter of images, gladly lent their aid to the Bœotians. They ravaged all the sea-coast of Attica; and the Athenians were about to attack them in return, when they were stopped by the oracle of Delphi, which bade them wait till thirty years had passed from the time that the Eginetans did the wrong, and in the thirty-first year, having first set apart a precinct for Æacus, then to begin the war.[5] "So should they succeed to their wish," the oracle said; "but if they went to war at once, though they would still conquer the island in the end, yet they must go through much suffering and much exertion before taking it." On receiving this warning the Athenians set apart a precinct for

---

brooches; it was a long and full dress hiding the form, and reaching down generally to the feet. (Cf. Dict. of Ant., Articles *Peplu*, and *Tunica*.)

The poets frequently represented the *peplos* as made use of to blind persons. (Cf. Soph. Œd. Tyr. 1269; Eurip. Hec. 1153; Phœn. 60, &c.) Duris said (l. s. c.) that the Athenian women on this occasion first blinded the man, and then slew him (ἑντόρλωσαν, εἶτα ἀνέστειναν).

[2] This is another proof of the close connexion of the Carian and Greek races. (Vide supra, vol. i. pp. 548, 549.)

[3] The pottery of Athens was the most celebrated in ancient Greece. One whole quarter of the city was called Cerameicus, or "The Potteries." Earthenware was exhibited at the Panathenaic festival; and earthen vases were often prizes at the games. Athens, from her superior skill in the art of pottery, was sometimes represented as its inventor. (Plin. H. N. vii. 57.)

[4] This law perhaps amounted to a prohibition of the Attic pottery, and was really for the protection of native industry, though it may have been professedly a war measure, like a blockade or an embargo. Ancient protectionists, like modern ones, sought to exclude superior manufactures, sometimes by a high duty, sometimes by absolute prohibition.

[5] Did the Delphian priests foresee the probability of a Persian invasion, and wish to prevent the two great maritime powers from wasting each other's strength? Or was it only their wish to protect a Dorian state?

Æacus—the same which still remains dedicated to him in their market-place⁴—but they could not bear with any patience of waiting thirty years, after they had suffered such grievous wrong at the hands of the Eginetans.

90. Accordingly they were making ready to take their revenge when a fresh stir on the part of the Lacedæmonians hindered their projects. These last had become aware of the truth—how that the Alcmæonidæ had practised on the Pythoness, and the Pythoness had schemed against themselves, and against the Pisistratidæ; and the discovery was a double grief to them, for while they had driven their own sworn friends into exile, they found that they had not gained thereby a particle of good will from Athens. They were also moved by certain prophecies, which declared that many dire calamities should befall them at the hands of the Athenians. Of these in times past they had been ignorant; but now they had become acquainted with them by means of Cleomenes, who had brought them with him to Sparta, having found them in the Athenian citadel, where they had been left by the Pisistratidæ when they were driven from Athens: they were in the temple,⁵ and Cleomenes having discovered them, carried them off.

91. So when the Lacedæmonians obtained possession of the prophecies, and saw that the Athenians were growing in strength, and had no mind to acknowledge any subjection to their control, it occurred to them that, if the people of Attica were free, they would be likely to be as powerful as themselves, but if they were oppressed by a tyranny, they would be weak and submissive. Under this feeling they sent and recalled Hippias, the son of Pisistratus, from Sigeum upon the Hellespont, where the Pisistratidæ had taken shelter.⁶ Hippias came at their bidding, and the Spartans on his arrival summoned deputies from all their other allies,⁷ and thus addressed the assembly:—

"Friends and brothers in arms, we are free to confess that we did lately a thing which was not right. Misled by counterfeit

---

⁴ This would be the ancient ἀγορά, between the Acropolis and the Areopagus, where the statues of Harmodius and Aristogiton stood (Leake's Athens, p. 215); not the new one, which was north of the city, towards the church of Μεγάλη Παναγία.

⁵ The temple of Minerva Polias (vide supra, chs. 72 and 82.

⁶ Vide supra, ch. 65.

⁷ This was, so far as we know, the commencement of what afterwards became the regular practice — the established system on which Sparta treated her allies. Mr. Grote has some good remarks on the importance of the occasion (vol. iv. pp. 251, 252). The dispersion of the allies at the time of the last expedition (supra, ch. 75) had made the consultation necessary.

oracles, we drove from their country those who were our sworn and true friends, and who had, moreover, engaged to keep Athens in dependance upon us; and we delivered the government into the hands of an unthankful people—a people who no sooner got their freedom by our means, and grew in power, than they turned us and our king, with every token of insult, out of their city. Since then they have gone on continually raising their thoughts higher, as their neighbours of Bœotia and Chalcis have already discovered to their cost, and as others too will presently discover if they shall offend them. Having thus erred, we will endeavour now, with your help, to remedy the evils we have caused, and to obtain vengeance on the Athenians. For this cause we have sent for Hippias to come here, and have summoned you likewise from your several states, that we may all now with heart and hand unite to restore him to Athens, and thereby give him back that which we took from him formerly."

92. (§ 1.) Such was the address of the Spartans. The greater number of the allies listened without being persuaded. None however broke silence, but Sosicles the Corinthian, who exclaimed—

"Surely the heaven will soon be below, and the earth above, and men will henceforth live in the sea, and fish take their place upon the dry land, since you, Lacedæmonians, propose to put down free governments in the cities of Greece, and to set up tyrannies in their room.² There is nothing in the whole world so unjust, nothing so bloody, as a tyranny. If, however, it seems to you a desirable thing to have the cities under despotic rule, begin by putting a tyrant over yourselves, and then establish despots in the other states. While you continue yourselves, as you have always been, unacquainted with tyranny, and take such excellent care that Sparta may not suffer from it, to act as you are now doing is to treat your allies unworthily. If you knew what tyranny was as well as ourselves, you would be better advised than you now are in regard to it. (§ 2.) The government at Corinth was once an oligarchy—a single race, called Bacchiadæ, who intermarried only among themselves,³ held the

---

² Hermann remarks (Pol. Ant. § 32), that "it was chiefly by overthrowing the tyrants in the cities of Greece, that Sparta obtained her superiority over her neighbours;" and undoubtedly both Thucydides (l. 18, and Herodotus bear witness to the fact of her having pursued this policy. But it is difficult to collect many instances unless we regard the list in Plutarch (de Malign. Herod. ch. 21) as authentic. The expedition to put down the tyranny of Polycrates is the best attested case, and certainly proves that they would make great efforts with this object (supra, iii. 44-56).

³ Compare the case of the Roman patricians (Niebuhr's R. H. vol. ii. p. 280, &c.).

management of affairs.[1] Now it happened that, Amphion, one of these, had a daughter, named Labda,[2] who was lame, and whom therefore none of the Bacchiadæ would consent to marry; so she was taken to wife by Aëtion, son of Echecrates, a man of the township of Petra, who was, however, by descent of the race of the Lapithæ,[3] and of the house of Cæneus. Aëtion, as he had no child, either by this wife or by any other, went to Delphi to consult the oracle concerning the matter. Scarcely had he entered the temple when the Pythoness saluted him in these words—

'No one honours thee now, Aëtion, worthy of honour;—
Labda shall soon be a mother—her offspring a rock, that will one day
Fall on the kingly race, and right the city of Corinth.'

By some chance this address of the oracle to Aëtion came to the ears of the Bacchiadæ, who till then had been unable to perceive the meaning of another earlier prophecy which likewise bore upon Corinth, and pointed to the same event as Aëtion's prediction. It was the following:—

'When mid the rocks[4] an eagle shall bear a carnivorous lion,
Mighty and fierce, he shall loosen the limbs of many beneath them—
Brood ye well upon this, all ye Corinthian people,
Ye who dwell by fair Peirênê, and beetling Corinth.'[5]

(§ 3.) The Bacchiadæ had possessed this oracle for some time; but they were quite at a loss to know what it meant until they

---

[1] The tradition said, that after the Dorian conquest of Corinth (ab. B.C. 1040), the descendants of Aletes, the Heraclid conqueror, reigned for ten generations, when the monarchy was changed into an oligarchy by a process somewhat like that which may be traced at Athens, annual magistrates (Prytaneis) being substituted for monarchs, but the magistracy being confined to the royal family. About half-way in the list of kings, which is given by Eusebius (Chron. Can. 1. ch. xxxiv.), Syncellus (p. 179) and others, occurs the name of Bacchis, from whom the royal family is considered to have derived its appellation of Bacchidæ, or Bacchiadæ. (Heracl. Pont. v.; Pausan. II. iv. §§ 3, 4; Diod. Sic. ap. Sync. l. s. s.) The whole history, previous to the annual Prytaneis, must be considered as in the highest degree uncertain. Mr. Clinton, however, adopts it as authentic into his chronology. (Tables, Ol 9, 1, and vol. I. p. 129, note *.)

[2] Labda, according to the Etymologicum Magnum (ad voc. βλαισός), is the same as Lambda, and is a nickname given to indicate lameness (perhaps because the two legs of the old Greek lambda are of unequal length—Λ—this, at least, seems a better reason than that given in the Etym.—ὁ τοὺς πόδας ἐπὶ τὰ ἴσα διεστραμμένος).

[3] The mythic antagonists of Hercules (Apollod. II. vii. 7), whose king Cæneus is mentioned by Homer (Il. I. 264; Schol. ad loc.).

[4] There is a double pun here. Aëtion's name is glanced at in the word αἰετός (eagle), the place of his abode, Petra, in the expression ἐν πέτρῃσι (among the rocks).

[5] The fountain of Peirênê is described by Pausanias (II. III. 3); it was on the low ground, at the base of the Acro-Corinthus. The name, however, was sometimes applied to a spring of water in the citadel, which was supposed to communicate with the lower source (Ib. v. I.). Perhaps in this place the inhabitants of the lower town are indicated by the former, those of the upper by the latter part of the hexameter.

heard the response given to Aëtion; then however they at once perceived its meaning, since the two agreed so well together. Nevertheless, though the bearing of the first prophecy was now clear to them, they remained quiet, being minded to put to death the child which Aëtion was expecting. As soon, therefore, as his wife was delivered, they sent ten of their number to the township where Aëtion lived, with orders to make away with the baby. So the men came to Petra, and went into Aëtion's house, and there asked if they might see the child; and Labda, who knew nothing of their purpose, but thought their inquiries arose from a kindly feeling towards her husband, brought the child, and laid him in the arms of one of them. Now they had agreed by the way that whoever first got hold of the child should dash it against the ground. It happened, however, by a providential chance, that the babe, just as Labda put him into the man's arms, smiled in his face. The man saw the smile, and was touched with pity, so that he could not kill it; he therefore passed it on to his next neighbour, who gave it to a third; and so it went through all the ten without any one choosing to be the murderer. The mother received her child back; and the men went out of the house, and stood near the door, and there blamed and reproached one another; chiefly however accusing the man who had first had the child in his arms, because he had not done as had been agreed upon. At last, after much time had been thus spent, they resolved to go into the house again and all take part in the murder. (§ 4.) But it was fated that evil should come upon Corinth from the progeny of Aëtion; and so it chanced that Labda, as she stood near the door, heard all that the men said to one another, and fearful of their changing their mind, and returning to destroy her baby, she carried him off and hid him in what seemed to her the most unlikely place to be suspected, viz., a 'cypsel' or corn-bin.[e] She knew that if they came back to look for the child, they would search all her house; and so indeed they did, but not finding the child after looking everywhere, they thought it best to go away, and declare to those by whom they had been sent that they had done their bidding.[f] And thus they reported on their return home. (§ 5.) Aëtion's son grew up,

---

[e] Pausanias saw a corn-bin, said to have been that wherein Cypselus was hidden, in the temple of Juno at Olympia (v. xvii. § 2). It was of cedar, beautifully carved, and inlaid with gold and ivory. Perhaps the story grew up in part out of this offering, in part out of the name, Cypselus.

[f] Nicolas of Damascus makes the men repent of their errand, warn Aëtion, and then quit the country (Fr. 58).

and, in remembrance of the danger from which he had escaped, was named Cypselus, after the corn-bin. When he reached to man's estate, he went to Delphi, and on consulting the oracle, received a response which was two-sided. It was the following:—

'See there comes to my dwelling a man much favour'd of fortune,
Cypselus, son of Aëtion, and king of the glorious Corinth,—
He and his children too, but not his children's children.'

Such was the oracle; and Cypselus put so much faith in it that he forthwith made his attempt, and thereby became master of Corinth. Having thus got the tyranny, he showed himself a harsh ruler—many of the Corinthians he drove into banishment, many he deprived of their fortunes, and a still greater number of their lives. (§ 6.) His reign lasted thirty years, and was prosperous to its close; insomuch that he left the government to Periander, his son. This prince at the beginning of his reign was of a milder temper than his father; but after he corresponded by means of messengers with Thrasybulus, tyrant of Miletus, he became even more sanguinary. On one occasion he sent a herald to ask Thrasybulus what mode of government it was safest

---

[footnotes]

Yet Psammetichus, the grandson of Cypselus, mounted the throne. (Arist. Pol. v. 12.) He reigned however only three years, and then the tyranny was put down by Sparta (Plut. de Malig. Her. 21), or by a revolution (Nic. Damasc. Frag. 60): so that he could not be called properly "much favoured of fortune" (ὄλβιος).

A long account is given by Nicolas of Damascus, of the mode in which Cypselus established his power. According to this narrative, it was chiefly in the office of Polemarch, that he found means to ingratiate himself with the people. It was a part of the Polemarch's duty to exact legal fines, and former polemarchs had kept the condemned in prison until they were paid; but Cypselus would imprison no one. Sometimes he took security, sometimes he himself became security, and he always remitted the portion of the fine which belonged to him. Having thus made himself popular, he proceeded to extremities, slew Patroclides, the reigning Bacchiad, and was at once chosen king by the Corinthians Fr. 58).

In the "Economics" ascribed to Aristotle, there is a story (ch. ii.) that Cypselus had vowed the whole property of the Corinthians to Jupiter, if he obtained sovereign power; and that he acquitted himself of his vow by imposing a 10 per cent. property tax for ten years. But the authority of the Economics is very weak.

This account of the characters of Cypselus and Periander is not, perhaps, altogether at variance with the narrative of Aristotle. Aristotle (l. s. c.) informs us that Cypselus (like Pisistratus) was a leader of the popular party (δημαγωγός), and that his acceptability to the people enabled him to dispense with a body-guard; but that Periander was of a tyrannical disposition (τυραννικός). We may understand him to speak of Periander in his later years, and to give us one side of the character of Cypselus, to which Herodotus furnishes the other. Like the Pisistratids, the tyrants of Corinth were studiously mild towards the middle and lower classes (supra, ch. 62); but like them also (infra, vi. 39), they had to keep down the aristocracy by severe measures. Three Sosicles would naturally regard as atrocities, and would perhaps a little exaggerate. Nicolas says that Cypselus banished the Bacchiads, and confiscated their properties (l. s. c.).

to set up in order to rule with honour. Thrasybulus led the messenger without the city, and took him into a field of corn, through which he began to walk, while he asked him again and again concerning his coming from Corinth, ever as he went breaking off and throwing away all such ears of corn as over-topped the rest. In this way he went through the whole field, and destroyed all the best and richest part of the crop; then, without a word, he sent the messenger back. On the return of the man to Corinth, Periander was eager to know what Thrasybulus had counselled, but the messenger reported that he had said nothing; and he wondered that Periander had sent him to so strange a man, who seemed to have lost his senses, since he did nothing but destroy his own property. And upon this he told how Thrasybulus had behaved at the interview.[3] (§ 7.) Periander, perceiving what the action meant, and knowing that Thrasybulus advised the destruction of all the leading citizens, treated his subjects from this time forward with the very greatest cruelty. Where Cypselus had spared any, and had neither put them to death nor banished them, Periander completed what his father had left unfinished.[4] One day he stripped all the women of

---

[3] According to Aristotle (Pol. III. 8, p. 98, ed. Tauch.) it was Thrasybulus who sought, and Periander who gave this advice. The tale was transferred by some of the early annalists into Roman history. See Livy I. 54, where the annalist has compounded his story from this narrative and the history of Zopyrus. (Comp. Niebuhr's Rom. Hist. I. p. 503, E. T.) That Periander and Thrasybulus were really on very intimate terms, appears from l. 20.

[4] The cruel tyranny of Periander is agreed on by all writers. There is some difference of detail. He set up a body-guard of 300 men, made severe sumptuary laws, kept the citizens poor by means of fines and confiscations, shed abundant blood, and was frequently guilty of the grossest outrages. His private relations, which throw a light on the remainder of the chapter, have been already narrated (supra, III. 50-53). He was engaged in frequent wars; and the power of Corinth was never so great as in his day. (Compare Eph. Frag. 106; Ar. Pol. v. 12; Heraclid. Pont. v.; Nic. Damasc. Frag. 59; Diog. Laert. Vit. Periandr.) The following scheme of the Cypselid family may be gathered from Nicolaüs Damascenus. He differs from Herodotus in telling of Nicolas what the elder historian relates of Lycophron.

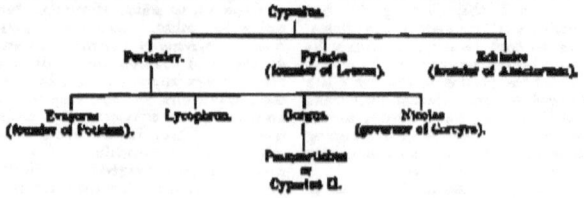

Strabo adds another member of the family—Tolgus, the founder of Ambracia—whom he calls a son of Cypselus (vii. p. 471). According to Aristotle

Corinth stark naked, for the sake of his own wife Melissa. He had sent messengers into Thesprotia to consult the oracle of the dead upon the Acheron° concerning a pledge which had been given into his charge by a stranger, and Melissa appeared, but refused to speak or tell where the pledge was,—'she was chill,' she said, 'having no clothes; the garments buried with her were of no manner of use, since they had not been burnt. And this should be her token to Periander, that what she said was true—the oven was cold when he baked his loaves in it.' When this message was brought him, Periander knew the token;° wherefore he straightway made proclamation, that all the wives of the Corinthians should go forth to the temple of Juno.° So the women apparelled themselves in their bravest, and went forth, as if to a festival. Then, with the help of his guards, whom he had placed for the purpose, he stripped them one and all, making no difference between the free women and the slaves; and, taking their clothes to a pit, he called on the name of Melissa, and burnt the whole heap.° This done, he sent a second time to the oracle; and Melissa's ghost told him where he would find the stranger's pledge. Such, O Lacedæmonians! is tyranny, and such are the deeds which spring from it. We Corinthians marvelled greatly when we first knew of your having sent for Hippias; and now it surprises us still more to hear you speak as you do. We adjure you, by the common gods of Greece, plant not despots in her cities. If however you are determined, if you persist, against all justice, in seeking to restore Hippias,—know, at least, that the Corinthians will not approve your conduct."

93. When Sosicles, the deputy from Corinth, had thus spoken, Hippias replied, and, invoking the same gods, he said,—"Of a surety the Corinthians will, beyond all others, regret the Pisistratidæ, when the fated days come for them to be distressed by the Athenians." Hippias spoke thus because he knew the prophecies[*] better than any man living. But the rest of the allies, who till Sosicles spoke had remained quiet, when they heard him utter his thoughts thus boldly, all together broke silence, and declared themselves of the same mind; and withal, they conjured the Lacedæmonians "not to revolutionise a Grecian city." And in this way the enterprise came to nought.

94. Hippias hereupon withdrew; and Amyntas the Macedonian offered him the city of Anthemûs,[1] while the Thessalians were willing to give him Iolcôs:[2] but he would accept neither the one nor the other, preferring to go back to Sigêum,[3] which city Pisistratus had taken by force of arms from the Mytilenæans. Pisistratus, when he became master of the place, established there as tyrant, his own natural son, Hegesistratus, whose mother was an Argive woman. But this prince was not allowed to enjoy peaceably what his father had made over to him; for during very many years there had been war between the Athenians of Sigêum and the Mytilenæans of the city called Achilleum.[4]

---

[*] Prophecies forged probably after the affairs of Epidamnus and Potidæa (Thucyd. i. 24–65), or at least after the battles in the Megarid (ib. 105–106). The bitter hostility of Corinth to Athens in the Peloponnesian war (ib. l. 119; v. 25, 27, 32, 48) contrasts remarkably with the friendly spirit here exhibited. It had its origin, first, in commercial jealousy, and secondly in the soreness engendered by the conduct of Athens on the above-mentioned occasions.

[1] Anthemus was a city of some note, on the borders of Macedonia, above Chalcidicê. It is difficult to fix with certainty its exact site. (See Leake's Travels in Northern Greece, iii. p. 450.) Stephen and Pliny (iv. 10) both mention it as a city; but Thucydides applies the name to a district (ii. 99, 100).

[2] Iolcos, the port from which the Argonauts were said to have sailed, was a place of still greater note than Anthemus. It lay at the bottom of the Pagasæan gulf (Scylax, Peripl. p. 60) in the district called Magnesia. All the geographers mention it (Ptol. p. 92; Strab. ix. p. 632; Plin. H. N. iv. 9, &c.). Its modern name is Volo (Leake's N. G. iv. p. 380).

[3] Supra, ch. 65.

[4] Achilleum, so called because it contained the tumulus of Achilles (Strab. xiii. p. 859), was within a very short distance of the town of Sigêum, on the promontory of the same name (Strab. l. s. c.; Steph. Byz. ad voc.; Plin. H. N. v. 30). See the plan of the country around Troy (infra, vii. 43). According to Demetrius, Achilleum was an ἀττείχισμα, or fort built near Sigêum by the Mytilenæans, for the purpose of vexing and harassing Sigêum, in the hope of ultimately recovering it. It appears that Mytilênê had, at an early date, made herself mistress of the Troad (Strab. xiii. p. 869).' Athens, about B.C. 620, sent out a colony under Phrynon, an Olympic victor (Strab. l. s. c.; Euseb. i. xxxvi.), to occupy Sigêum, a town already built by the Mytilenæans.

They of Mytilênê insisted on having the place restored to them: but the Athenians refused, since they argued that the Æolians had no better claim to the Trojan territory than themselves, or than any of the other Greeks who helped Menelaüs on occasion of the rape of Helen.

95. War accordingly continued, with many and various incidents, whereof the following was one. In a battle which was gained by the Athenians, the poet Alcæus took to flight, and saved himself, but lost his arms, which fell into the hands of the conquerors. They hung them up in the temple of Minerva at Sigêum;[3] and Alcæus made a poem, describing his misadventure to his friend Melanippus, and sent it to him at Mytilênê.[4] The Mytilenæans and Athenians were reconciled by Periander, the son of Cypselus, who was chosen by both parties as arbiter—he decided that they should each retain that of which they were at the time possessed; and Sigêum passed in this way under the dominion of Athens.

96. On the return of Hippias to Asia from Lacedæmon, he moved heaven and earth[1] to set Artaphernes against the Athenians, and did all that lay in his power to bring Athens into subjection to himself and Darius. So when the Athenians learnt what he was about, they sent envoys to Sardis, and exhorted the Persians not to lend an ear to the Athenian exiles. Artaphernes told them in reply, "that if they wished to remain safe, they must receive back Hippias." The Athenians, when this answer was reported to them, determined not to consent,

---

Phrynon took the place, and established himself in it; but a war followed of many years' duration between the Mytilenæans and the new colony, Achilléum being fortified by the former as a place from which to make their attacks. According to one account (Timæus, Fr. 49), Periander at this time assisted the Mytilenæans, and helped to fortify Achilléum by means of stones brought from Troy. Pittacus commanded on the side of the Mytilenæans; and it was in the course of this war that Alcæus lost his shield. Phrynon, B.C. 606 (Euseb.), challenged Pittacus to a single combat; the challenge was accepted, and Pittacus was victorious by means of the arts practised in later times by the *retiarius*. After this Periander was called in to arbitrate, and assigned Sigêum to Athens (Strab. l. s. c.; Diog. Laert. l. 74; Polyæn. l. 25; Plutarch.

H. p. 858; Suidas ad voc. Πιτταλδς, &c.). It would seem that the Mytilenæans must have afterwards recovered Sigêum, which was taken from them a second time by Pisistratus, probably about B.C. 535. This occasioned a renewal of the war.

[4] This temple is mentioned in the famous Sigean inscription, belonging to the reign of Antiochus Soter (Chishull's Inscr. Asiat. p. 52, § 35).

[5] Strabo seems to have quoted the first line of this poem, but the passage is hopelessly corrupt (xiii. p. 864). Compare with the fact of Alcæus writing on such a subject, the well-known ode of Horace (ii. 7).

[1] Literally "he moved everything"— an expression, the strength of which can only be given by some such idiom as that used in the text.

and therefore made up their minds to be at open enmity with the Persians.

97. The Athenians had come to this decision, and were already in bad odour with the Persians, when Aristagoras the Milesian, dismissed from Sparta by Cleomenes the Lacedæmonian, arrived at Athens. He knew that, after Sparta, Athens was the most powerful of the Grecian states.⁸ Accordingly he appeared before the people, and, as he had done at Sparta,⁹ spoke to them of the good things which there were in Asia, and of the Persian mode of fight—how they used neither shield nor spear, and were very easy to conquer. All this he urged, and reminded them also, that Miletus was a colony from Athens,¹⁰ and therefore ought to receive their succour, since they were so powerful—and in the earnestness of his entreaties, he cared little what he promised—till, at the last, he prevailed and won them over. It seems indeed to be easier to deceive a multitude than one man—for Aristagoras, though he failed to impose on Cleomenes the Lacedæmonian, succeeded with the Athenians, who were thirty thousand.¹ Won by his persuasions, they voted that twenty ships should be sent to the aid of the Ionians, under the

---

⁸ Compare I. 56.
⁹ Supra, ch. 49.
¹⁰ Supra, l. 147, and infra, ix. 97. The colonies, notwithstanding their political independence, counted on the aid of the mother city in time of need (see Thucyd. L 24).

¹ It has been generally supposed that this number is an exaggeration (Dahlmann's Life of Herod, p. 42, E. T.; Bœckh's Econ. of Athens, I. p. 48, E. T., &c.). Certainly in later times the actual number seems scarcely ever to have much exceeded twenty thousand. It was 19,000 in the year B.C. 444 (Plutarch, Pericl. c. 37; Philochor. ap. Schol. Arist. Vesp. 716), when Psammetichus sent the Athenians a present of corn, and 21,000 in B.C. 317, when Demetrius Phalereus made his census (Athenæus, vi. p. 272, B.). Aristophanes, in B.C. 422 (Vesp. 716), Plato, about B.C. 350 (Critias, p. 113, ed. Tauch.), and Demosthenes, in B.C. 331 (Aristog. L p. 785), make the same estimate, which is confirmed by the account given in Thucydides (II. 13) of the military force of Athens at the commencement of the Peloponnesian war. Still this estimate of Herodotus may be true for the period to which he refers. Clisthenes, it must be remembered, had recently admitted all the foreign inhabitants (ξένοι μέτοικοι) and enfranchised slaves of the same rank (δοῦλοι μέτοικοι) into the number of citizens; and them in after-times usually amounted to 10,000 (Athen. l. s. c.). No such general enfranchisement ever took place afterwards; and it is quite possible that the number of the citizens may have fallen, between B.C. 500 and B.C. 444, from thirty to twenty thousand. The vast number of colonists and cleruchs sent out from Athens during this interval would fully account for such a diminution. Ten thousand Athenians and allies were sent to Amphipolis in B.C. 465; 500 Athenians colonised Naxos a year earlier; 1000 went to the Chersonese between that date and B.C. 465; 250 went to Andros and 1000 to Chalcidicé about the same time; 500 to Sinope, some years afterwards; and a colony (number unknown) to Eubœa in B.C. 445. The whole policy of Pericles was to get rid of the superabundant population by encouraging the emigration of the poorer sort (see Plut. Vit. Pericl. c. 9, and 11, 20, 21, &c. &c.). On the general question of the population of Attica, see Clinton's F. H., vol. ii. App. ch. 22.

command of Melanthius, one of the citizens, a man of mark in every way. These ships were the beginning of mischief both to the Greeks and to the barbarians.

98. Aristagoras sailed away in advance, and when he reached Miletus, devised a plan, from which no manner of advantage could possibly accrue to the Ionians;—indeed, in forming it, he did not aim at their benefit, but his sole wish was to annoy King Darius. He sent a messenger into Phrygia to those Pæonians who had been led away captive by Megabazus from the river Strymon,[2] and who now dwelt by themselves in Phrygia, having a tract of land and a hamlet of their own. This man, when he reached the Pæonians, spoke thus to them:—

"Men of Pæonia, Aristagoras, king of Miletus, has sent me to you, to inform you that you may now escape, if you choose to follow the advice he proffers. All Ionia has revolted from the king; and the way is open to you to return to your own land. You have only to contrive to reach the sea-coast; the rest shall be our business."

When the Pæonians heard this, they were exceedingly rejoiced, and, taking with them their wives and children, they made all speed to the coast; a few only remaining in Phrygia through fear. The rest, having reached the sea, crossed over to Chios, where they had just landed, when a great troop of Persian horse came following upon their heels, and seeking to overtake them. Not succeeding, however, they sent a message across to Chios, and begged the Pæonians to come back again. These last refused, and were conveyed by the Chians from Chios to Lesbos, and by the Lesbians thence to Doriscus;[3] from which place they made their way on foot to Pæonia.

99. The Athenians now arrived with a fleet of twenty sail, and brought also in their company five triremes of the Eretrians;[4] which had joined the expedition, not so much out of goodwill

---

[2] Vide supra, chs. 15-17.

[3] Herodotus gives the name of Doriscus to the great alluvial plain through which the river Hebrus (*Maritza*) empties itself into the sea. Darius at the time of his invasion of Scythia had built a fortified post to command the passage of this river, to which the name *Doriscus* was also given (infra, vii. 59). It was a place of great strength (vii. 106), and continued to be known as an important stronghold down to the time of Philip, son of Demetrius (B.C. 200; cf. Liv. xxxi. 16).

[4] Eretria lay upon the coast of Eubœa, 12 or 13 miles below Chalcis. Its site is marked by extensive ruins (Leake, p. 266). The better situation of Chalcis prevented Eretria from competing with it successfully. By Strabo's time the superiority of the former city was clear and decisive (x. p. 653); and at present *Egripo*, which occupies its site, is the only place of any importance in the whole island.

towards Athens, as to pay a debt which they already owed to the people of Miletus. For in the old war between the Chalcideans and Eretrians, the Milesians fought on the Eretrian side throughout, while the Chalcideans had the help of the Samian people. Aristagoras, on their arrival, assembled the rest of his allies, and proceeded to attack Sardis, not however leading the army in person, but appointing to the command his own brother Charopinus, and Hermophantus, one of the citizens, while he himself remained behind in Miletus.

100. The Ionians sailed with this fleet to Ephesus, and, leaving their ships at Coressus in the Ephesian territory, took guides from the city, and went up the country, with a great host. They marched along the course of the river Caÿster, and, crossing over the ridge of Tmolus, came down upon Sardis and took it, no man opposing them ;—the whole city fell into their hands, except only the citadel, which Artaphernes defended in person, having with him no contemptible force.

101. Though, however, they took the city, they did not succeed in plundering it; for, as the houses in Sardis were most of them built of reeds, and even the few which were of brick had a reed thatching for their roof, one of them was no sooner fired by a soldier than the flames ran speedily from house to house, and spread over the whole place. As the fire raged, the Lydians, and such Persians as were in the city, inclosed on every side by the flames, which had seized all the skirts of the town, and finding themselves

unable to get out, came in crowds into the market-place, and gathered themselves upon the banks of the Pactôlus. This stream, which comes down from Mount Tmôlus, and brings the Sardians a quantity of gold-dust, runs directly through the market place of Sardis, and joins the Hermus, before that river reaches the sea." So the Lydians and Persians, brought together in this

[Ruins of Sardis. From a sketch by Rev. S. C. Malan.]

way in the market-place and about the Pactôlus, were forced to stand on their defence; and the Ionians, when they saw the enemy in part resisting, in part pouring towards them in dense crowds, took fright, and drawing off to the ridge which is called Tmôlus, when night came, went back to their ships.

102. Sardis however was burnt, and, among other buildings, a temple of the native goddess Cybêlê was destroyed; ' which was

---

" Two small streams descend from Tmolus, one on each side of the ruins of Sardis: "the western, which comes down the broader valley, and passes by the Ionic temple of Cybêlê, has generally been considered as the gold-bearing Pactolus" (Hamilton's Asia Minor, vol. I. pp. 146, 147.) Like most gold-fields, that of the Pactolus, so celebrated at an early period (Soph. Phil. 393; Strab. xiii. p 897), was soon exhausted. By the time of Augustus it had ceased to produce gold (Strab. l. s. c.)

' Cybêbê, Cybêlê, or Rhea, was the Magna Mater, or Mother of the Gods, a principal object of worship among all the Oriental nations. (Vide supra, i. 131, note ', and Essay x. pp. 495-497; and cf. Soph. l. s. c.; Catull. lxi.; Virg. Æn. vi. 785; ix. 617, &c. See also Selden, de Diis Syriis, ii. 2.) She may be identified with the Beltis of the Assyrian Inscriptions, the Mylitta of Herod.

the reason afterwards alleged by the Persians for setting on fire the temples of the Greeks.² As soon as what had happened was known, all the Persians who were stationed on this side the Halys drew together,³ and brought help to the Lydians. Finding however, when they arrived, that the Ionians had already withdrawn from Sardis, they set off, and, following close upon their track, came up with them at Ephesus. The Ionians drew out against them in battle array; and a fight ensued, wherein the Greeks had very greatly the worse.⁴ Vast numbers were slain by the Persians: among other men of note, they killed the captain of the Eretrians, a certain Evalcidas, a man who had gained crowns at the games, and received much praise from Simonides the Cean.⁵ Such as made their escape from the battle, dispersed among the several cities.

103. So ended this encounter. Afterwards the Athenians quite forsook the Ionians, and, though Aristagoras besought them much by his ambassadors, refused to give him any further help.⁶

[footnotes omitted]

Still the Ionians, notwithstanding this desertion, continued unceasingly their preparations to carry on the war against the Persian king, which their late conduct towards him had rendered unavoidable. Sailing into the Hellespont, they brought Byzantium, and all the other cities in that quarter, under their sway. Again, quitting the Hellespont, they went to Caria, and won the greater part of the Carians to their side; while Caunus, which had formerly refused to join with them, after the burning of Sardis, came over likewise.¹

104. All the Cyprians too, excepting those of Amathûs, of their own proper motion espoused the Ionian cause.² The occasion of their revolting from the Medes was the following. There was a certain Onesilus, younger brother of Gorgus, king of Salamis, and son of Chersis, who was son of Siromus,³ and grandson of Evelthon.⁴ This man had often in former times entreated Gorgus to rebel against the king; but, when he heard of the revolt of the Ionians, he left him no peace with his importunity. As, however, Gorgus would not hearken to him, he watched his

---

Greece, vol. iv. p. 390). There is no evidence to sustain such a view, which seems based upon a notion that the Athenians could not possibly do wrong. The truth seems to be, that on the first reverse Athens backed out of the war. Such conduct was certainly far more "open to censure" than the original embarking in the war, which was a very politic act. It is perhaps not going too far to say that if Athens and the other maritime states of Greece had given a hearty and resolute support to the Ionian cause, the great invasions of Darius and Xerxes might have been prevented.

² The Caunians had been brought under the Persian yoke by Harpagus with difficulty (supra, i. 176). For the situation of their country, see Appendix to vol. i. (Essay ii. p. 321). It is surprising that the Lycians did not take the opportunity, which now offered, to throw off the Persian yoke.

* Mr. Grote considers this revolt to have been confined to "the Greek cities in Cyprus," among which he even reckons Amathus (Hist. of Greece, vol. iv. p. 391); but Herodotus distinctly states that the Cyprians revolted generally. No doubt there had been a considerable Greek immigration into Cyprus before this period (vide infra, vii. 90), but the bulk of the population continued Phœnician till long afterwards. This is plain from Scylax, who calls all the inhabitants of the interior "barbarians," and notices as exceptional even the cases of Greek cities upon the coast. It would seem that in his time (the time of Philip of Macedon) there were in Cyprus no more than three Greek cities of note. These were Salamis, Soli, and Marium. We must therefore consider the revolt to have extended in a great measure to the Phœnician inhabitants, although the non-participation in it of the important and thoroughly Phœnician town of Amathus (Scylax, Peripl. p. 97; Theopomp. Fr. 111; Steph. Byz. ad voc.) would seem to imply that the Phœnician population entered into it less thoroughly than the Greek.

³ This name is clearly Phœnician, being identical with the Hiromus (Εἴρωμος) of Josephus, and the Hiram (חִירָם) of Scripture. (Compare vii. 98.) It is probable that the Greek princes of Cyprus intermarried with the Phœnicians.

⁴ The Evelthon of Bk. iv. ch. 162, seems to be meant; but it is difficult to understand how, within the space of thirty years, he could have been succeeded by a grown-up great-grandson. Still it is possible, if Evelthon at the time of Pheretima's visit (about B.C. 530) was a very old man.

occasion, and when his brother had gone outside the town, he with his partisans closed the gates upon him. Gorgus, thus deprived of his city, fled to the Medes; and Onesilus,[1] being now king of Salamis, sought to bring about a revolt of the whole of Cyprus. All were prevailed on except the Amathusians, who refused to listen to him; whereupon Onesilus sate down before Amathûs,[2] and laid siege to it.

105. While Onesilus was engaged in the siege of Amathûs, King Darius received tidings of the taking and burning of Sardis by the Athenians and Ionians; and at the same time he learnt that the author of the league, the man by whom the whole matter had been planned and contrived, was Aristagoras the Milesian. It is said that he no sooner understood what had happened, than, laying aside all thought concerning the Ionians, who would, he was sure, pay dear for their rebellion, he asked "Who the Athenians were?"[4] and, being informed, called for his bow, and placing an arrow on the string, shot upward into the sky,[5] saying, as he let fly the shaft—"Grant me, Jupiter,[6] to revenge myself on the Athenians!" After this speech, he bade one of his servants every day, when his dinner was spread, three times repeat these words to him—"Master, remember the Athenians."

106. Then he summoned into his presence Histiæus of Miletus, whom he had kept at his court for so long a time; and on his appearance addressed him thus—"I am told, O Histiæus, that thy lieutenant, to whom thou hast given Miletus in charge, has raised a rebellion against me. He has brought men from the other continent to contend with me, and, prevailing on the Ionians— whose conduct I shall know how to recompense—to join with this force, he has robbed me of Sardis! Is this as it should be, thinkest thou? Or can it have been done without thy knowledge and advice? Beware lest it be found hereafter that the blame of these acts is thine."

Histiæus answered—"What words are these, O king, to which thou hast given utterance? I advise aught from which unplea-

---

[1] The initial element of this name appears in that of the king of Limenia (*Himasiggutas*), who supplied labourers to Esarhaddon (supra, vol. i. p. 397, note [?].)

[2] Amathûs, one of the most ancient Phœnician settlements in Cyprus (Ἀμαθοῦντα, Steph. Byz.), was situated on the south coast, about 35 miles west of Citium (*Lamako*). Its ruins still exist near the village of *Limasol* (Engel's Kypros, vol. i. p. 109 et seqq.).

[4] Compare l. 153, and supra, ch. 73.

[5] Compare with this what is said of the Thracians (supra, iv. 94). The notion here seems to be, to send the message to heaven on the arrow.

[6] That is, "Ormazd." The Greeks identify the supreme God of each nation with their own Zeus (vide supra, I. 131; ii. 53, &c.).

saninees of any kind, little or great, should come to thee! What could I gain by so doing? Or what is there that I lack now? Have I not all that thou hast, and am I not thought worthy to partake all thy counsels? If my lieutenant has indeed done as thou sayest, be sure he has done it all of his own head. For my part, I do not think it can really be that the Milesians and my lieutenant have raised a rebellion against thee. But if they have indeed committed aught to thy hurt, and the tidings are true which have come to thee, judge thou how ill-advised thou wert to remove me from the sea-coast. The Ionians, it seems, have waited till I was no longer in sight, and then sought to execute that which they long ago desired; whereas, if I had been there, not a single city would have stirred. Suffer me then to hasten at my best speed to Ionia, that I may place matters there upon their former footing, and deliver up to thee the deputy of Miletus, who has caused all the troubles. Having managed this business to thy heart's content, I swear by all the gods of thy royal house, I will not put off the clothes in which I reach Ionia, till I have made Sardinia, the biggest island in the world,' thy tributary."

107. Histiæus spoke thus, wishing to deceive the king; and Darius, persuaded by his words, let him go; only bidding him be sure to do as he had promised, and afterwards come back to Susa.

108. In the mean time—while the tidings of the burning of Sardis were reaching the king, and Darius was shooting the arrow and having the conference with Histiæus, and the latter, by permission of Darius, was hastening down to the sea—in Cyprus the following events took place. Tidings came to Onesilus, the Salaminian, who was still besieging Amathûs, that a certain Artybius, a Persian, was looked for to arrive in Cyprus with a great Persian armament. So Onesilus, when the news

reached him, sent off heralds to all parts of Ionia, and besought the Ionians to give him aid. After brief deliberation, these last in full force passed over into the island; and the Persians about the same time crossed in their ships from Cilicia, and proceeded by land to attack Salamis;[2] while the Phœnicians, with the fleet, sailed round the promontory which goes by the name of "the Keys of Cyprus."[3]

109. In this posture of affairs the princes of Cyprus called together the captains of the Ionians, and thus addressed them:—

"Men of Ionia, we Cyprians leave it to you to choose whether you will fight with the Persians or with the Phœnicians. If it be your pleasure to try your strength on land against the Persians, come on shore at once, and array yourselves for the battle; we will then embark aboard your ships and engage the Phœnicians by sea. If, on the other hand, ye prefer to encounter the Phœnicians, let that be your task: only be sure, whichever part you choose, to acquit yourselves so that Ionia and Cyprus, so far as depends on you, may preserve their freedom."

The Ionians made answer—"The commonwealth of Ionia sent us here to guard the sea, not to make over our ships to you, and engage with the Persians on shore. We will therefore keep the post which has been assigned to us, and seek therein to be of some service. Do you, remembering what you suffered when you were the slaves of the Medes, behave like brave warriors."

110. Such was the reply of the Ionians. Not long afterwards the Persians advanced into the plain before Salamis,[1] and the

---

But that passage only states that Cilicians and Egyptians formed part of the naval force which three years afterwards attacked Miletus. The Persians seem scarcely ever to have drawn any part of their land force from either Cilicia or Egypt (comp. vii. 89-91; Arrian, II. 17). The only exception, so far as I am aware, is that of the Egyptian troops at Cunaxa, and even this is uncertain. (Αἰγυπτίοι δλίγοντο εἶναι, Xen. Anab. 1. viii. § 9.)

[2] The fleet probably collected at Nagidus or at Celenderis (Kelenderi), and crossing to Cerynela (Tcerines or Kkirneh), there disembarked the soldiers. The distance is about sixty miles (Leake's Asia Minor, p. 118). From Cerynela to Salamis is by land thirty-two miles; by sea, owing to the great projection of the eastern promontory, one hundred and thirty miles.

[3] The Keys were properly some small islands off the extreme eastern promontory of Cyprus, Cape Dinaretum (Iskler. ap. Plin. H. N. v. 31), the modern Cape Andrea. Strabo (xiv. p. 670) says they were two, Pliny (H. N. l. s. c.) four in number. The promontory is called by Ptolemy, from its shape, Cape Oxtail (Οὐρὰ βοός, v. 14).

[1] Salamis was situated on the eastern coast of Cyprus, at the mouth of the river Pedieus, the largest of the Cyprian streams. It did not occupy the site of the modern Famagosta, but lay on the north side of the river (Ptol. Geogr. v. 14, p. 157. Its ruins have been described by Pococke (Travels, vol. ii. part i. p. 314).

According to tradition Salamis was founded by Teucer, the son of Telamon and brother of Ajax, soon after the Trojan war (Mar. Par. 26; Strab. xiv. p. 973; comp. Theopomp. Fr. 111; and Clearch. Sol. Fr. 25). Hence it was supposed to

Cyprian kings ranged their troops in order of battle against them, placing them so that while the rest of the Cyprians were drawn up against the auxiliaries of the enemy, the choicest troops of the Salaminians and the Solians were set to oppose the Persians. At the same time Onesilus, of his own accord, took post opposite to Artybius, the Persian general.

111. Now Artybius rode a horse which had been trained to rear up against a foot-soldier. Onesilus, informed of this, called to him his shieldbearer, who was a Carian by nation, a man well skilled in war, and of daring courage; and thus addressed him:—
"I hear," he said, "that the horse which Artybius rides, rears up and attacks with his fore legs and teeth the man against whom his rider urges him. Consider quickly therefore and tell me which wilt thou undertake to encounter, the steed or the rider?" Then the squire answered him, "Both, my liege, or either, am I ready to undertake, and there is nothing that I will shrink from at thy bidding. But I will tell thee what seems to me to make most for thy interests. As thou art a prince and a general, I

think thou shouldest engage with one who is himself both a
prince and also a general. For then, if thou slayest thine adversary, 'twill redound to thine honour, and if he slays thee (which
may Heaven forefend!), yet to fall by the hand of a worthy foe
makes death lose half its horror. To us, thy followers, leave his
war-horse and his retinue. And have thou no fear of the horse's
tricks. I warrant that this is the last time he will stand up
against any one."

112. Thus spake the Carian; and shortly after, the two hosts
joined battle both by sea and land. And here it chanced that by
sea the Ionians, who that day fought as they have never done
either before or since, defeated the Phœnicians, the Samians
especially distinguishing themselves. Meanwhile the combat had
begun on land, and the two armies were engaged in a sharp
struggle, when thus it fell out in the matter of the generals.
Artybius, astride upon his horse, charged down upon Onesilus,
who, as he had agreed with his shieldbearer, aimed his blow at
the rider; the horse reared and placed his fore feet upon the
shield of Onesilus, when the Carian cut at him with a reaping-
hook, and severed the two legs from the body. The horse fell
upon the spot, and Artybius, the Persian general, with him.

113. In the thick of the fight, Stesanor, tyrant of Curium,[1]
who commanded no inconsiderable body of troops, went over with
them to the enemy. On this desertion of the Curians—Argive
colonists,[2] if report says true—forthwith the war-chariots of the
Salaminians followed the example set them, and went over
likewise; whereupon victory declared in favour of the Persians;
and the army of the Cyprians being routed, vast numbers were
slain, and among them Onesilus, the son of Chersis, who was the
author of the revolt, and Aristocyprus, king of the Solians. This
Aristocyprus was son of Philocyprus, whom Solon the Athenian,
when he visited Cyprus, praised in his poems[3] beyond all other
sovereigns.

---

[1] Curium lay upon the southern
coast, between Paphos and Amathus,
not far from the southernmost point of
the island (*Capo delle Gatte*), called
anciently Cape Curias (Strab. xiv. p.
972). Its exact site is variously conjectured, at *Piscopi* and at *Ardimo*. The
former position agrees best with Ptolemy's measurements (Geograph. v. 14,
p. 157).
[2] Strabo repeats this assertion positively (Κουρίους Ἀργείων κτίσμα, xiv. p.
972). Yet Stephen of Byzantium
ascribes the foundation of Curium to
Cureus, a son of Cinyras, the Syrian or
Phœnician conqueror of Cyprus (Steph.
Byz. ad voc. Κούριον. Cf. Apollod. III.
xiv. 3; and Theopomp. Fr. 111). He
believed it, therefore, to have been an
ancient Phœnician town.
[3] The poems of Solon were written
chiefly in the elegiac metre, and were
hortatory or gnomic. The fragments
which remain have been collected by
Bach (Bonn, 1825), by Brunck in his
Poetæ Gnomici, by Gaisford, and others.

114. The Amathusians, because Onesilus had laid siege to their town, cut the head off his corpse, and took it with them to Amathûs, where it was set up over the gates. Here it hung till it became hollow; whereupon a swarm of bees took possession of it, and filled it with a honeycomb. On seeing this the Amathusians consulted the oracle, and were commanded "to take down the head and bury it, and thenceforth to regard Onesilus as a hero, and offer sacrifice to him year by year; so it would go the better with them." And to this day the Amathusians do as they were then bidden.

115. As for the Ionians who had gained the sea-fight, when they found that the affairs of Onesilus were utterly lost and ruined, and that siege was laid to all the cities of Cyprus excepting Salamis, which the inhabitants had surrendered to Gorgus, the former king—forthwith they left Cyprus, and sailed away home. Of the cities which were besieged, Soli held out the longest: the Persians took it by undermining the wall in the fifth month from the beginning of the siege.

116. Thus, after enjoying a year of freedom, the Cyprians were enslaved for the second time. Meanwhile Daurises, who was married to one of the daughters of Darius, together with Hymeas, Otanes, and other Persian captains, who were likewise married to daughters of the king, after pursuing the Ionians who had fought at Sardis, defeating them, and driving them to their ships, divided their efforts against the different cities, and proceeded in succession to take and sack each one of them.

117. Daurises attacked the towns upon the Hellespont, and took in as many days the five cities of Dardanus, Abydos,

Percôté, Lampsacus, and Pæsus. From Pæsus he marched against Parium; but on his way receiving intelligence that the Carians had made common cause with the Ionians, and thrown off the Persian yoke, he turned round, and, leaving the Hellespont, marched away towards Caria.

118. The Carians by some chance got information of this movement before Daurises arrived, and drew together their strength to a place called "the White Columns," which is on the river Marsyas, a stream running from the Idrian country, and emptying itself into the Mæander. Here when they were met, many plans were put forth; but the best, in my judgment, was that of Pixodarus, the son of Mausôlus, a Cindyan, who was married to a daughter of Syennesis, the Cilician king. His advice was, that the Carians should cross the Mæander, and

fight with the river at their back; that so, all chance of flight being cut off, they might be forced to stand their ground, and have their natural courage raised to a still higher pitch. His opinion, however, did not prevail; it was thought best to make the enemy have the Mæander behind them; that so, if they were defeated in the battle and put to flight, they might have no retreat open, but be driven headlong into the river.

119. The Persians soon afterwards approached, and, crossing the Mæander, engaged the Carians upon the banks of the Marsyas; where for a long time the battle was stoutly contested, but at last the Carians were defeated, being overpowered by numbers. On the side of the Persians there fell 2000, while the Carians had not fewer than 10,000 slain. Such as escaped from the field of battle collected together at Labranda,[a] in the vast precinct of Jupiter Stratius[b]—a deity worshipped only by the Carians[1]—and in the sacred grove of plane-trees. Here they deliberated as to the best means of saving themselves, doubting whether they would fare better if they gave themselves up to the Persians, or if they abandoned Asia for ever.

120. As they were debating these matters a body of Milesians and allies came to their assistance; whereupon the Carians, dismissing their former thoughts, prepared themselves afresh for war, and on the approach of the Persians gave them battle a second time. They were defeated, however, with still greater

---

[a] Labranda was on the mountain range which separated the valley of the Marsyas from that of Mylasa (Strab. xiv. p. 943). It was a strong position. The site usually assigned is the modern village of *Iakler*, where there are important remains (Chandler, ch. lviii. p. 226). Col. Leake's conjecture, however (Asia Minor, p. 234), that these are the ruins of Euromus, and that Labranda is to be sought for on the high ground between *Melasso* (Mylasa) and *Arab-Hissar* (Alabanda), which was probable enough in itself, has received a striking confirmation from the researches of Sir C. Fellows. This traveller, on his way from Arab-Hissar to Melasso, discovered in the position anticipated by Col. Leake, some important ruins, evidently the remains of an ancient town; and also found considerable traces of an ancient paved road, leading from this town to Melasso (Lycia, p. 67). The latter circumstance exactly agrees with the account of Strabo, whose words are ὁδὸς ἐστρωμένη σχεδὸν τι ἑξήκοντα σταδίων μέχρι τῆς πόλεως ἱερὰ καλουμένη (l. s. c.).

[b] The temple of Jupiter Stratius at Labranda, is mentioned by Strabo (l. s. c.). He calls it πρὸς ἀρχαῖος. The paved road to which allusion was made in the last note, was a via sacra leading from Mylasa to this temple.

[1] Jupiter Stratius is thus entirely distinct from Jupiter Carius, who was worshipped by the Carians, Lydians, and Mysians in common (i. 171). He was called also Jupiter Labrandeus, either from his temple at Labranda, or (Plut. Quæst. Gr. ii. p. 301, F.) from the fact that he bore in his right hand a double-headed battle-axe (λάβρυς in the Lydian language). Such a representation of Jupiter is sometimes found upon Carian coins (Fellows's Lycia, Pl. 35, No. 5). And a similar axe appears frequently as an architectural ornament in the buildings of the country (ib. p. 75).

less than before; and while all the troops engaged suffered severely, the blow fell with most force on the Milesians.

121. The Carians, some while after, repaired their ill fortune in another action. Understanding that the Persians were about to attack their cities, they laid an ambush for them on the road which leads to Pedasus;[2] the Persians, who were making a night-march, fell into the trap, and the whole army was destroyed, together with the generals, Daurises, Amorges, and Sisimaces: Myrsus[3] too, the son of Gyges, was killed at the same time. The leader of the ambush was Heraclides,[4] the son of Ibanôlis, a man of Mylasa.[5] Such was the way in which these Persians perished.

122. In the meantime Hymees, who was likewise one of those by whom the Ionians were pursued after their attack on Sardis, directing his course towards the Propontis, took Cius,[6] a city of Mysia.[7] Learning, however, that Daurises had left the Hellespont, and was gone into Caria, he in his turn quitted the Propontis, and marching with the army under his command to the Hellespont, reduced all the Æolians of the Troad, and likewise conquered the Gergithæ,[8] a remnant of the ancient Teucrians.

---

[2] Vide supra, I. 175, note ⁹.

[3] This is probably the Myrsus mentioned in the third book (ch. 122), as carrying a message from Orœtes to Polycrates. He was a Lydian, and to judge from his own and his father's name (cf. I. 8, 9).

[4] Brother, probably, of the "Oliatus, son of Ibanolis," who was seized by order of Aristagoras (supra, ch. 37).

[5] Mylasa continues to exist in the modern Melasso, a town of some size. It still possesses considerable remains of antiquity, though the beautiful temple seen by Pococke has been destroyed (Pococke, vol. II. part 2, ch. vi.; Chandler, ch. 58. Its situation in a fertile plain, under the shadow of lofty and precipitous hills (Chandler, l. s. c.; Fellowe' Asia Minor, p. 259), agrees closely with the description of Strabo (xiv. p. 942), while its distance from the sea corresponds with the notice in Pausanias (viii. 10, § 3).

Scylax of Caryanda is said to have written a work entitled 'The History of the times of Heraclides, king of Mylasa' (Suidas ad voc. Σκύλαξ). The person intended is probably this Heraclides; but it may be questioned whether the work was not a forgery.

[6] Cius lay at the extreme recess of the Cianean gulf, the modern gulf of Moudania, upon the river of the same name, which bore to the sea the waters of Lake Ascania (Lake of Isnik). It was destroyed by Philip, son of Demetrius, but rebuilt by his ally Prusias, who called it after his own name (cf. Strabo, xii. p. 814; Polyb. xv. 22, 23; Steph. Byz. ad voc. Πρoύσα; Scylax, Peripl. p. 84.. The modern village of Kemlik nearly occupies the site. Cius, like most other towns upon this coast, was a colony of the Milesians (Schol. in Apoll. Rhod. I. 1178).

[7] So Scylax (Peripl. l. s. c.), who assigns to Mysia the whole peninsula between the gulfs of Moudania and Ismid, which tract is more usually reckoned to Bithynia. (Cf. Ptol. Geograph. v. 1; and Strabo, xii. p. 812, who, however, remarks on the difficulty of distinguishing the boundaries of the several tribes in these parts, p. 815.)

[8] These Gergithæ seem to have inhabited the mountains south of Lampsacus, between the Scamander, the Granicus, and the coast (infra, vii. 43). According to Strabo (xiii. p. 851), Stephen (ad voc. Γέργις), Livy (xxxviii. 39), and others, there was a city called Gergis, Gergithus or Gergetha, in these parts. Perhaps we may connect the

He did not, however, quit the Troad, but, after gaining these successes, was himself carried off by disease.

123. After his death, which happened as I have related, Artaphernes, the satrap of Sardis, and Otanes, the third general,[ ] were directed to undertake the conduct of the war against Ionia and the neighbouring Æolis. By them Clazomenæ in the former,[1] and Cymé in the latter,[2] were recovered.

124. As the cities fell one after another, Aristagoras the Milesian (who was in truth, as he now plainly showed, a man of but little courage), notwithstanding that it was he who had caused the disturbances in Ionia and made so great a commotion, began, seeing his danger, to look about for means of escape. Being convinced that it was in vain to endeavour to overcome King Darius, he called his brothers-in-arms together, and laid before them the following project:—"'Twould be well," he said, "to have some place of refuge, in case they were driven out of Miletus. Should he go out at the head of a colony to Sardinia,[3] or should he sail to Myrcinus in Edonia, which Histiæus had received as a gift from King Darius, and had begun to fortify?"

125. To this question of Aristagoras, Hecatæus, the historian, son of Hegesander, made answer, that in his judgment neither place was suitable. "Aristagoras should build a fort," he said, "in the island of Leros,[4] and, if driven from Miletus, should go there and bide his time; from Leros attacks might readily be made, and he might re-establish himself in Miletus." Such was the advice given by Hecatæus.

126. Aristagoras, however, was bent on retiring to Myrcinus. Accordingly, he put the government of Miletus into the hands of

one of the chief citizens, named Pythagoras,⁵ and, taking with him all who liked to go, sailed to Thrace, and there made himself master of the place in question. From thence he proceeded to attack the Thracians; but here he was cut off with his whole army, while besieging a city⁶ whose defenders were anxious to accept terms of surrender.

---

⁵ Aristagoras, it is evident from this, had not really divested himself of the supreme authority in his native town (vide supra, ch. 37). Little regard seems, however, to have been paid to his nominee and successor.

⁶ It appears from Thucydides (iv. 102), that this city was on or near the spot called Nine-Ways ('Εννέα 'Οδοί), where Amphipolis was afterwards built (infra, vii. 114). The Thracians who defeated Aristagoras, were the Edonians. It would seem they not only succeeded in protecting their own cities, but made themselves masters of Myrcinus, which is called in Thucydides, an Edonian city ('Ηδωνική πόλις, iv. 107).

APPENDIX TO BOOK V.

ESSAY I.

ON THE EARLY HISTORY OF SPARTA.

1. Spartans, immigrants into the Peloponnese. 2. Supposed migrations of the Dorians. 3. Their occupation of the Peloponnese according to the ordinary legend. 4. The true history unknown. 5. Probable line of march. 6. Date of the occupation. 7. The conquest gradual. 8. Spartan Dorians—Sparta and Amyclæ—early wars. 9. Internal history—origin of the double monarchy—troubles of the early period. 10. Condition of Sparta before Lycurgus—the three classes—i.) Spartans—(ii.) Perioeci—(iii.) Helots. 11. Succession of the early kings. 12. Original constitution of Sparta— Kings—Senate—Ecclesia. 13. Constitutional changes of Lycurgus, slight. 14. His discipline—question of its origin. 15. Causes of its adoption. 16. Supposed equalisation of landed property. 17. Arguments which disprove it. 18. Effects of Lycurgus' legislation—conquests, and increase of Perioeci. 19. Messenian wars. 20. Causes of the rupture. 21. Outline of the first war. 22. Date and duration. 23. Internal changes consequent on the first war—"Partheniæ" and "Inferiors"—"Small" and "Great Assembly" —colonisation of Tarentum. 24. Interval between the wars. 25. Outline of the second war. 26. Its duration. 27. War with Pisatis. 28. War with Arcadia. 29. Gradual diminution of the kingly power at Sparta, and continued rise of the Ephors. 30. Rapid decrease in the number of Spartan citizens.

1. THAT the Spartans of history were not original inhabitants of the Peloponnese, but invaders from northern Greece, who established their dominion over a large portion of the peninsula by a conquest of its previous occupants, is a fact which even the most sceptical of modern historians has not hesitated to admit as certain.[1] A uniform tradition,[2] supported by the representation of antique times contained in the earliest Greek writer,[3] and remarkably in unison with the actual condition of the population of the country when its circumstances first become known to us,[4] constitutes

---

[1] See Mr. Grote's History of Greece, vol. II. part. ii. ch. 4 (pp. 408-442).

[2] Cf. Hesiod. Fr. vii.; Tyrtæus ap. Strab. viii. p. 536; Pind. Pyth. v. 92-96, and Fragm. ed. Böckh, vol. I. p. 577; Herod. I. 56, vi. 52, viii. 43, and 73; Thucyd. i. 12, 18, 107; Isocrat. Panath. p. 256; Archidam. p. 194; Aristid. Orat. 46, vol. II. p. 284; Ephor. Fr. 10-20; Apollodor. II. 8; Strab. Ch. 528 et seqq.; Strab. viii. p. 530, &c.; Diod. Sic. iv. 37-60; Pausan. III. i., &c., iv. iii. § 3, &c.; (Enom. ap. Euseb. Præp. Ev. v. 20, p. 210, C.

The only writer who gives an account essentially different is Plato, by whom the Dorians are represented as expelled Achæans returning to their own country under the conduct of one Dorieus (Leg. iii. p. 682, E.).

[3] Homer has no Dorians in the Peloponnese, the inhabitants of which, according to him, are Achæans, Argives, or Danaans. He has, indeed, a single insignificant town Dorium (Il. ii. 594) on the west coast near Pylos; but the Dorians only appear in his writings as a Cretan race. (Od. xix. 177.)

[4] See below, pp. 278-280.

evidence the weight of which is altogether irresistible. It may be assumed therefore that the Dorian Spartans, whose history is now to be traced, unlike their rivals, the Athenians, were immigrants into an occupied country—settlers among a people from whom they differed to a greater or less extent,[1] whom they conquered and held in subjection. Regarding thus much as allowed on all hands, we have in the first instance to consider—1. whence they came, and why they left their primitive seats; 2. in what way they effected the conquest.

2. According to Herodotus, the Dorians, whom he identifies with the Hellenes, had dwelt originally in Achæa Phthiôtis,[2] the country immediately east of the Pagasæan Gulf, lying both north and south of the chain of Othrys. Hence they had removed to a tract called Histiæôtis in Upper Thessaly, which Herodotus seems to place near Tempé, since he tells us that it lay "at the base of Ossa and Olympus."[3] From this region they had been driven by the Cadmeians, whereupon they had fled into Pindus; and while there had taken the name of "Macedni" (or Macedonians).[4] After a time they had quitted this refuge and gained possession of Dryopis, the tract between Parnassus and Callidromus, consisting of the valleys of the Pindus and certain other streams which form the head-waters of the great Cephissus river. From this country, which in the historical age was known as Dôris, they had entered the Peloponnese, and subjugated the previous inhabitants.

It has been observed by K. O. Müller in reference to this account of the early migrations of the Dorian race, that "no one can consider it as flowing immediately from ancient tradition; it can only be viewed as an attempt of the father of history to arrange and reconcile various legends and traditions."[4] This remark appears to be just. Whatever value we may be inclined to attach generally to the account which a nation without a literature gives of its origin, it is impossible to imagine that a people driven about in the way described would orally preserve for centuries so exact an account of its many wanderings. Herodotus, or those from whom he drew his information, must be considered to have thrown together and blended into a single narrative stories current in different parts of Greece, which it required some ingenuity to harmonise. The Dorians had to be placed originally in Phthiôtis, because that was in Homer[5] the country of the Hellenes, with whom the Dorians were identified: they must be given seats in Histiæôtis, since Upper Thessaly was the abode of the Lapithæ, with whom Ægi-

---

[1] Widely different opinions have been held on this point. Mr. Grote says (Hist. of Greece, vol. ii. p. 451), "So little is known of the previous inhabitants of the Peloponnese, that we cannot at all measure the difference between them and their Dorian invaders, either in dialect, in habits, or in intelligence." He inclines, however, to think, at least with regard to their language, that it "did not differ materially from the Doric" (p. 452). K. O. Müller, on the other hand, speaks of "the difference between the language, religion, and customs of the two nations" as "strongly and precisely marked." (Dorians, vol. i. p. 56.)

[2] Herod. i. 56.

[3] Ibid. τὴν ὑπὸ τὴν Ὄσσαν τε καὶ τὸν Ὄλυμπον χώρην.

[4] Ibid. loc. cit., and compare vii. 43.

[5] Dorians, vol. i. pp. 21, 22.

[6] Iliad, ii. 683, 684.

mius, their mythic ancestor, was said to have contended;[1] and since, according to some accounts,[2] the Dorian colonies in Crete proceeded from that region: they must descend l'indus that they might reach Dryopis, their well-known habitation in later times; and they must be called Macedonians, in order to give a foundation to those claims of Hellenism which the Macedonians were in the habit of preferring, not only for their royal family, but for their whole nation.[3] The very lowest degree of credit must be considered to attach to these legends, which receive no support from Homer,[4] and are full of internal improbabilities. All that can be said to be ascertained of the Dorians before they settled in the Peloponnese, is the fact that they previously inhabited the "small and sad region"[5] known in historical times as Doris, or the Doric *metropolis*, where they had a confederacy of four townships, Pindus, Bœum, Citinium, and Erineus,[6] all situated in the valley of the Pindus river. Of this country they were reported to have gained possession by the expulsion of the Dryopes, one of the most ancient races of Greece, which may be regarded as a sister-tribe to the Pelasgi, Leleges, Caucônes, Dolopes, &c.; but this expulsion does not seem to rest upon such evidence as entitles it to take rank among the established facts of history.[7]

3. According to the prevailing legend, the Dorians were induced to leave their seats under Parnassus by the entreaties of a band of fugitives from the Peloponnese, who begged their aid in order to effect a return to their native country. These fugitives were the Heraclidæ, or descendants of Hercules, by hereditary right the royal family of Argos, but expelled from the Peloponnese by a usurper of their own house (Eurystheus), and at his death superseded by another ancient Peloponnesian family, the Pelopidæ, or descendants of Pelops. Received with open arms by the Dorians and adopted into their body, the Heraclidæ became the ruling family of the nation whose aid they had sought, and imparted the name of Hylleans to their principal tribe.[8] After various attempts to force

Essay I. DORIAN CONQUEST OF THE PELOPONNESE. 269

their way into the peninsula by the Isthmus of Corinth, which were met and defeated by the inhabitants,[1] the Dorians under their Heracleid leaders at last effected the passage of the Corinthian Gulf near its mouth, in ships which they had built at Naupactus, a port granted to them by the Ozolian Locrians. They were accompanied on their expedition by Oxylus, an Ætolian chief,[2] who was desirous of possessing himself of the rich country of Elis, where he had recently passed a year of exile; and who was thus qualified by acquaintance with this part of the Peloponnese to serve as guide to the invaders. He conducted the fleet from Naupactus to Molycrium at the mouth of the gulf, and thence crossing to Panormus, led the Dorians through Arcadia, against the Achæan force, which was collected under Tisamenes, the son of Orestes, near the isthmus. A battle was fought in which the Dorians were completely victorious, and the inheritance of the Heraclidæ was recovered. As the family of Hyllus had now divided into three branches,[3] a threefold division of the ancient Achæan territory was made. Lots were drawn for the kingdoms of Argos, Sparta, and Messenia, the first of which fell to Temenus (the eldest of the sons of Aristomachus), the second to Eurysthenes and Procles, the infant children of Aristodemus (the second son), and the third to Cresphontes (the third son), who had craftily contrived to obtain this fertile territory for himself by placing in the urn an unfair lot.[4] Elis was given to Oxylus, according to previous agreement. A portion of the Achæans refused to submit to the conquerors, and leaving their country entered Ionia—the northern tract of the Peloponnese extending along the gulf of Corinth—where they overcame and expelled the inhabitants, who sought a refuge in Attica. Thus the

---

[1] Three such attempts are narrated: the first under Hyllus, after the death of Eurystheus, in which Hyllus was slain by Echemus (Herod. ix. 26; Schol. Pind. Ol. x. 79); the second under Cleodæus, the son of Hyllus, who also fell in an engagement (Œnom. ap. Euseb. Præp. Ev. v. 20, p. 210, C.; Schol. ad Pind. Isth. vii. 18); and the third under Aristomachus, the son of Cleodæus, which had the same ill success (Apollod. II. viii. § 2; (Enom. l. s. c., &c.).

[2] The legend ran—that the Delphic Oracle bade Temenus take as guide for his army a three-eyed man. Soon after, chancing to meet Oxylus, who had lost an eye, riding on horseback, he at once recognized in him the necessary "three-eyed guide." (Apollod. II. viii. 3.) Another account assigned the loss of an eye to the animal on which Oxylus rode (Pausan. v. iii. § 5).

[3] The mythic genealogy of the Heraclidæ was as follows:—Hercules had four sons by Deianira, of whom Hyllus was the eldest. Hyllus left a son, Cleodæus, who was the father of Aristomachus. Aristomachus had three children, Temenus, Aristodemus, and Cresphontes. Aristodemus, according to some accounts, reigned at Sparta (Herod. vi.

52); according to others, he was killed by lightning at Naupactus, leaving behind him twin sons, Eurysthenes and Procles. (Apollod. II. viii. § 2, ad fin.) The genealogy may be thus exhibited:—

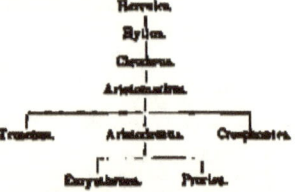

[4] The three parties were to draw lots for the three kingdoms by placing each their pebble in a jar of water, from which an indifferent person was to draw them forth. The first whose stone was drawn out was to receive Argos, the second Sparta; Messenia would then fall to the third. Cresphontes, in order to obtain the third lot, which he preferred to the others, instead of a stone placed in the jar a lump of clay, which forthwith dissolved. (Apollod. II. viii. § 4.)

new arrangement of the Peloponnese was complete: the country previously held by the Achæans passed into the hands of the Dorians; Ionia became Achæa; the Epeans of Elis were merged in the Ætolians; only the Arcadians and Cynurians remained undisturbed in their ancient abodes, the former in the central mountain tract, the latter in a sequestered valley on the eastern shore.

4. Such is, in outline, the legendary story that has come down to us concerning the mode whereby the Dorian conquests in the Peloponnese were effected. It is related consecutively by Apollodorus and Pausanias, with whose statements the fragmentary notices in Herodotus, Thucydides, and other early writers appear in the main to agree. Certain isolated traditions have, however, descended to us, which are thought to militate against the general truth of this tale, and to indicate that the conquest was the result of at least two separate and independent attacks, one proceeding from the Maliac gulf by sea against Argos and the eastern coast, the other directed from Ætolia by way of Elis against Messenia and Sparta. But the writers from whom these notices come appear themselves to have been entirely unconscious of any discrepancy between the traditions in question and the common legend, which they accept and adopt unhesitatingly; and the facts which they record, even if admitted to be true, would seem to be quite insufficient for the establishment of any definite hypothesis. Perhaps we must be content to acquiesce in the conclusion of Niebuhr, that the conquest of the Peloponnese by the Dorians is a fact, but that "we do not possess the slightest historical knowledge of the

circumstances accompanying it."⁵ The legendary tale above given seems to be the invention of poets, who, when all memory of the mode wherein the conquest was effected had faded away, composed a narrative which might seem to account for the state of things existing at the time when they wrote.

5. The tradition of the place at which the Dorians effected their entrance may, however, be accepted, since it is one which would not be likely to be invented, as the Isthmus is the natural door of ingress to the Peloponnese,⁶ and since it accords with certain circumstances in the character of the people, and in the position of their earliest settlements. The Dorians were at all times unskilful in the attack of walled places;⁷ and if the Pelasgic population of the Peloponnese, so famous for its Cyclopian architecture, had established (as is not impossible⁸) a rampart across the isthmus at this early date, or even if they had blocked with walls the difficult passes of the Oneia,⁹ it may readily be conceived that the Dorians would have found it impossible to force an entrance. And the settlements at Stenyclērus and Sparta, which are certainly among the very first in which the conquerors established themselves, are (as has been shown⁸) readily accessible from the western side of Greece, by a route which passes through Elis and Pisatis, up the valley of the Alpheus, and thence into that of the Eurotas, over a pass of no great height. It appears to be on the whole more probable that the entire migration took this direction than that two distinct lines were followed, as Mr. Grote supposes. The theory that the Dorians were "the Normans of Greece," and setting out in fleets of "piratical canoes," proceeded from the Maliac Gulf by sea against the distant Peloponnese,¹ has great difficulties, and is destitute of any solid foundation.¹ The Dorians, despite some brilliant examples to the contrary in later times, are an essentially un-

---

⁵ Lectures on Ancient History, vol. i. p. 230, E. T.

⁶ See Thucyd. i. 13, and note in this connexion the inability of the Spartans to conceive of the Persians entering in any other way (Herod. vii. 40, ix. 7, 8, &c.). The word "Isthmus" is by some derived from the root i-, which appears in the Greek ἴθμα, the Latin ire, &c. (See Scott and Liddell's Lexicon, ad voc. 'ἰσθμός, and Smith's Dict. of Gk. and Rom. Geography, ad voc. Corinthus.)

⁶ Cf. Herod. ix. 70, and note, as illustrations, the long siege of Ithômê (Thucyd. i. 103) and the blockade of Plataea (ibid. ii. 78).

⁸ It is true that "the first Isthmian wall mentioned in history, was the one thrown up in haste by the Peloponnesians when Xerxes was marching into Greece" (Dict. of Gk. and Rom. Geograph. i. p. 684); but we may suspect that this was really the restoration of an old defence. Could the Spartans otherwise have accomplished the task—a bulwarked wall, at least 3½ miles in length—

within the space of a few months?

⁷ There are remains of walls in these passes (Chandler's Travels, ii. ch. 58, p. 273); but I am not aware if they are Cyclopian. That passes were early guarded by walls is shown in Herod. vii. 176.

⁸ See Grote's History of Greece, vol. ii. p. 439.

⁹ Grote, ii. p. 417; Müller's Dorians, i. p. 90, E. T.

¹ Mr. Grote (ii. p. 416, note ⁷) finds a foundation for it not only in the supposed colonisation of Crete from Doris, but also in the explanation which Aristotle gave of the proverb, Μηλιακὸν πλοῖον. (See Phot. Lex. Synag. p. 594, 9.) He considers Aristotle to represent Hippotes (the father of Aletes—the mythic founder of Corinth), as "having crossed the Maliac Gulf in ships for the purpose of colonising." But Aristotle makes no mention at all of the Maliac Gulf; and it is quite uncertain to what time he meant the story to refer. (See C. Müller's note in the Fragm. Hist. Gr. vol. ii. p. 150.)

nautical people. Their towns are built at a distance from the coast—they are slow to colonise—at sea they feel out of their element—their system discourages voyaging: they are thorough landsmen, and if it be said that nevertheless they are found at a very early period in situations which they could only have reached in ships; we may reply that, in the first place, the evidence of the fact is doubtful; and, secondly, that at best the cases adduced are so rare as to present all the appearance of exceptions to a general rule.[1] An examination of the supposed parallel case of the Dryopians[2] shows very strikingly the improbability of the Dorian conquests having been effected by sea. The Dryopians undoubtedly started on shipboard from their original country upon the Maliac Gulf, and the consequence is that we find their settlements widely dispersed, and universally *upon the coasts*. They are found at Hermioné, Eion, and Asiné on the coast of Argolis, at Styra and Carystus of Euboea, in Cythnos, in Cyprus, and again in the Messenian Asiné, inhabiting either actual seaports, or towns removed but a very short distance from the shore. The Dorians, on the contrary, occupy a single continuous territory, and all their chief cities are inland, as Sparta, Stenyclèrus, Argos, Troezen, Corinth, Megara, and Sicyon. Results so widely different can only be accounted for by a difference in the manner of the two migrations.

6. With respect to the time at which the conquest was made, the tradition usually followed[3]—which first appears in Thucydides[4]—placed the event in the eightieth year after the Trojan war, and the twentieth after the migration of the Boeotians from Arné in Thessaly. No great reliance can be placed on a tradition of this sort, which even if accepted fails to furnish a definite date, since the Trojan war, though probably a real event, is one the time of which cannot be fixed within two centuries.[5] The question whether the Greeks had any means of accurately estimating the lapse of time before the institution of the Olympic festival is one of great difficulty; and the answer to it will vary according to the belief that is entertained of the nature of those public records which were preserved from a remote period in many Greek cities.[6] If the *anagraphs* of the Spartans, for instance, contained, besides the names

---

[1] The mention of Dorians in Crete by Homer (Od. xix. 177) shortly after the Trojan war is the most remarkable notice bearing on this subject. If we believe the fact, we must suppose either that the Dorians had sailed at this early time from Greece proper to Crete, or else that at a still more remote era they had passed into Crete from Asia. They may have done so on their way to Europe. Perhaps, however, Homer is guilty of an anachronism, and assigns to the time of the Trojan war what did not really take place till some time after the Dorian conquest of the Peloponnese. There was no settled tradition concerning the colonisation of Crete (see Strab. x. p. 693).

[2] See Grote's History of Greece, vol. ii. p. 417.

[3] The interval of eighty years was adopted by Eratosthenes (ap. Clem. Alex. Strom. vol. i. p. 402), by Apollodorus (ap. Diod. Sic. l. 5), by Crates (ap. Tatian. 48, p. 107), by the Pseudo-Plutarch (De vit. Hom. k. 3, p. 720, ed Wytt.), by Velleius Paterculus (i. 2), by Syncellus (pp. 321 and 333), by Tzetzes (Chil. xii. 193), and others. There were, however, conflicting accounts. Clearchus tells us (l. s. c.) that some reckoned 120 and others 180 years between the two events.

[4] Thucyd. l. 12.

[5] See note " on Book ii. ch. 145.

[6] See the Essay on the Life and Writings of Herodotus, prefixed to vol. i. (ch. ii. pp. 43, 44).

of their kings, the number of years that each king reigned—which is a probable conjecture of Ottfried Müller's[a]—a means of calculating back with exactness to the first settlement of the Dorians in Sparta would have existed. Even if the names only were preserved, together with the relationship of each king to the preceding monarch, it would have been easy to make a rough estimate, which could not be far wrong, of the date in question. The number of generations from Aristodemus to the invasion of Greece by Xerxes, is given by Herodotus (who traces the descent of both the Spartan kings at that time[b]) as seventeen; and hence we obtain as an approximate date for the Dorian conquest, the year B.C. 1046.[c] The establishment of the Olympic contest about midway in the list of Spartan kings, which is an independent tradition,[d] confirms this estimate, since it furnishes a date for the reign of Theopompus, the ninth ancestor of Leotychides, almost exactly 300 years before Leotychides; whence we might conclude that the ninth ancestor of Theopompus would reign about 300 years earlier, or B.C. 1080. On the whole it may be assumed as probable that the first lodgment of the Dorian invaders in the Peloponnese belongs to the middle or the earlier half of the eleventh century before our era, and that it followed on the Trojan war within one, or at most two centuries.

7. Various tales were current concerning the manner of the conquest. According to the most poetical (which was also the most popular) legend, a single defeat produced the general submission of the Achæans; and the realms of the Atridæ were at once partitioned out among the three sons of king Aristomachus, Temenus, Cresphontes, and Aristodemus, the last-named being represented by his infant-children. Other accounts, however, told of a longer and more doubtful contest. The story of the Temenium, however we understand it,[e] seems to show that even in Argolis there was a prolonged resistance to the invaders; and in Laconia it would appear that the conquest was only effected after a fierce and bloody struggle, which lasted for above three centuries. The independence of Amyclæ, a strong town little more than two miles distant from Sparta, till within fifty years of the first Olympiad, is a fact established upon ample evidence;[f] and this fact, even if it stood alone, would sufficiently indicate that the Spartan Dorians were confined within very narrow limits during the first two or three centuries after their establishment in the valley of the Eurotas.

---

[a] Dorians, vol. i. p. 150, E. T. Mr. Clinton thinks that, if the years had been registered, "there would have been less uncertainty in the date of the Trojan war" (F. H. vol. i. p. 332). But the uncertainty might partly arise from different estimates of the time between the fall of Troy and the settlement of the Dorians at Sparta (see above, note [1]), partly from the calculations being based upon other and conflicting data.

[b] See Herod. vii. 204, and viii. 131.

[c] Seventeen generations, calculated according to the estimate of Herodotus at three to the century, will produce a total of 566 years. This sum, added to the date of the battle of Salamis (B.C. 480 + 566 = B.C. 1046), gives the year mentioned in the text.

[d] Diod. Sic. ap. Euseb. Chron. Can. Pars i. c. 35.

[e] Supra, p. 270.

[f] Pausan. III. ii. 6, iii. 7, &c. Comp. Ephor. Fr. 18; Conon. 36; Nic. Damasc. Fr. 36; Serv. ad Æn. x. 564, &c.

We learn, however, from Pausanias and other writers[a] that many cities of Laconia besides Amyclæ were first reduced to subjection about the same period; Pharis and Geronthræ in the reign of the same monarch who captured Amyclæ, Ægys on the borders of Arcadia in the reign of his father, Helos in the plain near the mouth of the Eurotas in that of his son. In Messenia too there were independent towns till near the close of the eighth century B.C., as is evidenced by the list of Olympic victors preserved in Eusebius.[b] It thus appears that the Achæans, instead of yielding upon a single defeat, and either quitting their country or becoming the willing subjects of the conquerors, maintained with great tenacity their hold upon the territory, and were only dispossessed by slow degrees and after centuries of contest.

8. The Dorian settlement at Sparta was the lodgment of a band of immigrants, forced to seek new abodes by the straitness of their own limits, in a portion of a valley easily defensible, which at once gave them a secure home, and enabled them to threaten a city of importance, the metropolis of a considerable kingdom. This was Amyclæ, which is with reason believed to have been "the ancient capital of Lacedæmon,"[1] being in tradition the home of Tyndareus and his family,[2] and the seat of the court of Agamemnon;[3] and possessing the tombs of that monarch and of Cassandra, as well as all the most ancient and venerated sanctuaries.[4] Whether a foreign invitation coincided with the desire of the Dorians to emigrate, and determined their settlement to the particular site actually preferred, which is a conclusion drawn by some modern writers from a tradition mentioned in Ephorus,[5] or whether the position itself decided them, is open to question. The site of Sparta, though not so striking as that of Athens, Corinth, or even Thebes, was one possessing most of the features regarded as important in ancient times. The Eurotas, which, from its source on the southern flank of the Arcadian highland to its junction with the Œnus a little above Sparta, is a more rapid mountain-stream running in a narrow valley, emerges shortly after the junction upon an open space, the modern plain of *Misra*, which is again closed towards the south by the approach of the mountains on both sides to the edge of the stream, at a distance of about six miles from the point where the plain commences. In this open space, surrounded on all sides by lofty mountains, the flanks of which are scarped and precipitous, stands a cluster of lesser elevations, from 50 to 60 feet above the level of the plain, guarded on the north and south by torrent-courses, and on the east protected by the stream of the Eurotas, in

---

[a] The capture of Pharis and Geronthræ is mentioned by Pausanias (III. ii. 7), that of Ægys by the same writer (ibid. § 5), that of Helos by him (ibid. § 7), and Philpon of Tralles (Fr. i.).

[b] Chron. Can. Pars I. c. 33. Oxythemis the Cnossian is a native of Cardut in Messenia, not of Coronea in Bœotia. (See Grote's Greece, vol. ii. p. 444, note.)

[?] Niebuhr's Lectures on Ancient History,
vol. i. p. 293, E. T. Compare Thirlwall's History of Greece, vol. i. ch. vii. p. 267, and Müller's Dorians, vol. i. pp. 106-108, E. T.

[2] Pausan. III. l. § 3, 4.
[3] Simonides, Fr. 177; Stesichor. ap. Schol. Eurip. Orest. 46.
[4] Cf. Pausan. III. xix.
[5] Fr. 18. See Grote, vol. ii. p. 441.

ORIGINAL LIMITS OF THE TERRITORY.

this place rarely fordable.' Here, upon these hills, at the upper end of this remarkable basin—the "hollow Lacedæmon" of Homer'—was built the cluster of villages, Limnæ, Pitané, Mesoa, and Cynosura, which formed in the aggregate the town of Sparta.' Near the lower extremity of the plain—most probably on an isolated hill overlooking the Eurotas, where now stands the church of *Aia Kyriaki*'—was the strong citadel of Amyclæ, the city itself extending to the north and west amid groves and gardens,' nearly to the stream called the Tiasus. The settlement at Sparta was clearly an ἐπιτείχισμα, or position occupied for purposes of offence, against Amyclæ, standing in nearly the same relation to that place in which the original Rome upon the Capitoline and Palatine hills stood to the Sabine settlement upon the Quirinal. That Amyclæ succeeded in maintaining its independence for three centuries—a fact concerning which there can be little doubt'—was owing, in part to the strength of its position, in part to its walls and the inexpertness of the Dorians at sieges. So long as it withstood the attacks of the Spartans, it would block against them the lower valley of the Eurotas, the whole of which down to the sea-coast must have remained in the hands of the Achæans.' At the same time the scarped chains of Parnon and Taÿgetus would confine the Spartans on the right and on the left, so that they could expand freely only towards the north, where the upper valleys of the Eurotas and the Œnus gave them a ready access to the territories of their neighbours. Accordingly we find wars with these northern neighbours distinctly assigned to this period of the Spartan history by writers of high authority.' The possession of Cynuria was disputed with Argos;' distant expeditions were conducted into Arcadia;' and quarrels began with the sister state of Messenia, between which and Sparta there had existed at first very close relations of friendship.' The stubborn resistance of the Achæan capital, while it checked the progress of Sparta towards the south, favoured perhaps, rather than hindered, its growth in the opposite direction.

9. The internal history of Sparta during these centuries is involved in great obscurity, and presents, indeed, difficulties of no common kind. The peculiarity of the double monarchy is the first thing that attracts attention when the early Spartan constitution is brought under review. It is obvious that the popular tradition furnishes no satisfactory explanation of this remarkable anomaly, to which the annals of the world do not present a parallel. We can scarcely doubt that the arrangement either arose out of a struggle for the crown between two families of almost equal power and influence, or was a contrivance of the nobles to weaken the royal authority. In either case the real history of the institution is lost, and has been superseded by fables which furnish no clue to the truth. Again, great doubt is thrown even upon the bare genealogy of the early kings, by the fact that the two royal houses were known in actual history, and from very remote times, by the names of Agids and Eurypontids, instead of Eurysthenids and Procleids. The explanations attempted of this circumstance are conflicting, while no one of them is very probable; and it cannot but be suspected that Agis and Eurypon were respectively the first kings of their houses, and that their predecessors in the genealogy, Eurysthenes in the one case, Procles and Sous in the other, were either of a different race, or else belong to the class of purely fictitious personages. Thirdly, it is difficult to understand what exactly was that state of sedition or lawlessness (στάσις or ἀνομία) under which the Lacedaemonians are said to have groaned during those centuries, and from which they were delivered by the legislation of Lycurgus. The explanation offered by some writers, that it was merely a departure from the ancient Dorian institutions—a casting off, under the influence of success, of the rigid discipline which had originally prevailed, and through which a clan of mountaineers had had strength and energy enough to overthrow the mighty kingdoms of the Atridae—can scarcely be received as true, since it is based upon an unproved and very questionable supposition, viz. that the institutions of Lycurgus were the mere revival of a primitive system, and it is far from harmonising with the expressions by which the ancient writers describe the condition of things anterior

to the Lycurgean legislation. That condition is distinctly declared to have been one of tumult and disturbance,¹ not merely one of luxury and relaxed discipline. So far indeed from discipline having been relaxed under the early kings, we have the direct testimony of Aristotle to the fact, that the way was prepared for the strict regulations of Lycurgus by the hardy life and warlike habits to which the Spartans had been accustomed for some time previously.² According to some accounts, the disorders in question consisted in the main of struggles between the "people"—by which we are probably to understand the Dorian inhabitants of Sparta—and their kings,³ who at one time made rash concessions, and at another stiffly maintained, or even unduly exalted their prerogative.⁴ If we accept this view, they would resemble in some measure the disturbances in Cyrênê, which Demonax was called in to end,⁵ but which his legislation, less felicitous than that of the Spartan lawgiver, only tended to aggravate.

10. According to some writers, however, the early disputes at Sparta were not so much between the kings and their Dorian subjects, as between the Dorian conquerors and the submitted Achæans. These last were, we are told, admitted in the first instance to full or qualified citizenship; but after a while a jealousy against them arose, and they were deprived of their rights, and reduced to the condition of freemen without political privilege.⁶ Great discontent followed, sometimes bursting out into revolts,⁷ which furnished an excuse for fresh severities, rebellion being punished by loss of freedom.⁸ Thus it would seem that the three classes were formed into which the Lacedæmonians are divided in the historical age—1. Spartans, 2. Perioeci, and 3. Helots—the first the sole possessors of political rights and privileges, the second free but without franchise, the third serfs attached to the soil, cultivating it for the benefit of their masters.

It is unnecessary to describe at length the condition of these three classes. Bishop Thirlwall in the eighth chapter of his History,¹ Mr. Grote in his second volume,² and writers of repute in various works upon Greek antiquities, have treated the subject in such a way as to exhaust it, and are agreed in the main as to the facts. A few leading points however may be noticed, which have not always been given sufficient prominence.

(i.) The Spartans were the free inhabitants of Sparta itself, not all the Dorian population of the country. They were themselves chiefly, but not exclusively, of Doric blood, having among them Ægidæ from Thebes, who were probably (admeians,) Heraclidæ and Talthybiadæ, who were Achæans. They were originally all landed proprietors, possessed of considerable estates in the richest part of the territory, which they cultivated by means of their serfs or Helots. They were gentlemen and soldiers, it being impossible for them—at least from the time of the Lycurgean legislation—to engage in trade, or even to superintend their estates, their whole lives being passed in the performance of state duties, either with the army or in the capital.

(ii.) The Periœci were the free inhabitants of the towns and country districts around Sparta. Their share of the territory was small and of little value. Trade, however, and commercial enterprise generally, manufactures, art, &c., were altogether in their hands; and thus they often acquired wealth, and occasionally were even employed by the Spartans in offices of considerable dignity. They formed an important element in the Spartan army, where they served not only as light-armed but also as heavy-armed; and thus they must have been called upon to undergo a good deal of severe exercise and training, though they were free from the oppressive burthen of the Lycurgean discipline. They were probably for the most part descendants of the conquered Achæans, but with a slight Doric infusion, and perhaps some further intermixture of races foreign to the Peloponnese.'

(iii.) The Helots were the slave population of Laconia. Their name may best be regarded as equivalent to *Halôti* (ἅλωτοι), "captives."¹ Their existence is probably coeval with the conquest of the country by the Dorians, who would retain as slaves those whom they took prisoners in battle. At first they would be insignificant in number; but the conquest of rebel towns,² and perhaps in some cases of Achæan cities which made a prolonged resistance,³ greatly increased them; and finally, upon the reduction of Messenia and the general enslavement of its inhabitants, they became the preponderating element in the population.¹ A considerable number of them dwelt in Sparta, where they were the attendants⁴ of their masters, and were subject to their caprices; but by far the greater portion lived scattered over the country, cultivating (like the Russian serfs) their masters' lands, but paying (instead of a definite amount of labour) a certain proportion of the produce of the land —probably one half⁵—as rent to the owner. Happier than the Russian serfs, these rustic cultivators were not brought into any direct contact with their masters, who dwelt at Sparta; but enjoyed their homes and indulged their family affections in security. With hearths inviolate and self-respect intact; with free social intercourse among each other, and no cold shadow of neighbouring greatness to awe or oppress them; with a firm hold on their lands from which they could not be ejected; with a fixed scale of rent which the lord had no power of augmenting; with a possibility of acquiring property by industrious exertion, and some prospect of obtaining freedom by purchase⁶ or by services to the state,⁷ the Spartan Helots must be considered, as a rustic class, to have been singularly favoured, and to have occupied a position which will in

---

selves as the dominant race. The supposed migration of the Achæans into the Peloponnesian Ionia can refer only to a small section of the nation; for that narrow region cannot possibly have received more than a portion of the great race which was spread through the three countries of Argolis, Lacedæmon, and Messenia. Herodotus, it must be allowed, seems to regard the Perioeci as Dorians when he mentions the several nations of the Peloponnese in his eighth book (ch. 73); but it is not quite certain that he does not merely omit them from his list as not forming, like the Cynarians, a separate people; and farther, it is worthy of remark that his early Spartan history is very indifferent (cf. i. 65, and note ad loc.).

² See Ephorus, Fr. 18; Herod. iv. 145.

¹ Harpocration (ad voc. εἱλωτεύειν) and Pausanias (iii. 20, § 6), derive Helot from the town "Ἕλος"; but this is wrong both historically and etymologically. The derivation given above—which was known to the ancients (see Schol. ad Plat. Alcib. I. p. 76, ed. Bekk.; Apostol. vii. 62)—is approved by

K. O. Müller (Dorians, ii. p. 30) and by Drs. Liddell and Scott.

² As Ægys (Pausan. iii. 2, § 5).

³ As is related of Helos (Pausan. iii. 2, sub fin., and iii. 20, § 6. Compare Ephor. Fr. 18).

¹ Clinton calculates the Helots at 170,000, and the rest of the population at 90,000 (F. H. ii. p. 508); K. O. Müller makes the former 224,000, the latter 156,000. These calculations cannot, of course, pretend to be more than rough guesses; but they sufficiently express the fact noted in the text (On the number of the Helots, cf. Thucyd. viii. 40).

² Xen. Rep. Lac. vi. 3; Arist. Pol. ii. 2, &c.

³ This was at any rate the proportion paid by the Messenians (Tyrtæus, Fr. 5), who were probably placed on the same footing with other Helots.

⁴ Plut. Cleom. c. 23.

⁵ Thucyd. iv. 26, and 80; Xen. Hell. vi. 5, § 28; Myron. ap. Athen. vi. p. 271, F.

many respects compare favourably with that of the modern day-labourer. Had it not been for one terrible institution—the barbarous practice of the "Crypteia"—by which the bravest and most aspiring of the Helot class were from time to time secretly made away with, at the mere will of the government,[e] their position might have been envied by the peasantry of almost any other country. This cruel and inhuman system, sanctioned by law[f] and frequently carried out in act,[g] must have greatly diminished from that comfort in which the country Helot would otherwise have lived; and, while devised to lessen the danger of a servile rising, must in reality have been the chief cause of that hostile feeling which the Helots entertained against their Spartan lords, and which showed itself on various occasions in disaffection and even in open revolt.[h]

11. The order of succession in the two royal houses at Sparta from Agis I. in the one, and from Eurypon in the other, may be regarded as tolerably certain;[i] but the characters of the early kings and the events assigned to their reigns cannot be considered to have much historic foundation. The *anagraphs* of the Spartans, even if they commenced so early, would be likely to contain at most a bare notice of the wars,[k] and would neither descend to personal traits, nor even give the details of military operations. And tradition on such points would be a very unsafe guide, more espe-

---

[e] Thucyd. iv. 80; Aristot. Fr. 80; Heraclid. Pont. Fr. II. 3; Plut. Vit. Lycurg. c. 28.

[f] Aristotle's statement that the Ephors, as a part of the regular formula on entering office, proclaimed war upon the Helots (Fr. 80), has been needlessly called in question by Müller (Dorians, ii. p. 41), Thirlwall (Hist. of Greece, vol. i. p. 311), Grote (vol. ii. p. 510, and others. On such a point Aristotle's authority is decisive; and all difficulty is removed if we regard the proclamation as secret, being intended (as Aristotle said) merely to satisfy the consciences of those in power in case they thought it expedient to have recourse to the Crypteia during their year of office (ὅπως εὐαγὲς ᾖ τὸ ἀνελεῖν).

[g] See Thucyd. iv. 80; Plut. Leg. I. p. 633; and the authorities quoted in the last note but one.

[h] Thucyd. I. 101, iv. 41; Xen. Hell. vii. 2, § 2, &c.

[i] The line of descent is commonly given as follows:—

(i.) ÆGIDÆ:—

Eurysthenes
|
Agis (his son)
|
Echestratus (his son)
|
Labotas (his son)
|
Doryssus (his son)
|
Agesilaus (his son)
|
Archelaus (his son)

(ii.) EURYPONTIDÆ:

Procles
|
Sous (his son)
|
Eurypon (his son)
|
Prytanis (his son)
|
[Eunomus (his son)]
|
Polydectes (his son)
|
Charilaus (his son)

Some suspicion attaches to the name of Eunomus, whose position in the list is not altogether settled. It is thought to have been originally a mere epithet applied to the king who was reigning when Lycurgus introduced his *cosmia*. (See Clinton's F. H. vol. i. p. 144, note.)

[k] They would not be likely to contain more than the primitive Roman Fasti, such as we see three in the fragments dug up on the site of the Forum.

cially during a time admitted to have been one of continued struggle and disturbance. Spartan history, in its connexion with real and genuine personages whose deeds and characters are known to us, must be considered therefore to begin with Lycurgus, who, though presented to us in somewhat mythical colours,[1] is to be accounted an actual man, the true founder of the greatness of his country. What Sparta became was owing entirely to the institutions of this famous lawgiver, who stands without a rival in the history of the first state in Greece, as the author of a system which endured nearly unaltered for five centuries, and which raised a small and insignificant country to a proud and wonderful eminence.

12. Great as were the services of Lycurgus to Sparta, they have undoubtedly been in one respect exaggerated. Not contented with viewing him as the introducer of the discipline known by his name, and as the improver in certain points of the previously existing constitution, the ancient writers are fond of ascribing to him the entire constitution of Sparta as it existed in their own day. Thus Herodotus and Plutarch speak of his "establishing the Senate;"[2] and in one of the Rhetræ which he was said to have procured from Delphi all the main points of the constitution are made to be of his institution.[3] As however Sparta certainly existed as a separate state for several centuries before Lycurgus, there must have been an established form of government anterior to him; and hence, before we can determine how much or how little of the framework existing in later times was of his creation, we must endeavour to find out what the constitution of the Spartan state was in the interval between the original settlement and the Lycurgean legislation. Now it is evident from the Homeric poems that in all really Hellenic states the form of government was from the earliest times a species of limited monarchy.[4] A royal race, generally regarded as possessing a divine right,[5] stood at the head of the nation; and the crown descended from father to son according to the ordinary law of primogeniture. But the Greek king, unlike the Asiatic despot, was controlled and checked by two powers coordinate with himself, and equally a part of the established constitution. A council of chiefs or elders (γέροντες) is invariably found

in attendance upon the monarch, with a power to offer advice which he cannot safely disregard; and all decisions of importance must be submitted to the assembly of the people (ἀγορά), whose consent was generally presumed, but to whose dissent, when plainly manifested, it was absolutely necessary to yield.* It is impossible to suppose that the Spartan monarchy was without these checks in the early times, more especially as the device of a double royalty is indicative of the successful exertion, at the period when it originated, of aristocratic jealousy and influence. When therefore Herodotus and Plutarch tell us that Lycurgus "instituted the Senate," we must either disregard altogether their authority, or at least look upon them as greatly exaggerating the real facts of the case.* A senate in Sparta must have been coetaneous with the monarchy; and even the details of number, which have been ascribed to Lycurgus in modern times,¹ being in all probability based upon the primitive divisions of the people, may with more reason be regarded as original than as later arrangements.

The Spartan Senate appears to have consisted from the first of thirty members, inclusive of the two kings, who acted as its presidents. This number is reasonably connected with the ancient threefold division of the people into tribes—Hylleans, Pamphylians, and Dymanians or Dymanatæ—which was common to all Dorian settlements.* In Sparta we know that besides this division there was another into Obæ, the number of which was thirty *—probably ten to each tribe. We may conclude, from the identity of number and from numerous analogies, that these Obæ, called also Phratriæ,⁴ had the right—possessed at Rome by the Gentes*—of each furnishing a member to the Senate. As two Obæ of the Hylleans were represented on the hereditary principle by the two kings, so it is likely that the other Obæ were originally represented each by its hereditary chief or head. The Senate, thus composed, formed a perpetual council which the kings were bound to consult, and through which alone they could exercise any great political influence. As its presidents they convoked, dissolved, or adjourned its meetings, proposed measures and put them to the vote, and otherwise took the lead in its proceedings; but the actual powers which

---

* Aristotle says of the old monarchies, οἱ βασιλεῖς ἦ μοιλασντο ἀπηγγέλλον τῷ δήμῳ (Eth. Nic. iii. 3, § 18). But Weiss seems to be right in supposing that when the opinion of the people declared itself distinctly against a proposition, the kings had neither the power nor the right to force it upon them. (See Hermann's Pol. Ant. § 55, note 13.)

* See note ⁷ on Book I. ch. 65.

¹ Grote's History of Greece, vol. ii. p. 453.

² These tribes can be distinctly traced at Argos (Steph. Byz. ad voc. Δυμᾶν), Sicyon (Herod. v. 68., Tzetzes Steph. Byz. ad voc. Ὑλλεῖς), Megara (Bœckh, 1073), and Corcyra (Bœckh's Staatshaltung, vol. ii. p. 404), as well as at Sparta. A triple division, probably the same, appears also in Crete (Odyss. xix. 177) and Rhodes (Iliad, ii. 668).

³ See note ⁵ on the preceding page. Mr. Grote (Hist. of Greece, vol. ii. p. 461, note ⁶) prefers the punctuation which connects τριάκοντα with γερουσίαν σὺν ἀρχαγέταις. But this is very harsh, and contrary to the best critics. (See Müller's Dorians, vol. ii. p. 87, E. T.; Bœckh, ad. Corp. Ins. Pars iv. § 3, p. 609; Hermann's Pol. Ant. § 24, note ¹, &c.) Had τριάκοντα referred to the later clause γερουσίαν it would certainly have taken the place of γερουσίαν.

⁴ Athenæus, iv. p. 141, F.

⁵ See Niebuhr's Hist. of Rome, vol. i. p. 333, E. T., where the Romans and Spartans Senates are compared.

they possessed above other members were limited to the right of voting by proxy,' and giving a casting vote in case of an equal division.

The Ecclesia, or general assembly at Sparta, must be considered to have contained originally all the free males who dwelt within the city and were of the legal age. Its proper name was "Apella."

All changes in the constitution or the laws, and all matters of great public import, as questions of peace or war, of alliances, and the like, had to be brought before it for decision; but it had no power of amending, nor even of debating a proposition, the right of addressing the assembly being probably limited in the early times to the kings. It met once a month—on the day of the full moon, or more frequently if summoned; and decided the questions put to it by acclamation.

13. If such was—as there is every reason to believe—the constitution of Sparta before Lycurgus, it is evident that he introduced no sweeping or fundamental changes into the government. He may have fixed the legal age of a senator at sixty, and have introduced the principle of election by the general assembly from the Oba in lieu either of hereditary right or of appointment by the Oba; but otherwise he can have made scarcely any alteration even of detail respecting the Senate, whose number, functions, and position with regard to the kings, remained such as above described throughout the whole of the historical period. The two slight changes which have been conjecturally assigned to him would tend, the one to increase the weight and influence of the Senate by making them the representatives of the whole body of the citizens, the other to strengthen the conservative character of the government by putting the entire direction of the state into the hands of men of advanced age—both objects in complete harmony with the general spirit and intention of Lycurgus's legislation.

With respect to the Apella, or general assembly of the citizens, if Lycurgus made any change, it was probably to increase the weight and importance of this element in the state. In the famous Rhetra already so often quoted, which was regarded as embodying his institutions, a special stress is laid upon the authority to be exercised by the people.' And the assembly, as if it had gained strength by his legislation, soon afterwards proceeded to assert rights, which it was found necessary to restrict by new enactments.' The unusual limitation of age too, by which Spartans only became entitled to take part in the public assemblies on the completion of their thirtieth year,' is likely to have been instituted by him, since it plainly stands connected with that prolonged education which was one of the leading features of the Lycurgean system.

The institution of the Ephoralty, which is ascribed to Lycurgus by Herodotus and Xenophon, and which may fairly be regarded as in all probability a part of his system, offers an apparent rather than a real exception to the general character of insignificance which marks (as has been observed above) all his constitutional innovations. Important as this element in the state ultimately became, it was in its origin harmless and trivial enough. The Ephors of Lycurgus were petty magistrates, empowered to hold a court, and to punish by fine and imprisonment; and probably appointed for the special purpose of *watching over* the Lycurgean discipline, and punishing those who neglected it. From this general supervision or superintendence they received their name, and to it their powers were confined in the earlier times. Their political influence had an entirely different source, and grew out of circumstances which arose later, and were probably little foreseen by the inventor of the magistracy. The election by the assembly, the number five, and even perhaps the monthly oath interchanged between them and the kings, may have dated from Lycurgus; but the origin of their political power must be sought in events which happened a century after his decease.

14. It is not, therefore, in the political changes introduced by Lycurgus—however well adapted to put an end to the internal troubles from which Sparta was suffering—that we must look for traces of that originality and genius which entitle him to his reputation as one of the master minds of Greece. His true glory is to be found in the introduction of that extraordinary system of training and discipline by which the Spartans were distinguished from all the nations of continental Greece, and through which there can be no doubt that they attained their vast power and influence. Whether this system was originally conceived in his own mind, or whether it (or something like it) had been in force from a remote period among all Greeks of the Doric stock, or whether finally it was copied by the Spartan lawgiver from institutions which had pre-

viously existed only in Crete, there is scarcely sufficient evidence to determine. While the hypothesis that the Lycurgean legislation was a mere revival of primitive Dorian customs, tends to lessen in some degree the marvel of its successful establishment, and has some of the greatest of modern names in its favour,[1] the fact—noted by Mr. Grote[2]—that no traces of such a system appear in any other Dorian state, unless it be in Crete, and the further fact that not a single ancient writer views the matter in this light, interpose almost insuperable obstacles to its reception. The balance of ancient authority is strongly in favour of the derivation of the whole Spartan system from Crete;[3] but it may be questioned whether on such a point a balance of authority is of much value, and whether probability is not upon the whole a better guide. Granting the close resemblance of the Cretan and Spartan systems, which it seems over-bold to deny,[4] it would appear to be at least as likely that the institutions travelled from the continent to the island as from the island to the continent. Very little is really known of early Cretan history;[5] and it may be doubted whether the Dorian cities in Crete were not, one and all, colonies from the Peloponnese,[6] who carried with them into their new homes institutions and practices found beneficial in the mother-country. In this way the spread of the system is natural, and has numerous analogies; while the contrary story, that Lycurgus sought and found in the remote,

---

[1] As Ottfried Müller, Heeren, Niebuhr, K. F. Hermann, and Bishop Thirlwall.

[2] Hist. of Greece, vol. ii. p. 456. Niebuhr anticipates this objection, and to meet it declares he considers it more probable that the ancient Doric institutions had been given up by the other Dorians than that they were newly invented and instituted by the Spartans (Lectures on Ancient History, vol. i. p. 259, E. T.). But the opposite view may be maintained with at least as much reason.

[3] This is the view of Heraclides (i. 85), who expressly gives it as the Spartan tradition, of Aristotle (Pol. ii. 7, ad init.), of Ephorus (Fr. 64), of Plutarch (Vit. Lycurg. c. 4), and of Strabo (x. p. 706; comp. xvi. p. 1084). The last-mentioned writer regards it as an admitted fact (ὁμολογεῖται). Tyrtæus, however, the most ancient authority, by assigning the Lycurgean institutions to the Delphic oracle, seems to ignore their Cretan origin.

[3] Mr. Grote says the Cretan institutions were "dissimilar" to the Spartan "in those two attributes which form the mark and pinch of Spartan legislation, viz. the military discipline and the rigorous private training" (Hist. of Greece, l. s. c.). But there are exactly the points in which all the ancient writers declare the resemblance to have been most close. (See Plut. Leg. p. iii.; Ar. Eth. i. 13, § 3; Pol. vii. 2, § 5; Ephor. Fr. 64; Hermi Id. Poss. Fr. 3; Nic. Damasc. Fr. 115.) Even Polybius, who maintains the dissimilarity of the Cretan and Spartan institutions (vi. 45) by his silence with regard to these points, is a witness in favour of their being common to the two systems.

[4] "Crete," says Niebuhr, "is the most mysterious of all the countries that belong to the empire of Greece" (Lectures, vol. i. p. 251, E. T.). Ephorus seems to have been the first writer who distinctly treated of Cretan customs and history, and his judgment was very defective.

[5] The earliest notice of Dorians in Crete is the well-known passage in the Odyssey—

ἐν μὲν Ἀχαιοί,
ἐν δ' Ἐτεόκρητες μεγαλήτορες, ἐν δὲ Κύδωνες,
Δωριέες τε τριχάϊκες, καὶ τε Πελασγοί.
(Od. xix. 176-177.

But the value of this must depend on the date of the Odyssey, which is probably a good deal later than the Iliad, and perhaps little, if at all, anterior to Lycurgus. Andron's story of a migration of Dorians to Crete from Histiæotis, which K. O. Müller admits to be "wonderful," and to "present a striking anomaly in the history of the ancient colonies" (Dorians, vol. i. p. 37, E. T.), is quite unworthy of credit, the minute "accuracy" of its statements betraying its origin. Even the colony of Altherment (Eph. Fr. 62) is open to grave doubts; and it may be questioned whether the Lacedæmonian colonies of Lyctus and Lampe were not really the first settlements made by the Dorians in the island.

insignificant, and scarcely Hellenic Crete⁶ a set of institutions which he transferred bodily to his native Sparta, is—to say the least—as improbable a tale as any that has come down to us on respectable authority.

15. But from whatever quarter the Lycurgean discipline was derived, whether from Crete, from Delphi, or (as is most probable) from the genius of Lycurgus himself, it must always remain one of the most astonishing facts of history, that such a system was successfully imposed upon a state which had grown up without it. To change the customs of a nation, even in single points, is proverbially difficult; to introduce strictness of living in the place of laxity, unless under the stimulus of strong religious feeling, is almost unprecedented; but without such stimulus, or at least with a very low degree of it, to induce a nation voluntarily to adopt an entirely new set of institutions, and those of so strict and self-denying a character as the Spartan, is a triumph of personal influence exceeding anything with which ordinary experience makes us acquainted, and one which could only have been possible under very peculiar circumstances. Nothing less than the combination of great genius and great personal weight on the one hand, with imminent and extreme peril on the other, can account for the submission of the Spartans to a new and untried system, which compressed all within its iron grasp, and which to every man not bred up in it must have been felt as a scarcely endurable slavery. Perhaps the continued resistance of Amyclæ, and the hardships and miseries consequent on a perpetual warfare with so very near a neighbour, may have been found so intolerable as to render any change acceptable which held out a prospect of relief; or it may be that the very existence of Sparta was threatened by the growing power of the unsubdued Achæans, and that the legislator made his appeal not so much to the desire of ease or the lust of conquest as to the instinct of self-preservation.

The details of the Lycurgean discipline are so well known, they have been so fully discussed in the ordinary histories, and there is so little dispute concerning them, that it is unnecessary to swell the present Essay by introducing an account of them in this place. The reader is especially referred to the description given by Mr. Grote,⁷ as at once the most copious and the most exact which exists in our language.

16. On one point, however, in the legislation of Lycurgus a very important difference of opinion exists, into which it will be necessary to enter. Most modern writers,⁸ following the detailed and circumstantial statements of Plutarch,⁹ have represented Lycurgus

---

⁶ Niebuhr has remarked on the strangeness of the Cretan inscriptions (Lectures, vol. i. p. 252). They mark the presence in the population of a large barbaric element, probably in part Pelasgic, in part derived from Asia. The 'Ετεόκρητες, or "true Cretans," of the Odyssey appear to represent the Asiatic inhabitants to whom Herodotus alludes (Book i. ch. 171-173).

⁷ History of Greece, vol. ii. pp. 512-529.
⁸ As K. F. Hermann (Pol. Ant. of Greece, § 28), Manso (Sparta, i. 1, § 110), Bp. Thirlwall (Hist. of Greece, vol. i. pp. 302-305), Schömann (Ant. Jur. Publ. p. 116), Tittmann (Griech. Staatsalterthümer, § 28), and Clinton (F. H. vol. ii. p. 495, note *).
⁹ Plut. Vit. Lycurg. c. 8.

as resuming the whole land of Sparta, and allotting it out afresh in equal portions to the inhabitants. According to this view, one of the chief objects of the lawgiver was to produce and maintain a general equalization of property; and hence various provisions are ascribed to him having for their object to prolong the equality, which, without such provisions, would have disappeared in one or two generations. He is supposed to have forbidden the subdivision or alienation of lots, entailing them strictly upon the eldest son, or the eldest daughter, if there were no son; in the case of childless persons to have only allowed their lots to be bequeathed to citizens not possessed of any land; and in the case of heiresses to have provided that they should be married only to such persons.¹ By these means it is thought that the number of the lots was maintained intact, and the near equality of possessions preserved, from the original institution of Lycurgus down to the close of the Peloponnesian war.

17. Against this view, which had come to be generally received, Mr. Grote has argued with irresistible force in the second volume of his History.² He has shown, first, that no knowledge of any such equalization, or of the provisions to maintain it, is possessed by any of the earlier writers, Herodotus, Thucydides, Xenophon, Plato, Isocrates, or Aristotle, whose statements are often in direct opposition to the theory;³ secondly, that in the historic times there is as much inequality of property in Sparta as elsewhere⁴ in Greece; thirdly, that the provisions assumed as part of the Lycurgean system are for the most part pure modern inventions, and rest upon no ancient authority; and fourthly, that the account in Plutarch is absurd on the face of it, since it assumes an extent of Spartan dominion in the time of Lycurgus which was not acquired till some centuries later.⁵ He also with great ingenuity accounts for the original

---

¹ Thirlwall, vol. I. p. 324; Manso's Sparta, b. I, § 121, and b. 2, § 129-134; Müller's Dorians, vol. ii. pp. 202-205.

² Pp. 530-560.

³ Aristotle calls Phaleas of Chalcedon, and not Lycurgus, the inventor of Communism (Pol. ii. 4). He also makes the levelling tendency of the Lycurgean legislation consist entirely in the system of συσσίτια (τὰ περὶ τὰς συσσίτια ἐν Λακεδαίμονι τοῖς συσσιτίοις ὁ νομοθέτης ἐκοίνωσε. ibid. ii. 2. Compare Theophrastus, ap. Plut. Lycurg. c. 10). Instead of regarding Lycurgus as having established equality of possessions, he complains that he had not taken sufficient precautions against the accumulation of property in a few hands. Xenophon, who is the unqualified eulogist of Lycurgus' legislation, knows nothing about his having established any forced equality of property, but praises him for removing the motives which led men to seek wealth, by his laws with regard to diet and dress (Rep. Lac. c. vii.). Isocrates mentions "the re-division of lands" among the evils from which Sparta had always been free (Panath. xii. p. 287). The silence of Plato as to Lycurgus in his Laws is also of great importance.

⁴ Herodotus seems to consider that wealth was distributed at Sparta as unequally as elsewhere. He speaks of the wife of Agetus as "the daughter of wealthy parents" (ἀνθρώπων ὀλβίων θυγατέρα, vi. 61), and of Sperthias and Bulis as "among the wealthiest men in the place" (χρήμασι ἀνήκοντες ἐς τὰ πρῶτα, vii. 134). Thucydides, referring to a more distant date, observes that "the richer Spartans, in the simplicity of their dress and in their whole style of living, conformed themselves to the ordinary standard" (i. 6). Xenophon contrasts the "opulent" with the other Spartans (Rep. Lac. v. 3, and Hell. vi. 4, § 11). Plato says that there was more gold and silver in Sparta than in all the rest of Greece (Alcib. I. p. 122, E.).

⁵ Plutarch makes Lycurgus divide the land about Sparta into 9000 equal lots for the Spartans, and the rest of Laconia into 30,000 similar lots for the Perioeci. The modern writers who profess to follow him, almost all admit that the latter statement

formation of the story which we find in Plutarch and for the currency obtained by it, attributing the former to certain antiquarian dreamers contemporary with Agis III. (B.C. 250), and the latter to the enthusiastic partisans of that monarch, who perished in an attempt to carry into effect at Sparta a communistic scheme almost identical with that ascribed by Plutarch to Lycurgus.

The whole notion then of Lycurgus having interfered with property requires to be set aside. Whatever the principle on which the Dorian conquerors had originally partitioned among themselves the lands of the Achæans—which may or may not have been that of equality, and whatever the changes which time had wrought in this original distribution—Lycurgus made no new arrangement. We are not entitled to assign to him the credit or discredit—as we may regard it—of inventing communism. He did not seek to deprive the rich of their wealth, which has never yet been attempted without its leading to a bloody struggle. He left property as he found it, contenting himself with imposing, alike on rich and poor, the same strict system of training and discipline—the same stern round of perpetual toil and privation—the same simple dress, plain fare, hard couch, unceasing drill, life-long restraint. He prevented any very rapid accumulation of wealth by forbidding his citizens to engage either in commerce or in the pursuit of agriculture; and, by attaching citizenship to the due payment of the prescribed quota to the public mess-table (or perhaps by an express law), he made it disgraceful to alienate the land from which that quota could alone be drawn; but, having thus furnished some checks against the extremes of riches and penury, he left the citizens free within those limits to indulge their natural tastes, not aiming at an impracticable equality, but satisfied if wealth could be deprived of its power to enervate.

18. The immediate effect of the Lycurgean legislation was to enable the Spartans to rise with a sudden bound from comparative insignificance to great power and prosperity. In the century following Lycurgus a most rapid advance may be traced. Teleclus (who succeeded Archelaus, the contemporary of Lycurgus) besieged and took Amyclæ, which had so long resisted the Spartan arms; received the submission of Pharis and Geronthræ, whose Achæan inhabitants quitted the Peloponnese; and thus opened a way for further conquests on the lower Eurotas and the sea-coast. Alca-

menes, his son, reduced Helos, defeated the Argives, and began the first war with Messenia.* We do not know by whom, or exactly at what time, the other towns upon the Laconian Gulf—Gythium, Teuthrônê, Aoriæ, Asôpus, &c.—were brought under, nor when the country to the east of l'arnon, and that immediately to the west of Taÿgetus, became Spartan territory; but probably the conquest of these tracts followed closely upon the full possession of the Eurotas valley, which was completed by the capture of Helos. Thus it would seem that Sparta, within the space of a century after Lycurgus, more than quadrupled her territory, and acquired nearly those limits which constituted Laconia Proper through the whole period of Grecian independence.

It is the opinion of Mr. Grote that "the formation of the order of Periœci" was subsequent to the introduction of the Lycurgean system at Sparta, and arose entirely out of the career of conquest sketched in the preceding paragraph. He conceives that in the time of Lycurgus there were in Lacedæmon two classes only—Dorian warriors and their Helot subjects—and that it was not until after the successes of Teleclus that Periœcic townships were formed, and a new class introduced between the full citizen and the Helot. But in this view he runs counter alike to tradition and to probability, which unite in throwing back the order of Periœci to the time of the original conquest. Isocrates* and Ephorus,* differing in many particulars, agree in this; while the circumstances of the case are such as almost to necessitate the early establishment of the class in question. Whatever view we take of the Periœci, whether we regard them, with the great bulk of modern authorities, as submitted Achæans, or, with Mr. Grote, conceive of them as consisting in the main of Dorian subjects of Sparta occupying the towns and villages throughout her territory, they will equally date from the time of the first settlers. The original Spartan territory must not be confined to the tract in the immediate neighbourhood of the city: it included undoubtedly the valley down which the invaders came, and probably extended up the courses of all those streams which unite above Sparta with the Eurotas. Thus Belemna, Pellana, Ægys, Œnus, Sellasia, Sciros, Caryæ, &c., would be within the Spartan dominion from the first; and the free dwellers in those places would hold the rank and condition of Periœci during the centuries which intervened between the invasion and the legislation of Lycurgus. Nor is there any reason why we should set aside the concurrent testimony of Isocrates and Ephorus, that these primitive Periœci were in the main submitted Achæans. Mr. Grote has clearly shown—and no one will now attempt to deny—that a Doric element was intermixed with an Achæan in certain Periœcic townships; but it is too much to argue from the few known cases of this kind* that a similar element existed in a greater or less proportion in all of them. Sparta, where the Dorian race was always inclined to dwindle,* can scarcely have furnished colonists for the hundred

---

* Pausan. III. ii. ad fin. Amyclæ (Pausan. III. ii. § 6). Pharis
* Pausihen. p. 270, 271.   * Fragm. 18. (Ibid.), and Geronthræ (ib. xxii. § 5).
* The only known cases are those of * Vide infra, p. 299.

dependent townships' which were scattered through her territory, or even for that portion of them which belonged to Laconia Proper; and the probability is that the Doric element in the periœcic class was really very small, and but slightly affected the general character of the body.

Although, however, the order of Periœci must date from the time of the first settlement made in Sparta by the Dorians, it is of course quite true that its great development belongs to the century immediately following Lycurgus. By the conquests of Teleclus and Alcamenes the Spartan territory was, as has been observed, quadrupled; and the Periœci must have increased proportionately; while the subjugation of Messenia, which belongs to the succeeding reigns, again nearly doubled the habitable territory, and caused a further extension of the Periœcic element, though not in the same proportion. The inhabitants of Messenia were for the most part Helotised, their principal cities being destroyed; but some seem to have been more favourably treated, since places in Messenia are occasionally reckoned among the Periœcic townships.

19. The history of the Messenian wars has only come down to us in anything like a detailed or complete form in the work of Pausanias. The authorities which this writer followed were (as he tells us') Myron of Priéné, who had written a prose history of the earlier war, and Rhianus of Bené in Crete, who had made the later one the subject of an epic. Neither of these two writers can be regarded as an authority of much weight, the poet being absolved by the nature of his work from any obligation to respect historical truth, and the prose writer being expressly declared untrustworthy by Pausanias himself. How little dependance can be placed on accounts derived from these sources appears from the circumstance that the two writers were not agreed as to which war it was wherein Aristomenes took part, each claiming him as the leader in that portion of the struggle which he had undertaken to commemorate. From this circumstance, and from the fact that the details assigned to the two wars have so great an amount of resemblance, it might naturally have been suspected that there was but a single contest, and that the process of duplication, whereto the early fabulists had recourse so often to complete the meagre outline of history, which was all that tradition furnished, had formed two wars out of one. The Fragments, however, of the contemporary poet Tyrtæus disprove this conclusion, and make it absolutely certain that there were two distinct struggles—divided by an interval, which seems to have been of about forty years.

20. The causes assigned for the rupture between Sparta and Messenia are of a trivial nature—especially those immediately preceding it. A dispute between two herdsmen upon the frontier,

followed up by a murder on the one part, and then by reprisals on the other, is made by Pausanias the actual provocative of hostilities.* We know, however, that border-quarrels do not involve nations in war unless they are otherwise disposed to it; and we may be sure that neither the violence of Polychares, nor even the slaughter of king Teleclus at the temple of Diana Limnatis⁵ (which act had evidently been condoned by Sparta),ʳ would have produced an outbreak, had not Sparta been disposed, as a matter of policy, to attack her neighbour. The Messenian version of the matter—which was, that these private wrongs were mere pretexts, and that Sparta only brought them forward to cloke her covetousness⁷—may be the whole truth; or possibly, the lust of conquest may have been sharpened by political animosity, the policy of conciliation pursued by the Dorian conquerors of Messenia⁸ standing in marked contrast with the exclusiveness of Sparta, and tending to rouse a spirit of discontent among the subject population of the latter country.

21. Sparta is accused of having opened the war by an act of treachery, similar to that by which the Bœotians commenced the great Peloponnesian struggle,¹ or to that by which Louis XIV. in 1681 began his attack upon Germany.² Ampheia, a Messenian town upon their borders, was seized in time of peace, a Spartan army having entered by night through the open gates, and massacred the inhabitants in their beds.³ The war was then carried on from this basis. Sparta ravaged the open country and besieged the towns,⁴ but met with the ill-success which always marked her attempts upon walled places.⁵ Meanwhile the Messenians, who were superior at sea, plundered the Lacedæmonian coasts. In the fourth year of the war the Messenian monarch ventured to take the field for the protection of his territory; and the Spartans, unwilling to assault the position where he had entrenched himself, were forced to retire without their usual booty. Reproached on their return home for this failure, they made in the next year a great effort: both kings took the field, and a desperate battle was fought, but without any decided result, neither party even claiming the victory.⁶ However, about this time the strength and resources of the Messenians are said to have been so exhausted, that they were forced to

adopt the plan of abandoning most of their cities and occupying the high mountain of Ithômé, where they fortified themselves.¹ At the same time they sent to Delphi to ask advice, and were bidden to offer to the infernal gods a virgin of the royal race of Æpytus. In obedience to this oracle, Aristodemus, an Æpytid, sacrificed his daughter;² and the Spartans, alarmed at such bloody rites, made no further attack upon the Messenians for the space of six years.³ At last, in the twelfth year of the war, they took heart, and marched against Ithômé. A second battle was now fought, which was as little decisive as the former, though the Messenian king (Euphaës) was slain in it. Another pause followed. During the first four years of Aristodemus, the successor of Euphaës, no operations of importance were attempted on either side;¹ his fifth year, however, was signalised by a third engagement, in which the Spartans were assisted by the Corinthians, while Arcadia, Argos, and Sicyon gave their aid to the Messenians; and after a stoutly contested fight the Spartans were completely defeated, and forced to retreat in confusion to their own country.⁵ Sparta now in her turn sent for advice to Delphi, and was recommended to have recourse to craft—a counsel which she was not slow to follow. No particular success attended her efforts;⁶ but at last, in the twentieth year of the war, the Messenians being hard pressed for provisions, and alarmed by portents and oracles, gave up all hopes of resistance, and, deserting Ithômé, scattered themselves to their homes, or took refuge in foreign states.⁶ The Spartans razed Ithômé to the ground, and rapidly overran the whole country; the inhabitants were treated with extreme severity; the entire population was reduced to the condition of Helots, becoming serfs upon the land, which was regarded as forfeited, and paying to their masters as rent a full half of the produce.⁶

22. The first Messenian war, which lasted (as Tyrtæus declared⁶) exactly twenty years, began certainly, and probably ended, within the single reign of Theopompus.⁷ According to Pausanias, it com-

¹ Pausan. IV. ch. ix. § 1. Thirlwall (Hist. of Greece, vol. I. p. 348) regards Ithomé as occupied for the purpose of "covering the region which lay beyond it," i. e. the rich vale of the Pamisus. But Pausanias has no such notion.

² Ibid. ch. ix. § 5.
³ Ibid. ch. x. § 1.
⁴ Ibid. ch. xi. § 1.
⁵ Ibid. ch. xi. § 3.
⁶ Ibid. ch. vii. §§ 1, 3.

⁴ Arcadia and Argos received the bulk of the refugees (Pausan. IV. xiv. § 1). Some of the priestly families are said to have taken up their abode at Eleusis (ibid.).

⁵ See the well-known fragment (Fr. 5) in which Tyrtæus describes their condition:—

"Ὥσπερ ὄνοι μεγάλοις ἄχθεσι τειρόμενοι,
δεσποσύνοισι φέροντες ἀναγκαίης ὕπο λυγρῆς
Ἥμισυ πᾶν, ὅσσόν περ ἐπὶ ἀρουραν φέροι."

This cannot be considered a very oppressive

burthen. In our own country the rent is commonly reckoned at one-third of the produce. In Russia the serf gives half his time to his lord, and in addition pays an annual tax of eight roubles for each male in his family (De Hell, p. 109).

⁶ Tyrtæus, Fr. 4:—

'Αμφ' αὐτῷ δ' ἐμάχοντ' ἐννέα καὶ δέκ' ἔτη,
Νωλεμέως, αἰεὶ ταλασίφρονα θυμὸν ἔχοντες,
Αἰχμηταί, πατέρων ἡμετέρων πατέρες·
Εἰκοστῷ δ' οἱ μὲν κατὰ πίονα ἔργα λιπόντες
Φεῦγον Ἰθωμαίων ἐκ μεγάλων ὀρέων.

⁷ See Pausan. IV. iv. § 3, and § 6. As Mr. Grote observes, Pausanias's authority, Tyrtæus, does not positively affirm that Theopompus brought the war to a close (Hist. of Greece, vol. ii. p. 570, note ⁷). His words, however, certainly convey that impression:—

"Ἡμετέρῳ βασιλῆϊ θεοῖσι φίλῳ Θεοπόμπῳ,
Ὃν διὰ Μεσσήνην εἵλομεν εὐρύχορον."
(Fr. 3.)

menced in the second year of the ninth Olympiad,* or B.C. 743, and consequently terminated in B.C. 724. These dates cannot be considered to have any high historical value, but they harmonize sufficiently with all that is known on the subject. There can be little doubt that the war fell into the latter half of the eighth century B.C., following within a century the legislation of Lycurgus.

23. It is conjectured, with a good deal of probability,² that important internal changes grew out of this war and conquest, which so greatly altered the external position of Sparta. Political acts of no small consequence are assigned to both the kings engaged in it;¹ and it seems certain that the unusual circumstance of the founding by Sparta of a real colony out of her own citizens belongs to the period immediately following the close of the struggle.³ Perhaps there are scarcely sufficient data on which to reconstruct the true history of the period; but the view taken by Bishop Thirlwall of the changes made, and the circumstances which led to them, is at once so ingenious and so consistent with probability, that it well deserves at least the attention of the student.

Bishop Thirlwall supposes that, to supply the losses which Sparta sustained in the course of the war, a number of new citizens were admitted at its close from the Periœci and Helot classes; but that between these new citizens and the old ones a distinction was made, the new forming a lower grade and being therefore designated "Inferiors" ('Υπομείονες),' while the old citizens, who had certain exclusive privileges, were termed 'Ομοιοι—"Peers" or "Equals." The assembly of the whole body of citizens he considers to have constituted the ordinary "Assembly" (ἡ ἐκκλησία—οἱ Ἐκκλητοι), while that of the Peers only was the "Little Assembly" (ἡ μικρὰ ἐκκλησία). This last-named body elected the Senators (γέροντες); but the possessors of the lower franchise had a vote in the general assembly which elected the Ephors. Hence the Ephors had from the time of Theopompus a new position—they became the representatives, and the sole representatives, of the *whole* people. They were therefore able to assume a tone, and gradually to take a position, far above that which they had held under the original constitution of Lycurgus; and from this circumstance arose the mistaken view which assigned the original creation of the Ephoralty to Theopompus. The colonization of Tarentum grew out of the admission of the new citizens. A portion were discontented

* Pausan. IV. v. § 4.
² Thirlwall's Hist. of Greece, vol. I. pp. 352-357.
¹ Theopompus is said by writers of great authority to have instituted the Ephors (supra, vol. I. p. 161, note ⁹). Polydorus, the king of the other house, was reputed by some to have added 3000 lots—and therefore 3000 citizens—at the close of the war (Plut. Vit. Lycurg. c. 8). The two kings conjointly were said to have procured from Delphi the ordinance limiting the powers of the assembly to the simple rejection or acceptance of propositions (ibid. c. 6).

³ See the Fragments of Ephorus and Antiochus quoted by Strabo (vi. pp. 402, 403), and compare Arist. Pol. v. 6. It may be doubted whether Crotona, Locri, and the other cities of Magna Græcia which were said to have received colonies from Sparta (Pausan. III. iii. § 1), are not more properly regarded as settlements of the exiled Achæans (see Hermann's Polit. Ant. § 50).
⁵ Compare the "Gentes minores," at Rome—a later addition to the citizen body, according to both Livy (l. 35) and Cicero (De Repub. ii. 20).

with the inferior grade which they occupied, and—like the Minyæ at an earlier period¹—claimed more complete equality of privileges. Their demands being resisted, they attempted a revolution; and the government was fain to disembarrass itself of them by adopting "one of the usual means of getting rid of disaffected and turbulent citizens." As the Minyæ were led out to Thera, so the discontented "Inferiors" were induced to take up their abode at Tarentum. Hence the stories of Theopompus and Antiochus—misrepresentations of the real history, which are yet correct in the main facts—the connexion of the colonisation with the Messenian struggle, and the discontent in which it originated.

Such is the view suggested by Bishop Thirlwall. Mr. Grote, without examining it formally, by implication rejects it, since he regards the distinction between "Equals" and "Inferiors" as equivalent to that between the fully qualified citizens, who paid their due quotas to the syssitia, and the disfranchised poor, whose means were insufficient for that purpose;² while his explanation of the two assemblies is, that the larger was that of the "Equals" only, while the lesser (ἡ μικρά) was *the same with the Senate*!³ With regard to the colonisation of Tarentum, he allows that it took place at this time, and that it was connected with serious disturbances at Sparta;⁴ but he contents himself with simply repeating the account given by Antiochus of the matter, without any attempt to explain its difficulties, or to harmonise it with the statements of other writers. These statements are so various and conflicting,⁵ while their authority is so nearly equal, that they seem to be fairly regarded as one and all "distortions of a historical fact."⁶ Bishop Thirlwall's conjectural restoration of the fact is on the whole satisfactory, and if not history, deserves to be regarded as the best substitute for history that is possible, considering the scantiness and contradictory character of the data.

24. The second Messenian war broke out, according to Pausanias, thirty-nine years after the close of the first.¹ It has been argued that this interval is too short to suit the expression of Tyrtæus— the only writer of authority on the subject—that the second war was carried on by those whose "fathers' fathers" carried on the

---

¹ Herod. iv. 146.
² History of Greece, vol. ii. p. 489.
³ Ibid. p. 481. Mr. Grote quotes the authority of Lachmann (Spart. Verfass. § 12, p. 216), and refers to Xen. Hellen. iii. iii. § 8 as decisive. But this passage does not really determine anything. I cannot think that in any Greek State the name of ἐκκλησία—ordinarily understood to mean the general assembly of the people— would have been applied to a body consisting of twenty-eight members.
⁴ Ibid. p. 574, note; and vol. iii. pp. 512-515.
⁵ Antiochus and Ephorus related that Tarentum was colonised by the Spartans, called Parthenii, the progeny born during the absence of the men in the Messenian war by the wives and daughters of the Spartans engaged in it. Despised and deprived of the rights of citizens, they plotted a revolt, which was discovered and crushed, the detected conspirators being compelled to seek another country (Strab. l. s. c.). Diodorus, on the contrary, traces the foundation to the Ἐπευνάκται (Excerpt. Vat. lib. vii. 10, Fr. 12, Mail), who, according to Theopompus (Fr. 180), were Helots married to the widows of those Spartans who had fallen in the war. There are considerable differences between the narratives of Antiochus and Ephorus.
⁶ See the article on *Parthenia* in Smith's Dict. of Antiquities, p. 871.
¹ Pausan. IV. xv. § 1.

first." The objection, however, is of no great weight;* and, on the whole, the numbers of Pausanias have a better claim to be considered historical than any others which have come down to us.* We may therefore place the great revolt, and the commencement of the second war, in B.C. 685; regarding this date, however, like those of the former war, as no more than approximate.

25. The events of the second Messenian war, as recorded in Pausanias, have a more poetic colouring than those of the first, as might have been expected, considering that they are probably drawn entirely from the epic of Rhianus. They consist principally of the wonderful exploits of Aristomenes, who takes the place occupied by Aristodemus in the first war, but is a still more conspicuous figure. His daring ventures and hair-breadth escapes, his skilful stratagems and reckless bravery, form the staple of the narrative; which has too little the air of an authentic account to deserve much notice in this brief summary of Sparta's early history. As in the first war, so in this, there were said to have been three battles; the first, in which the two foes contended singly, took place in the first year, at Derœ in Messenia, and had no decisive result;* the second, in which the Messenians were assisted by the Argives, the Sicyonians, the Arcadians and the Pisatæ, while the Spartans had the aid of the Corinthians and the Lepreatæ, was fought in the second year on the plain of Stenyclerus, at a place called the "Boar's Tomb," and was a very complete Messenian victory;* the third, in which Messenia had (nominally) the help of the Arcadians, while Sparta stood alone, fell in the third year, and was a still more complete Messenian defeat, through the treachery of the Arcadians, who drew off their troops in the middle of the battle.' This last fight took place at the spot called "the Great Trench," which seems to have been in the plain between Stenyclerus and Andania—the birthplace of Aristomenes. This general after his defeat betook himself, with the shattered remains of his army, to the mountain called Eira; which was occupied and fortified in the same way that Ithome had been in the first war,* and became thenceforth the head-

quarters of the resistance. The Messenians maintained this position for at least eleven years,[1] sometimes under their enterprising leader making forays deep into the heart of Laconia,[2] and bringing an ample spoil to their stronghold. Finally, however, Aristomenes being disabled by a wound, and discipline becoming relaxed, Eira was taken by surprise during a stormy night, and the war came to an end by its capture.[3] Aristomenes, with a considerable number of his countrymen, escaped into Arcadia, whence he emigrated to Rhodes, where he passed the remainder of his days with Damagetus, his son-in-law.[4] Such of the inhabitants as did not fly their country were reduced once more to the condition of Helots;[5] and Messenia became an integral portion of the Spartan territory, from which it was not severed until the time of Epaminondas.

26. The duration of the second Messenian war, according to the dates contained in Pausanias, was seventeen years; his details, however, only allow for fourteen years. Other writers[6] furnish an estimate beyond the higher of those two numbers. On the whole we may safely conclude that the contest terminated before the middle of the seventh century B.C., and probably lasted from about B.C. 685 to B.C. 668.

27. The conclusion of the Messenian struggle was closely followed by an invasion of Triphylia and Pisatis,[7] the inhabitants of which had assisted the Messenians in the war. These countries, which intervened between Messenia and the "hollow Elis"—consisting of the valleys of the Alphens and some minor streams—were conquered and made subject to the Eleans, who had rendered services to the Spartans during the contest.

28. The second Messenian war had been conducted by the two kings, Anaxander, the grandson of Polydorus, and Anaxidamus, the great-grandson of Theopompus. During the reign of their successors Eurycrates II. and Archidamus, the war with Arcadia, which Herodotus mentions,[8] appears to have broken out. The attack had been provoked by the assistance lent to Messenia in both her struggles, and seems to have been commenced with extensive views of general conquest.[9] It soon however settled into a struggle with the single town of Tegea, which resisted all attempts against its independence for two generations, but in the third, having lost its palladium,[10] suffered several defeats, and sank into the condition of

---

[1] arrival of Arcadian succours, as well as to render a retirement into that region, in case of defeat, comparatively easy.

[2] Pausan. IV. xx. § 1. Pausanias makes the war last seventeen years, but only accounts in his details for fourteen of them—viz. three years, while the Messenians kept the field, and eleven years after they shut themselves up in Eira.

[3] Ibid. IV. xviii. and xix.

[4] Ibid. IV. xx. and xxi.

[5] Ibid. iv. xxiv. § 1.

[6] Ibid. § 2.

[7] As Plutarch, who makes the actual siege of Eira last "above 20 years," and who would therefore certainly assign to the war a duration of 24 or 25 years (see his treatise "De Sera Numinis Vindicta," p. 548, F.), and Isidore ad voc. Τρυγαίος, who speaks of the war in which this part took part having lasted 20 years.

[8] Pausan. VI. xxii. § 2; Strabo, viii. p. 515.

[9] Herod. I. 66. Compare Pausan. III. iii. § 5.

[10] The Spartans consulted the Delphic oracle "in respect of all Arcadia" (ἐπὶ πάσῃ τῇ 'Ἀρκάδων χώρῃ, Herod. l. a. c.).

[11] Herod. i. 67, 68; Pausan. III. iii. § 6.

a dependant ally of Sparta, entitled however to peculiar honours.¹ About the same time or a little earlier, Sparta conquered the Thyreatis from Argos,² and thus extended her dominion over the entire southern half of the Peloponnese. The external history of Sparta from this point is traced with sufficient distinctness by Herodotus, and will not therefore be further pursued in this place. It only remains to notice certain internal changes of importance, which intervened between the time of Theopompus and the reigns of Cleomenes and Demaratus.

29. It was the boast of Sparta that her form of government underwent no material alteration from its original foundation by Lycurgus till after the close of the Peloponnesian struggle.³ And this boast was so far just, that she certainly continued during the period indicated remarkably free from those sudden and complete revolutions which afflicted almost every other Greek state. It was not possible, however, that she should escape altogether the silent and gradual alterations which the hand of time imperceptibly works; and accordingly we observe in her history that little by little the original constitution was modified, and that finally a state of things was introduced almost as different from that which Lycurgus designed, as if the government had at some time or other been changed by violence. Lycurgus preserved not only the forms but the essential spirit of the ancient monarchy. His Sparta was to be governed by her kings.⁴ Before the commencement of the Persian war, the kings had sunk into mere cyphers—they "reigned but did not govern." Honour and dignity were theirs; but power was lodged in a different quarter. The principal kingly functions are found to have been transferred to the Ephors, who were the true rulers of the Spartan state during the time of which Herodotus and Thucydides treat. The Ephors in Herodotus receive embassies,⁵ direct the march and give the command of armies,⁶ issue their orders to the kings,⁷ act as their judges and condemn or absolve them,⁸ accompany them abroad as a check,⁹ interfere in their domestic concerns¹⁰—in all respects have the real management of affairs; while the king is a nonentity, possessing little more political power than a senator,¹¹ and obliged to have recourse to the Ephors before he can force a foreigner to quit the town.¹² In Thucydides the Ephors recall the kings from abroad¹³—imprison them, and even put them to death¹⁴—act as presidents of the assembly, though the king is present¹⁵—conduct the foreign affairs of the country¹⁶—and control

---

¹ Herod. ix. 26-28. The Tegeatæ had the privilege of occupying one of the wings in the armies of Sparta.
² Ibid. i. 82; Strab. viii. p. 346.
³ Thucyd. i. 18.
⁴ Tyrtæus, Fr. 2, ll. 5, 6.
⁵ Herod. ix. 7.
⁶ Ibid. v. 39, 40.
⁷ Ibid. ix. 76.
⁸ Ibid. ch. 10.
⁹ Ibid. vi. 82.
¹⁰ Ibid. v. 39-41.
¹¹ The only real superiority which the king possessed over a senator in Sparta, seems to have been the double vote (Herod. vi. 57, ad fin.), which itself was probably nothing more than a casting vote (see note ad loc.).
¹² Herod. iii. 148. Compare, however, the case of Aristagoras (v. 50), whom the same king sends away without consulting the Ephors.
¹³ Thucyd. i. 131.
¹⁴ Ibid. and l. 134.
¹⁵ Ibid. l. 87. ἐπεψήφιζεν αὐτὸς (ὁ Σθενελαΐδας), ἔφορος ὤν.
¹⁶ Ibid. v. 36, vi. 88, viii. 6 and 12. Remark also that while the Ephors' names are essential to a treaty those of the kings

the monarch on foreign expeditions by means of a body of councillors." It is clear that by a slow and silent process of continual usurpation the Ephors had, by the time of Thucydides, completely superseded the kings as the directors of affairs at Sparta; while the kings' military pre-eminence—which was the last of their prerogatives that remained to them—had begun to be viewed with jealous eyes, and was already in danger of passing from them."

If it be asked how this gradual change was brought about—what inherent strength there was in the Ephoralty enabling it to make and maintain these usurpations—the answer is to be found, first of all in the fact that the Ephors were annually elected by the whole mass of Spartan citizens, and thus felt themselves the representatives of the nation; and, secondly, in the misconduct of the kings on various occasions, which caused them to be regarded with continually increasing distrust. The Ephors, it is probable, first assumed royal functions during the Messenian wars, when in the absence of both kings from the city it would naturally fall to them to convoke the assembly and the senate, to receive embassies and reply to them, to send out troops, and in fact to take the chief conduct of public affairs. They were able to establish themselves above the kings by means of their general right of supervision and correction of offenders, which entitled them to summon the kings themselves before their tribunal, to censure and to fine them; and especially by their power of intermeddling with the king's domestic concerns, under pretence of watching over the purity of the race of Hercules, with which the existence of Sparta was supposed to be bound up. The humiliating subjection in which the kings were thus kept, led naturally to their entertaining from time to time treasonable projects; and the discovery of these projects favoured the further advance of the Ephors, who in transferring to themselves the royal prerogatives seemed to be adding to the security of the commonwealth.

30. Another gradual change in the Spartan state—and one which ultimately destroyed the Lycurgean constitution—was effected by the working of regulations which Lycurgus had himself instituted. The perpetual diminution in the number of citizens, which is to be traced throughout Spartan history,[1] arose in part from the infanticide which he enjoined, in part perhaps from the restraints which he placed upon the free intercourse of young married persons, but chiefly from the disqualification under which he laid all those whose means did not allow them to furnish from their estates the necessary quotas for the *syssitia*, which acted as a discouragement to marriage,[2] and gradually reduced, not only the number of the *full* citizens, but that of the whole Dorian body, to a mere handful in the population of the city.[3] An exclusive possession of political rights, which (according to Greek ideas) was fairly enough enjoyed by a Demus of some 10,000 men controlling an adult male population of 50,000 or 60,000,[4] became intolerable, when its holders had dwindled to a few *hundreds*, and were scarcely a visible element among the inhabitants,[5] or an appreciable item in the strength of the country.[6] The general disaffection which arose from this disproportion, first showed itself at the time of the conspiracy of Cinadon, B.C. 397, which was with difficulty suppressed.[7] It afterwards caused Periœci as well as Helots to join with the Thebans in their invasion of Sparta.[8] Finally it robbed the community of all real national spirit, producing a state of internal struggle and disunion which took away from Sparta all her influence in Greece,[9] and tempted the young and enthusiastic Agis to his great experiment—fatal at once to himself and to what remained of the Lycurgean system.

---

[1] The original number of the full Spartan citizens was, according to one account, 10,000 (Ar. Pol. ii. 6). In the division of the territory, ascribed by some to Lycurgus, by others to Polydorus (Plut. Vit. Lycurg. c. 8), they are estimated at 9000. Demaratus (B.C. 480), describing their numbers to Xerxes, and probably exaggerating a little, laid them at 8000 (Herod. vii. 234). If the 5000 sent to Platæa were, as is generally supposed, τὰ δύο μέρη (comp. Thucyd. ii. 10), they would have amounted really at that time to 7500. After this they rapidly diminished. Not more than 700 Spartans were engaged at Leuctra (Xen. Hell. vi. iv. § 15). Isocrates probably gives the number in his own time, when (Panath. p. 286, C.) he estimates the original conquerors at 2000 (see Clinton, F. H. i. p. 408, note *). This would be about B.C. 350. Aristotle (about B.C. 330) declares that they did not amount to 1000 (οὐδὲ χίλιοι τὸ πλῆθος ἦσαν, Pol. ii. 8). Eighty years later, in B.C. 244, the whole number was 700 (Plut. Vit. Agid. c. 5).

[2] Polybius notes that in his time three or four Spartan brothers had often the same wife (Collect. Vet. Script. vol. ii. p. 384), the truth being, probably, that only the eldest brother could afford to marry (see Müller's *Dorians*, vol. ii. p. 236, note ¹).

[3] It is the whole Spartiate body which is in the reign of Agis 700. Of these not more than 100 were full citizens (Plut. Vit. Agid. l. s. c.).

[4] See Clinton on the Population of Ancient Greece, F. H. vol. ii. Appendix, ch. 22. pp. 401-505.

[5] Xen. Hellen. III. iii. § 5.

[6] Thirty Spartans only accompanied Agesilaus into Asia (Xen. Hellen. III. iv. §§ 2, 3). The same number went with Agesipolis to the Olynthian war (ibid. v. iii. § 8). The 700 who fought at Leuctra are an unusually large contingent for the time.

[7] Xen. Hellen. III. iii. §§ 5-11.

[8] Ibid. vi. v. § 25; Ages. ii. 24.

[9] Plut. Vit. Agid. c. 5, et seqq.

ESSAY II.

ON THE EARLY HISTORY OF THE ATHENIANS.

1. Obscurity of early Athenian history. 2. Primitive inhabitants of Attica unwarlike. 3. Causes of her weakness—no central authority—Pelasgic blood. 4. First appearance of the Athenians in history—stories of Melanthus and Codrus. 5. Blank in the external history. 6. Ionian migration conducted by sons of Codrus. 7. Internal history. 8. Early tribes—*Teleontes, Hoplites, Ægicoreis,* and *Argadeis.* 9. Clans and phratries—importance of this division. 10. Trittyes and Naucraries. 11. Political distribution of the people—*Eupatridæ, Geomori,* and *Demiurgi.* 12. First period of the aristocracy—from Codrus to Alcmæon, B.C. 1050-752. 13. Second period—from Alcmæon to Eryxias—B.C. 752-684—rapid advance. 14. Mode in which the usurpations were made—substitution of the Eupatrid assembly for the old Agora. 15. Power of the old Senate. 16. Full establishment of oligarchy, B.C. 684. 17. First appearance of the democratical spirit—legislation of Draco. 18. Revolt of Cylon, crushed. 19. Sacrilege committed—widespread discontent. 20. Solon chosen as mediator—his proceedings. 21. Date of his archonship. 22. His recovery of Salamis. 23. His connexion with the Sacred War. 24. His legislation—the *Seisachtheia* and debasement of the currency. 25. Prospective measures. 26. Constitutional changes—Introduction of the four classes, *Pentacosiomedimni, Hippeis, Zeugitæ,* and *Thetes.* 27. Arrangement of boribens—income tax—military service. 28. Pro-Bouleutic council. 29. Importance of these changes—Dicasteries. 30. Solon the true founder of the democracy. 31. Solon confined citizenship to the tribes. 32. Laws of Solon—(i.) Penalties for crimes—(ii.) Stimulus to population—(iii.) Law against political neutrality. 33. Results of his legislation—time of repose—revival of discontent—Solon leaves Athens. 34. Reapperance of the old parties—Pedieis, &c.—return of Solon—his courage. 35. Tyranny of Pisistratus.

1. THE early history of Athens is involved in even greater obscurity than that of Sparta, owing to the comparative isolation and seclusion, which were the consequence of its geographical position, and of the character of its soil.[1] Lying, as Attica did, completely out of the path of the armies which proceeded from Northern Greece to the Peloponnesus by way of the Isthmus or the Straits of Rhium, and possessing little to tempt the cupidity of conquerors, it scarcely came into contact with the other nations of Greece till just before the Persian War, and is consequently almost unheard of through the opening scenes of the Hellenic drama. No doubt this security might have tended with some races to foster a great power, which would have forced itself into notice by aggressions upon others; but the primitive Athenians appear to have been an unwarlike people, who were quite content to be left to themselves, and had no thought of engaging in foreign enterprises. The genius of the nation was from the first towards luxury and towards the arts;

---

[1] Compare Thucyd. i, 2. τὴν γοῦν Ἀττικὴν ἀνασίαστον οὖσαν ἄν- 'Αττικὴν ἐκ τοῦ ἐπὶ πλεῖστον διὰ τὸ θρώπων ᾤκουν αἱ αὐτοὶ ἀεί.

when they engaged in war, it was forced upon them, and for many centuries they were content to repel the aggressions which, at long intervals, were made upon their independence.

2. A marked indication of this temper is to be found in the part which they are made to play in the Trojan war by Homer. Menestheus, the Athenian chief, commands a contingent of 50 ships[1]—a number which is surpassed by only six of the confederates;[2] yet neither he nor his troops are ever spoken of as earning the slightest distinction in the field. On the contrary, in the only place where the war rolls his way, Menestheus "shudders," and hastily invokes the aid of the Ajaces, who come and save him from his danger.[3] "Athens and Arcadia," as it has been well observed,[4] "may justly be regarded as the only two undistinguished in Homer among those states of Greece which afterwards attained to distinction." They alone "fail in exhibiting to us signs of early pre-eminence in the arts of war."[5] Thus Athens neither made a history for herself in the primitive times, like Sparta and Argos, nor was brought into notice, like the Messenians, Arcadians, and others, by being mixed up with the history of more powerful countries.

3. One cause of the weakness of Athens—or, to speak more accurately, of Attica—in the early ages, may be found in the want of a common centre, and single governing authority; another, in the inferior character of the Pelasgic race. "Attica," we are told "until the time of Theseus, was divided into a number of petty states, each under its own ruler, which in ordinary times were quite independent of one another. It was only when danger threatened that a certain precedency and authority was conceded to the Athenian king, who was then placed at the head of a species of confederacy."[6] Twelve of these little communities are named by a writer of fair repute,[7] viz.:—Cecropia (by which we must understand Athens herself), Tetrapolis, Epacria, Decelea, Eleusis, Aphydna, Thoricus, Brauron, Cythêrus, Sphêttus, Cêphisia, and Phalêrus; and of these one, Tetrapolis, was itself a confederacy of four towns or villages—(Œnoë, Marathon, Probalinthus, and Tricorythus[8]—like the "Three Leagues" of the Grisons, which together form a Swiss Canton. According to the legend, Theseus, who is made a little anterior to the Trojan War, put an end to this state of things, compelling or persuading the several communities to forego their independence, and to elevate Athens into the position of a real capital. It may however be doubted whether the consolidation of the Athenian power was really effected at this early date. There are not wanting indications[9] of the continuance of cantonal

---

[1] Hom. Il. II. 556.
[2] Namely, Argos, Mycenæ, Pylos, Sparta, Arcadia, and Crete.
[3] Il. xii. 331, et seqq.
[4] See Mr. Gladstone's Homer and the Homeric Age, vol. I. p. 139.
[5] Ibid. l. s. c.
[6] Thucyd. ii. 15: ἐπὶ γὰρ Κέκροπος καὶ τῶν πρώτων βασιλέων ἡ Ἀττικὴ ἐς Θησέα ἀεὶ κατὰ πόλεις ᾠκεῖτο πρυτανεῖά τε ἔχουσα καὶ ἄρχοντας, καὶ ὁπότε μή τι δείσειαν, οὐ ξυνῇεσαν βουλευσόμενοι ὡς τὸν βασιλέα, ἀλλ' αὐτοὶ ἕκαστοι ἐπολιτεύοντο καὶ ἐβουλεύοντο.
[7] Philochorus, Fr. 11, quoted by Strabo (ix. p. 577).
[8] Strabo, viii. p. 383; ix. p. 579; Steph. Byz. ad voc. Τετράπολις.
[9] In the Homeric Hymn to Ceres (Demeter), which is supposed by some to have been composed as late as B.C. 650, Eleusis appears to be regarded as quite independent

sovereignty to times long subsequent to Theseus; and considering the strong affection of the Greeks for autonomy,[a] and the special love of the Attic race in the historical age for their country towns,[b] it may fairly be suspected that the rise of Athens to the headship which she ultimately obtained, was far more gradual than either Thucydides or Philochorus imagined.

The Pelasgic origin of the Athenians is stated as an undoubted fact by Herodotus,[c] and is fairly regarded as implying a certain degree of military incapacity.[d] Whatever we take to be the difference between Pelasgi and Hellenes, it is at least clear that the latter were the stronger, the more enterprising, and the more warlike race. The peaceful and agricultural people, who built their towns away from the sea for fear of attacks from corsairs, and protected them with massive walls against land foes, was not indeed devoid of a certain sturdy and passive courage, which showed itself occasionally in a heroic resistance,[e] but had no spirit of active enterprise, and apparently no power of self-development. So long as Attica was purely or even mainly Pelasgic, she naturally remained weak and unwarlike. It was only when, by a gradual influx of Hellenic refugees, she lost the Pelasgic and assumed the Hellenic character,[f] that a military spirit grew up, and Attic armies ventured across the frontier.

4. The first appearance of the Athenians upon the stage of Grecian history is connected with that invasion of the region immediately north of Attica by the Bœotians from Arné in Thessaly, which Thucydides placed at the distance of sixty years after the Trojan war.[g] At that time it appears that Attica furnished a refuge to many of those who fled from before the conquerors—Cadmeians, Minyans, Gephyræans,[h] &c.; in consequence of which she drew the attacks of the Bœotians on herself, and had some difficulty in maintaining her independence. After the death however of the Bœotian

king Xanthus, in single fight with Melanthus,¹ she again enjoyed a period of tranquillity, till the stream of Dorian conquest, which had overflowed from the Peloponnese, and spread itself over Corinth, Egina, and the Megarid, set her way, and Athens found her very existence threatened by the powerful race which had destroyed the kingdoms of the Atridæ, and now sought to master the whole of Greece. This expedition, of which we have one of the earliest notices in Herodotus,² was certainly unsuccessful; it failed, as we are told, through the self-sacrifice of Codrus,³ Melanthus' son and successor, who devoted himself for his country in a manner which reminds us of the stories of the Decii, and thereby assured the victory to his own side. The Dorian army retreated; and Athens, released from this peril, entered upon that long period of profound and unbroken repose, which contrasts so remarkably alike with her own later struggles, and with the contemporary history of her great foe and rival, Sparta.

5. The death of Codrus is said to have taken place about the middle of the eleventh century before our era.⁴ From that time to the age of Solon (B.C. 600), a period of four centuries and a half, the external history of Athens is almost a blank. She had wars undoubtedly with her neighbours, Bœotia and Megara; but they were of small importance, and left the respective positions of the three countries almost unchanged.⁵ She also may have taken part in the struggle between Chalcis and Eretria, in which it is said that most of the Greeks participated;⁶ but there is no distinct evidence that she did so, and at any rate she did not obtain at that time any important increase of territory or of reputation.

6. The most important event—or rather series of events—belonging to this early period, which may properly be regarded as forming a portion of the external history of the country, is the great movement which proceeded from Attica to Asia, known commonly by the name of the Ionian migration. It appears that in the troublous times which followed on the passage of Mount Pindus by the Thessalians, when nation pressed upon nation, and three-fourths of the inhabitants of Greece seem to have changed their abodes, Attica received with open arms the refugees from all quarters, and thereby acquired a population which her scanty and sterile territory was quite incapable of permanently supporting. While there was danger of a Dorian invasion, the inconvenience was endured; but no sooner had the attempt at conquest been repulsed, and the Dorians forced to relinquish their enterprise, than means were taken to get rid of the superfluous population by finding them abodes elsewhere. The principal mass of the refugees was formed of the Ionians from

---

¹ Pausan. IX. v. § 8; Strab. ix. p. 570; Schol. ad Plat. ad. Ruhnk. p. 49.
² Book v. ch. 7d.
³ Strab. ix. p. 570; Pausan. II. xxxix. § 4; Justin. ii. 7; cf. Pherecyd. Fr. 110.
⁴ Two hundred and ninety-three years before the first Olympiad, according to Eusebius (Chron. Can. ii. pp. 304-318), or B.C. 1069.

⁵ Athens gained somewhat from Bœotia. Eleutheræ, in the woody range of Cithæron, but on the southern side of the main ridge, is said to have been originally Bœotian, but to have become Attic at an early period (Pausan. I. xxxviii. § 8.) The same seems to have been the case with Oropus.
⁶ Thucyd. i. 15. Compare Herod. v. 99, and note ad loc.

the northern coast of the Peloponnese, who had been compelled to yield their narrow but fertile valleys to the expelled Achæans,[1] and to seek an asylum among their kindred in Attica. With them, however, were intermingled Greeks of various other tribes, Pylians, Phocians, Cadmeians, &c.,[2] whom the migratory movements in progress, and perhaps other causes, had made fugitives from their homes. According to the tale commonly believed by the Greeks, Neleus, a son of Codrus, having quarrelled with his elder brother, Medon, to whose throne he had aspired, led out the first body of emigrants from Attica,[3] and, passing through the Cyclades, many of which were occupied upon the way,[4] conducted his followers to the Asiatic coast, where he settled them at Miletus. Androclus, another son of Codrus, soon afterwards made a settlement at Ephesus,[5] Andræmon,[6] or Andropompus,[7] at Lebedus, Damasichthon and Promethus at Colophon,[8] and other sons of Codrus elsewhere; until in the course of a few years twelve cities were founded, and the confederacy established which formed the Ionia of historic times.

There is scarcely a doubt that the legendary writers, from whom the details above given were originally derived, "invested" with an undue "unity," the great event of which we are here speaking.[9] The occupation of the islands, and of the Asiatic coast from Miletus to Phocæa, must assuredly have been spread over a certain number of years. No parallel, however, is to be drawn between the formation of these settlements and that of the later colonies, owing to the essential difference which exists between *migration* and *colonisation*. The latter is naturally slow and gradual, being connected with the regular advance and growth of the colonising power; the former is bound by no such laws, being abnormal and irregular, the result of a sudden need or a sudden impulse, and therefore rapid, startling, marvellous—in a brief space effecting vast changes, and often beginning and ending within ten or twenty years. Whatever may be the true history of the origin and formation of the Ionian confederacy— which it is not the object of the present Essay to trace further—it is reasonable to suppose that the movement, so far as Attica was concerned, was one of short duration. A vent once found, the surplus population would have drained off rapidly; and accordingly we find that all the Attic traditions connected with the Ionian towns, point to the single reign of Medon as their era, and that in the subsequent history there is no appearance of a recurrence to the policy which was found necessary at that time.

7. The internal history of Athens from Codrus to Solon, while it

---

[1] Herod. I. 145; vii. 94; viii. 73.
[2] Ibid. I. 146; Pausan. VII. ii. § 2.
[3] Pausanias gives the history at full length (VII. ii. § 1, et seqq.,; also Ælian (Var. Hist. viii. 5). An infinite of writers agree in their brief notices (Herod. ix. 97; Hellan. Fr. 63; Thucyd. i. 12, 95, &c.; Ephor. Fr. 32; Strab. xiv. p. 907; Eustath. ad Dionys. Perieg. 823; Clitoph. Fr. 3; Tzetzes ad Lycophr. 1378, &c.).
[4] Herod. vii. 95; viii. 46, 48; Thucyd. I. 12; vii. 57; Ælian, l. s. c.; Plutarch de Ex.

[5] ii. p. 603, B.; Eustath. ad Dion. Per. 525.
[6] Strab. l. s. c.; Pausan. VII. ii. § 4, &c.
[7] Pausan. VII. iii. § 2.
[8] Strab. l. s. c.
[9] Pausan. VII. iii. § 1. Mimnermus, however, the Colophonian poet (about B.C. 600), made Andræmon the founder, and brought him straight from Pylos, without mentioning Athens (ap. Strab. xiv. p. 909).
[10] See the remarks of Mr. Grote (Hist. of Greece, vol. iii. p. 229, and p. 232).

partakes in some degree of the quiet and negative character of the external history of the same period, presents nevertheless a series of slight but significant changes, by which the ancient heroic monarchy was gradually transformed into an oligarchy on a narrow basis. There are also assigned to this period a certain number of institutions, broadly marked upon the surface of Athenian history by the sections into which the nation was split, which are at once interesting in themselves, and important as for the most part continuing in a modified form to the time of Clisthenes, or even later. These institutions will be first considered; after which a sketch of the growth and history of the oligarchy, to the time when it received its first great check from the hand of Solon, and a short account of that statesman's measures, will complete the "Early History" of the country, and bring us to the date at which Athens first comes before us in the pages of our author.

8. The earliest known division of the Attic people was that into *Teleontes* (or *Geleontes*), *Hopletes*, *Ægicoreis*, and *Argadeis*.[?] These four tribes—common apparently to the whole Ionic race [1]—are regarded by some as simply parallel to the triple division of the Dorians into Hyllæi, Dymanes, and Pamphyles—that is to say, as an ultimate fact which we cannot analyse, and into the inner significance of which it is idle to inquire.[2] The more usual,[1] however, and perhaps the more correct opinion, sees in these remarkable names a distinct trace of the early condition of society in Attica, regarding them as plainly indicating the existence in early Greece, as in India and Egypt, of the system of *caste*. This subject has been already discussed in a foot-note,[4] and scarcely needs any further notice. The Attic castes, if they existed, belong to the very infancy of the nation, and had certainly passed into tribes long before the reign of Codrus. In the historic times no superior honour, or dignity even, seems to have attached to one tribe over another; and it may be doubted whether the origin of the division, or the primitive import of the names, was at all present to the consciousness of those who used them at this period. They were then more political divisions, forming a convenient basis for a double organisation, which, pervading the whole community, tended to break down local barriers, and to unite into one the scattered members of what had till recently been a confederation of independent towns.

[?] Julius Pollux, a writer of the second century after Christ, tells us that there had been various divisions before this. Under Cecrops there had been four tribes, Cecropis, Autochthon, Acteea and Paralus; under Cranaüs the names had been Cranaïs, Atthis, Mesogaea, and Diacris: under Erichthonius, Dias, Athenaïs, Poseidonias, and Hephaestias (viii. 109.). At last, in the time of Erechtheus, the names Teleontes, Hopletes, Ægicoreis, and Argadeis, were adopted. I cannot regard this statement as historical, or even attach to it any particular value. Of the four divisions there is no evidence that any was really in use but the last.

[2] It is to mark this that the names are said to have been taken from the four sons of Ion (Herod. v. 66; Eurip. Ion, 1579; Pollux, l. s. c.). They are found in inscriptions belonging to various Ionic cities (Böckh. Corp. Inscrip. 5078, 5079, 5663, 3664, 3685, &c.).

[3] See Mr. Grote's Hist. of Greece, vol. ii. p. 70, and compare Wachsmuth, Alterthumsk. i. 1, § 43; G. Hermann, Praef. ad Eurip. Ion, pp. 27-30, &c.

[1] For the arguments on this side of the question see K. F. Hermann's Pol. Ant. of Greece, § 5 and § 94; Schömann, de Com. Ath. p. 351, et seqq.; and Thirlwall's Hist. of Greece, vol. ii. pp. 4-8.

[?] See note [4] on Book v. ch. 66.

9. The more important, and probably the earlier, division of the tribes, was into φρατρίαι, "Brotherhoods," and γένη, "Clans," or "Houses." Each tribe is said to have contained three "brotherhoods"—each "brotherhood" thirty "clans." Each "clan" again comprised thirty γεννῆται, or "heads of families."[a] Thus a total is produced of 360 clans, and 10,800 families. These numbers, below that of the brotherhoods or phratries, are no doubt more ideal than real; like the actual number of the Roman Gentes,[b] they must have varied at different times, the clans in a brotherhood continually diminishing, since there was no means of replacing such as became extinct; and the families in a clan rising or falling, according as the particular races proved prolific or the contrary.

It is the opinion of Mr. Grote that the family was the unit in this system, and that the process by which the arrangement was made, was one of "aggregation." He regards the clan, and still more the brotherhood, as artificial formations arising out of the mere will of the legislator, who arranged the families which he found existing into certain groups, which he denominated "clans," aggregated the clans into "brotherhoods," and finally put the "brotherhoods" into "tribes."[c] Granting in one place[d] that the transaction which he thus describes is involved in deep obscurity, and that "we have no means of determining to what extent the Gens at the unknown epoch of its first formation was based upon relationship" or otherwise, he nevertheless assumes throughout his whole account the absence from the gentilitial and phratric ties of the principle of relationship, and their purely arbitrary and factitious character. In this view he re-asserts a theory of Niebuhr's[e] not generally accepted in Germany,[f] which has a basis in assertions of the grammarians,[g] expressive of the state of belief in their own day, but which is contrary to the opinions of earlier and more philosophical writers,[h] as well as to the probabilities of the case. It has

---

[a] This view rests chiefly on a fragment of Aristotle (Fr. 3) quoted by a Scholiast (in Plat. Axioch. p. 465, ed. Bekker). It is confirmed by Pollux (viii. 111), and Harpocration (sub voc. γεννῆται).

[b] See Niebuhr's Roman History, vol. i. p. 393, K. T.

[c] Hist. of Greece, vol. iii. pp. 73-77.

[d] Ibid. p. 78.

[e] Roman History, vol. i. pp. 305-309, E. T.

[f] The opposite side of the question is maintained by Meier (De Gentilitate Attica) by Wilda (Das Deutsche Strafrecht, p. 123), and by K. F. Hermann (Pol. Ant. of Greece, § 99, &c.).

[g] As Pollux, who says the γεννῆται were γένει μὲν οὐ προσήκοντες, ἐν δὲ ταῖς συνόδοις οὕτω προσαγορευόμενοι" (viii. 9); Hesychius (sub. voc. γεννῆται); and the author of the Rhetorical Lexicon, published by Bekker (Anecdot. i. p. 227, 229).

[h] As Aristotle (Pol. l. 1), who, according to Niebuhr (R. H. i. p. 303), "in an unguarded moment gave way to the illusion;"

and his pupil Dicaearchus, who very distinctly maintains the blood-relationship, not only of the γεννῆται, but even of the φράτορες (ap. Steph. Byz. sub voc. πάτρα). In order to escape the weight of this argument it is assumed that Pollux "drew his account of the Athenian constitution from Aristotle's Politics" (Niebuhr, vol. i. p. 303; Grote, vol. iii. p. 78), and therefore that Aristotle must have contradicted himself upon the point. But though Pollux certainly had the work of Aristotle before him, and quotes from it occasionally (iv. 174; ix. 801 n. 165, &c.), yet, as it is clear that he had many other authorities, we cannot possibly tell with regard to any particular statement which he makes whether it came from Aristotle or no. Mr. Grote candidly admits in one place that Aristotle would have rejected his theory (p. 80), and, indeed, that the ancient Greeks generally believed the members of a gens to have had a common ancestor (p. 79.)

been well observed by K. F. Hermann,[a] that "all the forms and institutions, as well as the names, of the phratriæ and clans, bear every appearance of family distinctions;" and it should be noted, that, while experience furnishes instances of a national organisation, similar to that of Athens, being based upon real relationship,[b] there is no evidence that such a purely artificial arrangement as Grote and Niebuhr suppose was ever actually carried into effect in any country.[c] It seems therefore most reasonable to regard the division into brotherhoods, clans, and houses, as having resulted originally from the extension of family ties, and therefore as having proceeded downwards, not upwards; by separation, not by aggregation; from the tribe to the house, and not in the reverse order.

In addition to the bond of consanguinity, which as time went on became continually weaker, a religious principle which never lost its strength, and social advantages of considerable value, held together the various portions of the organisation which we are considering. Each tribe had its own special sacred rites,[d] celebrated once a year under the presidency of the tribe-king (φυλοβασιλεύς); each phratry held similar meetings,[e] probably more frequently; finally, each clan or house had exclusive religious ceremonies, a priesthood belonging only to themselves, and a private burial-place where none but members of the clan could be interred.[f] Again, the members of a clan possessed an interest in the property of all their brother clansmen. In the early times property was vested absolutely in the clan, and could not be willed away from it;[g] if a man died without children, his clansmen succeeded necessarily to all the property that he left behind him. Even after Solon, they enjoyed this privilege, if any one died intestate.[h] They could also claim the right of marrying any heiress of the clan, who had the misfortune to be left an orphan; though this privilege was counterbalanced, after the time of Solon, by a corresponding obligation upon them to marry poor orphans, or provide them with suitable portions.[i] Some clans moreover certainly, and perhaps all, had common property, which was administered by a treasurer of their own.* There was also a general duty on the part of all members of the clan to help, defend, support, and, in case of need, avenge other members who required their assistance;* which, though not exactly a privilege, was a strong bond of union, and, in an unsettled state of society, must have been felt rather as an advantage than as a burthen.

It resulted in part from the material advantages accruing to the members of a clan from their membership, in part from the religious feeling which regarded rites as polluted by the participation in them of persons of a different blood, that admission to a clan was jealously guarded by the law, and narrowly watched by the existing members.* Foreigners admitted to citizenship did not thereby become γεννῆται, or φράτορες;* nor did their descendants, unless born of women who were citizens. In that case they were enrolled in the clan and phratry of their mother. The children of foreign women, or of any women who were not citizens, were also excluded.* Thus "the preservation of legitimacy and purity of descent among the citizens," may be considered as the main "political object and import"* of the whole organisation; though, even apart from this, it must have possessed a high value in the eyes of a wise statesman, as tending to establish a close union of different classes, based upon the double foundation of religious communion and consanguinity.

10. The other ancient division of the tribes was that into Trittyes and Naucraries. As each tribe (φυλή) contained three Phratries or "Brotherhoods," so it also contained three Trittyes, or "Thirdings." It is uncertain whether these divisions were really distinct and separate; according to some writers the Phratry and the Trittys were two names of the same body.* But if so, the identity of the classifications ceased at this point, the Naucraries having no connexion whatever with the γένη, or "clans." While in each Phratry there were thirty "clans," in a Trittys there were but four Naucraries. The Naucraries existed solely for political, and not at all for religious or social purposes. They are properly compared with the later συμμορίαι,* and consisted of a number of householders (ναύκραροι, or ναύκληροι) associated together for the purpose of undertaking state burthens, as the providing of soldiers, of money, and in later times of ships.* Each Naucrary had its head, or Prytanis, who,

until the institution of the Polemarch, were the chief military officers.¹ Nothing is known as to the manner of their appointment; but the probability is that, like the φυλοβασιλεῖς, or heads of the tribes, they were nominated by the nobles,² not elected by the people.

Of the two distributions here considered, it is evident that the former was by far the more important. The Naucraries existed merely for state purposes, and touched nothing but material interests. The Phratries and Clans were private as well as public unions, and had the closest connexion with all the deepest feelings and most sacred associations of the people. With the one the Athenian came into contact on rare occasions, and merely in the way of business: the other was an element of his daily life, and entwined itself with his social and domestic affections, with his ordinary duties, and with his religious feelings. Hence the latter outlived the Clisthenic constitution,⁴ and continued to exist and flourish through the whole period of the subsequent history, while the former, if not formally abolished, sunk at any rate very shortly into entire desuetude.⁵

11. It is remarkable that political privilege does not appear to have been attached in the early times to either of these two organisations. In that of the Clans and Phratries, a rough resemblance may be traced to the old Roman organisation into Gentes and Curies; but nothing in ancient Athens corresponds to the Comitia Curiata of antique Rome, nor to the original Senate of 300, one from each of the 300 gentes.⁶ Again, in the Trittyes and Naucraries we seem to have a division analogous to that of the Roman Centuries (which had reference at once to taxation and to military liability); but Athens has no Comitia Conturiata, where privilege is apportioned to service, and the citizen who has done most for the state compensated by the largest share of power. All important political privilege is engrossed by the Eupatrids,⁷ who consist of a certain number of "clans" claiming a special nobility, but not belonging to any single tribe, or distinguishable from the ignoble clans, otherwise than by the possession of superior rank and riches.⁷ The rest of the citizens constitute an unprivileged class,⁸ personally free, but with no atom of political power, and are roughly divided,

---

¹ This is perhaps the meaning of Herodotus where he says in connexion with Cylon's revolt (L. s. c.) that "the Heads of the Naucraries at that time bore rule in Athens."

² Pollux. viii. 111 and 120.

⁴ For the many passages above quoted from the orators, especially Dem. c. Neaert. p. 1054, and Isæus, de Circ. Hered. c. 19.

⁵ Photius says (s. v. Ναυκραρία) that Clisthenes raised the number of Naucraries from 48 to 50, making 5 in each of his 10 tribes; and the fact of the Athenian navy amounting soon after to 50 ships (Herod. vi. 89) is some confirmation of this. But with the rise of the system of trierarchy, all trace of the Naucraries disappears.

³ I mean that neither the early Senate at Athens, nor the early Assembly, was based upon the organisation of the clans. No doubt the Assembly of the Eupatrids did in some degree resemble the Comitia Curiata.

⁷ The author of the Etymologicum defines the Eupatrids as οἱ αὐτὸ τὸ ἄστυ οἰκοῦντες, καὶ μετέχοντες τοῦ βασιλικοῦ γένους, καὶ τὴν τῶν ἱερῶν ἐπιμέλειαν ποιούμενοι. But these are rather the consequences than the sources of their pre-eminence.

⁸ Dionysius of Halicarnassus seems to be right in recognising but two real orders in ancient Athens (ii. 8). There was no difference of rank or privilege between the γεωμόροι and the δημιουργοί.

according to their occupations, into γεωμόροι (yeomen-farmers) and δημιουργοί (artisans).[a]

12. The union of the Eupatrids in the same tribes and phratries with the Geomori and Demiurgi, seems to show that the aristocracy of Athens was not original, like that of Rome, but grew out of an earlier and more democratical condition of things—such, in fact, as we find depicted in the Homeric poems. A real monarchy, like that of the heroic age, tends to level other distinctions; for kings always use the people to check the power and insolence of the nobles. Thus at Athens, as elsewhere, in the heroic times, there was undoubtedly the idea of a public assembly (ἀγορά), consisting of all freemen; but this institution seems entirely to have disappeared during the centuries which intervened between Codrus and Solon.[1] The power of the nobles gradually developed itself during this period, increasing at the expense of the kingly prerogative on the one hand, and of popular rights upon the other. We are told that at the death of Codrus, the Eupatrids, in pretended honour to that monarch's self-sacrifice, formally abolished the name of king, substituting that of Archon, or Ruler.[2] Such a change undoubtedly implied more than it asserted. The alteration of title would symbolize, and thereby tend to produce, a diminution of authority; and the nobles, who had made the change, would, by that very fact, have set themselves up above the sovereign, and asserted their right to control and limit his prerogatives. Still the royal power appears to have been but slightly diminished. The Archons held their office for life,[3] and though nominally responsible,[4] can have been subject to no very definite restraints, and, when once appointed, must have ruled pretty nearly at their pleasure. The old royal family was moreover maintained in a quasi-royal position, the archonship being confined to the Medontidæ, or descendants of Medon, the son and successor of Codrus. On the other hand, hereditary right, as previously understood, was abolished; and at the death of an Archon, the Eupatrids chose his successor out of those descendants of Medon who were of an age to govern.

It is remarkable that, according to the traditions, this state of things maintained itself, without further change, for three centuries. Medon had twelve successors in the office of life-archon,[5] whose united reigns are said to have covered the space of 296 years.[6] This period is a blank in Athenian history. Nothing is known of the life-archons beyond their names; and we can only gather from the silence of ancient authors, that the time was one of peace abroad, and of tranquillity—perhaps of comfort and contentment

---

[a] Pollux, viii. 111; Hesych. ad voc. Ἀγροιῶται; Etym. Magn. ad voc. Εὐπατρίδαι. Cf. Arist. Fr. 3.

[1] Mr. Grote speaks of there being "traces" of the continued existence of "general assemblies of the people with the same formal and passive character as the Homeric Agora," in the interval between Theseus and the Solonian legislation (vol. iii. p. 97). But I can find no proof of this assertion.

[2] Justin. ii. 7; comp. Lyc. c. Leocr. 20.
[3] Pausan. iv. v. § 10.
[4] Pausan. iv. ii. § 4, and vii. ii. § 1.
[5] These were Acastus, Archippus, Thersippus, Phorbas, Megacles, Diognetus, Pherecles, Ariphron, Thespieus, Agamestor, Æschylus, and Alcmæon.
[6] Euseb. Chron. Can. pars ii. p. 306-320. But comp. pars i. c. 30, where the number of years is only 272.

—at home.' The Asiatic colonisation, it must be remembered, had carried off unruly spirits, and left the land with a deficient rather than a surplus population; labour was probably well paid; above all, the yearning after free institutions and the excitement of political life, had not yet commenced. The state was in its boyhood, unconscious, satisfied with life; free from those fierce cravings, in part noble, in part selfish and brutalising, which in the nation, as in the individual, mark the period of adolescence.

13. On the termination of this long interval of almost complete rest and inaction, the advance of the aristocracy was rapid. In the first year of the seventh Olympiad (B.C. 752), the life-archonship was brought to an end, and the duration of the office was limited to ten years,' but without infringement on the right of the Medontidæ to its exclusive possession. By this change, not only was the dignity diminished, but the responsibility of the Archon was rendered a reality; for he could be actually called to account for any abuse of his authority at the close of his ten years of office. Thus the Eupatrids obtained a power over the nominal sovereign, which they were not slow to use; and we find that in the reign of the fourth decennial Archon (B.C. 714) they took advantage of an act of cruelty which he had committed,' not only to depose him individually, but to declare that the Medontidæ had in him forfeited their claim to rule; upon which it naturally followed that the office should be thrown open to all Eupatrids. The decennial term of office was still continued for thirty years longer;' but at the end of that time (B.C. 684) the mask was altogether thrown off, and the last remnant of the monarchy disappeared before the assaults of the aristocrats. The decennial (sole) archonship was abolished; and in lieu of it a governing board was set up, consisting of nine persons, who were to share among them the kingly functions, and to hold office only for a year. Thus was a form of government established, such as an oligarchy especially affects, with numerous magistrates and a short term of office, whereby that equality among its own members is best produced, which is as dear to an exclusive aristocracy as the destruction of all antagonistic powers.

14. Such are said to have been the steps whereby the Athenian

Eupatrids obtained the complete possession of the sovereign power. The means and instruments wherewith they worked are more obscure, and require investigation. It has been noticed[?] that from the earliest times there was in every Greek monarchy an Assembly or Agora, which exercised a certain amount of control over public affairs. This assembly rightfully consisted, according to the idea universally prevalent, of all the freemen capable of bearing arms in the state. It would seem, however, that at Athens the Eupatrids contrived gradually to substitute for this body the mere assembly of those of their own order. The effect was as if at Rome the Patricians had at any time succeeded in suppressing the Centuries, and replacing them on all occasions by the Curies. The Eupatrids thus certainly obtained the power of nominating the Phylo-Basileis, or Tribe-Kings,[?] who must have originally received their appointment from the whole people; and they probably also named the Prytaneis of the Naucraries,[?] as they undoubtedly did afterwards both the decennial and the annual Archons. Through the Phylo-Basileis they would at once exercise a very important influence over the monarch; for the Phylo-Basileis were from the first assessors of the king, without whom he could not deliver sentence in the Prytaneum.[?] They would also, if they appointed the Prytaneis of the Naucraries, have had a hold both over the military force and over the revenue, which would fully account for the inability of the monarchs to resist their aggressions.

15. Still another institution remains to be noticed, by means of which it is probable that their power was mainly advanced. A Council (βουλή), or Senate (γερουσία), is as essential an element of the ancient monarchy as an Assembly (ἀγορά),[?] and must have existed at Athens from the remotest times. There is no reason to think that the Athenian kings ever acquired such a preponderance in the state as could have alone enabled them to abrogate this primitive institution. Weakness is the characteristic of the Athenian monarchy, in which the king was never much more than "the first of the nobles;"[?] and we may therefore assume that throughout the monarchical period there was from first to last a Senate, possessing as much weight as the Roman, and acting as a most influential check upon the king, and a most powerful instrument for the aggrandisement of the Eupatrids. It is with reason that many critics and historians identify this primitive council with the "Senate of Areopagus,"[?] which, after the time of Solon, was distinguished by that affix from the new Council established by him. The bulk of ancient writers, indeed, (if we may believe Plutarch[?]), ascribed the institution of both Senates to Solon; but we have already seen, in connexion with Lycurgus,[?] how little stress can be laid in such a case upon a preponderance of authority. To the first known lawgiver of

---

[?] Supra, Essay i. pp. 281, 282.
[?] See Pollux, viii. 111 and 120.
[?] Grote, vol. iii. p. 90.
[?] Pollux, viii. 111, and Plut. Vit. Solon. c. 19.
[?] Supra, Essay i. pp. 281, 282.
[?] See Thirlwall, vol. ii. p. 11.

[?] As Meier (Der Attische Process, Einleitung, p. 10), Schömann (ibid.), Matthiæ (De Jud. Ath. pp. 142-148), and Mr. Grote (vol. iii. p. 97).
[?] Vit. Solon. c. 19.
[?] Supra, Essay i. p. 282.

ESSAY II.   ESTABLISHMENT OF OLIGARCHY.   313

a country all its ancient institutions are popularly assigned, however antique and primitive they may in fact be; and this is done the more uniformly the further men are removed from the period. Against the authority of Plutarch's "majority of writers," most of whom were undoubtedly of a late date, may be set as an equipoise the single name of Æschylus, who, coming within a century of Solon, was so far from making him the author of the Areopagite Council, that he represented it as already existing in the time of Orestes—more than 500 years earlier.[3] If Solon had instituted the Areopagus, it is probable that its powers would have been more definite, and its weight less. It is also very unlikely that it would have borne the name of βουλή, since from his time its functions were far more those of a court than of a council.[3] But if it was an ancient institution, continued with diminished powers by Solon, we can easily understand its retaining its ancient name, even when that name had become inappropriate, and we can account for the indefiniteness of its powers, the vastness and vagueness of its claims, and the strong hold which it had upon great numbers of the Athenians. If we regard it as almost the sole relic of the ancient constitution which survived the sweeping reforms of Solon and Clisthenes, we can understand how it should draw to itself the affectionate regard of the more conservative portion of the Athenian people; how the traditions of the past should cling around it; and how it should finally become the watchword and the rallying point of that party which was the determined opponent of democratic progress.[4]

16. Such then would seem to have been the instruments whereby the Athenian Eupatrids effected their usurpations — usurpations which issued in the establishment, about the year B.C. 684, of an oligarchy even closer[5] than that which existed at Rome before the institution of the Tribunate. The noble clans not only monopolised office, but confined even the franchise to members of their own body;[6] they both furnished and elected the Archons, Phylo-Basileis, and heads of the Naucraries; they also occupied all the priesthoods of any account;[7] and there is reason to believe that they held almost exclusive possession of the territory of the state, either directly, in their own names, or indirectly, as mortgagees of the small properties belonging to the poorer landowners.[8] The unre-

---

[3] Eumen. 651 et seqq. Aristotle, it must be added, made the Areopagus anterior to Solon (Pol. ii. 9).
[3] See Hermann's Pol. Ant. § 105.
[4] In the time of Ephialtes and Pericles. (See Arist. Pol. ii. 9; Diod. Sic. xi. 27; Plutarch, Vit. Pericl. c. 9, &c.)
[5] Aristotle (l. s. c.) calls the oligarchy λίαν δεσποτική, and speaks of the people as held in slavery under it (δουλεύοντες..
[6] Whereas at Rome, in the worst times, the Plebeians had a voice in the election of one consul.
[7] So much, at least, may be gathered from the definition of the Eupatrids in the Etymologic. Magn.

Εὐπατρίδαι, οἱ αὐτὸ τὸ ἄστυ οἰκοῦντες, καὶ μετέχοντες βασιλικοῦ γένους, καὶ τὴν τῶν ἱερῶν ἐπιμέλειαν ποιούμενοι. Compare Plut. Vit. Thes. c. 24, where Theseus is said to have made the Eupatrids ἱερῶν καὶ ἱερέων ἡγεμόνας.

[8] The poverty which Solon was required to remedy must have been an evil of long standing, which very gradually came to a head. It appears that in his time the whole land was covered with mortgage pillars, whence he himself represents the earth itself as reduced to slavery (Fr. 28, quoted at length, p. 322).

strained power which they enjoyed had the effect—seen commonly to result from it—of stimulating their selfishness, and rendering them harsh and unjust towards all those who were beyond the charmed circle of their own order. We may gather from a name afterwards borne by the democratical party in Attica,[1] that in the distributions of territory which were made from time to time under Eupatrid influence, as Athens passed from the pastoral life to the agricultural,[2] it was only the poorer and less desirable lands that were allotted to the small cultivators. Again, the demand for written laws, which is the first symptom of life manifested on the part of the unprivileged classes, is indicative of sufferings arising from an abuse of power,[3] and seems to imply that undue severity was shown towards the humbler criminals, while those of a higher grade were allowed comparative impunity. The universal poverty, moreover, which it was one of the objects of Solon's legislation to remedy, proves incontestably the prevalence of a tyrannical and oppressive spirit, which had ground down the humbler classes to the lowest point whereat existence was possible, and which was prepared to ruin the state by enforcing the primitive law of debt in the full rigour of its archaic severity.

17. It appears that during the space of nearly sixty years (from B.C. 684 to B.C. 624), the Eupatrids continued in the undisputed possession of all the powers of the state, and disposed almost at their will of the lives and properties of the citizens. The Archons—their representatives—not only administered but made the laws, deciding all matters by their θεσμοί, or edicts;[4] they tried causes of every kind,[5] and punished the accused at their discretion. We have no means of measuring the sufferings or the patience of the unprivileged Athenians during this interval; but we find that towards its close discontent at the existing condition of things began to manifest itself in a shape felt to be dangerous, and the oligarchy became convinced, that in order to secure the maintenance of their power active steps must be taken. The popular discontent assumed the shape, which is not unusual under similar circumstances, of a demand for written laws—*i.e.* of a requirement that the penalties of offences shall no longer be fluctuating and arbitrary, dependent upon the

---

[1] "Highlanders" (διάκριοι or διακρίων). The aristocrats were at the same time known as "Lowlanders" (πεδιείς or πεδιακοί). It is plain that in allotting territory, the nobles had taken to themselves all the rich and fertile plains, while they had assigned the hilly tracts, with their light and shallow soil (τὸ λεπτόγεων, Thuc. i. 2), to the unprivileged classes.

[2] If the ancient tribes' names be taken to signify priests, warriors, goatherds, and mechanics, the goatherds alone will represent those who got their living by the land; and the transition from the pastoral to the agricultural life will be marked by the substitution after Theseus of the term γεωμόροι for the earlier αἰγικορεῖς.

[3] Compare the similar demand in Rome (Liv. iii. 9), and see Niebuhr's remarks on it (Hist. of Rome, vol. ii. pp. 278, 279, E. T.).

[4] The name "Thesmothetae" applied to every Archon; only as the first three were ordinarily designated by other titles, the six who had no special designation came to be regarded as θεσμοθέται κατ' ἐξοχήν. Θεσμός is properly a law (comp. θεμίστες), and was so used by Solon (Fr. xxiv. l. 8). In early times the distinction between laws and decrees or edicts is unknown.

[5] The Ἄρχων ἐπώνυμος judged all disputes connected with the family and with the gentilitial and phratric tie; the Βασιλεὺς decided cases of sacrilege and homicide; the Polemarch was judge in disputes between citizens and non-citizens; the other six archons had a general jurisdiction.

caprice or interest of the presiding magistrate; but be fixed by a positive enactment, to which all judges shall be bound to conform their sentences. When this demand became so general and so urgent that it could no longer be safely met by a mere passive resistance, the Eupatrids resolved to deal with it in another way. Professing to consent to what was required of them, they appointed one of their body—a noble who has come down to us as Draco [5]—to the office of chief Archon, and empowered him to produce a written code of laws, according to which justice should thereafter be administered. The legislator was, however, no doubt instructed, instead of mitigating the severity of the ancient and traditional scale of punishments, to heighten and aggravate it; and so thoroughly did he act in this spirit, that his laws were said in later times to have been written, not with ink, but with blood.[6] Death was made the penalty, not only for murder and sacrilege, but for adultery, for homicide in self-defence, and even for petty thefts, while idleness, or the attempt to change one of his laws, was to be visited with perpetual disfranchisement.[7] It was probably thought that "such a code was likely to be a convenient instrument in the hands of the ruling class, for striking terror into their subjects and stifling the rising spirit of discontent which their cupidity and oppression had provoked."[8] To crush by terror, or drown in blood, the nascent democracy, which at its very birth they at once feared and hated, seems to have been the aim and intention of the Eupatrids at this crisis: that they did not succeed was perhaps owing rather to casual circumstances than to any miscalculation on their part, either of their own strength, or of the weakness of their adversaries.

18. The spirit which had murmured at the "whips" of the ante-Draconic government was not very likely to submit tamely to the "scorpions" of Draco. Discontent, if repressed, must have burnt still more fiercely in men's hearts; and probably it was soon evident that there would be an outbreak. Unfortunately our authorities for this period—one of the very greatest interest—are scanty and fragmentary;[9] and in default of trustworthy guides we are thrown to a great extent on conjecture and probability for the interpretation which we shall assign to the mere outline of facts which has come down to us. It is certain that within twelve years of Draco's archonship, a violent commotion took place at Athens, which was near destroying the whole framework of the constitution, and which had permanent results of a most important nature. Cylon, a Eupatrid of the highest rank and position,[1] a victor at the Olympic games,[2] and a man of such wealth and eminence, that he had been selected by Theagenes, tyrant of Megara, as a fitting husband for

---

[5] The name is suspicious from its peculiar epithet. It is perhaps really a nickname which has ousted the true appellation.
[6] Demades ap. Plutarch. (Vit. Sol. c. 17).
[7] See Lysias de Cæd. Eratosth. c. 11; Demosth. c. Aristocrat. p. 637; Aul. Gell. xi. 18; Plut. Vit. Solon. c. 19; Pausan. IX. xxxvi. § 4.
[8] Thirlwall, vol. ii. p. 19.

[9] They are principally Herod. v. 71; Thucyd. i. 126; and Plutarch. Vit. Solon. c. 12. All three writers treat of the history merely incidentally.
[1] Thucydides says he was ἀνὴρ Ἀθηναῖος τῶν πάλαι εὐγενής τε καὶ δυνατός (l. a. c.).
[2] He had gained the δίαυλος, or double foot-race (Plut. l. a. c.).

his daughter, suddenly appeared in arms against the government, and made himself master of the Acropolis. He is said to have been assisted by a body of troops lent him by his father-in-law;[a] but it is evident that his real strength lay in the discontent of the Athenians themselves with their existing constitution, which led great numbers to welcome any change. Whether the motives of Cylon were selfish or patriotic; whether (like Spurius Cassius and Titus Manlius) he was urged to his enterprise by real sympathy with the sufferings of the lower orders, or, like Pisistratus, and his own father-in-law, Theagenes,[b] merely sought to make the advocacy of popular rights a stepping-stone to power, is perhaps open to question. Most modern writers decide the doubt unfavourably to the character of Cylon, and it must be admitted that in the brief accounts of the ancients the same view seems to be taken;[c] but on the other hand it appears that the statue of Cylon was preserved to the close of the Republic, among those of other public benefactors, in the Acropolis;[d] so that the Athenians of the democratic times must certainly have regarded his attempt with favour, and have considered its bearing to have been on the side of progress.[e] At the rumour of revolt the Eupatrids and their supporters flocked from all parts of Attica to the capital,[f] and invested the Acropolis, which long resisted their efforts. The siege had to be turned into a blockade, which was conducted by the heads of the Naucrariae under the direction of the nine Archons,[g] and pressed to a successful issue. Provisions and water alike failed the besieged; and, despairing of success, Cylon secretly escaped,[h] while his partisans still continued the defence; till at length, when several had actually died of starvation, resistance was abandoned, and the remnant of the besieged, quitting the walls, took refuge in the temple of Minerva Polias, and assumed the sacred character of suppliants. Megacles,[i] the chief Archon, on entering the citadel, found these persons ready to perish of hunger in the holy ground, and, anxious to avoid the pollution of the place by their death, induced them to remove from it by entering into an engagement that at least their lives should be spared.[1] The prisoners do not seem to have felt much confidence in the pledge given them; but, having only the alternative of starving where they were or of accepting it, they agreed to quit their shelter and began to descend from the height. In order, however, to keep themselves still under the protection of the goddess, they tied a long rope to the image, and holding this in their hands commenced the descent.[2] They had not gone far when the rope broke or was cut; and immediately their foes fell upon them.[3] Many were slain on the spot; the rest fled to the altar of the Eumenides, which was at hand,[4] and to various other shrines in the neighbourhood. But the sword once drawn, religious scruples lost their force, and the fugitives were pursued and slain wherever they could be found; even the Eumenides were not permitted to screen those who had sought their protection; a universal massacre was commanded or allowed; and the blood of their suppliants stained the altars even of the "Awful Goddesses."[5]

19. The victory was complete. Cylon, though he had escaped, undertook no fresh enterprise; and all the boldest and bravest of the party which had supported him had suffered death in the massacres. The Eupatrids probably congratulated themselves on having annihilated their opponents, and looked forward to the quiet enjoyment of a fresh lease of power. But if so, they had miscalculated. In Athens, at all times religious almost to excess,[6] the spiritual had far greater weight than the physical. Their enemies were fled or dead; but in smiting them the Eupatrids had done a deadly injury to themselves. They, or at least many of them, had incurred the guilt of sacrilege, and in this way brought themselves under a curse, which was believed to rest, not on the actual criminals only, but on the remotest generation of their descendants.[7] Moreover, as the government for the time being, they had involved the state in their guilt; and gloomy apprehensions settled down upon the mass of the people,[8] combined with a bitterness of feeling against those whom they regarded as the authors of their

disquietude. It shortly became evident that, unless active steps were taken to quiet the superstitious fears which had obtained possession of men's minds, and at the same time to remove the causes of that settled aversion with which they regarded the existing constitution of their country, an outbreak of a desperate character was to be expected. Already dissensions of an alarming nature manifested themselves; and parties were formed whose *geographic* basis threatened the state with disruption. The men "of the Highlands," "of the Plain," and "of the Coast," became banded together, and formed factions of a novel kind,[1] with which it was most difficult to deal. The great body of the Eupatrids must have been convinced of the seriousness of the danger when they put themselves into the hands of Solon, and allowed him to prescribe and apply the remedies which in his judgment were necessary to meet the crisis.

20. Solon was indeed a Eupatrid, and descended from the royal line of Codrus;[2] but the extravagance of his father, Execestides, had so reduced his inheritance, that in his youth he was forced to engage in trade,[3] a circumstance which could not but tend to weaken in his mind those exclusive notions in which persons of his class were ordinarily nurtured. He had also shown himself in his writings the fearless denouncer of the wrongs committed by his own order, and the energetic advocate of the just claims of the people.[4] In common times he would have been actively persecuted for such conduct, or at least punished by scorn and neglect; but, amid the perils which now beset the state, he presented himself to the terrified nobles as their best protection — perhaps as their only possible saviour. For some time it appears that his advice was sought and adopted, and he was allowed to have the main direction of affairs, without being invested with any distinct office, or placed in a position to act with real authority. It was while he occupied this ambiguous position that he is said to have "persuaded"[5] Megacles and his accomplices to stand their trial on the charge of sacrilege, and to submit to the decision which made them exiles from their country. This step (if really taken) not proving sufficient to allay the general disquietude, he seems, while still without office, to have devised his second

---

[1] Plut. Vit Solon. c. 13. Mr. Grote says these factions "had prevailed before" (vol. iii. p. 125.; but I know no authority for such a statement. The divisions of the territory mentioned by Pollux (supra, p. 305, not.[1]), even if regarded as authentic, would be far from a proof.

On the character of these factions, see below, pp. 333, 354.

[2] Ibid. c. 1. The relationship of Philaetius to Solon, and the connexion of the former with the Codridae, are generally admitted (Herod. v. 65, and note ad loc.,..

[3] Ibid. Hence Aristotle regards him as belonging to the "middle classes." (Pol. iv. 9; Ἐκμείνον δὲ ... τὸ τοὺς διαλλάσσοντας ἡγήσαντας ὅλως τῶν μέσων πολιτῶν. Σόλων τε γὰρ ἦν τοιοῦτος.)

[4] The scanty fragments of Solon were edited by Dr. Gaisford in his Poetae Minores Graeci, vol. i. They have been published in a separate form by Bach (Bonn, 1825). His strong language on the subjects mentioned in the text is particularly remarkable in Fr. 21. of Gaisford's edition.

[5] Plut. Sol. c. 12; ὁ Σόλων ἔπεισε τοὺς ἐναγεῖς διάγνωσιν ὑποσχεῖν. The tale, however, is somewhat apocryphal, and perhaps grew out of proceedings under Pisistratus. At any rate if the Alcmaeonidae made a show of submission, and retired, they soon returned, and were as powerful as ever. Alcmaeon, the son of the guilty archon, commanded in the sacred war (infra, p. 321), which was from about B.C. 600 to B.C. 591. And Megacles, his son, appears at the head of a political party in B.C. 500 (Herod. i. 59.).

measure — the purification of the city by Epimenides.⁴ Finally, after this proceeding had been attended with a very large amount of success, and the religious apprehensions of the community had been tranquillised thereby, but the political horizon continued still clouded, it was resolved to put all power formally into his hands; he was invested with the dignity of chief archon, and given full authority to arrange the state at his pleasure, to frame a new constitution, and to repeal, confirm, or modify the Draconian code of laws.⁷

21. The archonship of Solon is fixed by most chronologists to the year B.C. 594,⁵ eighteen years after the insurrection of Cylon, and thirty from the attempt of Draco to crush the rising spirit of democracy by severity. Before proceeding to consider the enactments by which Solon met the dangers of the crisis, it is important to review the circumstances whereby he had acquired weight in the state, more especially as those circumstances bring before us in a tolerably distinct manner the external position of Attica and her relations with neighbouring countries, of which we have obtained no glimpse since the date of Codrus.

22. It appears that, during the troubles of the Draconian and Cylonian period, the little state of Megara on the western borders of Attica took advantage of her internal disorders to commence an aggressive war, and succeeded in it so well as to dispossess their rivals of the island of Salamis, to which they had, or professed to have, a claim of long standing.⁶ Repeated attempts were made by the Athenians to recover their lost despondency; but on these occasions they were so roughly handled by the Megarians that they had at last desisted from the war, and, convinced of its impolicy, had even passed a decree forbidding, under penalty of death, any pro-

---

⁴ The invitation to Epimenides is not distinctly said to have proceeded from Solon; but there can be little doubt that it was in fact his doing. Plutarch mentions the friendly terms on which Epimenides was with Solon while at Athens (L. s. c.); and Laertius (i. 110) notes that the intermediary upon the occasion was the Delphic oracle, between which and Solon there was evidently a good understanding.

On the history and character of Epimenides see the treatise of Heinrich, *Epimenides aus Kreta*, Leipsic, 1801; and compare Thirlwall, vol. ii. pp. 27-30; Grote, vol. iii. pp. 112-117; and the article on the subject in Smith's Biographical Dictionary. On his prescription of human sacrifices, asserted by Neanthes of Cyzicus (Fr. 24), and denied by Polemo (Fr. 53), see Mr. Grote's note ³, p. 114. The time of his visit to Athens cannot be exactly fixed, but it was probably in or about the year B.C. 600. (See Clinton's F. H. vol. i. p. 225; Ol. 46.)

⁷ Ἤρεθη ἄρχων ... ὁμοῦ καὶ διαλλακτὴς καὶ νομοθέτης (Plut. Vit. Solon. c. 14). Cf. Herod. i. 29.

⁵ Clinton's Fasti Hellenici, vol. ii. Appendix, ch. 17. But it must be remembered that Demosthenes — by far the earliest authority — gave a much later date, viz., B.C. 580 (De Fals. Leg. p. 420). I cannot agree with Mr. Clinton that Demosthenes distinguishes Solon's death from his archonship, and counts from that. Solon's archonship was his death. (Cf. Ding. Laert. ἤκμασέ ποτὶ τὴν τεσσαρακοστὴν ἕκτην Ὀλυμπιάδα, ἧι τῷ τρίτῳ ἔτει ἦρξεν Ἀθήνησιν, i. 62.)

⁶ Plut. Vit. Sol. c. 8. It is likely enough that the Megarians may have held possession of Salamis during a considerable portion of the time intervening between Codrus and Solon, since Megara was a powerful naval state from the middle of the eighth to the middle of the seventh century B.C. During this period she founded colonies in Sicily, in the Propontis, on the Bosphorus, and (probably) in the Black Sea. That she had really possessed the island in ancient times is indicated by her appeal to the graves of her peculiar method of interment as apparent in many of the old tombs (Plut. Vit. Sol. c. 10).

posal to renew the struggle.¹ Solon, however, himself a Salaminian,² took a different view of the course proper under the circumstances; and making up his mind to risk the consequences, he one day feigned madness, and rushing into the forum, where the people (i.e. the nobles) were assembled, he recited in an impassioned tone a poem of his own composition, in which the Athenians were exhorted to make another effort for the reconquest of the island. The venture succeeded. Many of the nobles—among them Pisistratus,³ who was his kinsman—seconded his efforts: and the decree was repealed, an expedition voted, and Solon himself appointed to the command of it.

The details of the expedition by which Solon carried out his project are variously related,⁴ and rest on no very good authority. It seems certain that Pisistratus, though very young at the time, was engaged in the war,⁵ and gained considerable distinction in it: and there is no doubt that Salamis was recovered; but more than this bare outline can scarcely be said to be known. The war was terminated by an appeal to Sparta on the chief matter in dispute between the combatants, namely, the possession of Salamis, which was adjudged to Athens on the combined evidence of oracles and mythic traditions.⁶

21. Solon shortly afterwards engaged Athens in another dispute, which he likewise carried to a successful issue. Perhaps he thought by involving his countrymen in foreign wars to make them forget their domestic differences. A quarrel had arisen between the Delphians and the people of Cirrha, the port from which Delphi was ordinarily reached by travellers from the west. In a meeting of the Amphictyonic Council, Solon, as Athenian deputy, urged the armed interference of the League on behalf of the Delphians,⁷ and per-

---

¹ Demosth. de Fals. Leg. (l. s. c.); Diog. Laert. i. 46; Plut. Vit. Sol. c. 8.

² According to Diogenes Laertius (L 45), who says that the fact was recorded on his statue at Athens. Mr. Grote suggests that he was not really born at Salamis, but only revived an allotment there after the conquest of the island (Hist. of Greece, vol. iv. pp. 210, 211). The story of the dispersion of his ashes over the island seems to be connected with the tradition of its being his true country (Plut. Vit. Sol. ad fin.; Diog. Laert. i. 62; Arist. p. 230, ed. Dindorf.

³ So Plutarch (l. s. c.). Yet, as Mr. Grote observes (p. 121), at this time (about B.C. 600-594, according to the ordinary chronology), he could scarcely have been more than a boy. He died B.C. 527, and as he is never said to have attained to an extreme old age, we can scarcely suppose him born before B.C. 607. Yet he is represented by Plutarch as aiding Solon in getting the war voted, and by Herodotus (i. 59) as greatly distinguishing himself in it. These are grounds, however, not for distrusting the facts, but for questioning the ordinary dates,

which rest only upon late authority (Sosicrates, Laertius, Clemens, &c.). The difficulty would be to a great extent removed by adopting the chronology of Demosthenes (see above, p. 319, note ª).

⁴ According to one authority he was not personally engaged in the war at all (Polemarch. Fr. 7). According to others (Plutarch, Laertius, Polyaenus, Ælian, &c.) he had the sole management of it; and took the city of Salamis by stratagem in the first year. The stratagem, moreover, is reported variously. (Compare Polyaen. L 20, with Ælian, V. H. vii. 19.) The Megarians, again, gave a completely different account of the mode by which they lost this island (Pausan. i. xl § 4).

⁵ Herod. I. 59, and note ad loc. The testimony of Herodotus would be decisive on such a point, even if more weight attached to the ordinary chronology than I should be inclined to assign to it.

⁶ Plut. Vit. Sol. c. 10. Compare Ar. Rhet. i. 15 (p. 63, ed. Tauchn.).

⁷ Aristot. Fr. 263.

suaded the Council to adopt his proposition. A force consisting of Thessalians, Sicyonians, and Athenians, was collected,* and the first Sacred War commenced, probably in the year B.C. 600.* It was conducted by Eurylochus the Thessalian,† with the assistance of Clisthenes, tyrant of Sicyon,‡ and of Alcmæon, son of the Archon Megacles, who commanded the Athenian contingent.§ According to one account,‖ Solon himself accompanied the army in the capacity of counsellor, and actually contrived the stratagem through which Cirrha was captured;¶ but such a position does not belong to the simplicity of the time,* and the part taken by Solon in the war was probably limited to a warm advocacy of it in the first instance, and a recommendation at its close that Cirrha should be destroyed and its lands given to the Delphians.

24. Such were the chief public actions of Solon at the time of his selection as "lawgiver." He was known as a skilful leader, a bold man, and a warm patriot. Connected by birth with the high aristocrats, by occupation with the commercial classes, and by sympathy with the oppressed commons, he had friends in every rank, and might be expected to deal fairly by all. His abilities were great, his moderation greater; and probably Athens possessed at the time no other citizen half so fitted for the difficult office which he was urged, and at last consented, to undertake. The nobility felt that he would not sacrifice his own order; the commons knew that he approved their cause, and would have the courage to see justice done them; the trading class, which was just beginning to feel its strength,† had hopes from one who had been personally engaged in commerce, and did not regard it as a degradation. The task, however, which had been committed to him, was one of no ordinary difficulty. He had not only to remodel a barbarous code, and frame a constitution suitable to the existing state of the community, which were the usual duties of a lawgiver;‡ but he had to meet a financial crisis in the shape which such matters commonly took in ancient times—he had to acknowledge and relieve a wide-spread insolvency, to prevent a war between rich and poor, to put a stop to the oppression of the one, and to save, so far as practicable, the just rights of the other. The measure by which he effected these objects—his

---

* Plut. Vit. Sol. c. 11; Æsch. c. Ctes. p. 69; Schol. ad Pind. Pyth. Proleg.; Schol. ad Pind. Nem. ix. 2; Pausan. ii. ii. § 6, and x. xxxvii. § 4.

* See Clinton's F. H. vol. i. p. 224, Ol. 46, 2; and vol. ii. pp. 239, 240. This date depends chiefly on the Parian marble, which makes the capture of Cirrha fall into the year B.C. 591. According to Callisthenes (ap. Athen. xiii. p. 560, C.), the war lasted ten years.

† Schol. ad Pind. Pyth. Proleg.; Strab. ix. pp. 418-421; Polyæn. vi. 13; comp. Pausan. ii. ii. § 6.

‡ Pausan. x. xxxvii. § 4; Frontin. Strateg. iii. 7.

§ Plut. Vit. Sol. c. 11.

‖ Pausan. l. s. c.

* The poisoning of the river Pleistus, which supplied Cirrha with water (Pausan. x. xxxvii. § 5). Polyænus and Frontinus (l. s. c.) ascribe this stratagem to Clisthenes; Thessalus, to a certain Nebrus.

† To send a ξυμβουλος or ξυμβουλοι with a general, was a practice commenced by Sparta about the year B.C. 445.

‡ The Paralii of Plutarch (Vit. Sol. c. 13) and Herodotus (i. 59) seem to represent this trading class. They dwelt chiefly along the southern sea-board, where the principal ports lay, and perhaps included the workers of the silver mines towards the extremity of the peninsula.

§ Νόμους θέσθαι και πολιτείας καταστήσαι (cf. Arist. Pol. ii. 9, &c.).

Seisachtheia—has been differently understood and estimated. According to some[a] it consisted of two points—a reduction in the rate of interest, which was made retrospective, and thus extinguished a number of debts—and a debasement of the currency to the extent of above one-fourth, whereby all outstanding obligations were diminished in that proportion. According to others[b] its chief proviso was the positive and complete abolition of all debts, or at least of those where the debtor had borrowed on the mortgage of his estate or the security of his person. The old Athenian law of debt, like the Roman,[c] and indeed like the primitive law of debt in almost all countries,[d] allowed the poor man to borrow "on his body."[e] In this case, if he did not repay the debt at the stated time, he became the slave of his creditor, and was thenceforth employed by him in servile labours. His children, too, and even his unmarried sisters, passed with him into slavery, unless he had sold them previously, which the law allowed him to do.[f] Such sales and forfeitures had, it is said, taken place to a large extent in Attica before Solon's appointment, while the lands of the small proprietors were almost universally mortgaged, and the whole class of free agriculturists was in imminent danger of becoming absorbed into the slave population, or being forced to emigrate. It is certain that Solon's legislation effectually remedied this wretched condition of things; that it freed all those who were in slavery for debt; that it swept off the mortgage pillars from the lands, and entirely cleared them of all burthens.[g] A mere diminution in the rate of interest, even though retrospective, would not have done this, for it would have affected recent debts but very slightly: there is, moreover, distinct evidence that Solon did not reduce the legal rate of interest, but by a distinct enactment declared it free.[h] We are therefore necessitated to conclude that the relief which Solon's legislation confessedly gave was not effected in this way; and consequently we must regard the *Seisachtheia* as (at least to some extent) an actual abolition of debt, which is what the word itself, notwithstanding its euphemistic cast," evidently means. Solon regarded the circumstances of the time as justifying, or rather requiring, a departure from the ordinary law of contracts, a relaxation of hard and strict justice, a concession to poverty and necessity, with which moderns cannot consistently find fault, so long as no objection is made to insolvent debtor courts and bankruptcy courts, which render such general abolitions of debts unnecessary among ourselves, by continually doing on a small scale for individuals what otherwise has to be done from time to time on a grand scale for the community. On the other hand, Solon evidently took care not to go beyond the needs of the occasion. He was far from abolishing all debts; otherwise there would have been no object at all in that debasement of the currency, which is an undoubted portion of his scheme.[a] Where and how he drew the line we have no evidence to show; it is quite possible that, as at Rome on one occasion,[b] proof of insolvency may have been required on the part of the debtor; or debts of a particular kind and class may (as Mr. Grote thinks[c]) have been excused, being known to be such as only the extremely poor had contracted. The benefit extended to the debtor, who was in no danger of losing his freedom, amounted to little more than one-fourth of his obligation[d]—a sensible alleviation doubtless, but one which did not greatly injure the creditor. To assert, however, as Androtion did, that the creditor suffered no loss at all by the arrangement,[e] is absurd; since, had that been the case, the debtor could have experienced no relief. Every lowering of the standard is a fraud upon creditors in the same proportion that it is a boon to debtors, and though admitting of justification by circumstances, on the great political principle "*salus publica suprema lex*," requires, in order to carry the approval of right-judging minds, that such justification shall be distinctly made out. In the case before us there seems no reason to doubt that a wise discretion was exercised, and that the sacrifice required of the richer citizens was one imperatively called for by the circumstances of the time, and amply compensated to them by the dangers which it warded off, and the security and tranquillity to which it conduced.

25. In legislating on this difficult subject Solon was not content (as the Romans were in too many instances[f]) to deal only with the

actual evils before him, but wisely looked to preventing their recurrence. He at once abolished servitude for debt,¹ which was not done away with at Rome till a century and a half after the first legislation on the subject;² and at the same time he made it illegal to sell a child or a sister.³ He redeemed from slavery—by what means we are not informed—the citizens who had been sold into foreign countries, and compelled the immediate emancipation of such as were still in Attica.⁴ To obviate a return of the general poverty, which had required such severe remedies, he thought it enough in the first place to incline the burthen of taxation upon the rich,⁵ and in the second to turn the attention of the Athenians to manufactures, requiring every father, on pain of losing his claim to be supported by his sons in old age, to teach them in their youth a handicraft,⁶ and empowering the Areopagus to examine into every man's means of subsistence, and to punish those who had no definite occupation.⁷ It may be questioned whether these provisions would have been very effectual for their purpose had the general condition of Greece continued unchanged; the rapid advance in the material prosperity of Athens, which commenced soon afterwards, arose from causes wholly unconnected with the Solonian legislation; first, from the vast increase in the yield of the Attic silver-mines;⁸ secondly, from the value of the Persian plunder;⁹ thirdly, and mainly, from the establishment of the empire of Athens over her subject allies; and the prosperity thus produced prevented Solon's safeguards against poverty from being subjected to any searching test. It also precluded all temptation to repeat the process which he had sanctioned—a process necessary perhaps once or twice in the lifetime of a state, but ruinous if allowed to become a habit—and thus enabled Athens to enjoy the benefits without suffering the evils which usually attend upon the repudiation of money engagements.⁹

26. Having thus met and remedied the principal difficulty of the time, the lawgiver applied himself to the comparatively easy tasks of framing a constitution and introducing a code of laws. The *timocratical* constitution of Solon is too well known to require more than the briefest notice here. He divided the whole body of Athenian *citizens*—i.e. all the members of the old hereditary tribes—

into four classes, according to their property.¹ Those whose income amounted to 500 *medimni* of corn, or *metretes* of wine or oil, formed the first class,² and were called *Pentacosiomedimni*, a term significative of their wealth. Those whose income ranged between 500 and 300 such measures constituted the second class, and bore the name of *Hippeis* (horsemen), or *Hippada-teluntes* (belonging to the horseman class), being persons who could afford to keep a horse. Those who had less than 300 measures a-year, and more than 200,³ were called *Zeugitæ* (yokemen), because they could support a yoke of oxen; these made the third class. Finally, there was a fourth class, composed of all whose income was under 200 measures; this class bore the name of *Thetes* (hirelings), because it was presumed that their poverty would in general necessitate their employment as the hired labourers of others.⁴ The chief difference in the rights of the several classes seems to have been that the archonship and the Court of the Areopagus (which was composed of ex-archons⁵) were confined to the Pentacosiomedimni;⁶ that offices of inferior dignity were open to the Hippeis and Zeugitæ; and that the Thetes were made incapable of any office at all.⁷ All ranks, however, voted in the Ecclesia, or General Assembly of the People, which Solon re-established, and to which he committed the election of all officers, including the archons and the members of the pre-considering council.

27. The distribution of state burthens was proportioned to that of state privileges. Direct taxation had probably existed in Athens from the earliest times; but hitherto it may have been a mere poll-tax, the most oppressive mode of raising a revenue. Solon absolutely exempted the Thetes from direct burthons, and established a graduated income-tax, pressing most heavily on the wealthiest. The Pentacosiomedimni were taxed at the full value of their property, or at twelve times their income; the Hippeis at one-sixth less than the full value, or at ten times their income; the Zeugitæ at one-half the rate of the Hippeis, or at five times their income.⁸ The rate of tax demanded varied from time to

---

¹ Plut. Vit. Sol. c. 18, et seq.; Arist. Pol. ii. 9, and Fr. 9; Pollux, viii. 130; Argum. ad Aristoph. Eq. sub fin.; and the Lexicographers, passim.

² It is supposed by some that the income was to be in every case *derived from land*, but I agree with Mr. Grote (vol. iii. p. 159) that this is very unlikely.

³ I agree with Mr. Grote that we are bound to follow the authority of the ancients on this point, rather than the speculations even of so ingenious a person as Böckh. (See the History of Greece, vol. iii. pp. 157, 158, note.) Bp. Thirlwall inclines to follow Böckh (vol. ii. p. 37). So Hermann (Pol. Ant. § 108).

⁴ Mr. Grote denies that the fourth class can really have borne this appellation, because "it is not conceivable that a proprietor whose land yielded to him a clear annual return of 100, 120, 140, or 180 drachms, could ever have been designated by that name" (vol. iii. p. 159). But a class is named from the general character of those composing it, without reference to a few exceptional cases. And all the best authorities (Aristotle, Plutarch, Pollux) are unanimous on the point.

⁵ Idem. c. Androt. p. 598; Plut. Vit. Sol. c. 19.

⁶ Plut. Vit. Aristid. c. 1.

⁷ Ar. Pol. ii. 9.

⁸ See Pollux, viii. 130, with the explanation of Boeckh (Econom. of Athens, vol. ii. pp. 269-273), which is followed by Bishop Thirlwall (vol. ii. pp. 38, 39), by Mr. Grote with one exception (vol. iii. pp. 156, 157), and by Dr. Schmitz (Smith's Dict. of Antiq., sub voc. *Censu*).

time, according to the needs of the state; but whatever the rate fixed for the year, the Hippeus paid a double income-tax compared with the Zeugitæ, and the Pentacosiomedimnus more than such double tax by two-fifths. To illustrate familiarly, if the Zeugitæ had been called on in any year for fivepence in the pound upon his income, the Hippeus would have had to pay tenpence in the pound, and the Pentacosiomedimnus a shilling. Besides this general burthen, the occasional and irregular expenses of the Liturgies or State Services were thrown entirely upon the rich citizens,[a] among whom they were distributed according to some system which has not come down to us.

Had the revenue of the state been derived solely, or even mainly, from the property-tax, great dissatisfaction would probably have been felt at its graduation, as well as at the exemption from it of the mass of the citizens. But the chief and only permanent sources of revenue at Athens were the state-property,[b] which was no burthen on any one, and the duties on imports,[c] to which all alike contributed. The Eisphora, or property-tax, was rarely levied, and only upon occasions of difficulty;[d] so that it corresponded rather to the forced loans of modern states, which have always been exacted from the rich, than to any part of the regular taxation.

There is some indication that in the timocratical scheme of Solon at Athens, as in that of Servius Tullius at Rome, not taxation only, but military duties also, were apportioned according to wealth, and therefore according to privilege. But the graduation in this case is not completely made out. It is clear that the second class furnished the cavalry of the Athenian army,[e] and the third class its heavy-armed infantry;[f] while the fourth formed no part of the regular army, only serving as light troops upon an emergency.[g] But nothing is said concerning the military obligations of the first class; and we are left to conjecture whether they were legally exempt from all service, or acted as cavalry without being called Hippeis, or merely furnished the officers of the cavalry and infantry, as has sometimes been supposed.[h] The first supposition is precluded by the whole spirit of Greek antiquity, which attached the profession of arms to the upper classes especially;[i] the last may be true to some extent, but will not be a sufficient account to give of the whole body.[j] We must therefore conclude that there was no exact

---

[a] On the antiquity of the Liturgies, cf. Aristot. Œconom. ii. 5. In later times, no one contributed to them whose property was under three talents (Lysias de Pyrrh. c. 80; Isæ. c. Aphob. p. 833). If this was the original rule, they can have fallen only upon Pentacosiomedimni. Mr. Grote says, that they " were distributed between the *zeugitæ* of the (first) three classes " (vol. iii. p. 160); but he does not quote his authority.

[b] Böckh, vol. ii. pp. 9-23.

[c] Ibid. pp. 23 et seqq.

[d] Thucyd. iii. 19; Lycurg. de Dicæog. c. 57; Antiph. Tetral. i. 12. Compare Böckh, vol. ii. p. 227, and K. F. Hermann; § 162.

[e] Plut. Vit. Solon, c. 18; Aristoph. Eq. 548-563.

[f] This evidently follows from the ordinary exemption of the Thetes (see the next note), combined with the cavalry service of the Hippeis.

[g] Xen. Hell. ii. iii. § 20; Thucyd. vi. 43; Harpocration, ad voc. Θῆτες.

[h] Thirlwall, vol. ii. p. 38.

[i] Cf. Hermann's Pol. Ant. § 57 and § 67.

[j] Unless we believe that the Hippeis were in the time of Solon under 100 (I, as Andocides declared (de Pace, p. 92); in which case the Pentacosiomedimni would have been scarcely so many.

line of demarcation between the first and second classes in respect of military service, but that both alike served in the cavalry,[ ] and probably with the same equipment.

28. Besides introducing this new organisation, and thereby really establishing a species of moderate democracy,[ ] Solon instituted the Pro-Bouleutic Council,[ ] a sort of committee of the Ecclesia, consisting of 400 citizens, 100 from each of the tribes, whose business it was to prepare all measures before they could be submitted to the Assembly, to convoke it when necessary, to direct its proceedings, and see to the execution of its decrees. The election of these 400 persons, as well as that of the archons, was entrusted to the free vote of the people,[ ] who had further the power of sitting in judgment on the archons after their year of office,[ ] and refusing or allowing their admission into the Areopagus.[ ]

29. These are the chief points of Solon's constitution on which modern writers are agreed. They constitute an immense advance from the strict oligarchy which he found established, and amply account for the opinion which prevailed widely in later times that Solon was the true founder of the democracy at Athens. The extension of real citizenship from the Eupatrids, who alone can be truly said to have possessed it previously, to all members of the tribes; the substitution of the standard of wealth for that of birth, with reference even to the highest offices of the state; the change in the mode of appointing the archons from nomination by the Eupatrids to free election by the Assembly of the People; the practical introduction of the εὔθυνα, whereby the archons became really accountable for their conduct while in office; and the institution of an elective council, with the right of taking the initiative in legislation and in the conduct of affairs, must, even if unaccompanied by any other changes, have conferred on the Athenians a measure of liberty and self-government which, compared with their former condition, could not but seem absolute democracy, and which, even regarded in itself, was substantial freedom. It is possible, however, that Solon may have gone further. Plutarch[ ] and Aristotle[ ]

expressly ascribe to him the institution of the Dicasteries or popular law-courts; and the Attic orators connect his name with almost the whole machinery of democracy, as it existed in their own day.' No doubt there is in such statements more or less of incorrectness—a tendency to concentrate under one name what was really scattered over a larger surface, and at the same time to dignify with antiquity what the speakers regard as important in the democratical system; in many instances too it is clear (as Mr. Grote has well shown) that the particular points of the system which are ascribed to Solon belong to a far more refined and advanced age; but on the other hand it seems over bold to set aside the direct, positive, and circumstantial statements of writers like Aristotle and Plutarch, who both make the establishment of the law-courts a leading feature in the Solonic changes, and to pronounce that he did absolutely nothing in this matter, because the entire complex system which existed in the time of Pericles cannot have come from him. We are bound to believe, on two such authorities, that the idea of popular trial originated with Solon, and that some machinery was introduced by him for the purpose. It would thus appear that the entire democratical system of later times had its germs in his legislation, with only two exceptions of any importance—viz. ostracism and election by lot.

30. If the democratic character of the Solonian constitution has been insufficiently apprehended by some of our writers, by others it has undoubtedly been exaggerated to a still greater extent. To ascribe to Solon (as Bishop Thirlwall does) the full organisation of the Heliæa, as it appears in the time of the orators, the institution of the Heliastic oath, of the Nomothetæ and Syndics, and of that bulwark of the later constitution, the γραφὴ παρανόμων, is to misunderstand altogether his position in Athenian constitutional history, and to fail in distinguishing the spirit of his legislation from that of Clisthenes. The democracy is born under Solon, but it is born an infant—not, like Minerva, full grown. Under Clisthenes it attains to adolescence, under Pericles to maturity. It is an error of the most serious kind to ascribe to the sim-

ple and comparatively rude time of Solon what have truly been called "the last refinements and elaborations of the democratical mind of Athens."* These refinements no doubt grew up gradually between the ages of Clisthenes and Pericles, being the inventions of various authors during the gradual development of the democratic idea.

31. It may be doubted whether in one respect even Mr. Grote has not given Solon credit for a more liberal legislation than can be rightly assigned to him. He considers him to have recognised as citizens, not the members of the four old tribes only, but all the free inhabitants of Attica, except actual aliens. Such persons, he says, though not eligible for councillors, nor for archons, and therefore incapable of entering the Areopagus, "were citizens, and could give their votes for archons and senators, and also take part in the annual decision of their accountability, besides being entitled to claim redress for wrongs in their own persons."* To me it seems that the admission of these persons to citizenship at this time is highly improbable, and that, if it had been a part of the Solonian scheme, we must have found distinct mention of it.¹ I cannot but regard it as one of the main differences between the Solonian and Clisthenic constitutions, that the former left untouched the conditions of citizenship, and merely made alterations in the rights and privileges of those already acknowledged to be citizens; while the latter admitted into the citizen body classes never before recognised as worthy of belonging to it. Mr. Grote in his account of the Clisthenic legislation seems to admit all that is here contended for; but his statements in that place appear to me wholly inconsistent with those contained in his account of the Solonian laws and constitution.* The point is one of importance in any estimate that we

---

* Grote's Hist. of Greece, vol. iii. p. 164.
* Ibid. pp. 175, 176.
¹ As we do find in the case of Clisthenes, though so much less is told us of him than of Solon. (See Arist. Pol. iii. 1; καθ-ίστησι μετὰ τὴν τῶν τυράννων ἐκβολὴν πολλοὺς ἐφυλέτευσε ξένους καὶ δούλους μετοίκους.)

* In the eleventh chapter of his third volume, Mr. Grote discusses the "status, under the Solonian constitution, of persons not included in the gentes and phratries" — and having decided that they could not be members of the Pro-Bouleutic Council, nor Archons, nor (consequently) members of the Court of Areopagus, he says:—"There remained only the public assembly, in which an Athenian, not a member of these tribes, could take part; yet he was a citizen, since he could give his vote for archons and senators, and could take part in the annual decision of their accountability, besides being entitled to claim redress for wrong from the archons, in his own person, while the alien could only do so through the intervention of an avouching citizen or Prostates. It seems,

therefore, that all persons not included in the four tribes, whatever their grade of fortune might be, were on the same level in respect to political privileges as the fourth and poorest class of the Solonian census." But in the thirty-first chapter of his fourth volume (p. 169) Mr. Grote expresses himself as follows:—"The political franchise, or the character of an Athenian citizen, both before and since Solon, had been confined to the primitive four Ionic tribes, each of which was an aggregate of so many close corporations or quasi-families—the gentes and the phratries: none of the residents in Attica, therefore, except those included in some gens or phratry, had any part in the political franchise."

Bp. Thirlwall is consistent, but (as I think) wrong. He regards Solon's system as having made "room for all freemen" (vol. ii. p. 39); and Clisthenes as only having enfranchised a number of "aliens" and "slaves" (ibid. p. 74). On the true meaning of the passage in Aristotle to which he refers (quoted above in note ¹), see Mr. Grote's note, vol. iv. pp. 170, 171.

attempt to form of the true character of either system, and it is to be regretted that without necessity a doubt should be allowed to rest upon it.

32. To give a complete account of the laws of Solon would expand this Essay beyond all reasonable limits. It is also entirely unnecessary, as an admirable digest is contained in the work of Mr. Grote.[a] Reference will here be made only to those cases where his enactments had a special bearing upon the existing condition of parties, or had otherwise a political rather than a social import.

(i.) The outcry raised by the severity of Draco's laws was met by their abolition, except in the case of homicide, where his enactments were maintained.[b] Capital punishment was probably limited to this single case, or, if extended beyond it, was attached only to one or two other crimes of especial heinousness.[c] Solon's penalty for theft was to force the robber to restore twofold.[d] Inferior offences, as libel, seduction, &c., were punished by fines of greater or less magnitude.[e] Even rape was only made punishable by a fine;[f] but adulterers might be killed by any one who caught them in the act.[g] Adulteresses also were placed under certain disabilities, constituting a species of infamy (ἀτιμία).[h]

(ii.) A certain number of Solon's regulations seem to have been aimed especially at increasing the population of Attica. Marriage was encouraged by a law which released illegitimate children from the necessity of supporting their parents.[i] Cohabitation after marriage was made compulsory in certain cases.[j] Dowries were secured to females as a matter of right.[k] That Attica might be able to support a larger population, no agricultural produce was allowed to be exported, except olive-oil; all the rest was to be consumed at home.[l] Trade and manufactures were honoured and encouraged, to furnish a means of subsistence to a larger number than could have drawn their living from the soil.[m] Foreigners were invited to settle permanently in Attica by the hope of enfranchisement, if they entirely gave up their native country, and brought with them a useful trade.[n] It is evident that the legislator sought both to attract settlers from abroad and to stimulate the growth and increase of the native population. He saw that Attica, with her narrow limits and poor soil, could never be great so long as she was purely or even

---

[a] Hist. of Greece, vol. iii. pp. 177-194.

[b] Plut. Vit. Sol. c. 17.

[c] According to Æschines (c. Timarch. p. 40) the procurer in a case of seduction was punished by death. Perhaps sacrilege was so punished, as it certainly was both earlier and later (comp. Plut. Sol. c. 17 with Lys. pro Call. p. 183).

[d] Aul. Gell. xi. 18. The old Roman law was the same (Cat. de Re Rust. Procem.).

[e] Seduction by a fine of twenty drachms, as some understand Plutarch (Vit. Sol. c. 23. See Mr. Grote's Greece, vol. iii. p. 185, and Langhorne's Plutarch, vol. i. p. 278); libel, by a fine of five drachms (Plut. Sol. Vit. c. 21).

[f] Plut. Vit. Sol. c. 23. The fine in this case was 100 drachms, or one mina, a fifth of the yearly income of a Pentacosiomedimnus.

[g] Ibid. l. s. c.

[h] Æschin. c. Timarch. pp. 176, 177, ed. Reiske.

[i] Plut. Vit. Sol. c. 22.

[j] Ibid. c. 20.

[k] Isæus de Pyrrh. c. 39; Harpocrat. ad voc. οἶκος. Solon forbade expensive trousseaux (φερνάς, Plut. Sol. c. 20); but this law did not affect the dowry (προῖκα).

[l] Plut. Vit. Sol. c. 24.

[m] Ibid. c. 22.

[n] Ibid. c. 24.

mainly agricultural. He conceived the idea of a manufacturing and commercial development of his state, being aware, from the example of Corinth, and perhaps of Megara, that by such means a scant territory might be made to shelter a great power.

(iii.) The law of Solon which has provoked most comment[a] is that which punished with infamy (ἀτιμία) the man who remained neuter in a sedition. In the free states of modern Europe partisanship is viewed generally with disfavour, and the public safety is supposed to depend in a great degree on the number of moderate citizens who eschew party and look with a dispassionate eye on the strife of those engaged in political life. But the case was different in the communities of ancient Greece. There indifference was disliked; to keep aloof from state affairs was considered a dereliction of duty; to take no side in politics was thought to prove a cold and selfish temper, careless of the welfare of others.[b] The cause of the difference lies partly in the far greater size of the modern states, which renders it at once impossible for the bulk of the citizens to occupy themselves in political life, and safe for them to abstain, since their mass is too great to be readily overpowered by the violence of a small knot of agitators. It lies partly also in the different conception entertained by the ancients and the moderns of the relation between the state and the individual.[c] With us the individual is paramount—the state is a mere machinery for his convenience; with them the state was all in all, and the individual existed only because the state could not exist without him.[d] Solon therefore did nothing strange in the eyes of his contemporaries, or of his countrymen (so long as they continued Greeks, and were not Romanized[e]), when he enacted the law in question. He did but attach a legal penalty to conduct already condemned by public opinion. And the penalty was not one of great severity.[f] There is no reason to believe that it was perpetual ἀτιμία, or more than that gentle pressure which was often used as a means of compelling a man to submit to the laws.[g] No doubt the sufferer could at any moment terminate it, simply by choosing his side. And it must be remembered that the law only came into force *when there was an actual sedition*.[h] Public opinion was opposed to all abstinence from

---

[a] Plutarch calls it τῶν αὐτοῦ νόμων ἴδιον μάλιστα καὶ παράδοξον (Vit. Sol. c. 20), and in one place condemns it altogether (de Ser. Num. Vind. ii. p. 550). Aulus Gellius, on the other hand, warmly commends it in his Noctes Atticae (ii. 12). Montesquieu in his *Esprit des Lois* (xxix. 3), and Mr. Grote in his History (vol. iii. pp. 190-194) defend it as *necessary under the circumstances of the time*.

[b] Hence in a great measure the unpopularity of Socrates, and of the philosophers generally. (See Aristoph. Nub. ; Plat. Gorg. p. 485, B, C.; Repub. vi. § 4-10; Xen. Mem. i. vi. § 15; &c.)

[c] K. F. Hermann has some judicious remarks on this subject (Pol. Ant. § 51).

[d] Ar. Pol. i. 1. (p. 4, ed. Tauchn.)

[e] Plutarch (Vit. Sol. c. 20) speaks as a Roman—and not only so, but as a Roman of the time of the Empire, when such a law would no doubt have seemed " strange."

[f] Aulus Gellius undoubtedly exaggerates, when, professing to give the exact words of the law (N. A. ii. 12), he speaks of the man who came under its operation as losing his houses, his country, and his estates; and also as sent into exile. The punishment was, at the utmost, ἀτιμία, which did not involve either exile or loss of property.

[g] Cf. Dict. of Antiq. ad voc. ἀτιμία (p. 169, a).

[h] Νόμον δ᾽ ἔθηκεν ἄτιμον εἶναι τὸν ἐν στάσει μηδετέρας μερίδος γενόμενον (Plut. Vit. Sol. i. 20).

politics, even in the quietest times; but Solon did not make such abstinence penal until the state was in danger. Indifference at such a time might well be regarded as not blameworthy merely but criminal. And Solon no doubt looked as much to expediency as to justice. He wished to end such seditions by throwing a decisive weight on one side or the other, judging rightly that the mass of calm and dispassionate persons would probably decide alike, and, when compelled to choose, would go over in a body to one of the competitors, whose influence would thus become irresistible. He saw too, we may be sure, that their accession would commonly be to the more moderate of the rivals, who would attract to him those of a like temperament.

33. The legislation of Solon was followed by an interval[6] of profound repose. His changes were accepted—even those which pressed most hardly upon certain classes—if not with full satisfaction, yet with general and complete acquiescence.[7] The council and the archons, as representatives of the nation, swore to maintain them;[8] and no opposition showed itself from any quarter. Objections, however, after a while began to be felt against portions of the system. As no party had been violently offended by the alterations, so none had been much gratified. Solon's Fragments are enough to show that during his lifetime he derived but little credit from his labours. Some called him a fool for not having made himself tyrant;[9] others accused him of undue concessions to the mob; others again maintained that he had not given any real relief to the poorer classes.[10] Solon complains of the impossibility of pleasing every one,[1] of the angry looks which former flatterers cast at him, and of the general hostility which he saw in men's countenances.[2] He labours to defend himself from opposite attacks, insisting on the moderation of the course which he had pursued, and the value of the protection which he had afforded.[3] It seems that at length he grew weary of defending himself and his legislation from attack, and, quitting Athens about the year B.C. 570, proceeded upon his travels, having first (according to some[4]) taken an oath of the nation that for ten years they would make no change in his laws. He trusted that by the expiration of the period named they would have become fami-

---

[6] If we accept B.C. 594 as the date of the Solonic legislation, we must suppose a space of 34 years—above a generation—during which the history of Athens is a blank. If the more probable date of B.C. 583 be taken, we shall reduce the interval to 23 years.

[7] Plut. Vit. Sol. c. 16, and c. 25.

[8] Ibid. c. 25.

[9] See Fragment xxv. of Gaisford's edition, which begins thus—

Οἷοι ἠδη ἰδίαν ἐκόμισσαν, αἰεὶ φοιτέοντι δυοῖν, [illegible]

In another place Solon defends his conduct in declining to seize the sovereignty, and says he is not ashamed of it (Fr. xxvii.).

[10] Plutarch says, ἔφασαν ὀνδυνέροντ,

ἀλλ' ἐλόγησε μὲν τοὺς πλουσίους διελῶν τὰ συμβόλαια, καὶ μᾶλλον ἔτι τοὺς πένητας, ὅτι γῆν ἀναδασμὸν οὐκ ἐποίησεν (Vit. Sol. c. 10).

[1] Fr. vii.: ἔργμασιν ἐν μεγάλοις πᾶσιν ἁδεῖν χαλεπόν.

[2] Fr. xxvi.:—

χαίτοι μὲν τότ' ἐπλεύνεσαν, νῦν δ' ὁμὸς χολού- μενοι

λοξὸν ὀφθαλμοῖς ὁρῶσι πάντες ὥστε δήιον.

[3] See Fragments xi. and xii.

[4] Herod. i. 29. Plutarch says nothing of any pledge at the time of his going abroad, but relates that his laws were originally made to continue in force 100 years (Vit. Solon. c. 25, ad init.).

liarised with his system," and would have ceased to wish for alteration. In this confidence he left them, feeling that were he to stay he might be asked to dispense them from their oath—a request which, if preferred by the general voice, he could not possibly have resisted.

34. On the departure of Solon, the factions which he had taken no measures to suppress, but which his personal influence had sufficed to keep in abeyance, immediately revived. The parties of the plain, the sea-coast, and the highlands, again showed themselves, and resumed their contentions.* It may be conjectured that the aim of the Pedieis was to abolish the timocratical constitution of Solon, and to reinstate the Eupatrids in their sole and undivided authority. They would consist of the great mass of the Eupatrids themselves, the proprietors of the fertile lands about Athens and Eleusis, together with their hangers-on and friends, and would form the party of the Reaction, which dreamt of cancelling the past by a few strokes of the pen or of the sword, and of returning to the good old days of Megacles and Draco. Their leader was a certain Lycurgus,* a member of a Eupatrid family otherwise unknown to us, but which Herodotus seems to regard as familiar to his readers*—the family of the Aristolaids. Against them were ranged the Paruli, or party of the sea-coast, the mercantile and commercial class in Athens and in the various ports, consisting in part of Eupatrids, but mainly of those who owed everything to the legislation of Solon, and whom his timocratical system especially favoured. These had at their head the Alcmæonid Megacles, a grandson of the archon, and formed the Conservative party of the time, which was content with the existing constitution, and wished for nothing but to maintain it. The Hyperacrii were the party of the Movement, consisting chiefly of the poor yeomen and labourers who with difficulty got a living from the land in the barren cantons of the east and north, and consequently only recognised in the Solonian constitution as Thetes, debarred from office under his system, and perhaps disappointed that he had done no more for them than to cancel their debts;* they were anxious for change in the opposite direction to those desired by the Pedieis, demanding probably some such reforms

as those which Clisthenes, half a century later, accomplished. As frequently happens with the democratical party in its earlier struggles, they were at a loss for a head, and hence they readily accepted the offer of Pisistratus to lead them, though he was previously known only by his military talents[1] and by his relationship to Solon, which can scarcely have been at this time a ground of popularity. The three parties were organised, we are told, and had begun a furious contention, when Solon returned from his travels.[2] He saw the danger of the crisis, detected the ambition of his kinsman, and strenuously exerted himself, both by entreaties addressed privately to the leaders,[3] and warnings given openly to the people,[4] to avert the coming revolution. But his efforts were unavailing. His long absence and his advanced age alike tended to weaken his authority; the chiefs paid no heed to his prayers, and the people thought little of his warnings. He was compelled to witness sorrowfully the fulfilment of his worst anticipations by the success of the artifice which made Pisistratus tyrant of Athens.[5] Even then he did not compromise his character or bate his freedom of speech. During the short time that he survived the usurpation, which seems to have been little more than a year,[6] he continued to reproach the Athenians with their tameness and folly, and to remind them that their own hands had placed the yoke of servitude upon their necks.[7]

35. The tyranny of Pisistratus and his sons occupied a space of almost exactly half a century.[8] As Herodotus gives a tolerably full account of this period,[9] and as it has been amply discussed by modern writers, no attempt will be made to give a connected view of it here. The "*early*" History of Athens—its dark and unfamiliar period—may indeed be considered to end with Solon, who stands at the close of the archaic state of things, and at the commencement of that new phase which has been forcibly and truly said to be more *modern* than ancient. For this latter period, so far as it falls within the space covered by our author, such illustration as seemed necessary is given in the foot-notes.[1] Those who require more are referred to the thirtieth and thirty-first chapters of Mr. Grote's History, which contain the most accurate digest of the ancient authorities, and the most philosophical comment upon them, to be found in the whole range of modern literature.

---

[1] Supra, page 320.
[2] Plut. Vit. Sol. c. 29. Laertius follows a different tradition. He makes Solon quit Athens on account of the tyranny of Pisistratus, and refuse to return thither (i. § 50, and § 67).
[3] Plut. Sol. l. s. c.
[4] See Fragments xvii. and xviii., and compare Plut. Vit. Sol. c. 30; Diog. Laert. i. § 49.
[5] Herod. i. 59; Plut. Vit. Sol. l. s. c.
[6] Plut. Vit. Sol. ad fin. Compare Clinton, F. H. ii. p. 368, and Grote, iii. p. 208.
[7] See Fragment xix:—

Εἰ δὲ πεπόνθατε δεινὰ δι' ὑμετέρην κακότητα,
Μή τι θεοῖς τούτων μοῖραν ἐπαμφέρετε.

[8] From B.C. 560 to B.C. 510. It was not, however, continuous. On the probable arrangement of the several reigns and exiles of Pisistratus, see Clinton, F. H. vol. ii. Append. c. ii.
[9] Book i. chs. 59-64, and Book v. chs. 55-65. Compare also, v. 94; vi. 103; vii. 6; &c.
[1] See especially the notes to Book i. chs. 63-64; Book iii. ch. 50, note [*]; Book v. chs. 56, 65, 66, 69, 97; Book vi. ch. 103; and Book viii. ch. 79.

THE SIXTH BOOK

OF THE

HISTORY OF HERODOTUS,

ENTITLED ERATO.

1. ARISTAGORAS, the author of the Ionian revolt, perished in the way which I have described. Meanwhile Histiæus, tyrant of Miletus, who had been allowed by Darius to leave Susa, came down to Sardis. On his arrival, being asked by Artaphernes, the Sardian satrap, what he thought was the reason that the Ionians had rebelled, he made answer that he could not conceive, and it had astonished him greatly, pretending to be quite unconscious of the whole business. Artaphernes, however, who perceived that he was dealing dishonestly, and who had in fact full knowledge of the whole history of the outbreak, said to him, "I will tell thee how the case stands, Histiæus : this shoe is of thy stitching ; Aristagoras has but put it on."

2. Such was the remark made by Artaphernes concerning the rebellion. Histiæus, alarmed at the knowledge which he displayed, so soon as night fell, fled away to the coast. Thus he forfeited his word to Darius ; for though he had pledged himself to bring Sardinia, the biggest island in the whole world, under the Persian yoke,[1] he in reality sought to obtain the direction of the war against the king. Crossing over to Chios, he was there laid in bonds by the inhabitants, who accused him

---

[1] Vide supra, v. 106. "An expedition against Sardinia," as Mr. Grote observes, "seems to have been among the favourite fancies of the Ionic Greeks of that day." (Hist. of Greece, vol. iv. p. 400; and compare supra, L 170, v. 124, and Pausan. iv. xxiii. § 4.) It is curious that it was never realised. While the coasts of Sicily, Italy, Gaul, and Spain were studded with colonies from Greece, and even Corsica had at least one settlement of some note (Alalia), Sardinia, notwithstanding its great fertility (Strabo, v. p. 318; Cic. Leg. Man. 12; Polyb. I. 79) and convenient position, appears (unless we believe the tale of Iolaus, Pausan. x. 17; Steph. Byz. ad voc. 'ΟΛΒΙα) never to have attracted a single Hellenic colony. Perhaps the power of Carthage was fully established there, before the Greeks became familiar with the locality.

of intending some mischief against them in the interest of Darius. However, when the whole truth was laid before them, and they found that Histiæus was in reality a foe to the king, they forthwith set him at large again.

3. After this the Ionians inquired of him for what reason he had so strongly urged Aristagoras to revolt from the king, thereby doing their nation so ill a service. In reply, he took good care not to disclose to them the real cause, but told them that King Darius had intended to remove the Phœnicians from their own country, and place them in Ionia, while he planted the Ionians in Phœnicia, and that it was for this reason he sent Aristagoras the order. Now it was not true that the king had entertained any such intention, but Histiæus succeeded hereby in arousing the fears of the Ionians.³

4. After this, Histiæus, by means of a certain Hermippus, a native of Atarneus,³ sent letters to many of the Persians in Sardis, who had before held some discourse with him concerning a revolt. Hermippus, however, instead of conveying them to the persons to whom they were addressed, delivered them into the hands of Artaphernes, who, perceiving what was on foot, commanded Hermippus to deliver the letters according to their addresses, and then bring him back the answers which were sent to Histiæus. The traitors being in this way discovered, Artaphernes put a number of Persians to death, and caused a commotion in Sardis.⁴

5. As for Histiæus, when his hopes in this matter were disappointed, he persuaded the Chians to carry him back to

---

³ The readiness with which this was believed proves, even better than historical instances, how frequent such transfers of population were in the great oriental empires. (Vide supra, iv. 204, note ⁸, and compare vol. ii. p. 467, note ⁹.)

³ Atarneus, in Herodotus, is not a city, but a tract. It lies opposite Lesbos, between the range of Cand and the sea. It is reckoned in Mysia, but belongs to the Chians, being the reward which they received from Harpagus for delivering up Pactyas. (Cf. i. 160; vi. 28; vii. 42; viii. 106.) In after times there seems to have been a town of the same name upon the coast. (Scylax, Peripl. p. 86; Xen. Hellen. iii. ii. 11; Strab. xiii. pp. 834, 865.)

⁴ I cannot accept Mr. Grote's account of this transaction. (Hist. of Greece,

vol. iv. p. 401.) According to him, Histiæus laid a trap into which Artaphernes fell. The letters written were "false," and Hermippus was instructed to take care that Artaphernes got possession of them. The suspected conspirators were quite innocent, and Artaphernes damaged his own cause by killing them. It is unnecessary to point out how irreconcilable such a view is with the entire story of Herodotus.

Probably Mr. Grote was led to depart from his authority by perceiving the improbability of any Persians having joined, or thought of joining, the rebels. This is a real difficulty, which I should explain by supposing that the persons alluded to, though Persian subjects, were in reality Lydians. The event would then indicate the near approach at this time of a Lydian outbreak.

Miletus; but the Milesians were too well pleased at having got quit of Aristagoras to be anxious to receive another tyrant into their country; besides which they had now tasted liberty. They therefore opposed his return; and when he endeavoured to force an entrance during the night, one of the inhabitants even wounded him in the thigh. Having been thus rejected from his country, he went back to Chios; whence, after failing in an attempt to induce the Chians to give him ships, he crossed over to Mytilênê, where he succeeded in obtaining vessels from the Lesbians. They fitted out a squadron of eight triremes, and sailed with him to the Hellespont, where they took up their station, and proceeded to seize all the vessels which passed out from the Euxine, unless the crews declared themselves ready to obey his orders.

6. While Histiæus and the Mytilenæans were thus employed, Miletus was expecting an attack from a vast armament, which comprised both a fleet and also a land force. The Persian captains had drawn their several detachments together,[1] and formed them into a single army; and had resolved to pass over all the other cities, which they regarded as of lesser account, and to march straight on Miletus. Of the naval states, Phœnicia showed the greatest zeal; but the fleet was composed likewise of the Cyprians (who had so lately been brought under),[2] the Cilicians, and also the Egyptians.[3]

7. While the Persians were thus making preparations against Miletus and Ionia, the Ionians, informed of their intent, sent their deputies to the Panionium,[4] and held a council upon the posture of their affairs. Hereat it was determined that no land force should be collected to oppose the Persians, but that the Milesians should be left to defend their own walls as they

---

[1] Hitherto the Persian forces had operated in distinct detachments, and upon distant points at the same time. Daurises, Hymees, and Otanes, had been at the head of three distinct armies (supra, v. 116-123).

[2] Supra, v. 115, 116.

[3] Mr. Grote considers the Egyptians, Cilicians, and Cyprians to have formed the land army, and ascribes the entire fleet of 600 vessels to the Phœnicians. (History of Greece, l. s. c.) Herodotus clearly means that the four great naval powers of Asia (infra, vii. 89-91) combined to furnish the fleet. (Vide supra, v. 108, note 6.)

The special zeal of the Phœnicians, who may perhaps have furnished half the fleet, arose probably from their jealousy of the naval power and commercial prosperity of Ionia.

[4] Supra, i. 141 and 148. It would appear that on the departure of Aristagoras (v. 126) the revolt entered upon a new phase. Hitherto Miletus had been a sort of dominant power, and Aristagoras had directed all affairs. On his departure, the old confederacy seems to have been restored. Probably no confidence was felt in Pythagoras, his nominee and successor, who can scarcely have retained much authority even at Miletus. Otherwise Histiæus would not have been refused admission (ch. 5).

could;[9] at the same time they agreed that the whole naval force of the states, not excepting a single ship, should be equipped, and should muster at Ladé,[10] a small island lying off Miletus—to give battle on behalf of the place.

8. Presently the Ionians began to assemble in their ships, and with them came the Æolians of Lesbos; and in this way they marshalled their line:—The wing towards the east[1] was formed of the Milesians themselves, who furnished eighty ships; next to them came the Prienians with twelve, and the Myusians with three ships;[2] after the Myusians were stationed the Teians, whose ships were seventeen; then the Chians, who furnished a hundred. The Erythræans and Phocæans followed, the former with eight, the latter with three ships; beyond the Phocæans were the Lesbians, furnishing seventy; last of all came the Samians, forming the western wing, and furnishing sixty vessels.[3] The fleet amounted in all to three hundred and fifty-three triremes.[4] Such was the number on the Ionian side.

---

[9] There is no reason to suppose that the Ionians came to this decision from "jealousy of Milesian influence" (Blakesley, ad loc.). They always recognised the sea as their own proper element (compare I. 28, and v. 109), and they knew, as well as the Persians (infra, ch. 9), that so long as they could maintain the mastery at sea, Miletus and the other maritime towns were safe.

[10] Ladé is now a hillock in the plain of the Mæander (Chandler's Travels, ch. liii. vol. I, p. 206). The deposits from the river have extended the coast to a distance of several miles west of Miletus (supra, i. 142, note[7]). The whole scene of the sea-fight is now land.

[1] The fleet formed in front of Miletus, and thus faced the north. (See the chart, vol. i. p. 216.) "The wing towards the east" would therefore be the right wing—the post of honour (vi. 111; ix. 28; &c.).

[2] Myus and Priene, which "had the same dialect" with Miletus (i. 142), and lay in its immediate neighbourhood, were probably little more than dependancies on "the glory of Ionia" (v. 28). Hence their ships are drawn up next to hers.

[3] It is remarkable that four of the Ionian cities, Ephesus, Colophon, Lebedus, and Clazomenæ, furnished no vessels to the combined fleet. The defection of Clazomenæ may be accounted

for, since it had been recently recovered by the Persians (supra, v. 123). But why the other three cities sent no contingents is not so clear. Perhaps the army of Otanes had taken them on its march from Clazomenæ to Miletus. They all three lie upon the route.

The number of ships furnished is a good indication of the relative importance of the several states. Chios, Miletus, Lesbos, and Samos are the four leading powers. This is very remarkable with respect to Samos, which was said to have been so utterly ruined not twenty years previously. (See note[8] on Book iii. ch. 149.) Phocæa, once the rival of Miletus, is now, in consequence of her great migration (supra, i. 165-167), miserably reduced. Still the nautical superiority of her inhabitants is shown by the fact that the leader of her small contingent is felt to be the fittest man to command the united fleet. Teos and Priene have recovered from the shock of the Persian conquest (i. 161 and 168) far more than Phocæa. Samos and Miletus are regarded as possessing the greatest nautical skill, and therefore occupy the wings, the posts at once of honour and of danger.

[4] It must be noticed as remarkable, that the sum total here given by Herodotus exactly tallies with his separate items, which is very rarely the case. (See Introductory Essay, vol. i. pp. 80, 87.)

9. On the side of the barbarians the number of vessels was six hundred.[1] These assembled off the coast of Milesia, while the land army collected upon the shore; but the leaders, learning the strength of the Ionian fleet, began to fear lest they might fail to defeat them, in which case, not having the mastery at sea, they would be unable to reduce Miletus, and might in consequence receive rough treatment at the hands of Darius. So when they thought of all these things, they resolved on the following course:—Calling together the Ionian tyrants, who had fled to the Medes for refuge when Aristagoras deposed them from their governments, and who were now in camp, having joined in the expedition against Miletus, the Persians addressed them thus: "Men of Ionia, now is the fit time to show your zeal for the house of the king. Use your best efforts, every one of you, to detach your fellow-countrymen from the general body. Hold forth to them the promise that, if they submit, no harm shall happen to them on account of their rebellion; their temples shall not be burnt, nor any of their private buildings; neither shall they be treated with greater harshness than before the outbreak. But if they refuse to yield, and determine to try the chance of a battle, threaten them with the fate which shall assuredly overtake them in that case. Tell them, when they are vanquished in fight, they shall be enslaved; their boys shall be made eunuchs, and their maidens transported to Bactra;[2] while their country shall be delivered into the hands of foreigners."

10. Thus spake the Persians. The Ionian tyrants sent accordingly by night to their respective citizens, and reported the words of the Persians; but the people were all stanch, and refused to betray their countrymen, those of each state thinking that they alone had had overtures made to them. Now these events happened on the first appearance of the Persians before Miletus.

11. Afterwards, while the Ionian fleet was still assembled at

[1] This was something less than the full force which the four powers (Phœnicia, Egypt, Cyprus, and Cilicia) were able to furnish. See the account of the fleet of Xerxes (infra, vii. 89-95), where they contribute 750.

[2] One would have expected Susa, rather than Bactra, here; as the captive maidens would of course be carried to the court (vide infra, ch. 32, ἀνασπάστους παρὰ βασιλέα). But perhaps the remote and savage Bactra was introduced of set purpose into the threat, as fitter to terrify the Greeks.

Not many early writers speak of the city Bactra (the modern Balkh), from which the province Bactria obtained its name. Herodotus, however, mentions it both in this place, and in another passage (infra, ix. 113). It afterwards became well known through the conquests of Alexander (Arrian, Exp. Alex. lib. 29; Strab. xi. p. 752, &c.). The Zendavesta makes it the fourth earliest settlement of the Arian race.

Ladé, councils were held, and speeches made by divers persons—among the rest by Dionysius, the Phocæan captain, who thus expressed himself:—"Our affairs hang on the razor's edge, men of Ionia, either to be free or to be slaves; and slaves, too, who have shown themselves runaways. Now then you have to choose whether you will endure hardships, and so for the present lead a life of toil, but thereby gain ability to overcome your enemies and establish your own freedom; or whether you will persist in this slothfulness and disorder, in which case I see no hope of your escaping the king's vengeance for your rebellion. I beseech you, be persuaded by me, and trust yourselves to my guidance. Then, if the gods only hold the balance fairly between us, I undertake to say that our foes will either decline a battle, or, if they fight, suffer complete discomfiture."

12. These words prevailed with the Ionians, and forthwith they committed themselves to Dionysius; whereupon he proceeded every day to make the ships move in column, and the rowers ply their oars, and exercise themselves in breaking the line;[7] while the marines were held under arms, and the vessels were kept, till evening fell, upon their anchors,[8] so that the men had nothing but toil from morning even to night. Seven days did the Ionians continue obedient, and do whatsoever he bade them; but on the eighth day, worn out by the hardness of the work and the heat of the sun, and quite unaccustomed to such fatigues, they began to confer together, and to say one to another, "What god have we offended to bring upon ourselves such a punishment as this? Fools and distracted that we were, to put ourselves into the hands of this Phocæan braggart, who does but furnish three ships to the fleet! He, now that he has got us, plagues us in the most desperate fashion; many of us, in consequence, have fallen sick already—many more expect to follow. We had better suffer anything rather than these hardships; even the slavery with which we are threatened, however harsh, can be no worse than our present thraldom. Come, let us refuse him obedience." So saying, they forthwith ceased to obey his

---

[7] This was the most important naval manœuvre with which the Greeks were acquainted. It is supposed to have had two objects; one, the breaking of the oars of the two vessels between which the ship using the manœuvre passed, and the other, the cutting off of a portion of the enemy's fleet from the rest. It is not quite certain, however, that it had this latter object. (For the value set upon the manœuvre by the most skilful of the ancient sailors, see Thucydides, L. 49; li. 89; vii. 36; Xen. Hellen. L. vi. 31; Polyb. i. ii. 9, and xvi. iv. 14. This last passage is particularly important as showing the nature of the operation.)

[8] Instead of being drawn up on shore, as was the usual practice.

orders, and pitched their tents, as if they had been soldiers, upon the island,[1] where they reposed under the shade all day, and refused to go aboard the ships and train themselves.[1]

13. Now when the Samian captains perceived what was taking place, they were more inclined than before to accept the terms which Æaces, the son of Syloson, had been authorised by the Persians to offer them, on condition of their deserting from the confederacy. For they saw that all was disorder among the Ionians, and they felt also that it was hopeless to contend with the power of the king; since if they defeated the fleet which had been sent against them, they knew that another would come five times as great.[2] So they took advantage of the occasion which now offered, and as soon as ever they saw the Ionians refuse to work, hastened gladly to provide for the safety of their temples and their properties. This Æaces, who made the overtures to the Samians, was the son of Syloson, and grandson of the earlier Æaces.[3] He had formerly been tyrant of Samos, but was ousted from his government by Aristagoras the Milesian, at the same time with the other tyrants of the Ionians.[4]

14. The Phœnicians soon afterwards sailed to the attack; and the Ionians likewise put themselves in line, and went out to meet them. When they had now neared one another, and joined battle, which of the Ionians fought like brave men and which like cowards, I cannot declare with any certainty, for charges are brought on all sides; but the tale goes that the Samians, according to the agreement which they had made with Æaces, hoisted sail, and quitting their post bore away for Samos, except eleven ships, whose captains gave no heed to the orders of the commanders, but remained and took part in the battle. The state of Samos, in consideration of this action, granted to these men, as an acknowledgment of their bravery, the honour of having their names, and the names of their fathers, inscribed

---

[1] Ladé was capable of accommodating a considerable body of men. Alexander, when he attacked Miletus, disembarked upon the island a detachment of 4000 Thracians. (Arrian, Exped. Alex. L. 18.)

[1] It adds a value to these graphic details, to consider that they may have been preserved by Hecatæus, who was likely an eye-witness of the proceedings (supra, v. 36, and 124).

[2] On this exaggeration, see the Introductory Essay, vol. I. p. 63. To judge by the fleet of Xerxes, the greatest naval force that Persia could collect was a fleet of 1200 triremes (infra, vi. 89).

[3] The family tree of the Samian Æacidæ is the following:—

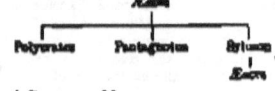

[4] Supra, v. 38.

upon a pillar, which still stands in the market-place.¹ The Lesbians also, when they saw the Samians, who were drawn up next them, begin to flee, themselves did the like; and the example, once set, was followed by the greater number of the Ionians.

15. Of those who remained and fought, none were so rudely handled as the Chians, who displayed prodigies of valour, and disdained to play the part of cowards. They furnished to the common fleet, as I mentioned above, one hundred ships, having each of them forty armed citizens, and those picked men, on board; and when they saw the greater portion of the allies betraying the common cause, they for their part, scorning to imitate the base conduct of these traitors, although they were left almost alone and unsupported, a very few friends continuing to stand by them, notwithstanding went on with the fight, and ofttimes cut the line of the enemy, until at last, after they had taken very many of their adversaries' ships, they ended by losing more than half of their own. Hereupon, with the remainder of their vessels, the Chians fled away to their own country.

16. As for such of their ships as were damaged and disabled, these, being pursued by the enemy, made straight for Mycalé, where the crews ran them ashore, and abandoning them began their march along the continent. Happening in their way upon the territory of Ephesus, they essayed to cross it; but here a dire misfortune befell them. It was night, and the Ephesian women chanced to be engaged in celebrating the Thesmophoria —the previous calamity of the Chians had not been heard of¹—

---

¹ No doubt Herodotus had seen this pillar. His descriptions of Samos are throughout those of an eye-witness. (Compare iii. 54 and 60). Suidas relates (ad voc. 'Ἡρόδοτος) that he fled to Samos from the tyranny of Lygdamis, the grandson of Artemisia, and continued there a considerable time—long enough to learn accurately the dialect of the place. But it has already been shown that we cannot trust these statements (Introductory Essay, vol. i. pp. 11-13).

² For a description of Mycalé, vide supra, i. 148. It was the name given to the mountainous headland which runs out from the coast in the direction of Samos, separating the bay which receives the waters of the Mæander (or Great Mender) from that into which the Cayster (or Little Mendere) flows. The range is now called Mount Samsun, from Samsun, the modern name of Priené.

⁷ In this fact we seem to have another indication that Ephesus kept aloof from the revolt (supra, ch. 8, note ⁹). The Thesmophoria was a festival in honour of Demeter, or Ceres Thesmophorus (i. e., the lawgiver), in which women only participated, and which was celebrated in various parts of Greece with similar rites, but not everywhere at the same time of the year. At Athens the festival took place in autumn, in the month Pyanepsion ('October¸); but elsewhere it seems to have been generally celebrated in the summer. It lasted for some days. The places where it is known to have been held are the following: Sparta, Athens, Thebes, Eretria, Drymæa in Phocis, Delos, Miletus, Ephesus, Syracuse, and Agrigentum. For a full account of the ceremonies with which it was accompanied at Athens, see Smith's Dictionary of Antiquities, pp. 964, 965.

so when the Ephesians saw their country invaded by an armed band, they made no question of the new-comers being robbers who purposed to carry off their women;[*] and accordingly they marched out against them in full force, and slew them all. Such were the misfortunes which befell them of Chios.

17. Dionysius, the Phocæan, when he perceived that all was lost, having first captured three ships from the enemy, himself took to flight. He would not, however, return to Phocæa, which he well knew must fall again, like the rest of Ionia, under the Persian yoke; but straightway, as he was, he set sail for Phœnicia, and there sunk a number of merchantmen, and gained a great booty; after which he directed his course to Sicily, where he established himself as a corsair,[*] and plundered the Carthaginians and Tyrrhenians, but did no harm to the Greeks.

18. The Persians, when they had vanquished the Ionians in the sea-fight, besieged Miletus both by land and sea, driving mines under the walls, and making use of every known device, until at length they took both the citadel and the town,[1] six years from the time when the revolt first broke out under Aristagoras. All the inhabitants of the city they reduced to slavery, and thus the event tallied with the announcement which had been made by the oracle.

19. For once upon a time, when the Argives had sent to Delphi to consult the god about the safety of their own city, a prophecy was given them, in which others besides themselves were interested; for while it bore in part upon the fortunes of Argos, it touched in a by-clause the fate of the men of Miletus. I shall set down the portion which concerned the Argives when I come to that part of my History,[2] mentioning at present only the passage in which the absent Milesians were spoken of. This passage was as follows:—

"Then shalt thou, Miletus, so oft the contriver of evil,
Be, thyself, to many a feast and an excellent booty;
Then shall thy matrons wash the feet of long-haired masters;—
Others shall then possess our lov'd Didymian temple."

Such a fate now befel the Milesians; for the Persians, who wore their hair long,[3] after killing most of the men, made the women and children slaves; and the sanctuary at Didyma,[4] the oracle no less than the temple, was plundered and burnt; of the riches whereof I have made frequent mention in other parts of my History.[5]

20. Those of the Milesians whose lives were spared, being carried prisoners to Susa, received no ill treatment at the hands of King Darius, but were established by him in Ampé, a city on the shores of the Erythræan sea, near the spot where the Tigris flows into it.[6] Miletus itself, and the plain about the city, were kept by the Persians for themselves, while the hill-country was assigned to the Carians of Pedasus.[7]

21. And now the Sybarites,[8] who after the loss of their city occupied Laüs[9] and Scidrus,[1] failed duly to return the former kindness of the Milesians. For these last, when Sybaris was taken by the Crotoniats,[2] made a great mourning, all of them, youths as well as men, shaving their heads; since Miletus and Sybaris were, of all the cities whereof we have any knowledge,

---

of the Persians is conspicuous in the sculptures of Persepolis and Behistun. Æschylus, on account of it, called the Persians *Συδραξανθριχες* (ap. Athen. Deipn. xiv. 23, p. 627, D.). For a representation of the manner in which it was worn, see the woodcuts, vol. i. p. 221.

[4] Didyma was the name of the place called also Branchidæ. In the territory of Miletus, where the famous temple of Apollo stood. (Strab. xiv. p. 927. τοῦ ἐν Διδύμοις ναοῦ; Steph. Byz. Διδύμα τόπος Μιλήτου.) The temple itself was sometimes called "the Didymæum" (Quint. Curt. vii. 5, § 28), and the Apollo worshipped there "Apollo Didymeus" (Strab. xiv. p. 910; Plin. H. N. v. 29; Macrob. Sat. i. 17; Etym. Mag. ad voc. Διδυμαῖος).

The temple and its site have been already described (supra, i. 157, note [9]).

[5] Supra, i. 92; v. 36. Strabo (l. s. c.) seems to think that the temple was first burnt, and its riches carried off by Xerxes; but this statement is of no weight against the clear testimony of Herodotus.

[6] The city Ampé is known only to Herodotus and Stephen. (See Steph. Byz. ad voc.) It is impossible to fix its site, since the course of the rivers have changed, and the coast-line has advanced considerably. (See vol. i. p. 466.)

[7] Supra, i. 175. It is probable that the Pedasians had continued faithful to

the Persians, when the other Carians revolted from them, and were now rewarded for their fidelity. Mylasa, which lay nearer the Milesian hill-country (Mount Latmus), had, we know, taken a leading part in the insurrection (supra, v. 121).

[8] For the situation of Sybaris, and its history, see above v. 44, note [9].

[9] Laüs was about 35 miles from Sybaris. It was situated on the western coast of Italy, near the mouth of the river of the same name (Strab. vi. p. 364; Plin. H. N. iii. 5; Steph. Byz. ad voc.), which is still known as the *Lao* (Swinburne, vol. ii. p. 474). It had ceased to exist by the time of Strabo, and no traces seem now to remain of it.

[1] Stephen of Byzantium (ad voc.) is the only other writer who has preserved to us a notice of this town. He calls it a city of Italy, and records that its inhabitants were mentioned by Lycus 'of Rhegium', one of the historians of Alexander, about B.C. 300. It was probably situated at no great distance from Laüs, either in the mountain region between that place and Sybaris (cf. Schiller de Thuriorum Rep. p. 8), or, perhaps, on the coast, like Laüs. According to some, its site is marked by the ruins at *Sapri*, six miles east of *Policastro*. (See the article on Scidrus in Smith's Geograph. Dict.)

[2] Supra, v. 44.

the two most closely united to one another.³ The Athenians, on the other hand, showed themselves beyond measure afflicted at the fall of Miletus, in many ways expressing their sympathy, and especially by their treatment of Phrynichus.⁴ For when this poet brought out upon the stage his drama of the Capture of Miletus, the whole theatre burst into tears; and the people sentenced him to pay a fine of a thousand drachms,⁵ for recalling to them their own misfortunes. They likewise made a law, that no one should ever again exhibit that piece.

22. Thus was Miletus bereft of its inhabitants. In Samos, the people of the richer sort were much displeased with the doings of the captains, and the dealings they had had with the Medes; they therefore held a council, very shortly after the sea-fight, and resolved that they would not remain to become the slaves of Æaces and the Persians, but before the tyrant set foot in their country, would sail away and found a colony in another land. Now it chanced that about this time the Zancleans of Sicily had sent ambassadors to the Ionians, and invited them to Calé-Acté,⁶ where they wished an Ionian city to be founded. This place, Calé-Acté (or the Fair Strand) as it is called, is in the country of the Sicilians, and is situated in the part of Sicily which looks towards Tyrrhenia.⁷ The offer thus made to all the Ionians was

---

³ The historian Timæus (Fragm. 60) asserted, 'that this close union resulted from the commercial intercourse between the two cities. According to him the wool of Miletus was the chief material used by the Sybarites in their dress; and as they thus depended on Miletus for one of their most valued luxuries, the Sybarites regarded its inhabitants with special affection. But Timæus has the air of exaggerating the Sybaritic luxuriousness (vide infra, ch. 127).

⁴ Phrynichus, the disciple of Thespis (Suidas, ad voc.), began to exhibit tragedies about the year B.C. 511. He is said to have been the first who "dropt the light and ludicrous cast of the original drama, and dismissing Bacchus and the Satyrs, formed his plays from the more grave and elevated events recorded in the mythology and history of his own country." His tragedies were of great merit. (Aristoph. Thesmoph. 164.) Æschylus, his junior by about ten or fifteen years, was accused of borrowing largely from them. (Aristoph. Ran. 1728, ed. Bothe; Glauc. Rheg. in Introduct. ad Æschyl. Pers.) His Phœnissæ was on the same subject as the Persæ of Æschylus, and appears to have gained the tragic prize in the year B.C. 476. He was especially famed for the excellency of his choruses. (Aristoph. Av. 716; Vesp. 220, 269; Aristot. Prob. xix. 31.)

⁵ Twice the income of a Pentacosiomedimnus. The same story is told by Strabo (xiv. 911), Ælian (xii. 17), Plutarch 'Præcept. Reipubl. ger. ii. p. 814, B.., Libanius (t. p. 506), Ammianus Marcellinus (xxviii. 1), and others.

⁶ This place became afterwards known as Calacté, or Calacta. (Cic. in Verr. ii. iii. § 43; Ptolem. Geograph. iii. 4, p. 78; Sil. Ital. xiv. 251.) It lay on the north coast of Sicily, between Halæsa and Haluntium. The probable site is the modern Caronia (long. 14° 27', lat. 38° nearly). The coast in this part is very beautiful, thickly wooded with oak, elm, pine, and ash, clothing a series of rocky hills. (Smyth's Sicily, pp. 96, 97.) Perhaps, however, the "Fair Strand" derived its name rather from the productiveness of its fisheries. Silius Italicus (l. s. c.) calls it "litus piscosa Calacté."

⁷ That is, on the north coast, Mr.

embraced only by the Samians, and by such of the Milesians as had contrived to effect their escape.

23. Hereupon this is what ensued. The Samians on their voyage reached the country of the Epizephyrian Locrians,[a] at a time when the Zanclaeans and their king Scythas were engaged in the siege of a Sicilian town which they hoped to take. Anaxilaüs, tyrant of Rhegium,[b] who was on ill terms with the Zanclaeans, knowing how matters stood, made application to the Samians, and persuaded them to give up the thought of Calé-Acté, the place to which they were bound, and to seize Zanclé itself, which was left without men. The Samians followed this counsel and possessed themselves of the town; which the Zanclaeans no sooner heard than they hurried to the rescue, calling to their aid Hippocrates, tyrant of Gela,[c] who was one of their allies. Hippocrates came with his army to their assistance; but on his arrival he seized Scythas, the Zanclaean king, who had just lost his city, and sent him away in chains, together with his brother Pythogenes, to the town of Inycus;[d] after which he

came to an understanding with the Samians, exchanged oaths with them, and agreed to betray the people of Zanclé. The reward of his treachery was to be one-half of the goods and chattels, including slaves, which the town contained, and all that he could find in the open country. Upon this Hippocrates seized and bound the greater number of the Zancleans as slaves; delivering, however, into the hands of the Samians three hundred of the principal citizens, to be slaughtered; but the Samians spared the lives of these persons.

24. Scythas, the king of the Zancleans, made his escape from Inycus, and fled to Himera; whence he passed into Asia, and went up to the court of Darius. Darius thought him the most upright of all the Greeks to whom he afforded a refuge; for with the king's leave he paid a visit to Sicily, and thence returned back to Persia, where he lived in great comfort, and died by a natural death at an advanced age.

25. Thus did the Samians escape the yoke of the Medes, and possess themselves without any trouble of Zanclé, a most beautiful city. At Samos itself the Phœnicians, after the fight which had Miletus for its prize was over, re-established Æaces, the son of Syloson, upon his throne. This they did by the command of the Persians, who looked upon Æaces as one who had rendered

them a high service and therefore deserved well at their hands. They likewise spared the Samians, on account of the desertion of their vessels, and did not burn either their city or their temples, as they did those of the other rebels. Immediately after the fall of Miletus the Persians recovered Caria, bringing some of the cities over by force, while others submitted of their own accord.

26. Meanwhile tidings of what had befallen Miletus reached Histiæus the Milesian, who was still at Byzantium, employed in intercepting the Ionian merchantmen as they issued from the Euxine.[5] Histiæus had no sooner heard the news than he gave the Hellespont in charge to Bisaltes, son of Apollophanes, a native of Abydos, and himself, at the head of his Lesbians, set sail for Chios. One of the Chian garrisons which opposed him he engaged at a place called "The Hollows," situated in the Chian territory, and of these he slaughtered a vast number; afterwards, by the help of his Lesbians, he reduced all the rest of the Chians, who were weakened by their losses in the sea-fight, Polichné, a city of Chios,[6] serving him as head-quarters.

27. It mostly happens that there is some warning when great misfortunes are about to befall a state or nation; and so it was in this instance, for the Chians had previously had some strange tokens sent to them. A choir of a hundred of their youths had been despatched to Delphi; and of these only two had returned; the remaining ninety-eight having been carried off by a pestilence. Likewise, about the same time, and very shortly before the sea-fight, the roof of a school-house had fallen in upon a number of their boys, who were at lessons; and out of a hundred and twenty children there was but one left alive. Such were the signs which God sent to warn them. It was very shortly afterwards that the sea-fight happened, which brought the city down upon its knees; and after the sea-fight came the attack of Histiæus and his Lesbians, to whom the Chians, weakened as they were, furnished an easy conquest.

28. Histiæus now led a numerous army, composed of Ionians and Æolians, against Thasos,[7] and had laid siege to the place when news arrived that the Phœnicians were about to quit Mile-

---

[5] Supra, ch. 5. From the time that Miletus refused to receive Histiæus back (supra, ch. 5), his policy seems to have become purely selfish. His proceedings at Byzantium must have injured the Greeks far more than the Persians. And now he proceeds openly to attack his own countrymen. Contrast his conduct with that of Dionysius (ch. 17).

[6] There were two other places of this name, one in Crete, and one in the Troas (Steph. Byz. ad voc.). The site of the Chian Polichne is unknown.

[7] The gold mines of Thasos perhaps formed the chief attraction. (Vide infra, ch. 46, and supra, iii. 44.)

tus and attack the other cities of Ionia. On hearing this, Histiæus raised the siege of Thasos, and hastened to Lesbos with all his forces. There his army was in great straits for want of food; whereupon Histiæus left Lesbos and went across to the mainland, intending to cut the crops which were growing in the Atarnean territory,* and likewise in the plain of the Caïcus,² which belonged to Mysia. Now it chanced that a certain Persian named Harpagus¹ was in these regions at the head of an army of no little strength. He, when Histiæus landed, marched out to meet him, and engaging with his forces destroyed the greater number of them, and took Histiæus himself prisoner.

29. Histiæus fell into the hands of the Persians in the following manner. The Greeks and Persians engaged at Malêna,² in the region of Atarneus; and the battle was for a long time stoutly contested, till at length the cavalry came up, and, charging the Greeks, decided the conflict. The Greeks fled; and Histiæus, who thought that Darius would not punish his fault with death, showed how he loved his life by the following conduct. Overtaken in his flight by one of the Persians, who was about to run him through, he cried aloud in the Persian tongue that he was Histiæus the Milesian.

30. Now, had he been taken straightway before King Darius, I verily believe that he would have received no hurt, but the king would have freely forgiven him. Artaphernes, however, satrap of Sardis, and his captor Harpagus, on this very account,—because they were afraid that, if he escaped, he would be again received into high favour by the king,—put him to death as soon as he arrived at Sardis. His body they impaled at that place,³ while they embalmed his head and sent it up to Susa to the king. Darius, when he learnt what had taken place, found great fault with the men engaged in this business for not

---

* As master of Chios, he would consider the Atarnean plain his own (l. 160).
² The whole valley of the Caïcus was most rich and beautiful (σφόδρα εὐδαίμονα γῆν, σχεδὸν τὴν ἀρίστην τῆς Μυσίας, Strab. xiii. p. 895; compare Fellows, Asia Minor, p. 29); but the part near Pergamum, about the junction of the Cateius with the Caïcus, was called κατ' ἐξοχὴν "the Caïcian plain," and is probably the tract here indicated (Strab. l. s. c. and xv. p. 984). This plain is not more than ten or twelve miles from the coast.
¹ This is a not unusual name among the Arians. Harpagus the Mede, in Book i., was clearly a different person; and both are probably distinct from the Harpagus of the Lycian inscriptions.
² This place is wholly unknown to the geographers. Wesseling would read "Carina," from the mention of that place in vii. 42; but that passage shows Carina to have been beyond the limits of Atarneus.
³ According to the Persian custom with rebels. See Behistun Inscription, col. ii. para. 13, 14, col. iii. para. 8; and supra, iii. 159, infra, vii. 238.

bringing Histiæus alive into his presence, and commanded his servants to wash and dress the head with all care, and then bury it, as the head of a man who had been a great benefactor to himself and the Persians.⁴ Such was the sequel of the history of Histiæus.

31. The naval armament of the Persians wintered at Miletus, and in the following year proceeded to attack the islands off the coast, Chios, Lesbos, and Tenedos,⁵ which were reduced without difficulty. Whenever they became masters of an island, the barbarians, in every single instance, netted the inhabitants. Now the mode in which they practise this netting is the following. Men join hands, so as to form a line across from the north coast to the south, and then march through the island from end to end and hunt out the inhabitants.⁶ In like manner the Persians took also the Ionian towns upon the mainland, not however netting the inhabitants, as it was not possible.

32. And now their generals made good all the threats wherewith they had menaced the Ionians before the battle.⁷ For no sooner did they get possession of the towns than they chose out all the best favoured boys and made them eunuchs, while the most beautiful of the girls they tore from their homes and sent as presents to the king, at the same time burning the cities themselves, with their temples.⁸ Thus were the Ionians for the third time reduced to slavery; once by the Lydians, and a second, and now a third time, by the Persians.

33. The sea force, after quitting Ionia, proceeded to the Hellespont, and took all the towns which lie on the left shore as one sails into the straits. For the cities on the right bank had already been reduced by the land force of the Persians. Now these are the places which border the Hellespont on the European side;

---

⁴ Of a piece with this mildness is the treatment of Metiochus (infra, ch. 41), of the Milesian prisoners (supra, ch. 20) and of the Eretrians (infra, ch. 119). A still more signal instance of clemency on the part of Darius is recorded by Ælian (Hist. Var. vi. 14). Compare Cæsar's conduct on receiving the head of Pompey.

⁵ Nothing had been said of the participation of Tenedos in the revolt; but as the Ionians had had the command of the sea, it is probable that all the islands of the coast had taken part in it.
Tenedos retains its name absolutely unchanged to the present day. It is a small but fertile island, producing an excellent wine. Its situation off the mouth of the Hellespont, and its safe port, have at all times made it a place of some consequence. (See Chandler, ch. vi. vol. l. p. 19.)

⁶ Supra, iii. 149.

⁷ Supra, ch. 9.

⁸ Mr. Grote (Hist. of Greece, iv. p. 414) observes, with reason, that the account of these severities must be exaggerated. The islands continue to be occupied by a Greek population; and the towns upon the mainland appear shortly as flourishing as ever. Within fourteen years the Greeks of Asia are found furnishing 290 ships (which would imply near upon 60,000 men) to the fleet of Xerxes (infra, vii. 93-95).

the Chersonese, which contains a number of cities, Perinthus, the forts in Thrace, Selybria, and Byzantium. The Byzantines at this time, and their opposite neighbours, the Chalcedonians, instead of awaiting the coming of the Phœnicians, quitted their country, and sailing into the Euxine, took up their abode at the city of Mesêmbria. The Phœnicians, after burning all the places above mentioned, proceeded to Proconnêsus and Artaca, which they likewise delivered to the flames; this done, they returned to the Chersonese, being minded to reduce those cities which they had not ravaged in their former cruise. Upon Cyzicus they made no attack at all, as before their coming the inhabitants had made terms with Œbares, the son of Megabazus, and satrap of Dascyleium, and had submitted themselves to the king. In the Chersonese the Phœnicians subdued all the cities, excepting Cardia.

34. Up to this time the cities of the Chersonese had been under the government of Miltiades, the son of Cimon, and grandson of Stesagoras, to whom they had descended from Miltiades, the son of Cypselus, who obtained possession of them in the following manner. The Dolonci,³ a Thracian tribe, to whom the Chersonese at that time belonged, being harassed by a war in which they were engaged with the Apsinthians,⁴ sent their princes to Delphi to consult the oracle about the matter. The reply of the Pythoness bade them "take back with them as a colonist into their country the man who should first offer them hospitality after they quitted the temple." The Dolonci, following the Sacred Road,⁵ passed through the regions of Phocis and Boeotia; after which, as still no one invited them in, they turned aside, and travelled to Athens.

35. Now Pisistratus was at this time sole lord of Athens; but Miltiades, the son of Cypselus, was likewise a person of much distinction. He belonged to a family which was wont to contend in the four horse-chariot races,⁶ and traced its descent to

seems the best, that it was the old Scythic (*i. e.* Cymric) appellation (Steph. Byz. ad voc. Καρδία). Accordingly we may trace in the word the Celtic *Caer*, which is so common in the Welsh names, and which is found likewise in Carcinitis (supra, iv. 55) and Cardamus (Hecat. Fr. 157), both *Scythian* cities.

³ The Dolonci almost disappear from among the Thracian tribes. No further mention of them is made by the Greek historians. The only trace, I believe, which we possess of their continued existence is the occurrence of their name in the catalogues of Pliny (H. N. iv. 11), and Solinus (c. 10). They may perhaps have been ethnically connected with the Dolones of Cyzicus, and the Dolopes of Thessaly (cf. Marcellin. Vit. Thucyd. p. viii., where the Dolonci are called "Dolopes").

⁴ The Apsinthians or Apsynthians were a Thracian people who occupied the tract immediately north of the Chersonese, as is plain both from ch. 37. and from a fragment of Hecataeus (Fr. 135). It is impossible to fix their limits with exactness, either eastward or westward. Stephen of Byzantium (ad voces Ἀλτοι and Νιψαιοί) seems to extend them westward to the Hebrus. They are but little known in history.

Stephen and Suidas (ad voc. Ἀψυνθος) have a town Apsynthus, which they confuse with the Oenus of Herodotus (infra, vii. 58). Dionysius Periegetes has a Thracian river of the same name (l. 575), from which Eustathius (ad loc.) says that the Apsynthians derived their appellation.

⁵ By "the sacred road" is meant apparently the road which led from Delphi eastward, in the direction of Lebadea and Orchomenus. Along this road would come all the processions from the principal states of Greece.

⁶ As the keeping of a horse indicated some considerable wealth, both in Greece and Rome, whence the social rank of ἱππεῖς, ἱπποβόται, *equites*, &c., so still more did the maintenance of such a stud as could entitle a man to contend with any chance of success in the great games, mark the owner as a person of ample fortune. Hence the constant allusions in Pindar to the wealth and munificence of those who had won the chariot-races (Ol. ii. 53; Pyth. i. 50, 90, v. 1, 99; Nem. ix. 32; Isth. i. 42), and hence the force of what Herodotus says below of Callias (ch. 122). First-rate horses sold at enormous prices, as appears by the well-known instance of Bucephalus, who fetched a sum equal to 3000*l.* sterling (Aul. Gell. v. 2). Skilful charioteers were highly paid; and no expense was spared in the decoration of the chariots and equipment of the coursers. The expensiveness of the pur-

Æacus and Egina, but which, from the time of Philæas, the son of Ajax, who was the first Athenian citizen of the house, had been naturalised at Athens. It happened that as the Dolonci passed his door Miltiades was sitting in his vestibule, which caused him to remark them, dressed as they were in outlandish garments, and armed moreover with lances.[1] He therefore called to them, and, on their approach, invited them in, offering them lodging and entertainment. The strangers accepted his hospitality, and, after the banquet was over, they laid before him in full the directions of the oracle, and besought him on their own part to yield obedience to the god. Miltiades was persuaded ere they had done speaking; for the government of Pisistratus was irksome to him, and he wanted to be beyond the tyrant's reach. He therefore went straightway to Delphi, and inquired of the oracle whether he should do as the Dolonci desired.

36. As the Pythoness backed their request, Miltiades, son of Cypselus, who had already won the four-horse chariot-race at Olympia, left Athens, taking with him as many of the Athenians as liked to join in the enterprise, and sailed away with the Dolonci. On his arrival at the Chersonese, he was made king by those who had invited him. After this his first act was to build a wall across the neck of the Chersonese from the city of Cardia to Pactya,[2] to protect the country from the incursions and ravages of the Apsinthians. The breadth of the isthmus at this

part is thirty-six furlongs, the whole length of the peninsula within the isthmus being four hundred and twenty furlongs.

37. When he had finished carrying the wall across the isthmus, and had thus secured the Chersonese against the Apsinthians, Miltiades proceeded to engage in other wars, and first of all attacked the Lampsacenians; but falling into an ambush which they had laid he had the misfortune to be taken prisoner. Now it happened that Miltiades stood high in the favour of Crœsus, king of Lydia. When Crœsus therefore heard of his calamity, he sent and commanded the men of Lampsacus to give Miltiades his freedom; "if they refused," he said, "he would destroy them like a fir." Then the Lampsacenians were somewhile in doubt about this speech of Crœsus, and could not tell how to construe his threat "that he would destroy them like a fir;" but at last one of their elders divined the true sense, and told them that the fir is the only tree which, when cut down, makes no fresh shoots, but forthwith dies outright. So the Lampsacenians, being greatly afraid of Crœsus, released Miltiades, and let him go free.

38. Thus did Miltiades, by the help of Crœsus, escape this danger. Some time afterwards he died childless, leaving his kingdom and his riches to Stesagoras, who was the son of Cimon, his half-brother. Ever since his death the people of the Cher-

sonese have offered him the customary sacrifices of a founder; and they have further established in his honour a gymnic contest and a chariot-race,[1] in neither of which is it lawful for any Lampsacenian to contend. Before the war with Lampsacus was ended Stesagoras too died childless: he was sitting in the hall of justice when he was struck upon the head with a hatchet by a man who pretended to be a deserter, but was in good sooth an enemy, and a bitter one.

39. Thus died Stesagoras; and upon his death the Pisistratidæ fitted out a trireme, and sent Miltiades, the son of Cimon, and brother of the deceased, to the Chersonese, that he might undertake the management of affairs in that quarter. They had already shown him much favour at Athens, as if, forsooth, they had been no parties to the death of his father Cimon—a matter whereof I will give an account in another place.[2] He upon his arrival remained shut up within the house, pretending to do honour to the memory of his dead brother; whereupon the chief people of the Chersonese gathered themselves together from all the cities of the land, and came in a procession to the place where Miltiades was, to condole with him upon his misfortune. Miltiades commanded them to be seized and thrown into prison; after which he made himself master of the Chersonese, maintained a body of five hundred mercenaries, and married Hegesipyla,[3] daughter of the Thracian king Olorus.

40. This Miltiades,[4] the son of Cimon, had not been long in the country[4] when a calamity befel him yet more grievous than

was the issue of the former, Cimon of the latter marriage (cf. infra, ch. 103). Marcellinus makes Stesagoras, the successor of Miltiades, himself the half-brother of that king (Vit. Thucyd.).

[1] See b. 167, and compare the similar honours paid to Brasidas at Amphipolis (Thucyd. v. 11).

[2] Infra, ch. 103.

[3] The Thracian princes were not averse to giving their daughters in marriage to the Greeks upon the coast. Teres, the founder of the great kingdom of the Odrysæ, married one of his daughters to Nymphodorus, a Greek of Abdera (Thucyd. ii. 29). Hegesipyla, the daughter of Olorus, is said to have accompanied her husband to Athens, and after his death to have married another Athenian, by whom she had a son who was named Olorus, after his grandfather. This Olorus was the father of Thucydides, who seems to have inherited, through his grandmother, the

Hegesipyla here mentioned, a considerable property in Thrace (Thucyd. iv. 104; compare Marcellinus, Vit. Thucyd., whose account, however, is very confused). Hegesipyla was probably, by her name, a half Greek, the daughter of a Greek mother. (Compare the case of Scylas, iv. 78.)

[4] There is here a curious laxity of expression, or a curious forgetfulness of dates. Miltiades cannot have entered upon his government much later than B.C. 512; for not only did he take part in the Scythian expedition of Darius, which was at latest in B.C. 507-500, but we are expressly told that he was sent from Athens to the Chersonese by the Pisistratidæ, who ceased to reign B.C. 510. Now his expulsion from the Chersonese by the Scyths falls, according to the account here given, into the year B.C. 495, so that he had been at least fifteen years in the country when the Scythians drove him out.

those in which he was now involved: for three years earlier he had had to fly before an incursion of the Scyths. These nomads, angered by the attack of Darius, collected in a body and marched as far as the Chersonese.[3] Miltiades did not await their coming, but fled, and remained away until the Scyths retired, when the Dolonci sent and fetched him back. All this happened three years before the events which befel Miltiades at the present time.

41. He now no sooner heard that the Phœnicians were attacking Tenedos[4] than he loaded five triremes with his goods and chattels, and set sail for Athens. Cardia was the point from which he took his departure; and as he sailed down the gulf of Melas,[7] along the shore of the Chersonese, he came suddenly upon the whole Phœnician fleet. However he himself escaped, with four of his vessels, and got into Imbrus,[8] one trireme only falling into the hands of his pursuers. This vessel was under the command of his eldest son Metiochus, whose mother was not the daughter of the Thracian king Olorus, but a different woman. Metiochus and his ship were taken; and when the Phœnicians found out that he was a son of Miltiades they resolved to convey him to the king, expecting thereby to rise high in the royal favour. For they remembered that it was Miltiades who counselled the Ionians to hearken when the Scyths prayed them to break up the bridge and return home.[9] Darius, however, when the Phœnicians brought Metiochus into his presence, was so far from doing him any hurt, that he loaded him with benefits. He gave him a house and estate, and also a Persian wife, by whom there were children born to him who were accounted Persians. As for Miltiades himself, from Imbrus he made his way in safety to Athens.

42. At this time the Persians did no more hurt to the Ionians; but on the contrary, before the year was out, they carried into effect the following measures, which were greatly to their

---

[3] This appears to have been a marauding expedition, to which the Scythians were encouraged by the success of the Ionian revolt up to that time. It took place the year before the fall of Miletus. This date explains the mistake, if mistake it be, of Strabo (xiii. p. 853), who thought the burning of the towns about the Hellespont, in B.C. 493 (supra, ch. 33), to have arisen from fear of a Scythic invasion of Asia. The anxiety of the Scythians to avenge the invasion of their land is indicated by the embassy to Sparta mentioned below (ch. 84).

[4] Supra, ch. 31.

[7] The modern gulf of Xeros, on the western side of the peninsula. It received its name from the river Melas, the small stream which flows into the gulf near Karatch, called by the Turks the Karatch Su.

[8] Imbrus is not more than ten or twelve miles from the coast. It is mentioned above (v. 26).

[9] Supra, iv. 137.

advantage. Artaphernes, satrap of Sardis, summoned deputies from all the Ionian cities, and forced them to enter into agreements with one another, not to harass each other by force of arms, but to settle their disputes by reference.[10] He likewise took the measurement of their whole country in parasangs—such is the name which the Persians give to a distance of thirty furlongs[1]—and settled the tributes which the several cities were to pay, at a rate that has continued unaltered from the time when Artaphernes fixed it down to the present day.[2] The rate was very nearly the same as that which had been paid before the revolt.[3]

---

[10] These provisions were common in the Greek treaties (compare Thucyd. I. 145, v. 18, 79, &c.); but it is difficult to imagine that the cities of Asiatic Greece had up to this time possessed the right of carrying on war with one another. Such a right seems incompatible with the Persian domination; and no instance appears of its exercise.

[1] Supra, ii. 6, and v. 53.

[2] Mr. Grote (Hist. of Greece, vol. v. pp. 454-456, note) denies that the Greek cities upon the coast paid any tribute to Persia from the date of the full organization of the Athenian confederacy (B.C. 476) till after the disasters at Syracuse B.C. 413. He thinks this passage only means that there was an assessment of the Ionic cities in the king's books, not that there was any payment of tribute. He supposes that Herodotus knew this fact of the assessment, from having access to the books themselves, and "might or might not know" whether the tribute was realised. To me it appears quite inconceivable that Herodotus should be ignorant of such a point, and very unlikely that he should have mentioned the continuance of the assessment in the way which he has, if all payment of it had ceased from the time when he was eight years old. There is, however, more direct evidence that the tribute continued to be paid. Mr. Grote admits that "Greek towns in the interior" paid their quotas, considering that point to be proved by the case of Magnesia, which Artaxerxes gave to Themistocles; but he has apparently forgotten that the revenues of Myus and Lampsacus, both cities of the coast, were assigned to the illustrious exile, in exactly the same way as those of Magnesia (Thucyd. i. 138). It is manifest therefore that Lampsacus and Myus were not only rated, but paid tribute, down to B.C. 465. Indeed this is confirmed by Mr. Grote in a previous note (vol. v. p. 385, note[2], strangely at variance with the later one. If so, there can be no reason for supposing that any of the towns upon the mainland were free from tribute.

The expressions of Thucydides (i. 18, 89, 95, &c.), which Mr. Grote quotes, concerning the Hellespontine and Ionian Greeks who had "revolted from Persia," and been "liberated from the king," must be understood, I think, of the cities on the European side of the Hellespont, and of the islands, Proconnesus, Cyzicus, Lesbos, Chios, Samos, &c.

It seems to me probable that the practical exemption from tribute of the Greek cities on the mainland commenced in B.C. 449, and was an express provision of the treaty of Cyprus. It was the equivalent which the Greeks received for agreeing to leave the Persians in undisputed possession of Cyprus and Egypt. Herodotus had perhaps at this time completed the first draught of his History. The facts were therefore, at the time of his writing, as he stated them. Afterwards at Thurii he neglected to alter the passage, which is not surprising, for he seems to have done little more than make additions to his History in his later years.

[3] Supra, iii. 90. What necessitated the new rating and measurement was the alteration of territory which had taken place in consequence of the revolt. Miletus we know had been punished for its share in the outbreak by the loss of a tract of mountain land which was given to the Carians of Pedasus (supra, ch. 20); and probably the remainder of the guilty cities had been treated in the same way. On the other hand, cities which abstained, as Ephesus (supra, ch. 16, note), may have received an increase of territory.

Such were the peaceful dealings of the Persians with the Ionians.

43. The next spring Darius superseded all the other generals, and sent down Mardonius, the son of Gobryas,[4] to the coast, and with him a vast body of men, some fit for sea, others for land service. Mardonius was a youth at this time, and had only lately married Artazôstra, the king's daughter.[5] When Mardonius, accompanied by this numerous host, reached Cilicia, he took ship and proceeded along shore with his fleet, while the land army marched under other leaders towards the Hellespont. In the course of his voyage along the coast of Asia he came to Ionia; and here I have a marvel to relate which will greatly surprise those Greeks who cannot believe that Otanes advised the seven conspirators to make Persia a commonwealth.[6] Mardonius put down all the despots throughout Ionia, and in lieu of them established democracies. Having so done, he hastened to the Hellespont, and when a vast multitude of ships had been brought together, and likewise a powerful land force, he conveyed his troops across the strait by means of his vessels, and proceeded through Europe against Eretria and Athens.[7]

44. At least those towns served as a pretext for the expedition, the real purpose of which was to subjugate as great a number as possible of the Grecian cities; and this became plain when the Thasians,[8] who did not even lift a hand in their defence, were reduced by the sea force, while the land army added the Macedonians to the former slaves of the king. All the tribes on the hither side of Macedonia had been reduced previously.[9] From Thasos the fleet stood across to the mainland, and sailed along shore to Acanthus,[1] whence an attempt was made to double

---

[4] This is another instance of the alternation of names among the Persians. (Compare iii. 160, &c.) Gobryas was the son of a Mardonius (Beh. Ins. col. iv. par. 18.)

[5] On marriages of this kind, see above v. 116, note [9], and compare vol. ii. p. 462, note [6].

[6] It would seem that the tale related by Herodotus in Book iii. (chs. 80-83), had appeared incredible to the Greeks themselves. Herodotus undoubtedly believed it to be true; but the story does not really derive any support from the policy here pursued by Mardonius. That policy was decidedly wise. The Persians had learnt, by dint of experience, that they lost more, through unpopularity, by upholding the tyrants, than they gained by the convenience of having the government of the Greek states assimilated to their own. To allow Greeks, in order to conciliate them, democratic institutions, was a very different thing from contemplating the adoption of such institutions among themselves.

[7] The aggressors in the late war (supra, v. 99).

[8] Thasos had hitherto escaped subjection. Megabazus, who carried his arms even farther west, seems to have had no fleet at his disposal. Otanes, who reduced Lemnos and Imbrus (supra, v. 26, 27.), did not venture so far as Thasos. [9] Supra, v. 18.

[1] Acanthus lay on the eastern side of the peninsula of Athos, as is plain both

Mount Athos. But here a violent north wind sprang up, against which nothing could contend, and handled a large number of the ships with much rudeness, shattering them and driving them aground upon Athos. 'Tis said the number of the ships destroyed was little short of three hundred; and the men who perished were more than twenty thousand.[2] For the sea about Athos abounds in monsters beyond all others; and so a portion were seized and devoured by those animals,[3] while others were dashed violently against the rocks; some, who did not know how to swim, were engulfed; and some died of the cold.

45. While thus it fared with the fleet, on land Mardonius and his army were attacked in their camp during the night by the Brygi,[4] a tribe of Thracians; and here vast numbers of the Persians were slain, and even Mardonius himself received a wound. The Brygi, nevertheless, did not succeed in maintaining their own freedom: for Mardonius would not leave the country till he had subdued them and made them subjects of Persia. Still, though he brought them under the yoke, the blow which his land force had received at their hands, and the great damage done to his fleet off Athos, induced him to set out upon his retreat; and so this armament, having failed disgracefully, returned to Asia.

46. The year after these events, Darius received information from certain neighbours of the Thasians that those islanders were making preparations for revolt; he therefore sent a herald, and

bade them dismantle their walls, and bring all their ships to Abdêra. The Thasians, at the time when Histiæus the Milesian made his attack upon them, had resolved that, as their income was very great, they would apply their wealth to building ships of war, and surrounding their city with another and a stronger wall. Their revenue was derived partly from their possessions upon the mainland, partly from the mines which they owned. They were masters of the gold-mines at Scapté-Hylé, the yearly produce of which amounted in all to eighty talents. Their mines in Thasos yielded less, but still were so far prolific that, besides being entirely free from land-tax, they had a surplus income, derived from the two sources of their territory on the main and their mines, in common years of two hundred, and in the best years of three hundred talents.

47. I myself have seen the mines in question: by far the most curious of them are those which the Phœnicians discovered at the time when they went with Thasus and colonised the island, which afterwards took its name from him. These Phœnician workings are in Thasos itself, between Cœnyra and a place called Ænyra, over against Samothrace: a huge mountain has been turned upside down in the search for ores. Such then was the source of their wealth. On this occasion no sooner did the Great King issue his commands than straightway the Thasians dismantled their wall, and took their whole fleet to Abdêra.

---

⁵ Megabazus had subdued the entire coast (supra, v. 10, ad fin.), and Abdêra had probably been occupied by a Persian garrison, like Eion and Doriscus (infra, vii. 106, 107). On its site, vide infra, vii. 109.

⁶ Supra, ch. 28.

⁷ The Thasians possessed a number of places on the coast opposite their island, as is plain from Thucydides (i. 100). One of these was Datum (Eustath. ad Dionys. Perieg. 517; Zenob. Prov. Gr. Cent. iii. 71), a place which combined so many advantages that it passed into a proverb for an abundance of good things (Zenob. l. s. c. Harpocration in voc.; Strab. vii. p. 331; see also infra, ix. 75, note). It possessed gold-mines, and was also a place of great fertility.

⁸ Scapté-Hylé is said by Stephen (ad voc.) to have been a town upon the Thracian coast, opposite Thasos. It was probably near Datum, to which its gold-mines seem sometimes to be ascribed.

The wife of Thucydides was, we are told, a native of this place, and the owner of some of its mines. Marcellin. Vit. Thucyd. p. ix.; and hither Thucydides himself retired when exiled from Athens, and wrote his history (ibid. p. x.; Plutarch, de Exil. ii. p. 605, C.). The name is sometimes written Σκαπτησύλη (Steph. Theophr.), and in Latin Sceptesula (Lucret.).

⁹ Thasos is said to have been called Chryse by the early Greeks, on account of its gold-mines (Arrian, Fr. 67; Eustath. ad Dionys. Perieg. 528).

¹ Supra, ii. 44. Compare Apollod. III. l. 1, § 7, 8. Thucydides makes Thasos a colony of the Parians (iv. 104).

² Bochart Geograph. Sac. 1. ii. p. 393, derives the word Thasos from the Syriac tas, "an amulet."

³ That is, on the south-east side of the island. Cœnyra still remains in the modern Keves. The site of Ænyra cannot be fixed.

48. After this Darius resolved to prove the Greeks, and try the bent of their minds, whether they were inclined to resist him in arms or prepared to make their submission. He therefore sent out heralds in divers directions round about Greece, with orders to demand everywhere earth and water for the king. At the same time he sent other heralds to the various seaport towns which paid him tribute, and required them to provide a number of ships of war and horse-transports.

49. These towns accordingly began their preparations; and the heralds who had been sent into Greece obtained what the king had bid them ask from a large number of the states upon the mainland, and likewise from all the islanders whom they visited.[ ] Among these last were included the Eginetans, who, equally with the rest, consented to give earth and water to the Persian king. When the Athenians heard what the Eginetans had done, believing that it was from enmity to themselves that they had given consent, and that the Eginetans intended to join the Persian in his attack upon Athens, they straightway took the matter in hand. In good truth it greatly rejoiced them to have so fair a pretext; and accordingly they sent frequent embassies to Sparta,[ ] and made it a charge against the Eginetans that their conduct in this matter proved them to be traitors to Greece.

50. Hereupon Cleomenes, the son of Anaxandridas, who was then king of the Spartans, went in person to Egina, intending to seize those whose guilt was the greatest. As soon however as he tried to arrest them, a number of the Eginetans made resistance, a certain Crius, son of Polycritus, being the foremost in violence. This person told him "he should not carry off a single Eginetan without it costing him dear—the Athenians had bribed him to make this attack, for which he had no warrant from his own government—otherwise *both* the kings would have come together to make the seizure." This he said in consequence of instructions which he had received from Demaratus.[ ] Hereupon Cleomenes,

---

[ ] Euboea is probably to be excepted from the list, and also Naxos, which it was intended to punish (infra, ch. 96). The rest of the Cyclades, without doubt, made their submission.

[ ] Mr. Grote has some excellent observations on the great importance of this appeal (Hist. of Greece, vol. iv. pp. 427-430). It raised Sparta to the general protectorate of Greece. Hitherto she had been a leading power, fre-

quently called in to aid the weaker against the stronger, but with no definite hegemony, excepting over the states of the Peloponnese (supra, v. 91). Now she was acknowledged to have a paramount authority over the whole of Greece, as the proper guardian of the Grecian liberties. It gave additional weight to the appeal that it was made by Athens, the second city of Greece.

[ ] This was the second time that Dema-

finding that he must quit Egina, asked Crius his name; and when Crius told him, "Get thy horns tipped with brass with all speed, O Crius!"[1] he said, "for thou wilt have to struggle with a great danger."

51. Meanwhile Demaratus, son of Ariston, was bringing charges against Cleomenes at Sparta. He too, like Cleomenes, was king of the Spartans, but he belonged to the lower house—not indeed that his house was of any lower origin than the other, for both houses are of one blood—but the house of Eurysthenes is the more honoured of the two, inasmuch as it is the elder branch.

52. The Lacedæmonians declare, contradicting therein all the poets,[2] that it was king Aristodemus himself, son of Aristomachus, grandson of Cleodæus, and great-grandson of Hyllus, who conducted them to the land which they now possess, and not the sons of Aristodemus. The wife of Aristodemus, whose name (they say) was Argeia, and who was daughter of Autesion,[3] son of Tisamenus, grandson of Thersander, and great-grandson of Polynices, within a little while after their coming into the country, gave birth to twins. Aristodemus just lived to see his children, but died soon afterwards of a disease. The Lacedæmonians of that day determined, according to custom, to take for their king the elder of the two children; but they were so alike, and so exactly of one size, that they could not possibly tell which of the two to choose: so when they found themselves unable to make a choice, or haply even earlier, they went to the mother and asked her to tell them which was the elder, whereupon she declared that "she herself did not know the children apart;" although in good truth

---

ratus had thwarted Cleomenes (vide supra, v. 75). The kings of the younger house had an inferior position; and their jealousy of the elder house found a natural vent in such petty annoyances as those which are recorded of Demaratus.

[1] Cleomenes puns upon the name Crius, which signifies "a ram" in Greek. Cicero indulges in *facetiæ* of the same kind with respect to Verres, *verres* being Latin for "a boar pig." (Cf. Cic. in Verr. Act. II. ii. 78, iv. 25 and 43. "Aistant in labores Herculis non minus hunc Immanissimum Verrem, quam illum aprum Erymanthinum referri oportere.")

[2] These poets are not those of the Epic cycle, which concluded with the adventures of Telegonus, the son of Ulysses, but either "those who carried on the mythological fables genealogically, as Cinæthon and Asius," or else "the historical poets, such as Eumelus the Corinthian" (Müller's Dorians, vol. I. p. 58, E. T.). Their views were adopted by the mythological prose-writers, as, for instance, Apollodorus (II. viii. 2, § 8) and Pausanias (III. i. 5), who both declare the death of Aristodemus to have taken place before the invasion of the Peloponnese. Herodotus follows the local Spartan tradition, as he himself states, which was that Aristodemus actually reigned at Sparta. Of this tradition we find another trace in Xenophon (Ages. viii. 7), the friend of Agesilaus, and so long a refugee in Laconia.

[3] Sister therefore, according to the myth, of Theras, the coloniser of Thera (supra, iv. 147).

she knew them very well, and only feigned ignorance in order that, if it were possible, both of them might be made kings of Sparta. The Lacedæmonians were now in a great strait; so they sent to Delphi and inquired of the oracle how they should deal with the matter. The Pythoness made answer, "Let both be taken to be kings; but let the elder have the greater honour." So the Lacedæmonians were in as great a strait as before, and could not conceive how they were to discover which was the first-born, till at length a certain Messenian, by name Panites, suggested to them to watch and see which of the two the mother washed and fed first; if they found she always gave one the preference, that fact would tell them all they wanted to know; if, on the contrary, she herself varied, and sometimes took the one first, sometimes the other, it would be plain that she knew as little as they; in which case they must try some other plan. The Lacedæmonians did according to the advice of the Messenian, and, without letting her know why, kept a watch upon the mother; by which means they discovered that, whenever she either washed or fed her children, she always gave the same child the preference. So they took the boy whom the mother honoured the most, and regarding him as the first-born, brought him up in the palace; and the name which they gave to the elder boy was Eurysthenes, while his brother they called Procles. When the brothers grew up, there was always, so long as they lived, enmity between them; and the houses sprung from their loins have continued the feud to this day.[1]

53. Thus much is related by the Lacedæmonians, but not by any of the other Greeks; in what follows I give the tradition of the Greeks generally. The kings of the Dorians (they say)— counting up to Perseus, son of Danaë,[2] and so omitting the god—

are rightly given in the common Greek lists, and rightly considered to have been Greeks themselves; for even at this early time they ranked among that people.³ I say "up to Perseus," and not further, because Perseus has no mortal father by whose name he is called,⁴ as Hercules has in Amphitryon; whereby it appears that I have reason on my side, and am right in saying, "up to Perseus." If we follow the line of Danaë, daughter of Acrisius, and trace her progenitors, we shall find that the chiefs of the Dorians are really genuine Egyptians.⁵ In the genealogies here given I have followed the common Greek accounts.

54. According to the Persian story, Perseus was an Assyrian who became a Greek;⁶ his ancestors, therefore, according to them, were not Greeks. They do not admit that the forefathers of

---

³ This cannot be held to be strictly true, since the name *Hellen* first entered the Peloponnese with the Dorians. If, however, we understand only that the earlier Peloponnesian princes were of no foreign race, but of one closely akin to the Hellenes, the statement may be accepted.

⁴ That is to say, he is uniformly declared to be the son of Jupiter.

⁵ Supra, ii. 91. Herodotus believes in the tale which brings Danaüs from Egypt.

(Many writers besides him ascribe the colonisation of parts of Greece to the uncolonising Egyptians. Danaüs led a colony from Egypt (Diod. i. 2); and not only was Danaüs said to have fled from Egypt to Argos, but Pausanias thinks the Nauplians a colony from that country in old times. (Bk. iv.) Diodorus and others say colonies went from Egypt to Athens, led by Cecrops from Saïs. Cadmus (the personification of the East) generally reported to have gone from Phœnicia to Bœotia (Her. v. 57), is said by Eusebius to have migrated from Egyptian Thebes with Phœnix, and to have founded Athens and Bœotian Thebes; and both he and Cecrops have the merit of leading a colony of Saïtes to Athens. (Schol. on Lycoph. Diod. i. 28.) Triptolemus again gave laws to Athens (Porph. de Abstin. iv.; Diod. i. 18, 29); and Erechtheus was also said to be an Egyptian. (Diod. i. 29.) But without giving full credit to these and similar statements, it is possible that some settlers, probably refugees, occasionally went from Egypt to Greece, and that, as Herodotus positively asserts,

a great number of barbarous people became united with them (Bk. i. c. 58); though no particular portion of the Greek race can be said to be of Egyptian, or any other foreign origin, subsequently to the great immigrations from Asia.—G. W.]

⁶ It has not been commonly seen that this is an entirely distinct story from that related below (vii. 150.—that Perseus, son of Danaë, had a son Perses, the progenitor of the Achæmenian kings —which latter the Greeks generally adopted (Plat. Alcib. I. p. 120. E.; Xen. Cyrop. I. ii. 1; Apollod. II. iv. 5, § 1). This tale denies any birth connexion between Perseus and the Greeks, bringing him originally from the East (strangely enough from Assyria), and making him settle in Greece and become naturalised.

Both stories seem to me pure inventions, based merely upon the similarity of name which the Persians found to exist between their own national appellation and a Greek mythological personage. They were willing to take advantage of this circumstance to encourage the belief in an early connexion between themselves and the Greeks; and they did not much care in what way the connexion was made out.

It is of course possible that the Greek hero Perseus may have come down to them from those primitive times when the Arian race had not yet split into sections, and thus the similarity of name may not be accidental. It may even indicate a real connexion of race, but not one of which either of the two tales is a proper exponent.

Acrisius were in any way related to Perseus, but say they were Egyptians, as the Greeks likewise testify.

55. Enough however of this subject. How it came to pass that Egyptians obtained the kingdoms of the Dorians,[1] and what they did to raise themselves to such a position, these are questions concerning which, as they have been treated by others,[2] I shall say nothing. I proceed to speak of points on which no other writer has touched.

56. The prerogatives which the Spartans have allowed their kings are the following. In the first place, two priesthoods, those (namely) of Lacedaemonian and of Celestial Jupiter;[3] also the right of making war on what country soever they please,[4] without hindrance from any of the other Spartans, under pain of outlawry; on service the privilege of marching first in the advance and last in the retreat, and of having a hundred[5] picked men for their body-guard while with the army; likewise the liberty of sacrificing as many cattle in their expeditions as it seems them good, and the right of having the skins and the chines of the slaughtered animals for their own use.

57. Such are their privileges in war; in peace their rights are as follows. When a citizen makes a public sacrifice the kings

---

[1] That is to say, the kingdoms of the Peloponnesus, afterwards conquered by the Dorians.

[2] It is uncertain to what class of writers Herodotus here alludes. He may intend the poets of the Epic cycle, with whom the adventures of Danaüs and his daughters were a recognised subject. (A poem, Ασωίς, is quoted by Clemens Alex. Strom. iv. p. 618, and referred to by Harpocration, ad voc. αὐτόχθων.) It is more probable, however, that he speaks of prose-writers, such as Acusilaüs, Hecataeus, and Hippys of Rhegium. The "genealogies" of the two former, and the Argolica of the latter author, might treat of the matters in question. Colonel Mure suggests that the reference is to the "Spartan magistrates" of Charon (Lit. of Greece, vol. iv. p. 306); but it is very unlikely that he went further back than the Dorian conquest.

[3] These are probably Achaean rather than Dorian priesthoods, and may have belonged to the Heracleid kings before their expulsion. The worship of Apollo especially characterised the Dorian tribes, that of Jupiter and Juno the Achaean (see Müller's Dorians, i. pp. 409-411, E. T.). Zeus Lacedaemon and Zeus Uranius would be respectively Jupiter the lord of the Lacedaemonian territory, and Jupiter the supreme god, or king of heaven. The necessary union of the priestly with the kingly office was an idea almost universal in early times (Müller, ii. pp. 101-104).

[4] Not the right of declaring war, which rested with the assembly, and might, we know, be exercised against the will of the king Thucyd. i. 87.), but the right of determining the general course and character of each campaign (ib. viii. 5).

[5] This is perhaps an error. The number of the knights who formed the king's body-guard is always elsewhere declared to be 300 (infra, vii. 205, viii. 124; Thucyd. v. 72; Xen. de Rep. Lac. iv. 3); and this number accords better with the other numerical divisions at Sparta, as, for instance, the three tribes, the thirty Obes, the thirty senators, &c. Possibly, however, the knights of the Hyllean tribe, who would be 100, were attached in a special way to the persons of the kings, and accompanied them as a body-guard on all expeditions, whereas the whole 300 may not have gone out unless upon special occasions.

are given the first seats at the banquet; they are served before any of the other guests, and have a double portion of everything; they take the lead in the libations; and the hides of the sacrificed beasts belong to them. Every month, on the first day, and again on the seventh of the first decade,[3] each king receives a beast without blemish at the public cost, which he offers up to Apollo;[4] likewise a medimnus of meal,[5] and of wine a Laconian quart. In the contests of the games they have always the seat of honour; they appoint the citizens who have to entertain foreigners';[6] they also nominate, each of them, two of the Pythians,[7] officers whose business it is to consult the oracle at Delphi, who eat with the kings, and, like them, live at the public charge. If the kings do not come to the public supper, each of them must have two chœnixes of meal and a cotyle of wine[8] sent home to him at his house; if they come, they are given a double quantity of each, and the same when any private man invites them to his table. They have the custody of all the oracles which are pronounced; but the Pythians must likewise have knowledge of them. They have the whole decision of certain causes, which are these, and them only:—When a maiden is left the heiress of her father's estate, and has not been betrothed by him to any one, they decide who is to marry her;[9] in all matters concerning the public highways

---

[3] On the division of the Greek month into decades, μὴν ἱστάμενος, μὴν μεσῶν, and μὴν φθίνων, see Smith's Dict. of Antiq. ad voc. CALENDARIUM, and comp. Hesiod, Op. et Dies, 788, &c. The seventh day of each month was sacred to Apollo, who was believed to have been born on the seventh of Thargelion (May). See Diog. Laert. iii. § 2, and comp. Hes. Op. et D. 771.

[4] The kings were at the head of the whole national religion, the Dorian Apollo-worship, as well as the Achæan cultus of Jupiter.

[5] On the size of the medimnus, and also of the chœnix, see vol. i. p. 264, note [6].

[6] The Proxeni, whose special duty was to receive and entertain ambassadors from foreign states. The chief states of Greece had generally a Proxenus at all the more important towns, who undertook this duty. He was always a native of the place, and, except at Sparta, was nominated to his office by the state whose proxenus he was. At Sparta, in consequence of the greater jealousy of foreigners, the state insisted on itself appointing the proxeni; and as the department of foreign affairs belonged, in an especial way, to the kings, committed to them the selection of fit persons.

[7] The Pythians at Sparta correspond to the ἐξηγηταὶ Πυθόχρηστοι at Athens, and to the permanent θεωροί of other states (Müller's Dorians, ii. p. 15, E. T.). They are mentioned as messmates of the kings by Xenophon (Rep. Lac. xv. § 4) and Suidas (ad voc. Πυθίοι). Many inscriptions place their names immediately after those of the kings (Mémoires de l'Académie des Inscriptions et Belles Lettres, tom. xv, p. 395). Müller thinks (l. s. c.) that they had seats in the senate.

[8] The cotyle is one of the Attic liquid measures: it contained about half a pint. Two cotyles made one ξέστης or pint. The Attic quart (τέταρτον) was the fourth part of a χοεύς—consequently only a quarter of a pint; but it may be suspected that the "Laconian quart" was a quarter ἀμφορεύς, or above two gallons.

[9] So at Athens the Archon Eponymus, who especially represented the ancient office of the king, had the guardianship of all orphans and heiresses

they judge; and if a person wants to adopt a child, he must do it before the kings. They likewise have the right of sitting in council with the eight-and-twenty senators; and if they are not present, then the senators nearest of kin to them have their privileges, and give two votes as the royal proxies, besides a third vote, which is their own.[1]

58. Such are the honours which the Spartan people have allowed their kings during their lifetime; after they are dead other honours await them. Horsemen carry the news of their death through all Laconia, while in the city the women go hither and thither drumming upon a kettle. At this signal, in every house two free persons, a man and a woman, must put on mourning,[2] or else be subject to a heavy fine. The Lacedaemonians have likewise a custom at the demise of their kings which is common to them with the barbarians of Asia—indeed with the greater number of the barbarians everywhere—namely, that when one of their kings dies, not only the Spartans, but a certain number of the country people from every part of Laconia are forced, whether they will or no, to attend the funeral. So these persons and the Helots, and likewise the Spartans themselves,[3] flock together to the number of several thousands, men and women intermingled; and all of them smite their foreheads

---

(Pollux, viii. 89). The disposal of heiresses and adoption of children were of more than common importance at Sparta, since the state looked with disfavour upon an undue accumulation of property.

[1] The meaning of this passage is very obscure. Müller (ii. p. 106, note 7, E. T.) thinks that Herodotus shared in the opinion which Thucydides says (i. 20) was current through Greece, and supposed each king to have the right of giving two votes. He would therefore consider Herodotus to mean that in the absence of the kings, the two senators nearest of kin to the two monarchs respectively, gave each a double vote for the monarch whose kinsman he was, after which he gave a third vote for himself. Schweighæuser regards Herodotus as speaking only of one senator, and using the plural *distributively*, meaning that the senators who were on each occasion most nearly related to the royal house, gave the royal votes (one for each king; and then gave their own. Whatever Herodotus means, there is little doubt that such was the actual practice (cf. Thucyd. l. s. c.; Plat. Leg. iii. 692, A.).

[2] That is to say, "wear squalid unwashed garments, or even cover themselves with mud and dirt;" for the Greeks, when they mourned at all, mourned in the Oriental fashion (see Hom. Il. xxiv. 164, 165). It is uncertain whether this mourning at the death of the Spartan kings was confined to the Perioeci, or whether it included the Spartans, who were forbidden by the laws of Lycurgus to mourn at the death of their own relatives (Plutarch, Inst. Lac. p. 238, D.).

[3] The three classes of which the Lacedaemonian population consisted are here very clearly distinguished from one another:— 1. The Perioeci, or free inhabitants of the country districts, the descendants in the main of the submitted Achæans; 2. The Helots, or serfs who tilled the soil upon the estates of their Dorian lords, descended in part from Achæans taken with arms in their hands, but chiefly from the conquered Messenians; and 3. The Spartans, or Dorian conquerors, who were the only citizens, and who lived almost exclusively in the capital.

violently, and weep and wail without stint, saying always that their last king was the best. If a king dies in battle, then they make a statue of him, and placing it upon a couch richly bravely decked, so carry it to the grave. After the burial, by the space of ten days there is no assembly, nor do they elect magistrates,[4] but continue mourning the whole time.

59. They hold with the Persians also in another custom. When a king dies, and another comes to the throne, the newly-made monarch forgives all the Spartans the debts which they owe either to the king or to the public treasury. And in like manner among the Persians each king when he begins to reign remits the tribute due from the provinces.[5]

60. In one respect the Lacedæmonians resemble the Egyptians.[6] Their heralds and flute-players, and likewise their cooks, take their trades by succession from their fathers. A flute-player must be the son of a flute-player, a cook of a cook, a herald of a herald; and other people cannot take advantage of the loudness of their voice to come into the profession and shut out the heralds' sons; but each follows his father's business.[7] Such are the customs of the Lacedæmonians.

61. At the time of which we are speaking, while Cleomenes in Egina was labouring for the general good of Greece, Demaratus at Sparta continued to bring charges against him, moved not so much by love of the Eginetans as by jealousy and hatred of his colleague. Cleomenes therefore was no sooner returned from Egina than he considered with himself how he might deprive

---

[4] Compare the Roman *justitium* usual at the death of an emperor or other great personage (Tacit. Ann. i. 16, ii. 82; Suet. Calig. 24; Lucan. Phars. ii. 16, &c.).

[5] The Pseudo-Smerdis, therefore, in remitting the tribute for three years, merely extended a species of largess, to which the subjects of Persia were already accustomed in some degree (supra, iii. 67).

[6] On the classes of the Egyptians see note on Book ii. ch. 164.

[7] The bearing of this passage upon the question of the existence of *caste* in Greece has been already noticed (supra, v. 66, note [1]). Priesthoods were hereditary in a large number of the Grecian states. Herodotus himself mentions the Iamids and Telliads of Elis (ix. 33, 34), the Talthybiads of Lacedæmon (vii. 134), and the Telliads of Gela in Sicily (vii. 153). Other writers furnish a very much larger catalogue of priestly families (cf. Histoire de l'Académie des Inscriptions, tom. xxiii. p. 51, et seq.). Nor are the indications of caste confined to the priesthood. Arts and sciences, too, often descended from father to son. Hence we hear of the family of the Asclepiads (physicians) in Cos and Cnidus ' Theopomp. Fr. 111), and of the Homerids in Chios (Hellan. Fr. 55) Acusil. Fr. 31); while ἱερῶν ναῶες, (κηρύκων παῖδες, and the like, are common periphrases for ἱερεῖς, (κηρύκες, &c. Thus the facts which are here mentioned with respect to Sparta have parallels in a number of other similar facts in various parts of Greece, all tending to establish the early prevalence of caste, of which the four Ionic tribes are the most marked and decisive indication.

Demaratus of his kingly office; and here the following circumstance furnished a ground for him to proceed upon. Ariston, king of Sparta, had been married to two wives, but neither of them had borne him any children; as however he still thought it was possible he might have offspring, he resolved to wed a third; and this was how the wedding was brought about. He had a certain friend, a Spartan, with whom he was more intimate than with any other citizen. This friend was married to a wife whose beauty far surpassed that of all the other women in Sparta; and what was still more strange, she had once been as ugly as she now was beautiful. For her nurse, seeing how ill-favoured she was, and how sadly her parents, who were wealthy people, took her bad looks to heart, bethought herself of a plan, which was to carry the child every day to the temple of Helen at Therapna,[1] which stands above the Phœbeum,[2] and there to place her before the image, and beseech the goddess to take away the child's ugliness. One day, as she left the temple, a woman appeared to her, and begged to know what it was she held in her arms. The nurse told her it was a child, on which she asked to see it; but the nurse refused; the parents, she said, had forbidden her to show the child to any one. However the woman would not take a denial; and the nurse, seeing how highly she prized a look, at last let her see the child. Then the woman gently stroked its head, and said, "One day this child shall be the fairest dame in Sparta." And her looks began to change from that very day. When she was of marriageable age, Agetus, son of Alcides, the same whom I have mentioned above as the friend of Ariston, made her his wife.

62. Now it chanced that Ariston fell in love with this person;

---

[1] Therapna was a place of some importance on the left bank of the Eurotas, nearly opposite Sparta, from which it was distant probably about two miles. It was strongly situated on the flat top of a high hill, and its towers made it a conspicuous object (Pind. Isth. i. 31, ὑψίπεδον Θεράπνας ἕδος; Alcman. Fr. i, εὔπυργοι Θεράπνα). Some think that it was the ancient metropolis of the Achæans, before Sparta became a great city (Bähr ad loc.; Müller's Dorians, I. p. 105, E. T.); but the claims of Amyclæ to this position are superior. (See the Essays appended to Book v. Essay i. p. 274.) There was a local tradition that Helen had been buried at Therapna (Pausan. III. xix. § 9); and both Helen and Menelaus were certainly worshipped there down to the time of Isocrates (Encom. Hel. xxvii. p. 231; compare Athenag. Leg. pro Christ. xii. p. 50). It is not clear whether the temple of Helen was distinct from that of the Dioscuri, which undoubtedly stood in the sacred enclosure called the Phœbeum (Pausan. III. xx. § 1). Therapna was regarded as their burial-place also (Pind. Nem. x. 55).

[2] A precinct sacred to Apollo, at a little distance from the town itself (Pausan. l. s. c. Θεράπνης δὲ οὐ πόῤῥω Φοιβαῖον καλούμενόν ἐστιν), but scarcely so far as Kiepert places it (Atlas von Hellas, Map xix. Plan of Sparta). Hence the Θεραπναῖαι Ἄιδι ὑπὲρ ὁδοῦ of Apollonius (Argon. II. 162).

and his love so preyed upon his mind that at last he devised as follows. He went to his friend, the lady's husband, and proposed to him that they should exchange gifts, each taking that which pleased him best out of all the possessions of the other. His friend, who felt no alarm about his wife, since Ariston was also married, consented readily; and so the matter was confirmed between them by an oath. Then Ariston gave Agêtus the present, whatever it was, of which he had made choice, and when it came to his turn to name the present which he was to receive in exchange, required to be allowed to carry home with him Agêtus's wife. But the other demurred, and said, "except his wife, he might have anything else:" however, as he could not resist the oath which he had sworn, or the trickery which had been practised on him, at last he suffered Ariston to carry her away to his house.

63. Ariston hereupon put away his second wife and took for his third this woman; and she, in less than the due time—when she had not yet reached her full term of ten months,[1]—gave birth to a child, the Demaratus of whom we have spoken. Then one of his servants came and told him the news, as he sat in council with the Ephors;[2] whereat, remembering when it was that the woman became his wife, he counted the months upon his fingers, and having so done, cried out with an oath, "The boy cannot be mine." This was said in the hearing of the Ephors; but they made no account of it at the time. The boy grew up; and Ariston repented of what he had said; for he became altogether convinced that Demaratus was truly his son. The reason why he named him Demaratus was the following. Some time before these events the whole Spartan people, looking upon Ariston as a man of mark beyond all the kings that had reigned at Sparta before him, had offered up a prayer that he might have a son. On this account, therefore, the name Demaratus[3] was given.

---

[1] Vide infra, ch. 69, note 4. The birth ordinarily takes place in the tenth lunar month. We are told below (ch. 69) that the wife of Ariston gave birth to Demaratus at the close of the seventh month.

[2] So Pausanias (l. s. c.), even more plainly, since he uses the expression ἐν βουλῇ καθημένῳ for the more ambiguous ἐν θώκῳ καθημένῳ of our author. The "council" intended would seem to be the Ephors' office (ἀρχεῖον, or simply ἀρχεῖον, Pausan. III. xi. § 8; Xen. Ages. I. § 36), where they held their daily meetings, which were attended occasionally by the kings themselves. (Cf. Xen. l. s. c., who says of Agesilaus, that when he was recalled from Asia to Lacedaemon, he "obeyed as readily as if he had been standing without retinue in the Ephors' office before the Five"—οὐδὲν διαφερόντως ἢ εἰ ἐν τῷ Ἐφορείῳ ἔτυχεν ἱστηκὼς μόνος παρὰ τοὺς πέντε.)

[3] Dem-aratus (ὁ τῷ δήμῳ ἀρατός) is the "People-prayed-for" king. Compare the Louis le Désiré of French history.

64. In course of time Ariston died; and Demaratus received the kingdom: but it was fated, as it seems, that these words, when bruited abroad, should strip him of his sovereignty. This was brought about by means of Cleomenes, whom he had twice sorely vexed, once when he led the army home from Eleusis,[4] and a second time when Cleomenes was gone across to Egina against such as had espoused the side of the Medes.[5]

65. Cleomenes now, being resolved to have his revenge upon Demaratus, went to Leotychides, the son of Menares, and grandson of Agis,[6] who was of the same family as Demaratus, and made agreement with him to this tenor following. Cleomenes was to lend his aid to make Leotychides king in the room of Demaratus; and then Leotychides was to take part with Cleomenes against the Eginetans. Now Leotychides hated Demaratus chiefly on account of Percalus, the daughter of Chilon, son of Demarmenus: this lady had been betrothed to Leotychides; but Demaratus laid a plot, and robbed him of his bride, forestalling him in carrying her off,[7] and marrying her. Such was the origin of the enmity. At the time of which we speak, Leotychides was prevailed upon by the earnest desire of Cleomenes to come forward against Demaratus and make oath "that Demaratus was not rightful king of Sparta, since he was not the true son of Ariston." After he had thus sworn, Leotychides sued Demaratus, and brought up against him the phrase which Ariston had let drop when, on the coming of his servant to announce to him the birth of his son, he counted the months, and cried out with an oath that the child was not his. It was on this speech of Ariston's that Leotychides relied to prove that Demaratus was not his son, and therefore not rightful king of Sparta; and he produced as witnesses the Ephors who were sitting with Ariston at the time and heard what he said.

66. At last, as there came to be much strife concerning this

---

[4] Supra, v. 75.
[5] Supra, chs. 50 and 51.
[6] The entire genealogy is given below (viii. 131), but with the difference that the grandfather of Leotychides is called Agesilaus instead of Agis. It is impossible to say which of the two is the right name. Bähr (ad loc.) prefers Agesilaus, and thereupon asserts that Demaratus and Leotychides were first cousins, since Agesilaus was, he says, the grandfather of Demaratus also; but the grandfather of Demaratus was Agasicles (supra, l. 65). The two lines of descent really parted at Theopompus, the eighth progenitor of Leotychides, and the seventh of Demaratus. (See Clinton's Table, F. H. vol. i. p. 255.)

[7] The seizure of the bride was a necessary part of a Spartan marriage. The young woman could not properly, it was thought, surrender her freedom and virgin purity unless compelled by the violence of the stronger sex. 'Cf. Plutarch, Lycurg. c. 15; Lac. Apophth. ii. p. 228, A.; and see Müller's Dorians, ii. p. 299, E. T.)

matter, the Spartans made a decree that the Delphic oracle should be asked to say whether Demaratus were Ariston's son or no. Cleomenes set them upon this plan; and no sooner was the decree passed than he made a friend of Cobon, the son of Aristophantus, a man of the greatest weight among the Delphians; and this Cobon prevailed upon Perialla, the prophetess, to give the answer which Cleomenes wished.[4] Accordingly, when the sacred messengers came and put their question, the Pythoness returned for answer, "that Demaratus was not Ariston's son." Some time afterwards all this became known; and Cobon was forced to fly from Delphi; while Perialla the prophetess was deprived of her office.

67. Such were the means whereby the deposition of Demaratus was brought about; but his flying from Sparta to the Medes was by reason of an affront which was put upon him. On losing his kingdom he had been made a magistrate; and in that office soon afterwards, when the feast of the Gymnopædia[2] came round, he took his station among the lookers-on; whereupon Leotychides, who was now king in his room, sent a servant to him and asked him, by way of insult and mockery, "how it felt to be a magistrate after one had been a king?"[10] Demaratus, who was hurt at the question, made answer—"Tell him I have tried them both, but he has not. Howbeit this speech will be the cause to Sparta of infinite blessings or else of infinite woes." Having thus spoken he wrapped his head in his robe, and, leaving the theatre,[1] went home to his own house, where he prepared an ox for sacrifice, and offered it to Jupiter,[2] after which he called for his mother.

68. When she appeared, he took off the entrails, and placing them in her hand, besought her in these words following:—

"Dear mother, I beseech you, by all the gods, and chiefly by our own hearth-god³ Jupiter, tell me the very truth, who was really my father. For Leotychides, in the suit which we had together, declared, that when thou becamest Ariston's wife thou didst already bear in thy womb a child by thy former husband; and others repeat a yet more disgraceful tale, that our groom⁴ found favour in thine eyes, and that I am his son. I entreat thee therefore by the gods to tell me the truth. For if thou hast gone astray, thou hast done no more than many a woman; and the Spartans remark it as strange, if I am Ariston's son, that he had no children by his other wives."

69. Thus spake Demaratus; and his mother replied as follows: "Dear son, since thou entreatest so earnestly for the truth, it shall indeed be fully told to thee. When Ariston brought me to his house, on the third night after my coming, there appeared to me one like to Ariston, who, after staying with me a while, rose, and taking the garlands from his own brows placed them upon my head, and so went away. Presently after Ariston entered, and when he saw the garlands which I still wore, asked me who gave them to me. I said, 'twas he; but this he stoutly denied; whereupon I solemnly swore that it was none other, and told him he did not do well to dissemble when he had so lately risen from my side and left the garlands with me. Then Ariston, when he heard my oath, understood that there was something beyond nature in what had taken place. And indeed it appeared that the garlands had come from the hero-temple which stands by our court gates—the temple of him they call Astrabacus⁵—and the soothsayers, moreover, declared that the apparition was that very person. And now, my son, I have told thee all thou wouldest fain know. Either thou art the son of that hero—either thou mayest call Astrabacus sire; or else Ariston was thy father. As

---

³ The Spartan king has an altar to Jupiter, whereon he sacrifices, within the walls of his own house. Hence Jupiter is his "hearth-god." (Cf. Servius ad Virg. Æn. II. 506; and Festus de Verb. Sign. viii. p. 174.)

⁴ Literally "ass-keeper," or "donkey-man." The name Astrabacus (see the next chapter) is connected with ἀστράβη, "a mule or ass" (according to some), and with ἀστραβηλάτης, "a muleteer." The scandal of the court gossips suggested that the pretended stable-god was in reality such a person.

⁵ The hero-temple (ἡρῷον) of Astrabacus is mentioned by Pausanias in his description of Sparta (III. xvi. § 5). An obscure tradition attaches to him. Astrabacus, we are told, and Alopecus his brother, sons of Irbus, grandsons of Amphisthenes, great-grandsons of Amphicles, and great-great-grandsons of Agis, found the wooden image of Diana Orthia, which Orestes and Iphigenia had conveyed secretly from Tauris to Lacedæmon, and on discovering it were stricken with madness (ib. § 6). The worship of Astrabacus at Sparta is mentioned by Clemens (Cohort. ad Gentes, p. 35). It is conjectured from his name, that he was "the protecting genius of the stable." See the foregoing note.

for that matter which they who hate thee urge the most, the words of Ariston, who, when the messenger told him of thy birth, declared before many witnesses that 'thou wert not his son, forasmuch as the ten months were not fully out,' it was a random speech, uttered from mere ignorance. The truth is, children are born not only at ten months, but at nine, and even at seven.[6] Thou wert thyself, my son, a seven months' child. Ariston acknowledged, no long time afterwards, that his speech sprang from thoughtlessness. Hearken not then to other tales concerning thy birth, my son: for be assured thou hast the whole truth. As for grooms, pray Heaven Leotychides and all who speak as he does may suffer wrong from them!" Such was the mother's answer.

70. Demaratus, having learnt all that he wished to know, took with him provision for the journey, and went into Elis, pretending that he purposed to proceed to Delphi, and there consult the oracle. The Lacedaemonians, however, suspecting that he meant to fly his country, sent men in pursuit of him; but Demaratus hastened, and leaving Elis before they arrived, sailed across to Zacynthus.[7] The Lacedaemonians followed, and sought to lay hands upon him, and to separate him from his retinue; but the Zacynthians would not give him up to them: so he escaping, made his way afterwards by sea to Asia,[8] and presented himself before King Darius, who received him generously, and gave him both lands and cities.[9] Such was the chance which drove Demaratus to Asia, a man distinguished among the Lacedaemonians for many noble deeds and wise counsels, and who alone of all the Spartan kings[1] brought honour to his country by winning at Olympia the prize in the four-horse chariot-race.

[6] Supra, ch. 63. Hippocrates gives it as the general opinion of his time, that children are born at seven, eight, nine, ten, and eleven months (τίκτειν καὶ ἐντάμηνα, καὶ ὀκτάμηνα, καὶ ἐννεάμηνα, καὶ δεκάμηνα, καὶ ἑνδεκάμηνα), but that the child born at eight months was sure to die (καὶ τοῦτον τὰ ὀκτάμηνα οὐ περιγίνεσθαι. De Septimestr. i. p. 447, ed. Kühn.). This is perhaps the reason why no mention is made here of an eight-months' child.

[7] Zacynthus is the modern Zante. It lay opposite Elis, at the distance of thirteen or fourteen miles. The enterprise of the Zacynthians is marked by their colonies in Crete (supra, lii. 59) and in Spain. Saguntum is said to have derived both its name and origin from Zacynthus (Liv. xxi. 7).

[8] In B.C. 486 (infra, vii. 3). Ctesias (Persic. Exc. § 23) made Demaratus first join the Persians at the Hellespont (B.C. 480), on occasion of its passage by Xerxes; but no weight attaches to this statement, which clearly contradicts Herodotus (cf. infra, vii. 3, and 239).

[9] Compare the treatment of Themistocles (Thucyd. I. 138), who received from Artaxerxes the revenues of three cities, Magnesia, Myus, and Lampsacus. The places given to Demaratus seem to have been Pergamus, Teuthrania, and Halisarna, which were in the possession of Eurysthenes and Procles, his descendants in B.C. 399. (See Xen. Hell. iii. l. § 6.)

[1] Wealth was the chief requisite for success in this contest (Schol. ad

ACCESSION OF LEOTYCHIDES.

71. After Demaratus was deposed, Leotychides, the son of Menares, received the kingdom. He had a son, Zeuxidamus, called Cyniscus² by many of the Spartans. This Zeuxidamus did not reign at Sparta, but died³ before his father, leaving a son, Archidamus. Leotychides, when Zeuxidamus was taken from him, married a second wife, named Eurydamé, the sister of Menius and daughter of Diactorides. By her he had no male offspring, but only a daughter called Lampito,⁴ whom he gave in marriage to Archidamus, Zeuxidamus' son.

72. Even Leotychides, however, did not spend his old age in Sparta, but suffered a punishment whereby Demaratus was fully avenged. He commanded the Lacedæmonians when they made war against Thessaly,⁵ and might have conquered the whole of it, but was bribed by a large sum of money.⁵ It chanced that he was caught in the fact, being found sitting in his tent on a gauntlet, quite full of silver. Upon this he was brought to trial and banished from Sparta; his house was razed to the ground;

and he himself fled to Tegea,¹ where he ended his days. But these events took place long afterwards.

73. At the time of which we are speaking, Cleomenes, having carried his proceedings in the matter of Demaratus to a prosperous issue, forthwith took Leotychides with him, and crossed over to attack the Eginetans; for his anger was hot against them on account of the affront which they had formerly put upon him. Hereupon the Eginetans, seeing that both the kings were come against them, thought it best to make no further resistance. So the two kings picked out from all Egina the ten men who for wealth and birth stood the highest, among whom were Crius,² son of Polycritus, and Casambus, son of Aristocrates, who wielded the chief power; and these men they carried with them to Attica, and there deposited them in the hands of the Athenians, the great enemies of the Eginetans.

74. Afterwards, when it came to be known what evil arts had been used against Demaratus, Cleomenes was seized with fear of his own countrymen, and fled into Thessaly. From thence he passed into Arcadia, where he began to stir up troubles, and endeavoured to unite the Arcadians against Sparta. He bound them by various oaths to follow him whithersoever he should lead, and was even desirous of taking their chief leaders with him to the city of Nonacris,³ that he might swear them to his cause by the waters of the Styx. For the waters of Styx, as the Arcadians say, are in that city; and this is the appearance they present: you see a little water, dripping from a rock into a basin, which is fenced round by a low wall.⁴ Nonacris,

---

¹ According to Pausanias (III. v. § 6) he took sanctuary in the temple of Minerva Alea, as did Pausanias the younger and Chryris the Argive priestess. The peculiar sanctity of this asylum protected him.

² Supra, ch. 50. Crius is suspected to have been the Eginetan wrestler in whose honour Simonides composed a triumphal ode (Aristoph. Nub. 1301, ed. Both, et Schol. ad loc.). The honour in which wrestlers were held is evident from the story of Democedes (supra, iii. 137).

³ Nonacris was not far from Pheneus (see the end of the chapter, and compare Pausan. viii. xvii. § 18), an Arcadian city anciently of some note, but which had disappeared in the time of Strabo (Strab. viii. p. 363). Nonacris itself was in ruins when Pausanias wrote. Colonel Leake (Travels in the Morea, vol. iii. p. 169) places its site at Mesorughi, near Solos, about ten miles from Fonia (Phenous).

⁴ This description of the Styx differs greatly from that of most other writers, yet it has the appearance of being derived from personal observation. Pausanias (l. s. c.) describes the terrible water as "a stream falling from a precipice, the highest that he had ever beheld, and dashing itself upon a lofty rock, through which it passed, and then fell into the Crathis" (viii. xviii. § 2). Homer and Hesiod give similar descriptions 'κατειβόμενον Στυγὸς ὕδωρ —Il. xv. 37. Στυγὸς ὕδατος αἰπὰ ῥέεθρα —Ib. viii. 369. ὕδωρ δ᾽ ἐκ πέτρης κατα-λείβεται ἠλιβάτοιο—Hes. Theog.

where this fountain is to be seen,² is a city of Arcadia near Pheneus.

75. When the Lacedæmonians heard how Cleomenes was engaged, they were afraid, and agreed with him that he should come back to Sparta and be king as before. So Cleomenes came back; but had no sooner returned than he, who had never been altogether of sound mind,³ was smitten with downright madness. This he showed by striking every Spartan he met upon the face with his sceptre. On his behaving thus, and showing that he was gone quite out of his mind, his kindred imprisoned him, and even put his feet in the stocks. While so bound, finding himself left alone with a single keeper, he asked the man for a knife. The keeper at first refused, whereupon Cleomenes began to threaten him, until at last he was afraid, being only a helot, and gave him what he required. Cleomenes had no sooner got the steel than, beginning at his legs, he horribly disfigured himself, cutting gashes in his flesh, along his legs, thighs, hips, and loins, until at last he reached his belly, which he likewise began to gash, whereupon in a little time he died. The Greeks generally think that this fate came upon him because he induced the Pythoness to pronounce against Demaratus; the Athenians differ from all others in saying that it was because he cut down the sacred grove of the goddesses⁴ when

---

⁷⁸⁵). Colonel Leake (Morea, iii. p. 160) seems to have discovered the waterfall intended, near *Solos*, where "two slender cascades of water fall perpendicularly over an immense precipice, and, after winding for a time among a labyrinth of rocks, unite to form the torrent, which, after passing the Klukines, joins the river *Akrata*" (Crathis). Superstitious feelings of dread still attach to the water, which is considered to be of a peculiarly noxious character (cf. Pausan. l. s. c.; Plin. H. N. II. ciii. c. 111; Ælian, H. A. x. 4*), &c.). The following description of the Styx, from the pen of Mr. Clark (Peloponnesus, p. 302), is striking:—"In half an hour more we came in sight of the head of the glen—a grand specimen of mountain scenery. Mount Khelmos here breaks away in a vast wall of precipitous rock many hundred feet high, but choked with a heap of *débris* reaching half-way up, and sprinkled here and there with mesgre pines. Over the jagged line which marks the top of the precipice we see the higher slopes covered with snow, and from a notch in the mountain side a thin stream of water falls down the cliff on the rugged heap below. Every now and then the stream is lifted by wind and scattered over the face of the cliff, elsewhere grey with lichens and weatherstains, is, where thus washed, of a deep red tint. This thread of water is one of the sources of the full clear stream which flows through the glen, and joins the Crathis below Solos. The stream and the waterfall are both called Mavro-Nero, or Black-water, and are, beyond question, the same stream and waterfall which, in Pausanias's time, had the name of Styx."—A sketch is given in Wordsworth's Pictorial Greece, p. 388.

² It is quite conceivable that the Nonacrians may have conducted a rill of water from the main stream of the Styx into their own city, where oaths could be more conveniently taken than among the precipices of the *Mavro-Nero*.

³ Supra, v. 42.

⁴ The great goddesses, Ceres and Proserpine (vide supra, v. 82, note ⁴).

he made his invasion by Eleusis; while the Argives ascribe it to his having taken from their refuge and cut to pieces certain Argives who had fled from battle into a precinct sacred to Argus,[5] where Cleomenes slew them, burning likewise at the same time, through irreverence, the grove itself.

76. For once, when Cleomenes had sent to Delphi to consult the oracle, it was prophesied to him that he should take Argos; upon which he went out at the head of the Spartans, and led them to the river Erasinus.[6] This stream is reported to flow from the Stymphalian[7] lake, the waters of which empty themselves into a pitch-dark chasm, and then (as they say) reappear in Argos, where the Argives call them the Erasinus. Cleomenes, having arrived upon the banks of this river, proceeded to offer sacrifice to it, but, in spite of all that he could do, the victims were not favourable to his crossing. So he said that he admired the god for refusing to betray his countrymen, but still the Argives should not escape him for all that. He then withdrew his troops, and led them down to Thyrea,[8] where he sacrificed a

bull to the sea, and conveyed his men on shipboard[9] to Nauplia[10] in the Tirynthian territory.[1]

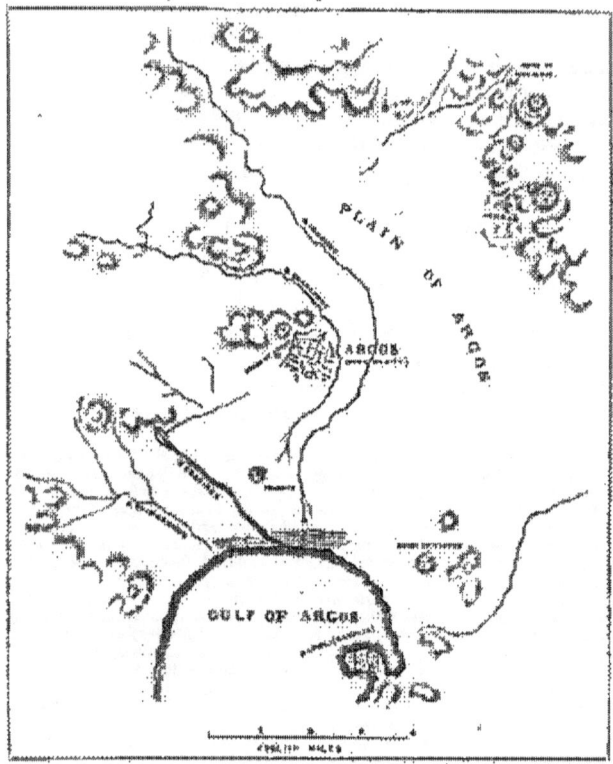

[9] See below, ch. 92, note [4].

[10] Nauplia, which is called in our maps by its Turkish name *Anapli*, is still known by its ancient appellation among the Greeks (Gell's Itin. p. 181). It stands at the extremity of the peninsula which forms the south-eastern angle of the bay of Argos. There are still at Nauplia some traces of Cyclopian walls, of a masonry very like those of Tiryns (Leake's Morea, ii. p. 357). Nauplia was the principal sea-port town of Argolis in the time of Scylax (Peripl. p. 43), but had fallen into ruins when Pausanias wrote (II. xxxviii. § 2).

[1] Tiryns was situated at a short distance from Argos, on the road which led from that city to Epidauria (Pausan. II. xxv. § 6, 7). It was removed a little from the sea (Scylax, Peripl. p. 43), being not quite a mile and a half from Nauplia (Strab. viii. p. 541). The Argives transferred the inhabitants to Argos, and let the city fall into ruins, soon after the close of the Persian war (Pausan. v. xxiii. § 3; II. xxv. § 7). Still, remains of the walls, which were Cyclopian, had been seen by Pausanias (l. proximè cit., and compare Strab. viii. 540).

There is no difficulty in fixing the site of Tiryns. The ruins at *Palæo-Anapli* correspond in all respects to the notices of Tiryns in ancient authors,

77. The Argives, when they heard of this, marched down to the sea, to defend their country; and arriving in the neighbourhood of Tiryns, at the place which bears the name of Sepeia,[2] they pitched their camp opposite to the Lacedæmonians, leaving no great space between the hosts. And now their fear was not so much lest they should be worsted in open fight as lest some trick should be practised on them; for such was the danger which the oracle given to them in common with the Milesians[3] seemed to intimate. The oracle ran as follows:—

"Time shall be when the female shall conquer the male, and shall chase him
Far away,—gaining so great praise and honour in Argos;
Then full many an Argive woman her cheeks shall mangle;—
Hence, in the times to come 'twill be said by the men who are unborn,
'Tamed by the spear expired the coiled terrible serpent.'"[4]

At the coincidence of all these things[5] the Argives were greatly cast down; and so they resolved that they would follow the signals of the enemy's herald. Having made this resolve, they proceeded to act as follows: whenever the herald of the Lacedæmonians gave any order to the soldiers of his own army, the Argives did the like on their side.

78. Now when Cleomenes heard that the Argives were acting thus, he commanded his troops that, so soon as the herald gave the word for the soldiers to go to dinner, they should instantly seize their arms and charge the host of the enemy. Which the Lacedæmonians did accordingly, and fell upon the Argives just as, following the signal, they had begun their repast; whereby

---

They occupy the summit of an isolated hill which rises out of the Argive plain to a height varying between 20 and 50 feet. This was plainly the acropolis, the Lycimna of Strabo (viii. p. 541). Some of the Cyclopian masonry still exists. It seems to have given Tiryns, at a very early time, its epithet of τειχιόεσσα (Hom. Il. ii. 559. Compare Gell, p. 182; Leake's Morea, ii. p. 350; Clark's Peloponnesus, pp. 86, 87).

[2] This place is mentioned by no other writer. It must have lain between Argos and Tiryns.

[3] Vide supra, ch. 19.

[4] It is hopeless to attempt a rational explanation of this oracle, the obscurity of which gives it a special claim to be regarded as a genuine Pythian response. Pausanias applies it to a repulse which Cleomenes and his army received, on attacking Argos after the victory, at the hands of Telesilla the poetess and the Argive women (ii. xx. § 7, 8; compare Plutarch, de Virt. Mul. ii. p. 245, D. E.; and Polyæn. viii. 33). But this story is incompatible with the statements of Herodotus; and, as Mr. Grote observes (Hist. of Greece, vol. iv. pp. 432, 433), probably grew up out of the oracle itself.

The conjecture that the female is Hérē, the protectress of Argos, and the male Sparta (Müller, Dorians, i. p. 197, E. T.; Grote, l. s. c. note [1]; Buhr. not ad loc.), may be received as probable.

[5] The favourable prophecy to Cleomenes (supra, ch. 76, ad init.), the warning to themselves, the invasion in an unexpected quarter, and perhaps some notion of connecting Sepeia, where they were stationed, with the "coiled terrible serpent" of the oracle. There was a serpent called commonly σηψ δίψ (Nicand. Th. 320), and σηψ ίς seems to have been used in the same sense in some parts of the Peloponnesos (Pausan. viii. xvi. § 2.)

it came to pass that vast numbers of the Argives were slain, while the rest, who were more than they which died in the fight, were driven to take refuge in the grove of Argus hard by, where they were surrounded, and watch kept upon them.

79. When things were at this pass Cleomenes acted as follows: Having learnt the names of the Argives who were shut up in the sacred precinct from certain deserters who had come over to him, he sent a herald to summon them one by one, on pretence of having received their ransoms. Now the ransom of prisoners among the Peloponnesians is fixed at two minae the man.⁶ So Cleomenes had these persons called forth severally, to the number of fifty, or thereabouts, and massacred them. All this while they who remained in the enclosure knew nothing of what was happening; for the grove was so thick that the people inside were unable to see what was taking place without. But at last one of their number climbed up into a tree and spied the treachery; after which none of those who were summoned would go forth.

80. Then Cleomenes ordered all the helots to bring brushwood, and heap it around the grove; which was done accordingly; and Cleomenes set the grove on fire. As the flames spread he asked a deserter "Who was the god of the grove?" whereto the other made answer, "Argus." So he, when he heard that, uttered a loud groan, and said—

"Greatly hast thou deceived me, Apollo, god of prophecy, in saying that I should take Argos. I fear me thy oracle has now got its accomplishment."

81. Cleomenes now sent home the greater part of his army, while with a thousand of his best troops he proceeded to the temple of Juno,⁷ to offer sacrifice. When however he would have slain the victim on the altar himself, the priest forbade him, as it was not lawful (he said) for a foreigner to sacrifice in that temple. At this Cleomenes ordered his helots to drag the priest

---

⁶ Vide supra, v. 77, note ³.

⁷ This temple of Juno, one of the most famous in antiquity, was situated between Mycenae and Argos, at the distance of less than two miles from the former place (Pausan. II. xvii.; Strab. viii. p. 535). It was burnt down in the ninth year of the Peloponnesian war, through the carelessness of Chrysis the priestess (Thucyd. iv. 133), but rebuilt shortly after, on a somewhat lower site, by Eupolemus, a native architect (Pausan. l. s. c.). The position is marked in the chart, supra, p. 378.

Col. Leake in 1806 failed to discover any traces of the Heraeum (Morea, ii. pp. 387-393). Its ruins, however, have since his time been identified, and have been visited by many travellers. A good plan and description will be found in the "Peloponnesus" of Professor Curtius (vol. ii. pp. 397-400, and Plate xvi.). Compare Mr. Clark's account (Peloponnesus, pp. 81-86).

from the altar and scourge him, while he performed the sacrifice himself, after which he went back to Sparta.

82. Thereupon his enemies brought him up before the Ephors, and made it a charge against him that he had allowed himself to be bribed, and on that account had not taken Argos when he might have captured it easily. To this he answered—whether truly or falsely I cannot say with certainty—but at any rate his answer to the charge was, that "so soon as he discovered the sacred precinct which he had taken to belong to Argus, he directly imagined that the oracle had received its accomplishment; he therefore thought it not good to attempt the town, at the least until he had inquired by sacrifice, and ascertained if the god meant to grant him the place, or was determined to oppose his taking it. So he offered in the temple of Juno, and when the omens were propitious, immediately there flashed forth a flame of fire from the breast of the image; whereby he knew of a surety that he was not to take Argos. For if the flash had come from the head, he would have gained the town, citadel and all;[1] but as it shone from the breast, he had done as much as the god intended." And his words seemed to the Spartans so true and reasonable, that he came clear off from his adversaries.

83. Argos however was left so bare of men,[2] that the slaves[1] managed the state, filled the offices, and administered everything until the sons of those who were slain by Cleomenes grew up. Then these latter cast out the slaves, and got the city back under their own rule; while the slaves who had been driven out fought a battle and won Tiryns. After this for a time there was peace between the two; but a certain man, a soothsayer, named Cleander, who was by race a Phigaleon[3]

from Arcadia,[2] joined himself to the slaves, and stirred them up to make a fresh attack upon their lords. Then were they at war with one another by the space of many years; but at length the Argives with much trouble gained the upper hand.

84. The Argives say that Cleomenes lost his senses, and died so miserably, on account of these doings. But his own countrymen declare that his madness proceeded not from any supernatural cause whatever, but only from the habit of drinking wine unmixed with water, which he learnt of the Scyths. These nomads, from the time that Darius made his inroad into their country, had always had a wish for revenge. They therefore sent ambassadors to Sparta to conclude a league, proposing to endeavour themselves to enter Media by the Phasis,[4] while the Spartans should march inland from Ephesus, and then the two armies should join together in one. When the Scyths came to Sparta on this errand Cleomenes was with them continually; and growing somewhat too familiar, learnt of them to drink his wine without water,[5] a practice which is thought by the Spartans to have caused his madness. From this distance of time the Spartans, according to their own account, have been accustomed, when they want to drink purer wine than common, to give the order to fill "Scythian fashion." The Spartans then speak thus concerning Cleomenes; but for my own part I think his death was a judgment on him for wronging Demaratus.

85. No sooner did the news of Cleomenes' death reach Egina than straightway the Eginetans sent ambassadors to Sparta to complain of the conduct of Leotychides in respect of their hostages, who were still kept at Athens. So they of Lacedæmon assembled a court of justice[6] and gave sentence upon Leo-

tychides, that whereas he had grossly affronted the people of Egina, he should be given up to the ambassadors, to be led away in place of the men whom the Athenians had in their keeping. Then the ambassadors were about to lead him away; but Theasides, the son of Leoprepes, who was a man greatly esteemed in Sparta, interfered, and said to them—

"What are ye minded to do, ye men of Egina? To lead away captive the king of the Spartans, whom his countrymen have given into your hands? Though now in their anger they have passed this sentence, yet belike the time will come when they will punish you, if you act thus, by bringing utter destruction upon your country."

The Eginetans, when they heard this, changed their plan, and, instead of leading Leotychides away captive, agreed with him that he should come with them to Athens, and give them back their men.

86. When however he reached that city, and demanded the restoration of his pledge, the Athenians, being unwilling to comply, proceeded to make excuses, saying, "that two kings had come and left the men with them, and they did not think it right to give them back to the one without the other." So when the Athenians refused plainly to restore the men, Leotychides said to them—

"Men of Athens, act which way you choose—give me up the hostages, and be righteous, or keep them, and be the contrary. I wish, however, to tell you what happened once in Sparta about a pledge. The story goes among us that three generations back there lived in Lacedæmon one Glaucus, the son of Epicydes, a man who in every other respect was on a par with the first in the kingdom, and whose character for justice was such as to place him above all the other Spartans. Now to this man at the appointed season the following events happened. A certain Milesian came to Sparta and having desired to speak with him, said,—'I am of Miletus, and I have come hither, Glaucus, in the hope of profiting by thy honesty. For when I heard much talk thereof in Ionia and through all the rest of Greece, and when I observed that whereas Ionia is always insecure, the Peloponnese stands firm and unshaken, and noted likewise how wealth is continually changing hands in our country,' I took counsel with my-

---

αὐτοῖς καὶ ἡ τῶν εἰκὰς Βασιλέως τῆς τρίβας). The ephors were at once accusers and judges in it.

² Connect this insecurity of property with the Lydian and Persian conquests, which were in the third generation from Leotychides.

self and resolved to turn one-half of my substance into money, and place it in thy hands, since I am well assured that it will be safe in thy keeping. Here then is the silver—take it—and take likewise these tallies, and be careful of them; remember thou art to give back the money to the person who shall bring you their fellows.' Such were the words of the Milesian stranger; and Glaucus took the deposit on the terms expressed to him. Many years had gone by when the sons of the man by whom the money was left came to Sparta, and had an interview with Glaucus, whereat they produced the tallies, and asked to have the money returned to them. But Glaucus sought to refuse, and answered them : 'I have no recollection of the matter; nor can I bring to mind any of those particulars whereof ye speak. When I remember, I will certainly do what is just. If I had the money, you have a right to receive it back; but if it was never given to me, I shall put the Greek law in force against you. For the present I give you no answer; but four months hence I will settle the business.' So the Milesians went away sorrowful, considering that their money was utterly lost to them. As for Glaucus, he made a journey to Delphi, and there consulted the oracle. To his question if he should swear,* and so make prize of the money, the Pythoness returned for answer these lines following:—

'Best for the present it were, O Glaucus, to do as thou wishest,
Swearing an oath to prevail, and so to make prize of the money.
Swear then—death is the lot e'en of those who never swear falsely.
Yet hath the Oath-God a son who is nameless, footless, and handless;
Mighty in strength he approaches to vengeance, and whelms in destruction
All who belong to the race, or the house of the man who is perjured.
But oath-keeping men leave behind them a flourishing offspring.'*

Glaucus when he heard these words earnestly besought the god to pardon his question; but the Pythoness replied that it was as bad to have tempted the god as it would have been to have done the deed. Glaucus, however, sent for the Milesian strangers, and gave them back their money. And now I will tell you, Athenians, what my purpose has been in recounting to you this history. Glaucus at the present time has not a single descendant; nor is there any family known as his—root and branch has he

---

* The Greek law allowed an accused person, with the consent of the accuser, to clear himself of a crime imputed to him, by taking an oath that the charge was false. (See Arist. Rhet. l. 15, p. 66, ed. Taucha.)

* The oracle, in this last line, quoted Hesiod (Op. et Dies, 285), or, rather, concluded with a well-known Greek proverb, older, perhaps, than Hesiod himself. The story of Glaucus is alluded to by Plutarch (ii. p. 556, D.), Pausanias (ii. xviii. § 2), Juvenal (xiii. 199-208), Clemens (Strom. vi. p. 749), Dio Chrysostom (Or. lxiv. p. 640), and others.

been removed from Sparta. It is a good thing, therefore, when a pledge has been left with one, not even in thought to doubt about restoring it."

Thus spake Leotychides; but, as he found that the Athenians would not hearken to him, he left them and went his way.

87. The Eginetans had never been punished for the wrongs which, to pleasure the Thebans, they had committed upon Athens.[1] Now, however, conceiving that they were themselves wronged, and had a fair ground of complaint against the Athenians, they instantly prepared to revenge themselves. As it chanced that the Athenian Theôris,[2] which was a vessel of five banks of oars,[3] lay at Sunium,[4] the Eginetans contrived an ambush, and made themselves masters of the holy vessel, on board of which were a number of Athenians of the highest rank, whom they took and threw into prison.

88. At this outrage the Athenians no longer delayed, but set to work to scheme their worst against the Eginetans; and, as there was in Egina at that time a man of mark, Nicodromus by name, the son of Cnoethus, who was on ill terms with his countrymen because on a former occasion they had driven him into banishment, they listened to overtures from this man, who had heard how determined they were to do the Eginetans a mischief, and

---

[1] Vide supra, v. 81, 89.

[2] The Athenian *theôris* was the ship which conveyed the sacred messengers (*theôroi*) to Delos and elsewhere (cf. Plut. Phæd. 58, B, C.). The *thalaminia* (Thucyd. iii. 33; vi. 53, 61) is said to have been specially set apart for this service (Suidas, sub voc. Ξαλαμινία ναῦς).

[3] If the reading πεντήρης (which is acquiesced in by Gaisford, Schweighaeuser, and Bähr) is allowed to be correct, we have here a proof that quinqueremes, or vessels of five banks of oars, were invented a century before the time usually assigned for them, which is the reign of the elder Dionysius (B.C. 400-368). See Diodor. Sic. xiv. 41, 42; Böckh's Urkunden über die Seewesen des Att. Staates, p. 76; Smith's Dict. of Antiq. p. 785. It is certainly remarkable, if quinqueremes were in use at Athens so early as B.C. 491, that no further mention of their employment by the Athenians occurs till the year B.C. 325. Perhaps the reading πεντηρικῆς, which is found in two MSS., should be adopted, which would give a very different sense. The passage, with this change, would have to be translated thus:—"It chanced that the Athenians were celebrating at Sunium a festival that recurred every fifth year: so the Eginetans, hearing it, set an ambush for them, and captured their holy vessel," &c. A πεντετηρίς would be a festival recurring at intervals of four years, like the Olympic and Pythian games. There is not, however (I believe), any other trace of this quadriennial festival at Sunium.

[4] The situation of Sunium, on the extreme southern promontory of Attica, has been already noted (supra, iv. 99, note [7]). Besides the remains of the Doric temple from which the cape derives its modern name of Cape Colonna, there are considerable traces of the ancient walls, the whole circuit of which may be distinctly made out (Leake's Demi of Attica, p. 63). The temple was sacred to Minerva Sunias (Pausan. i. i. § 1; Eurip. Cycl. 292). Sunium was a place of great importance in the time of the Peloponnesian war (Thucyd. viii. 4).

agreed with him that on a certain day he should be ready to betray the island into their hands, and they would come with a body of troops to his assistance. And Nicodromus, some time after, holding to the agreement, made himself master of what is called the old town.[6]

89. The Athenians, however, did not come to the day; for their own fleet was not of force sufficient to engage the Eginetans, and while they were begging the Corinthians to lend them some ships, the failure of the enterprise took place. In those days the Corinthians were on the best of terms with the Athenians;[6] and accordingly they now yielded to their request, and furnished them with twenty ships;[7] but, as their law did not allow the ships to be given for nothing, they sold them to the Athenians for five drachms a-piece.[8] As soon then as the Athenians had obtained this aid, and, by manning also their own ships, had equipped a fleet of seventy sail,[9] they crossed over to Egina, but arrived a day later than the time agreed upon.

90. Meanwhile Nicodromus, when he found the Athenians did not come to the time appointed, took ship and made his escape from the island. The Eginetans who accompanied him were settled by the Athenians at Sunium, whence they were wont to issue forth and plunder the Eginetans of the island. But this took place at a later date.

91. When the wealthier Eginetans had thus obtained the victory over the common people who had revolted with Nicodromus,[1] they laid hands on a certain number of them, and led them out to death. But here they were guilty of a sacrilege,

---

[6] Not (as Bähr says, not. ad. loc.) Œa, though that is very likely to have been the ancient capital, since all the early Greek capitals were built at some little distance from the shore (vide supra, v. 83); but rather a portion of the actual Egina, the part of the town which was the earliest settled and the most strongly fortified. Otherwise Nicodromus could scarcely have made his escape by sea (infra, ch. 90).

[6] Supra, v. 75; 92, 93. Perhaps Corinth was anxious to uphold Athens, as a counterpoise to Sparta. She may have feared Sparta becoming too powerful, and crushing the independence of her subject allies. Her own private wrongs induced her afterwards to abandon this policy (see note [6] on v. 93); but it was maintained even as late as B.C. 440 (Thucyd. L 41).

[7] This is confirmed by Thucydides (l. s. c.).

[8] In this way the letter of the law was satisfied, at an expense to the Athenians of 100 drachms (about 4l. of our money).

[9] Thus it appears that Athens at this time maintained a fleet of 50 ships. This number is supposed to be connected with that of the Naucraries, anciently 48, and increased to 50 by Clisthenes (supra, v. 71, note [8]).

[1] In Egina, as in most Dorian states, the constitution was oligarchical. The Athenians, it appears, took advantage of this circumstance, and sought to bring about a revolution, which would have thrown the island, practically, into their hands. This is the first instance of revolutionary war in which Athens is known to have engaged.

2 c 2

which, notwithstanding all their efforts, they were never able to atone, being driven from the island² before they had appeased the goddess whom they now provoked. Seven hundred of the common people had fallen alive into their hands; and they were all being led out to death, when one of them escaped from his chains, and flying to the gateway of the temple of Ceres the Lawgiver,³ laid hold of the door-handles, and clung to them. The others sought to drag him from his refuge; but, finding themselves unable to tear him away, they cut off his hands, and so took him, leaving the hands still tightly grasping the handles.

92. Such were the doings of the Eginetans among themselves. When the Athenians arrived, they went out to meet them with seventy ships;⁴ and a battle took place, wherein the Eginetans suffered a defeat. Hereupon they had recourse again to their old allies,⁵ the Argives; but these latter refused now to lend them any aid, being angry because some Eginetan ships, which Cleomenes had taken by force, accompanied him in his invasion of Argolis, and joined in the disembarkation.⁶ The same thing had happened at the same time with certain vessels of the Sicyonians; and the Argives had laid a fine of a thousand talents upon the misdoers, five hundred upon each: whereupon they of Sicyon acknowledged themselves to have sinned, and agreed with the Argives to pay them a hundred talents,⁷ and so be quit of the debt; but the Eginetans would make no acknowledgment at all, and showed themselves proud and stiff-necked. For this reason, when they now prayed the Argives for aid, the state refused to send them a single soldier. Notwithstanding, volunteers joined them from Argos to the number of a thousand, under a captain, Eurybates, a man skilled in the pentathlic contests.⁸ Of these

---

² Herodotus refers to the expulsion of the Eginetans by the Athenians in the first year of the Peloponnesian war, B.C. 431 (Thucyd. ii. 27).

³ Ceres Thesmophorus, in whose honour the feast of the Thesmophoria was celebrated in almost all parts of Greece (supra, ch. 16, note ⁷). Ceres was termed "the Lawgiver," because agriculture first forms men into communities, and so gives rise to laws. Hence Virgil calls this goddess *Legifera* (Æn. iv. 58. Compare Ovid, Met. v. 341; Calvus ad Serv. Æn. iv. 58; Claudian, de Rapt. Proserp. i. 30).

⁴ The collocation of the words seems to me to require this rendering, which is quite in accordance with probability,

though no translator, so far as I know, has adopted it. All suppose the 70 ships to be those of the Athenian assailants (supra, ch. 89, end).

⁵ Supra, v. 86.

⁶ Cleomenes, it appears, when he fell back upon Thyrea (supra, ch. 76), collected a fleet from the subject-allies of Sparta—among the rest from Egina and Sicyon—with which he made his descent upon Nauplia.

⁷ A sum exceeding 24,000*l*. of our money.

⁸ The πένταθλον, or contest of five games, consisted of the five sports of leaping, running, throwing the quoit or discus, hurling the spear, and wrestling. Hence the celebrated line, ascribed to

men the greater part never returned, but were slain by the Athenians in Egina. Eurybates, their captain, fought a number of single combats, and, after killing three men in this way, was himself slain by the fourth, who was a Decelean,[a] named Sophanes.[1]

93. Afterwards the Eginetans fell upon the Athenian fleet when it was in some disorder and beat it, capturing four ships with their crews.[2]

94. Thus did war rage between the Eginetans and Athenians. Meantime the Persian pursued his own design, from day to day exhorted by his servant to "remember the Athenians,"[3] and likewise urged continually by the Pisistratidæ, who were ever accusing their countrymen. Moreover it pleased him well to have a pretext for carrying war into Greece, that so he might reduce all those who had refused to give him earth and water. As for Mardonius, since his expedition had succeeded so ill, Darius took the command of the troops from him, and appointed other generals in his stead, who were to lead the host against Eretria and Athens; to wit, Datis, who was by descent a Mede,[a] and Artaphernes, the son of Artaphernes,[b] his own nephew. These men received orders to carry Athens and Eretria away captive, and to bring the prisoners into his presence.

Simonides, which enumerates as its elements—

ἄλμα, ποδωκείην, δίσκον, ἄκοντα, πάλην.

It was introduced into the Olympic games at the 18th Olympiad, B.C. 708 (Pausan. v. viii. § 3; Euseb. Chron. Can. t. xxiii. p. 144), and thence passed to the other Panhellenic festivals. Eurybates was a probable contest at the Nemean games (Pausan. t. xxix. § 4).

[2] Decelea was situated on the mountain-range north of Athens (Parnes), within sight of the city, from which it was distant 120 stades, or about 14 miles (Thucyd. vii. 19). The road from Athens to Oropus and Tanagra passed through it (infra, ix. 15). From these circumstances there can be little doubt that it was situated at or near the modern Tatoy. (See Leake's Demi of Attica, p. 18.)

[3] Sophanes, twenty-six years later (B.C. 465), was one of the leaders of the first expedition sent out by Athens to colonise Amphipolis (Thucyd. i. 100). He was slain at the battle of Drabescus (Pausan. i. xxix. § 4).

[2] The ἀδικτρόσιερια of the Eginetans was dated by some from this battle. Hence we read in Eusebius (Chron. Can. ii. p. 337)—"Decimo septimo loco maris imperium tenuerunt Æginetæ usque ad Xerxis transmissionem mais decem." (Compare Syncellus, p. 247, C.)

[3] Supra, v. 105.

[a] The occasional employment of Medes in situations of command has been already noticed (Appendix to Book iii. Essay iii., p. 470, note [b]). This is the most remarkable instance. Other instances are Mazares (i. 156), Harpagus (i. 162), Armamithres and Tithæus, sons of Datis (vii. 88), Tachamaspates (Beh. Inscrip. ii. xiv. 0), Intaphres (ib. iii. xiv. 3). No other conquered nation is considered worthy of such trust. The last two cases seem to have been unknown to Mr. Grote when he wrote, "We may remark that Datis is the first person of Median lineage who is mentioned as appointed to high command after the accession of Darius" (Hist. of Greece, iv. p. 412).

[b] Artaphernes the elder was a son of Hystaspes and half-brother of Darius (supra, v. 25). His son had probably

95. So the new commanders took their departure from the court and went down to Cilicia, to the Aleïan plain,¹ having with them a numerous and well-appointed land army. Encamping here, they were joined by the sea force which had been required of the several states, and at the same time by the horse-transports which Darius had, the year before, commanded his tributaries to make ready.² Aboard these the horses were embarked; and the troops were received by the ships of war; after which the whole fleet, amounting in all to six hundred triremes,⁴ made sail for Ionia. Thence, instead of proceeding with a straight course along the shore to the Hellespont and to Thrace,⁵ they loosed from Samos and voyaged across the Icarian sea⁶ through the midst of the islands; mainly, as I believe, because they feared the danger of doubling Mount Athos, where the year before they had suffered so grievously on their passage; but a constraining cause also was their former failure to take Naxos.⁷

96. When the Persians, therefore, approaching from the Icarian sea, cast anchor at Naxos, which, recollecting what there befell them formerly, they had determined to attack before any other state, the Naxians, instead of encountering them, took to flight, and hurried off to the hills.⁸ The Persians however succeeded

in laying hands on some, and them they carried away captive, while at the same time they burnt all the temples together with the town.⁴ This done, they left Naxos, and sailed away to the other islands.

97. While the Persians were thus employed, the Delians likewise quitted Delos, and took refuge in Tenos.⁵ And now the expedition drew near, when Datis sailed forward in advance of⁶ the other ships; commanding them, instead of anchoring at Delos, to rendezvous at Rhênea,⁶ over against Delos, while he himself proceeded to discover whither the Delians had fled; after which he sent a herald to them with this message:—

"Why are ye fled, O holy men? Why have ye judged me so harshly and so wrongfully? I have surely sense enough, even had not the king so ordered, to spare the country which gave birth to the two gods,⁷—to spare, I say, both the country and its inhabitants. Come back therefore to your dwellings; and once more inhabit your island."

Such was the message which Datis sent by his herald to the Delians. He likewise placed upon the altar three hundred talents' weight of frankincense, and offered it.

98. After this he sailed with his whole host against Eretria, taking with him both Ionians and Æolians. When he was departed, Delos (as the Delians told me) was shaken by an earthquake, the first and last shock that has been felt to this day.⁸

---

⁴ The Naxians pretended that they had repulsed Datis (Plut. de Malign. Herod. ii. p. 869). Naxos, the capital, was situated on the north-west coast of the island. Its site is occupied by the modern city of Axia.

⁵ Tenos (the modern Tino) was distant about 13 miles from Delos, in a direction almost due north. It lay in the direct line from Naxos to Eubœa, but the Delians might suppose that Datis would shape his course towards Attica by the islands of Paros, Siphnos, Seriphos, Cos, and Ceos.

⁶ The name of Delos (Dili) is now given to the island anciently called Rhênea, as well as to the rocky islet upon which the temple stood. Rhênea is styled "Great Delos" (Μεγάλη Δήλη), and Delos itself "Little Delos" (Μικρή Δήλη). The two islands are separated by a channel which in some places is not so much as half a mile wide. Considerable remains of the town and temple of Delos still exist (Tournefort, Lett. VII. pp. 240, 241; Ross's Inselreise, vol. i. p. 30, et seqq.). Opposite Delos, on the island of Rhênea, are the ruins of what seems to have been the acropolis of Delos (Strab. x. p. 709). Rhênea had been conquered by Polycrates, tyrant of Samos, and presented by him to the Delians (Thucyd. i. 13). It once possessed a capital city, whence ΡΗΝΙΑΝ and ΡΗΝΙΑΝ ΜΗΤΡΟΠΟΛΙΣ appear upon ancient coins; but by the time of Strabo it had ceased to be inhabited (l. s. c.), and has so remained probably ever since (Tournefort, p. 242; Ross, p. 36).

⁷ Apollo and Diana, whom the Persians may have thought it prudent to identify with the Sun and Moon, objects of reverence to themselves (supra, i. 131, and compare the Essays appended to Book i. Essay v. § 6). The mythological fable of their birth in Delos is found in Callimachus (Hymn. in Delum), Apollodorus (t. iv. § 1), and other writers.

⁸ It seems to me impossible that this can be the shock to which Thucydides alludes in the second book of his History (ch. 8). He would never have spoken of an event so recent (ὀλίγον πρὸ

And truly this was a prodigy whereby the god warned men of the evils that were coming upon them. For in the three following generations of Darius the son of Hystaspes, Xerxes the son of Darius, and Artaxerxes the son of Xerxes, more woes befell Greece than in the twenty generations preceding Darius;[1]—woes caused in part by the Persians, but in part arising from the contentions among their own chief men respecting the supreme power. Wherefore it is not surprising that Delos, though it had never before been shaken, should at that time have felt the shock of an earthquake. And indeed there was an oracle, which said of Delos—

"Delos' self will I shake, which never yet has been shaken."

Of the above names Darius may be rendered "Worker," Xerxes "Warrior," and Artaxerxes "Great Warrior." And so might we call these kings in our own language with propriety.[1]

(τούτων) which happened at a distance of sixty years. I should suppose that the Delians, whose holy island was believed to be specially exempt from earthquakes (Pind. Frag. p. 228 ed. Dissen), thought it to the credit of their god, that he should mark by such a prodigy the beginning of a great war. Accordingly, when Herodotus visited them, which must have been earlier than B.C. 443, they informed him that their island had experienced a shock a little previous to the battle of Marathon, but never either before or since. Twelve or thirteen years later, at the commencement of the Peloponnesian struggle, they again reported that a shock had been felt, and, forgetting what they had previously said, or trusting that others had forgot it, they, to make the prodigy seem greater, spoke of this earthquake as the first which had been felt in their island. Thucydides is unacquainted with the former, Herodotus with the latter story. (Cf. Müller's Dorians, i. p. 332, note[1], E. T.)

[2] This passage is thought to have been written after the death of Artaxerxes, which was in B.C. 425 (Thucyd. iv. 50). If so, it is perhaps the last addition to his History made by the author: at least there is no event known to be later than the decease of Artaxerxes, to which Herodotus can be shown to make any clear reference. Dahlmann (Life of Herod. pp. 31-33, E. T.) brings forward three such—the occupation of Decelea by Agis in B.C. 413, the revolt of the Medes from Darius Nothus in B.C. 408, and the death of Amyrtæus in the same year. With respect to the second of these, it has been shown (supra, i. 130, note[7]) that the revolt alluded to, is not that which took place in the reign of Darius Nothus, but the revolt from Darius the son of Hystaspes, in B.C. 518; with respect to the third, it has been remarked that Herodotus makes no mention of the death of Amyrtæus, but only alludes to his flight in B.C. 455 supra, iii. 15, note[9]. The passage which remains (ix. 73) is perverted from its plain meaning by Dahlmann. It alludes only to the sparing (actual or supposed) of Decelea from ravage during the earlier years of the Peloponnesian war (vide infra, note ad loc.).

While, however, I dissent from Dahlmann so far, I cannot assert positively with Mr. Grote (Hist. of Greece, iv. p. 306, note) that Herodotus alludes to no event in his history later than the second year of the Peloponnesian war. I think Herodotus does apparently "speak in this passage of the reign of Artaxerxes as past" (Dahlmann, p. 31, E. T.); I think, also, that several of the events to which he alludes, e.g. the flight of Zopyrus to Athens (iii. 160), and the cruel deed of Amestris in her old age (vii. 114), happened in all probability quite at the end of Artaxerxes' reign. And I should understand him to allude here in part to the calamities which befell Greece in the first seven or eight years of the Peloponnesian struggle, from B.C. 431 to B.C. 425 or 424. (See the Introductory Essay, vol. i. pp. 25-27.)

[1] On these and other Persian and Median names, see Appendix, Note A.

99. The Barbarians, after loosing from Delos, proceeded to touch at the other islands, and took troops from each,² and likewise carried off a number of the children as hostages. Going thus from one to another, they came at last to Carystus;³ but here the hostages were refused by the Carystians, who said they would neither give any, nor consent to bear arms against the cities of their neighbours, meaning Athens and Eretria. Hereupon the Persians laid siege to Carystus, and wasted the country round, until at length the inhabitants were brought over and agreed to do what was required of them.

100. Meanwhile the Eretrians, understanding that the Persian armament was coming against them, besought the Athenians for assistance. Nor did the Athenians refuse their aid, but assigned to them as auxiliaries the four thousand landholders to whom they had allotted the estates of the Chalcidean Hippobatæ.⁴ At Eretria, however, things were in no healthy state; for though they had called in the aid of the Athenians, yet they were not agreed among themselves how they should act; some of them were minded to leave the city and to take refuge in the heights of Eubœa,⁵ while others, who looked to receiving a reward from the Persians, were making ready to betray their country. So when these things came to the ears of Æschines, the son of Nothon, one of the first men in Eretria, he made known the whole state of affairs to the Athenians who were already arrived, and besought them to return home to their own land, and not perish with his countrymen. And the Athenians hearkened to his counsel, and, crossing over to Oröpus,⁶ in this way escaped the danger.

---

² Vide infra, ch. 133.
³ Carystus was one of the four principal cities of the ancient Eubœa ('the Egripo of our maps). These were Chalcis, Eretria, Carystus, and Histiæa (Scylax, Peripl. p. 50; cf. Strab. x. pp. 619-652). Carystus lay at the further end of a deep bay, with which the southern coast of the island is indented. It was celebrated for its marble quarries, and its temple of Apollo Marmoreus (Plin. H. N. iv. 12, p. 215; Strab. x. p. 630). The name *Κάρυστο* still attaches to the village which occupies its site (Leake's Northern Greece, vol. ii. p. 254).
⁴ Supra, v. 77.
⁵ A high mountain chain traverses Eubœa from its northern to its southern extremity, leaving in the whole island only three plains of any considerable extent. One of these is on the northern coast, near Histiæa and Artemisium; another opens out on the eastern near Port *Mandhúri*, the harbour of Cerinthus; while the third is that which has been already mentioned (supra, v. 77, note¹) between the cities of Chalcis and Eretria. The highest part of the mountain tract is near the centre of the island, between Chalcis and the nearest part of the opposite coast. The summits here attain an elevation of above 5000 feet.
⁶ There has been some doubt about the exact site of Oropus. Col. Leake was formerly inclined to place it at the modern *Orupó*, a small inland village situated on the right bank of the Asopus, at its issue from the rocky gorges of the hills which separate the plain of Oropus from that of Tanagra, where are

101. The Persian fleet now drew near and anchored at Tamynæ,[1] Chœreæ, and Ægilia,[2] three places in the territory of Eretria. Once masters of these posts, they proceeded forthwith to disembark their horses, and made ready to attack the enemy. But the Eretrians were not minded to sally forth and offer battle; their only care, after it had been resolved not to quit the city, was, if possible, to defend their walls. And now the fortress was assaulted in good earnest, and for six days there fell on both sides vast numbers, but on the seventh day Euphorbus, the son of Alcimachus, and Philagrus, the son of Cyneas, who were both citizens of good repute, betrayed the place to the Persians.[3] These were no sooner entered within the walls than they plundered and burnt all the temples that there were in the town, in revenge for the burning of their own temples at Sardis; moreover, they did according to the orders of Darius, and carried away captive all the inhabitants.[4]

---

the remains of a town of some considerable antiquity (Demi of Attica, 1st edition; Northern Greece, ii. p. 445). More recently, however (Demi of Attica, p. 116, 2nd edit.), he has admitted the weight of Mr. Finlay's arguments (Topography of Oropia, pp. 4-7) against this site. It seems certain that Oropus was anciently upon *the coast*. The present passage of Herodotus, several in Thucydides (iii. 91, viii. 60, 95), one in Strabo (ix. p. 585), one in Pausanias (i. xxxiv. § 1), and one in Diodorus (xiv. 77) indicate this. The last two passages are conclusive upon the point (compare also Ptolem. Geograph. iii. 15, p. 97, where Oropus is enumerated among the *maritime* cities of Attica). The true site then would seem to be not the modern *Oropó*, but the place called "the Holy Apostles," which is on the coast about two miles from *Oropó*. *Oropó* may have arisen from the later Oropus, the place to which the Thebans in B.C. 402 removed the inhabitants (Diod. l. s. c.).

Oropus had originally belonged to Bœotia (Pausan. l. s. c.; Steph. Byz. Ὠρωπός. πόλις Βοιωτίας.). We do not know at what time Athens got possession of it. It was for many years a perpetual bone of contention between the two states (Thucyd. viii. 60; Xen. Hell. VII. iv. § 1; Pausan. l. s. c.; Strab. i. p. 98), till at last Philip formally assigned it to Attica (Pausan. l. s. c.; Demad. Frag. iii. p. 488, Bekker.).

[1] Tamynæ or Tamyna is mentioned by Demosthenes (cont. Meid. p. 567, Reiske), by Æschines (c. Ctes. p. 480, Reiske), Strabo (x. p. 653), and Stephen (ad voc. Τάμυνα). No materials exist for fixing its site.

[2] Neither Chœreæ nor Ægilia is mentioned by any other author. The geographical notices of Eubœa, left us by ancient writers, are very scanty. Ægilia, the seaport town, must not be confounded with Ægileia the island, mentioned below (ch. 107).

[3] Xenophon, when giving an account of the expedition of Thimbron, speaks of a person named Gongylus as the only Eretrian who medised (*adver* Ἐρετριῶν μηδίσας ἔφυγεν, Hellen. III. 1, § 6). This person received as a reward from the Persians a district in Æolis containing *four* cities; but his medism cannot possibly have been at this time, since he was alive in B.C. 399, and joined in Thimbron's expedition. Pausanias (VII. x. § 1), and Plutarch (ii. p. 510, D.), agree with Herodotus.

[4] Some writers (Plato, Menex. p. 191, ed. Tauchn. Leg. iii. p. 104; Strabo x. p. 653; Diog. Laert. iii. 33) declare that the territory of Eretria was swept clean of its inhabitants by the process called "netting," which has been already spoken of (supra, iii. 149, vi. 131). But this process would have been futile unless applied to the whole of Eubœa, which is not pretended; and the whole story is discredited by the silence of Herodotus. No doubt a considerable number of the Eretrians escaped, and

CHAP. 101-103. PERSIANS LAND AT MARATHON. 395

102. The Persians, having thus brought Eretria into subjection after waiting a few days, made sail for Attica, greatly straitening the Athenians as they approached, and thinking to deal with them as they had dealt with the people of Eretria. And, because there was no place in all Attica so convenient for their horse as Marathon,[2] and it lay moreover quite close to

returning to their city after Marathon, raised it up once more from its ruins. Hence, in the war of Xerxes, Eretria was able to furnish seven ships to the Grecian fleet (infra, viii. 1, 46), and with its dependency Styra, 600 hoplites to the army (ix. 28). In former times, her hoplites had been at least 3000, and she had possessed 600 cavalry (Strab. x. p. 653).

[2] Attica has but three maritime plains of any extent, the Athenian, the Thriasian, and the plain of Marathon. The last of these is the clearest of trees, and the fittest for the movements of cavalry. Mr. Finlay's description of it is perhaps the best which has been given:—

"The plain of Marathon," he says, "extends in a perfect level along this

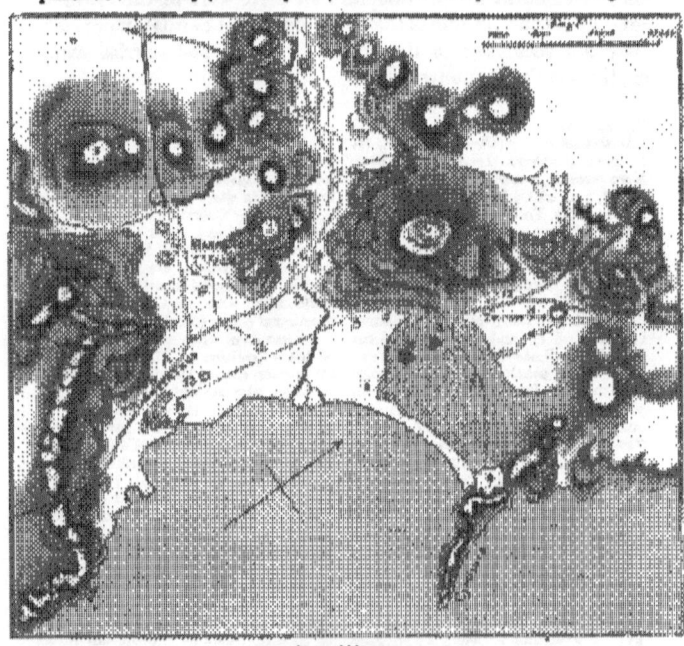

Plain of Marathon.

A.A. Position of the Greeks on the day of the battle.
B.B. Position of the Persians on the day of the battle.

1. Mount Argaliki.
2. Mount Aforismō.
3. Mount Kotroni.
4. Mount Kordiki.
5. Mount Dhrakonera.

6. Small marsh.
7. Great marsh.
8. Fountain Macaria.
9. Salt lake of Dhrakonera.
10. First position of the Greeks.
11. Temple of Athena Hellotis (?).
12. Village of Lower Suli.
13. Soro, or tumulus of Athenians.
14. Pyrgo, or monument of Miltiades.

Roads.
a a. To Athens between mounts Pentelicus and Hymettus, through Pallene.
b b. To Athens, through Cephisia.
c c. To Athens, through Aphidna.
d d. To Rhamnus.

Eretria,² therefore Hippias, the son of Pisistratus, conducted them thither.

103. When intelligence of this reached the Athenians, they likewise marched their troops to Marathon, and there stood on the defensive, having at their head ten generals,⁴ of whom one was Miltiades.⁵

Now this man's father, Cimon, the son of Stesagoras, was banished from Athens by Pisistratus, the son of Hippocrates. In his banishment it was his fortune to win the four-horse chariot-race at Olympia, whereby he gained the very same honour which had before been carried off by Miltiades,⁶ his half-brother on the

---

fine bay, and is in length about six miles, its breadth never less than a mile and a half. Two marshes bound the extremities of the plain: the southern is not very large, and is almost dry at the conclusion of the great heats; but the northern, which generally covers considerably more than a square mile, offers several parts which are at all seasons impassable. Both, however, leave a broad, firm, sandy beach between them and the sea. The uninterrupted flatness of the plain is hardly relieved by a single tree; and an amphitheatre of rocky hills and rugged mountains separates it from the rest of Attica, over the lower ridges of which some steep and difficult paths communicate with the districts of the interior." (Transactions of the Royal Society of Literature, iii. p. 364.)

Col. Leake (Demi of Attica, § 4, pp. 84, 85, remarks, that "as to the plain itself, the circumstances of the battle incline one to believe that it was anciently as destitute of trees as it is at the present day;" and relates, that "as he rode across the plain with a peasant of Vraná, he remarked that it was a fine place for cavalry to fight in. He had heard that a great battle was once fought here, but this was all he knew" (Ib. App. i. page 205, note).

² Much closer, that is, than either of the other plains upon the coast. The distance by sea between the bay of Marathon and Eretria, is not less than five-and-thirty or forty miles. Hippias probably thought that valuable time would have been lost by rounding Sunium, and that Marathon united, more than any other place, the requisite advantages for a landing. The large bay was capable of sheltering the entire fleet, the extensive beach allowed a rapid disembarkation, the rich plain afforded excellent pasture for horses, and its open character was most favourable for the operations of a cavalry force. Besides, he had himself already landed once upon this spot from Eretria, and made a successful march upon Athens (supra, i. 62), which he no doubt thought it would be easy to repeat with his hundred thousand or two hundred thousand Persians.

⁴ The Ten Generals (Strategi) are a part of the constitution of Clisthenes, who modelled the Athenian army upon the political division of the tribes, as Servius Tullius did the Roman upon the centuries. Each tribe annually elected its Phylarch to command its contingent of cavalry, its Taxiarch to command its infantry, and its Strategus to direct both. Hence the ten Strategi, who seem immediately to have claimed equality with the Polemarch or War-Archon.

The steps by which the Strategi became civil officers, no less than military, and the real directors of the whole policy of Athens, are well traced by Mr. Grote (Hist. of Greece, iv. pp. 180, 181, and 189-197). As representatives of the new system, they were able to encroach upon the Archons' office, which, sinking in importance, was first thrown open to all the citizens, and then determined by lot. This last step necessarily threw all matters of importance upon the Strategi, who were chosen for their personal merit by the free voice of the citizens.

⁵ Stesilaüs (infra, ch. 114) and Aristides (Plut. Vit. Aristid. c. 5) were also generals; and, perhaps, Themistocles (Plut. l. s. c.).

⁶ Miltiades, the son of Cypselus, the first king of the Chersonese. His Olympic victory is mentioned in ch. 36.

mother's side. At the next Olympiad he won the prize again
with the same mares; upon which he caused Pisistratus to be
proclaimed the winner, having made an agreement with him that
on yielding him this honour he should be allowed to come back
to his country. Afterwards, still with the same mares, he won
the prize a third time; whereupon he was put to death by the
sons of Pisistratus, whose father was no longer living. They set
men to lie in wait for him secretly; and these men slew him
near the government-house in the night-time. He was buried
outside the city,[7] beyond what is called the Valley Road;" and
right opposite his tomb were buried the mares which had won
the three prizes.[8] The same success had likewise been achieved
once previously, to wit, by the mares of Evagoras the Lacedæmonian, but never except by them. At the time of Cimon's
death Stesagoras, the older of his two sons, was in the Chersonese,
where he lived with Miltiades his uncle; the younger, who was
called Miltiades after the founder of the Chersonesite colony,
was with his father in Athens.

104. It was this Miltiades who now commanded the Athenians, after escaping from the Chersonese, and twice nearly
losing his life. First he was chased as far as Imbrus by the
Phœnicians,[1] who had a great desire to take him and carry him
up to the king; and when he had avoided this danger, and,
having reached his own country, thought himself to be altogether in safety, he found his enemies waiting for him, and was
cited by them before a court and impeached for his tyranny in
the Chersonese. But he came off victorious here likewise, and
was thereupon made general of the Athenians by the free choice
of the people.[2]

105. And first, before they left the city, the generals sent off
to Sparta a herald, one Pheidippides,[3] who was by birth an Atho-

---

[7] The tomb of Cimon was outside the gate of Melité, on the road leading through the demus Cœlé, north of the city. The place was known under the name of "the Cimonian monuments" (τὰ Κιμώνια μνήματα). Here Thucy-dides, whose connexion with the family of Cimon has been already mentioned (supra, ch. 39, note [9]), was said to have been buried (Marcellin. Vit. Thucyd. p. xi., and p. xv.; Anon. Vit. p. xviii. Bekker).

[8] Or " the road through Cœlé." Cœlé appears to have been the name of one of the Attic demes (Böckh, Corp. Inscr. 158, 275, &c.; Æsch. contr. Ctes. p. 584, Reiske).

[9] Compare Ælian (Hist. An. xii. 40), who mentions this fact, and likewise the honourable burial which Evagoras gave his mares.

[1] Supra, ch. 41.

[2] It is thought by some that the Strategi were not elected by their respective tribes, but by the whole mass of the citizens (Pollux, viii. 87; Hermann's Pol. Ant. § 152). This passage would favour such an opinion.

[3] Or Philippides, which is the reading of some MSS., and which has the support of Pausanias (i. xxviii. § 4).

nian, and by profession and practice a trained runner. This man, according to the account which he gave to the Athenians on his return, when he was near Mount Parthenium,[4] above Tegea, fell in with the god Pan, who called him by his name, and bade him ask the Athenians "wherefore they neglected him so entirely, when he was kindly disposed towards them, and had often helped them in times past, and would do so again in time to come?" The Athenians, entirely believing in the truth of this report, as soon as their affairs were once more in good order, set up a temple to Pan under the Acropolis,[5] and, in return for the message which I have recorded, established in his honour yearly sacrifices and a torch-race.

106. On the occasion of which we speak, when Pheidippides was sent by the Athenian generals, and, according to his own account, saw Pan on his journey, he reached Sparta on the very next day after quitting the city of Athens.[6] Upon his arrival he went before the rulers, and said to them—

"Men of Lacedæmon, the Athenians beseech you to hasten to

---

[4] Mount Parthenium bounded the Tegean plain upon the east and north-east. It was crossed by the road which led from Argos to Tegea (Pausan. VIII. liv. § 5). The modern name of this mountain is *Róïno*; but the pass through which the road goes is still called *Parthéni* (Leake's *Morea*, ii. p. 328). No remains have yet been discovered of the temple of Pan, built upon this spot in commemoration of this (supposed) appearance (Pausan. l. s. c.).

[5] The temple or rather chapel of Pan was contained in a hollow in the rock (ἐν σπηλαίῳ), just below the Propylæa, or entrance to the citadel (Pausan. I. xxviii. § 4). The cavern still exists, and has in it two niches, where the statues of Pan and Apollo (who was associated with Pan in this temple, as we learn from Pausanias) may have stood. In a garden, a little way from the cavern, a statue of Pan (now at Cambridge) was found (Leake's *Athens*, p. 170). This may be the statue dedicated upon this occasion, which was erected by Miltiades, and had the following inscription written for it by Simonides:—

Τὸν τραγόπουν ἐμὲ Πᾶνα τὸν Ἀρκάδα, τὸν κατὰ Μήδων,
τὸν μετ᾽ Ἀθηναίων στήσατο Μιλτιάδης.

The cave of Pan appears in coins representing the entrance to the Acropolis. (See the annexed figure.)

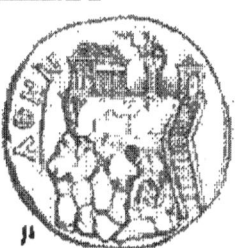

Cave of Pan.

[6] The distance from Athens to Sparta by the road is reckoned by Isocrates (Orat. Paneg. § 24, p. 171) at 1200 stades, by Pliny (H. N. vii. 20, p. 425), more accurately at 1140. Moderns estimate the direct distance at 135 or 140 miles. Pheidippides must therefore have travelled at the rate of 70 English miles a day. Kinneir says that this is a rate attained by the modern Persian foot-messengers (Geograph. Memoir, p. 44, but see above, vol. i. p. 186, note ⁹); and Pliny relates that two persons, Anystis a Lacedæmonian, and Philonides a courier employed by Alexander the Great, performed the extraordinary distance of 1200 stades (nearly 140 miles) in a single day (H. N. l. s. c.).

CHAP. 105-107.   DREAM OF HIPPIAS.   399

their aid, and not allow that state, which is the most ancient[7] in all Greece, to be enslaved by the barbarians. Eretria, look you, is already carried away captive; and Greece weakened by the loss of no mean city."

Thus did Pheidippides deliver the message committed to him. And the Spartans wished to help the Athenians, but were unable to give them any present succour, as they did not like to break their established law. It was then the ninth day of the first decade;[8] and they could not march out of Sparta on the ninth, when the moon had not reached the full.[9] So they waited for the full of the moon.

107. The barbarians were conducted to Marathon by Hippias, the son of Pisistratus, who the night before had seen a strange vision in his sleep. He dreamt of lying in his mother's arms, and conjectured the dream to mean that he would be restored to Athens, recover the power which he had lost, and afterwards live to a good old age in his native country. Such was the sense in which he interpreted the vision.[1] He now proceeded to act as guide to the Persians; and, in the first place, he landed the prisoners taken from Eretria upon the island that is called Ægileia,[2]

---

[7] It was the favourite boast of Athens that her inhabitants were αὐτόχθονες—sprung from the soil. Hence the adoption of the symbol of the grasshopper (Thucyd. i. 6; Aristoph. Eq. 1331; Nub. 985, ed. Bothe). Her territory had never been overrun by an enemy; and so her cities had never been overthrown or removed, like the cities in other countries (compare Herod. i. 56, vii. 171; Thucyd. i. 2; Plat. Tim. p. 10, ed. Tauchn.; Menex. pp. 186, 199; Isocrat. Paneg. § 4, p. 166).

[8] The Greeks divided their month of 29 or 30 days into three periods:—1. The μὴν ἱστάμενος, from the 1st day to the 10th inclusively; 2. The μὴν μεσῶν, from the 11th to the 20th; and 3. The μὴν φθίνων, or ἀνίων, from the 21st to the end. The ninth day of the first decade is thus the ninth day of the month itself. The battle of Marathon is said to have taken place in the month Boëdromion (Plutarch, de Malig. Herod. p. 861, E. &c.), which corresponded pretty nearly with our September.

[9] Mr. Grote believes that this was no pretence, but the "blind tenacity of ancient habit" (Hist. of Greece, iv. p. 460). We find such a feeling, he says, to abate, but never to disappear in the Spartan history; and he refers to the hesitation shown before the battle of Platæa (infra, ix. 7-10) as indicating the reality of this motive; but both that and the similar withholding of the bulk of their troops from Thermopylæ (vii. 206) may be explained on selfish grounds, and fail to show that the excuse was more than a subterfuge. I know but of one occasion in Spartan history where their own interests were plainly attacked, in which a religious motive is said to have had any share in preventing their troops from stirring. In the seventh year of the Peloponnesian war, at the first seizure of Pylos, the occurrence of a festival appears as one out of many reasons of their delay in making a resistance (Thucyd. iv. 5); but it is expressly stated that they made light of the occasion, and thought no hurry was needed.

[1] Compare the dream of Cæsar and its interpretation (Suet. Jul. Cæs. § 7, p. 16; Plut. Vit. Cæs. c. 32).

[2] The Ægileia here spoken of is not the island of that name near Crete, of which Stephen speaks (Steph. Byz. ad voc. Αἰγίλεια), and which is mentioned by Pliny under the name of Ægilia (H. N. iv. 12, p. 212), but an island, or rather islet, between Eubœa and Attica, at the entrance of what was called the

a tract belonging to the Styreans,² after which he brought the fleet to anchor off Marathon, and marshalled the bands of the barbarians as they disembarked. As he was thus employed it chanced that he sneezed and at the same time coughed with more violence than was his wont. Now, as he was a man advanced in years, and the greater number of his teeth were loose, it so happened that one of them was driven out with the force of the cough, and fell down into the sand. Hippias took all the pains he could to find it; but the tooth was nowhere to be seen: whereupon he fetched a deep sigh, and said to the bystanders—

"After all, the land is not ours; and we shall never be able to bring it under. All my share in it is the portion of which my tooth has possession."

So Hippias believed that in this way his dream was out.⁴

108. The Athenians were drawn up in order of battle in a sacred close belonging to Hercules,⁵ when they were joined by the Plataeans, who came in full force to their aid. Some time before,⁶ the Plataeans had put themselves under the rule of the Athenians; and these last had already undertaken many labours on their behalf. The occasion of the surrender was the following. The Plataeans suffered grievous things at the hands of the men of Thebes; so, as it chanced that Cleomenes, the son of Anaxandridas, and the Lacedaemonians were in their neighbourhood, they first of all offered to surrender themselves to them. But the Lacedaemonians refused to receive them, and said—

"We dwell too far off from you, and ours would be but chill

Myrtoan Sea. (Cf. Plin. H. N. iv. 12, p. 215, and Ptolem. Geograph. v. 2, p. 139, where Ægilia seems to be intended by Bexysalis.)

² Styra was a town of southern Euboea, not far from Carystus (Strab. x. p. 650). According to Pausanias it was a Dryopian settlement (iv. xxxiv. § 6). The modern *Stowra* retains the ancient name, and probably occupies nearly the ancient site.

⁴ On the *disappointing* fulfilment of dreams, see i. 114; and compare the Magian doctrine on the subject (i. 120).

⁵ Hercules was among the gods specially worshipped at Marathon. Tradition said that the hero had himself visited the place (Apollod. ii. v. 7), and that his sons had dwelt there during the greater part of their exile in Attica (ib. ii. viii. 2). The Marathonians claimed to have introduced the worship of Hercules into Greece (Pausan. i.

xxxii. § 4). Colonel Leake supposes that the remains of a temple near *Vrand* (which he regards as the ancient Marathon) are those of the Heracleium, and that the sacred precinct, or *temenus*, was in the plain below (Demi of Attica, p. 98; App. l. p. 211). See the plan of the Plain of Marathon, supra, p. 395.

⁶ Twenty-nine years before (B.C. 519). If we accept the date of Thucydides (ib. 68); but Mr. Grote (Hist. of Greece, iv. p. 222, note) has shown strong grounds for believing that Thucydides has for once fallen into error. If Herodotus has rightly represented the motive of Cleomenes, the transaction can scarcely have occurred during the reign of Hippias, with whom Sparta was on the most friendly terms (v. 63, 91). Mr. Grote supposes it to have taken place at the close of the second expedition of Cleomenes into Attica, B.C. 506 or 507 (supra, v. 72, 73).

succour. Ye might oftentimes be carried into slavery before one of us heard of it. We counsel you rather to give yourselves up to the Athenians, who are your next neighbours, and well able to shelter you."[7]

This they said, not so much out of good will towards the Platæans as because they wished to involve the Athenians in trouble by engaging them in wars with the Bœotians. The Platæans, however, when the Lacedæmonians gave them this counsel, complied at once; and when the sacrifice to the Twelve Gods was being offered at Athens, they came and sat as suppliants about the altar,[8] and gave themselves up to the Athenians. The Thebans no sooner learnt what the Platæans had done than instantly they marched out against them, while the Athenians sent troops to their aid. As the two armies were about to join battle, the Corinthians, who chanced to be at hand, would not allow them to engage; both sides consented to take them for arbitrators, whereupon they made up the quarrel, and fixed the boundary-line between the two states upon this condition: to wit, that if any of the Bœotians wished no longer to belong to Bœotia, the Thebans should allow them to follow their own inclinations. The Corinthians, when they had thus decreed, forthwith departed to their homes: the Athenians likewise set off on their return; but the Bœotians fell upon them during the march, and a battle was fought wherein they were worsted by the Athenians. Hereupon these last would not be bound by the line which the Corinthians had fixed, but advanced beyond those limits, and made the Asôpus[9] the boundary-line between the country of the Thebans and that of the Platæans and Hysians. Under such circumstances did the Platæans give themselves up to Athens; and now they were come to Marathon to bear the Athenians aid.

109. The Athenian generals were divided in their opinions; and some advised not to risk a battle, because they were too few

---

[7] The same account of the origin of the alliance is given briefly by Thucydides (iii. 55).

[8] The altar of the Twelve Gods at Athens has been mentioned before (ii. 7). It was in the Agora, near the statue of Demosthenes and the temple of Mars (Vit. X. Orat.; Plut. ii. p. 847, A.; Pausan. i. viii. § 5). Thucydides informs us that it was first dedicated by Pisistratus, the son of Hippias, during his archonship (vi. 54). It is mentioned by Lycurgus (contra Leocrat. p. 198, ed. Reiske), Plutarch (Nicias, c. 13), and the author of the Lives of the Ten Orators (l. a. c.). It seems to have been used as a point from which to measure distances (supra, ii. 7).

[9] The Asôpus is the modern Τοτίτσί, the great river of southern Bœotia. The situation of Hysiæ has been given above (v. 74, note). Platæa is undoubtedly the modern Κότλα (Gell's Itin. pp. 111, 112; Leake's Northern Greece, ii. 323-325).

to engage such a host as that of the Medes, while others were for fighting at once; and among these last was Miltiades. He therefore, seeing that opinions were thus divided, and that the less worthy counsel appeared likely to prevail, resolved to go to the polemarch, and have a conference with him. For the man on whom the lot fell to be polemarch[1] at Athens was entitled to give his vote with the ten generals, since anciently[2] the Athenians allowed him an equal right of voting with them. The polemarch at this juncture was Callimachus of Aphidnae;[3] to him therefore Miltiades went, and said:—

"With thee it rests, Callimachus, either to bring Athens to slavery, or, by securing her freedom, to leave behind thee to all future generations a memory beyond even Harmodius and Aristogeiton. For never since the time that the Athenians became a people were they in so great a danger as now. If they bow their necks beneath the yoke of the Medes, the woes which they will have to suffer when given into the power of Hippias are already determined on; if, on the other hand, they fight and overcome, Athens may rise to be the very first city in Greece. How it comes to pass that these things are likely to happen, and how the determining of them in some sort rests with thee, I will now proceed to make clear. We generals are ten in

---

[1] The Polemarch, or War-Archon, was the third archon in dignity, and before the time of Clisthenes had constitutionally the general superintendence of all military matters, having succeeded to the office of the kings as respected war. (Cf. Photius, ad voc. Πολέμαρχος.) It appears by the position of Callimachus on this occasion, that the legislation of Clisthenes, though it committed the general direction of military affairs to the Ten Strategi (supra, ch. 103, note⁹), yet did not at once deprive the Polemarch of his ancient office, but made him a sort of colleague of the generals, with certain special and peculiar privileges, as that of commanding the right wing (infra, ch. 111). There can be little doubt that Herodotus has fallen into error with respect to the mode in which the Polemarch was elected at this period, having, as Mr. Grote observes (Hist. of Greece, iv. p. 197, note⁷), "transferred to the year 490 B.C. the practice of his own time." It is difficult to believe that the office can have been assigned by lot, while it had such important duties belonging to it (cf. Arist. Pol. vi. 4, p. 198, ed. Taucha.). The change from open election to the lot most probably occurred shortly after Marathon, and in connexion with the great act of Aristides, the "throwing open to all citizens, without respect to tribe or property, of the archonship and all other public offices" (cf. Hermann's Pol. Ant. of Greece, § 112). Aristides himself, we are told, was in the year after Marathon elected archon by open vote (Idomeneus ap. Plutarch. Arist. c. 1).

[2] When Herodotus wrote, the polemarch had no military functions at all, but "attended to the personal and family interests of the metics and foreigners in general" (Hermann, § 138).

[3] Little is known of Aphidnae, except that it was a strong position between Phylé and Rhamnus (Dem. de Cor. § 12), and in the neighbourhood of Decelea (infra, ix. 73). Col. Leake places it conjecturally at the hill of Κοτρόνι, a strong height in the upper part of the valley of the river of Marathon, where are "considerable remains indicating the site of a fortified demus" (Demi of Attica, p. 21).

number, and our votes are divided; half of us wish to engage, half to avoid a combat. Now, if we do not fight, I look to see a great disturbance at Athens which will shake men's resolutions, and then I fear they will submit themselves; but if we fight the battle before any unsoundness show itself among our citizens, let the gods but give us fair play, and we are well able to overcome the enemy. On thee therefore we depend in this matter, which lies wholly in thine own power. Thou hast only to add thy vote to my side and thy country will be free, and not free only, but the first state in Greece. Or, if thou preferrest to give thy vote to them who would decline the combat, then the reverse will follow."

110. Miltiades by these words gained Callimachus; and the addition of the polemarch's vote caused the decision to be in favour of fighting. Hereupon all those generals who had been desirous of hazarding a battle, when their turn came to command the army, gave up their right to Miltiades.⁴ He however, though he accepted their offers, nevertheless waited, and would not fight, until his own day of command arrived in due course.⁵

111. Then at length, when his own turn was come, the Athenian battle was set in array, and this was the order of it. Callimachus the polemarch led the right wing; for it was at that time a rule with the Athenians to give the right wing to the polemarch.⁶ After this followed the tribes, according as they were numbered,⁷ in an unbroken line; while last of all came the

---

⁴ Aristides is said to have been one of the Strategi who recommended an immediate engagement (Plut. Vit. Arist. c. 5). Themistocles was on the same side; but it is uncertain whether he held the office of Strategus.

⁵ There seems to be some justice in Mr. Grote's remark (Hist. of Greece, iv. p. 463), that "Miltiades would not have admitted any serious postponement of the battle upon such a punctilio." Still it is clear that the Greeks were encamped for several days opposite to the Persians, unless we are to set aside altogether the narrative of Herodotus. We must therefore explain the delay in some way. (See on this point the remarks on the circumstances of the battle, in the Appendix to this book, Essay i. § 7.)

⁶ The *right* wing was the special post of honour (vide infra, ix. 27, where the Athenians dispute with the Tegeans the right of occupying it before the battle of Plataea). This arose from the greater exposure of those who fought at this end of the line, particularly when outflanked, from the shield being carried on the left arm (cf. Thucyd. v. 71). The Polemarch took the post as representative of the king, whose position it had been in the ancient times. (See Eurip. Suppl. 656.)

⁷ It would seem that the democratical arrangements of the Clisthenic constitution prevailed in the camp no less than in the city itself. Not only was the army marshalled by tribes, but the tribes stood in their political order, that is, in the order which had been determined by lot at the beginning of the civil year for the furnishing of the prytanes. The tribe Æantis had the right wing, because it was the prytany of that tribe at the time of the battle (Plat. Sympos. p. 628, D.). The tribes Antiochis and Leontis were in the centre, the former commanded by Aristides, the latter commanded or accompanied by Themistocles (ib. p. 628, E., F.).

Plataeans, forming the left wing. And ever since that day it has been a custom with the Athenians, in the sacrifices and assemblies held each fifth year at Athens,[a] for the Athenian herald to implore the blessing of the gods on the Plataeans conjointly with the Athenians. Now, as they marshalled the host upon the field of Marathon, in order that the Athenian front might be of equal length with the Median, the ranks of the centre were diminished, and it became the weakest part of the line, while the wings were both made strong with a depth of many ranks.

112. So when the battle was set in array, and the victims showed themselves favourable, instantly the Athenians, so soon as they were let go, charged the barbarians at a run.[b] Now the distance between the two armies was little short of eight furlongs. The Persians, therefore, when they saw the Greeks coming on at speed, made ready to receive them, although it seemed to them that the Athenians were bereft of their senses, and bent upon their own destruction; for they saw a mere handful of men coming on at a run without either horsemen or archers.[c] Such was the opinion of the barbarians; but the

---

The position of the other tribes is not known.

[a] The Panathenaic festival is probably intended. It was held every fifth year (i. e. once in every four years, half-way between the Olympic festivals), and was the great religious assembly (πανήγυρις) of the Athenians. The sacrifices with which it opened were of a magnificent character, for every town in Attica, and every colony of Athens, and in after times every subject city, sent a bull as an offering. After these victims were slain, and before the feasting upon their flesh began, the solemn prayer mentioned in the text seems to have been offered. (See Smith's Dict. of Antiquities, pp. 705, 706.)

[b] It is questioned by some writers what this really means. Col. Leake thinks that the Greeks can only have begun by a "quick step," the rapidity of which may have been increased as they approached the Persian line (Demi of Attica, App. I. p. 212). Mr. Finlay is of the same opinion. They suppose that a run of a mile must have disordered the troops, and unfitted them for engaging with the enemy. Mr. Grote admits this result, but still believes in the fact of the run, which, he observes, "was obviously one of the most remarkable events connected with the battle" (Hist. of Greece, iv. p. 470,

note). He ascribes the defeat of the Greek centre to the disorder produced by the rapid advance. But if this had been so, is it likely that Herodotus would have failed to notice it? Perhaps sufficient allowance has not been commonly made for the effect of athletic training upon the Greek frame. (See Professor Creasy's 'Fifteen Decisive Battles,' p. 34, where this point is noticed.)

[c] It was probably on account of the deficiency of the Greeks in archers and cavalry that the rapid charge was made. It took the Persians by surprise, and allowed their light-armed troops no time to act. There is reason to believe that the Persian horse was absent from the battle, having been sent on some other service. At least the explanation given by Suidas of the proverb, "χωρὶς ἱππεῖς," favours such a supposition. (See Appendix, Essay i. § 8.)

The sterile and mountainous character of Attica made it unfit to breed horses. Athens, however, was not absolutely without cavalry even in very early times. The requirement of two horsemen from each Naucrary (Pollux, viii. 108) must undoubtedly have been an ancient one, and would have given, in the times anterior to Clisthenes, 96, in those subsequent, 800 horse-soldiers. If the ἱππεῖς of the Solonian constitution (continued

Athenians in close array fell upon them, and fought in a manner worthy of being recorded. They were the first of the Greeks, so far as I know, who introduced the custom of charging the enemy at a run, and they were likewise the first who dared to look upon the Median garb, and to face men clad in that fashion.* Until this time the very name of the Medes had been a terror to the Greeks to hear.

113. The two armies fought together on the plain of Marathon for a length of time; and in the mid battle, where the Persians themselves and the Sacæ had their place,² the barbarians were victorious, and broke and pursued the Greeks into the inner country; but on the two wings the Athenians and the Platæans defeated the enemy. Having so done, they suffered the routed barbarians to fly at their ease, and joining the two wings in one, fell upon those who had broken their own centre, and fought and conquered them. These likewise fled, and now the Athenians hung upon the runaways and cut them down, chasing them all the way to the shore, on reaching which they laid hold of the ships and called aloud for fire.

114. It was in the struggle here that Callimachus the polemarch, after greatly distinguishing himself,⁴ lost his life; Stesilaüs too, the son of Thrasilaüs, one of the generals, was slain; and Cynægirus,⁵ the son of Euphorion, having seized on a vessel

of the enemy's by the ornament at the stern,⁶ had his hand cut off by the blow of an axe, and so perished; as likewise did many other Athenians of note and name.⁷

115. Nevertheless the Athenians secured in this way seven of the vessels; while with the remainder the barbarians pushed off, and taking aboard their Eretrian prisoners from the island where they had left them, doubled Cape Sunium, hoping to reach Athens before the return of the Athenians. The Alcmæonidæ were accused by their countrymen of suggesting this course to them; they had, it was said, an understanding with the Persians, and made a signal to them,⁸ by raising a shield, after they were embarked in their ships.

116. The Persians accordingly sailed round Sunium. But the Athenians with all possible speed marched away to the defence of their city, and succeeded in reaching Athens before the appearance of the barbarians:⁹ and as their camp at Marathon had been pitched in a precinct of Hercules, so now they encamped in another precinct of the same god at Cynos-

arges.¹ The barbarian fleet arrived, and lay to off Phalerum, which was at that time the haven of Athens;² but after resting awhile upon their oars, they departed and sailed away to Asia.

117. There fell in this battle of Marathon, on the side of the barbarians, about six thousand and four hundred men;³ on that of the Athenians, one hundred and ninety-two.⁴ Such was the

---

¹ Supra, v. 63. Cynosarges was situated very near the famous Lycæum, the school of Aristotle. Both seem to have been in the district called Cepi, or "the Gardens," which was on the south-eastern side of the city towards the Ilissus, and may have been in part within and in part without the walls (Pausan. I. xix. § 2-4, and xxvii. § 4; Plin. H. N. xxxvi. 5, p. 611; Liv. xxxi. 24). Cynosarges itself lay outside the city, a little way from the Diomeian gate (Diog. Laert. vi. 13; Plut. Them. c. 1). It was a grassy spot, thickly shaded with trees (Dicæarch. Fr. 59), situated upon rising ground (Plut. Vit. X. Rhet. ii. p. 834, B), and is placed with much probability by Colonel Leake "at the foot of the south-eastern extremity of Mount Lycabettus" (Athens, § vi. p. 277). It would thus both lie upon the common route from Athens to Marathon, and command a prospect of the sea and of the roadstead of Phalerum.

The temple of Hercules at Cynosarges is mentioned by a great number of writers. (See, besides the authorities already quoted, Aristoph. Ran. 612; Polem. ii. Fr. 78; Hesych. in voc.; Harpocrat. sub voc. 'Ἡράκλεια, &c.). Besides the temple, there was also a gymnasium, or public exercise-ground, at the place (Liv., Diog. Laert., Plutarch, Steph. Byz. ad voc. &c.).

² Supra, v. 63.

³ The moderation of this estimate contrasts remarkably with the exaggerated statements of later times. The inscription under the picture in the Poecilè put the number of the slain at 200,000.

Ἕλληνων προμαχοῦντες Ἀθηναίοι Μαραθῶνι
Ἐστόρεσαν Μηδων ἐνέα μυριάδας.
(Suidas, ad voc. Πανόφης.)

Others spoke of 300,000 (Pausan. IV. xxv. § 2) or of an innumerable multitude (Xen. Anab. III. ii. § 12; Plut. de Malign. Herod. II. p. 862). The great slaughter took place at one of the marshes, into which the flying Persians were driven by their conquerors. The picture at the Poecilè gave this incident

(Pausan. I. xv. § 4, and xxxii. § 6). The entire number of the Persians engaged is very uncertain. Justin (ii. 9) lays them at 600,000; Plato (Menex. p. 190, ed. Tauchn.) and Lysias (Orat. Fun. p. 82, ed. Reiske) at half a million; Plutarch (Parall. ii. p. 305) and Valerius Maximus (v. 3) at 300,000; and Cornelius Nepos at 210,000 (Miltiad. c. 4). This last estimate is perhaps not far from the truth. The 600 triremes must have carried at least 138,000 men (vide infra, vii. 184), and may probably have carried 150,000. The cavalry is not likely to have fallen short of 10,000, which is the estimate of Nepos (l. s. c.). And the names of the cavalry transports, together with the Greeks impressed into the service from the Cyclades (infra, ch. 132), may have easily amounted to 50,000. Thus we should have for the whole amount—

Crews of 600 triremes	120,000
Men-at-arms (Persians and Sacæ) on board them	30,000
Cavalry	12,500
Crews of the horse-transports	40,000
Greeks pressed into the service	12,000
	214,500

The Athenians are usually estimated at 9000, or, including the 1000 Platæans, 10,000. (See Pausan. x. xx. § 2; Plut. Parall. i. s. c.; Corn. Nep. Miltiad. c. 5.) Justin makes them 10,000 exclusive of the Platæan contingent (ii. 9). The light-armed would probably about double the number (infra, ix. 29). The Soros which marks the grave of the Athenian dead is still a conspicuous object on the plain of Marathon (Wordsworth's Pictorial Greece, p. 113; Leake's Demi of Attica, pp. 89; &c.).

⁴ The smallness of the loss sustained by a Greek army in a great engagement, unless in case of an utter rout, is very remarkable. At Platæa, where the troops engaged were above 70,000, Herodotus estimates the slain at 759, and of these 600 fell in a bye engagement, and no more than 159 in the main battle (infra, ix. 69, 70). With the Dorians

number of the slain on the one side and the other. A strange prodigy likewise happened at this fight. Epizelus,[1] the son of Cuphagoras, an Athenian, was in the thick of the fray, and behaving himself as a brave man should, when suddenly he was stricken with blindness, without blow of sword or dart; and this blindness continued thenceforth during the whole of his after life. The following is the account which he himself, as I have heard, gave of the matter: he said that a gigantic warrior, with a huge beard, which shaded all his shield, stood over against him; but the ghostly semblance passed him by, and slew the man at his side. Such, as I understand, was the tale which Epizelus told.[2]

118. Datis meanwhile was on his way back to Asia,[3] and had reached Myconus,[4] when he saw in his sleep a vision. What it was is not known; but no sooner was day come than he caused strict search to be made throughout the whole fleet, and finding on board a Phoenician vessel an image of Apollo overlaid with gold, he inquired from whence it had been taken, and learning to what temple it belonged, he took it with him in his own ship to Delos, and placed it in the temple there, enjoining the Delians, who had now come back to their island, to restore the image to the Theban Delium,[5] which lies on the

coast over against Chalcis. Having left these injunctions, he sailed away; but the Delians failed to restore the statue; and it was not till twenty years afterwards that the Thebans, warned by an oracle, themselves brought it back to Delium.

110. As for the Eretrians, whom Datis and Artaphernes had carried away captive, when the fleet reached Asia, they were taken up to Susa.[1] Now King Darius, before they were made his prisoners, nourished a fierce anger against these men for having injured him without provocation; but now that he saw them brought into his presence, and become his subjects, he did them no other harm, but only settled them at one of his own stations in Cissia—a place called Arderica[2]—two hundred and ten furlongs distant from Susa, and forty from the well which yields produce of three different kinds. For from this well they get bitumen, salt, and oil, procuring it in the way that I will now

---

town (πολίχνιον, Strab. l. s. c.; Steph. Byz. ad voc.) called Delium. The site of the latter seems to be occupied by the modern village of *Dhilisi*. The temple was much nearer the sea. (See Leake's Northern Greece, vol. ii. p. 450.)

[1] Damis, the friend and companion of Apollonius of Tyana, declared that Apollonius found the Eretrians still in the same place, and retaining their ancestral speech, in the first century of our era (ap. Philostr. Vit. Apoll. Tyan. i. 24). He reported their tradition to be, that the number of the captives in the first instance was 780, and consisted of men, women, and children—but that near one half died upon the journey, so that only four hundred men and ten women appeared before Darius at Susa. The Eretrians in his day occupied a strongly-fortified village, but suffered continually from the raids of their neighbours, who ravaged their cultivated land. Apollonius interceded for them with the Parthian king. There is nothing improbable in this narrative, which Mr. Grote discredits (Hist. of Greece, iv. p. 488, note) on account of the fictions wherewith the life of Apollonius is disfigured.

Strabo placed the captive Eretrians in Gordyêne or *Kurdistan*, the mountain region east of the upper Tigris (xv. p. 1048).

[2] This cannot be the Arderica which was mentioned in the First Book, for that was in the northern part of Babylonia, and lay on the Euphrates (i. 185). It must be sought for in Khuzistan, in the neighbourhood of one or other of the few places where bitumen is found. Sir H. Rawlinson places it at *Kir-Ab*, which is 3.5 miles (above 300 stades) from Susa, in a direction a little north of east.

"Among these steep ravines," he says, "I was surprised to detect the evident traces of a broad paved road, leading into the secluded plain of *Kir-Ab*, which appeared to come from the direction of *Sus* (Susa). I also found a heap of mounds in the plain, the remains of an ancient town; and uniting these indications with the bitumen pits, which abound in the neighbourhood, and from which the place has obtained its name, I could not but fancy that I beheld the site of the Eretrian colony of Arderica. It is true that the distance in a right line is too much to accord with the 210 stadia of Herodotus, and he seems to have actually visited the place himself; but in all other respects it will agree sufficiently well both with his account and with that of Damis (ap. Philostr. Vit. Apoll. l. s. c.). *The liquid bitumen is collected at the present day in the same way as is related by Herodotus*: the ground is impregnated with this noxious matter, and the waters are most unwholesome. The *Buledrud* may be the stream which was brought round the town to defend the Greek colonists from the attacks of the barbarians; and the rising ground behind the ruins is, at the present day, the part of the district chiefly under cultivation" (Journal of Royal Geographical Society, vol. ix. p. 94).

describe: They draw with a swipe, and instead of a bucket make use of the half of a wine-skin; with this the man dips, and after drawing, pours the liquid into a reservoir, wherefrom it passes into another, and there takes three different shapes. The salt and the bitumen forthwith collect and harden, while the oil is drawn off into casks. It is called by the Persians "rhadinacé," is black, and has an unpleasant smell. Here then King Darius established the Eretrians; and here they continued to my time, and still spoke their old language. So thus it fared with the Eretrians.

120. After the full of the moon two thousand Lacedæmonians came to Athens. So eager had they been to arrive in time, that they took but three days to reach Attica from Sparta.³ They came, however, too late for the battle; yet, as they had a longing to behold the Medes, they continued their march to Marathon and there viewed the slain. Then, after giving the Athenians all praise for their achievement, they departed and returned home.⁴

121. But it fills me with wonderment, and I can in no wise believe the report, that the Alcmæonidæ had an understanding with the Persians, and held them up a shield as a signal, wishing Athens to be brought under the yoke of the barbarians and of Hippias,—the Alcmæonidæ, who have shown themselves at least as bitter haters of tyrants as was Callias, the son of Phænippus, and father of Hipponicus.⁵ This Callias was the only person at Athens who, when the Pisistratidæ were driven out, and their goods were exposed for sale by the vote of the people, had the courage to make purchases, and likewise in many other ways to display the strongest hostility.

[122. He was a man very worthy to be had in remembrance by all, on several accounts. For not only did he thus distinguish

---

³ Isocrates says that the Spartans were three days *and three nights* on the road (Orat. Paneg. 24, p. 171, ed. Baiter). As the distance was not less than 130 miles (1140 stades, Plin. H. N. vii. 20), it is impossible that the march should have been accomplished in a shorter space of time.

⁴ Plato (Menex. p. 191, ed. Tauchn.) tells us that the Spartans arrived *the day after* the battle (τῇ ὑστεραίᾳ τῆς μάχης). As the Greeks did not leave the bodies of the Persians to infect the air, but buried them (Pausan. I. xxxii. § 4), probably as soon as they had entombed their own dead, this statement is in close accordance with Herodotus, and may be accepted as the truth.

⁵ Vide infra, vii. 151, where another Callias, the son of this Hipponicus, is mentioned. Hipponicus himself is said to have been one of the wealthiest Athenians of his day, which may account for this introduction of his name. (See Plut. Vit. Alcib. c. 8, and Athenæus, Deipnosoph. xii. 9. where, however, the story told of the mode in which he obtained his wealth is historically impossible.)

himself beyond others in the cause of his country's freedom; but likewise, by the honours which he gained at the Olympic games, where he carried off the prize in the horse-race, and was second in the four-horse chariot-race, and by his victory at an earlier period in the Pythian games, he showed himself in the eyes of all the Greeks a man most unsparing in his expenditure.⁹ He was remarkable too for his conduct in respect of his daughters, three in number; for when they came to be of marriageable age, he gave to each of them a most ample dowry, and placed it at their own disposal, allowing them to choose their husbands from among all the citizens of Athens,¹ and giving each in marriage to the man of her own choice.°]

123. Now the Alcmæonidæ fell not a whit short of this person in their hatred of tyrants, so that I am astonished at the charge made against them, and cannot bring myself to believe that they held up a shield; for they were men who had remained in exile during the whole time that the tyranny lasted, and they even contrived the trick by which the Pisistratidæ were deprived of their throne.⁹ Indeed I look upon them as the persons who in good truth gave Athens her freedom far more than Harmodius and Aristogeiton.¹ For these last did but exasperate the other Pisistratidæ by slaying Hipparchus,² and were far from doing anything towards putting down the tyranny; whereas the Alcmæonidæ were manifestly the actual deliverers of Athens, if

at least it be true that the Pythoness was prevailed upon by them to bid the Lacedæmonians set Athens free, as I have already related.

124. But perhaps they were offended with the people of Athens; and therefore betrayed their country. Nay, but on the contrary there were none of the Athenians who were held in such general esteem, or who were so laden with honours.[3] So that it is not even reasonable to suppose that a shield was held up by them on this account. A shield was shown, no doubt; that cannot be gainsaid; but who it was that showed it I cannot any further determine.

125. Now the Alcmæonidæ were, even in days of yore, a family of note at Athens;[4] but from the time of Alcmæon, and again of Megacles, they rose to special eminence. The former of these two personages, to wit, Alcmæon, the son of Megacles, when Crœsus the Lydian sent men from Sardis to consult the Delphic oracle, gave aid gladly to his messengers, and assisted them to accomplish their task. Crœsus, informed of Alcmæon's kindnesses by the Lydians who from time to time conveyed his messages to the god,[5] sent for him to Sardis, and when he arrived, made him a present of as much gold as he should be able to carry at one time about his person. Finding that this was the gift assigned him, Alcmæon took his measures, and prepared himself to receive it in the following way. He clothed himself in a loose tunic, which he made to bag greatly at the waist, and placing upon his feet the widest buskins that he could anywhere find, followed his guides into the treasure-house. Here he fell to upon a heap of gold-dust, and in the first place packed as much as he could inside his buskins, between them and his legs; after which he filled the breast of his tunic quite full of gold, and then sprinkling some among his hair, and taking some likewise in his mouth, he came forth from the treasure-house, scarcely able to drag his legs along, like any-

---

[3] What had become of Clisthenes? Probably he was dead, but when he died, and under what circumstances, history does not inform us. His tomb at Athens was among the sepulchres of those who had perished in defence of their country (Pausan. I. xxix. § 5). Apparently, therefore, he must have fallen in battle, and probably either in the Theban or the Eginetan war. The tomb of those who had perished in the latter was not far from his (Pausan. ibid.).

[4] Suidas makes Alcmæon, the son of Amphiaraus, the first founder of the family (in voc. 'Αλκμαιωνίδαι); but Pausanias (II. xviii. § 7) derives the Alcmæonidæ from Alcmæon, the son of Sillus, and descendant of Nestor, who was one of the Pylians expelled by the Heraclidæ when they conquered the Peloponnese. The families of Codrus and Pisistratus were said to have been derived from the same source (Pausan. ut supra; Herod. v. 65).

[5] Supra, i. 55.

thing rather than a man, with his mouth crammed full, and his bulk increased every way. On seeing him, Croesus burst into a laugh, and not only let him have all that he had taken, but gave him presents besides of fully equal worth. Thus this house became one of great wealth; and Alcmaeon was able to keep horses for the chariot-race, and won the prize at Olympia.[4]

126. Afterwards, in the generation which followed, Clisthenes, king of Sicyon, raised the family to still greater eminence among the Greeks than even that to which it had attained before. For this Clisthenes,[5] who was the son of Aristonymus, the grandson of Myron,[6] and the great-grandson of Andreas, had a daughter, called Agarista, whom he wished to marry to the best husband that he could find in the whole of Greece. At the Olympic games, therefore, having gained the prize in the chariot-race, he caused public proclamation to be made to the following effect:—"Whoever among the Greeks deems himself worthy to become the son-in-law of Clisthenes, let him come, sixty days hence, or, if he will, sooner, to Sicyon: for within a year's time, counting from the end of the sixty days, Clisthenes will decide on the man to whom he shall contract his daughter." So all the Greeks who were proud of their own merit or of their country flocked to Sicyon as suitors; and Clisthenes had a foot-course and a wrestling-ground made ready, to try their powers.

127. From Italy there came Smindyrides, the son of Hippocrates, a native of Sybaris—which city about that time was at

the very height of its prosperity. He was a man who in luxuriousness of living⁹ exceeded all other persons. Likewise there came Damasus, the son of Amyris, surnamed the Wise,¹⁰ a native of Siris.¹ These two were the only suitors from Italy. From the Ionian Gulf² appeared Amphimnestus, the son of Epistrophus, an Epidamnian;³ from Ætolia Males, the brother of that Titormus⁴ who excelled all the Greeks in strength, and who wishing to avoid his fellow-men, withdrew himself into the remotest parts of the Ætolian territory. From the Peloponnese came several—Leocedes, son of that Pheidon,⁵ king of the Argives,

---

⁹ Various tales were told of Smindyrides by later writers, illustrative of his character for luxuriousness. Timæus, a native of Sicily, well acquainted with the traditions of the cities of Magna Græcia, seems to have been the source from which they drew. One story was, that he was accompanied to Sicyon by a thousand fowlers and a thousand cooks (Athenæus, xii. 58, p. 541, C.), to which some added a thousand fishermen (Ælian, V. H. xii. 24); another, that he declared it made him feel tired to see a man hard at work in the fields (Senec. de Irâ, ii. 25; cf. Tim. Fr. 59,; a third, that he complained of the rose-leaves on which he slept having creases in them (Ibid.). He was regarded as the type of his nation, which carried luxury further than any other Grecian state. (See the long account of Athenæus, who follows Timæus and Phylarchus, Daipnosoph. xii. iii. pp. 519, B. 521.)

¹⁰ Is this Amyris the Sybarite, who alone understood the oracle which foretold the destruction of Sybaris, and therefore sold all that he had and quitted it, whence he was considered mad by his countrymen? See the story at length in Eustathius (Comment. ad Hom. Il. ii, p. 298), and Suidas (ad voc.); and compare Zenobius, who gives it differently (Cent. iv. 27). When it was found how wisely the supposed madman had acted, the proverb arose, "'Ἀμύρις μαίνεται."

¹ Siris, situated on a river of the same name, midway between Sybaris and Tarentum, was, according to different authors, a Trojan (Lycophr. Alex. 978), a Rhodian (Strab. vi. p. 380), or an Ionian settlement. Timæus (ap. Athen. xii. 5, p. 523, C.) ascribed its first origin to Troy, but related that it afterwards received a body of Colophonian colonists. The grounds upon

which Athens claims it as hers (infra, viii. 62) are very obscure. Siris was almost as celebrated for its luxury as Sybaris (see Athenæus, l. s. c., who quotes Timæus and Aristotle). It fell under the Tarentine colony of Heraclea (about three miles from it, and nearly the same distance from the sea), to which at first it served as a port, and in which eventually it was absorbed. (Strab. l. s. c.; Diod. Sic. xii. 37. Compare Scylax, Peripl. p. 11, where Heraclea is mentioned, but not Siris.) Some ruins of Heraclea remain, but none of Siris. The river, which bore the name of the latter city, is now called the Sinno. There is a roadstead at its mouth, where vessels may lie, but nothing that deserves the name of a harbour (Swinburne's Travels, vol. i. p. 279).

² By the Ionian Gulf, Herodotus means the Adriatic Sea (vide infra, vii. 20; ix. 92; and compare Thucyd. i. 24, &c.).

³ Epidamnus, a colony of the Corcyræans (Thucyd. i. 24), was situated on the Illyrian coast, between Apollonia (Polina) and Lissus (Alessio). The Romans changed its name to Dyrrhachium, which has been corrupted into Durazzo (cf. Strab. vii. p. 457; Plin. H. N. iii. 23).

⁴ Titormus is said to have contended with Milo, and proved himself the stronger. He lifted a stone up to his shoulders which Milo could scarcely move (Ælian, H. V. xii. 22). He also challenged Milo to a trial, which could the soonest devour an ox (Athenæus, x. 4, p. 412, F.).

⁵ Such is the reading of all the MSS. As, however, the Pheidon indicated flourished at least 150 years before Clisthenes (see Clinton's F. H. vol. i. pp. 247-250), it has been thought to be impossible that the text should be

CHAP. 127.   AGARISTA'S SUITORS.   415

who established weights and measures throughout the Peloponnese,⁴ and was the most insolent of all the Grecians—the same who drove out the Elean directors of the games, and himself presided over the contests at Olympia⁵—Leocêdes,⁶ I say, appeared, this Pheidon's son; and likewise Amiantus, son of Lycurgus, an Arcadian of the city of Trapezus;⁷ Laphanes, an Azenian of Pæus,⁸ whose father, Euphorion, as the story goes in Arcadia, entertained the Dioscuri at his residence,⁹ and thenceforth kept

sound. Various emendations have been suggested; but all of them involve so much alteration, that I should incline, with Müller (Æginet. p. 60), to regard the passage as sound, and the historical error as due to Herodotus himself, who applied what he had heard of one Pheidon, king of Argos, to another, the father of Leocêdes. That Herodotus was not well acquainted with Peloponnesian history is plain from the strange confusions of Book i. ch. 65.

⁴ Pheidon appears to have established a uniform system of weights and measures throughout his dominions (Marm. Par. 46, [τὰ μέτρα ἃ] νενόμικεν. Eph. ap. Strab. viii. p. 519; Plin. H. N. vii. 56. p. 478; Isidor. Etym. xvi. 25, § 2). His system continued for some time, and was known as the Pheidonian (Eph. ap. Strab. μέτρα τὰ Φειδώνεια καλούμενα; Pollux, Onomast. x. 179, τῶν Φειδωνίων μέτρων; Schol. Pind. Ol. xiii. 27, τὰ Φειδώνεια ἀγγεῖα). He is likewise said to have been the first (i. e. the first Greek, supra, vol. i. pp. 564, 565) to coin silver and other money, which he did in Egina, a portion of his dominions (Eph. ap. Strab. l. s. c.; Etym. Mag. ad voc. ὀβελίσκοι). He was the greatest of the Argive kings (supra, i. 82, note ⁸), but is accused by Aristotle of having changed the previously existing monarchy into a tyranny (Pol. v. 8, p. 178, ed. Taucha.).

⁵ Pausanias (vi. xxii. § 2) and Ephorus (ap. Strab. l. s. c.) give the circumstances of this transaction. According to the former, the Piseans, who wished to have the presidency of the Olympic games instead of the Eleans, invited Pheidon to their assistance. With his help they drove away the Eleans, and together with him presided at the festival. This was the 8th Olympiad (B.C. 748); and on account of the circumstances of the celebration, the Eleans omitted this Olympiad from their register, as they did also, for similar reasons, the 34th and the 104th. The Eleans afterwards applied for assistance to Sparta; and Sparta, with their aid, conquered Pheidon, and reinstated the Eleans in the presidency of the games, giving them at the same time Pisatis and Triphylis.

⁶ Leocêdes is probably the same person who is called Lacêdes by Pausanias (ii. xix. § 2), and by Plutarch (ii. p. 89, E) Lacydes. This latter represents him as an effeminate and luxurious prince.

⁷ Trapezus was one of the Arcadian towns doomed to be swallowed up in Megalopolis (Pausan. viii. xxvii. § 3). Its inhabitants, however, refused to remove, and so incurred the anger of the other Arcadians. The greater number were slain, and the rest removed to Trapezus on the Euxine (now Trebizond), which looked upon the Arcadian Trapezus as its mother city (Pausan. ut supra, § 4). Other writers make the Pontic Trapezus a Sinopian settlement (Xen. Anab. iv. viii. § 22; Steph. Byz. ad voc.; Arrian. Peripl. Pont. Eux. p. 113). In the time of Pausanias Trapezus was in ruins (viii. xxix. § 1). It lay on the left bank of the Alpheus (Ῥοῦφια), on the road which led from Megalopolis to Gortys (Atsicolo. Col. Leake identifies it with an ancient site near Mavria (Morea, vol. ii. pp. 27 and 293). Concerning the mythic origin of the name of Trapezus, cf. Apollod. iii. viii. 1, § 6.

⁸ Arcadia was divided into three regions, of which Azania was one (Pausan. viii. iv. § 2; Steph. Byz. ad voc. Ἀζανία). It seems to have been the northernmost portion (see Müller's Dorians, vol. ii. pp. 433, 434, E. T.). Pæus is not mentioned by any other writer, unless it be identical with the Paüs of Pausanias (viii. xxiii. § 9), which was in his time a ruined town to the north of the Ladon, in the district of Cleitor. (For the site of Paüs, see Leake, ii. p. 249, and Curtius, i. p. 380.)

⁹ Compare with this story the tale related by Pausanias of a certain Phormio, a Spartan, who, refusing the Dios-

open house for all comers; and lastly, Onomastus, the son of Agæus, a native of Elis. These four came from the Peloponnese. From Athens there arrived Megacles, the son of that Alcmæon who visited Crœsus, and Tisander's son, Hippoclides,[2] the wealthiest and handsomest of the Athenians. There was likewise one Euboean, Lysanias, who came from Eretria, then a flourishing city. From Thessaly came Diactorides, a Cranonian,[4] of the race of the Scopadæ;[3] and Alcon arrived from the Molossians. This was the list of the suitors.

128. Now when they were all come, and the day appointed had arrived, Clisthenes first of all inquired of each concerning his country and his family; after which he kept them with him a year, and made trial of their manly bearing, their temper, their accomplishments, and their disposition, sometimes drawing them apart for converse, sometimes bringing them all together. Such as were still youths he took with him from time to time to the gymnasia; but the greatest trial of all was at the banquet-table. During the whole period of their stay he lived with them as I have said; and, further, from first to last he entertained them sumptuously. Somehow or other the suitors who came from Athens pleased him the best of all; and of these Hippoclides, Tisander's son, was specially in favour, partly on account of his manly bearing, and partly also because his ancestors were of kin to the Corinthian Cypselids.[6]

129. When at length the day arrived which had been fixed for the espousals, and Clisthenes had to speak out and declare his choice, he first of all made a sacrifice of a hundred oxen, and held

a banquet, whereat he entertained all the suitors and the whole people of Sicyon. After the feast was ended, the suitors vied with each other in music and in speaking on a given subject. Presently, as the drinking advanced, Hippoclides, who quite dumbfoundered the rest, called aloud to the flute-player, and bade him strike up a dance; which the man did, and Hippoclides danced to it. And he fancied that he was dancing excellently well; but Clisthenes, who was observing him, began to misdoubt the whole business. Then Hippoclides, after a pause, told an attendant to bring in a table; and when it was brought, he mounted upon it and danced first of all some Laconian figures, then some Attic ones; after which he stood on his head upon the table, and began to toss his legs about. Clisthenes, notwithstanding that he now loathed Hippoclides for a son-in-law, by reason of his dancing and his shamelessness, still, as he wished to avoid an outbreak, had restrained himself during the first and likewise during the second dance; when, however, he saw him tossing his legs in the air, he could no longer contain himself, but cried out, "Son of Tisander, thou hast danced thy wife away!" "What does Hippoclides care?" was the other's answer. And hence the proverb arose.'

130. Then Clisthenes commanded silence, and spake thus before the assembled company:—

"Suitors of my daughter, well pleased am I with you all; and right willingly, if it were possible, would I content you all, and not by making choice of one appear to put a slight upon the rest. But as it is out of my power, seeing that I have but one daughter, to grant to all their wishes, I will present to each of you whom I must needs dismiss a talent of silver, for the honour that you have done me in seeking to ally yourselves with my house, and for your long absence from your homes. But my daughter, Agarista, I betroth to Megacles, the son of Alcmæon, to be his wife, according to the usage and wont of Athens."

Then Megacles expressed his readiness; and Clisthenes had the marriage solemnized.

131. Thus ended the affair of the suitors; and thus the Alcmæonidæ came to be famous throughout the whole of Greece. The issue of this marriage was the Clisthenes—so named after

---

' It is used as a proverb by Lucian in more places than one (Apol. pro merc. cond. ill. p. 285, and Philopatr. ix. p. 367), and noticed by Diogenianus (vii. 21), Zenobius (v. 31), and Suidas (ad voc. οὐ φροντὶς Ἱπποκλείδῃ, p. 2758, ed. Gaisford).

his grandfather the Sicyonian—who made the tribes at Athens, and set up the popular government.* Megacles had likewise another son, called Hippocrates, whose children were a Megacles and an Agarista, the latter named after Agarista the daughter of Clisthenes. She married Xanthippus, the son of Ariphron; and when she was with child by him had a dream, wherein she fancied that she was delivered of a lion; after which, within a few days, she bore Xanthippus a son, to wit, Pericles.*

132. After the blow struck at Marathon, Miltiades, who was previously held in high esteem by his countrymen, increased yet more in influence. Hence, when he told them that he wanted a fleet of seventy ships,[1] with an armed force, and money, without informing them what country he was going to attack, but only promising to enrich them if they would accompany him, seeing that it was a right wealthy land, where they might easily get as much gold as they cared to have [2]—when he told them this, they were quite carried away, and gave him the whole armament which he required.

133. So Miltiades, having got the armament, sailed against Paros, with the object, as he alleged, of punishing the Parians for having gone to war with Athens, inasmuch as a trireme of theirs had come with the Persian fleet to Marathon. This, however, was a mere pretence; the truth was, that Miltiades owed the Parians a grudge, because Lysagoras, the son of Tisias, who

---

* Supra, v. 69.
* The family tree of the Alcmaeonids, so far as it is known, may be thus exhibited:—

[family tree diagram]

[1] Seventy ships appear to have been the full complement of the Athenian navy, until the time when the number was raised by Themistocles to 200 (vide supra, ch. 89, and infra, vii. 144). Miltiades therefore took the whole Athenian navy on this expedition.

[2] Ephorus said that Paros was at this time the most prosperous and most powerful (εὐδαιμονεστάτη καὶ μεγίστη) of the Cyclades (Fr. 107). According to him Miltiades attacked several of the other islands besides Paros.

CHAP. 131-135. FAILURE OF THE PARIAN EXPEDITION. 419

was a Parian by birth, had told tales against him to Hydarnes the Persian.³ Arrived before the place against which his expedition was designed, he drove the Parians within their walls, and forthwith laid siege to the city. At the same time he sent a herald to the inhabitants, and required of them a hundred talents, threatening that, if they refused, he would press the siege, and never give it over till the town was taken. But the Parians, without giving his demand a thought, proceeded to use every means that they could devise for the defence of their city, and even invented new plans for the purpose, one of which was, by working at night to raise such parts of the wall as were likely to be carried by assault to double their former height.

134. Thus far all the Greeks agree in their accounts of this business; what follows is related upon the testimony of the Parians only. Miltiades had come to his wit's end, when one of the prisoners, a woman named Timo, who was by birth a Parian, and had held the office of under-priestess in the temple of the infernal goddesses, came and conferred with him. This woman, they say, being introduced into the presence of Miltiades, advised him, if he set great store by the capture of the place, to do something which she could suggest to him. When therefore she had told him what it was she meant, he betook himself to the hill which lies in front of the city, and there leapt the fence enclosing the precinct of Ceres Thesmophorus,⁴ since he was not able to open the door. After leaping into the place he went straight to the sanctuary, intending to do something within it—either to remove some of the holy things which it was not lawful to stir, or to perform some act or other, I cannot say what—and had just reached the door, when suddenly a feeling of horror came upon him,⁵ and he returned back the way he had come; but in jumping down from the outer wall, he strained his thigh, or, as some say, struck the ground with his knee.

135. So Miltiades returned home sick, without bringing the Athenians any money, and without conquering Paros, having done no more than to besiege the town for six and twenty days,

---

³ The Hydarnes meant is probably the conspirator (supra, iii. 70); as no other has yet been mentioned. Early in the reign of Xerxes he was in command of the whole Asiatic coast (infra, vii. 135); but at what time or in what way he came into contact with Miltiades is uncertain.

According to Strabo, a descendant of Hydarnes, by name Orontes, was on the throne of Armenia at the time of the defeat of Antiochus the Great by the Romans, B.C. 190 (xi. p. 771).

⁴ Supra, ch. 16.

⁵ He would feel that he was doing an act of great impiety, since the sanctuaries of Ceres were not to be entered by men.

2 E 2

and ravage the remainder of the island. The Parians, however, when it came to their knowledge that Timo, the under-priestess of the goddesses, had advised Miltiades what he should do, were minded to punish her for her crime; they therefore sent messengers to Delphi, as soon as the siege was at an end, and asked the god if they should put the under-priestess to death. "She had discovered," they said, "to the enemies of her country how they might bring it into subjection, and had exhibited to Miltiades mysteries which it was not lawful for a man to know." But the Pythoness forbade them, and said, "Timo was not in fault; 'twas decreed that Miltiades should come to an unhappy end; and she was sent to lure him to his destruction." Such was the answer given to the Parians by the Pythoness.

136. The Athenians, upon the return of Miltiades from Paros, had much debate concerning him; and Xanthippus, the son of Ariphron, who spoke more freely against him than all the rest, impleaded him before the people, and brought him to trial for his life, on the charge of having dealt deceitfully with the Athenians. Miltiades, though he was present in court, did not speak in his own defence; for his thigh had begun to mortify, and disabled him from pleading his cause. He was forced to lie on a conch while his defence was made by his friends, who dwelt at most length on the fight at Marathon, while they made mention also of the capture of Lemnos, telling how Miltiades took the island, and, after executing vengeance on the Pelasgians, gave up his conquest to Athena. The judgment of the people was in his favour so far as to spare his life; but for the wrong he had done them they fined him fifty talents. Soon afterwards his thigh

completely gangrened and mortified: and so Miltiades died;[*] and the fifty talents were paid by his son Cimon.[1]

137. Now the way in which Miltiades had made himself master of Lemnos was the following. There were certain Pelasgians whom the Athenians once drove out of Attica;[2] whether they did it justly or unjustly I cannot say, since I only know what is reported concerning it, which is the following: Hecatæus, the son of Hegesander, says in his History that it was unjustly. "The Athenians," according to him, "had given to the Pelasgi a tract of land at the foot of Hymettus[3] as payment for the wall with

---

We are told by Cornelius Nepos (Miltiad. c. 7), that it was fixed on, because it represented the cost of the expedition. Mr. Grote shows that, according to the usual process of law in the Athenian courts, it must have been the amount assessed by the friends of Miltiades as the penalty which he was content to pay. The first sentence must have gone against him; and then, on the question as to the amount of punishment, which always followed, Xanthippus must have proposed death, and the prisoner himself or his friends a fine of fifty talents. They may have been induced to fix this amount by its being what would clear the state from any pecuniary loss arising out of the misconduct of their client (Hist. of Greece, iv. pp. 492-494).

[*] Later writers (Corn. Nep. l. s. v.; Diod. Sic. x. p. 67; Plut. Cim. c. 4) related that Miltiades was cast into prison till he should pay the fine, and died there. But this was contrary to the usual course of Athenian justice, which allowed a fair time for the payment of all fines, and admitted of security being given for them (Hermann's Pol. Ant. § 143). The silence of Herodotus as to any imprisonment will outweigh in most minds the evidence of such writers as those referred to.

[1] The imprisonment of Cimon is another, more glaring, fiction of the anecdote-mongers. Cimon could neither by Athenian law be liable to imprisonment for his father's debts, as Cornelius Nepos supposes (Cimon, c. 1), nor would he have had any occasion to put himself in prison in order to obtain his father's body for burial, as Diodorus relates. Athenian law knew nothing of the arrest of the debtor's corpse. Even Plutarch discards these fictions. They grew probably out of the fact that Cimon remained destitute of civil rights (ἄτιμος) until the debt was discharged (Hermann, § 124).

[2] Supra, iv. 145, v. 26. (Compare Philochor. Fr. 5, ed. Didot; Pausan. I. xxviii. § 3; and see Appendix, Essay II. "On the Traditions respecting the Pelasgians.")

[3] The Pelasgic builders seem to have had two tracts of land given to them. One, which bore to a late date the title of Pelasgicum (τὸ Πελασγικόν), was situated at the foot of the acropolis, probably at its north-western angle (Thucyd. ii. 17; Lucian. Pisc. c. 47; Bis Accus. c. 9; and compare the remarks of Leake, Attica, § 8, pp. 318-315). This was most likely their abode while they were employed in building the wall. Afterwards the Athenians removed them to a greater distance from the town, giving them a portion of the plain on the left bank of the Ilissus, to the south-east of the city.

With respect to the Pelasgic wall itself, I have already mentioned (supra, v. 64) that it was built round the platform which forms the summit of the acropolis. It skirted the edge of the precipice, and consisted of a single line of wall on every side except the west, where the ascent though steep is not very difficult. Here it seems to have been more complicated. Nine gates are spoken of (Clitodem. Fr. 27), which must all have been at this end, and which seem to indicate nine successive barriers. The greater part of this fortification was thrown down by the Persians (infra, viii. 53; ix. 13), but perhaps some portions remained, as the Pelasgic work was of the most durable character. Certainly the wall at the summit of the acropolis continued to be called "the Pelasgic wall" centuries afterwards (cf. Aristoph. Av. 797, ed. Bothe, Schol. ad loc.; Callimach. Fragm. 287, &c.). Col.

which the Pelasgians had surrounded their citadel. This land was barren, and little worth at the time; but the Pelasgians brought it into good condition; whereupon the Athenians begrudged them the tract, and desired to recover it. And so, without any better excuse, they took arms and drove out the Pelasgians." But the Athenians maintain that they were justified in what they did. "The Pelasgians," they say, "while they lived at the foot of Hymettus, were wont to sally forth from that region and commit outrages on their children. For the Athenians used at that time to send their sons and daughters to draw water at the fountain called 'the Nine Springs,'[1] inasmuch as neither they nor the other Greeks had any household slaves in those days; and the maidens, whenever they came, were used rudely and insolently by the Pelasgians. Nor were they even content thus; but at the last they laid a plot, and were caught by the Athenians in the act of making an attempt upon their city. Then did the Athenians give a proof how much better men they were than the Pelasgians; for whereas they might justly have killed them all, having caught them in the very act of rebelling, they spared their lives, and only required that they should leave the country. Hereupon the Pelasgians quitted Attica, and settled in Lemnos and other places." Such are the accounts respectively of Hecatæus and the Athenians.

138. These same Pelasgians, after they were settled in Lemnos, conceived the wish to be revenged on the Athenians. So, as they were well acquainted with the Athenian festivals, they manned some pentecontors, and having laid an ambush to catch

---

Leake thinks that some remains of Pelasgic work may still be traced at the north-west angle of the acropolis (Athens, p. 313).

[1] The fountain of Enneacrunos, or "the nine springs," has been thought (Wheler's Travels, p. 383) to be the source which rises in front of the Propylæa on the western side of the acropolis, and joins the stream that issues from the grotto of Pan (supra, ch. 105), because Pausanias mentions it in connexion with the Ceramicus (t. iii. § 1, and xiv. §§ 1 and 5). But it is plain, both from this passage, from Thucydides (li. 15), and from other writers, that it lay exactly on the opposite side, in the direction of Hymettus, or nearly due east of the citadel. Thucydides tells us that it was near the temple of Jupiter Olympius, the ruins of which are so remarkable a feature in this quarter; and his statement is confirmed by Tarantinus (ap. Hierocl. Hippiatr. Præf. p. 4), and by the author of the Etymologicum Magnum, who places Enneacrunus near the Ilissus (ad voc.). Modern travellers have discovered a remarkable confirmation of this position. Enneacrunus, before the Pisistratidæ fitted it up with the nine pipes from which it derived its name, was called Callirrhoë (Thucyd. l. a. c.; Philosteph. Fr. 27), and Καλλιρρόη is still the name of a spring of excellent water in the bed of the Ilissus, as well as the name of the river itself (cf. Leake's Athens, pp. 172-178).

This portraiture of the simple customs of primeval times will not fail to recall the picture of Rebekah at the well of Padan-aram (Gen. xxiv. 13).

the Athenian women as they kept the festival of Diana at Brauron,[*] they succeeded in carrying off a large number, whom they took to Lemnos and there kept as concubines. After a while the women bore children, whom they taught to speak the language of Attica and observe the manners of the Athenians. These boys refused to have any commerce with the sons of the Pelasgian women; and if a Pelasgian boy struck one of their number, they all made common cause, and joined in avenging their comrade; nay, the Greek boys even set up a claim to exercise lordship over the others, and succeeded in gaining the upper hand. When these things came to the ears of the Pelasgians, they took counsel together, and, on considering the matter, they grew frightened, and said one to another, "If these boys even now are resolved to make common cause against the sons of our lawful wives, and seek to exercise lordship over them, what may we expect when they grow up to be men?" Then it seemed good to the Pelasgians to kill all the sons of the Attic women; which they did accordingly, and at the same time slew likewise their mothers. From this deed, and that former crime of the Lemnian women, when they slew their husbands in the days of Thoas,[*] it has come to be usual throughout Greece to call wicked actions by the name of 'Lemnian deeds.'"[7]

139. When the Pelasgians had thus slain their children and their women, the earth refused to bring forth its fruits for them, and their wives bore fewer children, and their flocks and herds increased more slowly than before, till at last, sore pressed by famine and bereavement, they sent men to Delphi, and begged the god to tell them how they might obtain deliverance from their sufferings. The Pythoness answered, that "they must give the Athenians whatever satisfaction they might demand." Then the Pelasgians went to Athens and declared their wish to give the Athenians satisfaction for the wrong which they had done to them. So the Athenians had a couch prepared in their townhall, and adorned it with the fairest coverlets, and set by its side a table laden with all manner of good things, and then told the Pelasgians they must deliver up their country to them in a similar condition. The Pelasgians answered and said, "When a ship comes with a north wind from your country to ours in a single day, then will we give it up to you." This they said because they knew that what they required was impossible, for Attica lies a long way to the south of Lemnos.[8]

140. No more passed at that time. But very many years afterwards, when the Hellespontian Chersonese had been brought under the power of Athens, Miltiades, the son of Cimon, sailed, during the prevalence of the Etesian winds, from Elæus[9] in the Chersonese to Lemnos, and called on the Pelasgians to quit their island, reminding them of the prophecy which they had supposed it impossible to fulfil. The people of Hephæstia obeyed the call;[1]

---

[7] Æschylus had observed before Herodotus, ἐπαινεῖν δέ τις τὰ δεινὰ ὧδ' Λημνίοις πήμασιν (Choeph. 622).

[8] Lemnos is two degrees (nearly 140 miles) north of Attica. An Athenian trireme might possibly have performed this distance in a long summer's day, if the condition "with a north wind" had not been added. The rate of motion in a trireme seems to have about equalled that of our ordinary steamers. (See Smith's Dictionary of Antiquities, p. 785, B. 2nd ed.)

[9] Elæus was situated at or near the extremity of the peninsula, as is plain from the notices in Scylax (Peripl. p. 68), Pliny (H. N. iv. 11, p. 209), and Mela (ii. 2). According to Scymnus Chius (l. 706) it was a colony from Teos. The site was near to that of the first European castle (Kilid Bahr), a little to the north-east. Some ruins remain; but they are not extensive (Chandler, vol. i. p. 18).

[1] By a felicitous emendation of a passage quoted by Stephen of Byzantium from the Chronica of Charax, we are enabled to fill up this history. It appears that Myrina was reduced first; and that then Hermon, the king of Hephæstia, fearing a similar fate, declared "that he acknowledged the Pelasgic promises, and gave himself up out of good-will to the Athenians." (Fr. 30.) Other writers tell us that a proverb arose from this circumstance. To

but they of Myrina,² not acknowledging the Chersonese to be any part of Attica, refused and were besieged and brought over by force. Thus was Lemnos gained by the Athenians and Miltiades.

"make a virtue of necessity," and give as a favour what you could not keep, was called Ἑρμόνιος or Ἑρμόνιος χάρις. (See Zenob. Cent. III. 86; Suidas ad voc. Ἑρμῶν. χάρ.) Mr. Blakesley's translation of the passage of Charax cannot possibly be received.

² Lemnos had but two cities of any note, Hephæstia and Myrina (Hecat. Fr. 102; Plin. H. N. iv. 12, p. 219; Ptolem. Geograph. iii. 13, p. 85; Etym. Magn. ad voc. Μυρίνα). Of these, Myrina was on the coast, Hephæstia inland (Ptol.). The former lay on the western, the latter towards the eastern side of the island (ibid.). It was said that Mount Athos at the solstice cast its shadow into the forum of Myrina (Plin. l. s. c.; Apoll. Rhod. l. 601-604). The site is probably marked by the modern Kastro, which is now the chief town in the island.

APPENDIX TO BOOK VI.

ESSAY I.

ON THE CIRCUMSTANCES OF THE BATTLE OF MARATHON.

1. Difficulties in the description of Herodotus. 2. Number of Persians engaged. 3. Numbers of the Greeks. 4. Proportion, five or six to one. 5. Landing of the army of Datis, and disposition of the troops. 6. Position occupied by the Greeks. 7. Motives inducing the Persians to delay the attack. 8. Causes of the original inaction of the Greeks, and of their subsequent change of tactics. 9. Miltiades' preparations for battle. 10. Description of the battle —re-embarkation of the invading army.

1. The description which Herodotus has given of the battle of Marathon is satisfactory to few moderns.[1] It is a bold and graphic sketch; but it is wanting in that accuracy of detail, and in those minute allusions to localities, which could alone have enabled the ordinary, or even the military, reader, to reproduce in imagination the struggle as it actually occurred. Herodotus omits to furnish any account of the numbers engaged on either side; he does not clearly mark the position of either army; he very imperfectly describes the disposition which the Greek general made of his troops, and takes no notice at all (unless incidentally) of the disposition made by the Persian leaders; above all, he is entirely silent on the subject of the Persian cavalry, neither telling us what part they took in the action, nor offering any explanation of their apparent absence from it. Again, he gives us no satisfactory account of the motives at work on either side; of the reasons determining both parties to delay so long, and Miltiades to strike when he did; nor even of the mode in which the two armies spent the interval. Further, besides these various omissions, there are certain inconsistencies in what he actually relates of the battle, which seem to show that his description is not even exact and correct so far as it goes, but requires, besides amplification, a certain degree of correction. Of this nature is the statement that the Persian centre "broke and pursued the Greeks into the inner country;"[2] to which there are two important objections—first, the smallness of the Greek loss, which is incompatible with such a rout of their troops; and

---

[1] Cf. Leake in his 'Demi of Attica' (Appendix, No. I.), and Mr. Blakesley in his edition of Herodotus (vol. ii. pp. 172-180) have written Essays upon the difficulties which beset the description of our author. Mr. Grote remarks on the deficiencies of his account (Hist. of Greece, vol. iv. p. 465, note).

[2] Herod. vi. 113. ἐδίωκον φεύγοντας ἐς τὴν μεσόγαιαν.

secondly, the subsequent account of the proceedings of the Greek wings. The existence of these and similar difficulties seems to constitute a call for some more sustained consideration of the battle and its circumstances than the exigencies of a running comment allow. It is therefore proposed to devote a few consecutive pages to the elucidation of this subject in the present Essay.

2. With regard to the number of troops engaged on the side of the Persians, the reader is referred to the long foot-note on ch. 117. The total strength of the expedition is there estimated at 210,000, a number which has in its favour the authority of a tolerable historian,[*] and the fact that it is the lowest estimate which has come down to us from any ancient writer. This number somewhat exceeds the calculation of Colonel Leake,[*] who supposes the cavalry to have been 7000 instead of 10,000,[*] and the crews of the horse-transports 20,000 instead of 40,000,[*] while he omits the Greek auxiliaries altogether. It is of course impossible to arrive at accuracy on a point where details are for the most part wanting, and where there is so much conflict of authority. Perhaps the whole that we have any right to conclude from our materials is, that the fleet conveyed to the shores of Attica *about* 200,000 men — but whether some thousands more or some thousands fewer we cannot say.

The next point to be considered is, how many of the 200,000 took part in the battle? Col. Leake proposes a deduction of nearly one-fourth of the "nominal strength" on account of "want of complement at the outset, desertion, sickness, accidents to ships, disabled horses, and garrisons at places on the way."[*] But Herodotus appears to regard the armament as increased rather than diminished on its way from Asia. No garrisons are said to have been left in the islands, while troops were taken from each,[*] probably at least enough to balance the losses from other causes. It is however far from probable that the whole 200,000 were engaged in the battle. Herodotus relates that Hippias "anchored the fleet off Marathon" at the time of the disembarkation;[*] and the circumstances of the re-embarkation seem to show that the ships were kept riding on their anchors, and ready for sea to the last. This would have involved the detention in the fleet of at least one-half of the crews,

---

[3] Cornelius Nepos (see his Miltiades, c. 5).

[4] Demi of Attica, Appendix I., p. 229. Col. Leake's numbers are as follows:—

Regular infantry, 50 in each of the 600 triremes	30,000
Cavalry (men mounted, with 3700 attendants)	1,800
Rowers of men-of-war, who were short of their complement	90,000
Boatmen of the triremes (30 to each)	20,000
Boatmen of the cavalry transports (estimated at 300)	30,000
	177,000

[5] This reduction is purely conjectural. I have not thought myself at liberty to depart from the statement of Nepos.

[*] Col. Leake's numbers here do not accord very well with one another. The crew of a horse-transport must be reckoned at 66 men and ½ (¼) for 300 transports to give 20,000 seamen; and the horse-conveying power of a transport must be reckoned at 11 horses and ⅔ (⅓) for 3500 horses to need 300 transports. I suppose 10,000 horses, 25 in a transport; therefore 400 transports and 100 men to each.

[7] Demi of Attica, p. 221.

[8] Herod. vi. 99.

[9] Ibid. ch. 107. This was a precautionary measure, in case a rapid re-embarkation should be necessary. The common practice was to draw up the vessels on the beach.

may 80,000 men, whereby the men landed would be reduced to 120,000. It is further doubtful (as has been already noticed more than once) whether the cavalry were present in the battle: if they were absent, the actual combatants would not have exceeded 110,000, of whom scarcely more than 30,000 could have been heavy-armed.[10]

3. On the side of the Greeks the number engaged was probably about 20,000. The earliest estimates of their force that we find are those of two Latin writers of the Augustan age, Trogus Pompeius and Cornelius Nepos. The former (whose work was epitomised by Justin) spoke of the Athenians as 10,000, and the Plataeans as 1000;[11] the latter agreed as to the Plataeans, but reduced the number of the Athenians to 9000.[12] This latter view is confirmed by Pausanias[13] and Plutarch,[14] and may therefore be regarded as that which possesses far the greatest weight of authority. It cannot, however, be accepted without one important correction. The light-armed must have been omitted from the calculation. This is distinctly evident in the case of the Plataeans, and highly probable in that of the Athenians. The former, who came "in full force" (πανδημεί) to Marathon,[15] cannot have furnished only 1000 men, since at Plataea, after their losses in the war and the destruction of their city by Xerxes,[16] they were able to furnish 1200.[17] The latter can scarcely be supposed to have sent to Marathon, when their very existence was at stake, no more than 9000 men, seeing that to the general rendezvous at Plataea they could send 16,000,[18] while they had at the same time a large fleet on the coast of Asia,[19] which must have absorbed 10,000 or 15,000 more. It is evident from the enrolment of slaves before Marathon—for the first time according to Pausanias[20]—that every effort was made, and as large an army levied as possible. The conjecture, therefore,[1] that the heavy-armed alone are reckoned in the estimates of Trogus and Nepos, is thoroughly entitled to acceptance; and we must add to the numbers reported by them a further estimate for the light-armed on the Greek side. Now the rule observed at this period with regard to the proportion of light to heavy-armed in a Greek army was, that the two should be equal in number;[2] and there is no reason to suppose that there was any departure from the rule on this occasion. We thus obtain

---

[10] The triremes in the fleet of Xerxes carried only 30 men-at-arms each (infra, vii. 184). If this was the complement in the fleet of Datis his heavy-armed would have been but 18,000. As, however, the fleet of Datis was specially intended for the conveyance of troops, whereas that of Xerxes merely accompanied his army, it must be supposed that the number of soldiers on board each trireme was greater. We find the Chians with 40 soldiers on board their vessels at the battle of Lade (supra, ch. 15), and the Greeks in the Peloponnesian war have sometimes as many as 50 (Thucyd. i. 61; iv. 129). We may suppose that Datis would embark at least this number. (See Leake's Demi, pp. 218, 219, where this point is well argued.)

[11] Justin, ii. 9.
[12] Corn. Nep. Vit. Milt. c. 5.
[13] Pausan. x. 12. § 2.
[14] Plut. Parall. ii. p. 305.
[15] Herod. vi. 109. [16] Ibid. viii. 50.
[17] Ibid. ix. 28, 29. Six hundred light-armed and six hundred heavy-armed.
[18] Ibid. Eight thousand of each description.
[19] Ibid. chs. 90 et seqq.
[20] Pausan. x. xxii. § 3.

[1] See Col. Leake's Essay (Demi of Attica, p. 232), and Thirlwall's Hist. of Greece, vol. ii. p. 242.
[2] Cf. Herod. ix. 29.

18,000 for the probable number of the Athenian and 2000 for that of the Plataean contingent; or 20,000 for the whole number engaged.

4. A comparison of the results now obtained will show that the disproportion between the two armies was far less than has generally been imagined. The Persian combatants were to the Greek as five to one, or possibly as six to one. This was about the proportion between the combatants at Plataea;⁴ and victories have often been gained against equal or greater odds, both in ancient and modern times.⁵ It is enough to mention the battle of Morgarten, which has been called "the Swiss Marathon," where 1600 mountaineers of Schwytz, Uri, and Unterwald, utterly defeated and overthrew an army of 20,000 Austrians."

5. The Persians, we are told, selected the plain of Marathon, or rather Hippias, their guide, selected it for them, on account of its fitness for the movements of cavalry.⁷ Col. Leake has remarked that the appearance of the plain is somewhat deceptive in this respect.⁸ With an average depth of two miles between the shore and the foot of the hills, it has an *apparent* width of about six miles between the ranges of *Dhrakonéra* and *Argaliki*; but the marshes at either extremity of the plain practically contract it as a battle-field, and leave in one place a width of only two miles, or two miles and a half, suitable for military evolutions or for encampment. The Persians probably landed upon the entire range of low coast, the length of which is above six miles,⁹ and anchored their ships off the shore in a single line,¹ extending to at least this distance. Their landing was unmolested; and they would easily place on shore, in the course of a few hours, the whole army with which they meant to engage, both horse² and foot. Advancing inland, they discovered

the existence of the two marshes, which obliged them to contract their front, but they would still have found, after passing the narrowest point, a space of nearly three miles in width, perfectly fit for a camping-ground, between the small marsh (θ on the plan) and the great marsh (δ on ditto), or between the former and the foot of Mount Korâki. Their front being thus placed at an average distance of about three quarters of a mile from the sea, sufficient room was obtained for the tents and pickets of 100,000 or 120,000 men. The heavy-armed, 30,000 in number, were probably arranged nearest the enemy, and must have been drawn up about four deep at the time of the engagement.[1] The Persians and Sacæ occupied the centre of the line, which is the usual post of honour in oriental armies—the less warlike auxiliaries were disposed to the right and to the left. The light-armed were undoubtedly arranged according to the usual Persian practice, behind the heavy-armed, and shot their arrows over their heads.[2] With regard to the cavalry, it was probably designed to be disposed upon the wings,[3] and here it may have had its station originally; but the silence of Herodotus as to any part which it took in the battle, together with the explanation offered by Suidas of the Athenian proverb χωρὶς ἱππεῖς, seems to show that when the engagement took place it was away from the field, either procuring forage or employed on some special service. Col. Leake supposes that, as the Persians were cramped for room, the cavalry was sent away at the first to "some neighbouring plain," where it had orders to remain "motionless in its cantonments."[4] But it is perhaps more probable that the absence was temporary and (so to speak) accidental. For the Persians to have sent away *permanently* that arm to which they mainly trusted for success, and on account of which they had chosen Marathon for their landing-place, would have been absolute madness. But if forage failed—and in the course of seven or eight days the requirements of 10,000 horse may easily have exhausted the crops standing in the Marathonian plain on the arrival of the expedition—it might be necessary to send them temporarily into neighbouring plains or valleys to supply themselves. The long inaction of the Greeks would have seemed to make the risk less, as it might have appeared to Datis that the enemy was determined to remain wholly on the defensive.

---

first, and that the intention was to send for them when the Athenians evacuated their position, and left the road open which led into the plain of Athens. But Marathon had been selected as the point of debarkation precisely because it was thought that the horse could act with peculiar effect there; and even if originally there had been a hesitation about landing them, yet, when the Persians were for above a week in full possession of the whole line of coast, the difficulty must have vanished, and the horse would have been sent for. My own belief is, that they were brought with the other troops and disembarked at once.

[1] By the nature of the ground it is evident that the Persian front had an extension of nearly three miles. Allowing two feet to a man, it would require a line of 7920 men to fill this space. Thirty thousand might then, by a very slight expansion of the ranks, have been ranged in the space four deep. According to Xenophon this was the regular depth of the Persian phalanx (Cyrop. VI. iii. § 24).

[2] Aristophanes notices the dense flights of the Persian arrows on this occasion (Vesp. 1049; ὑπὸ ἦ τῶν ταξιάρχων οἱκ ἆν ἴκοις τῶν ὀλομάρδων). Xenophon (l. s. c.) shows their position in the rear of the heavy-armed.

[3] As at Arbela (Arrian, Exp. Alex. iii. 11) and elsewhere.

[4] Demi of Attica, pp. 215, 216.

6. The Greeks on their part seem to have been originally drawn up at the entrance of the valley of *Vraná*, which is with good reason believed to represent the ancient Marathon. They here blocked up the direct road to Athens, which lay through the pass of *Stamáta* into the valley of the Cephissus, while at the same time they were in a position to defend the two other routes by which the capital might have been threatened. The Persians might have marched up the valley of the *Marathóna*,[?] through the modern village of that name and Œnoë (*Inói*), but the Greeks could then have met them at *Stamáta*, if they attempted to pass between that place and *Inói*, or at Decoleia, if they tried to reach Athens by way of the great northern road which connected the capital with Oropus. Or again, the Persians might have defiled to the left, and have proceeded to pass over the low spur from Mount Brilessus (*Argaliki*) which shuts in the Marathonian plain on the south, along the road which led to Athens by Pallêné and the valley of the Ilissus;[?] but in that case they would have laid open their flank—and not only so, but their *right* flank, which the shield did not cover—to an attack from the Greeks,[?] and would have risked the separation of their force into two bodies. At *Vraná* alone—in the central valley of the three—could a watch be kept upon all three routes: and here therefore the Greeks posted themselves. The position was one of great strength. The valley of *Vraná* is at its entrance less than a mile in width; so that, allowing two feet to a man, the Greek army might have been drawn up entirely across it, maintaining throughout a uniform depth of eight.[?] The right would rest upon the hill of *Argaliki*, which is lofty and covered with pines;[?] the left upon Mount *Kotróni*, which is barren and less elevated, but peculiarly rugged and difficult of access.[?] The Greeks were thus protected from what they principally feared—the attacks of cavalry upon their flanks; and they may even have taken steps to diminish the danger of such attacks in front, by felling trees and strewing them over the entrance of the valley.[?]

7. The Greek commanders, no doubt, expected to be at once attacked in their position, which they were prepared to defend as the Peloponnesians afterwards defended Thermopylæ. But the tactics of the Persians at this time were different. They had succeeded in reducing Eretria by internal treachery with little loss to themselves,[?] and were resolved to play the same game in Attica. They had probably no fear of the result of a battle, but felt they would please their master better if they accomplished the objects of the expedition without the effusion of blood. We may also give Hippias credit for a real wish to avoid the slaughter of his country-

men, like that which actuated Pisistratus nearly fifty years previously.⁶ Accordingly, negotiations were set on foot with the partisans of the exiled family at Athens, and perhaps in other parts of Attica,⁷ from which great things were expected: and in the mean time hostilities were suspended, and no attempt made even to molest the army in its position. Col. Leake has expressed surprise that, during the period which intervened between the landing of the Persians and the battle, they did not "spread on every side, occupy all the hills around the plain, and annoy the Greeks by attacks, especially from their archers, upon the flanks and rear."⁸ This would no doubt have been the conduct of an enemy anxious to push matters to extremities; but if the Persian commanders hoped to obtain the submission of Athens itself without a battle, it would have been natural for them to avoid movements the effect of which might probably have been to bring on a general engagement. They therefore remained within their lines, waiting to hear, either that Athens was ready to make submission, or at least that a civil war was begun there, which could not but have soon extended to the camp, and would then have broken up the Greek army.⁹

8. The delay on the part of the Greeks scarcely needs to be accounted for. Being in their own country, strongly posted, with abundant supplies at hand, excellently placed for the defence of their capital, and looking for the arrival within a short time¹ of important reinforcements, they had every strategic reason to remain quiet, at least until the Spartans should come to their assistance. Delay was sure to injure the Persians in many ways. They would suffer from their close packing, from the vicinity of the marshes, even from mere change of climate. Their stock of provisions moreover could not but have been in time exhausted, in which case they would have had to re-embark without striking a blow, or to have undertaken the perilous task of assaulting the Greek position. The most remarkable circumstance in the whole struggle is, that the Greeks should have assumed the offensive, especially at the time they did, when the arrival of the Spartans might almost hourly be expected. Two causes seem to have combined to produce the sudden change in the Greek tactics. The first is that mentioned by Herodotus⁸—the danger of an explosion at home. Miltiades was as well aware as Datis or Hippias that public opinion at Athens was in an unsettled state—that there were still many in the town who "loved tyranny better than freedom."⁹ This circumstance made it highly desirable that a battle should be fought soon; and, if matters had actually come to a crisis at Athens, there would have been

---

Herod. I. 63.
⁷ See Blakesley's Excursus, p. 176.
⁸ Levsi. p. 215.
⁹ This view rests chiefly on Herod. vi. 109. It receives some support from the story of the shield (ibid. chs. 121-124), which cannot have been without a foundation.
¹ When the Athenians first took up their position at Marathon they would have expected aid from Sparta in about five days.

When, about the time at which they had looked for this succour to arrive, the news reached them that Sparta would not move till the full moon, they found that they would have to wait five or six days more. Only eleven days seem to have intervened between the march of the Athenians to Marathon and the actual arrival on the field of the 2000 Spartans.
⁸ Herod. vi. 109. ⁹ Ibid. I. 62.

nothing surprising in the fact of the Greeks attacking. But this does not appear to have been the case. At least we hear of nothing more than the general danger which was fully known to Miltiades ten days earlier.* The question therefore arises, why did Miltiades, after remaining on the defensive so long, suddenly change his tactics and make the assault? Why, especially, did he do so when he must have known that the Spartans were on their road, and would probably arrive within a day or two? The fact mentioned by Suidas, and negatively confirmed by Herodotus, of the casual absence of the Persian horse on the day of the battle, exactly answers this question, and removes the difficulty. If the Persians, finding that forage grew scarce, and was not to be had in the immediate neighbourhood, and at the same time despising their enemy's inaction, and believing that he would never venture on attacking them, sent their horse on this day to forage for themselves in the plain of Tricorythus, or the valleys which open out of it; and if this movement was observed by the Greeks or reported to them by the Ionians;¹ nothing is more natural than that Miltiades should promptly take advantage of the capital error of his antagonist, and march upon him before it could be rectified. His knowledge of the Persian warfare made him confident that in the absence of the cavalry he could lead his Greeks to an assured victory; and he may not have been sorry to obtain for his own state the whole honour, which a few days later must have been shared with Sparta.

9. Miltiades had probably long determined on the mode in which he would attack if he should be compelled to do so, or should find a fitting opportunity. As he must necessarily in that case advance into the plain, he had resolved, in order not to be outflanked, to extend his line till it equalled, or nearly equalled, that of the Persians: and as even this arrangement would not, under the great

---

* Mr. Blakesley supposes that the battle was fought on the *fifth* day after the arrival of the Athenians at Marathon (Excursus, p. 177). He corrects, very properly, Mr. Grote's mistake in assuming that the nine other generals all resigned their command to Miltiades, and points out (what is undoubtedly true) that Herodotus only speaks of such a surrender on the part of four out of the nine (cf. Herod. vi. 110). But he improperly concludes from this that the battle was fought "on the fifth day." Herodotus does not say so. He merely says negatively that Miltiades did not fight on any of the days conceded to him, but waited for his own turn. He does not say that the conceded days were consecutive, and it is very unlikely that it would just happen that the four generals who gave up their turns should have had the right of command on four following days. We cannot really gather from this part of the narrative of Herodotus on which day he considers the battle to have been fought. We can, however, do so from other parts of his narrative. Herodotus tells us that Phidippides was sent off to Sparta before the generals left the city—doubtless on the morning of the same day. He arrived at Sparta on the evening of the day following. That was the ninth of the current Spartan month, six days before the full moon, which fell on the 15th. The Spartans marched out on the day after the full moon—*i. e.* on the 16th; and they arrived at Athens late on the third day, which was the 18th. This, according to Plato (Leg. iii. p. 104, ed. Tauchn.), was the day after the battle, which was consequently fought on the 17th of the Spartan month, the tenth day after Phidippides started for Sparta and the Athenians marched to Marathon. Herodotus confirms the fact of the Spartans arriving at this time by making them proceed to Marathon, and there view the Persian dead, which would certainly not have been left unburied longer than necessary, and would probably have been all interred by the end of the second day after the battle.

¹ As Suidas says.

disparity of numbers, offer complete security, he had determined further to give his wings a strength which would oblige him seriously to weaken his centre. A great boldness and originality is traceable in this handling of the troops under him. Hitherto Greek tactics had been of the simplest kind: they fought in phalanx order, with a uniform depth throughout, rarely falling short of eight. Miltiades suddenly conceived the idea of venturing, against Persians, to bring his troops *into line*. If he maintained on the wings for any distance a depth (say) of four files, a considerable portion of his centre must have consisted of a *single line* of Hoplites.* Behind these he may have placed a second, and possibly a third line of light-armed; but these would be rather for appearance than for strength, and would have been no match for Persians and Sacæ.

10. Having made this disposition of his troops as rapidly as possible, but assuredly not without attracting the attention of the Persians, and placing them to some extent upon their guard,¹ Miltiades sacrificed, and then gave the signal for an advance. The two armies were posted nearly a mile apart, and this space the Greeks are said to have passed "at a run."* Their object seems to have been to give the Persians as brief space as possible for preparation, and (in part) to shorten the time of their own exposure to missile weapons. For the latter purpose it would have been enough to run the last 100 or 150 yards; but the former may have been regarded as of sufficient importance to make the exertion—not perhaps a very great one to trained Greeks—advisable. The direct effect of the charge is not stated. It has been supposed that the Athenians were themselves disordered by the rapid movement, and that the defeat of their centre was in consequence of it;* but this is contradicted by the words of Herodotus, who says that the Athenians fell on the barbarians "in close array" (ἀθρόοι).¹ A prolonged and desperate conflict seems to have followed.* The Greeks were successful on both wings, where their main strength had been placed; but their weakened centre, being opposed to the best troops of the enemy, was borne back, and suffered considerably. Herodotus says that it was "broken and pursued into the inner country;" but this

---

* It has been observed that the Persian front must have had an extension of nearly three miles (supra, § 5, note *), which would require, at two feet to the man, a front line of nearly 8000 men. If we allow the Greek, with his larger shield, his larger and heavier weapons, and his greater self-reliance, a space of three feet, still, for a length of three miles, a line of 5280 men is requisite. The Greek heavy-armed were but 10,000. Supposing then the wings, for the space even of 200 yards, to have had a depth of four files, it would follow that above one-fourth of the centre had but a single line of heavy-armed.

¹ Professor Creasy supposes that the charge took the Persians by surprise. He imagines that the cavalry were present, but had not time to prepare their horses and mount before the Greeks closed with the Persian line (Fifteen Decisive Battles, Marathon). Mr. Blakesley also regards the charge as a complete surprise, assuming that the Greeks had descended into the plain, and drawn out in line opposite the Persians, on every previous day (Excursus, p. 177).

* Herod. vi. 112. Perhaps the δρόμῳ ἀδρόοι of Aristophanes (Vesp. 1041) is an allusion to this feature of the engagement.

* See Mr. Grote's History of Greece, vol. iv. p. 470, note ¹.

¹ Herod. l. s. c. 'Αθηναῖοι δ᾽, ἐπεί τε ἀθρόοι προσέμιξαν τοῖσι βαρβάροισι, ἐμάχοντο ἀξίως λόγου.

* Herod. vi. 113. Compare Aristoph. Vesp. 1050. ἀλλ᾽ ὅμως ἀντισχομεσθα ἐν ὅροις ὑπὲρ λεκιψε.

seems an exaggeration, arising from that rhetorical spirit and love of effect which has been noticed as one of his peculiar weaknesses.[a] As the entire loss on the Greek side was but 192, and as these seem to have fallen principally in the combat at the ships,[b] it is impossible that there can have been anything like a rout or disorderly flight of their centre or main body. It is also evident that, if the pursuit had been extended into the inner country, the latter part of the battle would have had a very different character from that which is assigned to it. If the Persians had really routed the Greek centre and pursued it across the plain into one or both of the two valleys lying behind—which is what the expression of Herodotus strictly taken implies—the Greek wings, when they united, would have found themselves *in the rear* of the Persian centre, interposed between them and their ships, and the Persians in order to escape must have charged and broken through their line.[c] But Herodotus clearly has no idea of this kind. He means to represent the wings as thrown across the *front* of the Persians—first checking their pursuit, then forcing them to give way, finally putting them to flight and driving them headlong to their ships. But if this was the true character of the movement made by the wings and of its result, the Greek centre cannot have been pursued to any great distance. Probably it was in difficulties, had yielded ground, and was about to suffer defeat, when it was saved by the arrival to its aid of the victorious wings. Then the tide turned—the barbarians were forced to begin a retreat, which perhaps became little better than a flight before they reached their ships. It can scarcely, however, have been the entire rout which Herodotus represents.[d] Here again his love of effect and of lively description has carried him away. The whole loss of the Persians was 6400 men out of above 100,000, a number indicative of a tolerably orderly retreat, rather than of a rout and an indiscriminate slaughter. The loss would have been still smaller had it not been for a peculiarity in the ground, which was of great detriment to the Persians. The large marsh at the north-east end of the plain was interposed between the army and a considerable portion of the fleet, which lay off the whole length of that narrow strip of beach by which the marsh is separated from the sea. In their haste to reach this portion of the fleet, the Persians pressed each other into the marsh; and here it was that they suffered their chief losses.[e]

---

[a] See the Introductory Essay, ch. iii. pp. 82, 83.

[b] Herod. vi. 114. Col. Leake regards the main loss as suffered by the centre, and attributes to this the position of the *Soros*, or tomb of the Athenians (Demi, p. 212); but he does not see that the expression, *ἐν τούτῳ τῷ πόνῳ*, at the beginning of ch. 114, refers to the struggle at the ships. See his paraphrase, p. 205.

[c] Mr. Blakesley is the only commentator who perceives this (Excursus, p. 178); and he accepts the consequences, believing that the Persian centre was "caught in a trap," and had to "force its way through" the victorious wings. Herodotus could hardly have thought this and given us no inkling of it. Plutarch, it must be borne in mind, does not even make the Greek centre retreat; it only has some difficulty in defeating the enemy (Aristid. c. 3).

[d] Mr. Blakesley has some good remarks on this point (Excursus, l. a. c.).

[e] In the picture of the battle which adorned the Pœcilè, or Painted Portico, at Athens—which was executed in the time of Pericles—while in the main battle the Persians were represented as fighting on equal terms with the Greeks, in the distance they were depicted as suffering great loss in the

There can have been no great confusion in the re-embarkation, or the Greeks would certainly have taken or destroyed more than seven triremes out of 600. Probably the portion of the force which had been retained on board acted in part as light-armed at this conjuncture, and protected the re-embarkation by clouds of missiles.

One other point seems to require a few words. What eventually became of the Persian cavalry? Messengers are almost sure to have been sent to recall it as soon as the fight began; but it seems certain, by the entire description of the battle, that it did not arrive till the whole struggle was over. Probably, however, it made its appearance before nightfall, when it may have been suffered to re-embark quietly. The Greeks would not have been anxious for a second encounter, and would by that time have either entrenched themselves on the plain, or have returned to the Heracleium. The Persian fleet was doubtless still in the offing, and, on noticing the arrival of the horse, would at once send the horse-transports to shore. Thus I should suppose the horse to have been re-embarked before Datis sailed to Ægileia, and to have accompanied him in his fruitless demonstration against Athens.

---

march (Pausan. L. iv. § 4). Pausanias says it was the current belief that almost the entire loss of the Persians took place there (L. xxxii. § 6).

ESSAY II.

ON THE TRADITIONS RESPECTING THE PELASGIANS.

1. Original population of Greece and Italy, homogeneous. 2. Kindred races in Asia Minor and the islands. 3. Characteristics of this ethnic group. 4. Position of the Pelasgi in it. 5. Extent of country occupied by the Pelasgians. 6. Their general movement from east to west. 7. Etymology of their name. 8. Lines of passage. 9. Migrations of the Tyrrheno-Pelasgians. 10. Pelasgic walls. 11. Absorption of the Pelasgians in other races.

1. THAT the various tribes which are presented to us by history as the earliest inhabitants of the Hellenic and Italic peninsulas were for the most part ethnically connected, and constituted in reality a single race, has been maintained by most modern writers of repute,[1] and is daily receiving fresh support from the progress of linguistic discovery. It now appears[2] that not only was there an element in the early Italian population undistinguishable in ethnic type from the race which inhabited Epirus and the Peloponnese, but that the *Italic* nations themselves, the Oscans, Umbrians, Sabellians, &c., were (with one exception[3]) of the same ethnic stock. A single homogeneous people was spread, at the earliest period to which history carries us back, over the whole, or by far the greater part, of the two peninsulas, reaching from the shores of the Egean to the borders of Liguria.

2. Nor was the race confined within the limits here indicated. Sicily, the islands of the Egean, and the western coast of Asia Minor, were certainly in the possession of the same people; and it is even doubtful whether we ought not to class with them the Phrygians, the Carians,[4] and the Lydians.[5] Sufficient materials do not perhaps

---

[1] Müller, Dorians, vol. I. (pp. 1-19, E. T.); Niebuhr, Roman History, vol. I. pp. 27-82, E. T.; Thirlwall, History of Greece, vol. I. ch. II.; Gladstone, Homer and the Homeric Age, vol. I. ch. ii. § 2.

[2] By the labours, chiefly, of Professor Lassen, Dr. Lepsius, and Dr. Aufrecht, who have very successfully analysed the remains of the Umbrian and Sabello-Oscan languages. It appears that there is the closest analogy between the grammatical forms in these tongues and those which prevailed in early times among the Romans and Latins generally. (See Lassen's paper *Beiträge zur Deutung der Eugubinischen Tafeln*, in the *Rheinisches Museum* for 1853-1854, Dr. Aufrecht's contribution to Bunsen's Philosophy of History, vol. III. pp. 84-109, and the various treatises of Lepsius.)

[3] That of the Etruscans, whose language is decidedly not even Indo-Germanic. It is surprising that so excellent a scholar and so acute a person as Dr. Donaldson should attempt to prove the Etruscan a "sister"

dialect to the other Italic languages by means of a certain number of similar roots (see Varronianus, ch. v.), when its entire structure is so different that it is impossible, even from the copious inscriptions that remain, to form a conjecture as to its grammar, or do more than guess at the meaning of some half-dozen words.

[4] According to Herodotus, the Carians were Leleges (i. 171); and the Leleges were certainly allied to the other races which peopled Greece. (Thirlwall, I. pp. 42-45.) Homer's epithet, βαρβαρόφωνοι, does not however we take it—prove the Carians of a different ethnic family; for a very slight diversity in speech would have been considered by the Greeks to constitute a people "foreign;" and the true meaning of the term, as applied to the Carians, seems to be that they spoke bad Greek. (See vol. I. p. 548.)

[5] The Lydians were of the same race as the Carians. (See Appendix to Book i. Essay xi. p. 548.)

yet exist to decide this question; but the Phrygian remains raise a strong suspicion of a close ethnic connexion between that people and the Greeks.⁶ If this affinity be admitted, we must extend the limits of the race in question to the mountain-chain of Taurus and the banks of the Halys.

3. Community of language was not the only tie which united the various tribes scattered over this vast space. A general resemblance in manners, habits, and religious belief characterised them, and distinguished them alike from their Semitic neighbours upon the south-east, and from the ruder and more savage races of Thracians and Illyrians who bordered them upon the north. Peaceful habits, agricultural pursuits, a love of navigation, and a taste for true art, seem to have been the leading features of the nation, or family of nations, of which we are here speaking.

4. What exact position the Pelasgians held in this ethnic group it is not easy to determine. The words Pelasgic and Pelasgian are used, both by ancient and modern writers, sometimes in a wider, sometimes in a narrower acceptation; on the one hand, as co-extensive with the entire ethnic group in question; on the other, as limited to a mere single tribe, on a par with Caucones, Leleges, Dryopes, Dolopes, and such minor divisions of the one great national family. It is observable, however, that the *earlier* writers, almost without exception, incline to give to the name a wide rather than a narrow meaning.⁷ Æschylus makes Pelasgus, king of Argos, rule over all Greece, from the Peloponnese on the south to the river Strymon upon the north.⁸ Herodotus says Greece was called anciently Pelasgia,⁹ and includes, under the common name of Pelasgi, the Athenians,¹⁰ the Arcadians,¹¹ the Ionians of Asia Minor,¹² the Lemnians,¹³ the Samothracians,¹⁴ and the Crestonians.¹⁵ Even Homer, who of all the early writers, makes least mention of the Pelasgians, yet seems to acknowledge their wide extent by connecting them at once with Crete,¹⁶ Dodona,¹⁷ and Thessaly.¹⁸ On the other hand, Thucydides distinctly states that the Pelasgic was only the most

numerous of the many connected races which peopled Greece;" and even the writers who dwell most upon their vast extent distinguish from them several other races,¹ who must yet be reckoned among the earliest inhabitants of Greece, and who may reasonably be regarded as sister tribes to the Pelasgian. We must therefore consider the appellation of Pelasgi, not as attaching properly, like Arian, Slave, or even Teuton, to all the various members of an entire ethnic family, but rather, like Hindoo or Saxon, as the name of a particular branch, itself split up into a number of subordinate tribes, each distinguished from the rest by a peculiar title. The Leleges, Curetes, Caucones, Dolopes, Dryopes, Bœotian Thracians, &c., are rather to be regarded as tribes parallel to the Pelasgic than as divisions of it. They bore probably the same relation to the Pelasgians that the Oscans did to the Umbrians in Italy, and the Lydians to the Carians in Asia Minor. We cannot pronounce that either flowed from the other, or determine which was the more ancient—we can only see that in the very earliest times on which history sheds any light Greece was inhabited by a people, homogeneous indeed, but separated into distinct tribes, and that one of these, which (on the authority of Thucydides) we may call the largest, was the Pelasgian.

5. It is interesting, however, to trace, so far as we may, the wanderings of this ancient race, which must be considered to have been among the earliest of those that passed from Asia into Europe.² They possessed, apparently, the western parts of Asia Minor at a very early date;³ and the two cities which bore the name of Magnesia have with reason been ascribed to them.⁴ They are enumerated by Homer among the allies of the Trojans;⁵ and they continued to possess places on the Asiatic side to a time later than Herodotus.⁶ They are found in many of the islands⁷ between the two continents; and

---

¹⁰ Thucyd. L. 3. κατὰ ἔθνη δὲ ἄλλα καὶ τὸ Πελασγικὸν ἐπὶ πλεῖστον.

¹ Herodotus, in speaking of the rapid growth of the Hellenic race, says that many other barbarous tribes besides the Pelasgians attached themselves to it (μάλιστα προσκεχωρηκότων αὐτῷ καὶ ἄλλων βαρβάρων συχνῶν, l. 58). And Strabo enumerates among the earliest inhabitants of Greece a large number of races which by means to place on a par with the Pelasgians in everything except power and extent of territory (vii. p. 465).

² The first wave of population which passed into Europe was, beyond a doubt, Scythic or Turanian. Traces of this race appear in the Pæonians of Lake Prasias (supra, v. 16, note ⁶), in the early dwellers upon the Swiss lakes (ibid.), in the Etruscans (and to some extent the Romans) in Italy (see vol. i. p. 482, and p. 486, in the neo-Celtic element of the (so-called) Celtic races of France and Britain, in the Basques in Spain, the Esthonians on the Baltic, the

Muscovs of Russia, and the Fins and Laps of the Arctic regions.

³ They originally held Cyzicus (Schol. ad Apoll. Rhod. i. 987). They preceded the Hellenes in Lesbos and Chios (Strab. v. p. 221, xiii. p. 621; and according to Menecrates (Fr. 1) were spread over the whole coast of Ionia before the commencement of the great migrations. (Compare Herod. vii. 95. Αἰολέες τὸ πάλαι καλεόμενοι Πελασγοί.)

⁴ Niebuhr's Kleine Historische Schriften, p. 371.

⁵ Il. II. 840. Ἱππόθοος δ' ἄγε φῦλα Πελασγῶν ἐγχεσιμώρων.

⁶ As Placia and Scylace on the Propontis (Herod. i. 57), and Tralles in Caria (Agathias. II. p. 54).

⁷ In Crete (Hom. Od. xix. 177), Andros (Conon. 41), Samothrace (Herod. II. 51), Lemnos and Imbros (Ib. v. 26), and anciently in the Cyclades generally (ib. vii. 95).

440   PELASGIC SETTLEMENTS.   App. Book VI.

on the mainland of the Hellenic peninsula they occupy a number of most important positions, very distant from one another, at a period of great antiquity. Of these the principal are Thessaly, Epirus, and the Peloponnese. In Thessaly their presence is marked by the Pelasgic Argos,[a] and the district called Pelasgiotis;[b] in Epirus Dodona was their special seat;[c] in the Peloponnese they seem anciently to have held undisputed sway,[d] and the Arcadians, Ionians, and even the primitive Argives, seem to have been, one and all, Pelasgian races.[e] They were not, however, limited to the three countries which have been mentioned. Attica was Pelasgic at a very remote period;[f] and a Pelasgian seems to have preceded an Illyrian population in Macedonia.[g] Nay, the Hellenes themselves, who in later times offered so remarkable a contrast to the Pelasgians, appear from the statement of Herodotus[h] to have been originally one of their tribes.

In Italy the nations which are most distinctly declared to be Pelasgians are the southern races, the Peucetians, Œnotrians, and Iapygians generally.[i] There is reason, moreover, to suspect that a Pelasgic element entered largely into the composition of the Latin people;[j] and it cannot be doubted that the population of Etruria was Pelasgian at one time to a very great extent. The Tyrrhenian Pelasgi, who are spoken of by more than one ancient writer,[k] must certainly have been connected in some way or other with the great people of northern Italy, whom the Greeks know only as Tyrsenians, or Tyrrhenians. And the traditional migration of Pelasgians westward into Etruria, of which Hellanicus spoke,[l] is confirmed by the

---

[a] Hom. Il. B. 681.
[b] Strabo, vii. p. 477.
[c] Hom. Il. xvi. 233; Æschyl. Suppl. 254; Hesiod, ap. Strab. vii. p. 475; Scymn. Ch. l. 449; Ephorus, Frag. 54.—Almost all the early tribes between the mouth of the Achelous and the Acroceraunian mountains seem to have belonged to the same stock. The Chaonians (Steph. Byz. ad voc. Xaovía), Thesprotians (Apollodor. III. vii. § 1; Steph. Byz. ad voc. Ἔφυρα), Taulantians (Apollod. l. s. c.), and indeed the Epirot nations generally (Strab. v. p. 313), are reckoned by authors of repute among the Pelasgians.
[d] This seems to have been the reason why the Peloponnese was specially called Pelasgia. (Ephorus, Frag. 54; Acusilaus, Frag. 12.)
[e] Herodotus calls the Arcadians a Pelasgic people (i. 146); and the old traditions generally connected the Pelasgi with Arcadia in some special way. Ephorus speaks of Arcadia as the earliest seat of the race (Frag. 54); and the myth in Apollodorus (I. s. c.) is to the same effect. Again, the Italian colonies were said to have been sent out from Arcadia. (Pherecyd. Frag. 85; Dionys. Hal. i. 11; Paus. Arcad. iii.). That Ionia 'afterwards Achæa' was Pelasgian we learn from Herodotus (vii. 94); and that Argolis

was so also originally, the names Argos and Larissa sufficiently indicate. (See Thirlwall, vol. i. ch. II. pp. 34 and 38.)
[f] Herod. i. 56.
[g] Æschyl. Suppl. 261; Apollodor. I. s. c.; Justin, vii. 1.
[h] Τὸ Ἑλληνικὸν [ἔθνος], ἀποσχιζόμενον ἀπὸ τοῦ Πελασγικοῦ, αὔξεται, κ. τ. λ. L. 58. 'Αποσχίζεσθαι is the word by which Herodotus expresses the branching off of a side stream from the main river. (See iv. 56.)
[i] Dionys. Hal. l. s. c.; Pherecyd. l. s. c. &c.
[j] It has generally been thought that the Latin language gives proof of this (see Niebuhr's Rom. Hist. i. p. 65; Marsh's Horæ Pelasgicæ, ch. iv.; and Mr. Gladstone's Homer, vol. I. pp. 299–301); but perhaps the resemblances between it and Greek might be otherwise explained. A better proof is furnished by the Pelasgic character of the Latin religious system.
[k] Sophocl. Inach. ap. Dionys. Hal. i. 25; Thucyd. iv. 109; Callimach. ap. Schol. Aristoph. Av. 832. &c.
[l] Hellanicus, Frag. 1. See also Strab. v. p. 312, where Agylla ('Cære') is called a Pelasgic settlement, and Dionys. Hal. L. 18.

remains of Etruscan art, where the language is often very closely akin to the Greek.¹

6. The general progress of the Pelasgian people may thus be traced from Asia Minor, by the Propontis and Egean, and again by Crete and the islands into Greece, and from Greece across the Adriatic into Italy. There is indeed no such distinct historical evidence of the former, as there is of the latter, movement; but while we have the strongest grounds for believing it from our general knowledge of the mode in which the earth was peopled, what history does show us is in entire accordance with such a view. For the Pelasgians of Asia are, at the earliest period to which history goes back, a declining people, bearing no resemblance to immigrants who have made settlements in foreign territory, but exhibiting the appearance of an oppressed remnant, with difficulty maintaining itself against more powerful races. Masters at an early time of the valleys of the Hermus and Mæander, in each of which they had Larissas or fortresses,² possessors of the entire coast from Mycalé northwards to the Hellespont³ and of the islands of Chios and Lesbos,⁴ they retain, when contemporary history opens, but a few scattered posts,⁵ the last strongholds of a people forced everywhere to yield to conquerors. The natural explanation of the historical phenomena is, that the Pelasgi were the original population of western Asia, and that their emigrations across the sea into Europe were occasioned by the pressure upon them of immigrants from the east, Lydians, Phrygians, and Carians, who forced them westward, and so caused their occupation of Greece and Italy.

7. The etymology of the name Pelasgi has been thought to confirm this view of their original seat. It has been regarded as equivalent to "swarthy Asiatics"—a title which is supposed to have been given them by the old inhabitants of Greece, to mark at once their proper country and their most striking physical characteristic.⁷ But this argument rests upon too insecure a basis to entitle it to much weight. The true etymology of the word Pelasgian is very uncertain;⁸ and the theory in question requires us to suppose European Greece already inhabited by a race similar in language to the Pelasgians, yet physically contrasted with them, at the time when the latter first made their appearance in Europe.

8. The order in which the European settlements were made, the

---

¹ As is the well-known legend "Ni Kaleira fuios" (αἰπὸς Καλαίρου παῖδας), given by Lanzi. (Epitafi scritti, No. 191.)
² Strabo, ii. p. 648, and xiii. p. 891.
³ Menecrates ap. Strab. xiii. p. 591.
⁴ Strabo, v. p. 313.
⁵ Tralles (Agath. l. s. c.), Placia, and Scylace (Herod. l. 57).
⁶ See Dr. Donaldson's Varronianus, pp. 24, 25. He regards Πελ- as equivalent to μελ-, "black," on the analogy of σίδη (= μερδ), and the meanings of μέλαος, μελάμβροτς, Πελάσγοι (Apollod. l. ix. § 3. &c. Δέγι might undoubtedly be equivalent to Δσσι, or Δσιοι, the people of Asia, as Bouth-

mann showed long ago. (Lexil. ad voc. Ἀσίη, p. 155, note. E. T.)
⁷ The ancients regarded Πελασγοί as a variant of πελαργοί, "storks," and said the name marked their wandering habits (Philoch. ad ferv. Æn. viii. 600; Strabo, v. p. 313). Moderns have suggested that it is derived from the Hebrew name Peleg, from the verb פלג, from the noun פלאים, and from the two words πέλας, "to till," and ἄγρος, "the field." (See Varronianus, l. s. c., and compare Mr. Gladstone's 'Homer,' vol. l. pp. 311-315.) Nothing is more difficult than to discover the original meaning of ethnic titles.

period at which they commenced, and the routes which the emigration followed, cannot with any accuracy be determined. Probably, while some were crossing by the Bosphorus and Hellespont, others passed from island to island across the Ægean, while the route of Rhodes, Carpathus, Crete, Cythēra, may have been pursued by a third stream of immigrants. To the first of these bodies, apparently, would belong the settlements in Lemnos, Imbros, and Samothrace, the ancient population of Macedonia, the Perrhæbians, the inhabitants of the Thessalian Argos, and the Epirots; to the second, the Pelasgi of the Cyclades and the early inhabitants of Attica; to the third, the Pelasgi of Crete, Cythēra, and the Peloponnesos. Subsequently, two great streams seem to have set into Italy; one, starting from Arcadia, proceeded into Iapygia,¹ and flowed northwards; the other skirted the Adriatic, spread over the plain of the Po, and thence extended itself towards the south.² To the former belong the Œnotrians, Peucetians, Messapians, Daunians, &c.; to the latter the Tyrrhenian Pelasgi and, perhaps, the Latins.

9. The later wanderings of the Tyrrhenian Pelasgi are capable of being traced with some approach to exactness. Driven from their own country by the inroads of an Alpine people, or impelled to seek new seats by a spirit of enterprise,³ they proceeded eastward, and are found, when we first catch sight of them, on the Greek side of the Adriatic, in Acarnania.⁴ After this they appear in Bœotia, where they assist the Bœotian Thracians against the Cadmians.⁵ Next we learn that they obtained settlements in Attica at the foot of Mount Hymettus, and assisted the Athenians to fortify their acropolis; but after a while were compelled once more to emigrate,⁶ and went some to the Hellespont,⁷ some to Lemnos,⁸ and some possibly to Mount Athos.⁹ In these places they continued to the time of our author, and bore the name of Tyrrhenian Pelasgi, to distinguish them from other branches of the same stock.

10. The skill of the Pelasgi in fortification was justly celebrated. The Pelasgic wall of Athens has been mentioned above. It was no solitary specimen, but one of a vast number of works which everywhere through Greece and Italy attested the presence of this people. These structures, the peculiar characteristic of which is that they are made of polygonal blocks fitted together without cement or mortar, are found in great abundance on the western coast of Asia Minor, in Epirus, the Peloponnese, and Italy. They are sometimes called Cyclopean, a name which marks well their grandeur and antiquity,

---

¹ This is the emigration of Pherecydes (Fr. 85), Pausanias (Arcad. 3l.), and Dionysius (Antiq. R. L. 11). Arcadian names occurred frequently in Southern Italy.

² See the famous fragment of Hellanicus (Fr. 1, Hist. Gr. Fragm. vol. i. p. 45.

³ If, with Niebuhr, we view the Pelasgic as the conquered element in the Etruscan nation, we must consider the Tyrrhenian Pelasgi as fugitives from Italy. If, with Dr. Donaldson, we believe the Pelasgi of Etruria to have conquered the former inhabitants, we may imagine that after the conquest they became marauders, like the Normans in later times.

⁴ See Pausan. l. xxviii. § 3.
⁵ Strabo, ix. p. 583.
⁶ Herod. vi. 137; Pausan. l. s. c.; Thucyd. iv. 109.
⁷ Herod. i. 57.
⁸ Ibid. vi. 137; cf. iv. 145.
⁹ Thucyd. l. s. c.

but which throws no light upon their real origin. It would seem that the unwarlike character of the Pelasgians led them, from the first, to trust to walls for their defence against the enemies who assailed them on all sides. Hence the numerous Larissas or strongholds by which their movements can be tracked,[1] defences which from the vast size of the separate blocks have defied the hand of time, and bid fair to outlast all the structures of later ages.

11. If it be asked what became of a people so numerous, and in ancient times so widely spread, the answer is that they were for the most part absorbed by races more or less nearly akin to them. In Greece Proper, the Hellenes, a daughter race, if we are to believe Herodotus,[2] swallowed them up, impressing upon them everywhere their own higher development and more advanced type of character. In Asia Minor they became mingled with the Carians, the Lydians, and the Phrygians; while in Italy they were either reduced to the condition of serfs, as the Œnotrians[3] and (probably) the Tyrrhenians,[4] or united with their conquerors to form a new people, as the Latins. Their whole character was plastic and yielding, not firm nor formative; and their fate was to furnish a substratum upon which stronger nationalities established and developed themselves.

---

[1] Of these Stephen enumerates twelve (ad voc. Λάρισσα), and Strabo (ix. p. 616) an equal number. Mr. Clinton has collected notices of sixteen (F. H. vol. i. pp. 25, 26, note).

[2] Herod. i. 56. I have already considered the question of the relation of the Hellenes to the Pelasgi in the essays appended to vol. i. (Essay xi. p. 546-547). To the authorities there quoted on the subject of their near connexion, may be added Dionysius of Halicarnassus, who regards the Pelasgians as included in the Hellenes (Ant. Rom. i. 9; τινὶ δὲ Πελασγοί τε καὶ τῶν ἄλλων Ἑλλήνων τινὲς ἀναμιχθέντες, κ. τ. λ.); and Strabo, who makes the Pelasgian occupants of Agylla speak Greek (v. p. 312).

[3] Steph. Byz. ad voc. Χίος.

[4] For the theory of Niebuhr as to the Etruscan nation appears to me preferable to that of Dr. Donaldson.

NOTE A.

ON THE DERIVATION AND MEANING OF THE PROPER NAMES OF THE MEDES AND PERSIANS.

[NOTE.—The published sources of the subjoined analysis are Sir H. Rawlinson's Vocabulary of the ancient Persian Language, contained in the Eleventh Volume (Part I.) of the Asiatic Society's Journal; M. Oppert's contributions in the Journal Asiatique; Pott's Etymologische Forschungen; Brockhaus's Glossary at the end of his edition of the Vendidad Sadé; and Benfey's Glossary in his Keilinschriften. These sources are indicated in the following way, viz.: Benfey's Glossary by the letter B.; Brockhaus's by Br.; Oppert's Mémoires by O.; Pott's Forschungen by P.; and Sir H. Rawlinson's Vocabulary by R. Voc. Additional communications from Sir Henry Rawlinson are marked H. C. R.; where there are no initials affixed, the conjecture is made by the Editor. When no authority is cited for the name, it occurs in Herodotus.]

ACHÆMENES (Old Pers. *Hakhámanish*) is either from Old Pers. *hakhá* (Sansk. *sakha*), "a friend," and an attributive affix, equivalent to the Zend and Sanscrit *mat*; "with," or "possessing," which makes the nominative in *man* (H. C. R. vide supra, vol. i. p. 211, note¹); or else, from *hakhá*, and a root like the Sanscrit *manas*, which is the Greek μένος, Latin *mens*, and our *mind*. In the former case the name means "possessing friends;" in the latter "friendly."

AMARDI (a Persian tribe, Strab. xi. p. 741) is thought to be from the Zend *ñu*, which is equivalent to the Sanscr. *nu*, and the Greek *vě*, and Mod. Pers. *merd*, "vir," or "heros."—P. As the old Persian word for "man," however, is *martiyn* (Zend *mereto*), and the meaning is "mortal" (from *mri* "to die") rather than "a hero," this etymology may well be doubted. It is better to refer both *Amardi* and *Mardi* to *mridh*, "to kill" or "fight." See under Mardonius. At any rate the first element in *Amardi* cannot possibly be *hu*, "good."—H. C. R. (See below, ANIOMARDUS.)

ANASPES (Xen.) is probably from Sanscr. *Ariya*, Zend *Airya*, "noble, excellent," and *aspa*, which in old Persian, as in Zend, meant "a horse." (See Sir H. Rawlinson's Vocabulary, *ad* voc. *U'vaspa*, p. 86.) The name means "having excellent horses."

ARBACES is a corrupt form of *Harpagus*, q. vide.

ARIABIGNES, from *Ariya*, "excellent," or here "the excellent One," i. e. Ormazd, and Sanscr. *bhaja*, "to serve:" therefore "serving the Excellent One."—H. C. R.

ARIACES (Arrian) is almost certainly *Ariya*, with a termination *ak*, which is either a diminutive, equivalent to the modern Persian *ek*; or, more probably a Scythic suffix, representing the terminal guttural so common in the primitive Babylonian, which may be compared with the Basque *c* at the end of names, and is perhaps, like that, a suffixed article.—H. C. R.

ARIÆUS (Xenoph.) seems to be simply the Greek rendering of *Ariya*, "excellent."

ARIARAMNES (Old Pers. *Ariyárámana*) from *Ariya* and *rámana*, akin to the Sanscrit *raman*, "a lover," and the Zend *ránum*, "pleasure" (R. Voc.), is perhaps "a lover of what is noble." Oppert says, from *ariya* and *aramna*, "joy."

NOTE A.   PROPER NAMES OF MEDES AND PERSIANS.   445

ARIARATHES (Polyb.), from *ariya* and *ratu*, which is Zend and Sanscrit, signifies "a chief."   Ariarathes = "noble chief."—P.

ARIMAZES (Q. Curt.), from *ariya*, and *maz*, "great."   (Compare Zend *maz* and Sanscrit *maha*, Gr. μεί(ζων, &c.)   Perhaps *Ari* here has the force of the Greek, ἀρι or ἐρι, in ἀρίζηλος, ἐριβῶλαξ, κ. τ. λ.

ARIOXABDUS (according to Pott) is from *ariya* and a root equivalent to the modern Persian *merd*, "vir," or "hero" (P.), whence the ethnic names Mardi (see vol. i. p. 345), Amardi, are thought to be derived. The name would thus mean "noble hero."

ARIZANTI (a Median tribe, Herod. i. 101) from *ariya* and (Zend) *zantu*, "stirps," therefore, "of noble stock," or "nobly descended."—P.

ARSACES (Æschyl.), from *arsa*, or *arsha* (Sanscr. *arshya*) "venerable," with the suffix *ak* (vid. supr. ad voc. ARIACES).

ARSAMENES, from *arsha* and (Sanscr.) *manas* (v. s. ad. voc. ACHÆMENES), "venerable-minded."—P.

ARSAMES (Old Pers. *Arshâma*) from *arsha* and *ma*, a suffix.—O.

ARSES (Diod. S.) is *arsha*, with the Greek nominatival ending.—R. Voc.

ARSITES (Diod. S.), a participial form, from a verb *ars* or *arsh*, equivalent to the Sanscrit *rish*, "to exalt."   Arsites is thus "exalted, elevated."—O.

ARTABANUS is probably for Atrabanus, or rather Atrapanus, and may be compared with Megapanus.   It is derived from *Atra* or *Adar*, "fire," and *pa* (which occurs in *khshatrapa*—"a satrap") "to protect."   The sense is "protecting the fire."—H. C. R.

ARTABARDES (Old Pers. *Artavardiya*), from the transcendental particle *arta*, which is connected with the Zend *areta*, or *ereta*, and *vardiya*, which is formed by the addition of the adjectival suffix *ya* to the root *vart* (compare Sanscr. *vritta*, Zend *vêrêto*, Pazend *vart*) "celebrated."   Thus the meaning of the name is "very celebrated."—H. Voc.

ARTABAZANES, or ARTABARZANES (which is preferable), from *arta* and Zend *berez* (which is the Sanscr. *bhraj*) "resplendent."   Artabarzanes = "very resplendent."—P.

ARTABAZUS.—*Arta* is here again probably by metathesis for *atra*, fire, as in Atradates.   (See above, vol. i. p. 201, note *.)   The name means probably "the worshipper of fire," from *Atra*, or *Adar*, "fire," and Sans. *bhaj*, "colere, venerari" (compare MEGABAZUS).

ARTACHÆES, or ARTACHÆUS, "very friendly," from the intensitive particle *arta*, and *hakhâ*, "a friend," or "friendly."—O.   (See above ad voc. ACHÆMENES.)

ARTÆUS is probably "great" or "famous."   (Compare Hesych. 'Αρτὰς, μέγας καὶ λαμπρός.)   It is of course connected with *arta*.—R. Voc.

ARTAMENES (Justin.) "high-spirited," from *arta*, intensitive, and Sanscr. *manas* = μένος.   (Comp. ACHÆMENES.)—P.

ARTAPATAS (Xen.) is either "powerful lord," from *arta*, intensitive, and Sanscr. *pati*, Zend *paiti*, "lord;" or "protected by fire," from *Atra*, "fire," and *pâta*, the past participle of *pa*, "to protect."   (Compare below, BAGAPATES, &c.)

ARTAPHERNES may not improbably be from *atra*, "fire," and the Sansc. *pri*, "to protect."   It would thus be equivalent to Artabanus, and would mean "protecting the fire."—H. C. R.

ARTASYRAS (Ctes.), "very bright," or "the bright sun;" from *arta*, intensitive, and *suru* (compare Sanscr. *surya*), or perhaps *thura*, "the sun." (The latter root seems to be contained in the name of the month *Thuravâhara*.   See Sir H. Rawlinson's Vocabulary, p. 160.)

ARTAXERXES (Old Pers. *Artakhshatrá*), from *arta*, and *khshatrá*, "a king." (Compare Sanscr. *kshatra*, and Zend *khshathra*, which have the same meaning.) *Khshatram* occurs frequently in the Behistun Inscription for "crown," or "empire." Herodotus is altogether in error when he supposes that the second element in this name is identical with the name of King Xerxes. His translation, however, μέγας ἀρήιος, may stand, for *kshatra* means both "king" and "warrior."—H. Voc.

ARTAYCTES is "celebrated," from *arta* intensitive, and Sanscr. *ukta* " said."— H. C. R.

ARTAYNTES and ARTAYNTA (*mul.*) from *arta* in the sense of "great" (compare ARTÆUS), and an adjectival termination—*vent* or *vant*. (Compare MARDONTES.)—H. C. R.

ARTEMBARES is probably, in Old Persian, *Atrambara*, from *atram*, the accusative case of *atra*, "fire," and *bara*, "bearer," as in Bubares, Œbares, &c. The signification is thus, "the bearer of fire."—H. C. R.

ARTOCHMES, "very strong," from *arta*, intensitive, and Zend *takhma*, "strong." (Compare SITSATACHMES and TRITANTÆCHMES.)

ARTÔNIS (Arrian) may compare with the Zend feminine *asaoni*, "caste."—O.

ARTOKABES (Plut.) is perhaps "rich in gold," from *arta*, intensitive, and Zend *zaru*, "gold."

ASPAMITRAS (Ctes.), "lover of horses," from Zend, *aspa*, Sanscr. *açva*, Mod. Pers. *asp*, "a horse" (comp. Old Pers. 'ινασπα, "rich in horses"), and *mitra*, or *mithra*, which is in Sanscr. not only the god Mithras, but also "a friend."—O.

ASPATHINES (Old Pers. *Aspachana*). The first element here is certainly *aspa*, as in *Aspimitras*; the second is conjectured to be an equivalent for the Sanscr. *dhanja*, "rich," in which case the signification of the name would be "rich in horses." This is the view of Pott (Forsch. p. lix.). M. Oppert derives the word from the Zend *açpathō*, "a horseman," with an appellative suffix *ina* (Journ. As. 4ᵐᵉ Série, tom. xviii. p. 369). Neither account seems to be aware that the native form is not Aspathines, but Aspachana (As. Journ. vol. xii. part ii. Note at the end, p. xx.).

ASTYAGES, or as the name is more correctly given by Abydenus (Fr. 7), Eusebius (Chron. Can. Armen. passim), and others, ASDAHAGES, represents beyond a doubt the Zend *Aj-dahak* (nom. *ajis-dahako*) "the biting snake," one element of which appears again in the name Deïoces, q. v. (Compare supra, vol. i. p. 331, note ¹, and p. 552, note ².)—H. C. R.

ATRADATES (Nic. D.).—This name has been already explained, vol. i. p. 201, note ⁵.

ATRINES (Old Pers. *Atrina*) is probably from the Zend *atar*, "fire;" with the appellative suffix -*ina*.—O.

ATROPATES (Arrian), from *atar* and Sanscr. *pati*, Zend *paiti*, "lord," would signify "the lord of fire"—a lofty title, which perhaps the satrap did not take till he became the real sovereign of the northern Media. Or the word may be from *atar* and *pāta*, the participle of *pa*, "to protect," which appears in *mitrapa*." (Compare ARTAPATAS.)

AZANES (Æschyl.) is conjectured to be either from the Zend *açnō*, "strength," and in that case to mean "strong," or else to be equivalent to the Sanscrit *su-jana*, "good, virtuous." It is probably the same name with the Oxanes of Ctesias.—P.

BADRES.—If this reading be taken, instead of Rares, in Herod. iv. 167, the word may be compared with the Sanscr. *badhra*, "fortunate."—P. It would be a simple adjective, and correspond exactly to the Roman "Felix."

BAGÆUS is explained by Pott as "fortunate," from Zend *bágha*, Sanscr. *bhága*,

NOTE A.   PROPER NAMES OF MEDES AND PERSIANS.   447

"fortune" (Forsch. l. s. c.); but by M. Oppert as "aimant Dieu" (Journ. As. ut supra, p. 357); from *baga*, "god," and (I presume) the Zend *yaz*, "colere, venerari."

BAGAPATES (Ctes.), according to Pott, is "lord of fortune," from Zend *bóghi*, "fortune," and Sanscr. *pati*, Zend *paiti*, "lord." (Forsch. p. xxxvii.) But M. Oppert's explanation seems preferable to this. He believes the derivation to be from Old Pers. *baga*, "a god," and *páta*, the past participle of *pa*, "to protect." The sense is then, "he who is protected by the gods." (Journ. As. 4ᵐᵉ Série, tom. xviii. p. 341.)

BAGABAZES is perhaps "strong as a God," from *bagn*, and Sanscr. *gnk*, "to be strong." Compare the sense of *Tritantæchmes*, infra, ad voc.

BAGOAS, according to Pott (Forsch. l. s. c.), represents the Sanscr. *bhagawat*, "happy, fortunate." According to M. Oppert, it is derived from *baga*, and the Zend verb *av*, "to protect." It would thus be the same in meaning as *Bagapates*.

BAGOPHANES (Q. Curt.) is regarded by Pott as the Sanscr. adjective *bhagawan*, "excellent." (Forsch. p. xxxvii.) M. Oppert explains it as "protégé par Dieu" (Journ. As. p. 357), deriving *-phanes* from the root *pa*, and apparently regarding it as having the same force with *-pates*. (See above, sub voc. BAGAPATES.) This, however, is scarcely possible. The form *-phanes* will represent the active participle, and give the sense of "protecting God," *i. e.* his worship.—H. C. R.

BARSINES, *mul.* (Arrian) is probably the Zend root *berez*, "resplendent," with the appellative suffix *-ina*.

BARZANES (Arrian) is the same root with a suffix *-ana*.

BARSENTES (Q. Curt.) or, BARSAENTES (Arrian) } is the participle *berez-vat*, "shining."—P.

BOGES appears to be either *Baga* simply, as M. Oppert thinks (Journ. As. 4ᵐᵉ Série, tom. xviii. p. 341), or the Zend *beykû*, Sanscr. *bhagí*, "fortunate."

BUBARES is probably from *bhu*, "the sacrificial fire" (Sanscr.), and *bara*, "bearing." Compare Zend *bere*, "ferre." The word would properly have been *Bhurubara*; but the *m* has lapsed before the cognate labial. Bubares is "the bearer of the sacrificial fire." Compare ARTEMBARES, which had probably the same meaning.—H. C. R.

CAMBYSES (Old Pers. *Kabujiya*) is thought to be from the Sanscr. *kub*, "to praise," and *uji*, "a speaker;" its signification, according to this view, is "a bard."—(R. Voc.) The μ in the Greek Καμβύσης arises from the difficulty which the Greeks have always experienced in expressing the sound of a real R. Hence we have Smerdis and Merdis for *Bardiya*, Megabyzus, Megadostes, Megasidres, for *Bagbukhsha*, *Bagadaushta*, *Bagachitra*, &c. Hence too in Modern Greek we have such words as φάμερμια for *fabrica*, Μαρίς for *Hri*, and the like.

CASPII.—The name of this people is thought to be derived from Old Pers. '*u* (which is the Sanscr. *su*, the Zend *hu*, and the Greek εὖ), "good," and *açpa*, a horse.—P. It may be doubted, however, whether the initial letter would not in that case have been χ instead of *c*.

CHOASPES (river) is the Old Persian word '*uaspa*, which is found in an inscription at Persepolis, and is an exact equivalent of the Greek εὔιππος. Its derivation from '*u* (= *hu*), "good," and *açpa*," may be regarded as certain.—R. Voc.

COMETES (Justin) is no doubt the Old Persian *Gaumata*, which would have been better rendered by Gomates or Gomates. The word is equivalent to the Sanscr. *gômat*, Zend *gaomat*, and means "possessing herds." It is derived from *gao*, "bos" (which is the German *kuh*, and our *cow*), and the common suffix *-mat*, "with" or "possessing."—R. Voc.

CRANASPES is, perhaps, "possessing active horses," from Sanscr. *karin*, "active" (compare Zend *kere*, "to do"), and *aspa*.

CYAXARES (Old Pers. *'Uvakhatara*) seems to be the comparative of *'Uvakhshi*, in which we have the element '*u*, "good" (compare *Choaspes*) joined with a root *akhsha*, which is perhaps the modern Persian *akkah*, Sanscrit *akshan*, Zend *aruna*, "oculus." The word would thus mean "beautiful-eyed," or literally, "more beautiful-eyed (than others)." Compare the name of the father of *Kai Khusru*, who is called *Siyáwakhsh* in Persian, *Cyavarsna* in Zend, i. e. "black-eyed."—R. Voc.

CYRUS (Old Pers. *Kurush*). This word was generally supposed by the Greeks to mean "the sun" (see Cats. Pers. Exc. § 49; Plut. vit. Artaxerx. Etym. Mag. ad voc. *Kúpos*, &c.); that is, it was identified with the Sanscr. *surya*, Zend *hware*, modern Persian *khur*. It is now suspected that this identification was a mistake, as the old Persian *k* never replaces the Sansc. *s*. The name is more properly compared with the Sanscrit *Kuru*, which was "a popular title among the Arian race before the separation of the Median and Persian branches," but of which the etymology is unknown.—R. Voc.

DADARSES (Old Pers. *Dadarshish*) is probably a reduplicated formation from the old Pers. *darsh*, "to dare," which appears in Sanscrit as *dhrish*, in Zend as *darsh*, and in Greek as *θαρσ-εῖν*.—R. Voc. *Dadarses* would thus represent the Greek Thraso, Thrasees, or Thrasius.

DARICS, or DARIEUS (Ctes.) is in old Persian *Daryavush*, a form well represented by the Hebrew דָּרְיָוֶשׁ, *Daryavesh*, and (if it be the true reading) by Strabo's Δαριαύης. It does not appear to mean either *ἐφεῖπς*, "the worker," as Herodotus states, or *φρόνιμος*, "the wise," as Hesychius asserts, or *πολέμιμος*, "the warlike," as the author of the Etymologicum says. The root seems to be the old Persian "dar," "to hold" or "possess," which is *dere* in Zend, *dhri* in Sanscrit, and *dar* in modern Persian. The remainder of the word is thought to be a mere appellative suffix, elongated on euphonic grounds; but no very satisfactory account can be given of it.—R. Voc.

DAMASPIA, *mul.* (Ctes.) is probably equivalent to the Greek *Ἱπποδάμεια*, being formed from a root *dam*, "to subdue," which is found in that exact form in Sanscrit, and appears in Greek as *δαμάω*, in Latin as *dom-o*, in German as *zähm-en*, and in English as "tame." The other element is the well-known *aspa*, "equus."—P.

DATAMES (Arrian) is perhaps the same as *Madates*, the two elements being merely transposed. Thus we have in Greek both Dorotheus and Theodorus. The word will mean on this hypothesis "given by the Moon," from *dáta*, the past participle of *da*, "to give," and *Máha* or *Mah*, "the Moon." (See *Madates*.)

DATIS is probably an adjectival form from *da*, and may compare with the Sanscrit *dadi*, "apt to give, liberal."

DEIOCES is best regarded as the Zend *dahâka* "mordens," which forms an element also in the name Astyages (q. vide). The Persian *Dhoháh*, Arabicised into *Zahak*, represents this name, or rather title. (See above, vol. I. p. 331, note '.)

EUPHRATES (Old Pers. *'Ufrata*) is explained as either equivalent to the Sanscrit *su-pratha*, which corresponds to the Greek *εὖ πλατύς* (O.), or as formed from '*u*, "good," *fra*, the particle of abundance, and a suffix of attribution. According to this latter explanation, the meaning of the word would be "the good and abounding (river)."—R. Voc.

NOTE A. PROPER NAMES OF MEDES AND PERSIANS.

GOBARES (Plin.). Pott suggests that Gobares is the Zend *howara*, Sanscr. *sawaru*, "valde desiderabilis" (Forschung. p. lxiv.). But this is very unlikely. At least there is no other known instance where the Greek *γ* replaces the Zend *h* and Sanscrit *s*. It may be doubted whether Gobares is a man's name at all. Pliny says he was the satrap who made the great canal (*Nahr-Malcha*). But as that canal was made by Nebuchadnezzar (Abyden. Fr. 9), and as its Semitic name was *Chobar* (cf. Ezek. i. 1), it is tolerably clear that Pliny has given to an imaginary satrap, what was in reality the appellation of the work ascribed to him. The Chobar was the "great" stream. Compare Heb. רָבָה, and the Cabiri, or "great gods" of the Phœnicians.

GOBRYAS (old Pers. *Gauharwca*). Of this word various etymologies have been given. Pott (Forschung. pp. xliv.-vi.) derives it from the Modern Persian *khub*, "pulcher," and *rui*, "facies;" but this conjecture is open to many objections. Sir H. Rawlinson suggests the Sanscrit *ga*, "speech," and *bru*, "to say," regarding the meaning of the word as "a speaker" (Voc. p. 135). M. Oppert makes the meaning "bull-browed," considering the elements to be the Zend *gao*, Sanscrit *gô*, "bos" or "taurus," and Zend *bruai*, Sanscr. *brhu*, "supercilium." (Journ. As. 4me Série, tom. xviii. p. 353.)

GOMATES (vide COMETES).

HARPAGUS is probably from an old Persian root akin to the Greek ἁρπ- in ἁρπάζω, and the Latin *rap-* in *rapere*. The adoption of the ἅρπη, or ἁρπάζων, as the dynastic emblem of the Harpagi on the Lycian coins (see vol. i. p. 250, note ^a) seems to indicate this connexion. The name is probably equivalent to the Greek ἅρπαξ.

HAUSTANES (Q. Curt.) is a name which appears under many forms. It is probably identical with the *Osthanes* of Pliny, the *Ostanes* of Tatian, the *Hystanes* of Herodotus, and even the *Histanes* of Arrian. There can be little doubt that the second element of the word is the Zend and Sanscrit *tanu*, modern Pers. *ten*, "corpus," which appears in *Otanes*, *Tanyoxarces*, &c. The first element is doubtful, but may compare with the modern Pers. *khush*, "good"—the name thus meaning "of good or strong body." —P. (Compare OTANES; and for the use of *u* prefix as instead of the ordinary *'u*, see Sir H. Rawlinson's 'Cuneiform Inscriptions,' vol. i. pp. 344, 345.)

HIRRAMENES (Thucyd.) is probably a Grecised form of a name derived from Sanscrit *vairya* (whence *vir*, *virtus*, &c.), "noble, manly," and "*manas*," "mind," as in Achœmenes, Artamenes, &c.

HYDARNES (Old Pers. *Vidarna*) is said by M. Oppert (Journ. As. ut supra, p. 544) to signify "a subduer." He does not give any derivation, but I presume he intends to suggest the common Sanscrit prefix *vi-* and *dharna*, from *dhri*, "to hold."

HYMEAS is perhaps the same with *Imæus* (Æschyl.). Both words may be compared with the hero Yima so often mentioned in the Zendavesta, who, as *Yimô-khshaêta* (or Yima the brilliant), became in Persian romance *Djemshid*. The etymology of the name is unknown.—P.

HYSTÆCHMES (Æschyl.) may be compared with *Artochmes*, the second element being the Zend *takhma*, "strong," while the first, which we have already seen in HAUSTANES, is *us*, used intensitively.

HYSTASPES (Old Pers. *Vishtaspa*) is "the possessor of horses," from the Zend *vista*, participle of *vid*, to "acquire," and (Zend *açva*) Sanscr. *açpa*, "a horse."—B. and D.

2 G

450   ON THE DERIVATION AND MEANING OF   App. Book VI.

INTAPHRNES (Old Pers. *Vidafra*), or INTAPHERNES (Old Pers. *Vidafrana*), is probably derived from Sanscr. *vida* (= *vidi*), "knowledge" (compare the Greek οἶδα, εἴδομαι; Lat. *videre*), and *pri*, "to protect." (See ARTA-PHERNES.) The name therefore means "protecting knowledge."— H. C. R.

ITHAMATRES or ITHAMITRES } is probably from the Old Persian *vitha*, which meant "house" or "palace," and *mitra* or *mithra*, "a friend," as in *Arya-mitrus*, q. v.—O.

MADATES (Q. Curt.) is "given by (or to) the moon," from old Persian *Māha* or *ma*, "the Moon." (Compare Sanscr. *masa*, Zend *mangha*, mod. Pers. *mah*), and *ddta*, the participle of *da*, "to give."—O. and P.

MAOÆUS (Plut.) is probably only another form of *Bagæus*, q. v.—O.

MARDONIUS (Old Pers. *Marduniya*) has been thought to represent an adjective like the Modern Persian *merdáneh*, which is "virilis, strenuus," from the root *merd* or *mard*, "vir," which appears in Mardi, Amanli, Ariomardus, &c.—P. But it is more probably from the Sanscrit root *mridh*, "to hurt," or "kill," from which is formed *mridham*, "battle;" and thus the signification of the name will be "a warrior."—H. C. R.

MARDONTES will also be from *mridh*, with the adjectival suffix -*vent* or -*vunt* (see above, ad voc. ARTAYNTA); and will have nearly the same meaning as *Murduniya*.—H. C. R.

MASISTES exactly renders the old Persian *mathista*, which is used throughout the Inscriptions for "a leader," but which is etymologically a superlative equivalent to the Zend *mazista*, and the Greek μέγιστος, "greatest."—P.

MASPII (a Persian tribe, Herod. i. 125). In this name we seem certainly to have the root *aspa*, "a horse." (See vol. i. p. 344.) It is conjectured that the initial letter represents the Sanscrit *meh*, "great" (Oppert), so that the Maspii are "those who have big horses," or possibly "the Big Horses," just as the Hyrcani are "the Wolves," the Persæ "the Tigers," the Medes "the Snakes," the Sacæ "the Dogs," the Cushites "the Eagles," the Maka or Myci "the Flies," the Derbicæ "the Wasps," and the Aswas of the Puranas "the Horses."

MAZACES (Arrian) MAZÆUS (Arrian) MAZARES } seem to be names formed from the root *maz*, "great" (compare Zend *mas*, Sanscrit *mahat*, Greek μεῖζ-ων), which appears again in *Oromasdes*, q. vide. Mazaces has the Scythic termination *ka* (supra, ad. voc. ARIACES); Mazæus is like Bagæus, &c.

MEGABATES is perhaps "enlightened by God" (O.), from *baga*, "God," and Sanscr. *bhâta*, "shone on," past participle of *bhá*, "to shine."—H. C. R.

MEGABAZUS is probably "a worshipper of God," from *baga*, "God," and the Sanscrit *bhaj*, "venerari, colere."

MEGABYZUS (Old Pers. *Bagabukhsha*) contains also the element *bagu*, which is here joined with (Zend and Sanscr.) *baksh*, "donare." The name means "God-given," and is equivalent to Theodotus and Theodorus.—H. C. R.

MEGADOSTES (In Old Pers., probably *Bagudausta*), from *baga*, "God," and *dausta*, which is found in the Behistun Inscription in the sense of "friend," would be "a lover of God," the Greek φιλόθεος.—O.

MEGAPANUS appears to be a mere variant of the name which Quintus Curtius gives as *Bagophanes*, q. vide.

MEGANDRAS is thought to represent an Old Persian name *Baguchitra*, which would mean "heaven-descended," or "of the seed of the Gods," from *bagu*, and *chitra*, "e stirpe, ortus, satus."—O.

NOTE A.   PROPER NAMES OF MEDES AND PERSIANS.   451

MEHERDATES (Tacitus) is a late form of the name which commonly appears as *Mithridates*, or *Mitradates*.—O. (The *Mithra* of the Achæmenian Persians became with their descendants first *Mitra*, and then *Mihr*. Similarly *chitra* became *chehr*, as in the name *Minuchehr*. See Sir H. Rawlinson's Cuneiform Vocabulary, ad. voc. *chitra*.)

MITHRENES (Q. Curt.) }
MITHRINES (Arrian)   } seem to be names formed from *Mithra*, each with an appellative suffix. (Compare *Atrines*, *Bagæus*,
MITRÆUS (Xenoph.)   } &c.)

MITHRAUSTES (Arrian) means "worshipper of Mithras," from *Mithra*, and Zend *ā́us*, "to worship."—O. (Compare Zend-*avesta*.)

MITHRIDATES (Xen.) } "given to Mithra" (see vol. I. p. 201, note ³).
MITHRADATES   }

MITHROBARZANES (Arrian), from *Mithra*, and *berez*, "resplendent"—therefore "resplendent as the Sun."—P. (Compare ARTABARZANES.)

MITROBATES (or less correctly METROBATES, Xen.), according to M. Oppert (Journ. As. 4ᵐᵉ Série, tom. xix. p. 52), signifies "enlightened by Mithras," from *Mithra* and *bhā́tas*. *bhā́ta*, "shone on." (Compare MEGABATES.)

NABARZANES (Arrian) is thought to be "with new splendour, newly splendid," from Zend *nava* (Greek νέος, Latin *novus*), "new," and *berez*, "resplendent."—P.

OCHUS (Plut.) is thought to be either from the Zend *rōhu*, "rich" (O.), or from *u*, and a root resembling the Modern Persian *khuj*, "temper" or "disposition." In the latter case the name would mean "of a good disposition, amiable."—P.

OEBARES was no doubt in old Persian *Ubara*. Its signification is declared by Nicolas of Damascus, who renders it ἀγαθάγγελος. It is therefore derived from *u* (Zend *hu*, Greek ἐύ), "good," and *bara* (Zend *ber*, Greek φέρω, Latin *fero*), our "bear." Its exact signification is "the bearer of good," *i. e.* of good tidings.

OEOBAZUS is explained as *Huhyabazush*, "strong-armed," from *bāzu*, which in Zend is "superior, better," and *bāzu* which is "the arm."—O.

OMARES (Arrian) which in old Pers. would be *Umanish*, is well compared with the Greek Εὐμένης (O.), to which it exactly answers.

OMARTES (Athenæus) would undoubtedly have been in Old Persian *Umartiya*. It corresponds with the Greek Evander, and, as the name of a man, probably meant no more than "brave" or "manly." It is applied to Persia in the Inscriptions (B. Voc.), and then means "having brave inhabitants."

ORMISDATES (Agathias) is clearly from *Ormazd*, a contracted form of the name of the great god Ormasdes or *Auramazdā* (see the next word), and *dāta*, the past participle of *du*, "to give." The ancient form of the word would be *Auramazdata*, and the signification "given to Ormazd."

ORMASDES (Old Pers. *Auramazdā*) has been variously derived, but is perhaps best regarded as composed of the three elements *Aura* (Sanscr. *asura*), from *aus*, "life," *mas*, which in Zend is "great," and *das* (from *da*, "to give"), "the giver"—the whole word thus meaning "the Great Giver of Life."

OXINES (Arrian) is derived from M. Oppert from *varkaha*, "a bear," with a suffix *-ina*, as in Athines, Nitibroes, &c.—O.

OTANES (Old Pers. *Utana*) is from the Old Pers. *u*, Zend *hu*, Sanscr. *su*, "well" or "good," and *tanu* (Zend and Sanscr.), "the body." The word thus signifies "strong of body" (εὐσώματος).—P.

452   ON THE DERIVATION AND MEANING OF   App. Book VI.

OTASPES is thought to be from the Sanscr. *vata*, "wind," and *aspa*, "a horse;" and the sense assigned to the word is "Storm-horse" (P.); but this is scarcely satisfactory.

OXATHRES (Diod. Sic.) is probably derived from the old Pers. 's, Zend *hu*, "well, good," and *khshathra*, which in Zend is "a king," or "chief." The word would have the sense of "good lord."—P.

PARETACENI (Median tribe, Herod. i. 101) are probably "mountaineers," from Sanscr. *parvata*, "a mountain," with an ethnic suffix *-kina*.—O.

PARYSATIS, muli. (Xen.), is conjectured to be from *paru*, which is compared with the Sanscr. *puru*, "much," and *shiti*, which in Zend is "land, earth." Parysatis would thus be "she who has much land."—O.

PATIRAMPHES may be "lord of pleasure," from *pati*, "lord," and Zend *rafno*, "joy, pleasure."

PATIKRITHES is perhaps "powerful lord," from *pati*, and Zend *syai*, "powerful."

PHARANDATES or PHERENDATES
{ This name, taken in conjunction with Pharnabazus, and one or two others, suggests the notion, that the genius *Behrum*, or *Varahran*, was known even to the Achæmenian Persians. (See Pott's 'Forschungen,' p. xlv.) He may have presided over the planet Mars, whose Arian title is otherwise unknown to us. In later times his name certainly appears in *Varanes*. Pharandates must be compared with Mithridates, Madates, Ormisdates, &c.; and must be explained as "given," or "dedicated to *Varahran*."—H. C. R. }

PHARNABAZUS seems to contain as its first element the same name *Farahran*, the second element being that which appears also in Megabazus, viz. *bhaj*, "colere, venerari." Its meaning is "Worshipper of *Varahran*."

PHARNACES. It is probable that *frana*—whatever its derivation, which was perhaps from *fra* (= Sanscr. *pra*), the particle of abundance, and *ni*, "to lead"—was used simply as an intensitive, like *arta*. In Pharnaces, and again in Pharnuches, we have this element, with the Keythic guttural suffix *-ka*. (Compare Artyces, and perhaps Artacmas.) The signification would be "chief," or "leader."

PHARNAPATES (Justin) is either from *frana* intensitive, and *pati*, "lord" (compare ANTAPATAS); or from *Varahran* and *pata*, the past participle of *pâ*, "to protect." In the one case it would mean "excellent lord;" in the other "protected by *Varahran*" (Mars?).

PHARNASPES is probably from the same *frana* intensitive, and *aspa*, with the meaning of "having excellent steeds;" or it may be simply from *fra* (= *pra*), the particle of abundance, and *aspa*, with a euphonic interposed; in which case it would mean "having many steeds."

PHARNASATHURS may compare with *Arta-khshatra*, the true form of Artaxerxes. The roots will be *frana* intensitive, and *khshatru* (Zend *khshathra*) a "king," or "warrior." (Compare ARTAXERXES.)

PHARNUCHES is perhaps only a variant of Pharnaces, q. vide.

PHRADASMENES (Arrian) is probably from *fradas* = Zend *frákhś*, "liberal" (which is itself from *fra*, the particle of abundance, and *da*, "to give"), and *menas* (= Greek μένος), as in *Acheamenes*, *Arsamenes*, &c. The word will thus mean "liberal-minded."

PHRADATES (Arrian) is simply *frákhś*, "liberal." (Compare PHRADASMENES.)

Note A. PROPER NAMES OF MEDES AND PERSIANS.

PHRAORTES (Old Pers. *Fravartish*) contains certainly in its first syllable the element *fra*, which is equivalent to the Greek προ-, the Latin *pro-*, and the German *ver-*. The other root is thought to be a verb equivalent to the German *wahren* in *verwahren* (O.), which corresponds to the French *garder*, and the English *ward*. The meaning would thus be "a protector."

PARXASPES is probably the same name with *Pourushaçpa*, the father of Zoroaster. The derivation of this latter word is undoubtedly from Zend *pouru*, Sanscr. *puru*, "abounding," and *açpa*, "a horse;" and the meaning is, "abounding in horses."—O. and P.

RHEOMITHRES (Arrian) is fairly enough explained as "fond of splendour," from the Zend *rayı*, "splendour," and *mithra*, which has the sense of the Greek φίλος.—O.

ROXANA, *mul.* (Arrian), may compare with the Zend *raç*, "splendere," and with the modern Persian *rushnd*, "lucidus."—P.

SAPTINE, *mul.* (Q. Curt.), is probably *Septima*, from the Sanscr. *saptan*, "seven."

SATASPES may be translated "hundred-horsed," from Zend *çata* (= Greek ἑκατόν, Latin *centum*), "a hundred," and *açpa*, "a horse."—P.

SATIBARZANES (Arrian) is thought to be derived from the Sanscrit *jāti*, "race," or "stock," and "*berz*," as in *Barsines*, *Barsanes*, &c. The name would thus signify "of splendid or illustrious race."—P.

SATROPATES (Q. Curt.) is almost certainly from Old Pers. *khshatram*, "the crown" (see Sir H. Rawlinson's Vocabulary, p. 115), and *páta*, the past participle of *pa*, "to protect." The name signifies "protected by the crown."

SISIMITHRES is perhaps from the Zend *çrira*, "beautiful," and *mitra*, or *mithra*, which corresponds to the Greek φίλος. The word might thus be rendered by φιλόκαλος.

SISAMNES } seem to be formed from the Zend *ça*, "lucere," with an
SISINES (Q. Curt.) } appellative suffix.

SITHATACHMES (Old Pers. *Chitratachma*) signifies "the strong leopard," from *chitra*, a root found in Sanscrit with the sense of "variegatus," whence modern Pers. *chitar*, "the leopard," and Zend *takhma*, "strong." (Compare ASTOCHMES, and vide supra, vol. i. p. 345.)

SMERDIS (Old Pers. *Bardiya*) is probably the Zend *berezya* (compare Vedic *barhya*), "elevated, glorious."—O.

SMERDOMENES must be the above, with the addition of the common element *manas* (= μένος), and will signify "of elevated mind."

SPAMITRAS (Ctes.) is either for *Aspamitras*, "fond of horses," from *aspa* and *mithra*, or else from *spak* (supra, vol. i. p. 202, note ^), "a dog," and *mithra*, "fond," with the meaning "fond of dogs."—O.

SPENDADATES (Ctes.) is "given to the Holy One," from Zend *çventa*, or *spenta*, "holy," and *dáta*, the past participle of *da*, "to give."—H. C. R.

SPITACES (Ctes.) is simply "holy," from *çpita* (= *çventa*. See the next name), with the Scythic guttural termination, as in Arsaces, &c.

SPITADRES (Ctes.) is from the same root. It is a peculiarity of Persian articulation to omit the nasal before the dental (see vol. i. p. 653, note ^), whence *çpenta* becomes *çpita* in almost all the names wherein it occurs. *Spitades* is probably "the Holy One gives," or "has given." (Compare the Hebrew *Nathanael*.)

SPITAMAS (Ctes.), "most holy," is the superlative of *çpenta*.—Dr. (Compare MASISTES.)

SPITAMENES (Arrian), "of holy temper," is formed from *spenta* and *menas*. —P.

SPITHROBATES (Diod. Sic.) is "enlightened by the Holy One," from *spenta* and *bhâta*, "shone on," the past participle of the Sanscr. *bhâ*, "to shine."

SPITHRIDATES (Xenoph.) is probably a mere variant of Spendadates, *spita* having become *spithri* from the influence of the better known name of Mithridates.

STAMENES (Arrian), "of steady mind," is formed from the root *sta*, "to stand," which runs through all the Indo-European languages, and *menas* (= μένος), "the mind," or "temper." (Compare SPITAMENES.)

STRABES (Justin) is probably the same as Œbares, and is at least as near the original name, which was 'Ubara. (See ŒBARES.)

SYSIMITHRES (Q. Curt.) is probably "one who loves light," from the Zend *çuç*, "lucere," and *mithra*, or *mitra*, "fond of."—O.

TABALUS is thought to come from the Zend *tan*, "fortis," and some root equivalent to the modern Pers. *jeleh*, "heros."—(P.) But this etymology is very doubtful.

TACHMASPATES (Old Pers. *Tachamaspâta*) contains evidently the root *takhma*, "strong," which appears also in Artochmes, Tritantæchmes, &c. Its second element, *pada*, is probably the Sanscr. *pati*, Zend *paiti*, "lord," which is found with the soft instead of the hard dental in *padishah*. The name will thus signify "the strong lord."

TANYOXARCES (Ctes.) is derived by M. Oppert from Zend and Sanscr. *tanu*, "body" (compare Hanslanes, Otanes, &c.), and the old Persian *vazarka*, "great, mighty," which is so common in the Inscriptions (Journ. As. 4me Série, tom. xvii. p. 262). He translates the name "fort de corps."

TEISPES (Old Pers. *Chishpaish*) is derived by Pott from the Zend *tevisi*, "strong" (Forschung. p. ix.). But this view was put forth before the discovery of the native form of the name. *Chishpaish* is probably from *chish*, "hair," the old Persian equivalent for the Sanscrit *kis*, and modern Persian *gis*, combined with the well-known element *pâ*, "to protect," or "nourish," -*ish* being an attributive suffix. The word would thus signify "hair-nourishing," or "long-haired."—R. Voc.

TERIBAZUS (Xenoph.), or TIRIBAZES (Plutarch), is composed of the two elements *Ter*, or *Tir*, the Old Persian name for the planet Mercury (see vol. i. p. 525), and *bhaj*, "venerari, colere." (Compare ARTABAZUS, MEGABAZUS, &c.) The name thus means "the worshipper of Mercury."—H. C. R.

TERIDATES (Ælian) or TIRIDATES (Q. Curt.) will signify "given," or "dedicated to Mercury." Compare MITHRIDATES, PHARANDATES, &c.

TIGRANES is probably "an archer," from *tigra*, with an attributive suffix. *Tigra* was in old Persian "an arrow," as is evident from the Nakhsh-i-Rustam Inscription, where the *Sakâ tigrakhudâ* are "Scythian archers."

TIGRIS (Old Pers. *Tigra*).—That the name of this river signified "an arrow," and that it was so called on account of its rapidity, is declared by various authors. (See among others Strab. xi. p. 529; Q. Curt. iv. 9; Plin. H. N. vi. 27.) The word *tigra*, "an arrow," seems to come from the Sanscr. *tij*, "to sharpen," whence Gk. θήγω, θηγάνη, a. r. λ.—R. Voc.

TRITANTÆCHMES seems to be "strong as Tritan," from Zend *takhma*, "strong," and *Tritan*, who, according to the Arian traditions, divided the world between his three sons, Selm, Tur, and Erij. In Persian romance Tritan became *Feridun*. (See vol. i. p. 264, note *.)

Note A. PROPER NAMES OF MEDES AND PERSIANS.

XATHRITES (Old Pers. *Khshathrita*) is apparently from old Pers. *khshatram*, "empire," with a suffix -*ita*, which may be compared with the Sanscr. participle *it*. The sense is "one who has obtained the empire."—R. Voc.

XERXES (Old Pers. *Khshayârshâ*) is derived by Sir H. Rawlinson from *khshaya*, "a king"—a form which may have existed together with *khshayathiya*, and which is represented by the modern Persian *shah*—and *arsha* (= Sanscr. *arshya*) "venerable." (Vocab. p. 120.) Benfey (Keilinschriften, p. 79) and Oppert (Journ. As. 4ᵐᵉ Série, tom. xix. p. 174) suggest *khshaya* and *arsha*, akin to the Sanscr. *akhsha* and the Zend *arssa*, "oculus." Benfey renders the word *König-Seher*, "King-Seer;" Oppert *œil dominatrice*, "Ruling Eye."

ZARIASPES (Q. Curt.) is exactly equivalent to the Greek "Χρύσιππος," being derived from Zend *zara*, "gold," and *aspa*, "a horse."—P. It means probably "having cream-coloured horses."

ZATHRAUSTES (Diod. Sic.) is the "lord of camels," from *kshatra* (= Zend *khshathra*), "king," or "lord," and Sanscr. *ushtra*, Zend *ustra*, "a camel."—P.

ZOPYRUS seems to be a very corrupted Greek form of the native *Daduhya*, which is found in the Behistun Inscription (Col. iv. Par. 18, 8). This last is a reduplicated form from *da*, "to give," and signifies (like Datis) "a giver."—H. C. R.

ZOROASTER.—It is uncertain to what family of languages this word belongs. Sir H. Rawlinson would seek its origin in the Semitic, and explain it as *Ziru-ishtar* (comp. Hebrew זרע and עשתרת) "the seed of Ishtar," or Venus (Notes on the Early History of Babylonia, in the Journal of the Asiatic Society, vol. xv. p. 246. Burnouf and Brockhaus prefer to regard it as Arian, and explain it, the latter as *Zarathrustra*, "golden star," the former as *Zaruth-ustra*, "having yellow camels" (Vendidad-Sade, p. 311).

END OF VOL. III.

LONDON: PRINTED BY W. CLOWES AND SONS, STAMFORD STREET AND CHARING CROSS.

C 42450

www.ingramcontent.com/pod-product-compliance
Lightning Source LLC
Chambersburg PA
CBHW022116300426
44117CB00007B/734